Studies in Church History

49

THE CHURCH ON ITS PAST

THE CHURCH ON ITS PAST

PAPERS READ AT
THE 2011 SUMMER MEETING AND
THE 2012 WINTER MEETING OF
THE ECCLESIASTICAL HISTORY SOCIETY

EDITED BY

PETER D. CLARKE

and

CHARLOTTE METHUEN

PUBLISHED FOR
THE ECCLESIASTICAL HISTORY SOCIETY
BY
THE BOYDELL PRESS
2013

First published 2013

A publication of the Ecclesiastical History Society
in association with The Boydell Press
an imprint of Boydell & Brewer Ltd
PO Box 9, Woodbridge, Suffolk IP12 3DF, UK
and of Boydell & Brewer Inc.
668 Mt Hope Avenue, Rochester, NY 14620-2731, USA
website: www.boydellandbrewer.com

ISBN 978-0-95468-101-2

ISSN 0424-2084

A CIP catalogue record for this book is available
from the British Library

The publisher has no responsibility for the continued existence or accuracy
of URLs for external or third-party internet websites referred to in this
book, and does not guarantee that any content on such websites is, or will
remain, accurate or appropriate.

Details of previous volumes are available from Boydell & Brewer Ltd

Produced by Toynbee Editorial Services Ltd
Typeset in Bembo Std

Papers used by Boydell & Brewer Ltd are natural, recyclable products
made from wood grown in sustainable forests

Printed and bound by CPI Group (UK) Ltd, Croydon, CR0 4YY

CONTENTS

CONTENTS

CONTENTS

PREFACE

Professor Sarah Foot's choice of 'The Church on its Past' as the theme for the fiftieth Summer Meeting of the Ecclesiastical History Society clearly struck a chord with the current consciously historiographical interests of many historians. Record numbers of communications and participants were attracted to this anniversary conference, ably conceived and chaired by Professor Foot and held at Christ Church, Oxford, in August 2011. A focus on the historiography of church-state relations made for a similarly excellent Winter Meeting in January 2012. The resulting volume offers the plenary lectures together with a selection of communications. The volume has a threefold structure: one group of essays considers the way that the church in the past has appealed to – and defined – its own past; a second group analyses the historiography of the past fifty years in relation to particular themes; and a third group addresses the historiography of church and state.

The editors wish to express their thanks to all those who chaired sessions at the Summer Meeting and peer-reviewed the communications, to the authors of the essays included in this volume for their prompt responses to requests for revisions, and particularly to Dr Tim Grass for his work as assistant editor. We are grateful to the society for continuing to fund his essential post. On behalf of the society, we would also like to thank our hosts: Christ Church, Oxford, for the Summer Meeting, and Dr Williams's Library, London, for the Winter Meeting. Professor Michael Walsh organized both meetings with his customary efficiency and also led the summer excursion, handling the last-minute changes to its programme with aplomb. We are very grateful to him for his contribution.

As this volume went to press, news was received of the unexpected death of Diana Wood, a former editor for the society. With Bill Sheils she co-edited five volumes (23–27), was sole editor for a further four (28–31), and also edited or co-edited three volumes of the Subsidia series. After relinquishing the editorship she remained a regular attender at EHS conferences for several years, and had communications accepted for two further volumes.

Peter D. Clarke
University of Southampton

Charlotte Methuen
University of Glasgow

CONTRIBUTORS

Jonathan ARNOLD
Chaplain and Senior Research Fellow, Worcester College, Oxford

David W. BEBBINGTON
Professor of History, University of Stirling

Liam CHAMBERS
Senior Lecturer and Head, Department of History, Mary Immaculate College, University of Limerick

Renie CHOY (*EHS postgraduate bursary*)
Postgraduate student, University of Oxford

Tony CLAYDON
Professor of Early Modern History, Bangor University

Alec CORIO (*EHS postgraduate bursary*)
Postgraduate student, The Open University

†John DORAN
Senior Lecturer, Department of History and Archaeology, University of Chester

Jessica Lee EHINGER (*EHS postgraduate bursary*)
Postgraduate student, University of Oxford

Sarah FLEW (*EHS postgraduate bursary*)
Postgraduate student, The Open University

Sarah FOOT (*President*)
The Regius Professor of Ecclesiastical History, University of Oxford

Luke GARDINER
Postgraduate student, University of Cambridge

Matthew GRIMLEY
Lecturer in Modern History, University of Oxford

Bernard HAMILTON
Professor Emeritus of Crusading History, University of Nottingham

Stephen Mark HOLMES (*EHS postgraduate bursary*)
Postgraduate student, University of Edinburgh

Robert G. INGRAM
Associate Professor of History, Ohio University

Rosalind JOHNSON (*EHS postgraduate bursary*)
Postgraduate student, University of Winchester

Andrew JOTISCHKY
Professor of Medieval History, Lancaster University

Judith M. LIEU
Lady Margaret's Professor of Divinity, University of Cambridge

Philip LOCKLEY
British Academy Postdoctoral Fellow, Faculty of Theology, University of Oxford

Andrew LOUTH
Professor Emeritus of Patristic and Byzantine Studies, Durham University

Diarmaid MacCULLOCH
Professor of the History of the Church, University of Oxford

Charlotte METHUEN
Lecturer in Church History, University of Glasgow

Anthony MILTON
Professor of History, University of Sheffield

Rosemary MOORE
Centre for Postgraduate Quaker Studies in association with the University of Birmingham

Conor O'BRIEN (*EHS postgraduate bursary*)
Postgraduate student, University of Oxford

Roger OTTEWILL
Postgraduate student, University of Birmingham

Kenneth L. PARKER
Associate Professor, Department of Theological Studies, Saint Louis University

Claudia RAPP
  Professor, Department of Byzantine and Modern Greek
  Studies, University of Vienna

Susan ROYAL (*EHS postgraduate bursary*)
  Postgraduate student, Durham University

Salvador RYAN
  Professor of Ecclesiastical History, St Patrick's College,
  Maynooth

Thomas W. SMITH (*EHS postgraduate bursary*)
  Postgraduate student, Royal Holloway, University of
  London

Andrew SPICER
  Professor of Early Modern European History, Oxford
  Brookes University

Chris WILSON (*EHS postgraduate bursary; Michael J. Kennedy
Postgraduate Prize*)
  Postgraduate student, University of Exeter

John WOLFFE
  Professor of Religious History, The Open University

ABBREVIATIONS

ActaSS	*Acta sanctorum*, ed. J. Bolland and G. Henschen (Antwerp, etc., 1643–)
AFP	*Archivum Fratrum Praedicatorum* (1931–)
AH	*Archivium Hibernicum* (1911–)
AHR	*American Historical Review* (1895–)
AHRC	Arts and Humanities Research Council
ARG	*Archiv für Reformationsgeschichte* (1903–)
BAV	Biblioteca Apostolica Vaticana
BJRL	*Bulletin of the John Rylands Library*, vols 1–50; *Bulletin of the John Rylands Library of Manchester*, vols 51–4; *Bulletin of the John Rylands University Library of Manchester*, vol. 55 on (1903–)
BL	British Library
Bodl.	Bodleian Library
CathHR	*Catholic Historical Review* (1915–)
CChr	Corpus Christianorum (Turnhout, 1953–)
CChr.CM	Corpus Christianorum, continuatio medievalis (1966–)
CCM	*Corpus Consuetudinum Monasticarum* (Siegburg, 1963–)
CHC	*Cambridge History of Christianity*, 9 vols (Cambridge, 2005–9)
ChH	*Church History* (1932–)
CQR	*Church Quarterly Review* (1875–1968)
CR	*Corpus Reformatorum* (Berlin, Leipzig, Zürich, 1834–)
CUL	Cambridge University Library
CYS	Canterbury and York Society
DBI	*Dizionario biografico degli Italiani* (Rome, 1960–)
DHGE	*Dictionnaire d'histoire et de géographie ecclésiastiques* (Paris, 1912–)
DOP	*Dumbarton Oaks Papers* (1941–)
EHR	*English Historical Review* (1886–)
EME	*Early Medieval Europe* (1992–)

ET	English translation
GCS	Die Griechischen Christlichen Schriftsteller
HistJ	Historical Journal (1958–)
HR	Historical Research (1986–)
HThR	Harvard Theological Review (1908–)
HZ	Historische Zeitschrift (1859–)
IER	Irish Ecclesiastical Record (1864–)
InR	Innes Review (1950–)
JBS	Journal of British Studies (1961–)
JEH	Journal of Ecclesiastical History (1950–)
JFHS	Journal of the Friends Historical Society (1903–)
JHI	Journal of the History of Ideas (1940–)
JMedH	Journal of Medieval History (1975–)
JMH	Journal of Modern History (1929–)
JRH	Journal of Religious History (1960–)
JRS	Journal of Roman Studies (1911–)
JSNT	Journal for the Study of the New Testament (1978–)
LCL	Loeb Classical Library
LPL	Lambeth Palace Library
LW	Luther's Works, ed. J. Pelikan and H. Lehmann, 55 vols (St Louis, MO, 1955–75)
MGH	Monumenta Germaniae Historica inde ab a. c. 500 usque ad a. 1500, ed. G. H. Pertz et al. (Hanover / Berlin, etc., 1826–)
MGH LdL	Monumenta Germaniae Historica, Libelli de Lite Imperatorum et Pontificum, Saeculis XI et XII conscripti (1891–7)
MGH SRG	Monumenta Germaniae Historica, Scriptores rerum Germanicarum in usum scholarum seperatum editi (1871–)
MGH SS	Monumenta Germaniae Historica, Scriptores (in folio) (1826–)
ODCC	Oxford Dictionary of the Christian Church, ed. F. L. Cross (Oxford, 1957; 2nd edn 1974; 3rd edn 1997; 3rd edn revised 2005); 2nd edn onwards with E. A. Livingstone
ODNB	Oxford Dictionary of National Biography, ed. H. C. G. Matthew and Brian Harrison, 60 vols + index vol. (Oxford, 2004)
OED	Oxford English Dictionary

OECS	Oxford Early Christian Studies
OECT	Oxford Early Christian Texts
OHCC	Oxford History of the Christian Church
OMT	Oxford Medieval Texts
P&P	*Past and Present: A Journal of Scientific History* (1952–)
PBA	*Proceedings of the British Academy* (1904–)
PH	*Parliamentary History* (1982–)
PL	Patrologia Latina, ed. J.-P. Migne, 217 vols + 4 index vols (Paris, 1844–65)
RQ	*Renaissance Quarterly* (1967–)
RSCHS	*Records of the Scottish Church History Society* (1923–)
s.a.	*sub anno* (under the year)
SCH	Studies in Church History
SCH S	Studies in Church History: Subsidia
SCJ	*Sixteenth Century Journal* (1970–2006)
SEHT	Studies in Evangelical History and Thought
s.n.	*sub nomine* ('under the name')
SNTS	Studiorum Novi Testamenti Societas / Society for New Testament Studies
Speculum	*Speculum: A Journal of Medieval Studies* (1925–)
s.v.	*sub verbo* ('under the word')
TNA	The National Archives
TRHS	*Transactions of the Royal Historical Society* (1871–)
TTH	Translated Texts for Historians
WA	*D. Martin Luthers Werke: Kritische Gesamtausgabe*, ed. J. K. F. Knaake, G. Kawerau et al. (Weimar, 1883–)
WABr	*D. Martin Luthers Werke: Kritische Gesamtausgabe. Briefwechsel*, 18 vols (1930–85)
WUNT	Wissenschaftliche Untersuchungen zum Neuen Testament

INTRODUCTION

Anniversaries represent occasions for reflection, retrospectively on the past but also towards possible futures. In 2011 the Ecclesiastical History Society celebrated its fiftieth year by publishing a history of its activities since its creation in 1961 written by the society's current honorary secretary,[1] and devoting the subject of its Summer and Winter Meetings to reflections on the church and its past. Members of the society were encouraged to think about the various ways in which churches have constructed and reinvented versions of their pasts in different periods, and also to contemplate how ecclesiastical history has evolved as a discipline over the past half-century. Plenary speakers at the Summer Meeting addressed specific areas of the writing of ecclesiastical history in the fifty years since the society's foundation, setting the debates and issues that have preoccupied church historians in the wider context of developments in history (and to some extent also theology) over the same period. Communications to the Summer Meeting were invited under two heads: historiographical reflections on particular areas of churches' histories; and discussion of specific eras in church history when churches have looked to the past to explain the present or to legitimate visions for the future. At the Winter Meeting, all three papers considered the shifts that have occurred in historical perceptions of the relations between church and state over the last fifty years.

The organization of this volume, which collects the proceedings of both Summer and Winter Meetings, reflects those three strands. It opens with my own presidential address, in which I asked – with deliberate provocation – whether church historians were in danger of losing their distinctive sense of mission and purpose. That ecclesiastical history no longer occupies the place that once it did within in the academy in Britain is undeniable; in university departments of history and theology (and in theological colleges and semi-

---

[1]   Stella Fletcher, 'A Very Agreeable Society': The Ecclesiastical History Society 1961–2011 (Southampton, 2011).

naries) numbers of church historians have declined significantly during the lifetime of this society. My lecture questions whether ecclesiastical historians have done enough to resist that decline and to respond to various shifts within the wider discipline of history that have occurred over the same period. It considers the effects on church history of the incorporation into historical enquiry of methods derived from other disciplines – including sociology, anthropology, literary theory, and cultural and gender studies – and the significant ways in which they have affected historians' approaches to the past. Coupled with the growing secularization of contemporary society (and the rise of the new atheism), these methodological shifts present serious challenges to the future of ecclesiastical history as conventionally understood and practised by this society. One possible way forward may lie in the adoption of the 'religious turn' manifest in some branches of historical and literary study and also in the history of science, where scholars have begun to take much more seriously the importance of religious belief in understanding and explaining cultures of earlier eras. Ecclesiastical historians could profitably do more to further this trend. I hope my polemical call to church historians to hold on to the fundamental plot that underpins and defines our branch of the discipline will serve as an inspiration to the society's members and help to reinvigorate church history in this country, inside and outside the academy. John Wolffe's essay (on the contribution that church history can make to the contemporary Church of England), which concludes part I of this volume, demonstrates to good effect how the ecclesiastical history of the last two centuries can be made to speak directly to contemporary parishes, priests and people in the diocese of London.

Several of those who offered communications to the Summer Meeting chose to explore specific instances when churches (or individual ecclesiastics) turned to the past in search of evidence to support a particular (often tendentious) reading of their own present, or to inspire or justify movements for restoration or reform of contemporary ecclesiastical institutions. Those essays, collected in part I, range chronologically from Luke Gardiner's analysis of Socrates Scholasticus's retelling of the events of the reign of Theodosius I (379–95) in the 440s, to John Wolffe's essay, already mentioned, on modern religious history and the contemporary church. Although the communications are spread fairly evenly across the two millennia of Christian history, a few cluster around particular periods. Given how contested an area the history of the Reformation has always proved, it is perhaps unsurprising that so many, in addition to Diarmaid MacCulloch's survey of fifty years of Reformation studies in part II, touch on aspects of early modern religious reform. But there are also groups of essays addressing European crusades to the Holy Land and different aspects of eighteenth-century church history.

Despite the existence of a separate International Conference on Patristic Studies, established ten years before the Ecclesiastical History Society in 1951 and convened every four years thereafter, the era of the early church has always been well represented among members – and indeed presidents – of the society and among published communications, and it also finds a secure place in this volume. Gardiner's consideration of Socrates' historical method considers how the fifth-century historian's tendentious decision to omit any mention of the massacre at Thessalonica in 391 in his account of the reign of Theodosius could equate with his self-professed ambition to write objective history. Andrew Louth looks at writings dating from the sixth century but attributed to the Dionysius who judged the court of the Areopagus and was converted by Paul. Louth considers how the pseudonymous author attempted to construct the apostolic or sub-apostolic church to which he purported to belong, what use he made of existing church histories (including Eusebius), and how far he may have tried to stand aloof from the doctrinal controversies which so disturbed the church of his own day. In her consideration of how seventh-century Christian writers tried to fit the rise of Islam into pre-existing methods of historical writing, Jessica Ehinger demonstrates how Muslims (identified with the demons and monsters prophesied in the Bible) came to be fitted into an overarching narrative of God's plan for humanity.

Long temporal perspectives also colour the essays on early medieval topics by Conor O'Brien and Renie Choy. O'Brien explores Bede's view of the 'Jewish church', showing how the eighth-century Northumbrian writer understood the roots of his own church to lie deep in the pre-Incarnation past, having developed out of the Jewish tabernacle and the temple. Attempting to define the essence of Carolingian monasticism, Renie Choy demonstrates that the monastic ideal promoted via reforming councils in the Frankish church early in the ninth century depended on a historical understanding of the nature of lives transformed by the search for God, which quest lay at the heart of their own spiritual endeavour. John Doran's essay encompasses a narrower time frame in assessing how Cardinal Boso, writing in the 1160s and 1170s, reappraised the pontificate of Gregory VII (1073–85) in order both to present him as an ideal model for Pope Alexander III (1159–81) and also thereby to vindicate the cardinal's own reforming strategies.[2]

Three communications, presented together at the conference, address aspects of the writing and rewriting of the history of the crusades. Thomas Smith asks how far the popes' decision-making was influenced by the memory of the actions of their predecessors, with specific reference to the policy of Honorius III (1216–27) over crusading in the Holy Land. He concludes that although Honorius knew of the involvement of the papacy in crusading in the twelfth century, he did not deem this relevant either to the planning of the Fifth Crusade or to that of Frederick II, in both of which he played a part. Andrew Jotischky explores how central were crusading and the Holy Land in the construction of fourteenth-century histories of the Carmelite Order and thus in the shaping of the Carmelites' identity. How the English Reformation altered understanding of the crusade movement from that held in the Middle Ages is the subject of Bernard Hamilton's essay, which looks at the *Historie of the Holy Warre* written in 1639 by the Anglican Thomas Fuller. He illustrates Fuller's close location of his account within a Christian historical framework, heavily influenced by the historical books of the Old Testament.

A cluster of essays on the Reformation period starts with Charlotte Methuen's analysis of the way in which Luther used church history to define and inform his critique of the papacy. As she argues, although Luther was not a church historian, he sought to explore the past as a means of vindicating his evangelical position, believing that his research into earlier eras illustrated the extent of the papacy's descent into corruption. Polydore Vergil, whose five books on the origins of Christian institutions (1521) are considered by Jonathan Arnold, was (amongst other things) an ecclesiastical

---

[2] Sadly, John Doran died as this volume was going to press. A tribute to him will appear in SCH 50, which he co-edited.

historian, who saw the recounting of the past as an act of faith; he hoped to discover the truth about the origins of church practices in order to strengthen the institution of the church in his own day. John Bale, England's first Protestant church historian, sought to reclaim England's true historical narrative, retrieving that truth from the false accounts related by medieval chroniclers. Susan Royal's assessment of Bale's work shows how Bale saw himself as a prophet as well as a historian; she argues for the prevalence of prophecy as a polemical tool during the Reformation.

After the Restoration of the English monarchy in 1660, the story of the Reformation looked rather different. A Catholic perspective comes in Salvador Ryan's analysis of the ecclesiastical history written by John Lynch (a priest-scholar from County Galway) in refutation of Gerald of Wales's twelfth-century condemnation of the Irish. Lynch's *Cambrensis Eversus* (1662) presented a new and confident narrative of Irish Catholicism to a continental audience, one in which loyalty to the papacy did not preclude loyalty to a legitimate monarch. Tony Claydon shows how the pro-Williamite ecclesiastical historian Gilbert Burnet devised a new periodization of the past, creating the Restoration era (1660–89) as a discrete period in British history. In Burnet's view, the events of 1689 did more than bring an end to the ills of James II's reign; they also served to save the Protestant Reformation. Yet, as Robert Ingram's essay illustrates, the nightmare of the Civil War was not forgotten in the eighteenth century but continued to be rewritten from different confessional perspectives. While Dissenters could rally around a shared history of persecution, Anglicans remembered the abuses they suffered at the hands of puritans, and so eighteenth-century polemicists continued to fight England's long Reformation. Chris Wilson's analysis of the use made of the Middle Ages by authors of early Methodist and anti-Methodist polemic widens the temporal lens, yet his communication also shows how the turbulence of England's recent past, and particularly its religious disputes, found reflection in the writing of histories designed to shape and define religious identities.

Similar considerations continued to affect attitudes towards the histories of the English churches in the later nineteenth and early twentieth centuries. As Andrew Spicer's essay reveals, accounts of the events of the Reformation era played a significant role in Archbishop Tait's defence of the French church in Canterbury in the

1860s, a defence he mounted in part on the historical ground that the Huguenot church provided an important symbol of the past tolerance of the Church of England. The Great Ejection of 1662 remained a formative moment in the history of Congregational churches; so in 1912, the 250th anniversary of that event became, as Rosalind Johnson and Roger Ottewill explain, a rallying call for the faithful and an opportunity to witness effectively to faith against a contemporary background of religious indifference. In the essays found in the first part of this volume, we see how successfully the churches have used their pasts in all historical eras to defend arguments about contemporary ecclesiastical practice; to suppress alternative, conflicting narratives; and to position their subjects and writers firmly within the Almighty's overarching plan for humanity.

The second part of the volume reflects the growth of interest in historiography among historians working in all aspects and periods of the discipline over the past half-century. From its former status as a marginal branch of history pursued only by a few, historiography has become a growing area of historical enquiry, taking a central place in undergraduate curricula in history and forming an essential part of postgraduate training programmes. Historians' increased reflexivity on their own discipline has arisen, in part, out of the substantial changes that history has experienced methodologically and conceptually over the second half of the twentieth century, as it has adopted the practices of other disciplines, especially from the social sciences. These essays explore the extent to which those same shifts are visible in ecclesiastical history.

Judith Lieu's plenary address moves away from the question that has dominated so much of her previous work – what did the early church do for women? – to ask what women did for the early church, exploring the trends that have affected writing in this field in recent years. She locates her analysis in the context of developments in biblical studies and theology as much as in history, and shows how changing attitudes to women, gender and sexuality proved important influences on scholarly perceptions of women in the past. While realistic about the problems of rescuing women from the obscurity and erasure of early texts (almost exclusively written by men), and sensitive to the challenges to reconstructing a 'true' past posed by postmodernism, Lieu affirms confidently that women belong to the inner logic or deep grammar of the church's self-understanding. For her, contemporary debates about women's roles in the church have important implications for historians, whose challenge it is to recognize female agency and the multiple ways in which – often despite the expectations of their own societies – women have contributed to, and frequently transformed, the church.

Diarmaid MacCulloch uses his plenary address to challenge the Anglican, high church hegemonic narrative of the Reformation in England and present a picture of pluralized reformations. Also in part an autobiographical account, MacCulloch's essay traces developments in early modern church history from his own undergraduate days in Cambridge and his experiences as a research student. He locates a significant shift in historical representation of the Reformation around 1970, which he attributes to the ecumenical movement and the relaxation of denominational boundaries that followed the Second Vatican Council. New theological insights and the availability of a wider range of sources, including those of material culture, offered fresh perspectives on events in local and national contexts and led to more pluralized understandings of a Reformation whose history other historians have also come to take more seriously. MacCulloch's essay is complemented by two shorter communications: Stephen Mark Holmes's account of how Scottish Catholics fought back in the second half of the twentieth century against the dominant, Protestant, partisan history of the Reformation in Scotland; and Liam Chambers's exploration of the Irish colleges in early modern Catholic Europe and their contribution to maintaining the vitality of the Irish Catholic community, despite the persecutions.

For Evangelical history, as shown by David Bebbington in his plenary lecture, the past half-century has proved transformative. When the Ecclesiastical History Society was founded, Evangelicals had little time for history, which they perceived as a distraction from the imperative to preach the gospel. But from the early 1960s onwards, there has been an upsurge of interest in recording the history of Evangelical churches, at first from a denominational perspective, and with an emphasis on biographies of central figures, but latterly in a more scholarly fashion. Bebbington explores the evolution of this historical consciousness in Britain and in the United States, illustrating the relationship between theology and historical writing, the significance of the introduction of social scientific methods, and the ways in which a deeper historical consciousness has enabled Evangelicals to contribute more fully to national life. As he argues, this was an era in which Evangelicals made a discovery of their history.

Rosemary Moore looks at the history of the origins of the Quaker movement, and examines the different versions given of Quaker beginnings, and the tensions between the interpretations articulated by those who belong to the movement and those who write as outsiders. She argues for more diverse origins than many have accepted, and for the validity of plural understandings of the multiple facets of Quakerism. The discovery of the archives of the Panacea Society (a once thriving community of followers of the prophet Joanna Southcott) leads Philip Lockley to reflect on the ways in which church historians approach heterodoxy, arguing for the importance of tracing the full texture of the Christian experience of the past, encompassing unorthodox expressions such as those of the Southcottians.

Taking a longer chronological perspective than the other plenary speakers, Kenneth Parker examines tensions between Roman Catholic scholars and the Catholic church authorities over different historiographical understandings of the past between the first and second Vatican Councils. He takes four metanarratives of Catholic history and two case studies (birth control, and the place of women in the church) to illustrate his argument, showing how sharply drawn are the lines of these disputes and how entrenched the view that faith has something to fear from historical research. Different light on Catholic historiography is shed by Alec Corio's survey of G. G. Coulton's polemical historical writing directed against Cardinal Gasquet. This, he shows, was more than a debate about method, or about what could be known of the churches' pasts, but exposed contemporary social anxieties about the decline of the Anglican confessional state and a newly assertive spirit in Roman Catholicism. A final essay in part II by Sarah Flew offers a new perspective, demonstrating the neglect by church historians of the subject of religion and finance and showing, through an evaluation of the income of voluntary religious organizations in Britain, how significant a sphere of investigation money can prove to be, if only we can overcome our reticence in talking about it.

Proceedings of previous Summer and Winter Meetings of the society have conventionally integrated the plenary addresses given at the Winter Meeting into the general run of essays, but on this occasion we have determined to keep them separate. For the speakers at the Winter Meeting were asked to adopt a metahistorical view and discuss scholarship on church and state over the half-century of the society's existence. Claudia Rapp's lecture on church and state (or, as some medievalists prefer to say, 'religion' and 'power') in Late Antique and Byzantine scholarship, explores changing perceptions of the place of religion in society and politics in this period in a wide context. She traces the various social, cultural and historical shifts that affected approaches towards the writing of history since the 1960s and looks forward to likely future trends. In an increasingly globalized context, Byzantium is likely in the future to be explored in comparative perspective not with the Christian West but with its regional neighbours: Islam and even Asia. Anthony Milton's discussion of the same question in an early modern context reveals a similar sensitivity to questions of language and terminology, but also addresses related questions about modernity and the effect of modernization on the decoupling of church and state. His central focus is on the confessionalization paradigm, the relationship between religion and state formation and national identities. Although Milton expresses some confidence about scholarly recognition of the importance of religion in past cultures, he argues for the need for sensitivity to the changing meaning and significance of the religious discourses and symbols of earlier eras. Changes in the conception and role of both the church and the state in Britain over the past fifty years colour Matthew Grimley's assessment of religious history, politics and the state since 1961. Against a subtly drawn background of political, social and cultural change, declining church attendance and growing multiculturalism, Grimley shows how between the 1950s and 1980s the social history of religion in Britain became divorced from its political and intellectual history, bringing a temporary (and peculiarly British) eclipse of church and state as a subject for historical study. World political events in the 1980s and an increasing use of religious language in moralized political discourse helped in part to restore a historiographical connection between religion and politics and to revitalize the history of church-state relations from the 1990s onwards. Grimley's essay offers a sophisticated critique of simplistic readings of secularization theory and presents a narrative that does not always sit comfortably with some of the earlier essays in this volume.

★ ★ ★

The theme of the society's fiftieth anniversary conference sparked considerable interest among members and led to a well-attended and lively meeting in Oxford, which opened with a round-table, ecumenical discussion in Christ Church Cathedral on the question, 'What has Church history ever done for the Church?' Essays published in this volume show resoundingly how significantly ecclesiastical history has contributed to the churches' understandings of their own pasts since the time of the first apostles in Jerusalem. Yet they also illustrate the importance of a historical consciousness, not just to the formation and perpetuation of ecclesial identities, but to the understanding of relations between members of different Christian denominations and between Christians and representatives of other faiths, and of the place of the churches within political power-structures across time. In its second half-century, the Ecclesiastical History Society will need to demonstrate that it can respond sufficiently both to social, cultural and religious changes and to innovations within the wider historical profession, to enable it to contribute to contemporary debates and not merely comment on them retrospectively.

Sarah Foot
Christ Church, Oxford

HAS ECCLESIASTICAL HISTORY LOST THE PLOT?*

by SARAH FOOT

The Ecclesiastical History Society's fiftieth anniversary conference provides an opportunity both to celebrate the achievements of the society and to reflect on the current state of the discipline. In asking whether church historians have lost the plot, I do not mean to question colleagues' reason and sanity, but to wonder whether those of us who work in this field might have forgotten some of the objectives and principles that once distinguished our endeavour. Has ecclesiastical history lost its sense of purpose, its place at the heart of historical enterprise, to the extent that it has become not just marginalized and peripheral, but essentially irrelevant both to academic study and wider society?

Church history no longer enjoys the standing it once held within the historical profession. Over the last half-century, the number of established chairs of ecclesiastical history in British universities has dwindled from ten to two – the Regius chair in Oxford, and the Dixie Professorship in Cambridge.[1] Several contemporary historians who hold personal chairs in history have assumed titles that reflect their specialism in church history, but those posts are particular to the individual scholars, and will not necessarily be filled by ecclesiastical historians when the present incumbents retire. Church history might be expected to have a more secure status within departments of theology and in seminaries training ordinands for future ministry, but the redesignation of some university theology departments as schools of theology and religious studies has sometimes involved the loss of posts in church history (more properly seen as falling within history). We might want to ponder the implications of that for the future of

* I gave an earlier version of this essay as my inaugural lecture in Oxford on 18 May 2011: 'Thinking with Christians: Doing Ecclesiastical History in a Secular Age'.
    [1] David Bebbington, 'Response: The History of Ideas and the Study of Religion', in Alister Chapman, John Coffey and Brad S. Gregory, eds, *Seeing Things Their Way: Intellectual History and the Return of Religion* (Notre Dame, IN, 2009), 240–57, at 243–4.

church history, particularly against the background of the increasingly secular society in which we live.

Essentially, this address will explore why ecclesiastical history has become marginal to the contemporary understanding of history as a discipline. Perhaps we have just reached that point on the natural curve in the fortunes of our subject when it has fallen temporarily out of favour at the expense of a rise in prominence of other areas of study. All subjects or periods within any discipline naturally endure spells in the doldrums, when they seem to lie away from the mainstream, divorced from current fashionable trends; not all aspects of a discipline can be cutting-edge, innovative and exciting at the same time. But it does matter that those periods of relative downturn in one area do not pass entirely unnoticed, that complacency does not prevent critical introspection. And that seems to me precisely what is happening in church history: the crisis in ecclesiastical history is that there is no crisis. Or at least, there does not seem to me to be enough anxiety about the subject in Britain or within our society; elsewhere in Europe and perhaps especially in North America the matter is rather different. My remarks will, however, be directed to the British case.

DEFINING THE PLOT

To accuse today's church historians of having lost their sense of direction, to assert that they have lost the plot, is to presume that there was once a plot that shaped the writing of the history of the church that has since been forgotten. From its inception there was *indeed* an overarching narrative that conditioned church history; its plot was entirely obvious and readily understood both by those who wrote such histories and their audiences. From Eusebius onwards, historians of the church had a clear story to narrate, traceable back to the time of the apostles and to the narratives of the Book of Acts. They told the story of the salvation of humanity as revealed through the growth and development of the institution (latterly institutions) devoted to the worship of the Christian God, the church (or, in a modern world, churches). As the *Catholic Encyclopaedia* defines it, 'ecclesiastical history is the scientific investigation and the methodical description of the temporal development of the Church considered as an institution founded by Jesus Christ and guided by the Holy Ghost for the salvation of mankind'.[2] Essentially, if we take a generous definition of scientific investigation and method, that is what Eusebius thought he was writing, and also what the first historian of the English, the Venerable Bede, believed he wrote in his *Ecclesiastical History of the English People*, completed around 731.[3] Bede provided a clear account of the salvation of his own people; his central plot revolved around the narrative of the conversion of the separate English kingdoms and the creation of the first institutions of a national church. A major sub-plot of his history lay in the consequent invention of an identity for that English people as a single nation in the sight of God, a story that later generations of especially English Protestants would also prove keen to develop.[4] We need not doubt that patristic, medieval and early modern church historians, whether tracing universal narratives of the growth of ecclesiastical institutions or looking more parochially at the church or churches of their own regions, understood clearly the larger, overarching framework of salvation-history into which they set their accounts. The same conceptions and clear narrative understanding underpinned the work of those great monastic scholars, the Bollandists and the Maurists, who first began the collection and editing of sources for the study of saints, churches, monastic orders and ecclesiastical institutions.[5] To David Knowles, the great Maurist Jean Mabillon (1632–1707) 'stands next to the Venerable Bede, whom he resembles so closely in mind and character, as an embodiment of the ideal monk-scholar'.[6]

When history became a professional discipline in the nineteenth century, ecclesiastical history lay at its heart. Indeed, to Victorian

---

[2] *Catholic Encyclopaedia, s.v.* 'Ecclesiastical history', online at: <http://www.newadvent.org/cathen/07365a.htm>, accessed 2 April 2011.

[3] Eusebius, *The History of the Church*, transl. G. A. Williamson, rev. edn Andrew Louth, Penguin Classics (Harmondsworth, 1989); *Bede's Ecclesiastical History of the English People*, ed. and transl. Bertram Colgrave and R. A. B. Mynors, OMT (Oxford, 1969).

[4] Patrick Wormald, 'The Venerable Bede and the "Church of the English" ', in Geoffrey Rowell, ed., *The English Religious Tradition and the Genius of Anglicanism* (Wantage, 1992), 13–32.

[5] C. N. L Brooke, 'Problems of the Church Historian', in C. W. Dugmore and Charles Duggan, eds, *Studies in Church History* 1 (London, 1964), 1–19, at 1.

[6] David Knowles, 'The Maurists', in idem, *Great Historical Enterprises* (London, 1963), 33–62, at 50.

minds the study of history and the study of ecclesiastical history amounted in essence to the same endeavour. In the peroration to his inaugural lecture in Oxford as Regius Professor, not of ecclesiastical but of modern history, William Stubbs asserted:

> There is ... in the Study of living History, a gradual approximation to a consciousness that we are growing into a perception of the workings of the Almighty Ruler of the world; ... that we are coming to see, not only in His ruling of His Church in her spiritual character, but in His overruling of the world ... a hand of justice and mercy, a hand of progress and order, a kind and wise disposition ... bringing continually that which is good.[7]

The chair of ecclesiastical history, which Stubbs long coveted without success, had been established by Queen Victoria in 1842, together with a chair in pastoral theology as part of an attempt to improve the education of the mid-nineteenth-century Anglican clergy. The holders were to be in priest's orders and held (and indeed still hold) their posts in conjunction with canonries at Christ Church. As Thomas Gaisford, then dean of Christ Church, wrote to the archbishop of Canterbury, William Howley, in October 1840: 'the establishment of a professor of Ecclesiastical history would, I apprehend, meet with the approbation of all – and the duties such a professor would have to discharge need little or no specification'.[8]

Cambridge took longer to create its own chair in church history, with the establishment of the Dixie Professorship of ecclesiastical history in 1874. Its first holder, Mandell Creighton, had no doubts as to the nature of ecclesiastical history, or the means of studying it.[9] In his inaugural lecture he asserted unambiguously: 'One point cannot be too clearly stated ... : science knows

---

7   William Stubbs, 'Inaugural Lecture, 7 February 1867', in idem, *Seventeen Lectures on the Study of Mediaeval and Modern History and Kindred Subjects* (Oxford, 1900), 1–28, at 27.

8   Copy of letter from Dean Gaisford to Archbishop Howley, 28 October 1840, preserved in Oxford, Bodl., University Archives, MS N.W.21.5, 'Memoranda respecting the Professorships of Pastoral Theology and Eccl. History and the Statute De Disciplina Theologica', fol. 15 (in the handwriting of T. Gaisford, dean of Christ Church).

9   Frank Stubbings, *Forty-Nine Lives: An Anthology of Portraits of Emmanuel Men* (Cambridge, 1983), 37.

no difference of methods, and that ecclesiastical history must be pursued in exactly the same way, and with exactly the same spirit as any other branch of history. The aim of the investigator is simply the discovery of truth.'[10] He admired the historical turn taken by theology in his own day, but saw no need for church history to turn theological. He did, however, deplore the restricted nature of English views of church history (especially the failure to take the Roman church seriously after the Reformation and the narrow view church historians took of Nonconformity). He intended to work on a wider period 'to kindle a greater interest in the nature and influence of ecclesiastical organisation as a factor in European civilisation'.[11] For, he argued, 'till the end of the seventeenth century, ecclesiastical history is the surest guide to the comprehension of European history as a whole'.[12] In a later lecture delivered in 1887, he went further in arguing that ecclesiastical history could not safely be studied on purely ecclesiastical lines: 'The history of the Church cannot at any time be severed from the history of the nation, nor can ecclesiastical questions be considered apart from the background of the national life in which they were inextricably interwoven'.[13] His successor, H. M. Gwatkin, agreed: 'ecclesiastical history is simply the spiritual side of universal history'.[14]

For all these men, the study of church history did more than help its students to understand the present-day Christian churches,[15] or to provide time-depth to current doctrinal or ecclesiological controversies. Rather, at least in Britain, it explained the origins and the workings of the Protestant state.[16] It is not surprising that so many prominent church historians were experts in the medieval church when the history of the medieval church held so clear a

---

[10] Mandell Creighton, 'The Teaching of Ecclesiastical History' (Inaugural lecture delivered in Cambridge, 23 January 1885), in Louise Creighton, ed., *Historical Lectures and Addresses* (London, 1903), 1–28, at 5.

[11] Ibid. 2–3.

[12] Ibid. 15.

[13] Mandell Creighton, 'The Church and the Nation' (paper delivered at the Wolverhampton Church Congress, 1887), in Louise Creighton, ed., *The Church and the Nation: Charges and Addresses* (London, 1901), 156–65, at 156.

[14] Michael Bentley, *Modernizing England's Past: English Historiography in the Age of Modernism* (Cambridge 2005), 67; see also H. M. Gwatkin, *The Meaning of Ecclesiastical History: An Inaugural Lecture* (Cambridge, 1891), 8.

[15] Euan Cameron, *Interpreting Christian History: The Challenge of the Churches' Past* (Oxford, 2005), 3.

[16] Bentley, *Modernizing*, 46–9.

place in an overt grand narrative of state-making. When Zachary
N. Brooke (father of this society's distinguished former president,
C. N. L. Brooke) assumed the professorship of medieval history
in Cambridge in 1944, he noted that although he had only one
predecessor in that newly established chair (C. W. Previté-Orton,
appointed in 1937), medieval studies in Cambridge had long been
sustained by the Dixie professors of ecclesiastical history; he thus
named Creighton, Gwatkin and Whitney as his intellectual forebears.[17]

We should further recall that all these men, the holders of the
Dixie as well as the Oxford Regius chair, were clergymen. In
Britain and elsewhere in Europe, church history was largely written
from the inside, usually from a specific confessional perspective.[18]
The most visible change in ecclesiastical history since its late nineteenth-century glory is thus its increasing laicization, even though
there remain, of course, prominent and significant historians of the
church in monastic orders and among ordained ministers, many
of them active members of the Ecclesiastical History Society. To
explore how ecclesiastical history has changed since the Victorian
era, we need to consider it against the background of the shifts
made in the wider discipline of history over the second half of the
twentieth century.

SHIFTS IN THE HISTORICAL DISCIPLINE SINCE THE 1950S

Before the middle years of the twentieth century, church history
saw itself essentially as a form of institutional history, different
from other historical disciplines within theological studies (such
as the history of doctrine, historical theology, or the history of
liturgy), and a specific strand within historical studies through
its concern with the institutions of the Christian church (or
churches). This society's founder, Clifford Dugmore, defined the
business of church historians: '[t]o trace the origin and development of Christian ideas, customs, dogmas, liturgies, laws and institutions'.[19] Proper subjects for church historians to explore thus

[17] Z. N. Brooke, *The Prospects of Medieval History: An Inaugural Lecture Delivered at Cambridge 17 October 1944* (Cambridge, 1944), 3.
[18] Olwen Hufton, 'What is Religious History Now?', in David Cannadine, ed., *What is History Now?* (London, 2002), 57–79, at 58.
[19] Kings College London, College Archive, K/PP097, box 2: C. W. Dugmore, 'Ecclesiastical History No Soft Option', 25; quoted by Stella Fletcher, *A Very Agreeable*

included the papacy and papal government; monastic orders and individual monastic houses; bishops, priests and ministers; conventicles, synods and church councils (the 'pitched battles of ecclesiastical history', as A. P. Stanley described them).[20] The first presidents of the Ecclesiastical History Society all conformed to this conventional understanding of the nature of the subject. David Knowles was a noted historian of monasticism, especially of his own Benedictine order; Dugmore himself (trained in biblical studies), wrote on the Reformation; and Stanley Greenslade's expertise lay in the patristic period.[21] E. F. Jacob's work on the later Middle Ages extended far beyond church history, but his publications on ecclesiastical history included a four-volume edition of the register of the fifteenth-century archbishop of Canterbury, Henry Chichele.[22] Several of the early themed volumes of the society's proceedings, *Studies in Church History*, reflected the same sort of conception of the nature of the field: *The Province of York* (SCH 4); *The Mission of the Church and the Propagation of the Faith* (SCH 5); *Councils and Assemblies* (SCH 6).[23]

In the mid-twentieth century our discipline had a clear sense of its own distinctive identity and purpose. As it had been practised and understood in the generation before the founding of the Ecclesiastical History Society, the plot narrated by church history involved less the story of ideas, but rather the narrative of the development of the organization, the body of Christ, its growth, leadership and conflicts; one of its strongest elements lay in its diachronic coherence, the possibility it offered for cross-

---

Society: The Ecclesiastical History Society 1961–2011 (Southampton, 2011), 6. Dugmore's lecture was later published by SPCK: *Ecclesiastical History No Soft Option: An Inaugural Lecture* (London, 1959).

[20] A. P. Stanley, *Three Introductory Lectures on the Study of Ecclesiastical History* (Oxford, 1857), 39.

[21] David Knowles, *The Monastic Order in England: A History of its Development from the Times of St Dunstan to the Fourth Lateran Council, 940–1216* (Cambridge, 1940); C. W. Dugmore, *The Mass and the English Reformers* (London, 1959); Stanley Greenslade, *Schism in the Early Church* (London, 1953).

[22] E. F. Jacob, *The Register of Henry Chichele, Archbishop of Canterbury 1414–43*, 4 vols, CYS 42, 45–7 (Oxford, 1937–47); *Essays in the Conciliar Epoch* (Manchester, 1943); cf. also his contribution to the Oxford History of England, *The Fifteenth Century, 1399–1485* (Oxford, 1961); or *Henry V and the Invasion of France* (London, 1947).

[23] The first volume of SCH included an essay by Christopher Brooke reflecting on the problems of the church historian, covering many of the same issues raised by this paper: see n. 5 above.

temporal comparisons.[24] In England, as we have seen, that narrative was closely intermeshed with a story about the creation of a Protestant nation. Young scholars determined to work in the field of church history came to their research projects with well-established and clearly understood notions of the sorts of tasks on which they would be set to work. Peter Brown tells of his interview as a potential graduate student (in the mid-1950s) in Oxford by the then Regius Professor of Modern History, V. H. Galbraith. Galbraith's advice, he reports, was 'brusque and to the point. Vigorously poking the coal fire in his rooms in Oriel College, he barely looked up at me: "Brown. [he said] So you wish to do ecclesiastical history? Have you got a bishop? Everyone must have a bishop, you know. Go and read his register"'.[25] Brown, of course, followed that advice tangentially, by choosing to work first on that great bishop of Hippo, St Augustine, but not at all as Galbraith might have imagined.

Yet even at the point of the creation of the Ecclesiastical History Society, and while the first Summer Meetings took place in Herbert Butterfield's Peterhouse, the wider discipline of history had begun to change in ways which would come in time to threaten the securities on which ecclesiastical history had formerly rested. We might wonder whether there was something slightly defensive about the creation of an ecumenical organization devoted to the study of the church at the start of the 1960s. After all, as Stella Fletcher shows clearly in her history of this society, a number of organizations devoted to the history of different denominations among the English churches already existed: a flourishing non-denominational Scottish Church History Society had functioned since 1922; the American Society of Church History dated back to 1888, and the French Société d'histoire ecclésiastique de la France to 1914.[26] Looking for positive motives for the creation

---

[24] David Brakke, 'The Early Church in North America: Late Antiquity, Theory and the History of Christianity', *ChH* 71 (2002), 473–91, at 475. That has been one of the guiding principles underpinning the Society's annual publication, Studies in Church History, whose volumes survey particular themes across the two millennia of ecclesiastical history.

[25] Peter Brown, 'What's in a name?', lecture inaugurating the Centre for Late Antiquity in Oxford, online at: <http://www.ocla.ox.ac.uk/pdf/brown_what_in_name.pdf>, accessed 15 April 2011.

[26] Fletcher, *A Very Agreeable Society*, 2.

of the Ecclesiastical History Society, Fletcher has rightly stressed the optimism of the period, and especially the hopes then vested in ecumenism. She has located the society's foundation in 1961 in a series of related contexts: the launch of the *Journal of Ecclesiastical History* by Dugmore in 1950; F. L. Cross's invention of the International Conference on Patristic Studies in 1951; and the creation of the international commission on ecclesiastical history within the Comité International des Sciences Historiques.[27] In retrospect, however, one could also ask if the making of this society also (perhaps unconsciously) represented a last ditch attempt to save ecclesiastical history from the external threats presented both by changes within history and by the increasing secularization of lay society.

While it is possible to identify significant developments in ecclesiastical history in the first half of the twentieth century, especially as the field moved away from the constrictions imposed by purely confessional approaches, it faced both greater opportunities for evolution, as the wider discipline of history itself started to change from the late 1950s onwards, and also potentially greater problems. These would come to dent the confidence with which church history had once been pursued. The declining role of the church and of other forms of organized Christianity in Britain and elsewhere in the West across this period constitutes one element that helps to inform, and also a key context by which to explain, both methodological and disciplinary changes. It is striking that the now celebrated special number of the *Times Literary Supplement* entitled 'New Ways in History' which Geoffrey Barraclough put together in 1966 had much to say about new methods in history (for example, in Keith Thomas's essay on the tools and the job[28]), about the geographical expansion of the discipline outside the West, and about the relevance of technology to historians, but it had *no* essay on religion or the history of the churches.[29]

Let us look more closely at how those changes within history affected students of the history of the church. At first, moves

---

[27] Ibid. 3.

[28] Keith Thomas, 'The Tools and the Job', *Times Literary Supplement*, 7 April 1966, 275.

[29] This is the more surprising given Barraclough's own distinguished contributions to church history, especially papal history: cf. G. Barraclough, *The Medieval Papacy* (London, 1968).

towards the social, increased interest in studying history from below (looking not at kings, bishops and nobles but at people of lesser status, women as well as men), and the new availability of the sources and tools with which to do so, played readily into the hands of a new generation of church historians. Quantification and developing statistical methods opened routes into reconsideration of the economy of the church, for example Christopher Hill's *Economic Problems of the Church* (1956), Ian Kershaw's study of Bolton Priory, Edward Miller's work on Ely and that of his pupil, Edmund King, on Peterborough.[30] Similarly, Alan D. Gilbert's study of *Religion and Society in Industrial England* attempted a statistical analysis of the rise of Nonconformity.[31] Quite how far one could hope to get in testing the religious enthusiasms of past populations by counting, measuring or weighing evidence of their participation in religious life, for example through analysis of the quantities of wax candles offered to churches, or the numbers of new members who joined religious confraternities over a given period, is less clear.[32] Various *annaliste* efforts in this sphere were less than successful.[33]

Other ecclesiastical historians found new routes into the exploration of religious behaviour in the localities and from the perspective of the laity. Archbishop William Temple's decision to open diocesan registers to historical enquiry and the relocation of those materials from ecclesiastical archives to newly established county record offices provided a plethora of material; local studies in different periods of ecclesiastical (and secular) history

[30] Christopher Hill, *Economic Problems of the Church: From Archbishop Whitgift to the Long Parliament* (Oxford, 1956); Ian Kershaw, *Bolton Priory: The Economy of a Northern Monastery, 1286–1325* (Oxford, 1973); Edward Miller, *The Abbey & Bishopric of Ely: The Social History of an Ecclesiastical Estate from the Tenth Century to the Early Fourteenth Century* (Cambridge, 1951); Edmund King, *Peterborough Abbey, 1086–1310: A Study in the Land Market* (Cambridge, 1973).

[31] Alan D. Gilbert, *Religion and Society in Industrial England: Church, Chapel and Social Change, 1740–1914* (London, 1976).

[32] For a positive assessment of the value of such work, see Miri Rubin, 'Religion', in Ulinka Rublack, ed., *A Concise Companion to History* (Oxford, 2011), 317–30, at 318, quoting Pierre Chaunu, *La Mort à Paris XVIe, XVIIe et XVIIIe siècles* (Paris, 1978), and Jacques Chiffoleau, *La Comptabilité de l'au-delà: les hommes, la mort et la religion dans la région d'Avignon à la fin du Moyen Âge* (Rome, 1980).

[33] François Furet, 'Quantitative Methods in History', in Jacques Le Goff and Pierre Nora, eds, *Constructing the Past: Essays in Historical Methodology* (Cambridge, 1985), 12–27, at 18.

thus abounded in the 1960s and 1970s.[34] Many of today's leading church historians began their careers with such projects, including a number of our former presidents: Patrick Collinson encompassed a number of localities in his survey of the Elizabethan puritan movement, while Bill Sheils explored puritans in the diocese of Peterborough. In later historical periods we may discern a similar move towards the local in studies of Nonconformity; first, histories of individual Nonconformist groups, such as the four-volume *History of Methodism* edited by Rupert Davies and Gordon Rupp, or Clyde Binfield's work on Congregationalists, and latterly the more global work of David Bebbington on Evangelicalism from the eighteenth century onwards.[35] Nonetheless one may here, too, discern a parallel tendency towards increasing localism, one reflected in some of the papers in SCH 16, *The Church in Town and Countryside.*

Relevant of course to these changing intellectual currents were various shifts in contemporary religious culture. The churches began to articulate new attitudes towards the laity in the aftermath of the Second Vatican Council; all denominations started to encourage the full, conscious and active participation of Christian people in the liturgy, which may have helped inspire interest in lay devotion in earlier eras. Similarly, contemporary ecclesiastical debates about the participation of women in ordained ministry found reflection in historical enquiry into the roles taken by women in the early church and in later periods. Claire Cross's choice of theme in 1989, 'Women in the Church', thus proved highly topical. Yet I should concede that only in retrospect did I fully appreciate how much my study during the 1990s of the significance of women in Anglo-Saxon monasticism related directly to my engagement in debates about the place of women in the Church of England.[36] For all the public attention afforded to such matters, however, in contemporary society, religion – or at least church attendance – declined sharply. As Simon Green has shown recently, this represented no

---

[34] Christopher Haigh, 'A. G. Dickens and the English Reformation', *HR* 77 (2004), 24–38, at 29–30.

[35] David Bebbington, *Evangelicalism in Modern Britain: A History from the 1730s to the 1980s* (London, 1988); idem, *The Dominance of Evangelicalism: The Age of Spurgeon and Moody* (Leicester, 2005).

[36] The fruits of that research were published as Sarah Foot, *Veiled Women: The Disappearance of Nuns from Anglo-Saxon England*, 2 vols (Aldershot, 2000).

new development but one traceable back to the 1920s.[37] Further, Frank Prochaska has demonstrated how governmental reforms in the provision of education and welfare in the 1940s removed from the churches much of their role in social, educational and charitable provision, thus undermining the associational citizenship that went with church membership.[38] In this secular, or at least desacralized, environment, historians generally treated religious belief as one among many social or political phenomena, and not necessarily one that needed handling with especial care.[39]

Paralleling the focus on the local, and especially the laity in the localities, we may discern a growing historical interest in the 1970s and beyond in those who were outside the orthodox religious mainstream, and more generally in popular piety – lived religion – as opposed to the practices of elites or of ecclesiastical institutions. W. R. Ward chose 'Popular Belief and Practice' for his presidency in 1970–1. Stella Fletcher sees this conference as a watershed, 'privileging the popular over the elite and coming as close as the EHS ventured to the Marxist interests of that era'.[40] Eamon Duffy's approach to the same topic in 2004 – 'Elite and Popular Religion' – took a rather different line, urging consideration of the ways in which different expressions of piety have interacted rather than seeing them in opposition to one another.[41] Here the society responded outwardly to moves elsewhere in the discipline of history, but perhaps without fully recognizing just how secular historians had begun to talk about the religion of the people. From the 1970s onwards, popular religion came increasingly, as John Van Engen has argued, to be 'imagined and presented as an autonomous religious outlook, ancient in origin and belonging to the people', a phenomenon 'which could be explored as a set of indigenous sacred practices overtly or covertly resistant to the Christianising forces of the elite'; it may, he suggests, have owed something to Gramscian visions of resistance from below, and this new approach profitably opened up new ways of thinking

---

37 Simon Green, *The Passing of Protestant England: Secularisation and Social Change c.1920–1960* (Cambridge, 2011).

38 Frank Prochaska, *Christianity and Social Service in Modern Britain* (Oxford, 2008).

39 John Van Engen, 'The Future of Medieval Church History', *ChH* 71 (2002), 492–522, at 496–7.

40 Fletcher, *A Very Agreeable Society*, 34.

41 Ibid. 103.

about superstition and above all heresy. Freed from the confessional perspectives that had formerly dominated its study, heresy represented an ideal lens through which to explore manifestations of popular religious sentiment and fervour.[42] Now heresy could become – as it did perhaps most powerfully in Le Roy Ladurie's *Montaillou* (1975) – just another way of expressing the overlapping beliefs and practices of medieval peasant life; as Le Roy Ladurie put it: 'the sacred *is* only the social'.[43] R. I. Moore also developed a Durkheimian reading of the church's response to heresy (and other forms of deviance) classically articulated in his *The Formation of a Persecuting Society* (1987). Little of such trends emerged in the society's first venture into this area in 1971 with *Heresy, Schism and Religious Practice*, but later volumes of Studies in Church History (*Persecution and Toleration*, *Elite and Popular Religion* and *Discipline and Diversity*) testify more to a shifting agenda.

After the social turn, anthropology has perhaps had the greatest measurable impact on church history and the wider study of religion over the last five decades.[44] In a seminal article on the Balinese cock fight, Clifford Geertz offered a methodology for the analysis of culture as a signifying system, demonstrating how a dense web of symbols and meanings could be unravelled and decoded to discover and give meaning to complex cultural systems as well as individuals' expressions and actions.[45] Influenced by Geertz and also by the work of the French *Annales* school (itself drawing on Durkheim, Mauss and later Lévi-Strauss) as well as the growth of interest in *mentalités*, a school of historians emerged who looked not at the church and its institutions but at religion as a social and cultural phenomenon. By studying religion comparatively and with close reference to folklore, they found it possible to analyse a popular, oral and customary religious culture, quite distanced from the clerical and bookish expressions of formal, institutional

---

[42] Van Engen, 'The Future', 498.

[43] E. Le Roy Ladurie, *Montaillou: Cathars and Catholics in a French Village, 1294–1324* (London, 1978), 352; quoted in Peter Biller, 'Through a Glass Darkly: Seeing Medieval Heresy', in Peter Linehan and Janet L. Nelson, eds, *The Medieval World* (London, 2001), 308–26, at 320.

[44] Keith Thomas, 'History and Anthropology', *P&P*, no. 24 (1963), 3–24.

[45] Clifford Geertz, 'Deep Play: Notes on the Balinese Cockfight', in idem, *The Interpretation of Cultures* (New York, 1973), 412–53; see also Megan Vaughan, 'Culture', in Rublack, ed., *Concise Companion to History*, 227–45, at 233–4.

Christianity which used to be the preserve of the church historian.[46] Keith Thomas's *Religion and the Decline of Magic* (1971) used anthropological techniques to bring to light manifestations of popular religion reflecting widespread belief in magic and popular superstition both before and after the Reformation, drawing a distinction between elite and popular cultures with widely divergent religious views. For medievalists, opening up hagiography, accounts of the lives of saints, and miracle stories to new modes of enquiry, the popular and the cultural became evident.[47] Not everyone followed with such enthusiasm into these waters. John Bossy's inaugural lecture at the University of York, 'Some Elementary Forms of Durkheim', offered a sophisticated and linguistically turned critique of the Durkheimian proposition on which so much of this anthropologically inspired history has turned, that the object of religion is society.[48]

Amid these forces – the moves to the local, the popular, and even to the superstitious or frankly deviant – church history at first continued to thrive. For nothing in these methodological shifts to look at history from below, through sociological or anthropological lenses, threatened the basis on which all ecclesiastical history must rest: the inspired narrative of the origins and development of the churches since the days of Christ. Stella Fletcher has written engagingly about their impact on the society during the 1970s, 1980s and 1990s, and argued that during that period there was no dramatic difference in how the EHS 'did' history. Although not unaware of methodological shifts, she suggested that 'EHS stalwarts tended not to be much exercised by the latest academic fashions and many of them saw no reason to change'.[49] Flirtation with 'deliberately inclusive' themes such as 'Religion and humanism' and 'Religion and national identity' did not prove universally popular. Fletcher quotes James Cameron's insistence that the EHS should remain committed to specifically ecclesiastical history and

---

[46] Ibid. 235; see also Rubin, 'Religion', 317–8.

[47] e.g. Jean-Claude Schmitt, *The Holy Greyhound: Guinefort, Healer of Children since the Thirteenth Century* (Cambridge, 1983); Miri Rubin, Corpus Christi: *The Eucharist in Late Medieval Culture* (Cambridge, 1999); Carlo Ginzburg, *The Cheese and the Worms* (London, 1980).

[48] John Bossy, 'Some Elementary Forms of Durkheim', *P&P*, no. 95 (1982), 3–22.

[49] Fletcher, *A Very Agreeable Society*, 92.

resist the temptation to widen its remit to the history of religion.[50] Anthony Fletcher's conference on 'Gender and Christian religion' in 1996 might have started a move towards trendier, more fashionable topics, and Stuart Mews with his sociological training also had more sympathy for innovative approaches to church history,[51] but little in the following years points to a fundamental shift in method.

Meanwhile, however, in the late 1970s or early 1980s something had happened that profoundly disrupted the securities on which ecclesiastical history had always rested: the epistemological shift now loosely described as postmodernism. Most succinctly defined as a disbelief in meta- or grand narratives, postmodernism argues not against the notion that stories can be told, but against the confident understanding that one can construct overarching narratives of grand themes: the rise of a nation, the history of liberty or the story of Christianity. Rather, it argues, there must be plural narratives, multiple truths; there is no single Authorized Version, but many discourses about the past. All branches of history found the postmodern challenge to the availability of a true past that their careful, trained, disciplined investigation could uncover painful and difficult to reconcile; Marxist historiography, which depends on a different grand narrative, has struggled particularly. But to argue that there is no past there to recover — a corollary of relativizing epistemological claims — challenges most profoundly the foundations on which ecclesiastical history has always rested, and threatens to unpick the endeavour itself, unravelling the plot that lies at its heart.

Ecclesiastical historians responded to these challenges in a variety of ways, turning to literacy to explore modes of religious discourse; redefining the place of women in religious culture and using gender as a tool to analyse masculinity too; thinking about the body and asceticism, images and the ordering and use of sacred space, and the performance of religious ritual. In this ever more culturally turned understanding of the nature of historical enquiry, church history seems to have lost a good deal of what once made it distinctive, especially its former interest in the institutional context that regulates and sets limits to religious behaviour.

---

50 Ibid. 93.
51 Ibid.

Instead, it has allowed itself to be subsumed into cultural studies, in which religious behaviour has less to do with the sacred than with the construction of identity, or to become part of the wider – and extremely vibrant – branch of the study of religion. Instead of studying the church, historians began increasingly to look at Christianity in comparative focus beside other world religions, and indeed to talk not of Christianity, but of Christianities. Consider, for example, the recently published nine-volume *Cambridge History of Christianity*, not a complete chronological account of the history of the church (or churches) but rather a survey 'of the development of Christianity in all its aspects – theological, social, political, regional, global – from the time of Christ to the present day'.[52] Church history is here subsumed within the larger – and arguably healthier – umbrella of the study of religion, and Christianity is shown to be not a singular phenomenon. Several of the volumes indeed state overtly that they explore plural Christianities. As Tom Noble and Julia Smith argue in their preface to the third volume of this series, the plural 'denotes not chaos, confusion or disunity, but richness, creativity and complexity'; to them, Christianity is 'a lived experience as much as or more than a set of doctrinal formulations'.[53] Such work sheds important light on the social and cultural contexts for religion and reflects a wider displinary move away from institutional towards cultural history, but it contributes less to our understanding of spirituality and devotion in earlier eras.

In some spheres church historians have not only accepted this change of direction towards the cultural but affirmed their desire to redefine the field. Thus the Dutch journal *Nederlands archief voor kerkgeschiedenis* reinvented itself in 2006, shifting from Dutch to English language publication and renaming itself *Church History and Religious Culture*. The journal of the American Society for Church History also subtly moved away from the terms in which it had defined its objects on the foundation of *Church History* in 1932. In 1998 it added a subtitle 'Studies in Christianity and Culture' and announced the adoption of a new editorial strategy that sought to look not narrowly at the history of the church but

52   *Cambridge History of Christianity*, 9 vols (Cambridge, 2005–9).
53   Thomas F. X. Noble and Julia M. H. Smith, 'Preface' to *CHC*, 3: *Early Medieval Christianities, c.600–c.1100* (Cambridge, 2008), xvi.

rather to consider the intersection between Christianity and other faiths. It declared a self-conscious intent to draw on a wider range of historical approaches, including critical theory and the methods of the social sciences, along with more traditional modes of archival research and interpretation.[54] In the year 2000 the journal organized a conference to explore present trends in the study of Christian history, publishing the papers in a special issue. All raised serious methodological concerns about the state of church history in an increasingly secularized world and – as Hartmut Lehmann contended the most forcibly – a global environment in which Christianity plays substantially different roles in the northern and southern hemispheres. This is clearly the background against which we should understand the University of Cambridge's recent redefinition of the subject the Dixie Professor of ecclesiastical history should profess,[55] and the decision to appoint to it a historian of the social context of relations between African traditional religion and Christianity.

Beset by these conflicting cross-currents, where should ecclesiastical history go? Does it need to 'go' anywhere, or can it quietly go on doing what it has always done best? And what should be the role for our society in this post-ecclesiastical world? As decreasing numbers of people in the West participate in organized religion, fewer identify with specific ecclesial bodies. Christianity, once the bedrock of European civilization, has become increasingly remote from the daily experiences of most of its modern-day citizens. Although a central, defining feature of Europe's history, it resonates little with the cultural preoccupations of the modern age. Where does this leave a society devoted to ecclesiastical history? Who still wants to hear the stories that we can plot?

FUTURE PROSPECTS FOR ECCLESIASTICAL HISTORY

Hitherto, as already suggested, this society has not much favoured the adoption of innovative approaches to the study of the churches' past, and the Ecclesiastical History Society does not stand alone in

---

[54] 'Editorial', *ChH* 67/1 (March 1998), v–vi.

[55] The further particulars for the chair when it was advertised in 2010 situated the post within the expansion of ecclesiastical history in recent years 'to include the broader history of the Christian religion, which may include its relations with or comparisons to other major world religions'.

preferring a conventional understanding of the field. The editors of the *Journal of Ecclesiastical History* have not thought it necessary to adopt a new name for the journal, nor indeed did they choose to offer reflections on the direction of the discipline at the moment of its fiftieth anniversary, which coincided with the Millennium. One of those editors, Diarmaid MacCulloch, recently produced a highly acclaimed *History of Christianity* offering a magisterial survey over three thousand years.[56] Although his title implies a shift towards the sphere of the study of religion, and in places he talks overtly about Christianities, not a single, monolithic faith, in method the book owes much to his training in Cambridge with Geoffrey Elton. MacCulloch does not analyse belief systems as manifested in ritual or collective or individual Christian behaviour; he devotes little space to the beliefs or actions of lay Christian believers (although much to the history of theology). Centrally the volume supplies a history of the key figures and institutions of organized churches: popes, bishops, pastors and preachers; creeds and councils; theologians and theological controversy. He explores the relationship between shifts in theological understanding and the evolution of organized churches, and focuses overwhelmingly on the relationships between churches and secular political and military authority. This is church history, in other words, as traditionally understood, although accomplished on a vast and far from conventional scale, and with a mastery of a range of material and a geographical scope that few could equal. Its very success – as a well-received series of television programmes as well as a book – shows powerfully how a church historian can still tell a narrative of the evolution of the churches across time.

Others have, however, followed different methodological paths. The turn to the social which so dominated ecclesiastical history in the 1970s appears much reduced (indeed, to the extent, as Hugh McLeod and Simon Green have argued, that the social history of religion seems to have less and less to do with ecclesiastical and intellectual history).[57] In its place, it is the cultural history of religion that now dominates the historiography. Contributing

---

[56] Diarmaid MacCulloch, *Christianity: The First Three Thousand Years* (London, 2010).

[57] Hugh McLeod, 'Varieties of Victorian Belief', *JMH* 64 (1992), 321–37, at 322–3, 337; Green, *Passing of Protestant England*, 8–9.

the 'Religion' essay to a recently published concise companion to historical study, Miri Rubin argued for the value of anthropologically informed study of Christianity. She asserts that the historian should search for the inner logic to be found inside each religious culture and trace that logic through the narratives and rituals enacted collectively by members of that society, searching for explanation and meaning in all areas of their lives.[58] In her view, faith is no longer a prerequisite for the effective and illuminating study of the history of religion; indeed she seems positively to think disbelief an advantage: 'It is only when religion is understood as clusters of ideas and practices expressed and embedded with material objects, lived as stimuli to the senses, prompting memory and securing identity, that historians will be able to contribute to the understanding and interpretation of religion throughout the world.'[59] Thus historians should not, in her opinion, see religion as reflecting temporal avenues to the divine, nor as expressions of sanctity within the mundane world, but as 'cultural forms constitutive of the identities of individuals and groups'.[60]

Clearly, as Rubin's abundant examples demonstrate, this new cultural study of religion has shed fresh light on formerly neglected areas of the history of Christianity. I would follow her in accepting the enormous benefits that have followed from the move away from confessional histories that defended particular sectarian corners. Where I struggle is with the dogmatic assertion that disbelief is a positive advantage. For although this focus on ritual (and ritual agents), the spaces, sights, sounds, smells, rhythms and dramas of performed religious acts can reveal much, it readily descends into Durkheimian reductionism and functionalism. When it does, it becomes potentially as misleading as the confessional interpretation it eschews.[61]

Members of the Ecclesiastical History Society will not dissent from my own view that to write about any religion it is essential to take that religion seriously, to engage directly with the intrinsic nature of the belief systems which adherents espoused and thus to explore what those beliefs meant to their practitioners. The paral-

---

[58] Rubin, 'Religion', 319.
[59] Ibid. 329.
[60] Ibid.
[61] John Van Engen, 'The Christian Middle Ages', *AHR* 91(1986), 519–52, at 544.

lels here with Stuart Clark's arguments about the need to take demonology seriously as expressed in his *Thinking with Demons* are obvious.[62] It is not the purpose of ecclesiastical history, or the study of any other religion, to formulate twenty-first-century social theory, still less to use anthropology to explain away confessional ecclesiastical history in such a way as to make the study of religion legitimate aspects of our own present, and thus to support current notions of gender, identity, liberal humanism, secularization or globalization. Nor, of course, can the writing of church history merely to defend a particular confessional position any longer be accepted.

On the other hand, if church history has any hope of regaining any of the ground it has lost in recent decades, it will need to engage with these historiographical trends. It is not sufficient to say that we do not follow fashion and so ignore it. To counter the arguments of those critical of conventional ecclesiastical history and defend our own corner, we need not just to know what those critics are saying, but to locate our responses in a historiographically considered context. Specifically, church historians need to reclaim the importance of religious belief and practice from anthropological systems and reaffirm a commitment to making faith and spirituality matter in consideration of the past of the churches. But we cannot do so in a narrow-minded way that returns us to the old faith-based, confessionally determined models that used to dominate our subject. Rather we need to look for ways of engaging with the methodological shifts in the wider profession and challenging the reductionism from an informed standpoint.

One possible way forward here is suggested by what has come to be termed the 'religious turn'. This has emerged especially in early modern English literary studies but also in intellectual history, and in the history of modern Germany. Those who have advocated this turn to religion argue for the need to restore consideration of faith issues to the study of texts against the backdrop of the increasing secularization of the modern world. As John Coffey and Alister Chapman have argued, modernization and secularization have gone hand in hand in the West, so that reason and science have come to replace faith and dogma. Secularization has indeed been

---

[62] Stuart Clark, *Thinking with Demons: The Idea of Witchcraft in Early Modern Europe* (Oxford, 1997).

the dominant paradigm for understanding the religious history of modern Europe for some time. Charles Taylor demonstrated in *A Secular Age* that this results from a series of largely unrecognized assumptions that 'religion must decline ... because it is false ... because it is increasingly irrelevant ... and because religion is based on authority'.[63] Just as in the study of medieval and early modern religion, the study of religious history in the modern era has tended to analyse religious life in ways that the participants in religion find almost unrecognizable.[64] The secularization thesis is of course itself open to challenge; we need more nuanced readings of the relationship between the unquestionable decline in church attendance on the one hand and continuing public interest in, and espousal of, other articulations of religious and spiritual expression on the other. But we also need to recognize and respond to the damage that secularizing tendencies do to our own discipline.

The essays edited by Chapman and Coffey directly challenge the work of Quentin Skinner for its failure to engage with issues of faith (indeed their title 'seeing things their way' is one of Skinner's phrases). They also call into question the work of some of the Sussex school, for example the late John Burrow and Stefan Collini, whose visions of intellectual history have tended to be divorced from consideration of religion. Coffey and Chapman argue not that religious ideas should have a special status as the primary category of intellectual history, but that religious thought should have the same respect and be studied in the same way as scientific or political thought. Religious ideas should not be seen as a separate area left to specialists; indeed, they contend, in most historical periods it is anachronistic to separate religion from other parts of life: religion and church history should not be ghettoized, but more closely integrated.[65] As early as 1964, Henry F. May argued that American historiography had rediscovered religion,[66] and we might note the significant place that religion plays in much American historiography, just as it does in Amer-

---

[63] Charles Taylor, *A Secular Age* (Cambridge, MA, 2007), 428–9.

[64] Alister Chapman, 'Intellectual History and Religion in Modern Britain', in Chapman et al., eds, *Seeing Things Their Way*, 226–39, at 229.

[65] John Coffey and Alister Chapman, 'Introduction: Intellectual History and the Return of Religion', in Chapman et al., eds, *Seeing Things Their Way*, 1–23, at 4.

[66] Henry F. May, 'The Recovery of American Religious History', *AHR* 70 (1964), 79–92.

ican national life. Think, for example, of the work of Richard Carwardine, both his work on Evangelicalism in America before the Civil War and also the significance he gave to religious opinion in his biography of Lincoln.[67] In Britain, however, the turn to religion is a much more recent phenomenon; while its impact is now widely recognized in literary studies and increasingly in intellectual history, it might profitably be extended more obviously into the sphere of church history. Sarah Apetrei has energetically engaged with this new trend, locating her work on women in Enlightenment England in the framework of this religious turn, and urging the need 'for a fresh engagement with the mysterious, transcendent aspects of religious commitment and thought', in order to put religion at the centre of intellectual history.[68] One might also single out the recent collection of essays edited by Jane Garnett and others, which seeks consciously to take the study of religion, and of Christianity and the church specifically, out of the shadow of secularization theory into new light. Recent books by two of Garnett's co-editors, Matthew Grimley and William Whyte, also integrate church history and intellectual history with notable success, drawing on ecclesiastical sources in order to do so.[69]

If British ecclesiastical history has lost its way over the last half-century, this cannot be unrelated to the churches' own loss of direction. Bishops and clergy no longer occupy the central position in our public and intellectual life that they did in the nineteenth century; the church does not play the same role in the life of the nation; and the new forms of religious expression manifest in our society do not lend themselves towards the creation of new modes of church history. Our failure is to have lost sight of the fundamentals of church history and the elements that made it distinctive; we have allowed secularist historians – many of them seduced by fashionable trends in historical method – to reduce our field to one where religion has merely social or cultural meaning.

---

[67] Richard Carwardine, *Evangelicals and Politics in Antebellum America* (New Haven, CT, 1993); idem, *Lincoln: A Life of Purpose and Power* (New York, 2006).

[68] Sarah Apetrei, *Women, Feminism and Religion in Early Enlightenment England* (Cambridge, 2010), 42.

[69] Jane Garnett et al., eds, *Redefining Christian Britain: Post-1945 Perspectives* (London, 2007); Matthew Grimley, *Citizenship, Community, and the Church of England: Liberal Anglican Theories of the State between the Wars* (Oxford, 2004); William Whyte, *Oxford Jackson: Architecture, Education, Status, and Style 1835–1924* (Oxford, 2006).

Ecclesiastical history should not seek to identify current political or cultural fashions in the past, or to deploy past eras to legitimate our particular present and its current preoccupations. We need to cleave to our plot, the grand narrative of the inspired origins and continuous – if complicated – development of the churches since apostolic times. And the Ecclesiastical History Society ought to be ideally placed to do just that. If this society is to have a future, it needs to engage directly with where secular historians have taken the study of Christianity and the churches, and to challenge those readings on methodological grounds. We should be promoting the argument that ecclesiastical history must be practised on the basis of an understanding and tolerance of the belief-claims of its adherents, not against predetermined frameworks that dismiss those claims at the outset. The annual volumes of Studies in Church History already demonstrate the additional substantial benefit that derives from the study of the history of the churches over long periods.

One aspect of this society in which its members rightly take pride lies in the assistance given by the conference, and the published proceedings, to promoting the careers of young scholars. What more could the society do to encourage new scholars in this field and especially to persuade graduate students to stay in church history, and not be seduced away into secular fields? The demographics of the conference speak for themselves: young people do attend, but many just pass through; they come to communicate (to read their own papers), but not to confer; we do not fully succeed in presenting the conference as an occasion to share ideas across time and space. Our future will lie in the hands of these younger generations: we need to work harder to engage them more directly in our activities. Another problem we should address is that ecclesiastical history not only does not dominate the discipline of history any more, in many institutions it no longer even occupies the same physical space. In so far as it thrives at all in this country, as already argued, church history may do best in institutions devoted to ministerial training (and perhaps in some theology departments). Of course we can affirm the value of ecclesiastical history as taught and studied beside theology, and recognize that ignorance of, and an inability to engage with, an informed understanding of the church's past remain as dangerous for today's clergy as for those of the mid-nineteenth century for whose edification my own professorial chair was created. Yet there are dangers in allowing church history to become merely a small element in the collection of disciplines that make up theology, for it risks becoming there little more than a brief guide to Patristics and the Reformation. Because the history of the churches and the history of theology penetrate all areas of historical enquiry, ignorance of the significant role of the churches in the past, or an acquaintance only with an ecclesiastical history purged of its spirituality, diminishes all educated members of a civilized society.[70]

My own ambition in writing and teaching about ecclesiastical history has always been to restore to past Christian generations their present, and to recognize the subjects of my enquiries as thoughtful, sentient and often genuinely spiritual people, not the victims of an oppressive ideology. In such aspiration, I adhere closely to the principles followed by our earliest leaders. David Knowles, our first president, wrote to a friend in 1964 remarking on how his teaching and writing had changed as a result of his move to Cambridge: 'I felt that, having arrived most unexpectedly in a chair, and being a catholic priest, it was right to appeal to as wide an audience as possible, not with apologetics but with history in which Christianity was taken for granted as true.'[71] From my own lay perspective, I tend to articulate such a view only in my capacity as a canon when preaching in Christ Church Cathedral. But I do aspire to write and teach a history of Christianity in which I take it for granted that those whose pasts I study, unless they provide direct evidence to the contrary, accepted their faith as true. For, if we do not hold onto the fundamental plot that defines our discipline and teach an ecclesiastical past, how can we hope to have an ecclesial present? In narrating the significance of those ecclesiastical pasts to a wider public, the Ecclesiastical History Society has a key role to play.

---

[70] J. G. Dowling, *An Introduction to the Critical Study of Ecclesiastical History* (London, 1838), 2: 'an acquaintance with the facts of Ecclesiastical history is as indispensably necessary to the statesman and the philosopher as it is to the professional divine. ... Whenever it has been neglected, the consequence has uniformly been a melancholy increase of disorder and error.'

[71] David Knowles, letter to 'JHCA', 14 April 1964, quoted in Alberic Stacpoole, 'The Making of a Monastic Historian', *Ampleforth Journal* 80/2 (Summer 1975), 17–38, at 17.

As Stella Fletcher has reminded us, this is 'a very *agreeable* society'. I have been pleased to belong to it continuously since I first joined in 1988, to have been permitted to publish a small number of papers in Studies in Church History, and to have participated in several of its scholarly and convivial conferences, most recently in the company of some of my own graduate students. I was flattered to be asked to serve as the society's president in this anniversary year and am proud to do so. In our next fifty years, I sincerely hope we will be no less agreeable an organization. But I might further wish that we would engage more directly with the conceptual and methodological issues that concern the rest of the historical profession. Our reluctance to do so is not new. As early as 1964, David Knowles wrote about church historians, saying: 'No class of historian has found the presentation of its subject matter in terms of ideas so difficult and so perilous. … Church historians in general say too little about the changes of cultures and of mental climates.'[72] If we would address more obviously contemporary cultural changes and the mental climate of the wider discipline to which we belong, we would be better equipped to fulfil our stated charitable objects, of advancing public education by fostering and promoting the study of and interest in ecclesiastical history. Agreeableness need not condemn us to the avoidance of disagreement. It is time for ecclesiastical historians to speak out against the secularizing trends evident most obviously in the new cultural history, to show how powerfully a religious turn can illuminate both ecclesiastical and secular pasts, and to reassert our centrality within the historical profession.

Christ Church, Oxford

---

[72] David Knowles, 'Foreword' to Albert Mirgeler, *Mutations of Western Christianity* (Mainz, 1961; English edn London, 1964).

PART I

THE CHURCHES' USE OF THE PAST

INTIMATIONS OF A MASSACRE: THESSALONICA, THEODOSIUS I AND SELF-IRONIZATION IN SOCRATES SCHOLASTICUS'S *HISTORIA ECCLESIASTICA*

by LUKE GARDINER

From the vantage point of Constantinople in AD 440, under the rule of the orthodox Theodosian dynasty, Nicene Christianity may have appeared unassailable. Many of the most challenging of the heresies that had emerged in the century since Constantine's conversion seemed to be receding. Even the devastating Christological controversies that had erupted in the early 430s may (understandably, if wrongly) have looked, with Nestorius's deposition and the Formula of Reunion (433), to be under control. And yet Constantinople retained its confessional diversity, with members of numerous Christian sects – penalized by law theoretically, but often still visible and vocal in practice – living alongside members of the mainstream Nicene church.[1]

The reimposition of a Nicene hierarchy over the major churches of Constantinople had happened only from the 380s onwards. It had been a process fraught with difficulties – not least the survival in large numbers of groups polemically labelled as Arian, and the persistence of their intellectual, theological and historical traditions, even as their hopes of political or theological hegemony faded. From this milieu had come the Eunomian Philostorgius (c.368–439), and his highly sectarian – and anti-Nicene – *Church History* of the fourth and fifth centuries.

Conversely, from the Nicene community there emerged a broad, and often similarly sectarian, body of theological and historical writings and propaganda targeted at contemporary 'Arians' and their forebears.[2] Writing at this time was Socrates Scholasticus

---

[1] See Rochelle Snee, 'Gregory Nazianzen's Anastasia Church: Arianism, the Goths, and Hagiography', *DOP* 52 (1998), 157–86, esp. 157–8.
[2] On Constantinopolitan Nicene anti-Arian propaganda, see Rochelle Snee, 'Valens' Recall of the Nicene Exiles and Anti-Arian Propaganda', *Greek, Roman, and Byzantine Studies* 26 (1985), 395–419.

(c.380–?),[3] whose monumental *Church History* appeared around 440. Relatively little is known for certain of his background, beyond his literary education and his association with the circle of the sophist Troilus, but he was certainly a member of the Nicene community.[4] Socrates' historical project was underpinned by a deep concern to expose the numerous, often self-serving or self-deceiving, attempts of contemporaries to use texts to their own advantage, from the polemical citation of documentary evidence in sectarian disputes to the cynical usage of Scripture – both citations and physical text – by bishops during internecine disputes.[5] The misuse of texts was a perennial concern for church historians, going back to Eusebius of Caesarea (c.263–339), who had, in apologetic, exegetical and historical writings, defended aspects of Christian theology and pioneered influential visions of the Christian polity during the transition from persecution to triumph at the start of the fourth century.

In Socrates' *History*, among such manipulated, contested and perhaps dangerous narratives was history itself. Heretical historians such as Sabinus (*fl.* 370s) were criticized for sectarian, partial historical narratives.[6] But Socrates' historical project was not simply about exposing the tendentiousness of heretics. Rather, the narratives of (to him) orthodox church historians were often themselves understood as biased textual weapons, deployed in political or religious disputes by their authors and later generations.

Socrates depicted Eusebius of Caesarea as a heresy-hunter and a flatterer of the Christian emperor Constantine (306–37), more concerned with sycophancy than accuracy. Eusebius's *Life of Constantine*, he argued, was deformed by panegyrical praise; it required correction, not continuation.[7] Socrates also bore witness

---

3   For Socrates' *Church History* [hereafter: *HE*], I use *Sokrates. Kirchengeschichte*, ed. Günther Christian Hansen (Berlin, 1995); for the *Church Histories* of Rufinus and Eusebius [hereafter also: *HE*], *Eusebius Werke 2: Die Kirchengeschichte*, ed. Eduard Schwartz and Theodor Mommsen, 3 vols (Berlin, 1999).

4   On Socrates, see Theresa Urbainczyk, *Socrates of Constantinople: Historian of Church and State* (Ann Arbor, MI, 1997); Martin Wallraff, *Der Kirchenhistoriker Sokrates: Untersuchungen zu Geschichtsdarstellung, Methode und Person* (Göttingen: 1997); Peter Van Nuffelen, *Un héritage de paix et de piété. Étude sur les histoires ecclésiastiques de Socrate et Sozomène* (Louvain, 2004). On Socrates' supposed Novatianism, see n. 29 below.

5   e.g. Socrates, *HE* 1.6.41, 7.13.20.

6   e.g. Socrates, *HE* 1.8.24–8.

7   Socrates' text begins (*HE* 1.1.1–2) by noting the need to retell the origins of

to the ways in which such texts were deployed after their authors' deaths in theological disputes; he felt compelled to defend Eusebius's orthodoxy against 'Arian' attempts at appropriation, scouring his writings for statements of correct belief, and noting, conversely, that for some Nicenes, Eusebius remained a heretic, and one who had used his tendentiously edited account of the aftermath of Nicaea as a vehicle for legitimating Arianism.[8] Elsewhere, Socrates observed Nicene churchmen using the writing of history, and the authority that consequently accrued to them, as leverage in church politics against their Nicene co-religionists.[9] Historians always had to be aware of how their beliefs and desire for authority might influence others, especially given the possibility of an audience as exalted as an emperor.

Socrates' text was informed by broad and sophisticated methodological concerns over the writing of history, many of which have recently been explored by Peter Van Nuffelen and Martin Wallraff.[10] Important to Socrates was an openness about the limits of historical knowledge. Gone was the optimistic Eusebian desire to have God as co-author.[11] For Socrates, certainty over divine intervention in human history was circumscribed.[12] Similarly, the causes of earthly events often remained painfully irrecoverable, and choosing between alternative accounts of what happened in particular episodes impossible.[13] Absolutely central to composing balanced – and humble – historiography was an opposition to bias. The tendentious omission of inconvenient evidence was repeatedly excoriated in Socrates' assessments of other historians.[14] Yet despite his professed commitment to methodological rigour – expressed often through polemical exposure of perceived problems with other historical texts and those manipulating them – he proved, on some occasions, less than committed to playing by his

---

Arianism, as Eusebius's narrative was deformed by political, panegyrical concerns.

8 See ibid. 1.23.6. At 2.21, Socrates, at perhaps telling length, cited sections of Eusebius's *Contra Marcellum* to prove his orthodoxy.

9 e.g. Socrates, *HE* 7.26.

10 Van Nuffelen, *Héritage*, 163–242, 262–79, 290–303, 307–12; Wallraff, *Sokrates*, 135–207.

11 Eusebius, *HE* 1.1.3.

12 e.g. Socrates, *HE* 3.1.41.

13 e.g. ibid. 6.19.8.

14 e.g. ibid. 1.10.4.

own rules. How, then, are we to interpret incidents when theory and practice do not coincide?

My focus in this essay is on a series of conjoined passages dealing with the reigns of Valens (364–78) and Theodosius I (379–95), which distort the accepted chronological order of key events and repeatedly violate Socrates' explicit methodological commitment to avoiding bias. Specifically, I wish to explore the much discussed lack of an account of the infamous massacre at Thessalonica in Socrates' *History*.[15] Rather than seeing this as a case of genuine bias towards Nicene emperors, rendering discussed objectivity mere window-dressing, it will be argued that, in a number of ways, the narrative subtly highlights its own flaws, pressing the reader to question Socrates' claims to impartiality – and the possibility of true objectivity in historical narrative.

★ ★ ★

For what has become such a symbolic moment, it is surprisingly difficult to reconstruct what precisely occurred at Thessalonica, or why it did so. Excellent accounts of the massacre and its consequences include those of Neil McLynn,[16] Frank Kolb[17] and Robert Frakes.[18] To summarize and simplify: in 391 a group of Thessalonicans killed Butheric, the resident *magister militum* (military commander), for detaining a popular charioteer. Partly on Emperor Theodosius's orders, and partly as a result of opportunistic score-settling, imperial troops indiscriminately slaughtered thousands of civilians. In the aftermath, Theodosius was castigated by Bishop Ambrose of Milan (337/40–97), who refused to give him communion. Theodosius and Ambrose resolved the resulting impasse in a carefully calibrated scene of public repentance. Both in

[15] See, most recently, Urbainczyk, *Socrates*, 161–70; Daniel Washburn, 'The Thessalonian Affair in the Fifth-Century Histories', in Harold Drake, ed., *Violence in Late Antiquity: Perceptions and Practices* (Aldershot, 2006), 215–24; cf. Van Nuffelen, *Héritage*, 388–9.

[16] Neil McLynn, *Ambrose of Milan: Church and Court in a Christian Capital* (Berkeley, CA, 1994), 315–30.

[17] Frank Kolb, 'Der Bußakt von Mailand: zum Verhältnis von Staat und Kirche in der Spätantike', in *Geschichte und Gegenwart: Festschrift für K.-D. Erdmann*, ed. H. Boockmann, K. Jürgensen and G. Stoltenberg (Neumünster, 1980), 41–74.

[18] Robert Frakes, 'Butheric and the Charioteer', in idem, Elizabeth DePalma Digeser and Justin Stephens, eds, *The Rhetoric of Power in Late Antiquity: Religion and Politics in Byzantium, Europe and the Early Islamic World* (London, 2010), 47–62.

Ambrose's contemporary presentation and in the following historical accounts, 'the catastrophe [was turned] into a public relations
triumph for the emperor'.[19] For the most part, narratives of Theodosius and the massacre at Thessalonica – whatever their ideological
commitment to the subordination of emperor to church – are
ultimately narratives of triumphal repentance. As McLynn notes,
'no source records the massacre in isolation; it is everywhere set in
the context supplied by the emperor's penance'.[20]

In the account of Rufinus (340/5–410), the deeply unedifying
episode was reimagined, with Theodosius as 'the principal actor
in a saga of repentance'.[21] Ambrose's machinations are missing
and, as elsewhere, Theodosius crowns his repentance by issuing
a general law staying imperial punitive orders by thirty days to
permit time for reconsideration.[22] Theodosius is ultimately praised
as a noble Christian monarch rectifying his mistakes, and (particularly important for Rufinus) deferring to, and working in harmony
with, the Nicene church, by submitting in penance to an Italian
bishop. This transformation of the episode from a problematic
moment in Theodosius's reign into an ultimately redemptive
scene emphasizing Theodosius's exemplary qualities was echoed
by Socrates' fellow church historians and near contemporaries,
Sozomen (*c.*400–50) and Theodoret (*c.*393–457), both of whom
also converted this problematic moment into a display of exemplary 'episcopal action and imperial piety',[23] as well as infusing
their narratives with concerns particular to each.

Like Sozomen and Theodoret, Socrates was a Nicene Christian
writing under Theodosius II (401–50) – a Nicene grandson of
Theodosius I – and, like Sozomen, he lived in Constantinople
at a time when the city was still riven with numerous, sometimes mutually hostile, Christian sects. Expectations of a narrative
sympathetic to Theodosius (and hostile to heterodox emperors) are
therefore understandable. The glaring absence of the massacre at
Thessalonica from Socrates' *History* is consequently highly anomalous, warranting an explanation. Why not, if concerned like the

---

[19] McLynn, *Ambrose*, 323.
[20] Ibid. 328.
[21] Washburn, 'Thessalonians', 222.
[22] Cf. McLynn, *Ambrose*, 322–3.
[23] Washburn, 'Thessalonians', 218.

other church historians to portray Theodosius favourably, use the account of Thessalonica set out by Rufinus, which subtly transformed the episode from a disaster to an edifying moment? All the more so, since Rufinus has long been recognized as an important source for Socrates' *Church History*.[24] Indeed, throughout the text Socrates frequently alerted readers to his critical engagement with Rufinus.[25] Even in the absence of such explicit name-checking, it is clear (as in his narrative of Theodosius's reign), that Socrates broadly followed the pattern of events outlined by Rufinus. He moved (with some new material added) from Gratian's assassination to Justina's machinations and the overthrow of Magnus Maximus, and then (omitting the massacre) on to ecclesiastical affairs in Antioch, followed by Egypt and the destruction of the Serapaeum (the temple of the god Serapis in Alexandria).[26] Along the way, Socrates continued to engage critically with the substance of Rufinus's accounts – particularly, as discussed below, that of the destruction of the Serapaeum. Socrates thus indicated that he had read the corresponding sections of Rufinus's text, but also hinted tantalizingly at what was missing in his own narrative.

In dealing with the massacre at Thessalonica, Daniel Washburn has suggested that, for Socrates, even to follow a pre-existing sympathetic narrative of imperial penance here would damage the image of an emperor with whom (and with whose Nicene beliefs) he sympathized.[27] Portraying Theodosius as 'disclosing imperial regret, and by implication, culpability' would associate Theodosius with the sort of violence Socrates elsewhere abhorred, and would contradict his wish to portray Theodosius 'as an impressive monarch who quelled disturbances, not the sort of ruler who was guilty of causing a bloodbath'.[28] Washburn understands Socrates' treatment of the massacre, like Rufinus's, to reflect a partisan, pro-Theodosius and pro-Nicene agenda. Since Socrates' abhorrence of

---

[24] Cf. Wallraff, *Sokrates*, 188–90, 254–5; Hartmut Leppin, 'The Church Historians (I): Socrates, Sozomenus, and Theodoretus', in G. Marasco, ed., *Greek and Roman Historiography in Late Antiquity* (Leiden, 2003), 219–54, at 227.

[25] Socrates, *HE* 1.12.10; 1.15.10; 1.19.10; 2.1.1; 3.19.8; 4.24.8.

[26] Cf. ibid. 5.11–17; Rufinus, *HE* 11.11–22.

[27] Cf. Washburn's refutation of Urbainczyk's suggestion that the absence depended upon the overriding importance for Socrates of presenting positive, balanced emperor-bishop relations (i.e. Thessalonica might show Ambrose with the whip-hand over Theodosius): 'Thessalonians', 221–2.

[28] Washburn, 'Thessalonians', 223.

violence vitiated the possibility of offering a redemptive narrative of penance, his partisan agenda manifested itself instead in full and glaring omission of the massacre.[29] This explanation is, however, problematic. Certainly, Socrates emphasized the need for preserving public order, and deployed it frequently as a criterion for assessing individual worth. But he did not elsewhere eschew mentioning (unfavourably) violence associated with Nicene monarchs, including Theodosius. Whilst, for instance, Socrates introduced new sections praising Theodosius for such actions as imposing order at Rome[30] and marginalizing sectarianism at Constantinople,[31] he depicted Theodosius rather less favourably than Rufinus in describing his role in what was, for Socrates, the violent and unedifying spectacle of the destruction of Alexandria's Serapaeum (391/2).[32] Gone were Rufinus's emphases on the legitimate precedents for appropriating the temple (such a move had been permitted for the building decades earlier by Constantius), on Theodosius's authorization of the move (in alliance with Alexandria's bishop, Theophilus) to give a new purpose to an abandoned building as a house of prayer to cater for growing numbers of Christians, and on Theodosius's instrumentality in quelling the resulting riots and his mercy in doing so.[33] Rather, without background or precedent, Socrates' Theodosius endorsed, at the request of Bishop Theophilus,[34] an attempt to destroy all the pagan temples in Alexandria at once, actively instructing the bishop on the procedure for dissolution, whilst taking no part in quelling the consequent bloodshed.[35] Socrates could, then, nuance his generally favourable assessment of Theodosius's reign, and do

---

[29] Socrates' evasion of Rufinus's penitential model is also attributed to his supposed membership of the Novatianists, a Nicene schismatic sect which denied the efficacy of institutional penance: Wallraff, *Sokrates*, 235–56. The evidence for Socrates' membership is, however, not conclusive: cf. Leppin, 'Historians', 221–2. Indeed, in places Socrates may perhaps be seen as critical of the sect precisely because of their hostility towards institutional penance, e.g. in his giving prominence to Constantine's criticism of this hostility: *HE* 1.10.3–4. Socrates' attitude towards the efficacy of institutional penance elsewhere is far from being one of uncomplicated hostility.

[30] Socrates, *HE* 5.18.

[31] Ibid. 5.8, 10.

[32] Ibid. 5.16.

[33] Rufinus, *HE* 11.22.

[34] For Socrates, Theophilus was highly objectionable (e.g. *HE* 6.2) – not an ideal figure with whom to associate.

[35] Ibid. 5.16.11.

so through critical association of Theodosius with violence. Why, then, neither treat Thessalonica critically, nor – if he had genuinely wanted to put an exculpatory spin on the episode – follow the subtly and much less obviously tendentious narrative of repentance set out in the other church histories? Why appear more immediately and unsubtly tendentious through omitting the episode entirely?[36]

Or perhaps not entirely. Rufinus's account of the massacre at Thessalonica had a strikingly unusual beginning: 'At the same time the pious sovereign was vilely besmirched by the demon's cunning.' Demonic forces cause Theodosius's violent reaction to the murder of the *magister militum* Butheric. This is very unusual: as far as I know this is the only time when Rufinus himself depicted demons as intervening to change the course of historical events, and certainly the only time they act upon a Christian emperor. Rufinus's striking introduction was directly echoed in Socrates. Rufinus's Latin, 'Per idem tempus subreptione quadam daemonis, turpis macula religioso principi inusta' ('At the same time, by some insidious act of a demon, a shameful mark was branded onto the pious monarch')[37] was adapted by Socrates into Greek: "Ὑπὸ δὲ τὸν αὐτὸν χρόνον καὶ δαίμων τις ἀλάστωρ τῇ τοῦ βασιλέως ὠμότητι ἀπεχρήσατο' ('At the same time an avenging demon exploited the king's cruelty').[38] This allusive echo (which has not, to my knowledge, been noticed before) is arresting: beyond the directly translated temporal clause, the occurrence here of demons as active forces in history is effectively unparalleled elsewhere in Socrates' text.[39] That the target is a Christian emperor is all the more striking.

The line from Rufinus is redeployed to introduce Socrates' account of the magic and treason trials in Antioch of the emperor Valens in 371/2.[40] For Socrates, Valens was heterodox – indeed, a committed Arian Christian. In Socrates' account the magic trials are embedded within one of the longest continuous sections dedi-

---

[36] That Socrates was not committed slavishly to the Theodosian dynasty is clear also in his critical account of the relationship between Theodosius II and Nestorius: HE 7.29–33.

[37] Rufinus, HE 11.18.1.

[38] Socrates, HE 4.19.1.

[39] Cf. Wallraff, Sokrates, 261 (esp. on HE 3.21.15).

[40] Socrates, HE 4.19.

cated to depicting imperially sponsored violence and persecution within the *History*.[41] Elsewhere in his account of the emperor, Socrates presents a notably more measured description of Valens's actions. Yet here, in this relentless narrative of Valens's persecutions, balance seems to give way to hyperbole and tendentiousness, with chronological manipulation and compression deployed to imply an unremitting and extreme period of oppression. Nowhere is this impression clearer than in the account of the magic and treason trials.

In Socrates' version of the sordid events in Antioch a demon – the Rufinian echo – caused disturbances by exploiting Valens's anger on discovering that certain individuals had sought through magical divination to ascertain the identity of his imperial successor. The demon had revealed the first four letters of the next emperor's name: ΘΕΟΔ – enough for the conspirators to leap to conclusions. Knowledge of this prophecy quickly reached Valens, who, 'instead of committing the matter to God, who alone can penetrate the future',[42] also lent credit to the demonic prophecy and began summarily executing anyone whose name began with those letters.

Beyond the deliberate transposition of Rufinus's introduction to his narrative of the Thessalonian affair, Socrates's account of these purges is stylized to hint at Theodosius I and subtly to draw attention to the absence of the Thessalonian massacre in the account of Theodosius's reign, later in the *History*, in other ways. However ambiguous the demon's revelation was, it also turned out to be true: Theodosius I did succeed Valens. Theodosius's refracted presence here was augmented by Socrates' cryptic reference to one victim, 'Theodosiolus', a 'very brave man, descended from Spanish nobility'. This individual was mentioned nowhere else in

---

41 Listed consecutively (*HE* 4.15–22), with little attention paid to distinguishing chronological gaps and with the appearance of wilful distortion, are: Valens's execution of a number of Nicene presbyters at sea; Valens's persecution at Antioch of Nicenes, which can be dated to 370; next, the persecution at Edessa, implied as contemporaneous but most likely occurring in 375 (Noel Lenski, *Failure of Empire: Valens and the Roman State in the Fourth Century A.D.* [Berkeley, CA, 2003], 257); then the magic trials at Antioch in 371/2, followed by Athanasius's death, here placed in 371 rather than the well-attested 373 (in Rufinus's narrative, Athanasius's death correctly precedes the Edessene massacres). Finally, there follows the judicial and extra-judicial violence in Alexandria under the Arian Lucius, an episode, like the purges, concerned with the chaotic, disruptive consequences of abrogating justice and rushing to judgement.

42 Socrates, *HE* 4.19.4.

the *History*, nor in any other historical text. Regardless of who was signified directly, by his very name, his Spanish background, and the suggestion of a 'brave' military career, 'Theodosiolus' functioned for the reader as a prefigurement of the future emperor.

Strikingly absent, however, from Socrates' account is any discussion of the contemporaneous actions of Valentinian I – Valens's Nicene brother and co-emperor. For Valentinian had presided over similar, and equally infamous, trials in Rome. These trials, beyond their general notoriety, would clearly have been known to Socrates, given his use of Ammianus Marcellinus (325/30–91; the great Latin historian of the fourth-century West) or a common source for the reigns of both emperors.[43] Moreover, Socrates had earlier demonstrated an awareness of Valentinian's hostility towards magic-users in the third book of the *History*.[44] Socrates' dispassionate reference there to Valentinian's execution, for sorcery, of Maximus of Ephesus, heightens expectations that Valentinian's more extensive magic trials at Rome would later be mentioned These expectations were to be dashed: Socrates chose to portray Valens here as an angry tyrant, whilst refraining from showing the Nicene Valentinian's analogous misdeeds.[45]

Why, then, through the deliberate transposition of a striking line from Rufinus, was a massacre intimated that would then be omitted from the appropriate place in Socrates' *History*? And, crucially, what did embedding this intimation in the account of Valens's paranoid purges achieve? Encountered alone, a gruesome

---

[43] Peter Van Nuffelen, 'Dürre Wahrheiten: zwei Quellen des Berichts von Socrates Scholasticus über die Versorgungskrise in Antiochien 362/3', *Philologus* 147 (2003), 352–6, at 353; cf. idem, *Héritage*, 465 n. 15.

[44] Socrates, *HE* 3.1.16.

[45] Mirroring his portrayal of Theodosius, Socrates' depiction of Valens was not, aside from this series of episodes, uniformly hostile. This suggests here also an attempt to simulate the appearance of sectarian tendentiousness (this time unalloyed hostility to a heretical emperor). Whilst Socrates was generally critical of Valens, he was, when compared with his sources, more willing to introduce episodes into the church historical tradition favourable to Valens. After this series of events, Valens moderated persecution, not cynically, but persuaded by good advice; he permitted settlement of the Goths with uncharacteristic kindness; before the Adrianople debacle he even won victories; and (unlike in other accounts) he did not die as the result of divine punishment: *HE* 4.32.5, 4.34.2, 4.38. Earlier on, Socrates had praised Valens, with Valentinian, for refusing apostasy under Julian; in temporal matters, Valens reigned as well as Valentinian for a time: ibid. 4.1.8–11. Furthermore, despite being generally in favour of Valentinian (ibid. 4.1.12–13, 4.29.1), and omitting his magic trials at Rome, Socrates could be more nuanced elsewhere: ibid. 4.31.10–18.

narrative of the misdeeds of a heterodox emperor, or the omission of a major – and problematic – event like the Thessalonian
affair from the reign of an orthodox emperor might be best attributed to clumsily concealed sectarian bias. But the alignment of
the two suggests the absence of even an unsubtle attempt to pass
off surreptitiously a tendentious sectarian narrative as objective
historiography. Rather, partisanship – or the simulation of partisanship – appears positively and intentionally conspicuous here.
Further highlighting the issue of partiality at this juncture is the
broader texture of the narrative of the purges. For on one level the
episode offers an object lesson in human weakness and credulity
in the face of a cheap half-truth. The absurdly grotesque nature
of the episode is revealed as violence spirals out of control, based
upon the flimsiest information. Both conspirators and emperor
are satisfied with shadowy intimations and the slightest pretexts to
authorize their actions.

The longer version of the magic trials offered by the historian
Ammianus Marcellinus may also be of some help here.[46] Coming at
the head of often tangled narratives that recounted a much longer
series of trials in which half-truths and assumptions summarily
condemned innocent and guilty alike, the episode was ordered,
as Christopher Kelly has noted, to act as a lodestar for readers
in assessing the partial or perhaps unbelievable accounts of Valens
and Valentinian themselves that Ammianus himself provided. In
rushing to judgement,

> ... the reader was at risk of reiterating Valens's own behaviour
> ... the challenge to the reader is not to collude too closely
> with either emperors or conspirators. Rather, it is to seize
> upon the ambiguities and inconcinnities in the account, to
> resist the drive to fill in the gaps and make coherent sense
> of the material, and so assemble a definitive case against the
> emperors themselves.[47]

As with Ammianus, for Socrates, recounting the purges forced

---

[46] Ammianus, *Res Gestae* 29.1, on Valens's trials; cf. ibid. 28.1 onwards for Valentinian's.

[47] Christopher Kelly, 'Crossing the Frontiers: Imperial Power in the Last Book of
Ammianus', in J. Den Boeft et al., eds, *Ammianus after Julian: The Reign of Valentinian
and Valens in Books 26–31 of the* Res Gestae (Leiden, 2007), 271–92, at 290.

similar questions of partiality, incompleteness and judgement before the reader. With its focus on erroneous judgements and its omission of the expected account of Valentinian's trials, Socrates' account may perhaps be calling attention to the inadequacies of its narrative, and of its narrator – inadequacies that would render consequent assessments of the emperors under consideration problematic. It is not, I think, coincidental that Socrates should choose very soon after this episode to offer a concrete demonstration of precisely how sectarian bias might compromise historiographical objectivity. Concluding the series of persecutions – of which the purges were part – undertaken by Valens were Socrates' accounts of the violence inflicted by the emperor and his allies against the Nicene population of Egypt.[48] Here Socrates included an authorial aside on objectivity: 'Of the outrages perpetrated ... Sabinus takes not the slightest notice. In fact, half disposed to Arianism himself, he purposely veils the atrocities of his friends'.[49] The heterodox historian Sabinus cannot truthfully tell the full story about the violent excesses of Valens, his co-religionist. This sort of criticism, here and elsewhere, functioned as a standard against which Socrates' historiographical objectivity was articulated, naturally inviting comparison. Alongside the many ways in which partisanship and partiality had been placed in the foreground in this part of the *History*, this implicit invitation to critical comparison becomes almost an injunction. Socrates' omission of the misdeeds of his own co-religionists, Valentinian and Theodosius, is now returned to the fore. The question looms: can the reader trust the historian who devised a sophisticated methodology in order to lay bare the processes of historical writing to defuse its dangers – partiality, pretended certainty, self-aggrandizement – when his narrative, too, is defective?

By omitting the Thessalonian massacre Socrates made the appearance of tendentiousness unavoidable. The appearance was amplified as Socrates archly heralded and aligned this conspicuous void with his treatment of episodes in the reign of the Arian Valens, which itself appeared uncharacteristically tendentious in its unremitting hostility, and which was set against a reminder of how sectarian bias mutilated historical narrative. One way of understanding this unsubtle – and in a sense self-advertising – tenden-

---

[48] Socrates, *HE* 4.21–2, cf. 4.24.
[49] Ibid. 4.22.1.

tiousness is as evidence that Socrates valued, here, the appearance of being tendentious for the Nicene cause.

This glaring act of partisanship seems consonant neither with Socrates' wider critical approach to partisan historiography, nor with his generally favourable, but in places critical, approach to the reign of Theodosius. And even had Socrates genuinely wished, from Nicene sympathies or imperial loyalties – violating methodological commitments or cynically using them as a smokescreen – to put a positive gloss on the bloody affair at Thessalonica, absolute omission was not a sensible or natural approach. Indeed, a subtle exculpatory narrative model, developed by Rufinus and adapted by Socrates' Nicene successors, was already available, more apposite and, as I have argued, usable for Socrates. Tendentious narrative succeeds when it is artful – when it is not glaringly obvious, and does not call attention to itself. Had Socrates genuinely been writing tendentiously, to advance and naturalize a particular Nicene perspective, rather than to call attention to his tendentiousness, he would, I suggest, have followed the other church historians here.

Instead, Socrates carefully induced a moment of dislocation for the reader, a burst of concern that his narrative might be compromised by precisely those flaws he had sought to transcend, showing how the writing of history could never – whatever the pretences to objectivity – entirely be separated from sectarian agendas. The reasonableness and humility of Socrates' methodology might facilitate a renunciation of absolute certainty, partiality and self-serving claims to authority. But such a humble stance could itself, through generating a sense of seeming credibility, objectivity and moderation, dangerously inflate the value of the historical work for those perennially concerned with deploying historical narratives as justificatory texts in internecine church politics. It might also be adopted cynically by those composing historical narrative for their own advantage. For Socrates truly to be able to disrupt such potential misuse of church history, he had to attack the notion of the perfect – and perfectly objective – church historian. And only the sight of a historian, striving so hard, yet seemingly unable to live up to the promise of balance and neutrality on display in his methodology, could achieve that.

Corpus Christi College, Cambridge

CONSTRUCTING THE APOSTOLIC PAST: THE CASE OF DIONYSIUS THE AREOPAGITE

by ANDREW LOUTH

Somewhere around the 620s, there began to appear in the Byzantine world references to works allegedly by Dionysius the Areopagite, that is, the judge of the court of the Areopagus converted by Paul the apostle according to the account in Acts 17. The corpus of works consisted of two works, on the heavenly and earthly church respectively, the *Celestial Hierarchy* and the *Ecclesiastical Hierarchy*; a treatise called the *Divine Names*; a short treatise called the *Mystical Theology*; and ten letters, addressed to various people, arranged hierarchically, from a monk called Gaius, through lesser clergy, bishops (or 'hierarchs') such as Polycarp and Titus, to the apostle John.[1] Although they were initially cited by Monophysite theologians who rejected the Council of Chalcedon, there was little resistance to the acceptance of this body of texts; gradually in the course of the sixth century these works came to be regarded as genuinely belonging to the apostolic period.[2]

In a somewhat mystifying way, the author acquired a multiple identity: various known 'Dionysii' came to be identified with him. The name he assumed identified him with the judge of the Areopagus. Already, as we shall see, that Dionysius had been identified with an early bishop of Athens of the same name. There is no particular reason to doubt this identification. Later on, in the ninth century, the author was further identified with St Denys of Paris. The events of the life of Dionysius of Paris himself had already experienced some development: according to Gregory of Tours, he had been one of seven bishops sent to convert Gaul, and as bishop of Paris had been martyred on the 'hill of the Martyr',

---

[1] For a critical edition, see *Corpus Dionysiacum*, 1: *De divinis nominibus*, ed. Beate Regina Suchla [hereafter: *DN*]; 2: *De coelesti hierarchia, De ecclesiastica hierarchia* [hereafter: *EH*], *De mystica theologia, Epistulae* [hereafter: *ep.*], ed. Günter Heil and Adolf Martin Ritter, Patristische Texte und Studien 33, 36 (Berlin, 1990–1).

[2] For the early reception of Dionysius, see Andrew Louth, 'The Reception of Dionysius up to Maximus the Confessor', in Sarah Coakley and Charles M. Stang, eds, *Re-Thinking Dionysius the Areopagite* (Oxford, 2009), 43–53.

Montmartre, in Paris.[3] In the seventh century the relics of this martyr were translated to the royal abbey of St Denys, north of Paris. By the eighth century, it was believed that the first-century 'pope' Clement of Rome had sent him to Gaul. During the ninth century, in the course of diplomatic negotiations between the Carolingian court of Louis the Pious and the Byzantine court of Michael II, Denys of Paris was identified with Dionysius the Areopagite, and a *Life* was composed by Hilduin, abbot of St Denys, who wove together the lives of the Athenian judge and later bishop, the author of the Dionysian corpus and the apostle of Paris.[4] Later, this composite figure began to unravel: Abelard doubted that the Parisian saint was identical with the author of the Dionysian writings, and from the Renaissance onwards doubts were expressed about the idea that the disciple of Paul could have been the author of the treatises ascribed to him. Finally, at the end of the nineteenth century, two scholars, H. Koch and J. Stiglmayr, independently put it beyond doubt that the author of the *Corpus Areopagiticum* was indebted to the Neoplatonism of Proclus, and so could be no earlier than the late fifth century.

For the most part, the scholarly reaction to this has been to seek to crack the pseudonymity of 'Dionysius the Areopagite'. This has resulted in a long succession of attempts at identification that have generally satisfied no one other than the originator, though occasionally an identification has for a time found a following, most recently Peter the Iberian.[5] It seems that the one who wanted to be known as 'Dionysius the Areopagite' did such a good job in disguising his identity that it will never be uncovered now.

There is, however, another question we might ask, and it is one particularly appropriate to this volume: how did the author of the

3   Gregory of Tours, *History of the Franks* 1.30 (transl. Lewis Thorpe, Penguin Classics [Harmondsworth, 1974], 87).

4   On this, see Andrew Louth, 'St Denys the Areopagite and the Iconoclast Controversy', in *Denys l'Aréopagite et sa postérité en orient et en occident: Actes du colloque international, Paris, 21–24 septembre 1994*, ed. Ysabel de Andia, Collections des études augustiniennes, serié antiquité 151 (Paris, 1997), 329–39, esp. 336–7.

5   Already in 1969, Hathaway had listed twenty-two contenders: R. F. Hathaway, *Hierarchy and the Definition of Order in the Letters of Pseudo-Dionysius* (The Hague, 1969), 31–5. More recently, see the Introduction to Pseudo-Dionysius Areopagita, *Über die Mystische Theologie und Briefe*, intro., transl. and notes by A. M. Ritter (Stuttgart, 1994), 4–19; Beate Regina Suchla, *Dionysius Areopagita. Leben – Werke – Wirkung* (Freiburg, 2008), 24–5.

Corpus Areopagiticum go about constructing the apostolic or sub-apostolic past, to which he wanted to be thought to belong? Long ago, Hans Urs von Balthasar, in his chapter on Dionysius (Denys) in *Herrlichkeit*, remarked:

> He could not situate himself in the apostolic period on his own; he must transfer to that period his relationships, his theological and spiritual acquaintances. The person of his much-lauded teacher whom he calls Hierotheus and whom he regards as a disciple of Paul and to whom he maintains that he owes everything of importance is undoubtedly a real person ...

Von Balthasar goes on to suggest that the people to whom Dionysius refers throughout the *Corpus*, with names from the sub-apostolic period, are really contemporaries of the sixth-century author, 'only their names are transferred into the apostolic age'.[6] Perhaps something like that is the case, but it seems to me that the assignment of these sub-apostolic names was not a matter of arbitrary choice; they evoke associations that the reader is meant to be able to pick up. It must be the case that Dionysius, as I shall call the author of the *Corpus*, is constructing a picture of the apostolic past into which he projects himself and those with whom he is engaged in argument and dialogue, and in doing so finding these arguments already adumbrated in that past in some way. It seems to me at least interesting to try and work out how Dionysius sought to achieve this, for it may give us some more definite notion as to what he was attempting to achieve by his brazen, and successful, work of forgery. It is curious that the theme of multiple identity was already there as the unknown author put on the cloak of Dionysius, for his 'Dionysius' was both Athenian philosopher and Athenian hierarch; it is hardly surprising that his identity was to multiply further.

It would be most interesting to pursue this on the theological and philosophical level, and an attempt by Charles Stang to do this has recently been published;[7] an earlier article offers a sketch of

---

6 Hans Urs von Balthasar, *The Glory of the Lord. A Theological Aesthetics*, 2: *Studies in Theological Style: Clerical Styles* (Edinburgh, 1984), 150.
7 Charles M. Stang, *Apophasis and Pseudonymity in Dionysius the Areopagite: 'No Longer I'* (Oxford, 2012).

his argument.[8] In this brief essay what I want to do is to demonstrate that in building up his picture of the apostolic (or sub-apostolic) community to which he wanted to be thought to belong, Dionysius drew much of his material from Eusebius's *History of the Church*,[9] something that is betrayed by the various parallels that can be detected between Eusebius and Dionysius, which include not just parallels of substance but – perhaps even more telling – odd coincidences that can hardly be explained in any other way.[10]

We might start with Dionysius himself. Although there is nothing explicit in the *Corpus*, it is difficult to avoid the impression that Dionysius was a hierarch or bishop. However, the idea that the judge of the court of the Areopagus became bishop of Athens, though a natural conjecture, is no mere surmise: Eusebius asserts this twice, in both cases providing evidence, first in *History of the Church* 3.4 in which he deals with St Paul's immediate disciples, and again in 4.23, which deals with Dionysius, bishop of Corinth, whom Eusebius presents as an important second-century bishop, from whose letters he gleans various nuggets of information, including the assertion that Paul's Athenian convert became the first bishop of Athens.

Furthermore, it looks as if Dionysius (the author of the *Corpus*) paid careful attention to Eusebius's *History of the Church* 3.4. That chapter mentions various associates of Paul: Timothy and Titus, Luke the Evangelist, together with Linus and Clement, first and third bishops of Rome after Peter (Clement being identified with the Clement of Philippians 4: 3), as well as Dionysius himself. All of these, apart from Linus and Luke, are members of the imagined apostolic community of our Dionysius: Timothy as the recipient of all four of Dionysius's treatises; Titus of one of the letters (*ep.* 9); and Clement, 'the philosopher', mentioned as making a remark about the Platonic notion of *paradeigmata* of which Dionysius does not altogether approve (*DN* 5.9). It might seem strange to refer to Clement of Rome as 'the philosopher', though there are several

---

[8] Charles Stang, 'Dionysius, Paul and the Significance of the Pseudonym', in Coakley and Stang, eds, *Re-Thinking Dionysius*, 11–25.

[9] For a critical edition, see *Eusebius' Werke*, 2: *Die Kirchengeschichte*, ed. E. Schwartz and Th. Mommsen, 3 vols, GCS 9/1–3 (Leipzig, 1903–9) [hereafter: *HE*].

[10] This is an idea that came to me when I was writing my little introduction to Dionysius, *Denys the Areopagite* (London, 1989), just after editing for Penguin Classics a revised version of Eusebius's *History of the Church* (Harmondsworth, 1989).

passages in 1 Clement that draw on philosophical sources, notably
1 Clement 19–20.[11] Some have thought that there is some reference here to (or conflation with) Clement of Alexandria,[12] and
Dionysius may have made this association himself: which would
put some strain on the pseudonym he adopted – but more of that
later.

Other people mentioned by Dionysius are prominent in the
pages of Eusebius's *History of the Church*: the early second-century
bishop, Ignatius of Antioch (whose famous remark, 'My love was
crucified', is quoted in *DN* 4.12); and his younger contemporary, Polycarp, bishop of Smyrna (the addressee of *ep.* 7), to whom
Eusebius devotes a long chapter citing much of the text of the
account of his martyrdom.[13] It might be said that these figures are
so prominent in the history of the first half of the second century
that there is nothing striking about Dionysius's enlisting them. But
the truth is that our picture of the early church is still very much
that of Eusebius, not least when it comes to names and people.

There are other members of Dionysius's sub-apostolic confraternity whose presence becomes more understandable when one
recalls how Eusebius presents them. Bartholomew, for instance, is
evoked for the parallel he draws between theology – 'much and
most little' – and the Gospel – 'broad and great and yet concise'.
Bartholomew is a very shadowy apostolic figure; an apocryphal
'Gospel according to Bartholomew' is referred to by Jerome and
others, and some fragments of works associated with Bartholomew
survive. None of this sounds like Dionysius's Bartholomew. The
Book of Hierotheus mentions a Gospel of Bartholomew; but the
Book of Hierotheus is very likely dependent on Dionysius, the
only known attempt to extend his group of pseudonymous writings ('Hierotheus' is the name Dionysius gives to his mentor,
also presented as a disciple of Paul).[14] Eusebius, however, links

[11] See Andreas Lindemann, *Die Clemensbriefe*, Handbuch zum Neuen Testament 17,
Die Apostolischen Väter 1 (Tübingen, 1992), 67–77, esp. 76–7.

[12] e.g. I. P. Sheldon-Williams, in *The Cambridge History of Later Greek and Early
Medieval Philosophy*, ed. A. H. Armstrong (Cambridge, 1970), 457 n. 3. See also Beate
Suchla, in Pseudo-Dionysius Areopagita, *Die Namen Gottes* (Stuttgart, 1988), 119
(endnote 129).

[13] Eusebius, *HE* 4.14–15.

[14] For the apocryphal Bartholomew, see *New Testament Apocrypha*, ed. W.
Schneemelcher and R. McL. Wilson, 2 vols (London, 1963), 1: 484–508; *The Apocryphal New Testament*, ed. J. K. Elliott (Oxford, 1993), 654–76.

Bartholomew with Pantaenus.[15] Pantaenus, the 'Sicilian bee', was the teacher Clement found in Alexandria, and to whom he acknowledged much indebtedness.[16] Given the way in which some of the ideas of Neoplatonism were adumbrated in the 'Christian Platonism' of Alexandria, Pantaenus, presented by Eusebius as the source of this teaching, is someone with whom one might well expect Dionysius to feel some real affinity. Bartholomew, then, could well have been seen by Dionysius as the apostolic origin of the Alexandrian philosophy that chimed in so well with his own.

Another mysterious person is Gaius, the monk to whom the first four of Dionysius's letters are addressed. Gaius is also the addressee of 3 John, in which it is asserted that 'one who does evil has not seen God', and while it is true that the first letter of the four is about seeing God, it is not about the unexceptional point that evildoers are excluded from the vision of God, but rather about a mysterious darkness of unknowing, which is 'knowledge of the one who is beyond everything that is known'. It is, however, in the pages of Eusebius's *Church History* that we find a truly intriguing Gaius, the author, according to Photius,[17] of a work called by Theodoret the *Little Labyrinth*, from which Eusebius quotes extensively.[18] It is clear that Eusebius regarded Gaius as a man of great learning. If Dionysius is really enlisting Gaius, then his mask of pseudonymity is in serious danger of slipping, for Gaius belongs to the early third century (writing in the time of Pope Zephyrinus). However, Eusebius's first reference to him is in connection with Nero's persecution in the first century.[19] It is not impossible, therefore, that Dionysius mistakenly thought that Gaius was a figure of the late first century.

My suggestion is that, as well as enlisting those whom Eusebius associates with Paul, Dionysius is also attracted to what he may have regarded as the apostolic roots of the Alexandrian Platonism on which we know he drew,[20] and to which, as a Neoplatonist,

---

[15] Eusebius, *HE* 5.10.

[16] Clement of Alexandria, *Stromateis* 1.11.2; *Clemens Alexandrinus*, 2: *Stromata I–VI*, ed. O. Stählin, GCS 15 (Leipzig, 1906), 8–9.

[17] Photius, *Bibliotheca*, codex 48, ed. R. Henry (Paris, 1969), 34–5.

[18] Eusebius, *HE* 5.28.

[19] Ibid. 2.25, where he quotes from Gaius about the location of the relics of the Apostles Peter and Paul.

[20] The parallels between the treatment of love in Origen's preface to his *Commen-*

we would have expected him to have some affinity. Dionysius also found himself attracted by some of the mysterious learned men mentioned by Eusebius, not least Gaius. In both these cases there is clearly a danger of the Areopagite's pseudonymity being exposed: both Gaius and Clement of Alexandria (if he is Clement the 'philosopher': not, I think, a necessary deduction) are at least a century too late to have been contemporaries with Paul's Athenian convert, but if Bartholomew is invoked as the apostolic root of the teaching of Pantaenus, one might see Dionysius's strategy as one of creating a sense of different thinkers belonging to various early Christian traditions of philosophical learning amongst whom there was fruitful debate (Dionysius might have been attracted by the learning of the *Little Labyrinth*, but hardly, I think, by its content, and Clement 'the philosopher' is cited only to be criticized). But even if Dionysius runs the danger of anachronism, we need to remember that most Byzantines tended to telescope the past, and thus to have little sense of anachronism,[21] something that did not exclude occasional chronological acuity: to take an example from the later 'Dionysian' tradition, in his encomium of Dionysius based on Hilduin's *Vita*, Michael Syncellus corrects Hilduin's assertion that Dionysius was martyred under Domitian, as this would render impossible his knowledge of Ignatius's letter to the Romans, from which Dionysius had quoted in *De divinis nominibus*; Michael therefore has Dionysius martyred under the Emperor Trajan, like Ignatius.[22]

There are other figures who occur in Dionysius's writings and also in Eusebius, but in these cases either the link is very tenuous or they are much too well known to suggest any link. John the apostle, in exile on Patmos, is the recipient of *Epistula* 10; but John's exile on Patmos is evident from the Apocalypse – there would be no need for Eusebius's testimony.[23] Likewise, James the apostle is mentioned by Eusebius, but not in the context in which Dionysius locates him: the account of the Dormition of the Virgin Mary

---

tary on the Song of Songs and in Dionysius's DN 4.11–14 are too close to be coincidental.

[21] See, e.g., Cyril Mango, *Byzantium. The Empire of New Rome* (London, 1994), 189–200: ch. 10, 'The Past of Mankind'.

[22] Dionysius quoted from Ignatius, *ad Romanos* 7.2, at DN 4.12. For Michael's correction of Hilduin, see Louth, 'Denys and the Iconoclast Controversy', 338.

[23] Eusebius, HE 3.18.

(indeed James's prominence in Dionysius's account is at odds with the apocryphal accounts of the Dormition). Dionysius's Carpus seems to have nothing to do with the Carpus mentioned in Eusebius, even though he is mentioned in Eusebius's *Church History* at the end of the chapter devoted to Polycarp's martyrdom, as another martyr (not the monk of Dionysius's story: *ep.* 8.6); nor is it likely that there is any connection between the 'sacred Justus' mentioned by Dionysius and any of those mentioned by Eusebius. There are also five names that do not occur in Eusebius at all: Demophilus, Dorotheus, Elymas the magician, Sosipater and Hierotheus. The last mentioned is an enormously important figure for Dionysius, presented as being, like him, a disciple of the apostle Paul and also his own mentor, to whom various pieces of Dionysian teaching are attributed.

There is a further instance, however, where we can be confident that Dionysius is borrowing from Eusebius: his use of the term *therapeutes* for a monk. Throughout his writings, Dionysius consistently refers to monks as *therapeutai*. The first four letters are addressed to Gaius the *therapeutes*, and in *Epistula* 8 (to Demophilus the *therapeutes*), the members of the monastic order are consistently referred to as *therapeutai*. In the *Ecclesiastical Hierarchy* 6, Dionysius discusses the 'lay' rank in the ecclesiastical hierarchy – which consists of the monastic order; the order of laity, called the 'contemplative order'; and those preparing for initiation (catechumens) or who have spoilt their initiation and are seeking restitution (e.g. penitents) – and expounds the 'mystery' of monastic consecration. There he explains that 'our divine teachers' have deemed the members of 'the sacred order of monks'[24] worthy of 'sacred appellations, some of them calling them *therapeutai*, others monks, from their pure service and devotion (*katharas hyperesias kai therapeias*) to God and from the undivided and single life which through the sacred enfolding of things divided, as it were, makes them one in the deiform monad and God-loving perfection'.[25] As the term *monachos* refers to the monks' single life which draws all into unity, so the term *therapeutes* refers to their service and worship (*therapeia*) of God. The use of *therapeutes* in this sense is unique in Christian usage to Eusebius and

---

[24] The term *monachos* is only found in this chapter of *EH*, in contrast to *therapeutes*, which is found here and elsewhere in the *Corpus Dionysiacum*.

[25] Dionysius, *EH* 6.3 (*Corpus Dionysiacum*, 2, ed. Heil and Ritter, 116, lines 15–19).

Dionysius; otherwise it is mainly used by Christians to mean a healer
(from the Greek *therapeuein*, to heal).[26] Eusebius only uses the term
in one context in this distinctive sense: in *History of the Church* 2.17,
where he discusses Philo's *On the Contemplative Life*. In that work,
Philo gives an account of Jewish ascetics, whom he calls *therapeutai*
and (referring to the women ascetics) *therapeutides*, who are often
associated in scholarship with the Essenes (though Philo himself
seems to distinguish the contemplative *therapeutai* from the Essenes,
who lived an active life).[27] Eusebius takes Philo to be talking about
the early Christian community, and speculates that they were called
therapeutai because the term 'Christian' was not then in general
use.[28] What Eusebius is doing is to take Philo's account of the *therapeutai* as referring to the early Christians, as described in Acts 2:
42–7; 4: 32–5, who lived a simple life of prayer, worshipping in the
temple and breaking bread amongst themselves, having all things in
common and possessing nothing of their own. With hindsight, this
is extremely interesting, for those passages from Acts became classical
texts for the apostolic origins of, and inspiration for, the coenobitic
form of the monastic life. Eusebius's breathtaking assimilation of
the accounts in Philo and the Acts of the Apostles may not be so
utterly ahistorical as at first sight might appear; recent scholarship
has drawn attention to the links which both the apostolic community and Philo's *therapeutai* may have had with the community at
Qumran.[29] Dionysius uses the term *therapeutes* both on its own and
alongside the term *monachos*. It is ironic that he did not know that
the term *monachos*, applied to a monk, was a late fourth-century
coinage (hence Eusebius himself does not use it).[30] What he read
in the pages of Eusebius, however, was an unusual way of referring to the monastic order that belonged to the apostolic past, and

[26] See G. W. H. Lampe, *A Patristic Greek Lexicon* (Oxford, 1961), 644, *s.v.* θεραπευτής
1.b. Lampe cites a passage (1.a) from Clement of Alexandria that seems to use the word
of a contemplative (*Stromata* 7.24.8), which may reveal Clement's knowledge of Philo.
[27] On the meaning of the term *therapeutes* and the relationship of the *therapeutai* to
the Essenes, see most recently Joan E. Taylor, *Jewish Women Philosophers of First-Century
Alexandria: Philo's 'Therapeutae' Reconsidered* (Oxford, 2003), 54–73.
[28] Eusebius, *HE* 2.17.4, presumably alluding to Acts 11: 26.
[29] On the *therapeutai*, see E. Schürer, *The History of the Jewish People in the Age of
Jesus Christ, vol. 2*, rev. and ed. G. Vermes, F. Millar and M. Black (Edinburgh, 1979),
591–7.
[30] See E. A. Judge, 'The Earliest Use of Monachos for "Monk" (P. Coll. Youtie 77)
and the Origins of Monasticism', *Jahrbuch für Antike und Christentum* 20 (1977), 72–89.

this he incorporated into his vocabulary of the apostolic church.[31] Dionysius's predilection for the term *therapeutes* for a member of the monastic order is perhaps the most striking of his borrowings from Eusebius and is the more prominent because Eusebius himself was seeking to eke out his meagre sources for the apostolic period by drawing on Philo.

In dealing with influences and borrowings in late antiquity it is often difficult to reach absolute certainty; much has been lost. One thing we can be sure of is that the writers of late antiquity were acquainted with far more texts than we now have access to. However, it seems likely that Dionysius built up his picture of the apostolic confraternity with which he claimed affinity from his reading of the first few books of Eusebius's *History of the Church*. If so, it suggests that although, like anyone of his day, he had a 'tendency to telescope the past',[32] he nonetheless had some sense of the passage of time, some awareness that he could not project the concerns of the early sixth century without remainder on to the apostolic age.

It may well be, too, that he had a certain impatience with the divisive doctrinal disputes of his day, and wanted to stand aloof from the technical theological arguments about Christology, provoked by the Council of Chalcedon in 451 with its affirmation of the two natures, divine and human, united in the single person of Christ. Dionysius did this by taking refuge in a tradition that he believed went back to Plato and behind him to Moses, or even Adam. He would have found a great deal in Eusebius's own work about how to take such a perspective on theological matters.

Durham University

---

[31] It is possible that Dionysius took the term *therapeutes* directly from Philo. This seems unlikely for two reasons: first, Philo was not one of his sources for his philosophical ideas (at least, not directly: the role he ascribed to Moses does go back to Philo, but as Puech demonstrated long ago, Dionysius took it from Gregory of Nyssa: Henri-Charles Puech, 'La ténèbre mystique chez le Pseudo-Denys l'Aréopagite', in idem, *En quête de la gnose*, 2 vols [Paris, 1978], 1: 119–41, esp. 131–2); second, like Eusebius, he took the term *therapeutes* as referring to a Christian monk. He may, it is true, have known the pagan meaning of *therapeutes* as a worshipper (of God), and that may have influenced him.

[32] Louth, *Denys the Areopagite*, 10.

BIBLICAL HISTORY AND THE END OF TIMES: SEVENTH-CENTURY CHRISTIAN ACCOUNTS OF THE RISE OF ISLAM

by JESSICA LEE EHINGER

By the time of the rise of Islam in the early seventh century, Christian writers had already developed a complex methodology of historical writing, one that was not merely concerned with preserving the history of past events, but which viewed contemporary and past events through the lens of the biblical narrative of history, from creation to the ultimate end as prophesied in the eschatological books of the Bible. In this model, the history of the world could be traced from creation to follow the story of God's revelation of himself to humankind through the prophets, through inspired Scripture and, most importantly, through Christ.

Thus, at the rise of Islam, Christian writers understood themselves as preserving a history that was essentially set, which told a continuous story of the future as well as the past, defined by the biblical narrative and expanded by analysis of the scriptural text.[1] It was into this conception of world history that Christian writers

---

[1]   The classic example of early Christian historiography and its relationship to soteriology remains Eusebius's *Church History*. Although Eusebius's model of integrating the biblical narrative into his historical account was adopted throughout the Christian Near East, historians from the so-called 'heterodox' confessions often understood his history to have been corrupted by the Byzantine authorities, and so composed their own continuations in order to correct this, preserving a history that presented their understanding of the life of the church after the Councils of Ephesus and Chalcedon. For the development of the understanding of church history among Near Eastern sects in the sixth and seventh centuries, see Sebastian Brock, 'Syriac Views of Emergent Islam', in G. H. A. Juynboll, ed., *Studies on the First Century of Islamic Society*, Papers on Islamic History 5 (Carbondale, IL, 1982), 9–21, 199–203, repr. in Brock, *Syriac Perspectives on Late Antiquity* (London, 1984), VIII; idem, 'The Nestorian Church: A Lamentable Misnomer', *BJRL* 78/3 (1996), 23–36; Averil Cameron, *Christianity and the Rhetoric of Empire: The Development of Christian Discourse* (Berkeley, CA, 1991); Sidney H. Griffith, 'Anastasios of Sinai, the Hodegos, and the Muslims', *Greek Orthodox Theological Review* 32 (1987), 341–58; Hugh Kennedy, 'The Melkite Church from the Islamic Conquest to the Crusades: Continuity and Adaptation in the Byzantine Legacy', in *The 17th International Byzantine Congress: The Major Papers* (New Rochelle, NY, 1986), 325–43, repr. in idem, *The Byzantine and Early Islamic Near East* (Farnham, 2006), VI.

of the seventh century first attempted to integrate Islam, in order to understand how the rise of the new faith, and its fantastic military success over Christian lands, corresponded with the biblical history. In order to do so, they drew upon apocalyptic imagery to argue for Islam as a harbinger of the end, whose success heralded the imminence of the end times. This essay considers how Christian authors attempted to integrate the rise of Islam into the biblical narrative, and how, at the same time, Christian intellectual reliance on biblical narrative and eschatological imagery affected the Christian perception of Islam, resulting in the characterization of Muslims as non-human demons and monsters whose presence signalled the imminence of the end.

Over the last two decades there has been a great deal of academic interest in Islamic expansion and the period of transition from the sixth century to the ninth, particularly among late antiquarians and Byzantinists, as scholars continue to debate how the rise of Islam affected the cultural, social and political landscape of the Near East. The most recent works of Leslie Brubaker and John Haldon, James Howard-Johnston and the international project 'Change and Continuity in the Late Antique World', all demonstrate this current academic focus.[2] However, one of the central drives of this new academic focus has been a precise recalculation of the chronology of the Islamic expansion, as well as an interest in understanding exactly how and when a distinctly Muslim form of rule came into being. Modern scholarship has tended to rely heavily on chronicles and histories as sources, comparing these sources against other available material and archaeological evidence in order to understand the progress of Islam as a military and political entity. This focus is entirely reasonable for the questions these works have been asking, but taken as a whole it results in a biased perception of the first indigenous responses to the rise of Islam, firstly because

---

[2]   Leslie Brubaker and John F. Haldon, *Byzantium in the Iconoclast era c.680–850: A History* (Cambridge, 2011); James Howard-Johnston, *Witnesses to a World Crisis: Historians and Histories of the Middle East in the Seventh Century* (Oxford, 2010); as well as the proceedings of the 'Change and Continuity' project, funded by the AHRC and currently being undertaken as a joint research project between the universities of Leiden, Oxford and Paris, with publication of the first proceedings, from the 2010 conference in Leiden, expected in 2012. A similar trend can be seen in the slightly older work of John Haldon, *Byzantium in the Seventh Century: the Transformation of a Culture* (Cambridge, 1997); Averil Cameron, Lawrence I. Conrad and John Haldon, eds, *The Byzantine and early Islamic Near East*, 6 vols (Princeton, NJ, 1992–2004).

chronicles and histories often date from at least a century later and may not authentically preserve the perspective of the seventh-century population who first experienced the expansion, and secondly because these sources tend to downplay or omit entirely any consideration of the theological or cosmological significance of the rise of Islam.

As the theme of this volume is to focus particularly on how communities of Christians have understood their own history as representing the continued story of humanity's relationship to God, this essay intends to discuss this other side of the Christian response to the rise of Islam. The Near East of the seventh century, in which Islam first appeared, was far from a secular world. The church councils of the fifth and sixth centuries had created a series of sectarian communities, all of which understood themselves as preserving the one true faith in the face of the others' heresies. All of these communities – the pro-Chalcedonian Melkites, the anti-Chalcedonians or Monophysites, the so-called Nestorians or Church of the East (found primarily in Persia) and the pro-Monothelite Maronites – experienced the rise of Islam firstly as a military incursion, beginning in both the Levant and Mesopotamia in the 630s. Even as these communities began to consider the ramifications of Muslim victory, they continued to debate the doctrinal schisms of previous centuries. Thus, within the first few decades from the rise of Islam, there arose a series of works presenting a sometimes bewildering range of topics, discussing the rise of Islam but also the eschatological significance of contemporary events and the doctrinal debates of the church councils, as Christian writers of the seventh century understood these topics as essentially linked.

Many of these early works came, not surprisingly, from members of the church hierarchies, presumably as their congregations turned to them for an explanation of contemporary events. Sophorinus, the Chalcedonian patriarch of Jerusalem during the Muslim siege of the city, who also oversaw the city's capitulation after being besieged for a year and a half, preached on the Muslim expansion twice: on Christmas Eve 634, when the siege had just begun, barring the Christians of the city from their traditional pilgrimage to Bethlehem for Christmas Eve services, and for the Feast of

Epiphany, probably in 636, just before the city's capitulation.[3] In his Christmas Eve sermon, Sophronius made extensive use of the biblical narrative, in order to demonstrate how God's wrath, in the form of Muslim victory, had upset the story of peace and redemption which began with Christ's birth.

The most important example of Sophronius's use of biblical imagery in this sermon is his use of the Nativity story itself, which he used to set up a clear dichotomy between the story as it should be, on the one hand, in which the Incarnation offered redemption for humankind, and the story as it was, in which humanity was once again facing God's wrath because of sin. He began the sermon by recounting the story of Christ's birth in the manger, focusing particularly on the biblical phrase 'glory to God in the highest, peace on earth and goodwill to men'.[4] For Sophronius, this passage encapsulated the significance of the Nativity story, that Christ in his Incarnation 'descended from on high to lowliness to make you high and heavenly rather than earthly, and gave peace to us who were struggling in an unseen war, bringing us to his own Father'.[5] This is the story as it should have been, that through Christ's life, death and resurrection humanity was brought closer to God, so that there could be peace on earth and goodwill towards humanity.

It was with this context in mind that Sophronius then turned to describing his congregation's current condition, trapped in the city under Muslim siege. It was also in this context that Sophronius addressed the presence and persons of the Muslims themselves, and their role in the cosmic history preserved in the biblical narrative. By addressing the rise of Islam specifically in the context of the

---

3   The length of the siege of Jerusalem is one point of the chronology of the expansion that has received particular attention recently. James Howard-Johnston has argued persuasively that the siege should be dated as ending in 636, a dating which would also mean that Sophronius's second sermon on the Muslims coincided with the city's capitulation, which might help account for its dark tone. Howard-Johnston first developed this revised dating in his historical commentary on the Armenian chronicle attributed to Sebeos, and then expanded it in his more recent work on seventh- and eighth-century historiography: R. W. Thompson, James Howard-Johnston and Tim Greenwood, ed. and transl., *The Armenian History attributed to Sebeos*, 2 vols, TTH 31 (Liverpool, 1999), 2: 240–4.

4   'Weihnachtspredigt des Sophronius', ed. H. Usener, *Rheinisches Museum für Philologie* 41 (1886), 500–16, at 503.

5   Ibid. 504; translation mine.

peace and goodwill of the Nativity story, Sophronius created an image of Islam in which the Muslims stood outside the humanity brought to God through the Incarnation. For Sophronius, the story of peace and goodwill had been broken by the rise of Islam and the Muslims' victories in the Near East, which were caused, in turn, by the failings and sinfulness of Christians. Thus the only possible salvation for his congregation stood at the cost of the Muslims' defeat and death, which would only happen if God were to forgive the Christians:

> Thus I pray and plead and beseech you to entreat Christ God, in order that each of us, whatever our power, might reform ourselves and adorn ourselves with repentance, and turning around, might purify and curb the flow of deeds which are hateful to God. For if we were to live as is dear and pleasing to God, we might laugh at the fall of our adversaries the Saracens, and presently we might make their ruin feeble, and behold their final destruction.[6]

In this rather dark passage, Sophronius called for 'the final destruction' of the Muslims as necessary in order to restore the story as it should be, with peace on earth and goodwill to human-kind. In this way, Sophronius presented the Muslims as the phys-ical manifestation of God's wrath, with no clear interest in their humanity. Instead, they represented an anomaly in the biblical narrative, which must be removed for the story to return to its proper progression.

This use of biblical imagery to explain the role of Islam was expanded in the mid- and late seventh century through the devel-opment of the genre of apocalypses which recounted the rise of Islam and the Muslims' eventual defeat and overthrow in terms of the eschatological imagery of the Bible and particularly the book of Daniel.[7] Unlike Sophronius, who saw the Muslims as standing outside the biblical narrative, diverting the proper course of history, apocalyptic writers drew on eschatological imagery to argue that

---

[6] Ibid. 515; translation mine.
[7] For further details on the genre of apocalypses, see Paul J. Alexander, *The Byzan-tine Apocalyptic Tradition* (Berkeley, CA, 1985); Sebastian Brock, 'An Extract from the Apocalypse of Pseudo-Methodius', in Andrew Palmer, ed., *The Seventh Century in the West-Syrian Chronicles*, TTH 15 (Liverpool, 1993), 222–6.

Muslims and the rise of Islam should rather be understood as part of the biblical account of the end times, and that their victory in the Near East signalled the imminence of the end. As a genre, these apocalypses understood the history of Christianity as a continuous narrative stretching from creation and fall through the life of Jesus and the rise of the church to the *eschaton* and the future kingdom of Christ. By setting the rise of Islam within this larger narrative structure, authors of these apocalypses both presented an explanation for Muslim victory and lent the rise of Islam, and the subsequent suffering of the indigenous Christian communities the Muslims conquered, a cosmic significance.

These works also often served as apologies for the failure of the Byzantine army to defeat the Muslims, by painting the rise of Islam as a stepping-stone to the end, thus marking it as a necessary evil. In the Pseudo-Methodian apocalypse, which enjoyed wide circulation in the West in Greek and Latin, the author compared the rise of Islam to the punishment described by Paul, which would serve as a harbinger for the appearance of the Man of Sin (2 Thess. 2: 3).[8] In this way, the author excused the failures of the Byzantine military, because, if the Muslims were an aspect of the end, their defeat would be neither possible nor preferable in view of the greater purpose of bringing about the kingdom of God promised at the end.

One of the most serious challenges faced by the seventh-century authors who attempted to describe Islam and the Muslims as part of the biblical narrative was locating any relevant biblical passages that might prophesy the rise of Islam. For the Eastern church communities, who created the Syriac apocalypses, the potential pool of source material was even smaller, as the Eastern churches had never accepted Revelation as canonical, and therefore were forced to draw from Daniel for the bulk of their apocalyptic imagery. To this end, two Danielic images were called upon in these apocalypses: that of the fourth and final beast, 'terrifying and dreadful and exceedingly strong' (Dan. 7: 7), and that of the southern kingdom, from which 'a warrior king shall arise, who shall rule with great dominion and take actions as he pleases' (Dan. 11: 3).

---

8   Alexander, *Byzantine*, 46.

The imagery of the fourth beast appeared also in the Pseudo-Athanasian apocalypse, a Coptic apocalypse from the early eighth century which preserved a Coptic revision of the Syriac-style apocalypse. The author described the rise of Islam as a necessary punishment and harbinger of the end:

> After these things the good God will become angry, because they had altered His true faith. He will divide the unity of the kingdom of the Romans of their empire [*sic*] in return for their having divided His great Might into two natures ... He will give the power to the kings of Persia for a little while ... After this, God will remove the kingdom of the Persians and will stir up upon the earth a mighty people, numerous as the locusts. This is the fourth beast which the prophet Daniel saw.[9]

In this passage, the anti-Chalcedonian author presented a brief account of the history of the church, linking the sectarianism of the Christological debates to the defeat of the Romans (the Byzantines): 'in return for their having divided His great Might into two natures', God divided their kingdom, giving power to the Persians, who in turn would be defeated by the Muslims. In this way, the author integrated both the Persian empire and the rise of Islam into the biblical narrative, but also gave an explanation for the downfall of the Christian empire of Constantine, stressing the evil that had been created by the Chalcedonians as the essential source of both the Persian and Islamic incursions.

The imagery of the southern kingdom is developed in a Syriac work, *The Gospel of the Twelve Apostles*, which preserved three short and interrelated apocalypses, attributed to Simon Peter, James, and John the writer of Revelation. The three apocalypses each treated a separate period of church history, the first recounting the conversion of Constantine, the church councils and the Christological debates; the second narrating the rise of the Persians; and the third describing the rise of Islam and the end times. In this final section, the author described the rise of Islam as a southern wind, invoking the Danielic image of the southern kingdom:

---

[9]   Robert Hoyland, ed. and transl., *Seeing Islam as Others Saw It: A Survey and Evaluation of Christian, Jewish and Zoroastrian Writings on Early Islam* (Princeton, NJ, 1997), 282–3.

But there will be deniers of the truth, and men that know not God, and that do corruptly in their lasciviousness, those who provoke God, and then suddenly shall be fulfilled the prophecy of Daniel the pure and the desired, which he spake, that God shall send forth a mighty wind, the Southern one; and there shall come forth from it a people of deformed aspect, and their appearance and manners like those of women; and there shall rise up from among them a warrior, and one whom they call a prophet.[10]

Again, the author connected the rise of Islam and the imminence of the end with Christian sin and doctrinal failure, applying the Danielic imagery more directly to Islam, drawing on the dual roles of Muhammad as both military leader and prophet to present him as fulfilling the role of the southern king.

In the first instance, this Danielic imagery was used in order to provide a context for the rise of Islam. The Arabian peninsula had not traditionally featured in Christian eschatology, and the pre-Islamic Arabians were a mixture of Christians, Jews and polytheists, who had political and trade alliances with Byzantium, Persia, and the Himarite and Abyssinian kingdoms, so that no one pre-existent apocalyptic image remained clearly relevant to their appearance. Thus, at the rise of Islam, there was no established role for it to play in the biblical narrative, as there was by comparison for the Persian empire, which had featured regularly in Christian cosmology for centuries. In particular, the use of the figure of the king of the south, as employed by the *Gospel of the Twelve Apostles*, was presumably based in part on geographical realities, as clearly fitting the perspective of the indigenous Christian communities of the Levant and Mesopotamia, which first experienced Muslim incursion from the south.

However, these images served two further purposes, similar to the use of the biblical narrative in the sermons of Sophronius. Firstly, by casting the rise of Islam as part of that narrative, the authors of apocalypses lent a cosmic significance to contemporary events. This significance was undoubtedly bolstered by the realities of Muslim expansion: the Muslim military was fantasti-

---

[10] J. Rendel Harris, *The Gospel of the Twelve Apostles together with the Apocalypses of each one of them* (Cambridge, 1900), ιζ–ιη, translation at 36.

cally successful and, particularly in the Levant and Mesopotamia, executed several crushing defeats against both the Byzantines and the Persians, both empires which boasted larger, better organized and better equipped armies. By marking the Islamic expansion as a harbinger of the end, apocalypses could also act as apologetic for the failures of Byzantine military engagement.

Secondly, although the choice of Danielic images was partly determined by circumstance, in particular in the use of the figure of the king of the south, both the image of the fourth beast and that of the sons of the king of the south were also important in the Daniel vision itself as being the final harbingers witnessed by Daniel. By employing these images, apocalypse writers implied a particular understanding not only of the power and destructiveness of the Muslim incursion but also of the longevity of Muslim rule. By describing the Muslims as these specific figures, these authors demonstrated that the Muslims could be understood as the ultimate expression of human warfare and suffering, the worst but also the last. Indeed, many of these apocalypses also set an end date for Muslim rule, usually seen as lasting no more than a century, at which point the Muslims would be defeated and the end narrative itself begin, with the narrative turning to the cosmic battle between Christ and the powers of evil and the establishment of the kingdom of Christ on earth.

As in the sermons of Sophronius, the apocalypses' focus on the biblical narrative also gave a very specific image to the Muslims themselves. Both the fourth beast and the sons of the king of the south were described by Daniel as the most destructive of the monsters and warriors in the vision, destroying and subjugating the world and ruling as tyrants. For the communities who first experienced the expansion, it is not surprising that these images would resonate as potential descriptors for Muslim rule. Both the sermons of Sophronius and the apocalypses presented it as obvious that the Muslims would be as tyrannical as rulers as they were terrifying in battle. Thus the emphasis in the apocalypses on the Muslims as the final harbingers of the end was perhaps further intended to offer solace to the Christian audience of these works, attempting to mitigate somewhat the fear of Muslim rule by portraying it as terrible but also brief.

In reality, Muslim rule was neither tyrannical nor even particularly invasive for the indigenous Christian communities whom they conquered. Thus, in the centuries that followed, apocalyptic imagery disappeared from Christian writing, as these eschatological overtones must have appeared ridiculous to later Christian writers. The world had not ended, the end had not come, and the Muslims were not the demons and monsters that Christian authors of the seventh century feared they would be. For later Christian writers, history continued to convey the relationship between God and Christianity, but did so with little regard for Islam or for Muslim rule. Instead, Islam sank into the background of Christian writing, appearing in order to give context and environment but with little consideration for the theological significance of its continued presence. These later authors continued to understand contemporary history as playing out the biblical story, but returned to an understanding in which the biblical end was understood as a distant event; in so doing they came to write works which accepted Islamic rule as the new status quo.[11]

However, for the period of the seventh century, the presumed imminence of the end was central to Christian writing, and the resulting works melded together biblical history, eschatological future and doctrinal debate to account for the radical changes taking place in the Near East. In this way, these authors continued a Christian intellectual tradition that understood history as a concept that united past, present and future through the narrative preserved in the Bible. Although attempting first and foremost to account for the changes happening in their own time, these authors were simultaneously making a statement about how and where these changes stood in the biblical narrative, in the process also attempting to normalize the Islamic expansion and explain the Muslims' military victory over Christian forces. They were also making a statement about the Muslims themselves, characterizing them as the demons and monsters prophesied in the Bible. Thus the writings of the seventh century offer a unique perspective on

---

[11] The clearest example of this shift in perspective is the rise of the genre of Christian apologetics against Islam, which begin to appear in the late eighth century, and which often use a dialogue in the Muslim court between a Muslim ruler and Christian religious leader as their frame story, thus effectively accepting the current circumstance of Muslim rule as the norm; see, e.g., the Patriarch Timothy's dialogue with the caliph: A. Mingana, ed. and transl., *Woodbrooke Studies: Christian Documents in Syriac, Arabic, and Garshūni, Edited and Translated with a Critical Apparatus*, 2 (Cambridge, 1928), 15–162.

the earliest Christian attempts to integrate Islam and the Muslims into a Christian understanding of the world.

St Peter's College, Oxford

BEDE ON THE JEWISH CHURCH*

by CONOR O'BRIEN

We upon whom the ends of the ages have come can love with
sincere affection those faithful who were in the beginning of
the world, and receive them into the bosom of our love ...
and believe that we are also being received by them with a
charitable embrace.[1]

Bede (d. 735) is renowned as the first Englishman to write
seriously about the history of the church in England. But
the *Ecclesiastical History of the English People* was not the
only work of his to address the history of the church, and his
interest in the past extended far beyond that book's temporal and
spatial boundaries. He saw the Anglo-Saxon church as part of a
universal church whose origins lay in the pre-Incarnation past. The
above quotation from his commentary *On the Tabernacle*, a work
interested in the religious institutions of the Israelites, portrays
Jews from before the Incarnation as Bede's fellow members of
that church.

Bede certainly believed that the church existed on both sides
of Christ's coming in the flesh. Sometimes he emphasized that
more correctly there were two separate institutions: the synagogue
before the Incarnation and the church after the Incarnation.[2]
However this distinction blurred when he emphasized the essential
unity of both as Christ's church. But what did Bede actually mean

* I would like to thank Sarah Foot for her support and helpful comments on this
essay.

[1] Bede, *De Tabernaculo* [hereafter: *Tab.*] 2 (CChr.SL 119A, 62): 'nos in quos fines
saeculorum deuenerunt etiam eos qui in primordio saeculi fuerunt fideles sincero
affectu diligamus et ... in sinu nostri amoris suscipiamus et nos quoque ab illis per
amplexum caritatis suscipiendos esse credamus' (ET from *Bede: On the Tabernacle*, transl.
Arthur Holder, TTH 18 [Liverpool, 1994], 69). The following abbreviations are used
here for works by Bede: *Act.* = *Expositio in Actuum Apostolorum* (CChr.SL 121); *Cant.*
= *In Cantica Canticorum* (CChr.SL 119B); *Ezra.* = *In Ezram et Neemiam* (CChr.SL
119A); *Gen.* = *In Genesim* (CChr.SL 118); *HE* = *Historia Ecclesiastica Gentis Anglorum*
(*Ecclesiastical History of the English People*, ed. and transl. Bertram Colgrave and R. A. B.
Mynors, OMT [Oxford, 1969]); *Hom.* = *Homeliae Euangelii* (CChr.SL 122); *Luc.* = *In
Lucae Euangelium Expositio* (CChr.SL 120); *Temp.* = *De Templo* (CChr.SL 119A).

[2] *Tab.* 2 (CChr.SL 119A, 42–3); *Cant.* 1 (CChr.SL 119B, 190).

by the church before the Incarnation? This essay will argue that Bede thought of the church before the Incarnation as a 'Jewish church', and of the key institutions of the Jewish religion as being founded in Christ, possessing a sacramental power. This institution was remarkably similar in many ways to the contemporary, post-Incarnation Christian church. It will also be argued that Bede came increasingly to stress this view of the Jewish church's relationship with the Christian church in his later work as a response to changes in the ecclesiastical situation in northern Britain.

Previous scholars have shed light on Bede's interest in the Jews and the relationship between the church and Judaism. Of great importance is Glenn Olsen's work on Bede's concept of the primitive church.[3] Olsen argues that Bede believed that the church had developed through time; in its apostolic phase, when Gentile converts were as yet immature in the faith, the Christian community had retained much of the old Jewish religion. But as it grew and became stronger, it naturally changed and abandoned Jewish traditions. These had once been permissible but over time ceased to be licit for Christians.[4] Andrew Scheil has highlighted the complexity of Bede's thought, in which patristic anti-Jewish tropes sit side by side with a great sensitivity to the ultimate unity of Jews and Gentiles in the Christian church.[5] That Bede took the Augustinian idea of the community of the elect as existing before the Incarnation, and changed it slightly by identifying that pre-Christian community very definitely with the Jewish people themselves, has been argued by Georges Tugène.[6]

For Bede, the Jewish church possessed sacraments. Just like the contemporary church it had the power to bestow grace on individuals through rituals and rites. In particular Bede argued that circumcision was to the faithful of the Old Testament what baptism was to the faithful of the New: 'under the law, circumcision offered

[3] Glenn Olsen, 'Bede as Historian: The Evidence from his Observations on the Life of the First Christian Community at Jerusalem', *JEH* 33 (1982), 519–30.

[4] *Gen.* 4 (CChr.SL 118A, 241–2); *Act.* (CChr.SL 121, 67); *Tab.* 2 (CChr.SL 119A, 74); *HE* 3.25 (*Ecclesiastical History*, ed. and transl. Colgrave and Mynors, 300–3).

[5] Andrew Scheil, *The Footsteps of Israel: Understanding Jews in Anglo-Saxon England* (Ann Arbor, MI, 2004), chs 1–2.

[6] Georges Tugène, 'Le thème des deux peuples dans le *De Tabernaculo* de Bède', in Stéphane Lebecq et al., eds, *Bède le Vénérable entre tradition et postérité / The Venerable Bede: Tradition and Posterity* (Lille, 2005), 73–84.

the same help of a health-giving treatment against the wound of original sin that now, in the time of revealed grace, baptism is wont to do'.[7] Bede's problem was the question of how Gentiles could have been saved before the Incarnation if they did not receive circumcision. He suggested that sacrifices could have functioned to bestow grace, or that faith alone was in any case enough.[8] In giving the faithful before the Incarnation these options Bede may have been influenced by a comment of Gregory the Great.[9] But whereas in Gregory the three alternatives to baptism are listed together in a single compressed sentence, Bede expanded this and focused his interest on circumcision. In his view, it was circumcision which had been the official sacrament designed by God to remove original sin in ancient times, and it was consequently the Jewish church's equivalent to Christian baptism.[10]

The relationship of the animal sacrifices of the Jewish cult to the eucharist of Christians was somewhat more complicated. Bede certainly saw the former as a typological foreshadowing of the latter: Jewish sacrifice was a symbol of Christ's sacrifice on the cross.[11] But he also spoke of the ritual offerings of the temple cult as if they were the equivalent of the sacrament of the eucharist for the pre-Incarnation church: 'For they celebrated the sacrament of the Lord's passion (through which each of the two peoples has been redeemed) in the flesh and blood of sacrifices, but we celebrate it in the oblation of bread and wine.'[12] There is a definite sense here that the relationship is not one of typological subordi-

---

7   *Hom.* 1.11 (CChr.SL 122, 74): 'idem salutiferae curationis auxilium circumcisio in lege contra originalis peccati uulnus agebat quod nunc baptisma agere reuelatae gratiae tempore consueuit' (ET in *Bede the Venerable: Homilies on the Gospels*, transl. Lawrence T. Martin and David Hurst, Cistercian Studies 110, 111, 2 vols [Kalamazoo, MI, 1991], 1: 104); *Gen.* 4 (CChr.SL 118A, 206).

8   *Hom.* 1.11 (CChr.SL 122, 75); *Gen.* 4 (CChr.SL 118A, 234).

9   Gregory, *Moralia in Iob* 4.pref.3 (CChr.SL 143, 160): 'Quod uero apud nos ualet aqua baptismatis, hoc egit apud ueteres, uel pro paruulis sola fides, uel pro maioribus uirtus sacrificii, uel pro his qui ex Abrahae stirpe prodierant, mysterium circumcisionis' ('Certainly that which the water of baptism achieves amongst us, amongst the ancients either faith alone for children, or the power of sacrifice for elders, or, for those who had come from Abraham's line, the rite of circumcision achieved'; translation mine).

10   *Hom.* 1.11 (CChr.SL 122, 74–5).

11   *Tab.* 2, 3 (CChr.SL 119A, 77–8, 124).

12   *Tab.* 2 (CChr.SL 119A, 48): 'Nam passionis dominicae per quam utrique sumus redempti sacramentum illi in carne ac sanguine uictimarum nos in oblatione panis et uini celebramus' (*Tabernacle*, transl. Holder, 52); *Temp.* 1 (CChr.SL 119A, 158); *HE* 5.21 (*Ecclesiastical History*, ed. and transl. Colgrave and Mynors, 538–9).

nation but of sacramental equivalence: 'Bede could be considered to mean that only the form of the sacraments in the two testaments differed, and to permit the interpretation that the spiritual content of the Old Testament sacrifices and of the eucharist is the same.'[13]

Bede was rather less keen on suggesting equivalence between the institutional hierarchies of the Jewish religion and the Christian church; in particular, he was pleased to point out that priests were no longer simply chosen on account of biological descent from Aaron.[14] The appearance of the priest-king Melchizedek in Genesis, offering Abraham bread and wine, established the superiority of the Christian priesthood to the Jewish hierarchy.[15] However, alongside this line of argument, which derived scriptural authority from the letter to the Hebrews, there was also a tendency in Bede to equate the Jewish priesthood with that of the church. There was precedent for seeing the different ranks of Jewish priests as matching the different orders of the clergy, with Levites equivalent to deacons, for example.[16] More than that, Bede was perfectly willing to believe that when Exodus spoke of the priesthood of the sons of Aaron it was giving precepts which 'rightly pertain to the priests of the Church'.[17] God's promise that the Aaronic priesthood would last forever could not be literally understood, but in a spiritual sense it was true. Turning to his readers, who must have been substantially clerical, Bede declared: 'We are not born of the lineage of Aaron, but we have believed in him in whom Aaron also, with the saints of that age, believed.'[18]

---

[13] Mary Thomas Aquinas Carroll, *The Venerable Bede: His Spiritual Teachings*, Catholic University of America Studies in Medieval History, n.s. 9 (Washington, DC, 1946), 124–5.

[14] *Temp.* 1 (CChr.SL 119A, 150); *Luc.* 1 (CChr.SL 120, 27–8).

[15] *Gen.* 3 (CChr.SL 118A, 191).

[16] *Ezra.* 1 (CChr.SL 119A, 255, 262, 279–80); cf. Isidore, *Etymologiae* 7.12.22–3 (ed. W. M. Lindsay, Oxford Classical Texts [Oxford, 1911], unpaginated).

[17] *Tab.* 3 (CChr.SL 119A, 95): 'recte ecclesiae sacerdotibus congruit' (*Tabernacle*, transl. Holder, 109); see also *Tab.* 3 (CChr.SL 119A, 97); *Ezra.* 1 (CChr.SL 119A, 256, 277); ibid. 2 (CChr.SL 119A, 303).

[18] *Tab.* 3 (CChr.SL 119A, 139): 'nostra humilitas … non quidem de Aaron stirpe nascendo sed credendo in eum in quem et Aaron cum sanctis illius aeui credidit' (*Tabernacle*, transl. Holder, 162); cf. *Hom.* 1.4 (CChr.SL 122, 29). For the readership of Bede's commentaries as clerical, see Judith McClure, 'Bede's *Notes on Genesis* and the Training of the Anglo-Saxon Clergy', in Katherine Walsh and Diana Wood, eds, *The Bible in the Medieval World*, SCH S 4 (Oxford, 1985), 17–30.

This equivalence of sacramental rituals and of hierarchies, this sense of continuity between the institutions of the Jewish and Christian churches, was based on the fact that at heart Bede saw them as functioning in similar fashions. Old Testament Judaism may have been essentially an ethnic religion but the Jewish church was willing to share faith in the true God with Gentiles and conversions took place before, as well as after, the Incarnation.[19] This put the church before the Incarnation in the same tradition of preaching as the Christian church, possessing teachers until the end of time.[20] These Old Testament preachers and prophets were 'not in any way to be considered inferior' to the apostles.[21] After all, the synagogue was just as much founded on Christ as was the Christian church. When Moses was upon Mount Sinai God actually showed him 'the manifold sacraments of Christ and the Church': this was the pattern according to which the desert tabernacle was made.[22] David and the other prophets had seen Christ in vision; the leaders of the Jewish religion had all known of and earnestly awaited Christ's Incarnation.[23] Of course it had not been possible to make public the Christian nature of the ancient Jewish religion, for the common people would not have understood it.[24] But even this was not a fundamental difference between the Jewish and Christian churches: Bede seems to have accepted that contemporary Christians did not always understand what they believed either.[25]

Bede certainly subscribed to the Augustinian notion that faith in Christ was the same in both the Old and New Testaments; he frequently asserted that the church's faith had been one always, and only the *sacramenta* were different on account of the different

---

[19] Diarmuid Scully, Introduction to *Bede: On Tobit and On the Canticle of Habakkuk*, transl. Seán Connolly (Dublin, 1997), 17–37, at 23–5; *Ezra*. 1 (CChr.SL 119A, 255); *Hom*. 2.3 (CChr.SL 122, 203).

[20] *Tab*. 1 (CChr.SL 119A, 27–8, 31); ibid. 2 (CChr.SL 119A, 52–3, 65).

[21] *Temp*. 1 (CChr.SL 119A, 157): 'in nullo apostolis ... putandi sint esse minores' (ET in *Bede: On the Temple*, transl. Seán Connolly, TTH 21 [Liverpool, 1995], 18); *Gen*. 4 (CChr.SL 118A, 239).

[22] *Tab*. 1 (CChr.SL 119A, 40): 'multifaria Christi et ecclesiae sacramenta' (*Tabernacle*, transl. Holder, 44).

[23] *Temp*. 1, 2 (CChr.SL 119A, 159, 223). See also *Tab*. 1 (CChr.SL 119A, 22); *Temp*. 2 (CChr.SL 119A, 219); *Ezra*. 3 (CChr.SL 119A, 385).

[24] *Tab*. 1 (CChr.SL 119A, 31, 40); *Hom*. 2.15 (CChr.SL 122, 281).

[25] *Temp*. 1 (CChr.SL 119A, 191).

times.[26] Bede's historical understanding of the church was one of a developing institution. As the temple replaced the tabernacle, so in turn the temple was to be replaced as the church spread to the Gentiles.[27] The primitive church practised Jewish rites which over time were to be abandoned.[28] But this was not just a 'Whiggish' belief that the past had inevitably to change in order to bring about the present, the natural end-point of such a process. Bede was willing to acknowledge that the contemporary church was also just a phase and that it in turn would be surpassed. His spirituality was entirely focused on the Bible and the role of the institutional hierarchy in interpreting the Bible; yet he accepted as inevitable and good that there would be a time when 'we shall have no further need for Scriptures or for those who interpret them'.[29] The effect of this acknowledgement of development in the church's future as well as its past was to iron out the differences between the Jewish church of then and the Christian church of now, and to see them both as points along a line of continuous development towards the end times.

Some scholars have argued that all of Bede's ideas of development and change pale in the face of the one great leap forward in human existence, the Incarnation which changed darkness into light.[30] Certainly Bede's work is not entirely given over to celebrations of the equality of Jewish past and Christian present, nor did he always stress continuity rather than rupture. Many of his works display traditional anti-Jewish ideas, denigrating the Mosaic law and dismissing the Jewish past as a shadow to be dispersed by the light of the truth.[31] If one was to give equal status to all of Bede's comments on these matters in all his works, the result would be a very confusing one.

The rest of this essay will tentatively suggest one explana-

---

[26] *Act.* (CChr.SL 121, 26, 66–7); *Tab.* 2 (CChr.SL 119A, 86); *Cant.* 1 (CChr.SL 119B, 190); cf. Augustine, *Epistulae* 190.2.6 (CSEL 57, 142).

[27] *Act.* (CChr.SL 121, 37).

[28] *HE* 3.25 (*Ecclesiastical History*, ed. and transl. Colgrave and Mynors, 300–3).

[29] *Tab.* 1 (CChr.SL 119A, 28): 'nec scripturis ultra nec interpretibus earum opus habebimus' (*Tabernacle*, transl. Holder, 30); also *Tab.* 1, 3 (CChr.SL 119A, 39, 94); *Hom.* 2.25 (CChr.SL 122, 376).

[30] Carroll, *Spiritual Teachings*, 72–3; Glenn Olsen, 'From Bede to the Anglo-Saxon Presence in the Carolingian Empire', *Settimane di studio del Centro italiano di studi sull'alto Medioevo* 32 (1984), 305–82, at 363.

[31] *Hom.* 1.2 (CChr.SL 122, 10).

tion which may help make sense of this apparent confusion. A greater stress on continuity between the pre- and post-Incarnation churches appears in Bede's later work than in his earlier writings. He seems to have been more willing to recognize an Old Testament Jewish church, possessing grace-giving rituals and institutions fundamentally similar to those of the contemporary church, in the last fifteen years or so of his life. On this reading of his commentaries, the stress shifts from the difference between the law and the gospel to continuity and sameness. Things are complicated, of course, by the difficulty of dating all of Bede's works and the general lack of chronological precision one can bring to his corpus. Nonetheless, evidence can be cited here which supports this case.

As previously stated, on occasion Bede called the church before the Incarnation the synagogue, and that after the Incarnation the church. In his commentaries on Luke and the Song of Songs (both probably written by 716) he explained these terms by giving their etymologies: *sinagoga* means 'gathered together' and *ecclesia* means 'called together'. Inanimate objects and non-rational beasts could be gathered together, but only rational humans could be called together, he argued.[32] In the commentaries on the tabernacle and the temple (both written in the 720s), Bede provided the two names but did not provide this etymology which differentiated them by denigrating the Jewish church.[33]

The commentary on Mark was Bede's latest original work on the New Testament (written some time in the 720s); it is highly dependent on the earlier commentary on Luke, and Bede on occasion simply repeated himself verbatim. There are interesting changes, however. In both works Bede declared that God destroyed the temple in order to protect Christians weak in faith. In the commentary on Luke this destruction was necessary in case the beauty of the temple building and its rituals should entrance the Christian; in the later commentary on Mark the threat was the

---

[32] *Cant.* 1 (CChr.SL 119B, 190); *Luc.* 2 (CChr.SL 120, 101); cf. Isidore, *Etymologiae* 8.1.8. Unless otherwise indicated, I take the dates of Bede's works to be those suggested in the relevant CChr.SL volume. For the date of *Cant.*, see Arthur Holder, 'The Anti-Pelagian Character of Bede's Commentary on the Song of Songs', in Claudio Leonardi and Giovanni Orlandi, eds, *Biblical Studies in the Early Middle Ages* (Florence, 2005), 91–103, at 100–3.

[33] *Tab.* 2 (CChr.SL 119A, 42–3); *Temp.* 1 (CChr.SL 119A, 157).

Christian's knowledge that the temple had been established by God and used by holy prophets, which might cause backsliding into Judaism.[34] The change suggests an increased sense of the religious validity of the temple cult.

Bede provided two interpretations of Luke 2: 21 (the circumcision of Christ), one in the commentary on Luke's Gospel and one in *Homily* 1.11. The commentary (following Romans 4) emphasizes that Abraham was justified before his circumcision and not by it, thus undermining the sacramental powers of circumcision; the homily makes no reference to this.[35] The commentary also has an extended discussion as to why Joshua and not Moses circumcised the Israelites, which highlights the impotency of the law through a contrast between Christ (Jesus being the same name as Joshua) and Moses.[36] This contrast does not appear in the homily. The homily states that Jesus consented to be circumcised to teach that the 'decrees of the Law were most salutary', a much more positive attitude than that of the commentary, which sees Christ's circumcision simply as a figure of the moral renewal all individuals have to undergo.[37] The dates of Bede's individual homilies are unknown, but the commentary on Luke may well have been written first, serving as the basis for the homilies which addressed passages from Luke.[38]

The commentary on the temple was written more than a decade after the commentary on Luke. In the gospel commentary, Bede gave an interpretation of the bronze temple vessels which were formed in clay moulds that saw the moulds as the literal Old Testament that had to be broken to make way for the spiritual truth of the gospel.[39] When he later came to the temple vessels in the 720s he did not use this explanation; now the breaking of the clay moulds represented the move between this life and the next and not that between the Jewish and Christian Scriptures.[40] In the

---

34 *Luc.* 6 (CChr.SL 120, 364); Bede, *In Marcae Euangelium Expositio* 4 (CChr.SL 120, 595).

35 *Luc.* 1 (CChr.SL 120, 56); also *Cant.* 5 (CChr.SL 119B, 345).

36 *Luc.* 1 (CChr.SL 120, 59–60).

37 *Hom.* 1.11 (CChr.SL 122, 75): 'legis decreta suo tempore doceret esse saluberrima' (*Homilies*, transl. Martin and Hurst, 1: 106); *Luc.* 1 (CChr.SL 120, 57).

38 Eric Jay Del Giacco, 'Exegesis and Sermon: A Comparison of Bede's Commentary and Homilies on Luke', *Medieval Sermon Studies* 50 (2006), 9–29, at 10–11.

39 *Luc.* 6 (CChr.SL 120, 363).

40 *Temp.* 2 (CChr.SL 119A, 223–4).

720s Bede could happily see the relationship of Moses and Joshua as one not of contrast but of continuity; Jesus (in the figure of Joshua) could rightly be called Moses' servant as Christ submitted to the Mosaic law which he came to fulfil and not to abolish.[41] The major change is one of emphasis. Many of the important works which Bede wrote in the years up until 716/717 display a negative attitude to the Jews and focus on the end of the old ways and the beginning of the new through Christ.[42] In the 720s the commentaries on the tabernacle and temple display a consistent sense of unity between the Jewish and the Christian churches; for example, they frequently argue for the inherent sameness of the gospel and the law.[43] However, explaining why this shift in Bede's thought came about might be more difficult than suggesting that it happened. All the building blocks from which it seems to have arisen were in place quite early: in the early commentary on Acts Bede argued that the primitive church developed over time through a Jewish phase; he inherited the idea that the same faith had been expressed through different rites in different times from Augustine.

Bede's interest in the Jews and the Old Testament is often seen as a response to contemporary interests and his concerns over the election of his own people.[44] More work in relation to this may prove fruitful. The effort Bede made in his *Ecclesiastical History* to celebrate the role which heterodox missionaries, such as those from Iona to Northumbria, had in spreading the faith may be important here. The work argued that Northumbria's orthodox present evolved from a more heterodox past; more importantly Bede did not condemn those from the past, such as Aidan, whose opinions would be entirely unacceptable in his present.[45] Rather he stated that Aidan and the monks of Iona had 'a zeal of God but not according to knowledge', the phrase being Paul's description

---

[41] *Tab.* 1 (CChr.SL 119A, 6–7).

[42] Bede, *In Primam Partem Samuhelis* 2, 3 (CChr.SL 119, 108, 188); *Cant.* 1 (CChr. SL 119B, 191–2); ibid. 3 (CChr.SL 119B, 258, 271-2); *Act.* (CChr.SL 121, 36, 55).

[43] Tugène, 'Le thème'; *Temp.* 1 (CChr.SL 119A, 157–8, 182–3); *Tab.* 1, 3 (CChr.SL 119A, 19, 135).

[44] Scully, Introduction to Tobit, transl. Connolly Scheil, *Footsteps*, 43, 89–97; W. Trent Foley and Nicholas J. Higham, 'Bede on the Britons', *EME* 17 (2009), 154–85, at 168–9.

[45] *HE* 3.17 (*Ecclesiastical History*, ed. and transl. Colgrave and Mynors, 264–7); cf. Jennifer O'Reilly, Introduction to *Temple*, transl. Connolly, xvii–lv, at xxxvi–xxxvii.

of those who continued to believe in the old Jewish cult.[46] The incorrect Easter dating of the Ionans was seen as being equivalent to the outdated beliefs of the Jews.

When Bede began his writing career northern Britain was still divided in ecclesiastical practice. The key change was the conversion of Iona to the Roman Easter in 716; sometime in the years just before that King Nechtan of the Picts contacted Bede's abbot, Ceolfrith, asking for assistance in converting his nation to the Roman practice.[47] Thus, during the earlier part of Bede's career this was a live issue with an apparent push to bring the Ionan community, from which much of the Northumbrian church had received its origin, into the Roman fold. Exegesis which argued for a rejection of the old ways and the inferiority of the previous dispensation may be seen in a polemical light in such a context. It is quite possible that Bede was writing his exegesis with one eye on the ongoing Easter dispute.[48]

After 716/717 the issue changed; Iona and the Picts had accepted the Roman Easter and thus an assault upon antiquated customs was less necessary. But the origins of the Northumbrian church still lay in an era when Ionan missionaries had practised an 'incorrect' Easter. Hence perhaps the relevance of Bede's increased stress on the validity of Jewish religion in the past. Just as the Jewish church operated with sacramental power before the Incarnation, so too the Northumbrian church had possessed grace before the Synod of Whitby (when the Roman Easter was officially accepted). Both the Incarnation and the synod had changed things, but Bede's representation of the Jewish church implied that that change need not denigrate the previous state of affairs. This concept of the church may have proved helpful to the so-called 'middle group' in Northumbrian church politics, the party which embraced Roman practice without cutting all links with heterodox clerics.[49]

If a line were to be drawn through Bede's corpus based on the conversion of Iona, those works which seem to emphasize a break with the Jewish past would fall before it and those highlighting

---

[46] *HE* 3.3; 5.22 (*Ecclesiastical History*, ed. and transl. Colgrave and Mynors, 218–19, 552–5); cf. Rom. 10: 2.

[47] *HE* 5.21–2 (*Ecclesiastical History*, ed. and transl. Colgrave and Mynors, 532–55).

[48] Holder, 'The Anti-Pelagian Character', 101–3.

[49] Clare Stancliffe, *Bede, Wilfrid, and the Irish* (Jarrow, 2003), 10–11.

continuity between the Jewish and Christian churches after it. It is here, then, in the context of eighth-century Northumbria, that the cause of what has been discussed in this essay may be found. Bede argued that Old Testament Jews, seventh-century Ionan monks and contemporary Northumbrians all shared a unity of faith in the same God. That unity was related to a vision of the church as an institution developing in time, and it is perhaps appropriate, then, that it may shed some light on the development of Bede's own thought.

Queen's College, Oxford

THE DEPOSIT OF MONASTIC FAITH: THE CAROLINGIANS ON THE ESSENCE OF MONASTICISM

by RENIE CHOY

We live in an age wary of admitting that any institution has an essence, and this has posed a dilemma for the study of monasticism. Until relatively recently, historians of monasticism zealously sought out its timeless and immutable inner qualities rather than its many varieties. While acknowledging the changes in external form and circumstances, Adolf von Harnack's *Monasticism: Its Ideals and History* (1881), Dom Morin's *L'Idéal monastique* (1912), James Hannay's *The Spirit and Origin of Christian Monasticism* (1903) and Herbert Workman's *The Evolution of the Monastic Ideal* (1913) nevertheless pursued the stable qualities of monasticism which had survived the tides of time. Even in 1957 Jean Leclercq could still presume that monasticism had an 'essence', in a classic work translated into English under the title *The Love of Learning and the Desire for God: A Study of Monastic Culture*. To our twenty-first-century ears, such a monolith of a title, suggestive of the existence of a metahistorical 'monastic ideal', seems out of date. This essay approaches the subject of monastic historiography via an examination of Carolingian reflection on the monastic past, arguing that the significance of the ninth-century monastic programme lies in its effort to distil the entire received monastic heritage into a coherent and precise statement about the fundamental purpose of the monastic life. So we ask the question: when Eigil described Boniface and Sturm as spending a day away in a 'sweet discussion about the life and manners of monks', what exactly did he think they were talking about?[1]

The years from Charlemagne's *General Admonition* of 789 to the series of synods called by Louis the Pious between 816 and 819 were characterized by a concentrated effort to organize and regulate monasticism in the Frankish realm. The peak of monastic legislation occurred at Aachen in 816/17 under the leadership of

---

[1] 'suave colloquium inter se de vita et conversatione monachorum diutissime habuerunt': Eigil, *Vita Sturmi* 10 (MGH SS 2, 370).

Benedict of Aniane, when monasteries were placed under the sole
regulation of the *Rule of Benedict* and seventy detailed *capitula* were
issued, including additions to the divine office and the mass, restrictions on the privileges of abbots, and rules for strict enclosure,
clothing, bathing and eating. Over a decade ago, Richard Sullivan
observed that this intense legislative activity had left scholars somewhat bewildered about the goals of Carolingian monasticism, as
evidenced by the scarcity of scholarly studies expressly dedicated
to discussing its 'fundamental and essential features'.[2] The modern
consensus focuses on the desire of Charlemagne and Louis the
Pious to impose *uniformitas* in monastic rule, exhibit *correctio* in
practice, and organize monks as a separate *ordo* within society.[3]
These characteristics have led some scholars to regard the ceremonial accretions, legislative minutiae and rigid centralization of
Benedict of Aniane as the root of Dark Age ritualism of the most
disagreeable kind.[4]

The capitulary sources make it easy to focus on the external
forms of the monastic practice which the 'second Benedict' legis-
lated, rather than on the pastoral groundwork underpinning his
prescriptions. But if we are to take Ardo's biography at face value,
it was Benedict's discouragement at seeing many of his fellow
brethren 'retrace their steps they had walked on the road of salvation' and 'return like a pig to the dirt and a dog to his vomit' that
prompted his work as a monastic legislator: he was deeply troubled
(*turbatus*) by their unsteady faith.[5] Rebuked by Atilio for aban-
doning his brothers, Benedict made it his goal to become a teacher
of the way to salvation, to be a lamp for others. Toward this end,
Benedict zealously studied the key documents of the monastic
past, producing the *Codex Regularum*, a collection of coenobitic

---

2   R. Sullivan, 'What was Carolingian Monasticism? The Plan of Saint Gall and
the History of Monasticism', in *After Rome's Fall: Narrators and Sources of Early Medieval
History. Essays Presented to Walter Goffart*, ed. A. Murray (Toronto, ON, 1998), 251–87.

3   M. de Jong, 'Carolingian Monasticism: The Power of Prayer', in R. McKitterick,
ed., *The New Cambridge Medieval History*, 2: *c.700 – c.900* (Cambridge, 1995), 622–53.

4   e.g. A. Hauck, *Kirchengeschichte Deutschlands* (Leipzig, 1900), 2: 577–622, or (for
a more contemporary reading) A. Vauchez, *Spirituality of the Medieval West: From the
Eighth to the Twelfth Century* (Kalamazoo, MI, 1993), 11–33. Sullivan has offered a long
list of works portraying Carolingian monasticism negatively: 'What was Carolingian
Monasticism?', 259 n. 18.

5   'ut sus ad coenum canisque ad vomitum in calle salutis positum retraebant
pedem': Ardo, *Vita Benedicti abbatis Anianensis* 3 (MGH SS 15/1, 200–20).

rules, and the *Concordia Regularum*, which cited passages from these and other documents in parallel with the *Rule of Benedict*.[6] The two compilations are often viewed as evidence of the Carolingian obsession with uniformity and centralization: reformers, it is said, were eager to show how the entire monastic past culminated in the *Rule of Benedict* so as to convince reluctant monasteries to follow it exclusively.[7] But the true significance of the *Codex* and *Concordia* lies not in their being mere '*pièces justificatives*' for a uniform submission to the *Rule of Benedict*.[8] Rather, the compilations should be understood as an attempt to discern the essential nature of monasticism and to collate various textual units from the monastic past into a unified statement. Although monastic rules habitually borrowed from one another and frequently referred readers to patristic literature, we must still recognize that Benedict's act of compiling monastic literature was genuinely groundbreaking, for his compilations represent the first time that monastic rules from an extremely diverse array were brought together for the specifically stated end 'that one codex might exist out of many'.[9] He deemed it appropriate to bind together over twenty-five rules, spanning five centuries, from East and West, into one solid volume: we find here the diffuse and lengthy *Rule of the Master* alongside the spare and succinct *Second Rule of the Fathers*; rules intended for a single monastery (e.g. the *Rule of Ferreolus*) alongside those intended for several (e.g. the *Rule of Basil*); rules composed by a single author (e.g. Augustine's *Praeceptum*) alongside a rule decided by a synod of superiors (*Rule of the Four Fathers*);

---

[6]   The *Codex* is transmitted in the manuscript Munich, Bayerische Staatsbibliothek, Clm 28118 (*c*.800), and edited as *Codex regularum monasticarum et canonicarum* in PL 103, cols 393–702. In its complete form, the *Concordia* is transmitted in Orléans, Bibliothèque municipale, MS 233 (203), and Vendôme, Bibliothèque municipale, MS 60, of the ninth and eleventh centuries respectively. The authoritative edition is that of P. Bonnerue, *Benedicti Anianensis Concordia Regularum* (CChr.CM 168, 168a).

[7]   Accordingly, many studies are concerned with tracing the progress of early medieval monasticism into Benedictinism: see R. E. Sullivan, 'The Carolingian Age: Reflections on its Place in the History of the Middle Ages', *Speculum* 64 (1989), 267–306, at 277.

[8]   *Pace* D. Knowles, *The Monastic Order in England: A History of its Development from the Times of St. Dunstan to the Fourth Lateran Council, 940–1216* (Cambridge, 1940), 26–7.

[9]   'quatenus unus ex multis collectus existeret codex': Benedict of Aniane, *Concordia Regularum*, prose preface (CChr.CM 168a, 3). See C. Leyser, 'Late Antiquity in the Medieval West', in P. Rousseau, ed., *A Companion to Late Antiquity* (Chichester, 2009), 29–42, at 38.

a selection of sayings drawn from the *Vitae Patrum* alongside the extracts forming the *Regula Orientalis;* the ancient Eastern *Rule of Pachomius* alongside the seventh-century Irish *Rules of Columbanus* and the Iberian *Rule of Isidore.*[10] At the time of their original composition, monastic rules were not primarily texts of normative authority for general application, but were *ad hoc* apparati for the practical guidance of the specific communities for which they were written.[11] Benedict of Aniane brought together these diverse texts to assert the existence of a coherent body of monastic literature, using the classical 'plucking off various flowers' motif to indicate that he was weaving together one wreath.[12]

That there was a specific vision behind Benedict of Aniane's exercise is evident when we compare his compilations with two other ninth-century codices.[13] The manuscript Lambach Stiftsbibliothek 31 is, like that of Benedict, a *codex regularum*. It contains the Rules of Basil, Augustine and Columbanus, and pays particular attention to a set of rules ascribed to various Desert Fathers but actually composed in the fifth- and sixth-century West, such as the *Rule of Paul and Stephen*, the *Rule of Macarius* and the *Rule of the Four Fathers.*[14] The ninth-century compiler, working at either Gorze or

---

[10]   A. de Vogüé, 'The Cenobitic Rules of the West', *Cistercian Studies* 12 (1977), 175–83; M. Forman and T. Sullivan, 'The Latin Cenobitic Rules, AD 400–700: Editions and Translations', *American Benedictine Review* 48 (1997), 52–68.

[11]   The transformation of the monastic *regula* from an *ad hoc* instrument to a 'floating text' which could be collected into codices, and then finally to a tool of authority for monastic reform, is the subject of A. Diem, 'Inventing the Holy Rule: Some Observations on the History of Monastic Normative Observance in the Early Medieval West', in H. Dey and E. Fentress, eds, *Western Monasticism* ante litteram*: The Spaces of Monastic Observance in Late Antiquity and the Early Middle Ages,* Disciplina Monastica 7 (Turnhout, 2011), 53–84. He points particularly to the critical role of Caesarius of Arles and Columbanian monasticism in prioritizing textual observance as a feature of the monastic life.

[12]   Benedict of Aniane, *Concordia Regularum*, prose preface (CChr.CM 168a, 4); verse preface (ibid. 6). Smaragdus, abbot of St Mihiel present at the Aachen synods, also described his *Diadema Monachorum* in the same manner: PL 102, col. 593.

[13]   For a discussion about collections of rules, see A. Mundo, 'I "corpora" e i "codices regularum" nei tradizione codicologica delle regole monastiche', in *Atti del 7º congresso internazionale di studi sull'alto medioevo. 'San Benedetto nel suo tempo',* 2 vols (Spoleto, 1982), 1: 477–520. Information on the most important early medieval monastic rules, including the following two codices, has been compiled into an online database by A. Diem, in his Monastic Manuscript Project, at: <http://www.earlymedievalmonasticism.org>.

[14]   M. A. Claussen, *The Reforms of the Frankish Church: Chrodegang of Metz and the Regula canonicorum in the Eighth Century* (Cambridge, 2004), 153.

Münsterschwarzach, is primarily concerned with the textual transmission of monastic rules, and concentrates on preserving those
rules used in the two areas most famed for their monasticism: the
Rhône valley monasticism of the Gallic south and the Colum-
banus-initiated monasteries of the north. Another codex produced
in a monastery at Fleury at approximately the same time (BAV,
MS Reg. lat. 140), comprises texts of a much greater variety.[15]
Practically any type of document that has a bearing on any of the
various aspects of monastic life is admitted – for example, Ambro-
sius's tractate concerning fasting, Caesarius's sermon on the ten
virgins, Alcuin's sentences on the praise of psalmody, and extracts
from Isidore of Seville and Gregory the Great. Its purely pragmatic function as a supplemental guidebook for monks at Fleury
and its wide assortment of short texts are precisely what have
led scholars to posit that it was compiled by several distinct individuals over several periods of time.[16] These two codices reveal the
conventional purposes for compiling monastic texts: as a means
of textual transmission or as a means of spiritual exhortation in
which monastic rules were treated like any other form of spiritual
reading. Distinctively, the purpose of Benedict of Aniane's compilations is neither simply to record and transmit texts nor simply
to provide sources of spiritual reading. Rather, they exist to make
the assertion that the wide-ranging monastic traditions of the past
were bound together by a fundamental unity of spirit and formed
in aggregate a single message. Benedict of Aniane identified the
basis of this unity when he presented the purpose for his concordance of rules. Here, he cites the last chapter of the *Rule of Benedict*:
'[F]or anyone hastening on to the perfection of monastic life, there
are the teachings of the holy Fathers, the observance of which
will lead him to the very heights of perfection'.[17] For Benedict of
Aniane, the accumulation of monastic literature was a persuasive

---

[15] See Diem, 'Inventing the Holy Rule', 54; idem, *Das monastische Experiment:
Die Rolle der Keuschheit bei der Entstehung des westlichen Klosterwesens*, Vita Regularis,
Abhandlungen 24 (Münster, 2005), 379–80.

[16] L. Rudge, 'Texts and Contexts: Women's Dedicated Life from Caesarius to
Benedict', (Ph.D. diss., University of St Andrews, 2006), 142–9.

[17] 'Ceterum ad perfectionem conversationis qui festinat, sunt doctrinae sanctorum
patrum, quarum observatio perducat hominem ad celsitudinem perfectionis': *Concordia
Regularum* 1, 'De Concordia regularum' (CChr.CM 168a, 15–16); ET from *RB 1980:
The Rule of St Benedict in Latin and English with Notes*, ed. T. Fry et al. (Collegeville,
MN, 1981), 295.

presentation of the ascetic goal – moral conversion, the heights of perfection – and instruction on how to reach it.

When we appreciate Benedict's point – that the purpose of consolidating a monastic heritage was to help the monk reach the ascetic goal – the intention behind Carolingian monastic reform comes sharply into focus. One of the more subtle but significant acts of Benedict of Aniane's conciliar legislation was a direct appeal to the monastic heritage: the reinsertion of the third element of the monastic profession, the vow of *conversatio morum suorum*.[18] The original phrase from the sixth-century *Rule of Benedict*, meaning something to the effect of 'a way of life suitable for a monk', had become a point of confusion for monks in Merovingian Gaul and had been dropped from the profession formula, which now consisted only of a two-fold vow of stability and obedience.[19] In conjunction with the Aachen synods, a model *petitio* was issued with the phrase *conversatio morum* reinserted;[20] this revived three-fold profession formula was also included in Smaragdus's commentary on the *Rule of Benedict*.[21] Yet, although the authoritative text[22] of the *Rule of Benedict* distributed by Benedict of Aniane included the expression *conversatio morum*, Carolingian scribes evidently preferred to replace it with *conversio morum*, suggesting that the original phrase continued to prove puzzling or even meaningless.[23] Leaving aside Benedict of Nursia's original meaning and the ensuing confusion over the phrase, we can get some sense, from the routine replacement of *conversatio* with *conversio*, of what the

---

[18]   *Rule of Benedict* 58.17.

[19]   M. de Jong, *In Samuel's Image: Child Oblation in the Early Medieval West* (Leiden, 1996), 130.

[20]   D. Herwegen unequivocally credits Benedict of Aniane with the reinsertion of the *conversatio morum*, pointing to ch. 28 of the *Collectio capitularis*: 'Ut novitio non facilis monasterii tribuatur ingressus … ; expleto probationis suae anno secundum quod regula precipit inde faciat': *CCM 1*, 523. See D. Herwegen, *Studien zur benediktinischen Professformel* (Münster, 1912), 57–67; de Jong, *In Samuel's Image*, 104–5.

[21]   Smaragdus, *Expositio in Regulam S. Benedicti* 58 (*CCM* 8, 295).

[22]   Witnessed by St Gallen Codex 914 (see n. 23 below), in agreement with the oldest known manuscript of the *Rule of Benedict*, Oxford, Bodl., MS Hatton 48.

[23]   Manuscripts of Benedict's *Concordia Regularum* are inconsistent: several contain *conversatio*, others contain *conversio*: *Concordia* 65.1 (CChr.CM 168A, 550). The profession formula in St Gallen, Stiftsbibliothek, Cod. 914, reads *conversio* rather than *conversatio* (*CCM* 3, 177). The preference for *conversio* is also seen in the profession book of St Gall: *Das Professbuch der Abtei Sankt Gallen*, ed. P. Krieg (Augsburg, 1931), 16–19. See also Herwegen, 'Geschichte der benediktinischen Professformel', 57–60.

Carolingians intended when they reinserted this element into the monastic vow. Hildemar, writing about two decades after Benedict of Aniane's reforms, explains the full significance of the substitution:

> It must be known what is meant by *conversatio* and what by *conversio* … for some books have *conversio*, while others have *conversatio*. It seems to me that the books which say *conversio* are better than those which say *conversatio*, because *conversatio* refers to habit and life, whether good or bad. *Conversio*, however, refers to change, whether from bad to good, or from good to bad …[24]

What clearly appeals to Hildemar about the word *conversio* in place of *conversatio* is that it is a dynamic and pregnant term suitable for describing the passage from the sinful mediocre life to the virtuous glorious life.[25] It was the evidence of change and growth which the Carolingians attached to the monastic profession:

> The one (the genuine monk), increased by virtues, grows into something better, while the other (the spurious monk), grown lukewarm, deteriorates into something worse; the one grows strong in sacred virtues, the other grows lukewarm from the cares of the world; the one truthfully bears the name of monk, the other bears both the name and the tonsure of a false monk.[26]

---

[24] 'Sciendum est enim, quia aliud est *conversatio* et aliud est *conversio*. Conversatio enim attinet ad vitam et ad habitationem, conversio vero est de saeculo ad Deum, sicut in hoc loco dicitur. Quidam namque libri habent *conversionem*, quidam vero *conversationem*, sed sicut mihi videtur, melius habent illi, qui dicunt *conversionem*, quam illi, qui *conversationem*, eo quod conversatio attinet ad habitationem et ad vitam sive bonam sive malam, conversio autem ad mutationem sive de malo in bonum, sive de bono in malum': Hildemar, *Expositio Regulae Sancti Benedicti* 58, in *Vita et regula SS. P. Benedicti una cum expositione regulae a Hildemaro tradita*, ed. R. Mittermüller (Regensburg, 1880), 532–3.

[25] On this theme in medieval monastic exegesis, see H. de Lubac, *Medieval Exegesis: The Four Senses of Scripture*, transl. E. Macierowski, 2 vols (Grand Rapids, MI, 2000; first publ. as *Exégèse médiévale: Les quatre sens de l'Écriture*, 4 vols, Paris, 1959–64), 2: 143.

[26] 'unus virtutibus actus crescit in melius, alter tepidus factus decrescit in peius; unus pollet virtutibus sacris, alter tepescit saeculi curis; unus veraciter nomen monachi portat, alius falsatoris monachi nomen gestat pariter et tonsuram': Smaragdus, *Expositio* 1.6 (*CCM* 8, 59); ET from D. Barry, *Smaragdus of Saint-Mihiel: Commentary on the Rule of Saint Benedict*, Cistercian Studies 12 (Kalamazoo, MI, 2007), 120.

Smaragdus cites Isidore's etymological definition of 'life' to teach that growth was the essence of monasticism and the mark of a true monk seeking eternal life: 'Life is so called because of vigor, or because it has the power to be born and grow'.[27] Inasmuch as the Carolingian reformers felt that the monk's moral growth was the common vision behind all ancient monastic rules and the very reason for the monk's existence, Narberhaus has stated that the Carolingian insistence on the vow of *conversio morum* in the monastic profession 'strikes at the heart of the reform'.[28] Even though the majority of monks in Carolingian abbeys had been child oblates who had had no dramatic conversion of the type experienced by an adult novice, the fact that they had been consecrated to the Lord for a life of faith and virtue meant that their monastic training fundamentally concerned the shedding of vice and the accumulation of virtue.[29] An excerpt from the *Rule of Basil* which Benedict included in the section of his *Concordia Regularum* concerning child oblates commands that oblates be thrown out whose growth in spiritual diligence and fruit is not in keeping with their growth in age.[30] This was a point taken so seriously by Benedict of Aniane that the first document which he inserted into his *Codex* immediately after the *Rule of Benedict* itself was his tract on penance for monks who committed any of the four types of sins retarding spiritual growth.[31] To enforce the moral conversion of all monks was a fundamental task for this reformer who had

---

[27] Smaragdus, *Expositio*, Prologue 17, on the *Rule of Benedict*: 'Si vis habere veram et perpetuam vitam' (*CCM* 8, 30), citing Isidore *Etymologiae* 11.1.3: 'Vita dicta propter vigorem, vel quod vim teneat nascendi atque crescendi' (ET from Barry, *Commentary*, 82). On the theme of growth in Smaragdus, see also *Expositio*, Prologue 8, 49 (*CCM* 8, 24, 49).

[28] J. Narberhaus, *Benedikt von Aniane, Werk und Persönlichkeit* (Münster, 1930), 60: 'trifft den Kernpunkt der Reform'. This conclusion is in contrast with a strain of contemporary scholarship which views the medieval monastery as an impermeable locus of sanctity filled with monks and nuns deemed by society to be holy, a *septa secretiora* where holiness was more to be managed than pursued. See Diem, *Das monastische Experiment*.

[29] For the problem of the vow of *conversio morum* for those who had never known the secular life, see de Jong, *In Samuel's Image*, 131.

[30] Benedict of Aniane, *Concordia Regularum* 66.2, 'Ex Regula sancti Basilii' (CChr. CM 168a, 3): 'Si vero cum aetatis augmento nullus in eis depraehenditur profectus industriae, sed vaga mens et animus cassus ac tumens etiam post instituta probabilia infructuosus permanserit, huiuscemodi abici oportet'.

[31] Benedict of Aniane, *Excerptus diversarum modus paenitentiarum* (PL 103, cols 1417–20).

81

defined the 'path of the just' as 'a shining light proceeding and growing until it reaches the perfect day'.[32]

Precisely because of its effectiveness in taking monks along this path of progress, the *Rule of Benedict* was promoted as the exclusive rule for monasteries throughout the Frankish realm. Smaragdus's praise of the Rule rested solely on his confidence in its effectiveness in facilitating a monk's growth. The Rule, to paraphrase Smaragdus, admonishes the monk to seek the heavenly realms. It is a weapon against the darts of the wicked. It chastises the monk with love and nurtures him with a tender rod. It scrutinizes, shapes and adorns his behaviour. It weighs and compares monks. It files, weighs, polishes and shines. It removes faults, reproves, entreats, rebukes and amends. In doing these things, the Rule knows how to bring the monk all the way to eternal life.[33] But lest we mistakenly attribute finality to the Rule, the Carolingians, following St Benedict himself, made it clear that the Rule was 'not the whole fulfilment of justice'.[34] Rather, it was the entire deposit of the monastic faith which would encourage and facilitate the conversion of a monk's habits and nature, and bring him to his goal of perfection. This view is most clearly seen in the interest of Carolingian monastic writers in the final chapter of the Rule. The unique qualities of this section, such as its distinct language, introduction of new themes and independence from the *Rule of the Master* (an anonymous sixth-century monastic rule which most scholars agree was heavily used by Benedict for his own rule), have given rise to scholarly controversy about its authorship and original position within the *Rule of Benedict*.[35] At the hands of Carolingian monastics, this last chapter sometimes floated freely: Benedict of Aniane moved it to the beginning of his *Concordia Regularum*, and at least one manuscript from the early tenth century contains

---

[32] *De modis amiciciarum et vera amicicia*, ed J. Leclercq, in 'Les *Munimenta fidei* de saint Benoit d'Aniane', in *Studia anselmiana philosophia theologica*, 20: *Analecta monastica* 1 (Vatican City, 1952), 21–74, at 62, referring to Prov. 4: 18: 'Iustorum semita quasi lux splendens procedit et crescit usque ad perfectam diem'.

[33] Smaragdus, *Expositio*, metrical preface (*CCM* 8, 3–5; ET from Barry, *Commentary*, 43–5).

[34] 'De hoc quod non omnis iustitiae observatio in hac sit regula constituta': *Rule of Benedict* 73, referring to Matt. 3: 16.

[35] G. Penco, 'Ricerche sul capitolo finale della Regola di S. Benedetto', *Benedictina* 8 (1954), 25–42; E. Manning, 'Le chapître 73 de la Règle bénédictine est-il de S. Benoît?', *Archivium Latinitatis Medii Aevi* 30 (1960), 129–41.

only this section of the rule.[36] For the Carolingian commentators on the *Rule of Benedict*, this chapter was critical for specifying the common principle undergirding the entirety of the received monastic heritage, as they homed in on Benedict of Nursia's point that the teachings of Scripture, Cassian, Basil and other ancient Fathers would lead one to perfection, and that his own rule was only for beginners.[37] Smaragdus emphasized that the Old Testament prophets and the New Testament apostles presented the 'model and a norm' (*exempla et norma*) for all right-living monks of his time, who should also benefit from the 'universal discipline of the ancients' (*illam universam veterum disciplinam*) accessible through their precepts and biographies.[38]

This approach to the monastic past allows us to appreciate why Benedict of Aniane included as part of his *Codex Regularum* some texts which seem out of place. The sixth-century *Vita Pachomii Iunioris*, here ascribed to Jerome, stands apart in the *Codex* as the only narrative work.[39] Benedict of Aniane's interest in this *Vita* is possibly that it recounts the story about the *conversio* of Pachomius from paganism to Christian ascetic living, and his subsequent receipt of a coenobitic rule from an angel for leading monks through the transformation 'from the corruption of sin to the incorruption of life eternal'.[40] The two prayers of Pachomius praising God for the dramatic transformations which he effects (the blind see, the deaf hear, the lame walk, lepers are cleansed, the foolish made wise, and so on) make clear that the provision of a rule for monks is a divine gift to serve this purpose of *conversio*, the renovation of the soul.[41] Another text found in the *Codex* offers good indication that Benedict of Aniane's interest in compiling monastic literature was more sophisticated than simply pronouncing the triumph of

---

[36] El Escorial, Real Biblioteca de San Lorenzo, MS a I.13, part I, fol. 3.
[37] *Rule of Benedict* 73.1–2.
[38] Smaragdus, *Expositio* 63 (*CCM* 8, 336).
[39] For analysis and edition, see A. Diem and H. Müller, eds, '*Vita, Regula, Sermo*: Eine unbekannte lateinische *Vita Pacomii* als Lehrtext für ungebildete Mönche und als Traktat über das Sprechen', in R. Corradini, M. Diesenberger and M. Niederkorn-Bruck, eds, *Zwischen Niederschrift und Wiederschrift: Frühmittelalterliche Hagiographie und Historiographie im Spannungsfeld von Kompendienüberlieferung und Editionstechnik* (Vienna, 2010), 223–72.
[40] *Vita Pachomii* 11 (Diem and Müller, eds, '*Vita, Regula, Sermo*', 261).
[41] *Vita Pachomii* 35, 62–8 (Diem and Müller, eds, '*Vita, Regula, Sermo*', 262–4). Pachomius describes his conversion in terms of *anima renovata*.

the *Rule of Benedict.* Benedict appended to Fructuosus of Braga's *Regula Monastica Communis* a certain *pactum* which, emphasizing the right of monks to resist the authority of the abbot in the case of serious negligence or injustice, is at cross-purposes with the *Rule of Benedict*'s teaching on the absolute obedience owed by monks to abbots.[42] When viewed as a proof-text for the *Rule*, this *pactum*'s presence in the *Codex* makes little sense; when seen as a general reflection on the purpose of the monastic life, its inclusion is more readily appreciated. The pact argues that monks who have entrusted their souls to their abbot no longer have a reason to hold him as a spiritual father who fails to 'pronounce, teach, perform, reprimand, command, excommunicate, or correct in accordance with the Rule (of Fructuosus)' or to offer them to Christ 'spotless and unharmed'.[43] It was the essential purpose of monasticism to lead a monk to virtue and perfection, a fact which engaged Boniface and Sturm when they spent the day in conversation about the 'monastic life'.

The Carolingians approached their monastic history with the desire to show that the manifold sources all pointed to a single idea: that the work of a monk was 'to progress, to go forward, to tend towards perfection', in the words of Dom Paul Delatte.[44] That monasticism was about the transformation of a life in search of God, was a belief which guided their historiographical project: the monastic past presented them with a statement about what a transformed life looked like and how one could attain it. The larger Carolingian programme of *correctio* which occasioned this interest in monastic tradition was also concerned with other manners of cultural practice, including music, metalwork, and especially spelling, pronunciation and grammar. Significantly, Charlemagne's *De litteris colendis* made it clear that good grammar was not to be studied for its own sake.[45] A monk was to study the art of letters

---

[42]   Fructuosus of Braga, *Regula Monastica Communis* (PL 87, cols 1109–27); appended to the terminal chapter of the *Regula* is the *Pactum Fructuosi* (ibid., col. 1127). By comparison, see the chapter on 'obedience' in *Rule of Benedict* 5. See also C. J. Bishko, 'The Pactual Tradition in Hispanic Monasticism', in idem, *Spanish and Portuguese Monastic History* (London, 1984), I.

[43]   *Pactum Fructuosi* (PL 87, cols 1128, 1130; ET in *Iberian Fathers*, transl. C. W. Barlow, 2 vols, Fathers of the Church 62, 63 [Washington, DC, 1969], 2: 208–9).

[44]   P. Delatte, *The Rule of St. Benedict: A Commentary*, transl. J. McCann (New York, 1921; first publ. as *Commentaire sur la Règle de saint Benoît*, Paris, 1913), 491.

[45]   *Karoli epistole de litteris colendis* 29 (MGH Capitularia regum Francorum I

because it would point him to a world of grammatical categories and etymology outside of the immediate scriptural text which would allow him to understand the meaning behind the words: to understand figures of speech, tropes and other grammatical units was to penetrate deep spiritual mysteries. Thus the monk was to study grammar in order to attain a more substantial faith, 'so that whoever should desire to see you ... on account of the reputation of your holy way of life may be edified as much by your wisdom as by your appearance'.[46] Likewise the 'grammar' of the monastic past – the various units of monastic *regulae* which constituted the monastic entity – was put to the same use.[47] The texts pointed to a world of unified monastic categories outside of the immediate *Rule of Benedict* which would allow the monk to recognize the one purpose for which all the Rules existed, and in so doing to become a monk with a more substantial profession.[48] Recognizing the unity behind monastic rules, as with the rules of grammar, would allow the monk to penetrate the spiritual mysteries which bolstered his profession, facilitated his spiritual progress and led him to perfection. With this conviction, Benedict of Aniane wrote the following lines to introduce his *Concordia*:

> Whatever things the Fathers taught truly and in harmony,
> let me confess, are the very same words and one;
> although diverse, the meaning is never torn apart, for it is one.
> The spirit and the faith which it teaches is one,
> the fatherland to which it clings is one, the path which leads
> there is one,

[Hanover, 1883], 79).

[46] 'ut, quicunque vos propter ... sanctae conversationis nobilitatem ad videndum expetierit, sicut de aspectu vestro aedificatur visus, ita quoque de sapientia vestra': ibid.

[47] I am grateful to Luke Gardiner, who, in a response to the presentation of this communication at the Ecclesiastical History Society's Summer Meeting, suggested the similar function of grammar in the formation of an essential Christian or monastic identity. It is not surprising that we find the same Smaragdus who wrote a commentary on the *Rule of Benedict* also writing a commentary on Donatus's *Grammar*: Smaragdus, *Liber in partibus Donati* (CChr.CM 68).

[48] A. de Vogüé has argued that in producing the *Concordia*, Benedict of Aniane's purpose was to combat a certain '*paresse*' (laziness), indifference, and negligence of his contemporaries toward the monastic tradition apart from the *Rule of Benedict*: La Concordia regularum de Benoît d'Aniane: son vrai but et sa structure', in *Il monachesimo italiano dall'età longobardo all'età ottonianna (secc. VIII–X): Atti del VII Convegno di Studi Storici sull'Italia Benedettina, Nonantola (Modena), 10–13 settembre 2003*, ed. G. Spinelli (Cesena, 2006), 39–45, especially 40–1.

and so we rightly call the name of our book a Concordance. …
This is the true way, this goblet of life extends
sweet-flowing nourishments which are sweeter than honey.
This codex grants these things, grants that the worthy and
thankful
may merit to live with Christ blessed without end.[49]

University of Oxford

---

[49] 'Iam quidquid docuere Patres concorditer, atque | Verius ꞇ : fatear, eadem simul unus et ipsa | Verba, licet dispar sensus non scinditur unus, | Una fides cunctos docuit et spiritus unus, | Una tenet patria, trames qua duxit et unus, | Dicimus ergo libri nomen *Concordia* rite. … | Haec est vera via, porgit haec pocula v tae, | Pabula dulci-flua melle quae dulcius extant, | Haec tribuit codex, tribuit sine fine beate | Vivere cum Christo dignasque promere grates': Benedict of Aniane, *Concordia Regularum*, metrical preface (CChr.CM 168a, 6–7).

REMEMBERING POPE GREGORY VII:
CARDINAL BOSO AND ALEXANDER III

by JOHN DORAN[*]

In the conclusion to his masterly biography of Pope Gregory VII (1073–85), H. E. John Cowdrey notes the paradox that the pope so lionized by modern historians, to the extent that the age of reform bears his name, was largely forgotten in the twelfth century and made little impact on Christian thought, spirituality or canon law.[1] Cowdrey is not alone in his observation that Gregory 'receded from memory with remarkable speed and completeness'; when he was remembered, it was as a failure and as one who brought decline upon the church.[2] For Cowdrey, the answer to this conundrum lay in the fact that Gregory VII was in fact far closer to the ideals of the sixth century than of the twelfth; he was a Benedictine monk and shared the worldview and outlook of Gregory the Great (590–604) rather than those of the so-called lawyer popes Alexander III (1159–81) and Innocent III (1198–1216). Yet within a century of Gregory's death he was presented by Cardinal Boso as a model pope, who had overcome a schismatic emperor and the problems which his interference had precipitated in Rome. For Boso, writing for the instruction of the officials of the papal chamber, the very policies set out by Gregory VII were to be pursued and emulated. Far from being a peripheral and contradictory figure, with more in common with the distant past than the near future, Gregory was the perfect guide to the beleaguered Pope Alexander III, who was also struggling against a hostile emperor and his antipope.

Cardinal Boso composed his series of papal biographies during

[*]   Sadly, John Doran died as this volume was going to press. A tribute to him will appear in SCH 50, which he co-edited.

[1]   H. E. John Cowdrey, *Pope Gregory VII, 1073–1085* (Oxford, 1998), 683–4.

[2]   Thomas N. Bisson, *The Crisis of the Twelfth Century* (Princeton, NJ, 2009), 89–93, esp. 92; Geoffrey Barraclough, *The Medieval Papacy* (London, 1968), 89–90; John Gilchrist, 'The Gregorian Reform Tradition and Pope Alexander III', in Filippo Liotta, ed., *Miscellanea, Rolando Bandinelli, Papa Alessandro III* (Siena, 1986), 261–87, at 262–4; Colin Morris, *The Papal Monarchy: The Western Church from 1050 to 1250*, OHCC (Oxford, 1989), 109–21, esp. 121.

the 1160s and 1170s, after a long career as a curialist.[3] He seems to have arrived at the papal curia, certainly by 1135, under the patronage of Cardinal Guy of Pisa. Boso's association with Guy and his own words of praise for Lucius II (1144–5) for bringing canons regular from Lucca to Rome suggest that he was himself a canon regular, perhaps with links to S. Frediano in Lucca.[4] As a canon regular, Boso would have been perceived as an antagonist by the native Roman clergy, who were hostile to this mode of religious life, which was introduced to Rome from the early twelfth century, most notably in the Lateran basilica.[5] Symbolic of the dominance of the canons was the privilege they secured that every cardinal deacon of S. Maria Nova should come from the S. Frediano community, and this at a time when very few native Romans were being named as cardinals.[6]

Boso rose to prominence in the wake of his clerical protector. Cardinal Guy became chancellor of the Roman church under Eugenius III (1145–53) and, following his death in 1149, the role of chancellor was effectively occupied by Boso, who dated papal letters until Rolando, the future Alexander III, was appointed chancellor in 1153.[7] In 1154, under Adrian IV (1154–9), Boso became papal chamberlain (i.e. treasurer), while in 1157 he was elevated to the college of cardinals with the diaconal title of SS. Cosma e Damiano, previously held by both Guy of Pisa and Rolando.[8] As

---

[3]   Ian S. Robinson, *The Papacy 1073–1198: Continuity and Innovation* (Cambridge, 1990), 254–7; Zelina Zafarana, 'Bosone', in *DBI*, 13: 270–4; Fritz Geisthardt, *Der Kämmerer Boso* (Berlin, 1936); for a brief but thorough account, see *Le Liber Pontificalis*, ed. Louis Duchesne, Bibliothèque des Écoles françaises d'Athènes et de Rome, 2nd ser. 3, 2nd edn, 3 vols (Paris, 1955–7), 2: xxxvii–xliv.

[4]   *DBI*, 13: 271; *Liber Pontificalis*, ed. Duchesne, 2: 385–6.

[5]   Pietro Zerbi, '"Vecchio" e "nuovo" monachesimo alla metà del secolo XII', 3–24; Cosmo Damiano Fonseca, 'Monaci e canonici alla ricerca di una identità', 203–22; Luigi Prosdocimi, 'Germi di "modernità" nelle strutture ecclesiastiche del secolo XII', 721–31; all in *Istituzioni Monastiche e Istituzioni Canonicali in Occidente (1123–1215). Atti della settima Settimana internazionale di studio, Mendola, 28 agosto – 3 settembre 1977*, Pubblicazioni della Università Cattolica del Sacro Cuore 9 (Milan, 1980). See also Morris, *Papal Monarchy*, 240–62, 612–16.

[6]   Philippus Jaffé, *Regesta Pontificum Romanorum ad annum 1198*, ed. S. Loewenfeld, F. Kaltenbrunner and P. W. Ewald, 2 vols (Leipzig, 1885–8), no. 8480; renewed by Alexander III himself in 1160: ibid., no. 10637.

[7]   Johannes M. Brixius, *Die Mitglieder des Kardinalkollegiums von 1130–1181* (Berlin, 1912), 43, 56–7; Barbara Zenker, *Die Mitglieder des Kardinalkollegiums von 1130–1159* (Würzburg, 1964), 146–8, 86–8.

[8]   Brixius, *Mitglieder*, 58; Zenker, *Mitglieder*, 149–52.

papal chamberlain Boso pursued a concerted policy of restoring the fortunes of the church in central Italy, where much of his work involved personally receiving oaths from individuals and towns in the environs of Rome who had been induced to become papal vassals.[9] In pursuit of these efforts Boso compiled a *liber censuum*, a list of the claims of the Roman church to lands and rights, as a result of which his knowledge of the archival sources of the Roman church became very extensive. His series of papal biographies was essentially a private work, compiled in order to serve as a model for later chamberlains and others who sought to restore the fortunes of the papacy, such as Cencius Camerarius, later Honorius III (1216–27), and Cardinal Albinus, both of whom were active under popes Clement III (1187–91) and Celestine III (1191–8).[10]

The painstaking work undertaken by Boso in central Italy was destroyed by the disputed election of 1159 and the subsequent recognition by Frederick Barbarossa of the antipope Victor IV in preference to Alexander III.[11] The initial success of Victor forced Alexander to go into exile in France, but Boso remained an important adviser, and his promotion as cardinal priest of S. Pudenziana in 1165–6 was perhaps a reward for his part in garnering support in Italy and securing the return of Alexander III to Rome.[12] Few men in positions of such influence left eye-witness accounts, certainly during the Middle Ages, and the value of Boso's work has not been sufficiently appreciated by historians.[13] Boso was clearly involved in the formulation of policy at the highest level, and was denounced by the canons of St Peter's basilica as 'the first-born of Satan',

9 *Liber Pontificalis*, ed. Duchesne, 2: 397; Geisthardt, *Der Kämmerer Boso*, 441–59; Pierre Toubert, *Les structures du Latium médiéval: Le Latium méridional et la Sabine du IXᵉ siècle à la fin du XIIᵉ siècle*, 2 vols, Bibliotheque des Écoles françaises d'Athènes et de Rome 221 (Rome, 1973), 1048–51, 1060–5, 1075, 1170.

10 Paul Fabre, *Étude sur le Liber Censuum de l'Église romaine* (Paris, 1892), 16–21; Peter Munz, Introduction to *Boso's Life of Alexander III*, transl. G. M. Ellis (Oxford, 1973), 1, 25–9; Odilo Engels, 'Kardinal Boso als Geschichtsschreiber', in *Konzil und Papst. Festgabe für Hermann Tüchle*, ed. Georg Schwaiger (Munich, 1975), 147–68; *Liber Pontificalis*, ed. Duchesne, 2: xlii–xliii.

11 John Doran, '"At last we reached the port of salvation": The Roman Context of the Schism of 1159', in Peter D. Clarke and Anne J. Duggan, eds, *Pope Alexander III (1159–81): The Art of Survival* (Farnham, 2012), 51–98.

12 Zenker, *Mitglieder*, 151.

13 Engels, 'Kardinal Boso', 147; for an exceptional recognition of Boso's importance, see Arsenio Frugoni, *Arnaldo da Brescia nelle fonti del secolo XII* (Rome, 1954), 123–9.

and fomentor of the schism of 1159, yet there is little in his text which explicitly reveals his own role; it is here that his account of Gregory VII can provide important insights.[14] For Boso not only wrote biographies of his contemporary popes; he also drew upon other sources in order to explain the history of the papacy before his own time. Moreover, not content simply to copy from his sources, he made significant changes in his description of crucial events.[15] These changes show that Boso drew upon the past in order to inform the present, and when he found accounts which conflicted with his own perception of how a pope should behave, he altered them. They were given added significance because the cardinal was not writing for a general audience, but for a small group of administrators who were his assistants in the papal chamber, men who knew from the documents at their disposal that their task had indeed been begun under Gregory VII.[16] Boso's reappraisal of Gregory's pontificate was a direct appeal to the past in order to justify what he and his assistants were aiming to achieve in the present, a vindication of his own policy and of his own pope, Alexander III.

Boso's papal biographies present the historian with a number of problems. Firstly, there is no extant contemporary manuscript. Boso's original compositions, beginning with the pontificate of Paschal II, were copied into a version of the *Liber Censuum* of Cencius Camerarius, now at Florence, in 1254/5,[17] together with a series of excerpts from earlier sources. These appear as an attempt to provide an account of the papacy from the point at which the original *Liber Pontificalis* ended in the ninth century. Fabre reviewed the text for his edition of the *Liber Censuum* and expressed doubt as to whether Boso had compiled the earlier lives, although not doubting his authorship of the lives of Adrian IV and Alexander III.[18] Duchesne, who edited the text for inclusion in his edition of the *Liber Pontificalis*, noted that the compilation of the earlier lives was entirely consistent with Boso's original work and that it

14 Doran, '"At last we reached the port of salvation"', 87–91.
15 Engels, 'Kardinal Boso', 152.
16 Fabre, *Étude*, 21.
17 Paul Fabre, 'Les vies des papes dans les manuscrits du *Liber Censuum*', *Mélanges d'archéologie et d'histoire de l'École française de Rome* 6 (1886), 147–61, at 147–8; for an overview of the manuscripts of the *Liber Censuum*, see Fabre, *Étude*, 170–227.
18 Fabre, 'Les vies des papes', 155–7.

was thus reasonable to suppose that Boso had been responsible for the earlier compilation too. Both pieces were clearly intended to form part of his own *Liber Censuum*, the text of which has not survived, although it can be traced in the later compilation by Cencius Camerarius.[19]

The second problem with Boso's *Lives* is the attention which has been paid to one part of the manuscript, the life of Alexander III. Peter Munz stresses the dramatic element, noting that Boso was interested in writing a history of the Alexandrine schism which had a hero in Alexander, intent only on preserving the unity of the church, and a villain in Frederick Barbarossa, equally intent on destroying that unity.[20] Boso's model was the *Liber Pontificalis* and thus his lives were mainly concerned with the actions of the popes in the city of Rome.[21] To single out the biography of Alexander as a dramatic narrative is, however, to miss the point. The intention was to justify the consistent policy being pursued by the popes, and by Boso himself as chamberlain, which sought to restore the territorial fortunes of the papacy. The life of Alexander must be considered in the context of what came earlier in the manuscript.

Boso clearly saw his own era as a continuation of that of the reform. Adrian IV had made Boso responsible for the restitution of many towns and cities to the church and for the creation of new strongholds, the *castra specialia*.[22] The ultimate aim of this policy was to provide security for the pope in Rome.[23] That security was threatened, just as it had been in the eleventh century, by the assertive policies being pursued in Italy by a young emperor.[24] Significantly, Boso was at the forefront of a group of cardinals which supported the renewed alliance of Adrian IV with the Normans in

---

[19] *Liber Pontificalis*, ed. Duchesne, 2: xxxvii–lxiii; Enrico Stevenson, 'Osservazioni sulla "Collectio canonum" di Deusdedit', *Archivio della Società romana di storia patria* 8 (1885), 305–98, at 368–70.

[20] Munz, Introduction to *Boso's Life of Alexander III*, 1–3.

[21] Ibid. 4; for the *Liber Pontificalis*, see Duchesne's introductions to the first and second volumes and the additional notes provided by Mollat in the third volume; an accessible brief introduction is provided by *The Book of the Pontiffs (Liber Pontificalis)*, transl. and ed. R. Davis, TTH 6, rev. edn (Liverpool, 2000), xi–lxiii.

[22] *Le Liber Censuum de l'Église Romaine*, ed. P. Fabre and L. Duchesne, 3 vols (Paris, 1889–1910), 1: 385–400.

[23] Toubert, *Les structures du Latium*, 1051–81.

[24] Giovanni Tabacco, 'Northern and Central Italy in the Twelfth Century', in David Luscombe and Jonathan Riley-Smith, eds, *The New Cambridge Medieval History*, 4: *c.1024–c.1198* (Cambridge, 2004), Part 2, 428–34.

June 1156.[25] This political context explains the changes which Boso made to Bonizo of Sutri's *Liber ad amicum*, each of which can be explained as a deliberate attempt to correct the historical record in order to fit current preoccupations. The cardinal himself experienced the same problems which had faced Bonizo's popes.[26] Thus Boso included the Norman alliance of 1059, which demonstrated the vulnerability of the reform party in Rome, when Nicholas II (1059–61) was greatly disturbed that the Roman captains had 'through violence occupied and illegally retained the rights of the church and the rulership of the city'.[27] Nicholas went to Apulia in order to reconcile the Normans, who not only returned all the lands which they had seized, but forced the pope's contumacious vassals to return to their fealty. For Boso, the natural consequence of the pope's vassals returning to their fealty was the liberation of Rome from their tyranny and the restoration of the church.

In recounting the events of Christmas 1075, Boso revealed his own ideas about the role of the pope by altering Bonizo's account.[28] Cencius Stephani, a troublesome Roman nobleman, seized Gregory during the vigil mass of Christmas at S. Maria Maggiore and dragged him from the altar, Boso omitting that the pope was wounded as a result. He was then taken to a remarkable tower which Cencius had built in the city. In the morning the Romans released the pope and completely destroyed the tower. At this point the two accounts diverge significantly. Bonizo simply recounted that Gregory had prevented the Romans from killing Cencius; instead, they punished him and his accomplices with many blows and banishment. For Boso, however, the most significant thing was that following his ordeal Gregory returned immediately to his customary duties. Indeed, so keen was Boso to emphasize this that he deliberately transposed these events from

---

[25] Robinson, *Papacy*, 52–3, 79–83, 116, 389–91, 470–1; but see also Anne J. Duggan, '*Totius christianitatis caput*: The Pope and the Princes', in Brenda Bolton and Anne J. Duggan, eds, *Adrian IV, The English Pope (1154–1159): Studies and Texts* (Aldershot, 2003), 113–20.

[26] For Bonizo's 'Letter to a Friend', see Ian S. Robinson, *The Papal Reform of the Eleventh Century: Lives of Pope Leo IX and Pope Gregory VII* (Manchester, 2004), 36–63.

[27] *Liber Pontificalis*, ed. Duchesne, 2: 358; *Bonizonis episcopi Sutrini Liber ad amicum*, in MGH LdeL 1, 568–620, at 592–3; ET with extensive commentary in Robinson, *Papal Reform*, 158–262, at 232–3.

[28] *Liber Pontificalis*, ed. Duchesne, 2: 362; MGH LdeL 1, 606; Cowdrey, *Gregory VII*, 327–8.

Christmas to Easter, stating that the pope went to the Lateran palace to eat the customary meal with the cardinals and others.[29] These details do not appear in Bonizo's account, but they reveal the considerable importance which Boso attached to ceremonial and to the observation of customs. The disruptions of the twelfth century had led to the loss of the routine round of visits to the great basilicas and other stational churches, and of the communal meals which had their origin in the temporal administration of the eighth- and ninth-century popes.[30] The anxiety which Boso clearly felt about this is revealed towards the end of his *Life* of Alexander III, when he says that the pope wanted the Roman people to allow him to return to the city as shepherd and bishop of their souls in order that he and his brothers, the cardinals, could perform their customary offices in their churches.[31]

Boso's account of how the Romans dealt with Cencius is also revealing. While Bonizo simply reported that the Romans inflicted punishment and banishment on Cencius and his followers, Boso wrote that the Roman people judged Cencius and his accomplices in their own tribunal (*in rebus propriis*), condemning and imposing perpetual banishment from Rome upon them.[32] Here Boso placed a contemporary gloss on the events of 1075, reflecting the increased autonomy which the Romans had secured during the twelfth century with the development of their own commune, recognized by the popes but often at odds with them.[33] Significantly, he related that the rebels had been judged on Easter Monday, but Boso knew full well that this was the pope's ceremonial crowning day when he rode in procession from St Peter's to the Lateran, having received the customary oaths of fidelity from civic officials.

---

[29] *Liber Pontificalis*, ed. Duchesne, 2: 362; cf. MGH LdeL 1, 606; for this customary meal, see *Le* Liber Censuum, ed. Fabre and Duchesne, 1: 298.

[30] John Baldovin, *The Urban Character of Christian Worship: The Origins, Development and Meaning of Stational Liturgy*, Orientalia Christiana Analecta 228 (Rome, 1987), 105–268; Thomas F. X. Noble, 'Topography, Celebration, and Power: The Making of a Papal Rome in the Eighth and Ninth Centuries', in Mayke de Jong, Frans Theuws and Carine van Rhijn, eds, *Topographies of Power in the Early Middle Ages* (Leiden, 2001), 45–91, at 83–91.

[31] *Liber Pontificalis*, ed. Duchesne, 2: 426.

[32] Ibid. 2: 362; MGH LdeL 1, 606.

[33] Jean-Claude Maire Vigueur, 'Il comune romano', in A. Vauchez, ed., *Roma medievale*, Storia di Roma dall'antichità a oggi (Rome, 2001), 117–57.

Indeed, as chamberlain, Boso's task on that very day was to hand over the salaries of the officials in return.[34]

Boso's treatment of the third successive year in which Henry IV besieged Rome reveals once again that the interests of pope and Romans were not always identical.[35] By 1084 Gregory had lost much of his support in Rome, not only among the people, who had endured three years of hardship, but also among his own cardinals, who were critical of his intransigence.[36] Boso reported that the Roman people came to Gregory and implored him to crown Henry IV, begging him 'to have mercy on their almost lost homeland'. Gregory replied that he would rather die than renounce justice and the liberty of the church. He would only crown Henry if he guaranteed these things. Otherwise 'he ought not to and would not hear the Romans' plea'. Boso altered Bonizo's account of Gregory's words and chose to omit his inclusion of 'bishops, clerics, abbots and monks' among the imploring Romans. But Boso well understood the basis of the argument. Henry IV was exploiting the weakness of the pope in a city forced to suffer because of a quarrel in which it had little interest. In July 1167, after the Romans had been defeated outside Tusculum at Monte Porzio, Frederick Barbarossa was approaching Rome with an imperial army and a large number of Roman hostages.[37] In spite of the money expended by Alexander on the defence of the city, Frederick exploited this situation and secured the pope's flight from Rome, which must have been in Boso's mind as he wrote.[38]

According to Boso, Henry won over the Roman people with money and fear, inducing Gregory and his cardinals to move to Castel Sant'Angelo for greater security.[39] Boso made no attempt to hide the loss of local support related by Bonizo. Upon hearing that Gregory had sent for assistance to Robert Guiscard, Henry destroyed the houses on the Capitoline Hill and the Leonine City

---

[34] *Le* Liber Censuum, ed. Fabre and Duchesne, 1: 299–310; 2: 154.

[35] *Liber Pontificalis*, ed. Duchesne, 2: 367.

[36] Cowdrey, *Gregory VII*, 329; Robinson, *Papacy*, 36; for criticism of Gregory from the lower clergy of Rome, see Zelina Zafarana, 'Sul "conventus" del clero romano nel maggio 1082', *Studi Medievali* 7 (1966), 399–403.

[37] Doran, '"At last we reached the port of salvation"', 78–82.

[38] *Liber Pontificalis*, ed. Duchesne, 2: 417; ibid., xl for Boso writing his account in 1177–8.

[39] Ibid. 368.

before fleeing from Rome with Wibert (the antipope Clement III, 1080–1100). Here Boso followed Bonizo's account, but for him the destruction of houses on the Capitoline took on added significance.[40] At least since the establishment of the Roman Commune in 1143 the Capitol was regarded as a symbol of the Roman people.[41] Hence, for Boso, Henry's attack on the Capitol represented an attack on the Roman people. Although in 1084 the Capitol was probably a stronghold of the Corsi family, which continued to support Gregory after most other Roman families had abandoned him, Boso used this incident as an example of the hostility of the empire to the interests of the Romans.[42]

The assault of Robert Guiscard and the Normans on Rome in 1084 is often seen as an immense calamity for the city.[43] Although good reasons exist to believe that the severity of the sack which it occasioned has been exaggerated, Boso's concern was with the deserved punishment of the Romans for their abandonment of the legitimate pope.[44] At this point, he deviated markedly from his source. Bonizo related that, following the pope's liberation, Guiscard spent many days in the Lateran palace passing judgement upon the Romans, after which he took the pope with him to Salerno, the inference being that Gregory could not stay in a city in which he had lost support.[45] Boso, however, studiously avoided mentioning the Lateran palace as the place from which judgement was passed by Robert Guiscard. This is perhaps because the Lateran lost its judicial significance after the recognition of the Roman Senate by the popes in the 1140s, when such functions passed to the Capitol.[46] More plausibly, Boso was perhaps cautious about suggesting that Robert Guiscard had exercised judicial

---

[40] Ibid.; MGH LdeL 1, 614–15.

[41] Norberto Grammacini, 'La prima riedificazione del Campidoglio e la rivoluzione senatoriale del 1144', in *Roma, centro ideale della cultura dell'Antico nei secoli xv e xvi, da Martino V al sacco di Roma, 1417–1527. Convegno internazionale di studi su umanesimo e Rinascimento, Roma, 25–30 novembre 1985*, ed. Silvia Danesi Squarzina (Milan, 1989), 33–47.

[42] Richard Krautheimer, *Rome, Profile of a City, 312–1308* (Princeton, NJ, 1980), 149.

[43] Ferdinand Gregorovius, *History of the City of Rome in the Middle Ages*, transl. Annie Hamilton, 6 vols (London, 1894–8), 4: 237–54; L. Gatto, *Storia di Roma nel medioevo* (Rome, 1999), 314– 20.

[44] *Liber Pontificalis*, 2: 368; Louis Hamilton, 'Memory, Symbol, and Arson: Was Rome "Sacked" in 1084?', *Speculum* 78 (2003), 378–99.

[45] *Liber Pontificalis*, ed. Duchesne, 2: 368.

[46] Cesare D'Onofrio, *Un popolo di statue racconta* (Rome, 1990), 250–62.

power in Rome, especially in the place where papal justice was usually dispensed.[47]

Boso did, however, mention the Lateran palace, but in a context ignored by Bonizo, when he reported that following the Normans' liberation of Gregory, they left him and his brothers, the cardinals, 'sitting in peace in the Lateran palace, busy with ecclesiastical business from all parts of the world as their office demanded'. Only after 'a long time' did Gregory leave Rome voluntarily to join Robert Guiscard at Salerno.[48] Why did Boso falsify his historical account? It is clear that he believed that chastisement by the Normans had restored the Romans to their obedience. Elsewhere in his biographies he was a firm advocate of dealing harshly with the Romans to recall them from their errors.[49] But the main reason seems to be Boso's identification of the Lateran palace as the natural seat of papal jurisdiction. Gregory was the legitimate pope, and Wibert's flight from Rome after his unorthodox consecration was proof of this. Gregory could not then be seen to fly also. Wibert did in fact enjoy considerable support in Rome, and no fewer than twelve of Gregory's cardinals defected to him in 1084, enabling him to return to Rome and remain there until 1098.[50] Yet Boso made no mention of this. Indeed, after his account of Gregory's death at Salerno, he moved straight to the pontificate of Paschal II.

Why then did Boso feel impelled to rescue Gregory VII from the hard facts which Bonizo had related? Was it really so important to present him as pacifying Rome with the aid of his Norman allies and immediately returning to the business of administering the church universal from his traditional throne in the Lateran palace? And for what reason did he gloss over and disguise the unpalatable fact that the Romans, who had risen so heroically to rescue Gregory in 1075, simply abandoned him in 1084? Firstly, Boso was living through another papal schism, similar to that which had unfolded from 1080 onwards, and served a pope who was able to maintain himself in Rome only for brief interludes during a long pontificate. Boso was unable to present Gregory's failure in

---

[47] On the traditions of the Lateran palace, see Ingo Herklotz, *Gli eredi di Costantino. Il papato, il Laterano e la propaganda visiva nel xii secolo* (Rome, 2000), 41–94; for the judicial significance of the palace, see esp. 57 and 60–1.

[48] *Liber Pontificalis*, ed. Duchesne, 2: 368.

[49] Ibid. 424–5.

[50] Robinson, *Papacy*, 412; Cowdrey, *Gregory VII*, 321–3.

all its starkness because he feared a similar failure for Alexander III. Indeed, although Boso reported Alexander's flight as imperial troops approached Rome in July 1167, he avoided reporting the enthronement of Barbarossa's antipope 'Paschal III' and the subsequent imperial coronation.[51]

It should also be remembered that Boso represented a religious tradition which looked back favourably on Gregory VII in a way that the Roman people and clergy did not. He revealed this in a final intervention in the sources from which he copied Gregory's *Life*. Having described Gregory's rescue by Robert Guiscard, Boso inserted a passage from Bonizo's *Liber ad amicum* recounting the pope's success, early in his pontificate, in reforming St Peter's basilica.[52] This passage is of great interest, because it shows the reformed papacy turning against 'ancient and most wicked' customs in the city of Rome. Gregory was credited with having freed St Peter's basilica from the oppression of sixty lay lodgers (*mansionarii*), who had violently seized the altars and oratories of the basilica, except for the pope's own high altar, charging fees to those wishing to pray there, which they then kept for themselves. These Roman citizens, married or living with women, had shaved their beards and put on mitres, informing those who had come there to pray, and especially the gullible rustic pilgrims from Lombardy, that they were cardinal priests and could grant them indulgences and remission of their sins in return for money. They also lurked about at night, pretending to guard the basilica but in fact committing all sorts of filthy acts. Gregory had these men removed with great difficulty and committed the basilica to the care of honest clerics and priests.

Boso included this story because he found it in Bonizo of Sutri's work, but its anachronistic inclusion at this point emphasizes his conviction that the interests of the church could only fully be served when the city of Rome was under firm ecclesiastical control. He was also doubtless motivated by the fact that the canons of St Peter's had, in 1159, played a prominent part in ensuring the election of the antipope Victor IV (1159–64). In response, Boso appealed to history, his hope being that once Alexander III had

---

[51] *Chronica Regia Coloniensis (Annales Maximi Colonienses)*, MGH SRG 18, 117–18.
[52] *Liber Pontificalis*, ed. Duchesne, 2: 368; MGH LdeL 1, 603; Cowdrey, *Gregory VII*, 319.

secured the city of Rome and ended the schism, he would deal with entrenched and disruptive influences in Rome, just as his illustrious predecessor Gregory VII had done. If, as Munz suggests, Alexander was Boso's hero, this was because he was following in the footsteps of Gregory VII.[53] Far from being a pope who had left no legacy, for Boso Gregory VII was a model pope, wholeheartedly committed to his exalted office and determined, in spite of persecution and the malice of the Romans, to restore his city to its rightful place at the heart of the church universal. Yet by the 1170s Boso was one of the few people who remembered him this way.[54]

University of Chester

---

[53] Munz, Introduction to *Boso's Life of Alexander III*, 3.

[54] See *Liber Pontificalis*, ed. Duchesne, 2: xli, for admiration of 'this pope with few defenders' among the entourage of Pope Adrian IV.

HONORIUS III AND THE CRUSADE: RESPONSIVE PAPAL GOVERNMENT VERSUS THE MEMORY OF HIS PREDECESSORS*

by THOMAS W. SMITH

The medieval papacy was an institution steeped in its own history and traditions, but how far did the popes' recollection of their predecessors' 'blessed memory' influence their own political decision-making? Through access to earlier letter registers, combined with their memories of experiences at the curia before election to the papal throne, popes could potentially delve into their own institutional history when making contemporary political decisions. In 1977 James Powell suggested that, in negotiations with Emperor Frederick II (1220–50) over his Holy Land crusade vow, Pope Honorius III (1216–27) had reached decisions based on his memory of the negotiations between Pope Clement III (1187–91) and Frederick II's grandfather, Emperor Frederick I (1155–90).[1]

Powell's argument poses the question: how far was Honorius's decision-making regarding the Holy Land crusades influenced by the memory of his predecessors? Honorius, it will be remembered, was involved in preparations not only for the Crusade of Frederick II (1228–9) but also for the Fifth Crusade (1217–21). This question addresses the papacy's use and perception of the importance of its own past, and also forms part of a wider historiographical debate on whether the popes formulated policies or whether they were primarily responsive, even reactive, in their decision-making. Traditionally the medieval papacy has been interpreted as a policy-making (and policy-following) body, with a few notable exceptions, but the discourse has recently been reinvigorated by several important studies whose authors have begun to consider more critically how the curia operated, and to question the status of

* I wish to thank Brenda Bolton, Bernard Hamilton, Jonathan Phillips and the editors of Studies in Church History for commenting on this essay, and Barbara Bombi for several references.
[1] James M. Powell, 'Honorius III and the Leadership of the Crusade', *CathHR* 63 (1977), 521–36, at 528–9.

the popes as policy-makers.[2] This essay aims to contribute to that discussion by arguing that whilst Honorius was certainly aware of his predecessors' actions, and positive evidence of the influence of these recollections occurs in a small number of crusade letters from his first pontifical year, the subsequent memory of his predecessors exerted no discernible effect on his crusade decision-making. Instead, Honorius's letters were issued primarily in response to the initiative and will of the lay powers. Hence, he was neither making papal 'policy' nor following the 'policies' of his predecessors.

Before his election as Pope Honorius III on 18 July 1216 (consecrated 24 July), Cencius[3] served at the curia of Clement III, where he obtained a canonry in S. Maria Maggiore, and in 1188 was appointed as papal chamberlain. By 1192, he had compiled the *Liber censuum*, an administrative work detailing payments to the papacy.[4] Cencius's promising career continued to flourish under Celestine III (1191–8): in 1193 he became cardinal deacon of S. Lucia in Orthea, possibly in recognition of the completion of the *Liber*

---

[2] Geoffrey Barraclough criticized the search for 'high policy' in ecclesiastical history, yet it has persisted to the present day: see his *Papal Provisions: Aspects of Church History Constitutional, Legal and Administrative in the Later Middle Ages* (Oxford, 1935), 128–30. For an early view of responsive papal government, see Ernst Pitz, *Papstreskript und Kaiserreskript im Mittelalter* (Tübingen, 1971), 135–6; for a more balanced view, see Colin Morris, *The Papal Monarchy: The Western Church from 1050 to 1250*, OHCC (Oxford, 1989), 212–13, 217–19, 571. More recently, in favour of papal policy-making, see Rebecca Rist, 'Papal Policy and the Albigensian Crusades: Continuity or Change?', *Crusades* 2 (2003), 99–108; eadem, *The Papacy and Crusading in Europe, 1198–1245* (London, 2009), 3, 19, 84, 119. For similar views, although with a greater emphasis on petitioning, see Iben Fonnesberg-Schmidt, *The Popes and the Baltic Crusades, 1147–1254* (Leiden, 2007), 1, 2, 12, 16, 21, 149–51, 247–8. For an argument against policy-making, see Barbara Bombi, Novella plantatio fidei: *Missione e crociata nel nord Europa tra la fine del XII e i primi decenni del XIII secolo* (Rome, 2007), 24. Also on responsive papal government, although excluding crusades, see Patrick Zutshi, 'Petitioners, Popes, Proctors: The Development of Curial Institutions, c.1150–1250', in Giancarlo Andenna, ed., *Pensiero e sperimentazioni istituzionali nella 'Societas Christiana' (1046–1250)* (Milan, 2007), 265–93, at 268, 293. See also D. L. D'Avray, *Medieval Religious Rationalities: A Weberian Analysis* (Cambridge, 2010), 143. On the importance of outside initiative on decretal law, see Anne J. Duggan, 'Making Law or Not? The Function of Papal Decretals in the Twelfth Century', in *Proceedings of the Thirteenth International Congress of Medieval Canon Law, Esztergom, 3–8 August 2008*, ed. Peter Erdö and Sz. Anzelm Szuromi (Vatican City, 2010), 41–70, at 41.

[3] Cencius is no longer thought to have belonged to the Savelli family; his origins are obscure: Sandro Carocci and Marco Vendittelli, 'Onorio III.', in Manlio Simonetti et al., eds, *Enciclopedia dei papi*, 3 vols (Rome, 2000), 2: 350–62, at 350–1.

[4] Jane E. Sayers, *Papal Government and England during the Pontificate of Honorius III (1216–1227)* (Cambridge, 1984), 2.

censuum. He was further elevated as head of the chancery in 1194, combining this office with that of chamberlain. Cencius served frequently as an auditor hearing litigation at the curia throughout Celestine's reign; however, following Innocent III's accession in 1198 the combined position of chamberlain and chancellor was abolished. Although created cardinal priest of SS Giovanni e Paolo in 1200, Cencius's career under the new pontiff was somewhat unremarkable.[5] Nevertheless, by the time of his own election, he had a wealth of experience on which to draw, accumulated at the curia under no fewer than three noteworthy predecessors.

In addition to the memory of his predecessors, Honorius had access to their letter registers. Though no longer extant, the existence of papal registers from the late eleventh and twelfth centuries, and their survival down to his day, has been demonstrated by Uta-Renate Blumenthal, who noted the survival of 'registers' of Urban II (1088–99), Paschal II (1099–1118), Gelasius II (1118–19), Lucius II (1144–5), Eugenius III (1145–53), Anastasius IV (1153–4), Hadrian IV (1154–9) and Alexander III (1159–81), all of which we know were used at Honorius's curia because he had letters transcribed from them.[6] Furthermore, there is evidence that similar registers were kept under Clement III and Celestine III.[7] The registers were also being consulted for the compilation of thirteenth-century decretal collections, and Othmar Hageneder has drawn attention to the marks made in the margins adjacent to letters in Innocent III's registers which denote that they were being checked for inclusion in these collections.[8]

Anecdotes from the autobiography of Gerald of Wales (*c.*1146–*c.*1223) provide evidence not only for the survival of

5   Werner Maleczek, *Papst und Kardinalskolleg von 1191 bis 1216: Die Kardinäle unter Coelestin III. und Innocenz III.* (Vienna, 1984), 111–13.

6   Uta-Renate Blumenthal, 'Papal Registers in the Twelfth Century', in *Proceedings of the Seventh International Congress of Medieval Canon Law, Cambridge 23–27 July 1984*, ed. Peter Linehan (Vatican City, 1988), 135–51, at 135–6.

7   For evidence of Clement III's register, see Volkert Pfaff, 'Analekten zur Geschichte Papst Coelestins III. 1191–1198', *Historisches Jahrbuch* 109 (1989), 191–205, at 193–4. For Celestine III's lost register, see Constance M. Rousseau, 'A Prudent Shepherd and a Pastoral Judge: Celestine III and Marriage', in John Doran and Damian J. Smith, eds, *Pope Celestine III (1191–1198): Diplomat and Pastor* (Farnham, 2008), 287–304, at 288.

8   Othmar Hageneder, 'Die Register Innozenz' III.', in *Papst Innozenz III.: Weichensteller der Geschichte Europas, Interdisziplinäre Ringvorlesung an der Universität Passau, 5.11.1997–26.5.1998*, ed. Thomas Frenz (Stuttgart, 2000), 91–101, at 99.

twelfth-century registers, but also their common usage as reference works for curial officials during Innocent III's pontificate. Whilst pressing his case at the curia in 1200, Gerald was granted access to Eugenius III's registers. He not only had a letter copied from these but also witnessed Innocent referring to one of his own registers when discussing Gerald's cause in his chamber.[9]

It is clear, then, that the papal registers were in common use at the curia as important reference works serving a multitude of purposes. If Honorius desired to refer to the decisions of his predecessors, he could always check their registers, as he did on a large number of occasions when dealing with petitions on legal disputes and the renewal of privileges. Indeed, Honorius's letters on these matters explicitly refer to the decisions of previous pontiffs.[10]

Honorius certainly knew about the history of the papacy's involvement in crusading, something made clear by Eugenius III, his predecessor, in the famous letter *Quantum praedecessores* to the kingdom of France, which launched the Second Crusade on 1 December 1145.[11] The opening section of the letter reveals that Eugenius possessed a keen understanding of the efforts of his predecessors in their attempts to recover the Holy Land:

> We have learned from what men of old have said and we have found written in their histories how greatly our predecessors the Roman pontiffs have worked for the liberation of the eastern Church. Indeed our predecessor of happy memory, Pope Urban, sounding forth like a heavenly trumpet, took care to induce the sons of the Holy Roman Church from several parts of the world to free it.[12]

---

[9] *The Autobiography of Gerald of Wales*, ed. and transl. H. E. Butler, new edn (Woodbridge, 2005), 192–4, 182–3 respectively.

[10] Innocent III is explicitly cited in over two hundred letters issued throughout Honorius's reign, and dozens of letters cite Clement III, Celestine III and Honorius's other predecessors. For a small sample, see *Regesta Honorii Papae III*, ed. P. Pressutti, 2 vols (Rome, 1888–95; repr. Hildesheim, 1978), nos 336, 428, 549, 661, 866, 1887, 2247, 2296, 2497, 3633, 4223, 4772, 5066, 5178, 5190, 6186.

[11] The translation used here is from the reissue dated March 1146: Latin text in Peter Rassow, 'Der Text der Kreuzzugsbulle Eugens III. vom 1. März 1146, Trastevere (J.-L. 8796)', *Neues Archiv der Gesellschaft für ältere deutsche Geschichtskunde* 45 (1924), 300–5; ET in Louise and Jonathan Riley-Smith, *The Crusades: Idea and Reality, 1095–1274* (London, 1981), 57–9. See Jonathan Phillips, *The Second Crusade: Extending the Frontiers of Christendom* (New Haven, CT, 2007), 37 and n. 1.

[12] Riley-Smith and Riley-Smith, *Crusades*, 57.

In a similar vein Honorius not only drew on, but was in fact to an extent bound by, *Ad liberandam*, the constitution appended to the decrees of the Fourth Lateran Council (November 1215) which outlined Innocent III's plan to launch the Fifth Crusade, setting a muster deadline of 1 June 1217 and specifying Brindisi and Messina as the ports to be used.[13]

With such a distinguished history of papal involvement in crusading, with written documents in the registers and *Ad liberandam* to which to refer, it might be expected, then, that Honorius's crusade letters would make regular mention of his predecessors. However, of the large number of crusade letters issued during his pontificate, only a handful cite his predecessors' decisions using the same style of formulae as were employed in the plethora of papal documents on privileges and disputes. This by no means rules out the possibility that Honorius drew on his predecessors' memory for inspiration, or that he checked their registers without citing them in his letters, but the striking dearth of positive evidence for such behaviour suggests that most often when making decisions regarding the crusade, Honorius was attempting neither to imitate his forebears nor to continue a papal 'policy', but was responding as he saw fit at the time.

It is perhaps not surprising that, of the small number of letters that do provide positive evidence of the memory of his predecessors, most come from the first year of Honorius's pontificate – at precisely that time when he was assuming control over crusade business at the curia following the death of Innocent III. After consecration, Honorius's priority was the crusade: the first letter enregistered by his chancery was sent to John, king of Jerusalem (d. 1237), on 25 July 1216, with copies also being despatched to the patriarchs of Jerusalem and Antioch, the Hospitallers and Templars, and the Christians of the Holy Land. The letter reassured the recipients that despite Innocent's death, they were not to fear for the state of the Holy Land on account of his passing; 'his' crusade was still coming.[14]

---

[13] Norman P. Tanner, ed., *Decrees of the Ecumenical Councils*, 2 vols (London, 1990), 1: 267.

[14] 'Non ergo propter obitum prefati predecessoris nostri consternatur cor tuum neque formidet, quasi propter hoc Terre Sancte impediatur succursus': Vatican City, Archivio Segreto Vaticano, Registra Vaticana [hereafter: Reg. Vat.] 9, fol. 1r; *Regesta*, ed. Pressutti, no. 1.

In several other letters Honorius cited Innocent III's departure deadline of 1 June 1217. One letter, despatched to Odo, duke of Burgundy, and the other French crusaders on 7 August 1216, urged the recipients to leave on crusade by the deadline, hoping that their compliance might inspire others to follow their example.[15] Honorius sent a similar letter to the crusaders of Cologne on 27 January 1217, urging them not only to leave by the deadline, but also to set sail from the ports designated by Innocent so that the crusaders might receive the papacy's advice and support.[16] The letter also reverently noted the efforts that Innocent had invested in preparing for the Fifth Crusade, and Honorius spoke of his hope of bringing the crusade to fruition.[17]

Obviously Honorius intended to follow Innocent III's proposal, announced at the Fourth Lateran Council, to accompany the crusade armies in person to the ports of embarkation, and to appoint there a legate to represent the pope for the rest of the expedition. In the event this never came to pass (although Honorius did appoint Pelagius, cardinal bishop of Albano, as legate in July 1217), perhaps on account of the poorly coordinated passages of contingents leaving for the Holy Land, few of whom chose to use the ports designated by Innocent, and because even the more punctual crusade contingents missed the June deadline by several months.[18] But because *Ad liberandam* had been issued at Lateran IV, Honorius could hardly avoid following its instructions. Once the deadline of 1 June 1217 had passed, however, Honorius was released from Innocent's timetable for the crusade and the expectation that the pope should abide by the memory of his predecessor diminished.

[15] 'miramur quam plurimum quod neque bone memorie Innocentium Papam predecessorem nostrum, neque nos ipsos super passagio et apparatu navium requisisti, nec curasti exponere quod super hiis tue sedeat voluntati, cum in generali concilio ad transfretandum determinatum fuerit tempus certum': Reg. Vat. 9, fol. 2r; *Regesta*, ed. Pressutti, no. 14.

[16] 'ut cum eis Domino deducente in prefixo tempore perveniatis ad portus in concilio prefinito, ubi ad stabilendum vestrum propositum recipere possitis a nobis consilium et auxilium oportunum': Reg. Vat. 9, fol. 49v; *Regesta*, ed. Pressutti, no. 284.

[17] 'Quia licet ad palmam vos precesserit beate memorie Innocentus [*sic*] Papa predecessor noster huius sancti operis ferventissimus inchoator nos tamen licet indignos uncxit Dominus et pastorem constituit super suam familiam universam qui totis medullis totisque affectibus aspiramus, ad hoc excellentissimum ministerium consumandum': Reg. Vat. 9, fol. 49; *Regesta*, ed. Pressutti, no. 284.

[18] James M. Powell, *Anatomy of a Crusade, 1213–1221* (Philadelphia, PA, 1986), 111.

Another letter of January 1217 provides positive evidence of Honorius checking one of Innocent III's lost registers when making a decision on the crusade, albeit brought about through outside initiative in the form of a petition. On 25 January, Honorius wrote in response to a petition from Albert of Orlamünde, count of Holstein, informing him that permission was being granted to the bishop of Schleswig to allow ten of Albert's knights to commute their Holy Land crusade vows and to fight with him instead against pagans in Livonia.[19] Study of the letter's *narratio* – the section detailing the petitioner's version of the events prompting the issue of the papal letter – reveals that Albert was originally granted permission by Innocent to crusade in Livonia while on campaign there, a fact of which his unsuspecting vassals were unaware when they took vows to crusade in the Holy Land during his absence, thus creating a feudal tension.[20]

Although a fortunate coincidence meant that, in allowing this diversion of crusaders, Honorius was in effect supporting Innocent III's original decision which permitted Albert himself to fight in Livonia, it was by no means necessary for his decision to correspond with Innocent's. Despite considering the Livonian crusade a worthy cause, it is unlikely that Honorius would have chosen to divert crusaders away from the Holy Land when preparations for the fledgling Fifth Crusade were in full swing. In fact, the driving force in the issue of this document was not a supposed need to abide by Innocent's decision, but rather the influence of Albert's supplication, which epitomizes the responsive character of papal government and the power of petition over papal decisions. Jane Sayers observes of Honorius that 'no pope by the early

---

[19] 'Verum quia sicut tuis nobis litteris intimasti, te pro expeditione regia in remotis agente cum ad bone memorie Innocentium predecessorem nostrum litteras destinasses ut tibi liceret caracterem crucis accipere volenti contra paganos Livonicos proficisci, medio tempore multi de familia tua tuum propositum nescientes pro subventione terre Ierusolimitane crucis signaculum receperunt': Reg.Vat. 9, fol. 50r; *Regesta*, ed. Pressutti, no. 276. See also Angelo Forte, Richard Oram and Frederik Pedersen, *Viking Empires* (Cambridge, 2005), 388.

[20] At some time in the mid-thirteenth century, Innocent III's registers for most of year 3, and the entirety of years 4, 17, 18 and 19 were lost: Alfred J. Andrea, *Contemporary Sources for the Fourth Crusade*, rev. edn (Leiden, 2008), 8. Innocent probably wrote to Albert in 1215, see Rudolf Usinger, *Deutsch-dänische Geschichte, 1189–1227* (Berlin, 1863), 440 (no. 19). Honorius's reference implies that Innocent's letter was copied into the now-lost registers at the end of Innocent's pontificate.

thirteenth century could divorce himself entirely from the effect of his predecessor's rule'.[21] Whilst this rings true for Honorius's general curial business, it is possible to nuance this view slightly for the crusade by distinguishing between Honorius's first year in office and the rest of his reign. Once he had finished dealing with the immediate takeover of business from the preceding pontificate, when it proved impossible not to deal with Innocent's legacy on the crusade, Honorius clearly did not consider himself further bound by his predecessors' actions. His crusade correspondence with the lay powers after his first pontifical year (roughly demarcated by the departure deadline laid down in *Ad liberandam*) is almost devoid of citations of their decisions.

Even a close examination of the later evidence from 1219, cited by Powell in favour of the assertion that Honorius acted in the light of the memory of Clement III and Frederick I, reveals that although Honorius valued the motivational impact of invoking the memory of Frederick I, he appeared patently uninterested in his predecessor Clement, who received no mention whatsoever in Honorius's letter, issued on 1 October 1219 in response to Frederick II's request for yet another extension of his own crusade deadline. While granting him an extension until 21 March 1220, Honorius invoked the renowned memory of Frederick Barbarossa's crusade in an attempt to inspire the young emperor-elect at a time when previous papal exhortations were having little effect.[22]

Powell interpreted this invocation of the memory of Frederick I as explaining Honorius's approach to his entire negotiations with Frederick II, which he suggested was drawn from Honorius's experience at the curia under Clement III.[23] However, to try to interpret Honorius's approach to papal-imperial negotiations

---

[21] Sayers, *Government*, 194.

[22] 'festina si forte Dominus tanti consummationem negotii tue glorie reservavit, ut in dextera tua perficiat multorum manibus inchoatum. Certe clare memorie avus tuus Fredericus ad id se viribus totis accincxit, et quis scit si et tu Fredericus nepos ipsius illius memoriam non solum presentibus renovabis in nomine, sed etiam ad posteros prorogabis in opere, si quod ille ferventer in affectum assumpserat, tu salubriter produxeris ad effectum': Reg. Vat. 10, fol. 132v; *Regesta*, ed. Pressutti, no. 2207. For this passage, Powell relied on the edition in *Historia diplomatica Friderici secundi*, ed. J.-L.-A. Huillard-Bréholles, 6 vols (Paris, 1852–61), 1: 692–3. Huillard-Bréholles's edition contains a number of transcriptional errors, although they do not alter the sense greatly.

[23] Powell, 'Leadership', 528–9.

on the basis of this section of a single papal letter, which makes no mention of Clement, is perhaps to push the evidence too far. Holding up Barbarossa as a role model to his grandson was meant to inspire him to fulfil his vow rather than signalling Honorius's desire to copy Clement.

Honorius's attempts at motivation were not sufficient to move the emperor-elect to action, and Frederick continued to delay until the Fifth Crusade failed in 1221. In the aftermath of this disaster Frederick and Honorius began organizing a new expedition, and in March 1223 a papal-imperial conference was held at Ferentino, at which Frederick pledged to crusade by 24 June 1225. In response to this, in April 1223 Honorius issued letters calling the kings of Europe to crusade, offering the traditional remission of sins and papal protection to those who took the cross.[24] Honorius's register contains a transcript of the letter despatched to Philip Augustus of France (1180–1223) on 11 April, and records the customized wording that was included in the copy sent to Henry III (1216–72) on 27 April, which held out the prospect of the king of England being seen as a new Richard I (1189–99).[25] Powell suggested that in calling on Henry III and Philip II to join Frederick's crusade, Honorius was striving to replicate the triumvirate of royal crusade leadership witnessed in Clement III's time, on the Third Crusade (1189–92).[26]

However, it is important that these letters are not analysed in isolation. When those addressed to Henry III and Philip II are placed in the context of the rest of the batch issued on the same topic to lay powers across Europe, then they begin to lose their significance as evidence of Honorius's supposed aim to repeat the Third Crusade. Honorius's register records that a personalized copy was sent to King Andrew II of Hungary (1205–35), another

---

[24] 'Ecce ipsius inspiratione ut firmiter credimus karissimus in Christo filius noster Fridericus illustris Romanorum Imperator semper augustus et Rex Sicilie omissis multis arduisque negotiis quorum onus honorem Imperialis celsitudinis sequebatur, venit ad nos in Campaniam nobiscum de predicte Terre subsidio tractaturus': Reg. Vat. 12, fol. 52v; *Regesta*, ed. Pressutti, no. 4262.

[25] 'Sensit enim quis qualis et quantus ei fuerit illustris memorie Rex Riccardus cuius nomen sic in terrorem hostium fidei creverat quod exclamatio eius in prelio nonnumquam sufficiebat ad stragem': Reg. Vat. 12, fol. 53v; *Regesta*, ed. Pressutti, no. 4262. The original letter is preserved: Kew, TNA, SC 7/18/14. See also Simon Lloyd, *English Society and the Crusade, 1216–1307* (Oxford, 1988), 33.

[26] Powell, *Anatomy*, 108–9.

to the faithful of Tarantaise, and (crucially) that letters were also sent to other unnamed kings with customized wording that was personalized to the recipient.[27] We can identify two of these unspecified recipients from the original letters despatched to King Erik of Sweden (1222–9, 1234–50) and the faithful of Flanders and Brabant, and it is likely that given the general nature of the *in eundem modum* clause, there must have been more – too many to record in the register.[28]

Instead of being a unique call to repeat the Third Crusade, the letters appear as part of Honorius's attempt at pan-European crusade recruitment, designed to attract as many potential crusader kings as possible; the curia personalized the letters to increase the chances of success. Nicholas Vincent has written of the use of Henry III's crusading ancestry in papal letters: 'such ties were not unimportant, and would quite naturally be stressed by correspondents … anxious to recruit Henry's support'.[29] It is in this light that Honorius's deployment of the memory of crusading ancestors should be understood. Reviving the memory of Frederick I or Richard I was just a papal tool to stir the lay powers to action.

That Honorius rarely cited his predecessors in his crusade correspondence after his first pontifical year supports the case for responsive papal government that is emerging in the wider historiographical debate on the nature of papal government. Although the papacy had aims and attitudes, and did take the lead in issuing some letters, the overwhelming majority were issued in response

---

[27] 'In eundem modum aliis regibus quibusdam verbis mutandis competenter mutatis': Reg.Vat. 12, fol. 53v; *Regesta*, ed. Pressutti no. 4262.

[28] The original letter sent to Erik is now lost. First edited in 1623, it was probably destroyed in the fire of 1697 that gutted the Swedish royal archive: see *Vitis Aquilonia*, ed. Johannes Vastovius (Cologne, 1623), 172–4; *Regesta*, ed. Pressutti, no. 4304. For the letter to Flanders and Brabant, see *Sacrae antiquitatis monumenta historica, dogmatica, diplomatica*, ed. Charles Louis Hugo, 2 vols (Étival, 1725–31), 1: 122–3 (no. 136); *Regesta*, ed. Pressutti, no. 4388. The manuscript has since been lost, probably during the French Revolutionary wars: C. R. Cheney, 'Gervase, Abbot of Prémontré: A Medieval Letter-Writer', *BJRL* 33 (1950), 25–56, at 45–6, 46 n. 1. On 27 April 1223 a letter was also despatched calling on Count Thibaut IV of Champagne to crusade – possibly an *in eundem modum* copy, although this cannot be proven without consulting the manuscript: *Histoire des ducs et des comtes de Champagne*, ed. Henri d'Arbois de Jubainville, 7 vols (Paris 1859–69), 5: 197 (no. 1528); *Regesta*, ed. Pressutti, no. 4332. On the same day Honorius sent a different – although obviously connected – crusade exhortation to Duke Leopold VI of Austria: Reg.Vat. 12, fols 55v–56r; *Regesta*, ed. Pressutti, no. 4330.

[29] Nicholas Vincent, *The Holy Blood: King Henry III and the Westminster Blood Relic* (Cambridge, 2001), 22.

to someone else's initiative, whether a petitioner or a lay power. That the papacy was much more reactive than proactive elucidates why Honorius's crusade letters do not mention Innocent III with any frequency after the first year of his pontificate. To a great extent it was the lay powers who were setting the agenda of papal crusade diplomacy, while the context in which the crusade was unfolding had changed, and was continuing to change, from that in which Innocent had issued *Ad liberandam*. Generally, letters on the crusade flowing into Honorius's curia were more concerned with contemporary events than with the papacy's past, which explains why in turn Honorius did not mention his predecessors with any regularity in his outgoing crusade letters after mid-1217. Although Honorius was aware of the papacy's involvement in crusading during the previous century, he did not judge this knowledge to be relevant to the planning of either the Fifth Crusade or of Frederick II's crusade, in both of which he was centrally involved.

Royal Holloway, University of London

CARMELITES AND CRUSADING IN THE LATER MIDDLE AGES

by ANDREW JOTISCHKY

In contrast with their larger competitors, the Franciscans and Dominicans, the Carmelites seemed to eschew the Holy Land after its loss to the Mamluks in 1291. At first sight, the apparent lack of interest on the part of Carmelites in crusading and the Holy Land is surprising. Founded on Mount Carmel as an eremitical and contemplative community in the first decade of the thirteenth century, by the 1240s the Carmelites had begun to spread westward via Cyprus to England, France and Sicily, where they adapted their original Rule in order to become mendicants.[1] In 1291 they left the Holy Land altogether, but unlike the Franciscans, who negotiated a return in the 1330s through their custody of the Holy Places, and the Dominicans, who maintained missions in Mongol and Turkish territories, the Carmelites seemed to show little interest in returning to their original homeland.[2] Nor have they been generally associated with preaching the crusade in the systematic fashion of the larger mendicant orders. In fact, one could be excused for assuming that the order willingly lost touch with its geographical roots.

Although the Carmelites may not have been so obviously concerned with the Holy Land and crusading as the larger mendicant orders, it would be a mistake to assume that, once they had begun to migrate westwards, the Carmelites forgot their origins. Carmelite houses remained in the Holy Land until 1291, and their desire to remain permanently is visible in the letters to the West to which the Carmelite prior-general of the province of the Holy Land was a signatory in 1282.[3] In 1312 an English Carmelite

---

[1] Frances Andrews, *The Other Friars: Carmelite, Augustinian, Sack and Pied Friars in the Middle Ages* (Woodbridge, 2006), 9–36; J. Smet, *The Carmelites*, 2 vols (Barrington, IL, 1975–6), vol. 1.

[2] H. Fürst, *Die Custodie des heiligen Landes: Die Mission der Franziskaner im heiligen Land und im vorderen Orient* (Munich, 1981); R.-J. Loenertz, 'Les missions dominicains en Orient au XIVᵉ siècle', *AFP* 2 (1932), 1–83; idem, 'La societé des Frères Pérégrinants: Étude sur l'Orient dominicain', *AFP* 45 (1975), 107–45.

[3] Richard Copsey, 'Two Letters Written from the Holy Land in Support of the

friar, John de Boukhill, was sent to the Holy Land on pilgrimage 'for the health of the king and his subjects',[4] and although there are no surviving accounts of pilgrimages by fourteenth-century Carmelites as there are for Franciscans and Dominicans, there is no reason to suppose that they did not take place. Further interest in the Holy Land can be attested among Carmelites in the fifteenth century. A Flemish Carmelite was apparently martyred while preaching to the Turks in 1462, and a Carmelite pilgrimage to identify and perhaps attempt to resettle Mount Carmel took place at around the same time.[5]

The clearest indication of continuing Carmelite interest in the Holy Land, however, comes from the order's historical writing. From the 1280s onward, Carmelites began to develop a distinctive historical tradition, according to which the true founder of the order was the prophet Elijah. A complex and imaginative series of traditions evolved over the course of the fourteenth and fifteenth centuries, vigorously defended against critics and doubters, the purpose of which was to demonstrate the unbroken succession of hermits on Mount Carmel from the ministry of Elijah onwards.[6] By the late fifteenth century Carmel figured in the order's historical and devotional literature as a spiritual resource in which could be encompassed the careers of almost any supposed biblical, early Christian or medieval progenitor, from St Anne to Basil of Caesarea to Aimery, the twelfth-century patriarch of Antioch. Besides retrospectively claiming historical figures as Carmelites, Carmelite writers also invented a body of new characters who could be deployed to embody contemplative virtues thought to be specific to Carmel. At the same time, the Holy Land's own recent history, including the Crusades, could be garbled to form the subject of the Carmelite historical tradition. Thus, for example, in William of Coventry's *De adventu Carmelitarum ad Angliam*, written around the

Carmelite Order', in idem, ed., *Carmel in Britain. Studies on the Early History of the Carmelite Order, 3: The Hermits from Mount Carmel* (Faversham, 2004), 29–50.

4   *Calendar of Close Rolls Edward II 1307–27,* 4 vols (London, 1900–8), 1 (1307–13): 542.

5   Oxford, Bodl., Bodley MS 73, fol. 16v; Elias Friedman, 'Nicola Calciuri, O.Carm (d. 1466), a Genuine Witness to the Carmelite Monastery in wadi 'Ain as-Siah?', *Carmelus* 32 (1985), 60–73.

6   Andrew Jotischky, *The Carmelites and Antiquity: Mendicants and their Pasts in the Middle Ages* (Oxford, 2002).

middle of the fourteenth century, the arrival of the first Carmelites in England in 1242 is linked, reasonably enough, to the crusade of Richard of Cornwall (1239–41), but the account of the crusade itself elides its details with the events of the siege of Acre by the Third Crusade (1189–92).[7] Similarly, in Carmelite tradition Mount Carmel itself could assume a position of authority in the development of crusading. In a sixteenth-century collection of notes on Carmelite history, papal crusading strategy under Pope Gregory X, which included the commissioning of the first of the so-called 'recovery treatises', is attributed by implication to the visit by the soon-to-be pope to Mount Carmel while accompanying the army of the Lord Edward in 1270, as archdeacon of Liège, before the papal election.[8]

Although Carmelite interest in developing this historical narrative can first be detected in the 1280s, it was about a century later that it reached its peak. In one of the most original of all Carmelite historical inventions from this period, the *Life of St Angelo*, the order's putative prophetic history and the recent history of the Holy Land are fused. The first mention of St Angelo occurs in a manuscript of the 1360s, and the *Life* may date from this period or soon afterwards. Although the *Life* is most securely dated to the late fourteenth century, most manuscripts are from the fifteenth century, and it seems to have been especially in the second half of the fifteenth century that the *Life* circulated more widely. The manuscript tradition suggests circulation largely in Italian, German and Flemish Carmelite communities, but the *Life* was almost certainly first written in Sicily, where much of the action takes place, including Angelo's martyrdom, which forms the culmination of the narrative.[9]

The *Life* dates from a period when Carmelite interest not only in the Holy Land but in holy war was at its peak. In the second half of the fourteenth century two Carmelites became bishops in the Latin Empire of Constantinople: Thomas, appointed bishop of

7 William of Coventry, *De adventu Carmelitarum ad Angliam*, in A. Staring, ed., *Medieval Carmelite Heritage: Early Reflections on the Nature of the Order*, Textus et Studia Carmelitana 16 (Rome, 1989), 282–3.

8 Bodley MS 73, fol. 61v.

9 Ludovico Saggi, *Sant'Angelo di Sicilia. Studio sulla vita, devozione, folklore*, Textus et Studia Historica Carmelitana 6 (Rome, 1962). For discussion of dating and manuscript tradition, see ibid. 1–57.

Scutari in 1382, and, more prominently, the scholar Peter Thomas, made papal legate to the East in 1359 and Latin patriarch of Constantinople in 1364.[10] It was Peter who was responsible for the most active Carmelite involvement in crusading in 1365, when he preached and organized the expedition of Peter I of Cyprus that resulted in the capture of Alexandria.[11]

Carmelites, moreover, were also concerned with holy war outside the traditional arena of the eastern Mediterranean and their own place of origin. In 1389 the Norfolk Carmelite Walter Dysse was given papal dispensation for his part in preaching the 'crusade' of John of Gaunt undertaken to make good his claim to the kingdom of Castile – the so-called 'Despenser crusade'.[12] In 1419 another English Carmelite, the prior-general of the English province Thomas Netter, led an embassy on behalf of Henry V to mediate in the war between the Teutonic Knights and the kingdom of Poland-Lithuania. The Lancastrian house had a tradition of choosing Carmelites as confessors, of whom Netter was one. He had already become prominent as a Carmelite theologian, both for his role at the councils of Pisa in 1409 and Constance in 1415, and for his opposition to the Lollards in England that was to result in his anti-Wycliffite *summa,* the *Doctrinale fidei* (1421–30). From the few details that we know of the content of his diplomatic role in 1419, Netter seems to have been concerned to establish that the Teutonic Knights could not legitimately wage holy war against King Wladislav of Poland on the grounds which they adduced, namely that he was not a genuine Christian because he had used non-Christian soldiers against them.[13] This suggests that he was familiar with the arguments in Innocent IV's canon law

[10] Bodley MS 73, fol. ivr; *The Life of St Peter Thomas by Philippe de Mézières,* ed. J. Smet, Textus et Studia Historica Carmelitana 2 (Rome, 1954).

[11] Nicholas Coureas, 'Philippe de Mézières' Portrait of Peter Thomas as a Preacher', *Carmelus* 57 (2010), 63–80; R. Blumenfeld-Kosinski, 'Philippe de Mézières' Life of Saint Pierre de Thomas at the Crossroads of Late Medieval Hagiography and Crusading Ideology', *Viator* 40 (2009), 223–48.

[12] W. H. Bliss and J. A. Twemlow, eds, *Calendar of Entries in the Papal Registers Relating to Great Britain and Ireland, 4: Papal Letters 1362–1404* (London, 1902), no. 311.

[13] Jens Röhrkasten, 'Thomas Netter: Carmelite and Diplomat', in Johan Bergström-Allen and Richard Copsey, eds, *Thomas Netter of Walden: Carmel in Britain,* Studies on the Early History of the Carmelite Order 4 (Rome, 2009), 113–36.

commentaries on the limits of Christian holy war in relation to non-Christian peoples.[14]

In this context of heightened Carmelite interest in holy war, the *Life of Angelo* appears at first sight anomalous. The *Life* purports to have been written by Enoch, one of the saint's followers, and to date from the 1220s.[15] The introduction takes the form of an address by Enoch to thirty-six bishops assembled at a council in Jerusalem to hear an account of his martyrdom and to determine the question of his sanctity. The narrative then begins with an account of Angelo's birth and early years. Angelo and his twin brother John were born in Jerusalem in 1185 to parents who were both Jewish converts. After the early death of both parents, the boys were brought up in the household of the patriarch of Jerusalem, and both entered the monastic life, choosing the Carmelites in preference to the Rule of Basil – in other words, to a Greek Orthodox monastery. As the narrative progresses, it recounts how both boys show an appetite for the ascetic life, and both are eventually ordained. By the age of twenty-eight, Angelo has performed two miracles: saving his brother from drowning in the spring of Elijah on Mount Carmel, and calming the river Jordan so that seven thousand pilgrims are able to cross. He then raises a boy from the dead in Bethlehem, which proves to be the start of a spate of such miracles of healing on his part. While John is elected patriarch of Jerusalem, Angelo retires to the extreme solitude of Mount Quarantana for five years. Here he receives a vision from Jesus, who tells him that he has been called to go to Sicily to preach against the crimes of Berengar, count of Agrigento, who had committed incest with his sister, and that, although he will succeed in securing the repentance of the count's sister, he will be martyred at the count's hands. Jesus then delivers a prophecy about the fate of Jerusalem, the Christians in the Near East, and indeed the whole of the church. Angelo sails for Sicily with various relics, including the head of John the Baptist and the arm of St Katherine; after Angelo's prayers deliver the ship on which he is travel-

---

[14] James Muldoon, *Popes, Lawyers and Infidels: The Church and the Non-Christian World* (Liverpool, 1979), 29–48.

[15] *Vita Sancti Angeli*, in *ActaSS*, Mai II, 798–842. The following is taken from the longer *Vita*, first published in Benedict Gononus, *Vitae Patrum Occidentis* (Lyon, 1625), 227–56, ed. from Vatican City, BAV, Vat. lat. MS 3813, fols 1r–12v.

ling from Muslim pirates, he meets Pope Honorius III at Orvieto and then Francis and Dominic in the Church of St John Lateran in Rome. Both mendicant founders honour him, and he proceeds to Sicily, where he preaches and performs miracles of healing for fifty days. At last he confronts Berengar and his sister, who is repentant, but Berengar decides to kill Angelo, which he eventually does as the saint is preaching.

This story, far-fetched though it is in both the *mise en scène* and in many details, has a degree of verisimilitude in other respects. The list of forty bishops assembled at the council in Jerusalem in the introduction can be corroborated from other sources, even if the dating does not square with the presumed dates of the *Life*.[16] Something of the author's method can be seen in the use of the supposed patriarch of Alexandria, Athanasius, as one of the assembled bishops. The Greek Orthodox patriarch Athanasius (1276–1309) seems to have been the model for this character, but the author has given him a Sicilian background and family.[17] Specific influences can be seen in the recounting of Angelo's miracles. The rescue of his brother from drowning, and perhaps also the revival of the dead boy, seem to be drawn from Gregory's *Life of Benedict*, while stylistic parallels can be drawn with the *Acta S. Placidii* of the eleventh-century Monte Cassino monk Peter the Deacon.[18] The most prominent influence, however, is the *Life of Peter Martyr*, the Dominican friar murdered in 1252, of which at least three versions had been written before 1260. Common elements include the framing narrative, the role of preaching, the manner of death and the conduct of the martyr at the moment of death.[19] More broadly, the influence of mendicant spirituality can be seen in the concern, rather clumsily achieved, to locate Angelo within the orbit of Francis and Dominic.

I have drawn attention elsewhere to the purposeful lack of historical sense in the narrative, in particular regarding the account

---

[16] Saggi, *Sant'Angelo*, 154–61.

[17] Ibid. 115.

[18] Ibid. 121–2 (echoing Gregory the Great, *Dialogi* 2.32), 125; see U. Berlière, 'Le culte de S. Placide', *Revue Bénédictine* 33 (1921), 19–45.

[19] Saggi, *Sant'Angelo*, 126–8. See now Barbara De Marco and Jerry R. Craddock, 'St Peter Martyr and the Development of Early Dominican Hagiography', in *Études de langue et de littérature médiévales offertes à Peter T. Ricketts à l'occasion de son 70ème anniversaire*, ed. Dominique Billy and Ann Buckley (Turnhout, 2005), 141–52.

of the Holy Land in the period of Angelo's life between 1185 and 1220. Although this was a period of profound political change, with the loss of Jerusalem and much of the crusader kingdom to the Seljuqs, there is no trace of these events in the *Life*. The divisions in Christian society in the Holy Land at the time between Latins and Arabic-speaking Greek and Syrian Orthodox are ignored. Angelo and his brother are taught both Latin and Greek as boys, and consider professing in the religious life in Greek and Latin houses equally. Muslims make only fleeting appearances, for example as the pirates who try to capture Angelo and his companions en route for Italy. The general treatment of the background is reminiscent of *chansons de geste* in which deeds of valour and romance are located in flagrantly impossible settings. Yet underlying this insouciance about historical reality is a concern with the fate of the Holy Land and with Christian society more generally.

This concern is best appreciated in the long prophecy given to Angelo by Jesus himself while he is living in complete solitude on Mount Quarantana. Angelo's prayer for peace and security for the Holy Land is met by a prophecy of suffering and disruption. Jesus tells Angelo that Jerusalem, Judea and Samaria, along with Egypt, Armenia, Cappadocia and Phrygia, will all fall into the hands of the Saracens. At the same time Greece, Russia and Hungary will be overrun by a pagan people, while wars will take place in Italy. The Church will be divided and despoiled under two rival popes, and ruled by hypocrites. Angelo asks who will eventually free the holy city from the infidel, to which Jesus replies that a holy and powerful king would emerge from France, greatly loved by all, who will lead a passage overseas with a huge army, many of whom would give themselves to death for love of him, and achieve eternal glory.[20]

The prophecy is intriguing for a number of reasons, not least of which is its unexplained function in the narrative. Against the ahistorical, fictive backdrop in which the *Life* is set, a prophecy dealing with the fate of crusading and of the papacy takes the reader startlingly back to political concerns current at the time of its composition. The allusions to the papal schism date it to after 1378, while the lack of resolution in the prophecy regarding the ulti-

---

[20] *Vita S. Angeli*, 821–3.

mate fate of the papacy suggest that it may predate the election of Pope Martin V in 1417. Similarly, the knowledge of the incursions of pagans in the Balkans and as far into Europe as Hungary, with the mention of Othman in one manuscript of the *Life*, indicates a preoccupation with the threat of the Turks, and perhaps a specific allusion to the Nicopolis Crusade of 1396. But the main focus of concern in the prophecy is with Jerusalem and the Holy Land. Angelo's first thought after hearing Jesus foretell his own future is to pray for his homeland, Jerusalem; the prophecy concerning the disasters that would befall the Holy Land and Christendom in the eastern Mediterranean is Jesus's response to his prayer. Naturally, this part of the prophecy exposes the lack of any attempt at historical accuracy, since most of the regions that Jesus foretells as falling into the hands of the Saracens – Jerusalem itself, Judea and Samaria, Egypt and Asia Minor – were by the 1220s, the supposed setting of the *Life,* already under Muslim regimes. By the time the *Life* was written, the whole of the Holy Land had been out of Christian hands for over a century, and no crusading expedition to recover Jerusalem had gone farther than the planning stage.

The main themes of the prophecy are part of the standard repertoire of the eschatological literature of the period, which often focused on the delivery of the Holy Land by a heroic ruler as a signal of the end times.[21] Notwithstanding this generic interest reflected in the content of the prophecy, the use of these themes has particular resonance in the context of Carmelite involvement in crusading. Cypriot interest in reviving 'traditional' crusading, promoted by the Carmelite Peter Thomas and signalled not only in the capture of Alexandria in 1365 but also in a planned attack on Beirut a year later and raids on Tripoli in 1367, died with the assassination of King Peter of Cyprus in 1369 and the signing of a treaty with the Mamluks in 1370. By the turn of the fifteenth century crusading attention was largely divided between the Baltic and the Balkans. As early as 1375 Pope Gregory XI had advised Queen Joanna of Naples to contribute to war against the Ottomans rather than to a traditional recovery crusade.[22]

---

[21] The classic study is Marjorie Reeves, *The Influence of Prophecy in the Later Middle Ages* (Oxford, 1969).
[22] Noman Housley, *The Later Crusades from Lyons to Alcazar 1274–1580* (Oxford, 1992), 40–2; Peter Edbury, 'The Crusading Policy of King Peter I of Cyprus, 1359–

The wording of the prophecy, with its emphasis on the charisma and personal status of the king – 'he will be loved by all Christian kings' – but equally on the cost in human lives of the expedition – 'many will suffer death for love of me, and acquire eternal life for themselves'[23] – suggests Louis IX's disastrous attempt at conquering Egypt in 1249–50. At the time that the *Life* was written, the last French king to have been associated with the crusade was Philip VI, who, after the failures of crusading plans under his predecessors Philip V and Charles IV, in 1332 began to assemble the ill-fated crusading fleet that in 1336 was diverted instead to the war with England.[24] Not until a generation later was France to be involved in crusading to the East again. Peter of Cyprus's expedition of 1365 was preceded by a visit to the French court, at which King John II took the cross. John's death in 1364 put an end to the hopes of a French crusade, leaving Peter to undertake it on his own account. Nevertheless, what may look in retrospect like a one-off adventure on Peter's part, or a footnote to crusading in the eastern Mediterranean, was not seen as such at the time either by Peter Thomas or by his biographer Philip de Mézières, the chancellor of the kingdom of Cyprus. On the contrary, Peter Thomas argued before the fleet sailed for Egypt that the capture of Alexandria was the best way of achieving the recapture of Jerusalem – revisiting, in other words, the strategy of Louis IX.[25] Philip de Mézières, indeed, continued to argue for the recovery of Jerusalem by military means until his death in 1405; even planning the foundation of a new order of chivalry, the Knighthood of the Passion of Jesus Christ, to spearhead the conquest and resettlement of the Holy Land.[26]

Philip was, no doubt, a maverick but, as Norman Housley has shown, the Holy Land never quite disappeared from the thinking

1369', in P. M. Holt, ed., *Eastern Mediterranean Lands in the Period of the Crusades* (Warminster, 1977), 90–105.

[23] *Vita S.Angeli*, 822.

[24] Christopher Tyerman, 'Philip VI and the Recovery of the Holy Land', *EHR* 100 (1985), 21–51.

[25] Edbury, 'Crusading Policy', 94–5, discusses the likelihood of the 1365 crusade having been intended as a means of securing Jerusalem.

[26] Abdel Hamid Hamdy, 'Phillipe de Mézières and the New Order of the Passion', *Bulletin of the Faculty of Arts of the University of Egypt* 18 (1964), 1–104, edited from Oxford, Bodl., Ashmole MS 813; Andrea Tarnowski, 'Material Examples: Phillipe de Mézières' Order of the Passion', *Yale French Studies* 110 (2006), 163–75.

of Europeans concerned with the defence of Christendom against the Ottomans. From the recovery treatise of Emmanuel Piloti in 1420, to the planning of the Varna crusade in 1443, to the crusade proposals of King Manuel II of Portugal in 1505, we see the reiteration of the theory that the defeat of the Ottomans would lead to the recapture of Jerusalem from the Mamluks.[27]

Without knowing more about the authorship of the *Life of Angelo* it is impossible to know how closely related the prophecy in the text concerning the recovery of the Holy Land might be to the thinking of crusade theorists and planners. The *Life* almost certainly comes from a Carmelite community in Sicily, but whether its author was familiar with the revival of crusade planning between the 1360s and the end of the fourteenth century cannot be determined with any authority at present. Given that it plays no real part in the narrative of the *Life,* it is possible that the prophecy originated in a different text altogether, and was integrated into the *Life* as part of the bolstering of Angelo's sanctity. But if it is to be related in any way to a renewed interest in a traditional crusade, even one that only had any real force in Cyprus, it nonetheless provides another link between the Carmelites of the late fourteenth century and the Holy Land.

It is no coincidence that it was in the same period – the last quarter of the fourteenth century – that the Carmelite historical project was reaching its apogee, in the writing of the Catalan Felipe Ribot. It was Ribot's *De institutione et peculiaribus gestis religiosorum Carmelitarum* that provided the first systematic historical reconstruction of the Carmelites' alleged unbroken occupation of Mount Carmel.[28] In Ribot's hands, the history of the Holy Land, including the recent period of Frankish rule, became Carmelite history. Ribot took the supposed founding of the Carmelites as a prophetic order by Elijah as historical reality, and sought to fill in the narrative detail in between. By the last quarter of the fourteenth century, the need to 'prove' the Carmelite association with the Holy Land had become acute: Carmelite claims to special Marian status had been attacked by the Dominicans since the 1330s, and in 1374 a fresh assault had been launched by the Dominican theologian John Stokes at Cambridge. In public debate adjudicated

---

[27] Housley, *Later Crusades*, 45–8.
[28] Jotischky, *Carmelites and Antiquity*, 136–50.

by the University Chancellor, the Carmelite master John Hornby defended Carmelite claims not only to use the Marian title in their name but also to Elianic foundation on historical grounds. In 1379 Urban VI formally recognized the Carmelites' claims to their version of history. Powerful allies, including, in England, John of Gaunt, had been mobilized to petition the pope in favour of the Carmelites.[29]

By the 1370s, history – specifically, the history of the Holy Land – lay at the heart of the Carmelites' identity. The *Life of Angelo,* for all its historical vagaries, witnesses not only to this concern but also to Carmelite interest in a brief crusading revival in the later fourteenth century.

Lancaster University

---

[29] Ibid. 166–83; J. P. H. Clark, 'A Defense of the Carmelite Order by John Hornby, O.Carm, AD 1374', *Carmelus* 32 (1985), 73–106.

AN ANGLICAN VIEW OF THE CRUSADES: THOMAS FULLER'S *THE HISTORIE OF THE HOLY WARRE*

by BERNARD HAMILTON

T his essay is concerned with the ways in which the English Reformation changed the understanding of the crusade movement from that held in the Middle Ages. The papally inspired crusade movement was not an attractive subject to sixteenth-century Protestant scholars. As Christopher Tyerman has remarked in his study, *England and the Crusades*, it was not until 1639 that 'Thomas Fuller published his *Historie of the Holy Warre*, the first, and one of the more interesting histories of the crusades written by an Englishman'.[1] The only earlier post-Reformation English work which had touched on this subject was Richard Knolles' *The Generall Historie of the Turks* (1603).[2] Its first book was entitled 'The Generall Historie of the Turks before the Rising of the Ottoman Familie', and inevitably contained some account of crusading activity, though that was incidental to its main theme. Knolles' book proved popular and a second edition was published in 1610, showing that there was a public for works of this kind.

There were a variety of reasons for this interest in the Ottoman Empire in early Stuart England. Queen Elizabeth had conducted diplomatic relations with the Ottoman sultans Murad III (1574–95) and Mehmet III (1595–1603), hoping to facilitate trade between the two states and also to form an alliance against the Habsburg Empire. Although the latter objective did not succeed, the trade negotiations led to the foundation of the Levant Company in 1583. These exchanges involved the dispatch of many embassies from the English court to Constantinople. The envoys were not all diplomats, but were drawn from a wide social range, which included the instrument maker Thomas Dallas, who installed a clockwork organ which he had made in the Topkapi Palace as a gift from the Queen

---

[1]   All references in this article are to the second edition: Thomas Fuller, *The Historie of the Holy Warre* (Cambridge, 1640). See also C. Tyerman, *England and the Crusades 1095–1588* (London, 1988), 370.

[2]   Richard Knolles, *The Generall Historie of the Turks* (London, 1603).

of England. These official exchanges also encouraged individual English travellers such as Henry Cavendish to visit the Ottoman capital. The information which these men brought back generated a wide English interest in the Ottoman world.[3] Such an interest did not automatically lead to an interest in the crusades. Torquato Tasso's epic, *Gerusalemme Liberata*, published in 1580, was admired in Elizabethan literary circles and was translated into English by Edward Fairfax in 1600. Yet although the theme of this poem was the First Crusade, that was merely a setting for the study of love and honour, which were Tasso's central concerns. Knolles' work on the Ottomans made English readers aware of the crusading past, and it is arguable that the successful expansion of the Levant Company led to a further growth of interest in that field.[4] One of the most important factories established by that company was at Aleppo, the western terminus of caravans from Persia and Iraq. Fourteen English merchants were stationed there, and from 1613 their trade was carried on through the port of Alexandretta (Scanderoon) in north Syria, from which the road to Aleppo ran through the Amanus Mountains to Antioch, once the crusader capital of North Syria. It was natural that an interest in the history of Aleppo should lead to an interest in the history of the crusades, a period when the ports of Syria and Palestine had been under western rule. Considerations of this kind explain why there was an English public which welcomed the opportunity to read about the crusades, but the reason for Thomas Fuller's own interest in the subject is not known.

Fuller was born in 1608 and became a fellow of Sidney Sussex College, Cambridge, in 1629. He was ordained a priest in the Church of England in 1631 and until 1633 was perpetual curate of St Benet's, Cambridge. It was almost certainly during those years

---

3   G. MacLean, *The Rise of Oriental Travel: English Visitors to the Ottoman Empire* (London, 2004); idem and N. Matar, *Britain and the Islamic World* (Oxford, 2011); 'The Diary of Master Thomas Dallam, 1599–1600', in J. T. Bent, ed., *Early Voyages and Travels in the Levant*, Hakluyt Society ser. 1, 87 (Cambridge, 1893); 'Mr Harrie Cavendish. His Journey to and from Constantinople, 1589', ed. A. C. Wood, *Camden Miscellany* 17 (1940), 1–29; Lisa Jardine, 'Gloriana Rules the Waves', *TRHS* ser. 6, 14 (2004), 209–22.

4   Queen Elizabeth authorized the foundation of the Levant Company in 1581, but negotiations with the Ottoman authorities were not concluded until 1583: A. C. Wood, *A History of the Levant Company* (Oxford, 1935), 11–14; on the Aleppo factory, see ibid. 75–7; J. Mather, *Pashas: Traders and Travellers in the Islamic World* (London, 2009), 19–22.

that he began collecting material about the crusades, though his book about them was not completed until after he had become vicar of Broadwindsor, Dorset, in 1634.[5] He considered the study of history to be important, dedicating his book to two young noblemen, Edward Montagu and John Powlett, with the inscription: 'History maketh a young man to be old, without either wrinkles or gray haires; priviledging him with the experience of age, without either the infirmities or inconveniences thereof.'[6] Fuller did not explain how he had became interested in crusading history, but his work was well received, going into a second edition in 1640 and a third in 1647.

As a historian, not an antiquarian, Fuller's work raised wider issues which he addressed, and which will be considered below. Three are particularly significant: what was the relation of the Anglican church[7] to the medieval western Catholic church; what should the Christian attitude to aggressive, as opposed to defensive, warfare be; and what was the religious status of Islam?

Fuller's attitude to the medieval western church is fundamental to his work. He explained his position in his discussion of the Albigensian Crusade. Like all Protestant historians of his day he believed that the Albigensians, or Cathars, had been a group of reformers closely related to the Waldensians, who had been slandered by medieval Catholic writers.[8] Fuller said that amongst his contemporaries there were three views about the Cathars: the Roman Catholic view that they were terrible heretics; 'the opinion of some strict Protestants' that they and the Waldensians were 'the only true Church of God in that age'; and the third view, which he clearly shared, that held by those who considered the second view to be

---

5 *ODNB, s.n.* 'Fuller, Thomas'.

6 Fuller, *Holy Warre*, Epistle Dedicatorie, 4–5.

7 The Latin term *ecclesia anglicana* was used during the Middle Ages (e.g. in Magna Carta) to describe the English provinces of the western church. The word 'Anglican' is first attested in 1635, at the time that Fuller was writing, in a letter of James Howell (*c.*1593–1666), a royal official under Charles I. Howell used 'Anglican' and 'Gallican' to describe churches opposed to Rome, and that represents Fuller's own position. See *OED* (Oxford, 1931), 1: 327.

8 The first Protestant historian to challenge this view was Charles Schmidt in 1848–9, who asserted that the Cathars were dualists, not proto-Protestants; because Schmidt was a Protestant pastor, his views carried weight with his co-religionists: C. Schmidt, *Histoire et doctrine de la secte des Cathares ou Albiegeois*, 2 vols (Paris, 1848–9).

... trespassing on Divine providence; that God ... should be so long in lethargie ... for so many years together, leaving no true Church, but so small a company of such simple people. More modestly therefore they hold that these Albigenses were a purer part of the Church ... though guilty of some errors ... So that the main body of the Church visible at that time was much in dilapidation, whilest the Albigenses, as an innermost chapel thereof, was best in repair.[9]

Fuller thus saw the medieval western church as the same church, albeit unreformed, as the Anglican church to which he belonged. The crusades were therefore part of the history of his own church.

Fuller based his work on primary sources; indeed, there were no secondary works which he could use. By the 1630s a range of important texts were in print. He used the *Historia Ierosolimitana* of Albert of Aachen (*fl.* 1099–1119) as his chief source for the First Crusade, and William of Tyre's *Chronicle*, in the Basle edition of 1549, for the history of the Kingdom of Jerusalem from 1099 to 1186. For the Third Crusade he relied chiefly on the *Chronicle* of Roger of Howden (d. *c*.1202), while he found a good deal of material about crusading activity for the first half of the thirteenth century in the *Chronica Maiora* of Matthew Paris (*c*.1200–59). He also made full use of two important document collections: the compilation of medieval sources published at Basle by the Protestant Centuriators of Magdeburg between 1559 and 1574 as the *Historia Ecclesiae Christi*, which he read in the 1624 edition; and the *Annales Ecclesiatici* produced by Cardinal Baronius, librarian of the Vatican, in twelve volumes between 1588 and 1607, which he read in the Cologne edition of 1624. For the history of Byzantium in this period he used the *History* of Nicetas Choniates (*c*.1150–1215).[10] He did not cite any oriental source and few if any, I think, would have been available to him.[11]

The Historie of the Holy Warre is arranged in five books. Book 1

---

[9] Fuller, *Holy Warre*, 139–40 (3.18).
[10] Ibid., Qq3v, Qq4r [*sic*].
[11] This soon began to change. Edward Pococke was appointed to the Laudian chair of Arabic at Oxford in 1636, and in 1663, two years after Fuller's death, produced a Latin translation of Bar Hebraeus's history of the Near and Middle East, containing a good deal of information about the crusading period, entitled *Historia Compendium Dynastiarum* (this work is now generally called *Chronographia*): R. Irwin, *For Lust of Knowing: The Orientalists and their Enemies* (London, 2006), 93–7.

begins with the destruction of the Temple of Jerusalem by Titus in AD 70 and ends with the capture of Jerusalem during the First Crusade in 1099. Books 2–4 deal chiefly with the history of the Crusader States from 1099 to the capture of Acre by the Mamluks in 1291. The first seven chapters of Book 5 deal with the history of the military orders after the loss of the Latin Kingdom, and also with the vast number of claimants to the titular kingship of Jerusalem who were alive at the time when Fuller was writing.[12] The rest of Book 5 consists of what Fuller described as 'Observations', in which he analysed why the crusade movement was ultimately a failure. Fuller's main interest was in the history of the Crusader States. He mentioned the wars of the Spanish reconquest which prevented the Christian kings of Spain from taking a full part in crusades to the Levant, but he did not consider them a part of the crusades.[13] He discussed the Fourth Crusade, but said very little about Frankish Greece.[14] He did, nevertheless, hold the Fourth Crusade and its aftermath responsible for the schism between the eastern and western churches, which damaged the crusading cause and which, in his opinion, had not been present in the twelfth century.[15] The Baltic crusades received some consideration in Book 5, where he discussed the later history of the Teutonic Knights.[16] But the Albigensian Crusade was the only other area of crusading besides Syria and Palestine which Fuller examined in any detail.[17] This interested him as an Anglican clergyman, writing at a time when French Protestantism was officially recognized by the French crown under the provisions of the Edict of Nantes (1598). He remarked that 'in those parts of France where the Albigenses had been most cruelly handled, now the Protestants (heirs to most of their tenets) flourish most'.[18]

The underlying assumption in Fuller's work was that all human

---

[12] Fuller, *Holy Warre*, 278–82 (5.29).

[13] 'Spain was exercised all the time of this warre in defending her self against the Moores and Saracens in her own bowels': ibid. 266 (5.22).

[14] For the sack of Constantinople in 1204 and the creation of the Latin Empire, see ibid. 136–8 (3.17); for the recovery of Constantinople by the Byzantine emperor, Michael VIII, with a very brief summary of the history of the Latin Empire and the survival of Venetian rule in Greek lands, ibid. 171–2 (4.3).

[15] Ibid. 172–8 (4.4–6).

[16] Ibid. 234–6 (5.4).

[17] Ibid. 138–50 (3.18–22).

[18] Ibid. 150 (3.22).

history was determined by God's providence. He was certain that Islam had nothing whatever to be said in its favour. He dismissed it as a false religion,[19] although he treated some individual Muslims, for example Saladin, with sympathy.[20] Nevertheless, he was convinced that Islam had only prospered because God had used it as his instrument to pass judgement on the flawed Christian society of the Graeco-Roman world of late antiquity.[21] This was the background against which he discussed whether the crusading movement was justifiable. He set out the arguments in its favour quite fairly, but was not impressed by them. Its supporters urged that the land made holy by the presence of God incarnate should not remain in the hands of unbelievers, and that it was just to go to war to recover that land because it had formerly been part of the Christian Roman Empire. Fuller did not accept that pilgrimage to the Holy Places was an integral or even a desirable part of Christian practice and cited St Gregory of Nyssa and St Jerome in support of this view.[22] He thought the reason for considering crusades to be just wars was a weak one, because the Muslims had held the Holy Land for 460 years before the First Crusade, which surely gave them a secure title to it. He was more favourably impressed by the claim that the crusade was justified because it sought to prevent the Turks from expanding into the Byzantine Empire and thereafter into western Europe, a fear which had led Alexius Comnenus to ask for western help at the Council of Piacenza in March 1095.[23]

Fuller argued that the concept of the crusade originated with the papacy. This is uncontroversial, but he supposed that the popes had a hidden agenda: first that the holy war would be led by secular rulers, who thus would be unable to contest the growth of papal power in western Europe, and secondly that the war would also bring the eastern patriarchates under the authority of the Holy See. The second consideration was reflected in the

---

[19] Fuller described Islam as 'the scumme of Judaisme and Paganisme sod together, and here and there strewed over with a spice of Christianitie': ibid. 7 (1.6).

[20] [Saladin] 'wanted nothing to his eternall happinesse but the knowledge of Christ': ibid. 133 (3.14).

[21] Ibid. 7 (1.6).

[22] Ibid. 15 (1.10), 244 (5.9).

[23] Fuller knew from Baronius that this request had been made, though he did not himself consider it a very important cause of the First Crusade: ibid. 13 (1.9).

construction of Fuller's work. In Book 2 he devoted a chapter in his account of the reign of each king of Jerusalem to church affairs, although lack of adequate sources for the period after 1187 meant that he was unable to sustain this when writing about the thirteenth century. Fuller accepted the account in Albert of Aachen's *Chronicle* that the catalyst for the launching of the First Crusade was a letter from Patriarch Symeon II of Jerusalem, brought to Urban II by Peter the Hermit on his return from a pilgrimage, but suggested that the pope might have engineered this process by sending Peter to Jerusalem as an agent provocateur, charged with encouraging Symeon to appeal for help from the west.[24] Because the First Crusade was successful the papacy gained control of the patriarchates of Antioch and Jerusalem, and in Book 3 of his work Fuller argued that the Fourth Crusade was diverted to Constantinople in 1203 by Innocent III in order to put a pro-papal emperor on the Byzantine throne and thus bring the patriarchate of Constantinople into subjection to Rome, a simplistic view, but one not totally unrelated to the facts.[25]

Yet although he did not think that the crusades had been holy wars, Fuller's attitude towards them was ambiguous. He was not opposed to warfare per se, and he thought that fighting the Turks was a good thing in principle. 'Wars of Christians against infidels are like the heat of exercise which serveth to keep the body of Christianity in health', he wrote.[26] He could not, of course, accept the validity of the crusading indulgence offered by the papacy, which he dismissed as superstitious, leading men to believe that 'by dying for the Crosse [they did] crosse [out] the score of their own sinnes and score up God for their debtour'.[27] Yet although all

---

[24] Albert of Aachen, *Historia Hierosolimitana* 1.2–5; ed. and transl. S. B. Edgington (Oxford, 2007), 4–9; Fuller, *Holy Warre*, 11–12 (1.8).

[25] Fuller, *Holy Warre*, 136–8 (3.17); the degree of Innocent III's involvement in the diversion of the crusade to Constantinople remains controversial. The problems inherent in the sources are discussed by J. P. Phillips, *The Fourth Crusade and the Sack of Constantinople* (London, 2004).

[26] Fuller, *Holy Warre*, 211 (4.24).

[27] Ibid. 241 (5.9). At the Council of Clermont in 1095 Urban II had decreed: 'Whoever for devotion alone, not to gain honour or money, goes to Jerusalem to liberate the Church of God can substitute this journey for all penance [imposed for sins repented, and absolved in confession]': R. Somerville, *The Councils of Urban II. 1: Decreta Claromontensia*, Annuarium Historiae Conciliorum, Supplementum 1 (Amsterdam, 1972), 74; cited in the translation of L. and J. Riley-Smith, *The Crusades: Idea and Reality, 1095–1274* (London, 1981), 37.

crusaders received indulgences, Fuller was not prepared to belittle the spirit of religious devotion which inspired some of them: 'Let us not raise the opinion of our own pietie by trampling on our predecessours, as if this age had monopolised all goodnesse to itself. Some no doubt most religious and truly valiant (as fearing nothing but sinne) engaged themselves in this action.'[28] He sometimes showed a genuine admiration for individual crusaders, writing, for example, of Frederick Barbarossa, departing on the Third Crusade in 1189: 'Impute it not to the weaknesse of his judgment but the strength of his devotion, that at seventy years of age, having one foot in his grave, he would set the other on pilgrimage.'[29] Fuller was severe in his judgements of crusaders who lacked commitment. He wrote of Philip II of France, who left the Third Crusade prematurely: 'If it be true, what some report, that Saladin bribed him to return [to France] let him forever forfeit the surname of Augustus and the style of the Most Christian Prince.'[30] Similarly, he censured the War of St Sabas in 1256–61 between the Venetians, the Pisans and the Genoese in Acre and Tyre : 'these civil wars amongst themselves, like the heat of a feaver, [are] dangerous and destructive of religion'.[31]

Fuller shared with the medieval popes and chroniclers the view that military success in war against the infidel was a sign of divine approval and defeat in war a divine punishment for sin. All of these writers were, of course, influenced by the historical books of the Old Testament, in which similar considerations were shown to have determined the careers of the kings of Judah and Israel. On one occasion Fuller explicitly made this comparison, saying of Louis IX of France: 'This Lewis was the French Josiah, both for the piety of his life and woefulnesse of his death, ingaging himself in a needless war.'[32]

Fuller argued that crusader victories had been the gifts of God: 'True it is [that] God often gave them great victories, when they defended themselves in great straits.'[33] Yet just as medieval writers had been unable to find any other explanation than the sinfulness

---

[28] Ibid. 256 (5.16).
[29] Ibid. 113 (3.3).
[30] Ibid. 124 (3.9).
[31] Ibid. 211 (4.23).
[32] Ibid. 216 (4.27); cf. 2 Kings 22, 23: 1–10.
[33] Ibid. 67 (2.17).

of the participants for the failure of crusader armies who were fighting in God's name,[34] so Fuller explained the defeat of Hattin and the loss of Jerusalem in 1187 in the same terms: 'Thus Jerusalem, after it had fourscore and eight years been enjoyed by the Christians, by God's just judgement was taken again by the Turks. What else could be expected? Sinne reigned in every corner'.[35]

Book 4 ended with the fall of Acre in 1291 and Fuller summed up the crusade achievement: 'Thus after a hundred and ninety and four years ended the Holy Warre; for continuance the longest, for money spent the costliest, for bloodshed the cruelest, for pretences the most pious, for the true intent the most politick the world ever saw.'[36] In Book 5 Fuller considered the reasons for this failure. Many of those he identified were practical: the Crusader States were too distant from western Europe and too isolated from other Christian powers to receive help when they needed it.[37] Papal intervention was often detrimental to success: he cited the example of Cardinal Pelagius, papal legate on the Fifth Crusade, and his disastrous decision to march on Cairo during the time of the Nile floods.[38] One factor which Fuller identified as of central importance in the failure of the crusades was the frequent unwillingness of the Christian leaders to keep oaths which they had sworn to Muslim rulers. An important example of this was King Amalric's decision to invade Egypt in 1168 in contravention of the oath which his ambassadors had sworn to the Fatimid Caliph.[39] Fuller cited St Jerome's axiom: 'It mattereth not to whom, but by Whom we swear'. Fuller regarded such oath-breaking as blasphemous, and asked: 'How could Safety it self save this people and blesse this project so blackly blasted with perjury?'[40]

Yet, in Fuller's view, not all the consequences of the crusades had been bad. Two of the military orders founded to defend the Holy Land had survived the fall of Acre, and in his opinion they

---

[34] E. Siberry, *Criticism of Crusading 1095–1274* (Oxford, 1985).
[35] Fuller, *Holy Warre*, 106 (2.46).
[36] Ibid. 228 (4.32).
[37] Ibid. 251–3 (5.13).
[38] Ibid. 249–50 (5.12). For a full discussion of Pelagius's role, see J. Powell, *Anatomy of a Crusade 1213–1221* (Philadelphia, PA, 1986).
[39] Fuller, *Holy Warre*, 93 (2.37).
[40] Ibid. 248 (5.11).

had continued to do good work.[41] The Teutonic Knights, when they moved their activities to Prussia, defended eastern Europe against the Tartars and also converted the heathen Prussians.[42] Although Fuller did not believe in forced conversion, he thought it legitimate to use force against pagan rulers in order to allow the peaceful evangelization of their subjects.[43] His greatest praise was reserved for the Knights of St John. He related their relocation first to Rhodes and then to Malta after the fall of the Crusader Kingdom, and comments that they are 'the bulwark of Christendom to this day, giving dayly evident proof of their courage ... The Knights of Malta are at this day a good bridle to Tunis and Algiers.'[44] Tunis and Algiers were in Fuller's day the headquarters of the Barbary Corsairs, who were making an impact on the British Isles by extending their slave-raiding expeditions to the North Atlantic. As a West Country parson Fuller had good reason to feel apprehensive about them. In 1625 a party of Corsairs had landed at Mount's Bay in Cornwall one Sunday morning, rounded up the congregation in the parish church and taken them to Morocco to be sold into slavery.[45]

The Corsairs were the westernmost subjects of the Ottoman Sultan, whose power extended northwards into Hungary. The crusades had failed in the long term to contain the Turkish threat, and Fuller wryly remarked: 'At this day, the Turks, to spare the Christians their pains of coming so long a journey to Palestine, have done them the unwelcome courtesy to come more than half the way to give them a meeting.'[46] The divisions of Christendom, both political and religious, made any new crusade impractical: 'We may safely conclude', Fuller wrote, 'that the regaining of Jerusalem and the Holy Land from the Turks may better be placed among our desires than our hopes, as improbable ever to come

---

[41] The third military order, the Knights Templar, had been suppressed in 1311–12 by the Council of Vienne, and Fuller examined the reasons for this: ibid. 229–34 (5.1–3). For a full discussion of this matter, see M. C. Barber, *The Trial of the Templars* (Cambridge, 1978).

[42] Fuller, *Holy Warre*, 234–6 (5.4).

[43] 'If any object that Religion is not to be beaten into men with the dint of sword; yet it may be lawfull to open the way by force, for instruction, catechizing, and such other gentle means to follow after': ibid. 13 (1.9).

[44] Ibid. 237 (5.5).

[45] G. Milton, *White Gold* (London, 2004), 10.

[46] Fuller, *Holy Warre*, 228 (4.32).

to passe.'[47] But he entertained a more positive hope about the future of the Ottoman Empire. Although God alone knew when it would happen, 'we have just cause to hope that the fall of this unwelcome Empire doth approach'.[48]

In his attitude to war against the Muslims, Fuller had much in common with the medieval crusaders about whom he wrote, despite his reservations about some aspects of the crusading movement. He did not approve of what he considered had been a deliberate attempt by the papacy to manipulate the crusades for its own profit. He did not think it particularly important that the Holy Land should be ruled by Christians, because he saw no spiritual value in pilgrimage. He did not accept that crusading had had any value as a penitential exercise because he thought that this was an unacceptable attempt to bargain with God. Nevertheless, he did consider that wars intended to stem the political expansion of Islam were well-pleasing to God, and he assumed that God would always support Christians in their wars against unbelievers provided that they kept his commandments. If they failed to do so he would allow their enemies to triumph.

Fuller's *Holy Warre* is a work of sound scholarship, and marks the beginning of modern British crusading studies, but it differs from more recent work in one important way. Like the authors of the sources on which his book is based, Fuller was writing history in a Christian theological framework, and like them he was strongly influenced by the historical books of the Old Testament. He concluded his work with a statement which those medieval writers would have wholeheartedly endorsed: 'SOLI DEO GLORIA: TO GOD ALONE BE GLORY GIVEN.'[49]

University of Nottingham

---

[47] Ibid. 278 (5.28).
[48] Ibid. 285 (5.30).
[49] Ibid. 286.

USING THE PAST AGAINST THE PAPACY: LUTHER'S APPEAL TO CHURCH HISTORY IN HIS ANTI-PAPAL WRITINGS

by CHARLOTTE METHUEN

I t is well known that Martin Luther found ultimate authority *sola scriptura*. The evangelical endeavour which he initiated and exemplified focused on the return to the gospel and the rediscovery of a church modelled according to scriptural lines. For the Reformers, the truly catholic church was that church which adhered most closely to the church established by Scripture. The early church, being chronologically closest to that established in Scripture, was more authentic, not yet affected by innovation. But how were the details of that church to be discovered? Scripture was not always informative on practical questions of church life and ecclesiastical order, and for these an appeal to church history was necessary.[1] Drawing particularly on Scott Hendrix's study of Luther's attitude towards the papacy,[2] and the studies by John Headley and others of Luther's view of, and appeal to, church history,[3] this essay explores the ways in which Luther used his knowledge of church history to define and support his developing critique of the papacy. It focuses on his early writings to 1521, but will also consider the later work *Von den Consiliis und Kirchen*

---

[1]   There has been relatively little work done on the uses of history in the Reformation. For some notable exceptions, see the works on Luther's use of history in n. 3 below; cf. also John W. O' Malley, 'Historical Thought and the Reform Crisis of the Early Sixteenth Century', *Theological Studies* 28 (1967), 531–48; Geoffrey Dipple, *'Just as in the time of the Apostles': Uses of History in the Radical Reformation* (Kitchener, ON, 2005). For an account of history-writing in early modern England, see D. R. Woolf, *Reading History in Early Modern England* (Cambridge, 2000).

[2]   Scott H. Hendrix, *Luther and the Papacy: Stages in a Reformation Conflict* (Philadelphia, PA, 1981).

[3]   John M. Headley, *Luther's View of Church History* (New Haven, CT, 1963). This in turn draws on earlier works of German scholarship: Hanns Lilje, *Luthers Geschichtsanschauung* (Berlin, 1932); Walther Köhler, *Luther und die Kirchengeschichte nach seinen Schriften, zunächst bis 1521* (Erlangen, 1900); Ernst Schläfer, *Luther als Kirchenhistoriker* (Gütersloh, 1897); Headley argues that Luther was not a church historian, but nonetheless maintains that 'there exists in his thought a definite, if implicit, view of Church history', which 'represents a major expression of the Christian interpretation of history': *Luther's View of Church History*, 266.

(1539), a testimony to Luther's growing interest in the history of the church. Luther's first published appeal to the history of the church appeared in his *Explanations of the Ninety-Five Theses* (1518). The *Ninety-Five Theses* were directed against false attitudes towards piety. They also raised serious questions about the pope's power to forgive sin[4] and made some bold assertions about what Luther claimed must be the pope's true beliefs.[5] Some of Luther's contemporaries interpreted the *Ninety-Five Theses* as a highly provocative and serious challenge to papal authority. Nonetheless, in retrospect, writing in 1545, Luther remembered that he had been 'a most enthusiastic papist' at this time.[6]

Whitford suggests plausibly that Luther was shocked and somewhat dismayed by how quickly discussion of the *Ninety-Five Theses* became a controversy about papal authority.[7] As Hendrix observes, Luther regarded them as an extension of his efforts to reform the University of Wittenberg, and no one had challenged these university reforms as an attack on the papacy.[8] Lindberg thinks that Luther initially believed himself to be involved in 'an academic dispute in which he was entitled to engage due to his doctoral oath', whilst for the Dominicans appointed to engage with his case 'Luther's attack on indulgences appeared as an attack on Thomistic-scholastic theology, papal primacy, and the Dominican (or Curial) jurisdiction over heretics'.[9] Despite his dismay, Luther quickly rose to this challenge. In his *Explanations*, a defence of the *Ninety-Five Theses* written just months after he had composed the original text, he was already more explicit in his critique of papal authority. Over the months that followed, his thinking

---

4   See Luther, *Disputation on the Power and Efficacy of Indulgences*, Theses 25, 26 (*LW* 31, 27; *WA* 1, 234).

5   Ibid., Theses 48–51 (*LW* 31, 29–30; *WA* 1, 235).

6   *LW* 34, 328; *WA* 54, 179. Scholars have long debated the realities of Luther's attitude towards the papacy at this point in his career. In his study, *Luther and the Papacy*, Hendrix identifies seven phases in Luther's view of the papacy: ambivalence (1505–17); protest (October 1517 – June 1518); resistance (June–December 1518); challenge (1519); opposition (1520); conviction (1521–2); and persistence (1522–46).

7   David M. Whitford, 'The Papal Antichrist: Martin Luther and the Underappreciated Influence of Lorenzo Valla', *RQ* 61 (2008), 26–52, at 37.

8   Hendrix, *Luther and the Papacy*, 37.

9   Carter Lindberg, 'Prierias and his Significance for Luther's Development', *SCJ* 3 (1972), 45–64, at 50–1.

would develop further in response to his encounters with Thomas Cajetan, Johannes Eck, Sylvester Prierias and Johannes Tetzel.[10] In particular, their counters to his own assertions forced Luther to embark on a more careful study of the history of the church.

In his *Explanations*, Luther appealed to history for illustrations which might clarify the extent of papal authority. Elucidating the twenty-second of his ninety-five theses, 'Whereas [the pope] remits to souls in purgatory no penalty which, according to the canons, they would have had to pay in this life', Luther related the question of the pope's spiritual jurisdiction to the larger question of the historical and geographical jurisdiction of Rome:

> consider the Roman church as it was at the time of St. Gregory, when it had no jurisdiction over other churches, at least not over the Greek church. It is evident that canonical punishments were not binding upon the Greeks, just as they are not binding now for Christians who are not subject to the pope, as in the case of the Turks, Tartars, and Livonians. For these people, therefore, indulgences are not necessary, but only for those who come under the authority of the Roman church. If, therefore, they are not binding upon those who are living, much less are they binding upon the dead, who are not under the jurisdiction of any church.[11]

The historical example served to substantiate Luther's main point that there were, and always had been, those – including some living Christians, and all of the dead – who were outside the pope's jurisdiction.

Historical anecdote also played its part in Luther's *Explanations*. Considering the question of change, Luther noted the danger of falling away from the early church:

> For we read that at one time it seemed most dangerous to the holy fathers to teach anything beyond the heavenly rule, as

---

[10] For the significance of Luther's dispute with Prierias, see Lindberg, 'Prierias'. For Luther and Eck, see David Bagchi, *Luther's Earliest Opponents: Catholic Controversialists 1518–1525* (Minneapolis, MN, 1991), 69–91. For a recent discussion of the role of history in the debate between Luther and Eck, see Susan Schreiner, *Are You Alone Wise? The Search for Certainty in the Early Modern Era*, Oxford Studies in Historical Theology (Oxford, 2011), 152–65.

[11] *WA* 1, 571; *LW* 31, 152.

Hilary says; and the holy Spiridion, bishop of Cyprus, observed this discipline so strictly that he interrupted a person who used only one Greek word ambiguously, saying 'Take up your couch and walk' instead of 'Take up your pallet or your bed and walk,' finding fault with the word he used even though it did not change the meaning at all.[12]

Luther's main point was that the practice of indulgences represented a falling away from the proper practices of the church. In both these cases, Luther cited historical evidence, apparently simply assuming that ancient practice or an ancient saying must be authoritative.

The first of these examples, however, was viewed by Luther's opponents as contentious. They were not prepared to tolerate what they saw as a crass misrepresentation of the history of Roman primacy. At Augsburg, Cajetan drew on canon law to argue for the primacy of papal authority over the whole church from the earliest Christian centuries. Cajetan did not convince Luther; instead, the result was the opposite of what he might have hoped: Luther began to question the authority of the decrees and laws which made up canon law, commenting in his account of the disputation that 'the true and proper meaning of Scripture is not found in all the papal decretals'.[13]

Responding to Luther, Eck, like Cajetan, highlighted what he considered the inaccuracies of Luther's historical account, offering a counter-thesis: 'We deny that the Roman Church was not above the other churches before the time of Sylvester; rather, we have always acknowledged the one who held the seat and the faith

---

[12] *WA* 1, 572–3; *LW* 31, 155. Against Cajetan, Luther would later claim that 'according to Hilary, one should not read a meaning into the Holy Scriptures, but extract it from them': *WA* 2, 17; *LW* 31, 276. *LW*'s editors refer at these points to two different figures: the first is Hilary of Poitiers, who refused to sign a condemnation of Athanasius, and was banished by the Arian emperor Constantius (a son of Constantine) to Phrygia in 357; the other is Hilary of Arles, bishop of Arles from 428, who sought to exercise primacy in the province of Southern Gaul and in 444 was deprived of his rights to consecrate bishops, call synods, or oversee the church in the province by Pope Leo I. The former is the more likely since, had Luther been referring to Hilary of Arles, he would have been able to make good rhetorical use of the latter's conflict with the pope. Spiridion (more commonly Spyridon) was an archbishop of Tramathus (Trimythouse), Cyprus, who argued against the Arians at the Council of Nicaea (325). He was known for his simplicity, which makes Luther's anecdote surprising.

[13] *WA* 2, 22; *LW* 31, 284.

of the blessed Peter to be the successor of Peter and the general vicar of Christ.'[14] Luther's response to Eck's thesis – Proposition 13 – was published in 1519 under the title *Resolutio Lutheriana super propositione sua decima tertia de potestate papae*. In this short work he laid out his reasons – drawn from Scripture, history and reason – for disagreeing with Eck, claiming that, 'as history satisfactorily proves' (*ut satis probant historiae*), the Roman church was never set above the Greek, African or Asian churches.[15] Luther offered Eck a counter-proposition:

> That the Roman Church is superior to all others is proved by the feeblest [*frigidissimis*] decrees issued by the Roman pontiffs; against these stand the text of divine Scripture, the accepted history of the last fifteen hundred years, and the decree of the Council of Nicaea, the most sacred of all councils.[16]

The appeal to Nicaea would become characteristic; indeed Headley observes that Luther's use of Nicaea 'presents the most significant single example of the exploitation of the historical argument',[17] and Schreiner suggests that 'Canon VI of Nicea became the true touchstone for the debate about the antiquity of papal supremacy'.[18] However, in defence of his opinion that the authority of the bishop of Rome was not established until well into the sixth century, Luther drew on a range of sources. These included Cyprian's many letters asserting his authority to be independent of that of the bishop in Rome,[19] together with his affirmation that the unity of the church is founded 'in us' and not 'in Rome'.[20] Luther referred also to letters in which Pope Gregory the Great 'eulogised' the patriarch of Alexandria and, submitted to, the emperor and the patriarch of Constantinople at the time of Chalcedon.[21] Most particularly, he cited the councils of Nicaea and

---

14 'Rhomanam ecclesiam non fuisse superiorem aliis ecclesiis ante tempora Sylvestri negamus, Sed eum, qui sedem beatissimi Petri habuit et fidem, sucessorem Petri et vicarium Christi generalem semper agnovimus': Eck's proposition, as cited by Luther, *WA* 2, 185.

15 *WA* 2, 225.

16 *WA* 2, 185; cf. *WA* 2, 161; *LW* 31, 318.

17 Headley, *Luther's View of Church History*, 164.

18 Schreiner, *Are You Alone Wise?*, 155.

19 *WA* 2, 186, 231–2.

20 *WA* 2, 216.

21 *WA* 2, 201.

Chalcedon, which had neither been initiated by, nor accepted the authority of, the bishop of Rome.[22] Additionally, he suggested that Gregory IX, Boniface VIII and Clement V had all offered fictitious arguments for the primacy of the pope.[23] Luther conceded that the pope was head of the western church, but argued that this was a virtue of human law.[24] On the basis of his reading of early church history, viewed through the lens of his reading of Scripture, Luther rejected claims that papal primacy over the church was either divine or scriptural in origin.

Scripture for Luther had to be the arbiter of history. In the introduction to the publication of his lectures on Galatians (1519), Luther conceded that the pope had 'no one superior to him'; however the pope too must be 'subject to this unbreakable rule of the apostle (1 Thess. 5: 21): "Test everything, hold fast what is good".'[25] Such testing, argued Luther, reiterating the conclusion that he had reached against Cajetan, demonstrated the problem with the sources cited by the papacy:

> that even many decretals are inconsistent with the sense of the Gospel is clearer than light, so that the actual necessity itself compels us to flee for refuge to the most solid rock of Divine Scripture and not to believe rashly any, whoever they may be, who speak, decide, or act contrary to its authority.[26]

If history contradicted Scripture, Luther concluded, then premises based upon it must be countered. Consequently, in the course of the ongoing disputes over papal authority, the question of the proper interpretation of certain historical accounts became important. After the Leipzig disputation against Eck in the summer of 1519, Luther reported that Eck's defence of the primacy of the pope had 'rested on the words "You are Peter ..." [Matt. 16: 18] and "Feed my sheep, ... follow me" [John 21: 17, 22], and "strengthen

---

[22] *WA* 2, 216, 238 (Nicaea), 201, 232 (Chalcedon).

[23] *WA* 2. 226. These three popes were associated with canon law collections: the Decretals of Gregory IX, promulgated in 1234; *Liber Sextus*, promulgated by Boniface VIII in 1298; and *Clementinae*, the constitutions of Clement V, promulgated by his successor John XXII in 1317. This is presumably why Luther names them. I am grateful to Peter Clarke for this point.

[24] *WA* 2, 201–2. For more detailed consideration of the proposition, see Hendrix, *Luther and the Papacy*, 81–5.

[25] *WA* 2, 446–7; *LW* 27, 155.

[26] *WA* 2, 447; *LW* 27, 156.

your brethren" [Luke 22: 32]', along with 'many quotations from the church fathers'. Ultimately, however, Eck

> ... rested his case entirely on the Council of Constance which had condemned Huss's article alleging that papal authority derived from the emperor instead of from God. Then Eck stamped about with much ado as though he were in an arena, holding up the Bohemians before me and publicly accusing me of the heresy and support of the Bohemian heretics.[27]

Luther's immediate response was to reiterate the historical arguments which he had already gathered together in his repudiation of Eck's Proposition 13: 'In rebuttal I brought up the Greek Christians during the past thousand years, and also the ancient church fathers, who had not been under the authority of the Roman pontiff, although I did not deny the primacy of honor due the pope.'[28] However, in this case Luther went further, citing documents from the Council of Constance (1414–18) to show that in condemning Jan Hus, the council had itself been in error.[29] To the consternation of the conciliarists, Luther's reassessment of church history had brought him to reject the authority of the decrees of the church's councils if he believed them to stand in opposition to Scripture, just as by the same criterion he rejected that of papal decretals.

Eck's association of Luther with Hus spurred Luther to further investigation of Hus's position. He had introduced his Leipzig theses with a caveat, in which he seemed to distance himself from the Bohemian reformer's position:

> among the articles of John Huss one among several is to be found in which he states that the pre-eminence of the papacy came from the emperor, as Platina plainly wrote. I, however, undertook to prove that this power was derived, not from imperial, but from papal decrees. The Lateran Church itself in an inscription sings about the origin and the extent of its authority, stating that by papal and imperial decrees it is the mother of churches etc.[30]

[27] Luther to Spalatin, 20 July 1519: *WABr* 1, 422; *LW* 31, 322.
[28] Ibid.
[29] Ibid.
[30] *WA* 2, 158; *LW* 31, 315. Bartolomeo Platina (1421–81) was the author of the *Liber*

However, Eck's presentation convinced Luther that Hus's theology was 'Christian and evangelical', leading him to embark on a careful reading of the Bohemian's works. Early in 1520, Luther wrote to Spalatin commenting on the extent to which he had found himself in agreement with Hus:

> I have taught and held all the teachings of John Hus, but thus far did not know it. John Staupitz has taught it in the same unintentional way. In short we all are Hussites and did not know it. Even Paul and Augustine are in reality Hussites. ... I am so shocked that I do not know what to think when I see such terrible judgments of God over mankind, namely, that the most evident evangelical truth was burned in public and was already considered condemned more than one hundred years ago.[31]

In March 1520, Luther further urged Spalatin to read Hus's *De ecclesia* which had recently been published by Thomas Anshelm in Hagenau: 'Not only does the work please all people, but its spirit and learnedness are wonderful.'[32] Although, as Hendrix has argued, Luther's view of the church differed from that of Hus, and Luther would later distance himself from the earlier reformer,[33] his initial study of Hus had only confirmed what he was already convinced had been the flawed nature of the proceedings at Constance. Later that year, in his treatise *To the Christian Nobility of the German Nation concerning the Improvement of the Christian Estate*, Luther included in a long list of abuses within the church his interpretation of what had happened during the council:

> We must admit to the Bohemians that John Huss and Jerome of Prague were burned at Constance against the papal, Christian, imperial oath and promise of safe-conduct. This happened contrary to God's commandment and gave the Bohemians

---

pontificalis, a history of the popes: see n. 45 below.

[31] Luther to Spalatin, *c.*14 February 1520: *WABr* 2, 41–2; *LW* 48, 151; cf. Whitford, 'Papal Antichrist', 38.

[32] Luther to Spalatin, 19 March 1520: *WABr* 2, 72; *LW* 48, 155. Luther reported that two thousand copies of Hus's work had been printed. For a summary of Hus's *De ecclesia*, see Schreiner, *Are You Alone Wise?*, 139–46.

[33] Scott Hendrix, ' "We Are All Hussites"? Hus and Luther Revisited', *ARG* 65 (1974), 134–61; repr. in idem, *Tradition and Authority in the Reformation* (Aldershot, 1996), VII.

ample cause for bitterness. And although they should have acted as perfect Christians and suffered this grave injustice and disobedience to God by these people, nevertheless they were not obliged to condone such conduct and acknowledge it as just. To this day they would rather give up life and limb than admit that it is right to break and deal contrarily with an imperial, papal, and Christian oath. So then, although it is the impatience of the Bohemians that is at fault, yet the pope and his crowd are still more to blame for all the misery, error, and the loss of souls which have followed that council.[34]

Luther's study of the ideas of Jan Hus and of events at the Council of Constance added fuel to the fire of his criticism of the papacy and his fury at its dishonesty.[35]

At about the same time that Luther was reading Hus, he acquired a copy of Lorenzo Valla's *Oratio on the Forgery of the Alleged Donation of Constantine*, which had first appeared in 1440, in the second edition published by Ulrich von Hutten late in 1519.[36] Valla argued that the so-called *Donation of Constantine* – which purported to record Constantine's gift of the Western Empire, the Italian lands, and primacy over other patriarchal sees to Sylvester, bishop of Rome, in 314 or 315 – was actually a forgery, and that the idea that Constantine would have given away such authority, or Sylvester accepted it, was entirely implausible.[37] Luther's reading of Valla's work brought him to the devastating conclusion that one of the key sources cited by the successive popes to support their claims to primacy and much else was fraudulent. He wrote to Spalatin of his growing disquiet:

---

[34] *WA* 6, 454; *LW* 44, 196.

[35] Luther's interest in the Council of Constance did not abate: in 1536 he wrote the preface and *Nachwort* to Johannes Agricola's Latin edition and German translation of three letters by Jan Hus (*WA* 50, 23–39), and in 1545 his account of Constance was central to the treatise *Wider das Bapstum zu Rom vom Teuffel gestifft*: *WA* 54, 206–99.

[36] Hendrix, *Luther and the Papacy*, 98; Whitford, 'Papal Antichrist', 40.

[37] Valla's text has been edited by Wolfram Setz, *Lorenzo Vallas Schrift gegen die Konstantinische Schenkung. De falso credita et ementita Constantini donatione. Zur Interpretation und Wirkungsgeschichte* (Tübingen, 1975). For a summary of Valla's argument in the *Oratio*, see Salvatore I. Camporeale, 'Lorenzo Valla's "Oratio" on the Pseudo-Donation of Constantine: Dissent and Innovation in Early Renaissance Humanism', *JHI* 57 (1996), 9–26; Riccardo Fubini, 'Humanism and Truth: Valla writes against the Donation of Constantine', *JHI* 57 (1996), 79–86; Whitford, 'Papal Antichrist', 28–30.

I have in my hands Hutten's edition of Lorenzo Valla's *Confutation of the Donation of Constantine*. ... I am greatly tormented, I do not even doubt that the pope is properly the Antichrist, that even the whole world's popular opinion expects; everything which he does, lives, speaks, and declares fits perfectly.[38]

For Luther, Valla provided further evidence that the papal claims to primacy were fundamentally flawed. By the time he came to write *To the Christian Nobility*, he had become convinced by Valla's argument, referring to 'that impossible lie, the *Donation of Constantine*'.[39] Whitford and Hendrix agree that Luther's realization that the *Donation of Constantine* was a forgery was decisive in convincing him that the pope was the Antichrist,[40] in league with the 'prince of this world' against evangelical truth.[41]

Questions about the authority of the papacy were also raised by Luther's study of the Council of Nicaea. This showed him an emperor who, far from ceding authority over the church, exercised it himself, to the extent of calling councils to determine evangelical doctrine. In *To the Christian Nobility*, Luther described three walls which the papacy had built around itself: the distinction between spiritual and temporal powers; the claim that only the pope could correctly interpret Scripture; and the assertion that only the pope could call a council.[42] Against the third, Luther cited Acts 15, in which the council of apostles was not called by Peter, and the examples of Nicaea and subsequent ecumenical councils:

> Even the Council of Nicaea, the most famous of all councils, was neither called nor confirmed by the bishop of Rome, but by the emperor Constantine. Many other emperors after him have done the same, and yet these councils were the most

---

[38] Luther to Spalatin, 24 February 1520: *WABr* 2, 48; cf. Whitford, 'Papal Antichrist', 40.

[39] *WA* 6, 434; *LW* 44, 166. In 1537 Luther published an annotated translation of the *Donation*: *WA* 50, 60–89. It seems surprising that Luther only became aware of Valla's claim that the *Donation* was a forgery in 1520; however, he seems not to have engaged with questions of the authenticity of decretals until pushed into the discussion. Eck and Prierius both cited Marsilius of Padua in this connection (for Eck, see *WA* 2, 275; cf. *WA* 59, 461; *WABr* 1, 480; for Prierius, see *WA* 6, 336), but Luther himself never mentioned him.

[40] This is the thesis of Whitford, 'Papal Antichrist'.

[41] Hendrix, *Luther and the Papacy*, 98–9.

[42] *WA* 6, 406; *LW* 44, 126.

Christian of all. But if the pope alone has the right to convene councils, then these councils would all have been heretical.[43]

Luther exhorted the young and newly elected emperor, Charles V, to follow historical example and call a council to reform the church.[44]

Luther continued his study of church history, and particularly the Council of Nicaea, through the 1520s and 1530s.[45] His work *On the Councils and the Church* (1539) offered the fruit of two decades of engagement with the history of the church. Many of the earlier themes recurred. Councils – even Nicaea – must be judged according to Scripture:

> The pope's hypocrites have lapsed into such gross folly that they think that councils have the power and the right to set up new articles of faith and to alter the old ones. That is not true, and we Christians have to tear up documents like this too. No council ever did it or can do it; the articles of faith must not grow on earth through the councils, as from a new, secret inspiration, but must be issued from heaven through the Holy Spirit and revealed openly; otherwise, as we shall hear later, they are not articles of faith.[46]

However, the key, for Luther, was the proper reading of the sources, albeit with a carefully crafted definition of 'proper':

> Yet one sees in the histories that the Roman bishops have from the first sickened, ailed, wheezed, and gasped for sovereignty over all the bishops, but could not achieve it because of the monarchs. For even before the Nicene council they wrote many letters, sometimes to Asia, sometimes to Africa,

---

[43] *WA* 6, 413; *LW* 44, 137.

[44] In 1539, Luther would reiterate: 'History will have to bear me out, even though all the papists get mad, that if Emperor Constantine had not convoked the first council at Nicaea, the Roman bishop Sylvester would have been obliged to leave it unconvoked': *WA* 50, 522–3; *LW* 41, 24.

[45] Luther had access to a range of sources: Eusebius's *Historia Ecclesiastica* and its elaboration by Rufinus; the *Historia Tripartita* by Cassiodorus Senator, the standard Latin textbook on church history in the Middle Ages; Bartolomeo Platina's *Historia de Vitis Pontificum* (completed between 1471 and 1481); Peter Crabbe's newly published *Concilia Omnia* (Cologne, 1538); and collections of the writings of the Fathers and canon law: see 'Introduction', *LW* 41, 8.

[46] *WA* 50, 551; *LW* 41, 58.

and so on, demanding that nothing should be publicly decreed without the Roman See. But no one paid any attention to this at the time, and the bishops in Africa, Asia, and Egypt proceeded as though they had not heard it, although they addressed him with many fine words and humbled themselves, without, however, conceding anything. This is what you will find when you read the histories and compare them diligently. But you must pay no heed to their clamour or that of their adulators; rather, keep eyes and mind fixed on the story and the text.[47]

For Luther, this was the task of history: to read the histories and compare them diligently, and in doing so to ignore the 'clamour' of the medieval accounts which served only to obscure gospel truth.

In his study of the use of history by Giles of Viterbo (1469–1532), John O'Malley concludes that 'Giles's view of history certainly did not of itself preclude all valid insight into the problems of his age, but it undoubtedly tended to fit such insight into an already concluded argument and an already fabricated scheme of history',[48] and that this was typical for his era. Certainly, a similar claim could be made regarding Luther's appeal to history, and Headley observes that Luther 'often found historical facts which were in such profound agreement with the nature of the true church that he tended to make them tentative norms'.[49] The Council of Nicaea was one example of such a use. However, the example of his reading of Valla indicates that Luther's reading of history could also serve as a catalyst to his changes of conviction. Luther may never have been a church historian, but he was convinced that church history, properly read, revealed God's will for the church as laid down in Scripture – and he came to believe that this served to highlight the false claims of the papacy. The motivation for exploring the past, for Luther, was to vindicate his evangelical position. And the evidence yielded by his deepening historical knowledge convinced him that the papacy had become not only flawed but deeply and irredeemably corrupt.

University of Glasgow

---

47 *WA* 50, 523; *LW* 41, 24.
48 O'Malley, 'Historical Thought', 548.
49 Headley, *Luther's View of Church History*, 164.

POLYDORE VERGIL AND ECCLESIASTICAL HISTORIOGRAPHY IN HIS *DE INVENTORIBUS RERUM* IV–VIII

by JONATHAN ARNOLD

Polydore Vergil (*c.*1470–1555) was a controversial critic of the church of his day. As this essay will show, his radical solution to its problems was based upon his reading of the church's history. An Italian cleric on English soil for much of his life, Vergil is most famous for his *Anglica Historia* (1533), the first Tudor history of England. However, he was also responsible for another great (although now neglected) work, *De Inventoribus Rerum* ('on the inventors, or discoverers, of all things'). Consisting of eight volumes, it is an example of early encyclopaedic technique from original Latin and Greek sources, including the Bible, Josephus and Eusebius, as well as observation from contemporary life, in which 'invention' is depicted as a category of historiography and a means of examining scientific and cultural history.[1] The first three books were published in 1499 in Venice and deal mainly with scientific phenomena. The other five books, with which we are concerned here, consider the origins of Christian institutions (*initia institutorum rei Christianae*) and were published much later, in 1521, although Vergil continuously revised the entire *De Inventoribus Rerum* until his death. The topics covered range from early church history, baptism, clerical and religious orders, penance, prayers and simony, to heresies and schisms, martyrs and the triumph of Christianity.[2] An extremely popular work, with over forty editions in Vergil's lifetime, it was, nonetheless, censured for its criticisms of the church. Indeed, the purpose of Books IV–VIII was to demonstrate what was initiated by Christ and what the true nature of the church was, not by examining its doctrine but by seeking the origins of its practice.

This essay will argue that, in *De Inventoribus Rerum*, Vergil

---

[1] D. Hay, *Polydore Vergil: Renaissance Historian and Man of Letters* (Oxford, 1952), 58–9; C. Atkinson, *Inventing Inventors in Renaissance Europe: Polydore Vergil's* De Inventoribus Rerum (Tübingen, 2007), 97.

[2] Atkinson, *Inventing Inventors*, 102–3.

reflected upon many malpractices in the church of his day and that his explanation for their proliferation was not a doctrinal one, but a practical ecclesiological one, based upon the absence of ancient practice and in particular of the calling of regular general and provincial councils. It is this single and significant solution, hardly noticed in scholarship to date,[3] which features as the climax of Polydore's work, at the end of the last book (VIII), which reveals that Vergil imagined the body of Christ, the church, as the gathered people rather than a hierarchy of clergy engaged in performing ceremonies. Books IV–VIII are a strongly humanist work, for which Vergil consulted ancient classical and Christian sources in order to identify the *ecclesia* as a 'spiritual republic', a phrase reminiscent of the Florentine republic of Coluccio Salutati (1331–1406).[4] For Vergil, the solution to all ecclesiastical deficiencies was the calling of more councils, echoing the *Frequens* decree of the Council of Constance (1414–17).

This essay will briefly outline Polydore's career and some of the main themes of Books IV–VIII of *De Inventoribus Rerum*. Thereafter it will investigate how the work was received and how it became influential upon the works of contemporaneous and later

3   For scholarly discussion, see W. Busch, *England Under the Tudors: King Henry VII* (New York, 1895), 396–7, cited in P. I. Kaufman, 'Polydore Vergil's Fifteenth Century', *Historian* 47 (1985), 512–23, at 512; C. L. Kingsford, *English Historical Literature in the Fifteenth Century* (Oxford, 1911), 253; R. Flenley, ed., *Six Town Chronicles of England* (Oxford, 1911), 19; E. Fueter, *Geschichte der Neueren Historiographie*, 3rd edn (Munich, 1925), 164–5; T. D. Kendrick, *British Antiquity* (London, 1950); B. B. Adams, ed., *John Bale's King Johan* (San Marino, CA, 1969), 134; J. Ferguson, 'Notes on the Work of Polydore Vergil, *De Inventoribus Rerum*', *Isis* 17 (1932), 71–93; idem, 'Bibliographical Notes on the English Translation of Polydore Vergil's work *De Inventoribus Rerum*', *Archaeologia* 51 (1888), 107–41; M. T. Hodgen, 'Ethnology in 1500: Polydore Vergil's Collection of Customs', *Isis* 57 (1966), 315–24; A. B. Ferguson, *Clio Unbound* (Durham, NC, 1979), 19–21; F. J. Levy, *Tudor Historical Thought* (San Marino, CA, 1967); G. Watson, ed., *The New Cambridge Bibliography of English Literature*, 5 vols (Cambridge, 1969–77), 1: no. 2203; Hay, *Polydore Vergil*, 154; A. Stegmann, 'Le *De Inventoribus rei Christianae* de Polydor Vergil ou l'Érasmisme critique', in *Colloquia Erasmiana Turonensia* 1 (Paris, 1972), 313–22, esp. 319; B. Copenhaver, 'The Historiography of Discovery in the Renaissance', *Journal of the Warburg and Courtauld Institutes* 41 (1978), 192–214; Atkinson, *Inventing Inventors*, 11. The most complete English edition is *Beginnings and Discoveries: Polydore Vergil's De Inventoribus Rerum. An unabridged Translation and Edition with Introduction, Notes and Glossary*, ed. B. Weiss and L. C. Pérez (Nieuwkoop, 1997); this is based on the 1546 edition published by Gryphium in Lyon [hereafter: *DIR*].

4   *Beginnings and Discoveries*, ed. Weiss and Pérez, 527–8 (*DIR* 8.7); see also J. Arnold, *The Great Humanists: An Introduction* (London, 2011), 36–8.

historians and theologians, giving examples of how it was variously praised, mocked and censured. Having outlined some of the many ecclesiastical inadequacies cited by Vergil, we shall examine his call for more councils within the historical context of conciliarism, and how the issue reflects his fundamental concern for the church, its faith, authority and governance.

Vergil was a native of Urbino in Italy but lived from 1502 to 1553 in England where he was, until 1514, deputy of the papal tax, 'Peter's Pence', and from 1508 archdeacon of Wells. Like other humanists, Vergil got on the wrong side of Thomas Wolsey. In 1514/15 Wolsey decided no longer to support Vergil's patron, Cardinal Castelli, as collector of Peter's Pence, his new favourite being Andrea Ammonio. Ammonio had Vergil's correspondence seized in the hope of finding anti-Wolsey sentiments expressed therein, which indeed he did. Thus Polydore found himself imprisoned in the Tower of London for a few months in 1515–16, but was released after he had made an apology, and after Wolsey had been made a cardinal. Pope Leo X then summoned Vergil to Rome in 1516. On his return in 1517, Polydore resumed his post as archdeacon, taking a more cautious political stance, signing Henry VIII's articles of religion in 1536 and conforming to Edward VI's declaration that the eucharist should be received in both kinds in 1547. However, it appears that Vergil remained a faithful Roman Catholic and, once he had gained a life income from his archdeaconry and other benefices, he returned to Italy in 1553, dying there in 1555.[5]

Vergil's readership, or audience, was international, Latin-speaking and closely associated with the church. Of the many editions from Froben's press, only two were in German.[6] Of the dozens of editions issued in Latin, there was no comprehensive English version until 1997, when Weiss and Pérez translated and published the Lyon edition of 1546, helpfully marking those parts censored by the church authorities in bold type.[7] Prior to this version the only English translation was the very much abridged and altered

5   There are many biographical sketches of Vergil's life, including L. Galdieri in David A. Richardson, ed., *Dictionary of Literary Biography*, 132: *Sixteenth-Century British Nondramatic Writers, First Series* (Detroit, MI, 1993), 316–21; ODNB.

6   J. Benzing, *Die Buchdrucker des 16. und 17. Jahrhunderts im Deutschen Sprachgebiet* (Wiesbaden, 1963), 30, cited in Atkinson, *Inventing Inventors*, 94.

7   *Beginnings and Discoveries*, ed. Weiss and Pérez.

edition by Thomas Langley, published in 1546 with a considerable Protestant agenda. This became very popular and was reprinted several times, but it has perhaps contributed to Vergil's ambiguous reputation in the historiography. *De Inventoribus Rerum* remained in print for a hundred and seventy years and can only be regarded as a success. Even its inclusion in several indices of banned books can be interpreted as a mark of its value and popularity, given that the Catholic Church officially removed parts in order that it might be issued in an expurgated edition. It has thus been associated with Erasmian criticisms of the church. Hay rightly noted that '[i]t was, indeed, appropriate that Vergil should be detected as an Erasmian and join the honourable company of churchmen condemned by the Sorbonne'.[8] Erasmus himself admired Vergil's work, declaring it 'distinguished', whilst rather patronizingly recommending just before its publication that Polydore consult 'Thomas More, Cuthbert Tunstall, Thomas Linacre, William Latimer, *really* good scholars and friends'.[9] Vergil took the advice. His correspondence reveals his friendships with several English humanists and he must have known John Colet (1467–1519), dean of St Paul's, well; at one time they were both members of Doctors' Commons and had homes in St Paul's churchyard.[10]

De Inventoribus Rerum was included in the 1549 and 1551 Paris lists of censured books and the later 1559 Spanish index, the Roman index, the Tridentine index of 1564 and the Antwerp list of condemned books of 1569.[11] But Vergil's text was not found at

---

⁸ Hay, *Polydore Vergil*, 70.
⁹ Erasmus to Vergil, 30 April 1526: *The Collected Works of Erasmus* [hereafter: *CWE*], 12, ed. A. Dalzell and O. G. Nauert Jr (Chicago, IL, 2003), 183; Erasmus to Vergil, 23 December 1520: *CWE*, 8, ed. R. A. B. Mynors and P. G. Bietenholz (Chicago, IL, 1988), 188 (italics mine).
¹⁰ Hay, *Polydore Vergil*, 19; E. J. Davis, 'Doctors' Commons: Its Title and Topography', *London Topographical Record* 15 (1931), 36–50, at 38–9.
¹¹ Hay, *Polydore Vergil*, 70; Atkinson, *Inventing Inventors*, 252–3; J. M. de Bujanda, *Index de libres interdits: Thesaurus de la littérature interdite au XVIᵉ siècle*, 10 vols (Sherbrooke, ON, 1984–96), 1: 249–50. For the Roman index of 1559, see de Bujanda, *Index de libres interdits*, 3: 64–9 (no. 849). For the Spanish (Valdes) index, see ibid. 1: 102–3 (Vergil's works are nos 374 and 574 in this index); for the Tridentine and Antwerp indices, see ibid. 7: 122; F. H. Reusch, *Die Indices Librorum Prohibitorum des Sechszehnten Jahrhunderts*, Bibliothek des Litterarischen Vereins in Stuttgart 176 (Stuttgart, 1886), 110 (Sorbonne Index), 200 (Rome), 229 (Valdes), 276 (Tridentine), cited in Atkinson, *Inventing Inventors*, 253 n. 19.

fault on theological or doctrinal grounds, nor because the work was inaccurate or rationalist. It was condemned because 'he ventured to criticize the policy, prerogatives, and constitutional machinery of the Pope',[12] not least in the excised passage on councils. Vergil's work was viewed as valuable by the Catholic Church, as long as certain passages were expurgated, such as one on the proliferation of religious orders, which, he wrote, 'spring up like toadstools'.[13] Regarding clergy, Vergil's remarks concerning evil popes, the venality of offices in the papal administration, papal taxation, and the pomposity, vanity and lust for power in the higher clergy were expurgated following the Council of Trent.[14]

As for Protestant adherents, there were many, including the contemporaneous Lutherans Matthias Flacius Illyricus and Conrad Gesner.[15] It is plausible that Protestant Swiss exiles in the reign of Mary Tudor used Vergil's text as the basis for discussion regarding the true nature of the church, as the Protestant version was regularly reprinted in Basel.[16] Thomas Harding (d. 1572) demonstrated familiarity with *De Inventoribus Rerum*, as did John Jewel, bishop of Salisbury.[17] One contemporary author to poke fun at Vergil was François Rabelais (d. 1553), in his *Gargantua et Pantagruel* (1532/4).[18] Although he made no direct reference to Vergil, his depiction of the inventor 'Messer Stomach' demonstrates a knowledge of the encyclopedic genre that could only come from reading Vergil. The fictitious Stomach is described, satirically, as the first to do almost everything: till the soil, plant cereals, make bread, build cities, make weapons, and use plants for medicinal purposes; a reference to Polydore's work, and perhaps an affectionate tribute rather than an expression of disdain.[19] Maurice Scève made use of Vergil's text

---

[12] Hay, *Polydore Vergil*, 70; *Beginnings and Discoveries*, ed. Weiss and Pérez, 278 (*DIR* 4.6).

[13] 'Saepe more fungorum subito oriri solent': Hay, *Polydore Vergil*, 71, quoting the edition published by Daniel Elzevir: *Polydori Vergilii … De inventoribus rerum* (Amsterdam, 1671), 446 (*DIR* 7.2).

[14] Hay, *Polydore Vergil*, 72.

[15] Atkinson, *Inventing Inventors*, 257–60; C. Gesner, *Pandectarum Libri XXI* (Zurich, 1559), fols 50v, 104v, 168r, 169r.

[16] Atkinson, *Inventing Inventors*, 260.

[17] Ibid.; C. Coppens, *Reading in Exile: The Libraries of John Ramridge (d. 1568), Thomas Harding (d. 1572) and Henry Joliffe (d. 1573), Recusants in Louvain* (Cambridge, 1993), 5.

[18] Atkinson, *Inventing Inventors*, 269 n. 86.

[19] Ibid. 270 n. 88.

in his epic poem about the first days of the world, *Microcosme* (1562).[20] Another famous author to make use of it was Cervantes. In Part II of *Don Quixote* (1615), a clerk explains to the knight that he is working on a new text, a 'Supplement to Polydore Vergil, concerning the Invention of Things',[21] which will be far superior in its pedantry.

Vergil was commended by seventeenth-century Huguenot preachers such as Pierre du Moulin (d. 1658) for criticizing abuses in the church and, on the whole, until the eighteenth century, Protestants used the unexpurgated version, or Langley's abbreviated Protestant version, whilst the Catholics used the censured one, an example being Edmund Martène in his *De Antiquis Ecclesiae Ritibus* (*c.*1700), a work on the history of liturgy.[22] However, there was a general decline in interest in *De Inventoribus Rerum* until at the turn of the twentieth century the chemist John Ferguson extolled Books I–III as a history of science and Margaret Hodgen showed great interest in the anthropological aspect of Vergil's work as a collection of customs, leading to Copenhaver's recognition of Vergil's novel historiographical approach.[23] We turn now to consider Books IV–VIII and their context in more detail.

Although not published until 1521 (by the time of John Fisher's sermon against Luther at Paul's Cross and the burning of heretical books in May 1521, it was being printed by Froben), the prefatory letter to Books IV–VIII is dated December 1517, placing it shortly after Luther's ninety-five theses and before his interrogation by Cajetan in October 1518. However, Atkinson has plausibly suggested that Vergil 'pre-dated the letter to December 1517, thereby letting his work appear too early to be considered a reaction to Luther's call for Reform'.[24]

Polydore's main task, he wrote, was to make clear 'which practices derived from Christ our Saviour and which from the apostles'.[25] This often involved a passionate and often humorous

---

[20] V. L. Saulnier, *Maurice Scève*, 2 vols (Paris, 1948), 1: 410–20.

[21] Miguel de Cervantes, *The Ingenious Gentleman Don Quixote of La Mancha*, transl. P. A. Motteux, 4 vols (London, 1712), 2: 22, quoted in Hay, *Polydore Vergil*, 75–6.

[22] Hay, *Polydore Vergil*, 264; see also Caspar Calvör, *Rituale Ecclesiasticum* (Jena, 1705), which used Vergil's work on liturgy.

[23] See n. 3 above for references to these works.

[24] Atkinson, *Inventing Inventors*, 100.

[25] *Beginnings and Discoveries*, ed. Weiss and Pérez, 247 (*DIR* 4, preface).

critique of the church, as, for instance, when discussing the names of popes in Book IV:

> The first privilege given to a roman pontiff was to allow him to change his name upon taking office, if his given name was not respectable enough, such as, and the following is said tongue in cheek: if the pontiff had been an evil person, he would be called Boniface: if he had been fearful, Leo: if he had been a farmer, Urban: if wicked, Innocent: if arrogant, Clement: if people spoke ill of him, Benedict: in this way the pontiff would be known at least by a dignified name.[26]

Likewise, in a passage regarding the manner in which psalms are sung or chanted in worship, Vergil asserted: 'our cantors shriek to such an extent in our churches that nothing ... can be distinguished other than the sound of their voices ... in short, they are convinced that they are the only decorations in God's house'.[27] Vergil also attacked mendicant orders for always begging 'for alms when it is clear that Christ himself did not beg, nor did his apostles'.[28] He also criticized the sale of indulgences, claiming that in the time of Boniface IX 'they were sold everywhere and at any time with detriment to the vendors and buyers; so that by selling these remedies for the infirmity of the soul, many took less care against committing evil deeds. And the keys of authority [the Church] diminished in value'.[29] Thus Vergil considered probity and purity of practice as essential requirements in the operation of ecclesial authority. Despite the satire, the overall purpose of Books IV–VIII is quite serious: 'to show how Christ's original intent has been thwarted'.[30] As Vergil wrote: 'at the beginning, the mysteries handed down from Christ to the apostles were plain, simple, devoid of ceremonies and showed more devotion than pomp'.[31] He desired a return to such simplicity.

As already noted, much of Vergil's work was expurgated and gained a place on the indices of banned books, on account of his criticisms of the church. Polydore's two greatest criticisms, which

---

26 Ibid. 294 (*DIR* 4.10).
27 Ibid. 395 (*DIR* 6.2).
28 Ibid. 478–9 (*DIR* 7.6).
29 Ibid. 494 (*DIR* 8.1).
30 Ibid. 15.
31 Ibid. 16, 374 (*DIR* 5.10).

gave rise to much censure, were of clerical celibacy and the sale of indulgences.[32] On celibacy, Vergil quoted numerous passages from Scripture against it,[33] concluding that 'it would be useful for the Christian Church as well for religious orders, that the right to have a public marriage finally be restored to the priests'.[34] Regarding the sale of indulgences, Vergil observed the link to the doctrine of purgatory: 'When people did not worry about Purgatory, no one sought indulgences, because the entire value of indulgences comes from this belief in Purgatory.'[35] On this matter, he found himself tentatively, and dangerously, in alliance with Luther, whom he described as 'the best versed of his people in Theology'.[36]

However, it is Vergil's assessment of church councils, towards the end of the last book, that is perhaps his most illuminating criticism. For it was the lack of church councils that he blamed for all the unfortunate practices of the institution. At the Council of Constance, Pope Martin V had ordered that general councils ought to be held every ten years, but this had failed to be put into practice: 'the Roman Pope and all the princes of Christendom', Vergil reported, should have convened and attended such meetings, but this had not happened.[37]

At the end of his work, Vergil traced councils from the disciples in the Acts of the Apostles through Nicaea, Constantinople, Chalcedon and so on, until he reached a period when councils could only be called by the Roman pontiff, but also when pontifical negligence had caused serious damage to the church. He went on:

> When the lasting harm to the Christian religion, resulting from the discontinuation of convening councils, became clear, Martin V, as soon as he was made Pope by the Council of Constance ... decreed that at least once every ten years the Roman pontiff and all the Christian leaders were to convene in one place and consult on major issues. Until now this has not been observed at all, and for this reason, our Religion from

---

32 Ibid. 17–19.
33 Ibid. 334–5 (*DIR* 5.4): Matt. 19: 5–6 (Christ); 1 Tim. 3: 2, 12 (Paul); Titus 1: 5–6; 1 Pet. 1: 16; 1 Cor. 7: 5.
34 *Beginnings and Discoveries*, ed. Weiss and Pérez, 340–1 (*DIR* 5.4).
35 Ibid. 20, 494 (*DIR* 8.1).
36 Ibid.
37 Hay, *Polydore Vergil*, 73, quoting *De inventoribus rerum*, ed. Elzevir, 495–6 (*DIR* 8.5).

day to day goes from bad to worse. In short, this means that the significance of the Nicene Council's determinations was the issuing of a decree, that each year the Provincial Synods were to be convened, when necessary, in order to correct the questionable practices of the bishops and of the people.[38]

Of course, Vergil's call for a more frequent meeting of the general council was not new. In his sermon of 1511, Colet had called for more councils, which were 'to be oftener used for the reformation of the churche. For there never hapneth nothyng more hurtefull to the churche of Christe, than the lacke both of councell generall and provinciall'.[39] Likewise, Vergil's demand for more frequent councils raises the question of whether or not he possessed conciliarist tendencies, and therefore of whether or not *De Inventoribus Rerum* has, in part at least, a conciliarist agenda.

Conciliar theory, of course, held that the pope was not an absolute ruler but rather a constitutional monarch, and that final authority lay with the whole body of the church, or, in practice, with their representatives gathered in a general council.[40] Conciliarism had its roots in the early fifteenth century. The councils of Pisa (1409) and Constance (1414–18) had assembled in order to put an end to the great schism of 1378 between the Roman and Avignonese papacies, giving rise to the conciliarist movement.[41] At the next general council, convened at Basel (1431–7), radical conciliarists, led by a Paris University delegation, defied the authority of the pontiff, but failed to gain support from their hearers for a transfer of authority away from the pope and towards a council.[42] Thus, Vergil's call for more frequent councils seems to echo the conciliarist decree of *Frequens* resulting from the Council of Constance. As Mullett observed: 'conciliarism ... was a recipe

---

[38] *Beginnings and Discoveries*, ed. Weiss and Pérez, 513–14; *De inventoribus rerum*, ed. Elzevir, 495–6 (*DIR* 8.5).

[39] J. H. Lupton, *A Life of John Colet, D.D.* (London, 1887; 2nd edn, 1909), 302; S. Knight, *The Life of Dr. John Colet, Dean of St. Paul's* (London, 1724; 2nd edn, 1823), 248.

[40] F. Oakley, 'Almain and Major: Conciliar Theory on the Eve of the Reformation', *AHR* 70 (1965), 673–90, at 673.

[41] C. M. Bellitto, 'The Spirituality of Reform in the Late Medieval Church: The Example of Nicholas de Clamanges', *ChH* 68 (1999), 1–13, at 2.

[42] A. Black, *Council and Commune: The Conciliar Movement and the Fifteenth-Century Heritage* (London, 1979), 38.

for a running conflict between popes and councils'.[43] The *Frequens* decree was still in force at the end of the fifteenth century,[44] leaving the question of whether Vergil was advocating the implementation of *Frequens* itself.

The last council to meet without papal convocation was held at Pisa (1511–12), although a papal council, Lateran V, was convened soon after (1512–17). In Pisa, Vergil's contemporaries Jacques Almain (1480–1515), the Parisian theologian, and John Major or Mair (1467–1550), the Scottish scholastic, were conciliarism's chief apologists.[45] Almain believed that the ecclesiastical power residing within the church was not only more direct than that residing in the pope, and 'greater in extension' to it, but also that it was 'greater in perfection'.[46] For Almain, the church represented in a general council could not err in decisions because the Holy Spirit aided it. On this point, Almain was engaged in an ongoing debate with his Paris University colleague, Thomas de Vio Cajetan (1469–1534).[47]

Three common characteristics of conciliarism to emerge from the debates at Pisa were the demand for reform of the church by the periodic assembly of general councils; a vision of an oligarchic government consisting of bishops and cardinals; and the assertion of the superiority of a general council to the pope.[48]

Vergil's stance indicates his enthusiasm for the notion of *Ecclesia* as a gathered people, a 'spiritual republic', to use humanist language, transformed inwardly by their faith in Christ, rather than a clerical hierarchy enacting elaborate ceremonies. Indeed, at the very opening of his work, in Book IV, he denounced 'common people who call *Ecclesia* all sorts of priestly orders and all temples dedi-

---

43 M. A. Mullett, *The Catholic Reformation* (London, 1999), 2.

44 B. Gordon, 'Conciliarism in Late Medieval Europe', in A. Pettegree, ed., *The Reformation World* (New York, 2000), 31–50, at 45: 'In January 1497 King Charles VIII of France asked the theological faculty at Paris whether the decree *Frequens* was still valid, and the answer was an unequivocal yes'.

45 F. Oakley, *The Conciliarist Tradition: Constitutionalism in the Catholic Church, 1300–1870* (Oxford, 2003), 111–32.

46 Ibid. 125.

47 Ibid.; J. Wicks, 'Thomas de Vio Cajetan (1469–1534)', in C. Lindberg, ed., *The Reformation Theologians* (Oxford, 2002), 269–80, at 273.

48 Oakley, *Conciliarist Tradition*, 129–40; D. MacCulloch, *Reformation: Europe's House Divided, 1490–1700* (London, 2003), 88.

cated to God and to his saints'.[49] The Incarnation and Passion of
Christ had initiated this body of people and its regular gathering
was, in Polydore's view, the most authentic way for it to practise
its genuine purpose. Thus, *De Inventoribus Rerum* becomes not just
an encyclopaedic work, dry and dusty and humorously pedantic;
it is revealed as a work of faith, not of theological doctrine as such
but an expression of the simple correlation between Christ the
initiator of faith and the church's practice of that faith.

To conclude, Books IV–VIII of *De Inventoribus Rerum* are fundamentally theological in the sense that they are about the justification, or otherwise, for church practice. Like other humanist works
of this time, it was mistaken as being Protestant before its time,
avant le lettre. Vergil's life does not bear this out, and his preface to
the work distanced himself from Luther. Rather, Vergil's investigation of the church *ad fontes* was an effort to uncover the ancient
truths regarding the origins of all church practices, in order that
the institution of the church might be strengthened and sustained
rather than dismantled or replaced. Polydore's contribution to a
historicizing of the medieval church was based upon the work of
generations of Italian humanists who had prepared the ground in
philology, languages and a love of ancient sources. However, his
concern about general councils demonstrates that he combined
his knowledge of ancient sources with more recent ecclesiastical
history, such as the Council of Constance, and the work of his
contemporaries, such as Colet. Vergil's purpose was to use his
humanist skills to rediscover the original teachings and purpose
of Christ himself. He ordered the contents of his work by subject
rather than chronologically, thus freeing himself from long narrative history and creating a new humanist historiography which
required an impressive and profound grasp of the themes of
ecclesiastical history through the centuries. Vergil's analysis of the
church's ills and his historical survey led him to believe that the
cause of all the institutional problems lay in the lack of general
and provincial councils, an argument which, I suggest, is both the
climax and the main point of all five of his books. The only further
section after his pages on councils was a final message concerning
the triumph of faith in civilization. His main aim, therefore, was

[49] *Beginnings and Discoveries*, ed. Weiss and Pérez, 248 (*DIR* 4.1).

to show that faith had grown and won over the world. Vergil was worried that this dominance would be threatened by corruption, pomposity and complacency. His call for more frequent councils is intimately connected with the notion of faith as the supreme aspiration for humanity. By focusing on the origins of Christian practice rather than of doctrine, Vergil exposed where the purity of faith had been compromised and where that purity could be restored.

Worcester College, Oxford

HISTORIAN OR PROPHET? JOHN BALE'S PERCEPTION OF THE PAST*

by SUSAN ROYAL

The late medieval prophetic tradition played a significant role in how John Bale (1495–1563), England's first Protestant church historian, formulated his ideas about the nature of revelation, which would become a contentious issue in the course of the Reformation. It is the goal of this essay to examine this first-generation evangelical's views, which will bring us closer to understanding prophecy and its legitimacy in Reformation-era Europe. In an influential essay, Richard Southern illustrates the important role of the prophetical tradition in premodern historical writing: 'Prophecy filled the world-picture, past, present, and future; and it was the chief inspiration of all historical thinking.'[1] But while its significance is easy to pinpoint, the varied nature of prophetic revelation does not make for easy delineations or definitions. Southern names four types of prophecy in the Middle Ages: biblical (Daniel, Revelation); pagan (sibylline); Christian (such as that of Hildegard of Bingen); and astrological (stars and celestial events). Of course, even these are not clearly distinct categories; Southern notes that Merlin is 'half-Christian, half-pagan'.[2] Lesley Coote points out that the 'subject of political prophecy is king, people and nation',[3] separating this from theological, apocalyptic prophecy, though she also asserts that the two are closely related.[4] Bernard McGinn remarks that in the later Middle Ages, prophecy is 'seen as a divinatory or occasionally reformative activity – the prophet as the man who foretells the future, or the one who seeks to correct a present situation in the light of an ideal past or glorious

*   I wish to thank those who offered comments on this communication at the EHS Summer Meeting, and the society itself for a bursary that allowed me to attend. Innumerable thanks also go to Alec Ryrie for his insightful comments and suggestions on several drafts of this essay.

[1]   R. W. Southern, 'History as Prophecy', *TRHS* ser. 5, 22 (1972), 159–80, at 160.
[2]   Ibid. 168.
[3]   Lesley A. Coote, *Prophecy and Public Affairs in Later Medieval England* (York, 2000), 14.
[4]   Ibid. 4.

future'.[5] This notion of the prophet as reformer is also illuminating for the Reformation context. Robin Bruce Barnes writes:

> Lutherans conceived of the Reformation not as an unveiling of new truths but as a return to old ones. The essence of divine revelation, once preached openly, had been obscured for centuries; Luther had simply rediscovered it. Yet by the same token, the question now arose whether this recovery could blossom in further prophetic clarity among the faithful.[6]

The idea of prophecy as a direct personal revelation from God was problematic for most evangelicals, for whom *sola scriptura* had become one of the few shared tenets of their inchoate confederation. The reluctance of magisterial reformers to compose commentaries on the Book of Revelation reflects this unease: following Erasmus's concerns about the book's authority and authenticity, Martin Luther was originally sceptical of the work, until his growing belief in the pope as the Antichrist led him to explore the text.[7] John Calvin did not refer to it often and never offered a commentary.[8]

Mutual reticence about the book of Revelation was one of the few areas of agreement regarding this contentious topic. As first-generation reformers sought to demarcate the identity of the true church, the role of prophecy within it became an important focus. Luther identified two types of prophecy. The first explicated the words of the Old Testament prophets, and was 'the most necessary kind', because it taught the word of God; Luther wrote that it 'rules, preserves, establishes, and performs the preaching ministry'.[9] The prophecies of Revelation and of individuals affected by the Holy Spirit constituted a second, less significant, tier of prophecy,

---

[5] Bernard McGinn, *Visions of the End* (New York, 1998), 4; see also Robert E. Lerner, 'Medieval Prophecy and Religious Dissent', *P&P*, no. 72 (1976), 3–24.

[6] Robin Bruce Barnes, *Prophecy and Gnosis: Apocalypticism in the Wake of the Lutheran Reformation* (Stanford, CA, 1988), 95.

[7] Kevin Sharpe, 'Reading Revelations: Prophecy, Hermeneutics and Politics in Early Modern Britain', in idem and Steven N. Zwicker, eds, *Reading, Society, and Politics in Early Modern England* (Cambridge, 2003), 122–63, at 127; see also Irena Backus, *Reformation Readings of the Apocalypse* (Oxford, 2000), 3–36.

[8] Jaroslav Pelikan, 'Some Uses of the Apocalypse in the Magisterial Reformers', in C. A. Patrides and Joseph Wittreich, eds, *The Apocalypse in English Renaissance Thought* (Manchester, 1984), 74–92, at 75.

[9] Martin Luther, *Preface to the Revelation of St John*, in *LW* 35, 399–400.

which was 'concealed and mute'.[10] While Luther's opinions on prognostication were largely based on Scripture and centred on preaching, Philip Melanchthon believed in personal prophetic gifts and astrological augury (in which he had a longstanding interest, having studied it at Tübingen in the early 1510s).[11] Melanchthon also took an interest in biblical prophecy; an English translation of his exegesis of Daniel (Wittenberg, 1543) was included in George Joye's *The exposicion of Daniel* (1545).[12] *The exposicion of Daniel* was one of many texts in which prophecies pertained not merely to the past but to an increasingly imminent apocalypse. Francis Lambert's Marburg lectures on Revelation, published in 1528, offered a reading of St John's Apocalypse that directly reflected the course of church history.[13]

Calvin was more cautious about the value of prophecy, believing that Christ's Incarnation had ended the era of prophecy. His view of the prophetic office reflected the Erasmian and Zwinglian view of a prophet as one whose remit was restricted to the interpretation of Scripture.[14] Calvin went one step further, claiming that these interpreters could also apply their understanding of Scripture to their contemporary times, but he excluded predictive powers completely.[15] John Knox, on the other hand, held a more inconsistent theology that allowed him simultaneously to promote the notion of *sola scriptura* and to declare himself endowed with prophetic

---

[10] Ibid. 400.

[11] Barnes, *Prophecy and Gnosis*, 96–9; Euan Cameron, 'Philip Melanchthon: Image and Substance', *JEH* 48 (1997), 705–22, at 711; Sachiko Kusukawa, *The Transformation of Natural Philosophy: The Case of Philip Melanchthon* (Cambridge, 1995); Charlotte Methuen, 'The Role of the Heavens in the Thought of Philip Melanchthon', *JHI* 57 (1996), 385–403.

[12] George Joye, *The exposicion of Daniel the prophete gathered oute of Philip Melanchton, Iohan Ecolampadius, Chonrade Pellicane & out of Iohan Draconite. &c.* (Antwerp, 1545), fol. 5v. It is likely that Joye knew Bale and that Bale would have been familiar with his work: Joye's printer, Antonius Goinus, also published Bale's works (including the *Brefe Chronycle*) until 1546 in Antwerp, and although Bale's movements during his first period of exile remain obscure, it is believed that Joye was actually living in Antwerp and not editing from afar – so a direct personal connection is probable. On Bale's movements, see Peter Happé, *John Bale* (New York, 1996), 11; for Joye, see Charles C. Butterworth and Allan G. Chester, *George Joye 1495?–1553: A Chapter in the History of the English Bible and the English Reformation* (Philadelphia, PA, 1962), 205.

[13] Fairfield, *John Bale*, 73–5.

[14] Max Engammare, 'Calvin: A Prophet without a Prophecy', *ChH* 67 (1998), 643–61, at 648.

[15] Ibid. 644.

powers – a divisive position.[16] All reformers could agree, however, on the notion of preaching as a calling to prophesy the word of God.[17] It should also be noted that the reformers' reluctance to call themselves prophets did not extend to their followers: Theodore Beza bestowed this title upon Calvin;[18] Nicholas Bernard's biography of James Ussher placed him in this tradition;[19] and Augustine Bernher cast Hugh Latimer in this light in the introduction to his 1562 edition of Latimer's sermons.[20] Against this background of Reformation-era views of prophecy, we can explore its place in the polemical works of John Bale. When he converted to the evangelical faith around 1536, Bale turned his back on his Carmelite vows but maintained the interest in historical matters that the brotherhood had nurtured for centuries.[21] Historical manuscripts, including records of heresy trials kept by his erstwhile order as a record of their efforts against heterodoxy, now served as vital sources for Bale's enterprise to reclaim England's historical record from the 'corrupt' clerical chroniclers of the medieval past, and also served to recast former heretics, the Lollards, as spiritual exemplars.[22] To retrieve England's 'true' historical narrative, Bale used Scripture to determine the significance of past events, declaring about the Word: 'Yet is the text a light to the cronicles and not the cronicles to the texte.'[23] The key

---

[16] Dale Johnson, 'John Knox, Scripture, and Prophecy', in Helen Parish and William G. Naphy, eds, *Religion and Superstition in Reformation Europe* (Manchester, 2002), 133–53, at 147.

[17] Ibid.; Ute Lotz-Heumann, '"The Spirit of Prophecy Has Not Wholly Left the World": The Stylisation of Archbishop James Ussher as a Prophet', in Parish and Naphy, eds, *Religion and Superstition*, 124. The relationship between preaching and prophesying in the early Reformation is underscored by the establishment of the Prophezei in Zürich, where Scripture was interpreted and sermons were prepared: see Gottfried W. Locher, *Zwingli's Thought: New Perspectives* (Leiden, 1981), 27–30.

[18] Engammare, 'Calvin', 643.

[19] Lotz-Heumann, 'Archbishop Ussher', 119–32.

[20] *Sermons by Hugh Latimer*, ed. George Elwes Corrie (Cambridge, 1844), 320–1. I am grateful to Alec Ryrie for this reference.

[21] See Andrew Jotischky, *The Carmelites and Antiquity* (Oxford, 2002).

[22] For Bale's manuscripts, see James Crompton, 'Fasciculi Zizaniorum', *JEH* 12 (1961), 35–45, 155–66; W. T. Davies, 'A Bibliography of John Bale', *Oxford Bibliographical Society: Proceedings and Papers* 5 (1936–9), 201–79; Honor McCusker, 'Books and Manuscripts formerly in the Possession of John Bale', *The Library* ser. 4, 16 (1935–6), 144–65; John Bale, *Index Britanniae Scriptorum*, ed. Reginald Lane Poole and Mary Bateson, intro. Caroline Brett and James P. Carley (Woodbridge, 1990).

[23] John Bale, *The image of bothe Churches* (London, 1548), sig. Aiiiiv.

to the English past lay in the correct interpretation of Scripture, and in particular the prophecies therein. Bale's closely intertwined relationship between prophecy and history lies at the centre of this essay. Scholars have rightly emphasized the prophetic elements in Bale's historical works, citing his self-proclaimed affinity with John of Patmos (the exiled author of the Book of Revelation) and his belief that he was living in the 'latter days';[24] however, historians have largely overlooked the way Bale handled the medieval prophetic inheritance. By examining this element of Bale's writings and its place within his historical framework, this essay seeks to demonstrate that Bale's own prophetic voice rings clear through his characterization of medieval prophets – in particular, Sir John Oldcastle, the Lollard knight executed ignominiously for treason and heresy in 1417, who was the subject of Bale's martyrology, *A brefe chronycle concerninge the examinacyon and death of the blessed martyr of Christ syr Johan Oldcastell* (1544). Bale's influence on England's chief Protestant martyrologist, John Foxe (1516/17–87), was 'like a torch touched to dry kindling'.[25] Foxe's *Acts and Monuments* (1563) placed the Marian martyrs in a historical chronology that stretched from the early church to Elizabeth's succession, and Bale's emphasis on prophecy was often echoed in Foxe's work.[26]

As scholars have shown, Bale constructed his historical framework by mapping episodes in English history onto his reading of the Book of Revelation, which he saw as prophesying the struggle

---

[24] Leslie P. Fairfield, *John Bale: Mythmaker for the English Reformation* (Eugene, OR, 1976), 71; John N. King, *English Reformation Literature* (Princeton, NJ, 1982), 63; Gretchen E. Minton, '"Suffer Me Not to be Separated, and Let my Cry Come unto Thee": John Bale's Apocalypse and the Exilic Imagination', *Reformation* 15 (2010), 83–97.

[25] Elizabeth Evenden and Thomas S. Freeman, *Religion and the Book in Early Modern England* (Cambridge, 2011), 39.

[26] For instance, Foxe incorporated Bale's martyrology of Oldcastle nearly verbatim in the first edition of his *Acts and Monuments*: see John Foxe, *The Unabridged Acts and Monuments Online or TAMO* (1563 edn) (HRI Online Publications, Sheffield, 2011), 313–33, <http//www.johnfoxe.org>, accessed 1 July 2011. Foxe's characterization of Oldcastle, based on Bale's *Brefe chronycle*, caused polemical controversy in the sixteenth and seventeenth centuries: see Susannah Monta and Thomas S. Freeman, 'Holinshed and Foxe', in Paulina Kewes, Ian Archer and Felicity Heal, eds, *The Oxford Handbook of Holinshed's Chronicles* (Oxford, 2012), ch. 13. I am grateful to the authors for allowing me to see the manuscript prior to publication.

between two churches, true and false.[27] Bale interprets the true church, the remnant of Christ's apostolic congregation, as his fellow reformers and their theological predecessors, beleaguered throughout the ages by a dominant false church headed by the Antichrist; Bale understood this as the Roman church, led by the pope. By appropriating the Lollards, whose admonitions to the Roman church mirrored those of the reformers, as co-religionists, the reformer located England as an important battleground in the war between the churches.

Bale believed that England's history, like that of Israel in the Old Testament, was characterized by a series of sinful lapses that had come about because the people of the nation had not heeded the words of a prophet. Bale's understanding of the role of prophets was closely tied to history, implying that the roles of historian and prophet were not dissimilar, and his emphasis on the prophetic quality of historians was closely related to the medieval under-standing of history as inseparable from the moral actions of its people. Bale certainly saw the prophetic quality of the historian in his fellow countryman Gildas, writing of the sixth-century cleric, 'in hys dayly preachynges, both agaynst the clergye and layte, concernynge that vyce and soche other ... [he] prophecyed afore hande of the subuersyon of thys realme by the Saxons for yt, lyke as yt sone after folowed in effect'.[28] Divine punishment proved necessary again in the fifteenth century; in the *Brefe Chronycle*, Bale interpreted the turbulence of the Wars of the Roses as retribution from God for not heeding Oldcastle's call to a purer spirituality.[29] In the history of his own country, then, Bale saw direct paral-lels with the disobedience of the Israelites, whose 'abohminacions' forced God to send prophets such as Elijah to the Israelites on account of their idolatry and wickedness.[30] His narrative of the English past depicted a nation bound to God on a cyclical yet

---

[27] Richard Bauckham, *Tudor Apocalypse* (Abingdon, 1978), 38–90; Katharine R. Firth, *The Apocalyptic Tradition in Reformation Britain, 1530–1645* (Oxford, 1979), 32–68; Fairfield, *John Bale*.

[28] John Bale, *The actes of Englysh votaryes comprehendynge their vnchast practyses and examples by all ages* (Antwerp, 1546), Cvir.

[29] John Bale, *A brefe chronycle concerninge the examinacyon and death of the blessed martyr of Christ syr Johan Oldecastell* (Antwerp, 1544), Aviiir–Bir.

[30] John Bale, *The Vocacyon of Johan Bale* (Wesel, 1553), sig. Biv; see also Fairfield, *John Bale*, 110–11.

teleological path, revealed to Englishmen through the exegetical tool of Scripture.

Bale's exegesis of the opening of the seven seals recounted in the Book of Revelation shows clearly that he saw the increasing corruption of the church as concurrent with the rise of extra-biblical ceremonies in the liturgy. He interpreted the seven seals as the seven ages of the world, and believed that he was living in the sixth and penultimate age; he recognized this seal's opening as fulfilled in the dissemination of John Wyclif's teachings, the basis for Lollard belief. He interpreted the earthquake at the opening of the sixth seal (Rev. 6: 12) as a reference to the 'Earthquake Synod' of 1382, which condemned twenty-four propositions of Wyclif. The reformer noted that this latter age would bring on a renewal of martyrdom, and characterized the martyrs of his own day as fulfilling that prophecy.

Bale, then, read the Lollards' place in history as an essential step in the progression toward the end times, heralding the last age of tribulation on earth before the Antichrist's defeat. Investing Lollards with a special historical role was not without its problems, however; the sect had been tainted with heresy since Wyclif's day, and Oldcastle's own condemnation as a heretic only served to reiterate the reprobation. Undaunted by his task, Bale set out to demonstrate that the Lollards, in particular Wyclif and Oldcastle, had been condemned unjustly by a false church, and that they were not heretics but representatives of Christ's true flock. One way he tied the Lollards to his own movement, the true church manifest, was to interpret prophecy.

Before examining how Bale employed this tool in Oldcastle's case, it will be helpful to understand the way in which Bale saw the medieval prophetic inheritance and how he adjusted these ideas to fit into a reformed theological framework. Given Bale's dichotomous understanding of history and the place of the true and false churches within it, it is unsurprising that prophets were regarded throughout his writings as being either true or false. This view of prophecy adhered to a nearly comprehensive endeavour of history-rewriting by Protestants, which called into question miracles of the medieval era, in particular those associated with the cults of saints.[31]

Bale set about demonstrating the deceitful nature of some medieval prophets. He exhibited several approaches to this problem in his *Actes of the Englysh votaryes* (1546), which told the history of the English church (or rather the long history of papal interference with it). First, he associates the late medieval notion of prophecy as false prognostication with Archbishop Theodore of Canterbury (602–90), whose school at Canterbury was celebrated by Bede. Bale wrote: 'For hyther than brought he all vayne & craftye sciences, of countinge, calkynge, measurynge, syngynge, rymynge, reasonynge, arguynge, dyffynynge, shauinge, oylynge, exorcysynge, incantynge, & coniurynge.'[32] Later in the text, Bale attempted the same association of false prophets and magic, writing:

> Ethelstanus a monke, at one tyme takynge presthode with Dunstane and Ethelwolde, within a whyle after left all hys orders and toke hym to a wyfe. Wherfor they prophecyed of hym that hys ende shulde be myserable. And bycause they wolde apere no false Prophetes, they inchaunted hym, charmed hym, and changed hym in to an ele, and so he lyued in the water euer after with a great sort more of hys companye. Wherupon (they saye) that monasterye and towne hath euer sens bene called Elye.[33]

Here we see the taint of the miraculous with regard to false prophets. Through this story, Bale argued that both miracles and false prophecy were tools of the false church to deceive true believers. In another example, the reformer recalled Paul's prophecy that the latter days would see false prophets. When describing the synod of Thetford in Norfolk, where the reformer claimed that Hadrian of Canterbury (d. 710) published a book of Roman ordinances, Bale asked rhetorically: 'If this were not the departynge that Paule prophecyed to come … where shall we loke for any?'[34]

---

[31] Helen L. Parish, *Monks, Miracles and Magic: Reformation Representations of the Medieval Church* (Abingdon, 2005), 45–70.

[32] Bale, *The actes of Englysh votaryes*, E2v–3r; cf. Bede, *Ecclesiastical History of the English People* 4.2, ed. and transl. Bertram Colgrave and R. A. B. Mynors, OMT (Oxford, 1969), 332–5.

[33] Bale, *The actes of Englysh votaryes*, Gviv.

[34] Ibid., Eivr; cf. 2 Thess. 2: 1–12.

Of course, since Bale's sense of history was dichotomous, the examples of the false prophets were made to seem even more deceitful in light of their true counterparts. He urged people to read Gildas's writings alongside William Tyndale's *The obedience of a Christen man* (1528), thereby associating a Reformation martyr and translator of the English Bible with a medieval true prophet.[35] In other places, true prophets were those who lauded clerical marriage and who, in the latter age, had fought against the Antichrist, men such as Martin Luther, Francis Lambert and Philip Melanchthon.[36]

Bale's examples of true and false augurs were glossed with biblical passages that described the role of a prophet. It is noteworthy that these were drawn from both Testaments, offering continuity and a biblical basis by which believers should judge so-called prophets. Numbers 24 showed Balaam stressing his inability to articulate words of his own accord; rather, he was merely a vessel of the Lord;[37] in Micah 3, the Lord warned of prophets who would lead his people astray;[38] and in the New Testament, Paul warned the true church in 2 Thessalonians 2 about those who would prophesy falsely.[39]

Bale applied the prophecies of these men, and of others such as Hosea and John, retrospectively to English history. What is interesting in *The actes of the Englysh votaryes* is how Bale handled authoritative 'prophets' from the medieval era. For instance, Bale included Merlin's prediction that the Diadem of Brutus would one day be restored to the British kings; although elsewhere Bale cast Merlin as a false prophet, here the words were given authority by association with Balaam, who predicted Jesus's coming – and who also, as shown above, stressed that it was the message of God and not the vessel that counted.[40] Bede, a 'verye true prophet', served as another source of extra-biblical revelation.[41] In *The first examinacyon of Anne Askewe* (1546), Bale recalled Bede's predic-

35 Ibid., Cvir.
36 Ibid., Bir.
37 For a reference to this passage, see ibid., Fir.
38 Ibid., Diiir.
39 Ibid., Eivr.
40 See Geoffrey of Monmouth, *The History of the Kings of Britain*, ed. Michael D. Reeve, transl. Neil Wright (Woodbridge, 2007), 148 (Book VII).
41 John Bale, *The first examinacyon of Anne Askewe* (Wesel, 1546), Aiir.

tion of persecution in the coming ages, but tempered the monk's authority with instruction to read Bede's predictions with the aid of Scripture.[42] We see, then, Bale's acceptance of part of the medieval prophetic tradition, but with elucidation and in conjunction with biblical authority.

Bale's accommodation of certain medieval prophets and rejection of others reflects the larger Reformation process of history-rewriting, in which some medieval tropes and beliefs were accepted, others eschewed, and yet others re-presented – it appears that prophecy was no exception. Ultimately, Bale's attempt at identifying and categorizing medieval prophecy served as another example of his tireless correction of what he saw as the increasing evil of the pope and his false church, as characterized by fake miracles and false prophets. Additionally, he accommodated medieval prophetic notions to biblical precepts in an endless attempt to stress the tenet of *sola scriptura*.

From the general medieval prophetic tradition, we can now turn to examine how Bale used prophecy as one way to rehabilitate Oldcastle's reputation.[43] This was not a simple task: Oldcastle, condemned for his rejection of papal authority and disbelief in transubstantiation in 1414, then led a failed rebellion against Henry V, earning him the title of traitor in addition to that of heretic. In order to validate his membership in the true church, Bale painted Oldcastle as both a prophet and a fulfilment of prophecy.

The prophetic ability that Bale bestowed upon Oldcastle did not exhibit the hallmarks of medieval augury, as it was firmly rooted in Scripture and was conservative with regard to claims to direct personal revelation from God. During Oldcastle's interrogation, according to Bale, the knight claimed that he could know who was included in the true church (and, implicitly, who was excluded), citing Jesus's warning that an evil tree could be recognized by its ill fruit, and a false prophet by his works.[44] Later in his interrogation, he referred again to biblical prophecy:

---

[42]   Ibid., Aiijr; see Bede, *The Reckoning of Time* 68, ed. Faith Wallis, TTH 29 (Liverpool, 1999), 240–1.
[43]   Bale also sought to mend John Wyclif's reputation: see Margaret Aston, 'John Wycliffe's Reformation Reputation', in eadem, ed., *Lollards and Reformers: Images and Literacy in Late Medieval England* (London, 1984), 243–72, at 244–6.
[44]   Bale, *Brefe chronycle*, Dviv.

Both Daniel and Christ prophecyed, that soche a troublouse tyme shulde come, as hath not been yet sens the worldes begynnyng. And this prophecye is partlye fulfilled in youre dayes and doynges. For manye haue ye slayne alredye, and more will ye slee here after yf God fulfill not his promes. Christ sayth also, if those dayes of yours were not shortened, scarslye shuld anye fleshe be saued. *Therfore loke for yt iustlye, for God will shorten youre dayes.*[45]

Through this passage, Bale made two important points. Firstly, by rooting Oldcastle's revelatory powers in correct scriptural interpretation, Bale gave readers an example of a 'reformed' prophet, antithetical to the deceitful prognosticators of the medieval era. Secondly, by tying Oldcastle to Daniel, Christ and the apostles, Bale – as a correct interpreter of Scripture – cast himself in the light of a latter-day true prophet, bound through biblical revelation to exemplars of the true church. Thus, through prophecy Bale tied the Lollards to his own cause, bolstering the evangelical movement with historical legitimacy.

Bale also portrayed Oldcastle as a fulfilment of prophecy. In a passage where the Lollard was given divine help to answer his accusers, he referred to Revelation 6: 12, where John prophesied that darkness will block the sun, which Bale interpreted as the dawning of the penultimate age. In this age, the false church would be recognized as such, and the reformer highlighted Oldcastle as part of that historical process. Bolstering this point, Bale showed that Oldcastle's persecution had been prophesied by peppering the text with biblical references to the increased persecution of the last days. Even the title page of the *Brefe Chronycle* cited the most apocalyptic book of the Old Testament: 'In the latter tyme (sayth the Lorde vnto Daniel), shall manye be chosen, proued, and puryfyed by fyre', thus reinforcing his own historical framework through the medium of prophecy.[46]

Another paratextual element of the *Brefe Chronycle* further underscored the association between Oldcastle and prophecy. The apocalyptic tone of the work was mirrored in an addendum at the end of the piece, the 'Prophecyes of Joachim Abbas', which acted as a postscript for read-

---

[45] Ibid., Eir (my italics).
[46] Ibid., Giir.

ers.[47] These Joachimite predictions of the earth's end were printed on the verso side of the last leaf of the main text, leaving readers of Oldcastle's narrative with the final impression of a medieval true prophet. They came from a hostile source in Bale's possession, the *De Haeresibus* of Guido de Perpignan, a Carmelite bishop of the fourteenth century who advocated papal infallibility and condemned Joachim of Fiore's works. The prophecies announced that a law of liberty would be declared in the latter days; that the church of Rome was the synagogue of Satan; and that 'the holye ghost shall more perfyghtlye exercyse his domynyon in conuertynge peoples by the preachers of the later tyme, than by the Apostles'.[48] As Bale had set Oldcastle up as a prophet – which among the godly in the Reformation era was synonymous with 'preacher' – readers may have associated Oldcastle with one of these 'preachers of the later tyme'; they might also have understood the strong implication that Bale, as an accurate interpreter of Scripture and thus an apt historian, was a prophet as well.

Ultimately, the way Bale handled the medieval prophetic tradition can be seen as one part of a larger historiographical agenda of the Protestant movement, with the same concern to eradicate the deceit shown by the established church and the same emphasis on *sola scriptura*. That Oldcastle was a significant player in this process shows that, for Bale, Lollardy was a potential avenue to historical and theological validity. Although prophecy would prove yet another point of contention for Protestants, its value in terms of providing historical and theological legitimacy made it worth employing. Perhaps Bale's mediating position regarding this phenomenon (exhibited in his use of Balaam to show that it is the *word* and not the *vessel* of God that matters) reflects his knowledge of its contentious nature; still, there is an unmistakable implication that Bale thought of himself as a prophet. Nevertheless, prophecy, even in its modified form, proved to be a powerful polemical tool in the Reformation era.

Durham University

---

[47] The same type of paratextual component is also evident in an example from the Wittenberg press of Nickel Schirlenz, in which a work from the medieval prophetical tradition is appended to an evangelical text: a German translation of the Magdeburg prophecy serves as an appendix to pseudo-Pflaum's *Practica* (1532): see Barnes, *Prophecy and Gnosis*, 57; Robert E. Lerner, *The Powers of Prophecy: The Cedar of Lebanon Vision from the Mongol Onslaught to the Dawn of the Enlightenment* (Ithaca, NY, 2009), 166.

[48] Bale, *Brefe chronycle*, Gviiir.

'HOLDING UP A LAMP TO THE SUN': HIBERNO-PAPAL RELATIONS AND THE CONSTRUCTION OF IRISH ORTHODOXY IN JOHN LYNCH'S *CAMBRENSIS EVERSUS* (1662)

by SALVADOR RYAN

Competing confessional claims to the early church played a hugely significant part in the revival of the writing of ecclesiastical history during the period of the European Reformations. This question of Christian origins led rival religious groups to contest vigorously the right to claim to be the early church's legitimate heirs. Sixteenth- and seventeenth-century works of ecclesiastical history would, moreover, strive to attain and preserve the rigorous standards set by Renaissance humanist scholarship and, in turn, exploit any perceived weaknesses in the work of their opponents in this regard.[1] This essay examines a seventeenth-century Irish example of such ecclesiastical history-writing: *Cambrensis Eversus* ('Cambrensis Refuted'), written in Latin, largely for a continental audience, by a County Galway priest-scholar, John Lynch (1599/1600–73), and published in St Malo in 1662.[2] The work is ostensibly a reply to the twelfth-century works of Giraldus Cambrensis (*c*.1146–1223) on Ireland, which had attained a new importance in the confessional controversies of the late sixteenth and seventeenth centuries, cited afresh by scholars as evidence of the depraved nature of the medieval Irish (and, by extension, of medieval Irish Catholicism) and the need for their moral and religious reform. This had a particular resonance in the Reformation period: if medieval Catholicism could be proved to have been in a state of decay, then this would further legitimize the argument that it was in need of reform and would underscore the correctness of the Protestant return to a purer and more authentic early Christianity.

Whereas in his twelfth-century writings Giraldus took pains to stress the fantastic and the decadent in Irish Christianity,

[1] See esp. Katherine Van Liere, Simon Ditchfield and Howard Louthan, eds, *Sacred History: Uses of the Christian Past in the Renaissance World* (Oxford, 2012).

[2] John Lynch, *Cambrensis Eversus* (St Malo, 1662), ed. and transl. Matthew Kelly, 3 vols, Celtic Society 2 (Dublin, 1848–52).

emphasizing the gulf between its practices and those of mainstream (i.e. Roman) Christianity, Lynch would attempt, in turn, to highlight Irish Christianity's essential orthodoxy and its constant adherence to the authority of the papacy since its very beginning. However, in doing so he was faced with a somewhat inconvenient historical problem: that of the *Laudabiliter*, long believed to be a papal bull issued by the English pope, Adrian IV (1154–9), in 1155, in which he granted the lordship of Ireland to King Henry II with a view to its moral and religious reform, and thereby legitimized what would later become English rule in Ireland.[3] If Ireland had, indeed, displayed such fealty to the pope and to universal orthodox Christian practice, why should it have been necessary for the pope to intervene in this way? Lynch therefore concluded that the papal bull was in fact a forgery. The idea that Anglo-Norman intervention in Ireland was sponsored by the papacy on account of the abominable standards of Irish Christianity needed to be comprehensively challenged. To that end, Lynch pointed to a long history of fruitful and mutually respectful relations between Ireland and the papacy and the largely impeccable credentials of Irish Catholicism through the centuries.

There was a further complicating element to *Cambrensis Eversus*, however, which played its part in the rewriting of Irish religious and national history during this period, and that was the question of identity. What particularly characterized Irish Catholic examples of the rewriting of ecclesiastical history was the very question of defining who the Irish actually were. With the arrival of new and mainly Protestant English settlers to Ireland from as early as the 1550s and on through the Cromwellian Protectorate, the former late medieval categories of *Gael* and *Gall* (Irish and English) no longer worked. Now a distinction needed to be made between the 'Old English' of Ireland, who largely remained Catholic through

---

[3]   The putative bull's existence was known of from quite early on. In his *Meta-logicus*, written in 1159, John of Salisbury mentioned the *Laudabiliter* bull and claimed to have been the ambassador sent by Henry II to Pope Adrian IV to obtain it. However, the text of the bull first appears in Giraldus Cambrensis's *Expugnatio Hibernica* some thirty years later as one of Giraldus's five justifications for the invasion of Ireland: see esp. Michael Haren, '*Laudabiliter*: Text and Context', in Marie Therese Flanagan and Judith A. Green, eds, *Charters and Charter Scholarship in Britain and Ireland* (Basingstoke, 2005), 140–63; also Anne J. Duggan, 'The Making of a Myth: Giraldus Cambrensis' *Laudabiliter* and Henry II's Lordship of Ireland', *Studies in Medieval and Renaissance History* ser. 3, 4 (2007), 107–69.

the Reformation period, and these 'New English' Protestant settlers. This would see the descendants of the Anglo-Norman, now 'Old English', settlers make common cause with their native Irish Catholic counterparts, thus laying the groundwork for an 'Irish Catholic' identity. However, this would require historical legitimization, and Catholic writers of this period would need to revisit the circumstances which led to the arrival of the Anglo-Normans in Ireland in the later twelfth century. In particular, the question of papal involvement in the affair would need to be examined afresh, and especially the controversial bull *Laudabiliter*. The idea of such a papal donation (and its implication that the Irish church had been morally depraved), became increasingly repugnant to Irish Catholic historians in an environment in which Protestant polemic claimed that the medieval church had fallen into decay and that, in fact, an early figure such as St Patrick might best be regarded as a proto-Protestant. In the words of David Finnegan, 'Protestant commentators in Ireland – largely drawn from the new arrivals – looked to the past as a means of anticipating and justifying the transformations of the sixteenth century that shaped the political, economic, social and tenurial structures in the island'.[4]

Lynch followed in a line of seventeenth-century Irish Catholic scholars such as Stephen White (1574–1646) and Geoffrey Keating (*c.*1570–1644), who were responding to the works of a host of pro-English writers such as Richard Stanihurst (1547–1618), Edmund Spenser (1552–99), Meredith Hanmer (1543–1604), William Camden (1551–1623), Fynes Moryson (1566–1630) and 'saint-stealers'[5] such as the Scot Thomas Dempster (1579–1625), Dempster being taken to task by Lynch in a special chapter of *Cambrensis Eversus*. Later writers such as the Irish Roderic O'Flaherty (1629–1718) would respond to a new generation of detractors such as Edmund Borlase (1620–82), whose *The Reduction of Ireland to the Crown of England* was published in 1675. O'Flaherty responded to this with his *Observations on Dr. Borlase's Reduction of Ireland* (1682). In the same year, the Franciscan writer, Peter Walsh (*c.*1618–88),

---

4   David Finnegan, 'Old English Views of Gaelic Irish History and the Emergence of an Irish Catholic Nation, *c.*1569–1640', in Brian MacCuarta, ed., *Re-shaping Ireland 1550–1700: Colonization and its Consequences* (Dublin, 2011), 187–213, at 190.

5   This refers to the controversy over whether the word *Scotia* actually referred to Ireland or Scotland and the assertion among some Scottish writers such as Dempster that many early 'Irish' saints had not actually been Irish at all, but Scottish.

tackled Spenser's *View of the present state of Ireland* in his *A prospect of the state of Ireland*.[6] Meanwhile, Protestant writers such as the lawyer and later Lord Chancellor of Ireland Sir Richard Cox (1650–1753) dismissed Keating's writings as a pack of lies in the preface to his *Hibernia Anglicana* (1689).

What particularly galled Irish Catholic writers of this period, however, was the renewed influence of that *bête noire* of Irish historiography, Giraldus Cambrensis, whose *Topographia Hibernica* and *Expugnatio Hibernica* had lately been receiving a fresh airing in the writings of figures such as the Dublin-born Stanihurst, whose *De Rebus in Hibernia Gestis* was published at Antwerp in 1584, and also the English antiquarian Camden's publication of Cambrensis's works in his *Anglica, Hibernica, Normannica, Cambrica* … , published in Frankfurt in 1602. What followed was a series of responses to the re-emergence of Giraldus in the confessional controversies of the period, which largely came from members of the Old English community in Ireland. The Jesuit scholar Stephen White wrote his *Apologia pro Hibernia* as a direct response to Camden in 1610 and a second work, *Apologia pro innocentibus Ibernis*, in the 1630s in reply to Stanihurst's *De Rebus in Hibernia Gestis*.[7] The priest-scholar Keating, in his *Foras Feasa ar Éirinn* ('Compendium of Knowledge on Ireland'), written in Irish in the early 1630s, similarly sought to discredit Giraldus while also offering an updated origin legend for Ireland which fully incorporated the Anglo-Norman settlers; the emerging term Éireannach ('Irish-person') as used by Keating and others would describe those who were Irish-born and Catholic, whether of Anglo-Norman or native Irish stock.[8]

John Lynch's work would be the most comprehensive attempt to discredit Giraldus. Lynch was of Old English stock and a number of his extended family were bishops; he was educated on the Continent under the Jesuits at Douai and attended the Orato-

---

[6]   For the response to the earlier generation of writers, see Salvador Ryan, 'Reconstructing Irish Catholic History after the Reformation' , in Van Liere et al., eds, *Sacred History*, 186–205. For the continuing polemic after Lynch's *Cambrensis Eversus*, see Mark Williams and Stephen Paul Forrest, eds, *Constructing the Past: Writing Irish History, 1600–1800* (Woodbridge, 2010).

[7]   Jason Harris, 'A Case Study in Rhetorical Composition: Stephen White's two *Apologiae* for Ireland', in idem and Keith Sidwell, eds, *Making Ireland Roman: Irish Neo-Latin Writers and the Republic of Letters* (Cork, 2009), 126–53, at 127–9.

[8]   See Ryan, 'Reconstructing Irish Catholic History'.

rian College in Dieppe and the Irish seminary at Rouen in 1618. Ordained a priest around 1625, he was made archdeacon of Tuam in 1631, a benefice he held until 1670, even though he lived in the vicinity of St Malo from 1652, the year in which the Cromwellian siege of Galway ended.[9] Prior to this he had been chaplain for twenty-four years to Sir Richard Blake, lawyer, former mayor of Galway and leading Catholic confederate.[10]

Lynch was evidently an admirer of Keating's work, for he prepared a Latin translation of *Foras Feasa ar Éirinn* for circulation in Europe.[11] Although Keating and others had tackled Giraldus as part of broader *apologiae* for Ireland, Lynch 'would be the first to come to grips directly and exclusively with the fountain-head of English detractions'.[12] While White had some decades earlier attempted to tackle Giraldus, his work had not been published. In the first volume of his work, Lynch acknowledged White's contribution but went on to lament that works such as White's 'are not published and studied by the learned in order to block up that poisoned spring whence all other writers who hate Ireland imbibe their envenomed calumnies'.[13]

---

9 René D'Ambrières and Éamon Ó Cíosáin, 'John Lynch of Galway (*c.*1599–1677): His Career, Exile and Writing', *Journal of the Galway Archaeological and Historical Society* 55 (2003), 50–63; see also Ian W. S. Campbell, 'John Lynch and Renaissance Humanism in Stuart Ireland: Catholic Intellectuals, Protestant Noblemen, and the Irish *Respublica*', *Éire-Ireland* 45/3–4 (2010), 27–40.

10 On 7 June 1642 in Kilkenny, a meeting of lay and clerical leaders (drawn from native Irish and Old English backgrounds) formed a Confederation of Irish Catholics, who wished to assert their rights as loyal subjects of King Charles I. They set up a provisional executive and held nine general assemblies. Blake was to serve as Chairman to the Assembly. Major divisions would emerge between various factions within it, especially over the Ormond peace of 1646, which the papal nuncio Giovanni Battista Rinuccini rejected outright because it did not fully restore freedom of Catholic worship. He also had theologians who spoke in favour of the Ormond Peace excommunicated. It would be Blake, as Speaker of the Supreme Council, who would order the divisive Rinuccini to leave the country in October 1648: see Bernadette Cunningham, 'Representations of King, Parliament and the Irish People in Geoffrey Keating's *Foras Feasa ar Erinn* and John Lynch's *Cambrensis Eversus* (1662)', in Jane H. Ohlmeyer, ed., *Political Thought in Seventeenth-Century Ireland: Kingdom or Colony* (Cambridge, 2000), 131–54, at 134.

11 Bernadette Cunningham, 'Annalists and Historians in Early Modern Ireland', in Julia M. Wright, ed., *A Companion to Irish Literature*, 2 vols (Oxford, 2010), 1: 76–91, at 87.

12 Joep Leersen, *Mere Irish and fíor-Ghael: Studies in the Ideas of Irish Nationality*, rev. edn (Cork, 1996), 320.

13 Ibid. 97.

Lynch departed from Keating on one important element relating to the controversial bull of Adrian IV. Keating had argued that in 1092 Donnchadh Ó Briain, who was the disputed high king of Ireland, went on pilgrimage to Rome and, with the consent of many of the native ruling elites and ecclesiastics, entrusted sovereign authority over Ireland to Pope Urban II (1088–99) in an example of *translatio imperii* (transfer of rule).[14] For Keating, then, the arrival of the Anglo-Normans was not a conquest and the papal bull of 1155 only confirmed a process which had already been instigated by the Irish. Lynch, however, rejected the idea that Ireland had ever ceded sovereign authority to the pope, viewing the bull of 1155 as a forgery even as he assured his largely French readership that his stance on the bull was not to be understood as evidence of Irish disloyalty to the pope.[15] In contrast to Keating, then, Lynch rejected any papal claim to sovereignty in Ireland and regarded Anglo-Norman hegemony as a legitimate conquest. In seeking to decouple the monarchy and the papacy, perhaps Lynch sought to convince King Charles II, to whom *Cambrensis Eversus* was dedicated, that the Catholicism of the Old English was not an obstacle to their continued loyalty to the English Crown.[16]

In order to dismiss the notion that papal intervention was warranted in Ireland, Lynch would confront Giraldus point for point. In answer to Giraldus's claim that 'sailors saw men in some of the Connaught islands who went naked and knew nothing but fish and flesh, no distinctions of the seasons of Lent or festivals or the days of the week; who, in a word, were not Christians and never heard even the name of Christ',[17] Lynch responded: 'I could name all the islands on the Irish coast and mention the saints who dwelt

---

[14] See Brendan Bradshaw, 'Geoffrey Keating: Apologist of Irish Ireland', in idem, Andrew Hadfield and Willy Maley, eds, *Representing Ireland: Literature and the Origins of Conflict, 1534–1660* (Cambridge, 1993), 166–90.

[15] Cunningham, 'Representations', 142.

[16] Ibid. 143. Although Lynch was based in France, his audience was surely not solely a continental one. We know that Bishop Luke Wadding (1628–92) of Ferns in the south-east of Ireland possessed a copy of *Cambrensis Eversus* in his library, although the fact that Wadding had spent many years teaching in Paris weakens the significance of this evidence somewhat: see Jane Ohlmeyer, 'Introduction: For God, King or Country? Political Thought and Culture in Seventeenth-Century Ireland', in eadem, ed., *Political Thought*, 1–34, at 29; also Patrick J. Corish. 'Bishop Wadding's Notebook', *AH* 29 (1970), 49–113, at 56.

[17] Lynch, *Cambrensis Eversus*, 1: 325.

in them, for there was hardly one of them untenanted. There was no desert, scarcely a single corner or spot in the island, however remote, that was not thickly peopled by zealous convents and monasteries'.[18] Moreover, he stated: 'I cannot believe that any one of them had fallen so far from its primitive institution as that the people would not know at all events the name of Christ. Their nurses, or the old people, must have preserved some knowledge at least of the events formerly occurring on their islands'. Besides, he continued, 'what reliance can be placed on the authority of sailors?' He concluded that 'it is very improbable that sailors took the trouble of ascertaining the religious principles of an obscure tribe'.[19]

In contending with the claims of Giraldus that the Irish were filthy, profligate in morals and barbarous in laws, and that they paid neither firstfruits nor tithes and did not contract marriage legitimately, Lynch recognized elements borrowed from Bernard of Clairvaux's *Life of St Malachy* (c.1148–53)[20] but argued that what Bernard applied to just one region – the diocese of Connor – Giraldus extended to the whole of the island. Besides, he noted, by the time St Bernard wrote this life, these matters had been dealt with – the point being that Malachy had abolished them – whereas Giraldus represented them as continuing.[21] Connor was, for Lynch, merely a blip, uncharacteristic of Irish Christianity as a whole, and Malachy 'established in all the churches the apostolical decisions, and the decrees of the Holy Fathers and especially the customs of the Holy Roman Church'.[22]

The reputation of saintly and scholarly Irishmen on the Continent was employed by Lynch frequently in his work as disproving the need for reform of Irish Christianity in what might be called a *nemo dat quod non habet* ('one cannot give what one does not have') argument:

> Every person who has even a slight knowledge of the Christian religion is very well aware that it would be a crime to desert one's country when it is plunged in savage depravity

---

[18] Ibid.
[19] Ibid. 325–7.
[20] *Bernard of Clairvaux: The Life and Death of Saint Malachy the Irishman*, transl. Robert T. Meyer, Cistercian Fathers 10 (Kalamazoo, MI, 1978).
[21] Lynch, *Cambrensis Eversus*, 2: 337–41.
[22] Ibid. 343.

and universal ignorance of the rudiments of the faith, and to go plant an abundant harvest of virtue and religion on a foreign soil while barrenness and aridity wastes the whole extent of his native land ... the pope, after duly weighing those facts, would certainly have come to the conclusion that the Irish could not teach abroad what they had not learned at home.[23]

In fact, Lynch related how Adrian IV himself had been educated by an Irish scholar, Marianus Scotus, and had claimed to know no other who possessed such wisdom, eloquence and genius. If this was the case Lynch continued, then how could the same pope have possibly charged the Irish with depravity of morals?[24]

Lynch argued that additional proofs of the moral uprightness of Irish ecclesiastics could be found in the attendance of a number of Irish bishops at the Third Lateran Council of 1179:

> if their flocks were plunged in that hideous barbarism charged against all the Irish, how could they be worthy of being called to a distant place to sit in council on the important interests of the Catholic world, men who either could not or would not heal the infirmities of those whom they were bound by duty to protect?[25]

Moreover, when the popes appointed legates to Ireland to oversee ecclesiastical reform, they placed their confidence in Irishmen such as Gilbert of Limerick, Matthew O'h-Enni of Cashel and Lorcán (Lawrence) of Dublin.[26] Stressing once more the forged nature of the bull, Lynch pointed out that it 'represents a most virtuous pope as trampling on the laws of nature, on the laws of nations, and on all the laws of justice ... to rob not one man but a whole nation ... of their country, their fortunes and their lives, without hearing one word in their defence'.[27] Later in his work, he continued:

> can any man in his senses believe that the Supreme Pastor of

[23] Lynch, *Cambrensis Eversus*, 2: 405.
[24] Ibid. 401–5. This story refers to Marianus Scotus (d. 1088) who later became abbot of the monastery of St Peter at Regensburg.
[25] Ibid. 407.
[26] Ibid. 429.
[27] Ibid. 441.

the church would entrust the moral regeneration of Ireland
... to a king who surpassed William Rufus, Henry I and King
Stephen (immoral men all as I have shown) ... by intemper-
ately cherishing his great power to assail and destroy ... the
dignity of the church?[28]

Nothing was more common than to hear Henry II 'swear by
the eyes of God' and even Cambrensis admitted that he was more
given to hunting than holiness.[29] Placing the reform of Christians in Ireland in the hands of such a ruler, Lynch stated, would
be akin to 'throwing them from the limekiln into the coalpit'.[30]
Henry II's murder of Archbishop Thomas Becket, 'which struck
such deep and bitter grief into the pope's heart that, for eight
days, he never spoke, even to his domestics; and strictly ordered
that no Englishman should be admitted to his presence', clinched
the argument, for Lynch.[31] Why would the pope extend a grant
of such extraordinary importance to Henry II and, moreover, the
duty of reforming the immorality of the Irish? Lynch concluded:
'as well might you entrust him with the office of moral reformer
as fit a saddle on an ox'.[32]

However, there was also the record of Ireland's relations with
Rome over the *longue durée* to be elucidated. This Lynch set about
in chapter 25 of his work. A number of arguments in favour of the
persistent theological orthodoxy of the Irish were offered: why was
no indication given of Rome's displeasure with Irish practice before
1155?[33] Furthermore, Ireland stood apart from all other Catholic
kingdoms in never having been excommunicated or placed under
interdict by the pope.[34] Lynch quoted the testimonies of writers
such as Stanihurst, Cesare Baronio (1538–1607), Nicholas Sanders
(*c.*1530–81) and the Italian Oratorian priest Thomas Bozius (1548–
1610) as to the innate Catholicity of the Irish. He quoted Bozius
as stating that 'the very air of Ireland inspires no other religion; no

---

[28] Ibid. 473–5.
[29] Ibid. 479–81.
[30] Ibid. 553.
[31] Ibid. 487.
[32] Ibid. 483.
[33] Ibid. 579–81.
[34] Ibid. 581–3.

other is suggested by inanimate nature; the very beasts themselves appear to be impregnated with the Catholic faith'.[35]

The longevity of Irish Catholic ties to the papacy was somewhat stretched in Lynch's citing of André du Saussay (1589–1675) – bishop of Toul in Lorraine, publisher of the *Martyrologium Gallicanum* (Paris, 1637) – to the effect that St Mansuetus, an Irishman, went to Rome in AD 66 and was baptized by St Peter, prince of the apostles, and later served as bishop of Toul.[36] Lynch cited examples of a number of other Irish saints who had connections with Rome in the period before the arrival of St Patrick: Kieran of Saighir, who travelled to Rome in 382, and St Ailbhe, who (according to James Ussher), having been consecrated as bishop by the pope, set up a monastery in Rome which attracted fifty Irishmen in 397.[37] Such was the business between Ireland and Rome that some saints acquired the supernatural ability to travel to urgent meetings there and return within a day, as in the case of St Scothín.[38] Thus, for Lynch, there was 'no absurdity' in Prosper of Aquitaine's famous chronicle entry that Palladius was sent by Pope Celestine in 431 to the 'Irish believing in Christ'.[39] The work was completed, of course, by Patrick, who was commissioned by the pope.[40]

The intractable 'Easter question', which saw the Irish church observing Easter on a different date from Rome, would not be so easily papered over. Yet here too Lynch was prepared to make a defence, explaining that St Laurentius, successor to Augustine of Canterbury (d. 604), wrote a letter to the Irish imploring them to fall in line with universal observance and that St Tarannan, archbishop of Ireland, 'whose sanctity was so great that he is said to have raised three dead men to life', was convinced of the truth of Laurentius's plea and without fuss brought his flock back to unified observance.[41] A letter from Pope Honorius of about 629 on the Easter question also found favour with the southern Irish,

35 Ibid. 601–5.
36 Ibid. 623–5.
37 Ibid. 625.
38 Ibid. 627.
39 Ibid. 663.
40 Ibid. 675.
41 Ibid. 681.

although the northern Irish held out until 640.[42] Lynch noted that the Irish were never full-blown Quartodecimans for they always celebrated the feast of Easter on a Sunday 'like all Catholics', and never on the fourteenth day of the month on whatever day of the week it fell, as real Quartodecimans were prepared to do. On the question of the resurgence of the Pelagian heresy in Ireland, Lynch recalled a letter written by pope-elect John IV (640–2) to the northern Irish which addressed certain bishops, priests and abbots by name. This, he inferred, indicated that 'these holy men sent a complaint to the pope of the errors with which their flocks were tainted and implored the aid of his council to heal them, but that they themselves were not infected by these errors', the Irish hierarchy apparently being perfectly capable of policing their own church's orthodoxy.[43]

The interventions of the popes both on the Easter question and the Pelagian heresy are presented as having been utterly successful, to the extent that '[t]he Irish Church was now without a blemish and attained the summit of perfection. Under the care of the popes she was presented as a glorious church, not having spot or wrinkle, but holy and immaculate. The Irish, therefore, owe the whole glory of their church to the popes.'[44] Herein, however, lay some danger: 'But when the popes beheld the Irish church radiant with such surpassing splendour they relaxed for a considerable amount of time their ancient solicitude for the Irish, sending neither legates nor letters lest they might be said to be holding up a lamp to the sun.'[45] Thereafter, the glory of the Irish church was for a time darkened by the depredations of the Danes, who laid waste to the country, massacred the clergy and destroyed church buildings.[46] This allowed Lynch to bring the story up to the twelfth-century ecclesiastical reform in Ireland.[47] If there was need at all for such

---

[42] Ibid. 681–3. For a discussion of some of these earlier controversies regarding Irish orthodoxy, see Damian Bracken, 'Rome and the Isles: Ireland, England and the Rhetoric of Orthodoxy', *PBA* 157 (2009), 75–97.
[43] Lynch, *Cambrensis Eversus*, 2: 689.
[44] Ibid. 725.
[45] Ibid.
[46] Ibid. 727.
[47] See Marie Therese Flanagan, *The Transformation of the Irish Church in the Twelfth Century* (Woodbridge, 2010).

reform, this was attributed to the lingering effects of the Viking attacks:

> The torrent, however, which had so long deluged Ireland, left some of its slime and weeds on the national fame. To remove them, the popes exerted all their pastoral solicitude by sending legates in uninterrupted succession to Ireland who left no resource untried to repair the lost splendour of her religious fame. Gilbert, bishop of Limerick, was the first of those legates ...[48]

Thus any ecclesiastical problems which Ireland faced were not attributable to the depraved nature of her own Christians but rather were caused from outside. Moreover, the remedy for such ills was to be found within, in papal legates who were Irishmen 'and therefore better qualified than any others to inflame their countrymen with a love of virtue'.[49]

Lynch's assertion of healthy relations between the Irish church and the papacy over the centuries served a number of functions. Firstly, it countered any claims that Pope Adrian IV needed to take the moral reform of the Irish church into his own hands and, by extension, exonerated him from interfering in Irish sovereignty. Secondly, Charles II need have no fear, moreover, that Old English loyalty to the papacy might threaten the fidelity of this community to their rightful king. Lynch responded to the suggestion in the *Polycraticus* of John of Salisbury (1120–80) that the papal prerogative to confer on Henry II the right to annex Ireland rested on the fabled Donation of Constantine by asserting that 'now it is generally known that the temporal power of the pope is confined to certain territories in Italy and France, and theologians deny that it extends to countries subject to the dominion of other princes'.[50] While acknowledging Ireland's close adherence to the papacy in spiritual matters through history, Lynch's credentials were never-

---

[48] Lynch, *Cambrensis Eversus*, 2: 729. Gilbert of Limerick presided over the Synod of Rathbreasail in 1111 when the Irish church was first divided into dioceses.

[49] Ibid. 731.

[50] Ibid. 433–7. Lynch proceeded by the argument that even if such a donation had been made, Ireland had never been conquered by the Roman Empire and, furthermore, that there remained no evidence whatsoever of Constantine's authority in Ireland.

theless 'English and royalist to the core'.[51] Moreover, he regarded his exposure of the fallacies of Giraldus Cambrensis as following the rigorous standards of Renaissance humanist scholarship. He cited the unmasking of long-held 'fables' such as the existence of a Pope Joan and the capitulation of the early fourth-century Pope Marcellinus to idolatry, which 'circulated among the vulgar' for centuries as precedents.[52] *Cambrensis Eversus* presented a new and confident narrative of Irish Catholicism to a largely continental audience (in addition to the English monarch, Charles II, to whom Lynch professed his allegiance), in which loyalty to the papacy could peaceably coexist with loyalty to the legitimate monarch and a Catholicism in which both Old English and native Irish had a place at the table. After all, Lynch asked pointedly, '[a]re not five hundred years powerful enough to make one people of the English and the Irish?'[53] The intersection of questions of national identity with religious identity in post-Reformation Irish Catholic rewriting of ecclesiastical history thus makes Ireland a particularly distinctive case of the church reflecting on its past.

St Patrick's College, Maynooth

---

[51] Deana Rankin, *Between Spenser and Swift: English Writing in Seventeenth-Century Ireland* (Cambridge, 2005), 236.

[52] Lynch, *Cambrensis Eversus*, 1: 99–101.

[53] Ibid. iii, 161.

GILBERT BURNET: AN ECCLESIASTICAL HISTORIAN AND THE INVENTION OF THE ENGLISH RESTORATION ERA

by TONY CLAYDON

On the eve of the 1689 Revolution in England, Gilbert Burnet was best known as an ecclesiastical historian. Although he had had a noteworthy career as a Whig-leaning cleric, who had gone into exile at the start of James II's reign and had entered the household of William of Orange in the Hague, Burnet's reputation had been based on his magisterial *History of the Reformation*. This had appeared in its first two volumes in 1678 and 1683, and had rapidly become the standard work on the religious changes of the Tudor age.[1] Soon after the Revolution, Burnet also became notable as the chief propagandist of the new regime. He produced a steady stream of works justifying William's usurpation of James's throne, and played a major part in organizing such pro-Orange events as the fast days marking William's war with Louis XIV.[2] This essay explores a key intersection of these two roles. It suggests that Burnet's explicitly pro-Williamite understanding of church history gave rise to a new division of the past, and effectively invented the Restoration era as a distinct period of British history, running from 1660 to 1689.

As a historian-polemicist, Burnet had different ways of engaging with the past. One will not detain us long. In common with many contemporaries, he mined history for analogies for his current situation, treating distant events as timeless moral exemplars.[3] Elsewhere I have argued that this feature of Burnet's work led him to write like an earlier generation of Protestant, using biblical archetypes as parallels for God's dealings with England.[4] However, re-examining his works for this essay, I would now also stress his rich reference

---

[1] We lack a modern biography of Burnet, but see the classic by T. E. S. Clarke and H. C. Foxcroft, *A Life of Gilbert Burnet* (Cambridge, 1907), and Martin Grieg's article for the *ODNB*.

[2] See Tony Claydon, *William III and the Godly Revolution* (Cambridge, 1996).

[3] For such use of the past, see D. R. Woolfe, *Reading History in Early Modern England* (Cambridge, 2003).

[4] Claydon, *William III*, chs 1, 4.

to classical times for the purpose of analysing modern politics.[5] As Burnet − for instance − drew comparisons between William and virtuous emperors such as Trajan and Hadrian, or warned against emulating Roman reactions to the fall of Julius Caesar, he came closer to the style and concerns of his contemporary 'Augustan' writers than I have previously acknowledged.

Burnet's other approach to history went beyond example-hunting, and is more relevant to our purposes here. It was his tendency to think in eras. As we shall see, Burnet organized human experience into distinct stretches of time, each of which had its peculiar characteristics and was bounded by clear turning points. As an enthusiast for the Revolution of 1689, Burnet naturally saw it as one of these era-defining moments. To appreciate the importance of this, however, we have to realize that he saw 1689 as ending a number of different periods simultaneously. These ranged from the relatively short-term to the potentially apocalyptic, and they included his newly conceived Restoration epoch.

The shortest of Burnet's periods was the three-year rule of James II. To understand the stress on this brief timespan, we have to examine Burnet's political position. By 1688, he had wormed his way to the heart of Orange counsels. In the Netherlands, he acted as a political advisor to William and a close spiritual confidant of the prince's wife, Mary. In particular, he was respected as an expert on British public opinion.[6] He wrote pamphlets attacking James's rule; he was chosen to edit and translate William's manifesto to the English people; and he travelled in the prince's invasion force as chaplain, preaching some of the earliest sermons and penning some of the earliest tracts justifying Dutch actions.[7]

The prime task of such a propagandist during the Revolution was to secure a wide spectrum of support. This was a challenge, as the English political nation was already deeply divided into

---

[5] For these examples, see Gilbert Burnet, *A Sermon Preached at the Coronation of William III and Mary II* (London, 1689), 24–6; idem, *An Exhortation to Peace and Union* (London, 1689), 9.

[6] Gilbert Burnet, *The History of His Own Times*, 2nd edn, 6 vols (Oxford, 1833), 3: 135; N. Japikse, ed., *Correspondentie van William III en van Hans W llem Bentinck*, 5 vols (The Hague, 1927), 1: 33–4.

[7] For pamphlets against James, see, e.g., [Gilbert Burnet], *Reas ns against Repealing the Acts of Parliament Regarding the Tests* ([Amsterdam], 1687]); [idem], *Some Reflections on His Majesty's Proclamation* ([Amsterdam], 1687). For the manifesto and early propaganda pieces, see below.

Whigs and Tories.[8] The members of these two groups detested each other and had very different interpretations of recent history. In particular, Whigs blamed Tories for supporting James's right to accede to the throne in the last years of Charles II's reign, and for using their alliance with Charles to persecute their party after 1681. When, therefore, William's circle planned their justification for intervening in the Stuart realms, they had to decide when to suggest that things had begun to go wrong.[9] If they dated any problems before Charles's death in 1685, they would alienate the Tories, who believed that they had acted in good faith under Charles and that it was only after James came to the throne that he had clearly demonstrated his unfitness to govern. To maintain Tory support, therefore, William's analysis of England's troubles had to begin with 1685. The Orange court knew this, and Burnet accordingly stressed the unique evil of James's reign.

This short time-frame was most dramatically evident in the Orange manifesto.[10] In Burnet's version, this offered a comprehensive account of unconstitutional rule, which William had come to reverse, but whose legal enormities had had no manifestation before James's rule. The document thus denounced the king's attempts to pack Parliament with his supporters, his refusal to meet his legislature and his trampling on his subjects' rights – but the arguably similar actions of his predecessor were ignored. This left an impression of sharp divergence from English principles of government in 1685. Burnet reinforced this by writing two constitutional pamphlets in the interval between William's arrival in Devon on 5 November 1688 and Orange acceptance of the crown from a specially constituted convention on 13 February 1689. The first, *An Enquiry into the Measures of Submission*, stuck closely to the line of the manifesto, while the second, *An Enquiry into the Present State of Affairs*, concentrated on James's actions in the early winter of 1688–9 in order to demonstrate his probable abdication and his certain unfitness to rule.[11]

---

[8]   There has been dispute about the timing of party emergence, but Tim Harris, *Politics under the Later Stuarts* (Harlow, 1993), chs 3–4, gives a sensible account.

[9]   For the writing of the manifesto, see Lois Schwoerer, 'Propaganda in the Revolution of 1688–89', *AHR* 82 (1977), 843–74, at 850–4.

[10]   *The Declaration of His Highness William Henry, prince of Orange, of the Reasons Inducing Him to Appear in Arms in the Kingdom of England* (The Hague, 1688).

[11]   [Gilbert Burnet], *An Enquiry into the Measures of Submission to the Supreme*

Turning from Burnet's legal thought to his ecclesiastical understanding pulls us into a much grander time-frame. From numerous works, it is clear he thought that 1689 had rescued the entire European Reformation. But to understand the implied periodization, we need to know how long Burnet thought the movement had needed such salvation. The key here was the historian's 'two age' model of Protestantism. Throughout his writing, he argued that the reformed faith had fared very differently in the two ages (by which he meant centuries) since Luther had first proclaimed it. In the sixteenth century, Burnet believed, the Reformation had made rapid, indeed providentially miraculous, progress. In the seventeenth, by contrast, it had suffered disaster. This was superficially because Catholicism had fought back, but more fundamentally because Protestants themselves had lost the purity of their early vision. Instead of impressing with the simple and Scripture-based gospel of their message, they had fallen into division among themselves, and outdone papists in petty intolerance. The natural consequence was that the cause lost unity and drive. The spiritual effect was a God so disgusted with his supposed adherents that he punished them with defeat and persecution.[12] This message would be most clearly expounded in Burnet's *Discourse of the Pastoral Care* (1692) – a plea for clergymen to revert to community-based evangelism – but it was also prominent in early propaganda pieces for William. For instance, the chaplain's first published sermon for the prince after he arrived in London stressed that Protestants had made extraordinary advances in their first decades, but that 'in this present Age, the Reformation is not only at a stand, but going back'.[13]

Thus, for Burnet, the current era of Protestant misfortune had started around 1600. As an enthusiast for 1689, however, he soon presented the Revolution as a chance to end this epoch. William was a Protestant hero. From his coming to power in the Nether-

---

Authority (London, 1688); [idem], *An Enquiry into the Present State of Affairs* (London, 1688), esp. 5–7. A similar short-term and law-based analysis can be found in Gilbert Burnet, *A Pastoral Letter Writ by ... Gilbert, Lord Bishop of Sarum* (London, 1689).

[12] For more on the 'two age' theory, see Tony Claydon, 'Latitudinarianism and Apocalyptic History in the Worldview of Gilbert Burnet', *HistJ* 51 (2008), 577–97.

[13] Gilbert Burnet, *A Sermon Preached in the Chappel of St James ... 23 December, 1688* (London, 1689), 5. For similar sentiments, see idem, *A Sermon Preached before the House of Commons on 31 January, 1689* (London, 1689), 7.

lands in 1672, he had begun to halt the progress of the Counter-Reformation. Now his accession to the Stuart realms offered an extraordinary opportunity to roll back popery, especially if the English turned back to godly ways in gratitude for their deliverance, and so secured heaven's blessing. This was the burden, for example, of the numerous fast and thanksgiving sermons Burnet wrote for William's war with France.[14] To take a single example, the preacher told an audience in 1690 that Europe expected liberty and peace from the new English king, and 'the Reformation a recovery and a new lustre'.[15]

Such rhetoric produced a clear hundred-year period in the preacher's thought, but it ultimately hinted at a time-frame even longer than the century. For Burnet, the history of Protestantism was a microcosm of the entire Christian past. For the church universal, as for the Reformation, a pure faith had grown rapidly in its early period but had then lost its original shine as it sank into pride, intolerance and worldliness.[16] Christianity as a whole thus needed radical renewal, and William's example of godly zeal might provide this. Of course, such visions of the totality of church history have a tendency to turn apocalyptic, and Burnet's was no exception. In the immediate aftermath of the Revolution, the writer came close to suggesting that it might herald a new millennial age of religious perfection. Take, for instance, the following phrases from his first London sermon and his coronation sermon for William: the first talked of a potential 'new heavens and a new earth' if all responded appropriately to the Dutch deliverance; the second hoped that the 'New Jerusalem' might descend 'from heaven to settle among us' if the new monarch fulfilled his promise.[17]

So far we have looked at the two extremes of Burnet's perception of time. But perhaps the most interesting and innovative part of the Burnetine idea of history was a period between the short and long terms. This writer was, I argue, a major influence in the invention of the three decades since 1660 as a distinct 'Restoration' era. To start to see this, it is important to note that Burnet

---

[14] For the general tone of these sermons, see Claydon, *William III*, chs 3–5.

[15] Gilbert Burnet, *A Sermon Preached before the King and Queen … 19 October, 1690* (London, 1690), 26.

[16] Claydon, 'Latitudinarianism', 584.

[17] Burnet, *Sermon … 23 December, 1688*, 20–1; idem, *Sermon … Coronation*, 20.

saw the unfolding of the Reformation's fortunes in more detailed terms than the two ages outlined above. Within his grand pattern of advance followed by decline, there were shorter cycles. Protestantism had passed through repeated moments of crisis, which had engulfed the faithful across the European continent, before providential deliverances had brought at least temporary relief. As Burnet laid out in – for example – his sermon to Queen Mary in July 1690, these moments of crisis had included the 1550s, when Charles V had been defeating Protestants in Germany and Mary Tudor was suppressing the English Reformation, and the 1620s, when the Thirty Years War had been going badly in central Europe and the Huguenots had suffered defeat in France.[18]

In Burnet's mind, the 1680s had been another one of these crises. Not only had the decade seen James's attempts to promote Catholicism in England and Scotland, and to destroy the Protestant settlement in Ireland, but it had witnessed disasters abroad. There had been persecution in Savoy, the 1685 Revocation of the Edict of Nantes in France, and the consequent imposition of Louis XIV's intolerant popery both in his own realms and in a growing list of captured territories. Of course, Burnet saw the Revolution as an end to these latest troubles. Britain was rescued; William came to head a broad alliance against Louis.[19] This might bring us straight back to the short era in Burnet's thought (his fleeting years of crisis), but key passages in his post-Revolution works made it clear that there had in fact been a longer preamble to the latest danger. Crucially, the Reformation's descent into its most recent difficulties had started around the time of the Stuart Restoration. Once the immediate crisis of the revolution was over, once most Tories had been secured for the new regime, and once attention turned to William's war with France, the historian stressed events since 1660.

In the domestic sphere, Burnet was clear that the threat presented by James had been the culmination of developments starting soon after Charles II's return. First, the restored court, with its prominent Catholics and moral laxity, had become the entry-point for

[18] Gilbert Burnet, *A Sermon Preached before the Queen ... the 16th Day of July, 1690* (London, 1690), 24–9.

[19] For example, Burnet, *Sermon ... 16th July, 1690*; idem, *A Sermon Preached before His Majesty ... 31 October* (London, 1714), 8–27.

popery. Burnet condemned a regime which had tolerated popish agents and made irreligion fashionable.[20] Second, the British people had failed to respond as they should to the providence of the Restoration. Instead of showing penitential gratitude for a rescue from the enormities of the English republic, the populace had been infected by the sins of the court, and so had fallen into a cesspit of immorality, impiety and atheism.[21] As Burnet reminded multiple audiences after 1689, this mistake must not be repeated – a conviction which put him at the heart of a campaign for moral renewal.[22] Third, the Restoration settlement failed to accommodate the broad spectrum of England's Protestantism and so divided the nation's Reformation. Rather than showing Christian charity over minor differences, Anglicans and Dissenters had denounced one another and used what secular force they could secure to destroy their rivals.[23] This analysis explains Burnet's support for the measure of 1689 to suspend penalties against Nonconformity (the so-called 'Toleration Act'), and his exploration in *Pastoral Care* of a new pattern of charitable relations between establishment clergymen and parishioners of other denominations.[24] Taken together, Burnet thought Caroline failings had led to the crisis of James's reign. With Protestant England led by a popish court, infected by its luxury, and divided into warring sects, the dangers of James's reign were no surprise.

More importantly, the early 1660s also marked the start of the current era in the history of the European church. They were the point at which Louis XIV had taken personal charge in France; and Louis, as Burnet never tired of suggesting, was the great enemy of true religion. Presentation of Louis as a persecuting Antichrist was one of the most constant features of all of the historian's works. In the years 1685–7 Burnet had travelled through Europe, and had personally witnessed the sufferings of Protestants in France. Although his initial descriptions of this were brief, he later said that it had made the deepest impression on him, and it affected

---

[20] Claydon, *William III*, esp. chs 1, 3, 6.

[21] See Burnet, *Sermon ... 23 December, 1688*, 22–3; idem, *A Sermon Preached before the House of Peers ... 5 November* (London, 1689), 21–3.

[22] For this, see Claydon, *William III*, ch. 3; and esp. Gilbert Burnet, *Charitable Reproof: A Sermon Preached ... to the Societies for Reformation of Manners* (London, 1700).

[23] See, e.g., Burnet, *Exhortation*.

[24] Gilbert Burnet, *A Discourse of the Pastoral Care* (London, 1692), esp. ch. 8.

his thinking ever after.[25] In the post-Revolution era this produced a picture of profound and growing darkness in Europe, which had begun in 1661, and which was only rolled back upon William's triumph. Works in the immediate aftermath of the Revolution thus spoke of the French king as 'the cruel and barbarous enemy of mankind', as a man who had disturbed the peace of Europe 'beyond all former Examples', or as a scourge who had for 'so long' plagued his neighbours.[26] Louis' depredations abroad were linked to a pessimism regarding developments at home, because Burnet thought that France was behind what had gone wrong in England. Since the 1660s Louis had used Catholic agents at the Stuart court, and a deliberate campaign of moral corruption, to weaken English resistance. The nation, Burnet told the House of Commons in 1689, had been 'charmed by the Arts of a powerful but cruel Neighbour', and Louis had broken entirely into England's own counsels.[27]

Taken together, these elements of Burnet's thought defined a distinct period from 1660 to 1689. Moreover, they painted it with all the characteristics accorded to the 'Restoration' era in much of the succeeding historiography. For many later commentators, as for Burnet, the reigns of Charles II and James II saw a Catholically-affected and luxurious court presiding over a country which was losing its moral certainties and its religious cohesion, while across the Channel a new leviathan threatened to sweep all before it.[28] We therefore have to consider the central role of Burnet in shaping how we think about the temporal divisions of the Stuart age.

Of course one could object that the years from 1660 to 1689 marked a very clear period in England's story, and that it did not need a man with a peculiar view of the ecclesiastical past to point this out; 1689 represented the evident failure of the experiment started in 1660 – that of refounding the constitution and the

[25] Gilbert Burnet, *Some Letters Concerning What Seemed Most Remarkable* (Rotterdam, 1687), 227–30; idem, *A Sermon Preached ... upon the Reading of the Brief for the Persecuted Exiles* (London, 1704), 27–8.

[26] Burnet, *Exhortation*, 4; idem, *Sermon ... Coronation*, 29; idem, *Sermon ... 23 December, 1688*, 8.

[27] Burnet, *Sermon ... 31 January, 1689*, 8.

[28] This persistent historiographic mood is nicely summarized in the Introduction to George Southcombe and Grant Tapsell, eds, *Restoration Politics, Religion and Culture* (Basingstoke, 2010).

English church on early Stuart models after the republican 1650s. Yet there are problems with suggesting that this was an obvious or natural periodization, at least just after the Revolution. Even if it were true that the period from 1660 to 1689 was clearly defined as a failed experiment, it would have been hard to admit this. It would imply there was something inherently unstable about an ancient English establishment. This was a problem as William came to power, because (for continuity's sake) most people were maintaining that an ancient and virtuous settlement had been put back in place by Charles II at the Restoration, and preserved from James by the new Dutch king.[29] Thinking of 1660–89 as years of failure would also implicate much of the political nation. It would blacken most public careers as marked by acquiescence, or even complicity, in a long period of corruption. To avoid this, it was better to suggest a sudden disaster – the apocalypse of one man's wholly misguided rule; or alternatively to depict a good and traditional system struggling bravely against formidable opponents who had been trying to undermine it for centuries.

Looking beyond Burnet's prose, many contemporaries took one of these options at the Revolution. They thought in terms of eras far shorter, or far longer, than the thirty years Burnet was coming to emphasize. Consider for example, the historical sense of the men who gathered in the constitutional convention of 1689. They opened deliberations with a unanimous declaration that 'it hath been found by experience to be inconsistent with the safety and welfare of this Protestant kingdom to be governed by a popish prince'.[30] 'Experience' implied a long series of examples, which would stretch back to Mary Tudor, if not England's Catholic rulers before Henry VIII. Members of this convention went on to link celebration of the Revolution to the eighty-year-old thanksgiving for the discovery of the Gunpowder Plot, and to protest at James's breaches of a venerable English constitution perfected in the medieval period.[31] At the other extreme, we may instance the desperate

---

[29] This was, for example, the tenure of the main constitutional declaration to emerge from the constitutional convention of 1689, the 'Declaration of Rights', originally published as *The Declaration of the Lords and Commons Assembled at Westminster* (London, 1689).

[30] *Journal of the House of Commons* 10: 15; *Journal of the House of Lords* 14: 110.

[31] The liturgy for the 5 November thanksgiving was altered to include gratitude for the Revolution: see *Additional Prayers to be Used together with those Appointed in*

attempts to get everyone to forget everything that had happened before 1685. This was evident in William's manifesto, but also in attempts to obtain an act of indemnity for actions under Charles II, and in a pamphlet debate about the Revolution that restricted aspersions on royal action before James to a radical fringe.[32] In fact, in the early months after the Revolution the only group which seemed wholly comfortable with a thirty-year time-frame were not English: they were the Presbyterians of Scotland, who were happy to talk of the twenty-eight years' tyranny they had suffered since the imposition of the Restoration ecclesiastical settlement. Burnet had limited sympathy with this brand of his fellow countrymen, but he had objected to their persecution, and it is possible that he was importing some of their temporal sense across the border.[33]

With this exception, the concept of a Restoration era could be politically dangerous, and was widely avoided in 1689. In the mind of Burnet, however, a particular vision of church history demanded it. Thinking in medium-length cycles of the Reformation's progress, desperately disappointed at the ecclesiastical policies of Charles II, and above all convinced that Louis XIV was an anti-Christian threat, the writer saw the twenty-eight years after 1660 as a depressing whole. As a periodization, it was innovative and controversial – but it has proved durable.

Why this has been so is open for debate. Obviously, the immediate reasons for being suspicious of a 'Restoration' period faded with time; and we need to note the huge impact Burnet had in the 1690s. He published extensively in support of the new regime, and he led a group of prominent polemicists (most notably William's

---

the *Service for the Fifth of November* (London, 1689); for appeals to the medieval past, see Anchitell Grey, *Debates in the House of Commons from the Year 1667–1694*, 10 vols (London, 1769), 9: 8, 14, 19, 23, 57.

[32] Mark Goldie, 'The Revolution of 1689 and the Structure of Political Argument', *Bulletin of Research in the Humanities* 83 (1980), 473–564, stresses that the majority of post-Revolution pamphlets justified William's rule on grounds of conquest, providence, the necessity of resistance in the face of James's destructive tyranny, or a contract which James alone had broken – all short-term factors.

[33] For Burnet's Scottish origins and attitudes, see Claydon, 'Latitudinarianism'. The tendency of Presbyterians to think in 'Restoration era' terms was pointed out by Kathleen Middleton in a paper, 'Seeing off the Late Times: The Construction of the Revolution and the Preceding Decades in Scots Presbyterian Thought', given at the Bangor Conference on the Restoration, 27 July 2011.

new appointments to the bench of bishops, men such as John Tillotson, Edward Stillingfleet and Simon Patrick) who echoed his line in the pulpit and the press.[34] All these influential figures shared Burnet's sense that William's reign was an opportunity for moral and Protestant renewal after the corruptions of the post-Restoration era, and their propaganda campaign may well have set patterns for thinking about the chronological structure of history, both immediately and in the longer term. Perhaps, however, the grand scheme of Burnet's vision also helps explain its power. For him, 1689 ended not one but three or four different epochs which had operated over varying spans of time and at contrasting levels of experience. Indeed, although Burnet's various understandings of the past often mixed closely together to create some dizzying changes of historical perspective within a single work,[35] their focus on one world-changing event forged a consistency from those very different timescales, and added significance to each period of time considered. These periods included the newly minted sense that the Restoration era was a highly important division of the human experience.

Bangor University

---

[34] Claydon, *William III*, 65–70.
[35] For example, Burnet's coronation sermon in 1689 included classical analogy, implied apocalyptic, Reformation history and legal analysis of the period 1685–8, as well as a clear 'Restoration' sense.

THE MEDIEVAL CHURCH IN EARLY
METHODISM AND ANTI-METHODISM*

by CHRIS WILSON

John Wesley's sermon 'Of Former Times' (1787) provides just one example of his belief in the historical importance of the eighteenth-century Great Awakening. In its conclusion he noted that '[n]o "former time" since the apostles left the earth has been "better than the present"'.[1] In another sermon he argued explicitly that religious progress in the eighteenth century was greater than during the Reformation. Undecided about a more suitable comparison, he could not choose between the apostolic age and the rule of Constantine the Great.[2] In these arguments the early Methodists understandably afforded little time to the Middle Ages, which were seen as a dark period between the light of early Christianity and the brightness of their own movement. Yet this essay will argue that, despite this general approach to the history of the medieval church, there is an early Methodist medievalism worth recovering and that it can be best understood in the context of eighteenth-century religious polemic and debate.[3]

The Methodist approach to medieval church history was clearly coloured by the critique of Methodism forwarded by Anglican churchmen that attempted to link Wesley's followers to England's Catholic past. One example of the way in which this critique operated – a sustained attempt to paint the Methodists as 'new' thirteenth-century mendicants – will be discussed in the opening section of this essay. It will be followed by a discussion of the early

*   I would like to thank Sarah Scutts for her comments on this essay, Patricia Baker for helping track down a Wymeswold 'enthusiast' (see n. 10 below), and Colin Haydon, Bernard Hamilton, John Hargreaves and Peter Forsaith for helpful conversations at the EHS Summer Meeting in 2011.

[1]   John Wesley, 'Of Former Times', in *Sermons III*, ed. Albert C. Outler, vol. 3 of *The Bicentennial Edition of the Works of John Wesley* (Nashville: TN, 1976–), 442–53 (Sermon 102), at 453.

[2]   John Wesley, 'On Laying the Foundation of the New Chapel' (1777), in *Sermons III*, ed. Outler, 577–92 (Sermon 112), at 587.

[3]   For a recent introduction to the role that the medieval past played in debates about Britain's identity and its relationship with Europe, see Tony Claydon, *Europe and the Making of England* (Cambridge, 2007), 101–20.

Methodist reaction, focusing on John Wesley's treatment of one textbook of ecclesiastical history.

ANTI-METHODIST MEDIEVALISM

Historians of eighteenth-century religion have established that early anti-Methodist polemicists used two particular historical contexts for their attacks on the 'enthusiasts'. The first is neatly exemplified by a contributor to the *Gentleman's Magazine* in 1739, who noted the 'similitude' between the 'Risings of Enthusiastik Rant' and the 'Rise of those Troubles which at last overturn'd the Constitution and ruin'd the nation' in 'the last century'.[4] The extremist zeal of puritanism during the Civil War was a powerful reminder, so the argument went, of enthusiasm's ability to create 'disturbances in Church and State'.[5] The second context was just as vivid and even more contemporary. Anti-Catholicism, informed by the fear of Jacobite rebellion before 1745 and retribution afterwards, created a hostile confessional environment. In his analysis of the Pendle Forest Riots of 1758, Michael Snape has shown how this could contribute to local outbreaks of anti-Methodist violence.[6] Reginald Ward argued that English Methodism, unlike its American counterpart, developed under the shadow of that 'grossly-over-rated *incubus* of European Christianity, a Catholic church order which affected even those who resolved to do without it'.[7]

This shadow was famously at its darkest in the attack of George Lavington (1684–1762) on the Methodists, *Enthusiasm of Methodists and Papists Compar'd*, two volumes of which appeared anonymously in 1749, to be followed by a third in 1751.[8] Although the context of this work has been extensively discussed, little has been said about how Lavington – then bishop of Exeter – selected the historical examples which littered his polemic.[9] Where Lavington

4 Anon., 'Observations on the conduct of Mr Whitefield', *Gentleman's Magazine* 9 (1739), 239–42, at 241.
5 Ibid.
6 Michael F. Snape, 'Anti-Methodism in Eighteenth-Century England: The Pendle Forest Riots of 1758', *JEH* 49 (1998), 257–81.
7 W. R. Ward, 'Was there a Methodist Evangelistic Strategy in the Eighteenth Century?', in Nicholas Tyacke, ed., *England's Long Reformation, 1500–1800* (London, 1988), 285–306, at 305.
8 References here are to the first complete edition of the work: George Lavington, *Enthusiasm of Methodists and Papists Compared*, 3 vols (London, 1754).
9 See F. Baker, 'Bishop Lavington and the Methodists', *Proceedings of the Wesley*

went other, less studied, polemicists followed. Thomas Green (1704–76), a Leicestershire vicar, wrote a *Dissertation on Enthusiasm* (1755) which built on many of Lavington's themes and used some of his examples.[10] Green, like Lavington, did not shy away from setting out the historical context clearly: 'What advantage [he asked] did not Cromwell draw from Enthusiasm with respect to the path he chose to act?'[11]

These two works will form the basis of my more detailed comments below, but other polemicists also used medieval examples to attack Wesley and his followers. The anonymous author of *A review of the Policy, Doctrines and Morals of the Methodists* was typical in drawing a remarkable list of medieval parallels:

> Thus by opening a new and easy passage to heaven, it is no great wonder the [Methodists] meet with a number of votaries ... In one age of the church, men laid great stress on pilgrimages, on crusades, on hunting after the relics of saints and martyrs, and on expelling the infidels from the Holy Land. ... At other times the building of churches, and the endowment of religious houses, was a sufficient atonement for all sins, and the surest road to happiness; whilst a different class trusted their eternal salvation to the efficacy of these pardons and indulgencies ...[12]

This list seems broad, even arbitrary, but a closer analysis of Green and Lavington's work reveals that one particular group from within the medieval church was selected with disproportionate regularity: the thirteenth-century mendicants. In *Enthusiasm* the medieval mendicants and their founders are mentioned more than 130 times. Historians of the medieval church most often apply the term 'mendicant' to the followers of St Francis and St Dominic, who founded their orders in 1209 and 1214 respectively, but the term can be used to describe upwards of ten orders founded

---

Historical Society 34 (1963–4), 37–42.

[10] Thomas Green, *A Dissertation on Enthusiasm* (London, 1755). Green became vicar of Wymeswold on graduating from Trinity College, Cambridge, in 1728. In addition, he became rector of Walton-le-Wolds from 1758, holding both positions until his death.

[11] Green, *Dissertation*, 45.

[12] Anon., *A review of the Policy, Doctrines and Morals of the Methodists* (London, 1791), 10–11.

between 1209 and 1593. The Franciscans were also known as the Friars Minor and the Dominicans as the Order of Preachers, and both orders had separate identities and historiographical traditions to draw on. Yet it was not anachronistic for Lavington to refer to them as one group. Medieval commentators, historians and authors could also refer to them together, particularly in England where they arrived at roughly the same time in the 1220s, and this practice continued in Reformation polemic and modern scholarship.[13] There were a number of similarities. Both orders made claims to spiritual and economic purity, living off donations and begging (hence the term 'mendicant', from the Latin *mendicare*, to beg).[14] Both sent their members on preaching itineraries and established their houses on the edge of towns that were experiencing prodigious growth in the thirteenth century.[15] Both relied on the charismatic leadership of their founders and both preached outdoors.

Surveying this list, it is easy to see why eighteenth-century anti-Methodists identified the history of thirteenth-century mendicants as a fruitful source for their polemics.[16] Perhaps the most obvious parallel was the outdoor preaching of the friars, which could be neatly compared to the 'field preaching' of the Methodists. Field preaching was both a source of identity and vulnerability for Wesley's followers as, according to some jurists, it pushed the legal boundaries of the Toleration Act (1689).[17] This vulnerability was pounced on by Lavington. Some of the most vivid parallels that he drew between the medieval mendicants and Methodists relied on the selection and editing of material from collections of hagiography which celebrated the preaching of the friars. An example of this practice is his description of Anthony of Padua (d. 1231) – a Franciscan friar canonized less than one year after his

---

[13] See Wendy Scase, 'Antifraternal Traditions in Reformation Pamphlets', in *The Friars in Medieval Britain: Proceedings of the Harlaxton Symposium 2007*, ed. Nicholas Rogers, Harlaxton Medieval Studies n.s. 19 (Donington, 2010), 238–64.

[14] For a positive interpretation of the Dominican vows of poverty, see William A. Hinnebusch, 'Poverty in the Order of Preachers', *CathHR* 45 (1960), 436–53.

[15] Jacques Le Goff, 'Ordres mendiants et urbanisation dans la France médiévale', *Annales: Économies, sociétés, civilisations* 25 (1970), 924–87.

[16] It is worth noting that the medieval mendicants were not cited in other, similar polemics. When Lavington attacked the Moravians, for example, he used a completely different set of older historical examples, including the Valentinians and the Collyridians: George Lavington, *The Moravians Compared and Detected* (London, 1755).

[17] D. Hempton, 'Methodism and the Law', *BJRL* 70 (1988), 93–107.

death – in which he cited the *Flos Sanctorum* of Pedro de Ribadeneira (1527–1611), compiled between 1599 and 1610. Although this compilation became increasingly unfashionable as the work of the Bollandists began to be published from 1643, it seems that Lavington had access to the two-volume English translation of the work which had been published in 1730 under the title *The Lives of Saints*.[18] His use of this work in his description of Anthony is typical. According to Lavington, Anthony was 'forced to preach in the open fields and largest meadows, because people followed in such numbers, from cities villages and camps, that no church could contain them'.[19] The most imaginative comparison comes from Pedro's description of Anthony being guarded by men to prevent his audience crushing him as they tried to touch him or rip off his clothing.[20] Lavington compared this to stories he had heard about the Methodists and asked: 'Have not the Methodist-Preachers, as well as Saint Anthony, been attended with a sturdy set of followers, as their guards, armed with clubs under their cloaths, menacing and terrifying?'[21]

Lavington also used field preaching in his sustained attempt to link the mendicants and the Methodists to the medieval papacy. In one of his most direct attacks he quoted the canonization bull for St Francis, *Mira circa nos*, issued in 1228 by Pope Gregory IX.[22] After accurately recounting the pope's praise for Francis's simple preaching, he directly addressed the Methodists: 'If your peregrinations should lead you to Rome (whither you seem to be setting your faces) fail not to kiss his holiness' slipper for this honourable testimony of an itinerant field preacher'.[23]

For his part, perhaps stung by reports that a member of his own parish regularly travelled three hours 'the year round' to hear Walter Sellon (1715–92) preach at Breedon-on-the-Hill, Green concentrated on the quality of the Methodists' sermons and their ability

---

[18] Pedro de Ribadeneira, *Lives of Saints with other feasts of the year according to the Roman Calendar*, transl. W. P., 2 vols (London, 1730).

[19] Lavington, *Enthusiasm*, 1: 10.

[20] Ibid. 395.

[21] Ibid. 11.

[22] L. Auvray, ed., *Les Registres de Grégoire IX*, 4 vols (Rome, 1896–1955), 1: col. 130, no. 214. For a full introduction to the bull, see R. J. Armstrong, '*Mira circa nos*: Gregory IX's View of the Saint, Francis of Assisi', *Greyfriars Review* 4 (1990), 75–100 (first publ. 1984).

[23] Lavington, *Enthusiasm*, 1: xxxiii.

to preach without a book.[24] He noted that many in the established church preached in this manner but they did not claim 'the assistance of the Spirit'.[25] This reminded Green of the Dominicans who 'had boldly appropriated to their own order the Gift of Preaching, styling themselves *the preaching brothers*'.[26] He concluded, quoting 'a person who had frequently heard them', that he 'had scarce found any more unsuccessful than themselves in this part of the ministerial duty'.[27]

Claims to particular spiritual assistance also formed the basis of the comparison between St Francis and John Wesley, the most sustained individual analogy found in Lavington's treatise, with the possible exception of that made with Ignatius Loyola.[28] Green captured many elements of the comparison when he retold the story of Francis's attempt to preach to the sultan of Egypt in Italian, and Francis's offer to jump into the fire to prove his faith. The level-headed sultan sent Francis home, but the whole incident was, according to the author, testament to the 'great power of blind enthusiasm'.[29] The long established anti-Catholic critique of the *De conformitate vitae Francisco ad vitam Domini Nostri Jesu* by Bartholomew of Pisa (d. 1401) was the basis of many of these attacks.[30]

This assault on the over-confidence of Francis and Wesley was easily widened out to include their followers. Lavington drew his readers' attention to a book 'published about the middle of the thirteenth century' by 'the Mendicant Fryars called the Eternal Gospel or Gospel of the Spirit'.[31] This work showed that the mendicants, like the Methodists, believed that their success occurred at a God-

---

[24] Walter Sellon was closely associated with John Wesley and a group of Methodist preachers. For the reference to one of Green's flock attending Sellon's sermons, see J. B., 'The Church on the Hill: Recollections of Rev. Walter Sellon', *Wesleyan-Methodist Magazine* ser. 5, 2 (1856), 35–42, 133–40, 231–9, 332–40, at 337.

[25] Green, *Dissertation*, 16.

[26] Ibid.

[27] Ibid. Most of this section is extracted from the anonymous work *The Frauds of Romish Monks and Priests* (London, 1704).

[28] Modern scholars have also made the parallel. See Gwang Seok Oh, *John Wesley's Ecclesiology: A Study in its Sources and Development*, Pietist and Wesleyan Studies 27 (Plymouth, MA, 2008), 32–3.

[29] Green, *Dissertation*, 91–2.

[30] The English-language critique of this work can be dated back to the translation of the parody of it by Erasmus Alber (1500–53), *The alcaron of the barefote friers* (1550).

[31] Lavington, *Enthusiasm*, 1: 62.

appointed time in history. In this instance, Lavington's comparison was stretched and his lack of marginal notes is telling. Although the *Eternal Gospel* was originally penned by a Franciscan, it was opposed immediately by Pope Alexander IV, who ordered all copies to be burned, and the author was imprisoned for the rest of his life.[32] For its part, the Franciscan order prohibited the writing of works without leave at the General Chapter of 1260. In fact, almost all we know of the book is found in the refutation of its doctrines by the University of Paris.[33] Such details were at odds with Lavington's attempt to tie the mendicants, and by extension the Methodists, to the papacy and to Catholicism in general.

In addition to these parallels, the anti-Methodists tried to make a more complicated comparison between the perceived anti-clericalism of the 'enthusiasts' and the disruption of the secular clergy by the arrival of the friars in thirteenth-century England. The English context is important here because the stress placed on the Methodists' disruption of the established hierarchy reminded their readers of the two historical contexts described above. Green notes how the Friars 'formerly occasioned great disturbance, by going about preaching as they pleased, and encroaching upon the office of the parochial clergy … and by their insolent behaviour they made great confusion in this nation about five hundred years ago'.[34] This seems to be a deliberate echo of Green's explicit concern with the 'disorder and confusion in states and kingdoms' which 'our nation has formerly greatly suffered by', as outlined in his introduction.[35]

In order to make the analogy work, both Green and Lavington used the work of the Benedictine monk Matthew Paris (*c.*1200–59), who was notoriously critical of the behaviour of the mendicants in the first decades of their arrival in England.[36] Paris's work

---

[32] The work in question, Gherardo da Borgo San Donnino's *Liber introductorius ad Evangelium aeturnum* (1254), had contributed to the conflict between the secular masters and the mendicants at the University of Paris. See P. Péano, 'Gérard de Borgo San Donnino', *DHGE* 20: 709–21. These details would have been known to Lavington through the work of Matthew Paris, which he used in the compilation of *Enthusiasm*.

[33] Penn R. Szittya, 'The Antifraternal Tradition in Middle English Literature', *Speculum* 52 (1977), 287–313, at 291.

[34] Green, *Dissertation*, 168–9.

[35] Ibid., vi.

[36] Wiliel R. Thomson, 'The Image of the Mendicants in the Chronicles of Matthew Paris', *Archivum Franciscanum Historicum* 70 (1977), 3–34.

was available in a Latin edition published by William Wats in 1640 under the title *Historia Major*, and this is the version that Lavington cited.[37] Yet, even with the help of Paris's chronicle, the analogy was tricky to sustain. First, it required a movement away from seeing the mendicants as an integral part of the medieval church – something Lavington and Green also wanted to stress – in order to present their behaviour as a breach with working conventions. Second, it required a wilful misreading of Paris's chronicle, which neither flattered the parochial clergy nor presented them as the primary victims of mendicant malpractice.

In truth, Paris was heir to a historiographical tradition at the monastery of St Albans which was deeply ambiguous about the role of the clergy. The work of his predecessor, Roger of Wendover (d. 1236), was full of criticism of secular priests, which Paris copied into his work before adding his own accounts. The full extent of the St Albans reports of clerical malpractice cannot be detailed here, but for the years 1204 to 1234 alone priests were variously accused of carelessly handling a miraculous image of the Virgin, doing homage to the devil and incorrectly excommunicating villagers.[38] In short, Paris's chronicles did not present England as administered by a well-meaning and intelligent class of priests comparable to the image of the parish clergy in the eighteenth century put forward by the anti-Methodists. For Paris, the main victims of mendicant wandering were not parish priests but older monastic orders like his own. Paris described – at length – the usurpation of monastic rights in Bury St Edmunds (1258), Dunstable (1259) and Scarborough (1239 onwards), where the mendicants were 'despising the authentic orders which were instituted by the holy fathers St Benedict and St Augustine ... They look upon the Cistercian monks as clownish, harmless, half-bred ... and the monks of the black order [the Benedictines] as proud'.[39] Unsurprisingly, Lavington and Green did not

---

37 Matthew Paris, *Historia Major*, ed. W. Wats (London, 1640). As this is the version of the text that Lavington used, it, rather than the modern editions, will be cited below.

38 Paris, *Historia Major*, 211, 407, 408. An English translation of these passages can be found in Roger of Wendover, *Flowers of History*, transl. J. A. Giles, 2 vols (London, 1849), 2: 212, 599, 600.

39 Paris, *Historia Major*, 967–8; 986; 611–12; idem, *English History from the Year 1235–1275*, transl. J. A. Giles, 3 vols, (London, 1889), 3: 278, 324–5, 1: 247.

repeat Paris's concern about the impact of the mendicants on the monastic orders. Although some elements of Paris's description of the friars' relationship with the secular clergy (dating from 1246) were faithfully translated by Lavington, some phrases were creative embellishments. Such phrases as 'established clergy' and 'proper pastors', for example, did not accurately render Paris's Latin into English.[40]

EARLY METHODIST MEDIEVALISM

It goes without saying that eighteenth-century Methodists did not recognize the medieval comparisons drawn in these polemical accounts. The early Methodists were, in fact, very sensitive to accusations of popery. As John Walsh has shown, persecution of Catholics and Methodists was linked and the movement had to respond to sporadic rumours that the Wesleys, from a high church background themselves, had been bribed by the Spanish to raise an army in England.[41] As a result, early Methodist attacks on Catholicism could be as vicious as those of any other Protestant grouping, and the lack of sympathy shown by John Wesley to recent Catholic history in Ireland has been well documented.[42] However, the early Methodist reaction to the medieval past should be viewed in a more nuanced way than their attacks on contemporary Catholicism might suggest, for two reasons. First, there is the increasingly well documented and contested relationship between Wesley's theology and that of the medieval mystics.[43] This is outside the parameters of this essay, but adds a further layer to early Methodist medievalism. Second, there is the early Methodist response to the history of medieval heresy, which we shall explore with reference to John Wesley's Concise Ecclesiastical History (1781).[44]

[40] Lavington, Enthusiasm, 1: 169; Paris, Historia Major, 693–5; Paris, English History, 2: 135–40.

[41] John Walsh, 'Methodism and the Mob', in G. J. Cuming and D. Baker, ed., Popular Belief and Practice, SCH 8 (Cambridge, 1972), 213–27.

[42] See Colin Haydon, Anti-Catholicism in Eighteenth-Century England (Manchester, 1993), 65; Ward, 'Was there a Methodist Evangelistic Strategy?', 295–6.

[43] Jean Orcibal, 'The Theological Originality of John Wesley and Continental Spirituality', in Rupert Davies, A. Raymond George and Gordon Rupp, eds, A History of the Methodist Church in Great Britain, 4 vols (London, 1965–88), 1: 83–111; John Munsey Turner, 'Methodism, Roman Catholicism and the Middle Ages', One in Christ 38 (2003), 47–70; Gwang Seok Oh, John Wesley's Ecclesiology, 24–9.

[44] John Wesley, A Concise Ecclesiastical History, 4 vols (London, 1781).

Wesley's response to medieval heresy was complex. On one hand, it built on an established Protestant historiography that portrayed medieval heretics as persecuted proto-Reformers.[45] It seemed natural for Wesley to enhance this narrative to remind his detractors of the persecution of his own movement by the dominant church of the day. Equally, however, Wesley did not want to add fuel to the fire; his supporters were often labelled 'heretics' and his work betrays a marked sensitivity when dealing with elements of the past that reflected his movement's own position too acutely: 'heresy' was a loaded term for eighteenth-century Methodists. Responding to an outbreak of anti-Methodist violence in Exeter, an anonymous pamphleteer summed up their frustration:

> as to the charge of heresy and nonsense – give me leave to say, as to heresy it is a foolish and nonsensical word; and has been always made to signify any opinion contrary to that of angry fiery bigots. Thus all parties are hereticks to each other. At Rome, a Protestant is a heretick, in England a Roman Catholic is a heretick: And with an ignorant, hot, fiery Churchman a Methodist or Presbyterian is a heretick. Therefore, among all honest and wise men, Heresy is a foolish and non-sensical word …[46]

Wesley demonstrated a similar sensitivity when he dealt with the history of heresy in his *Concise Ecclesiastical History*. This four-volume history was a redaction of the work of the German Lutheran, John Lorenz von Mosheim (1693–1755), whose *Ecclesiastical History* was known to Wesley through a translation by Archibald Maclaine (1722–1804), published in 1765.[47] By looking at the editorial decisions Wesley made in regard to the composition of his work it is possible to gain an understanding of how he viewed the comparative value of particular areas of church history. A pattern first starts to emerge when one looks at Wesley's introduction to the text, where he notes that 'nine parts out of ten of what relates to the

---

[45] Euan Cameron, 'Medieval Heretics as Protestant Martyrs', in Diana Wood, ed., *Martyrs and Martyrologies*, SCH 30 (Oxford, 1993), 185–207.

[46] Anon., *A Brief Account of the Late Persecution and Barbarous Usage of the Methodists at Exeter* (Exeter, 1746), 36.

[47] John Lorenz von Mosheim, *Institutiones Historiae Ecclesiasticae* (1726); ET by Archibald Maclaine, *An Ecclesiastical History, Antient and Modern, from the Birth of Christ to the Beginning of the Present Century*, 2 vols (London, 1765).

heresies' was not edifying; they 'were the mere visions of senseless or self-conceited men ... It is not worth our while now to collect into one heap all the rubbish of seventeen hundred years'.[48] Tellingly, the only sentence omitted from Mosheim's introduction is a definition of heresy, which could easily have applied to Wesley and his followers, 'as denoting a person, who, either directly or indirectly, has been the occasion of exciting divisions and dissensions among Christians'.[49]

Yet it is also worth looking at the early Methodists' more sympathetic reaction to the heresies that Wesley copied into his *Ecclesiastical History*. Like many Protestants, Wesley looked back to Lollardy and Wycliffe, but this history could also be given a Methodist twist. In reply to Lavington's *Enthusiasm*, Wesley tried to cast the Anglican bishop in the light of the persecuting late medieval Catholic Church: 'would it be a satisfaction to his lordship if national persecution were to return? Does your lordship desire to revive the old law *De Haeretico Comburendo* [1401]?'[50] In a very different way, the Methodist preacher Joseph Sutcliffe (1762–1856) built on Protestant historiography about the medieval Piedmont Waldensians in his attempt to find historical precedents for Methodist prayer meetings.[51] Unsurprisingly, the persecutions of the Lollards and the Waldensians both featured in Wesley's history of the church.

Similarly, like many Protestant historians, Wesley demonstrated a profound sympathy with the Albigensians of Languedoc, victims of a twenty-year crusade in the thirteenth century (1209–29).[52] They

---

48 Wesley, *Ecclesiastical History*, 1: v.

49 Mosheim, *Ecclesiastical History*, transl. Maclaine, 1: xxiv.

50 John Wesley, *A Second Letter to the Author of Enthusiasm of Methodists and Papists Compared* (London, 1751), ix. Wesley's debates with Catholics about Wycliffe and the Council of Constance (1414–18) have occasioned considerable historical discussion: David Butler, *Methodists and Papists* (London, 1995), 60–9.

51 Joseph Sutcliffe, *The Mutual Communion of the Saints Exemplified* (London, 1796), 11–13. Sutcliffe's analysis relied on acceptance of the work of the seventeenth-century Waldensian pastor John Leger, whose mis-dating of several documents gave the Waldensians a doctrinally Reformed medieval past. The true picture was more complicated, and Euan Cameron has noted how 'slender' the evidence for this Protestant historiography actually is: Euan Cameron, *Waldenses: Rejections of Holy Church in Medieval Europe* (Oxford, 2000), 263, 129 respectively.

52 Wesley, *Ecclesiastical History*, 2: 272–9. The 'execrable crusades against the Albigensians' also featured in another of Wesley's works: *Popery Calmly Considered* (London, 1779), 23.

were 'persons of eminent piety and zeal for genuine Christianity
... ranked [as] heretics, merely on account of their opposing the
vicious practices and the insolent tyranny of the priesthood, and
their treating with derision that motley spectacle of superstition
that was supported by public authority'.[53] Mosheim's one note of
caution – that they thought church-building superstitious – was
'doubted' by Wesley in a rare footnote.[54] By comparing Mosheim
and Wesley it is possible to see the process by which the Albigensians' distinctive beliefs were watered down or ignored in order to
make them a more palatable precedent.[55]

This was in line with the genuine Protestant belief that Catholic
accusations against the Albigensians were untrue – a belief not
comprehensively challenged until the nineteenth century – but it
is interesting that the material on medieval heretics marked one
of Wesley's most significant departures from his source text (which
was, after all, compiled by a German Lutheran).[56] He removed the
details about the heresy of Leutard whose 'disciples made a part
of the sect that was afterwards known in France under the name
Albigenses'.[57] The description of the Manichaeans and Paulists
who fled to France in the eleventh century and became known as
'the Albigenses' was also deleted.[58] Finally, it is possible to detect
a contemporary context to Wesley's sympathy in his rendering of
Mosheim's summary of the Albigensian crusade. Mosheim wrote:
'thus ended a civil war, of which religion had been partly the

53   Wesley, *Ecclesiastical History*, 2: 209.
54   Ibid. 211.
55   A similar pattern of editorial behaviour can be noted in Wesley's treatment of
the Counter-Reformation French aristocrat Gaston de Renty: Eamon Duffy, 'Wesley
and the Counter-Reformation', in Jane Garnett and Colin Matthew, eds, *Revival and
Religion since 1700: Essays for John Walsh* (London, 1993), 1–19, esp. 11–12. Wesley was
not the only Protestant historian to use these tactics when it came to the Cathars or
Albigensians: Cameron, 'Medieval Heretics', 206.
56   C. Schmidt, *Histoire et doctrine de la secte des Cathares ou Albigeois*, 2 vols (Paris
/ Geneva, 1848–9). See Bernard Hamilton, 'The Legacy of Charles Schmidt to the
Study of Christian Dualism', *JMedH* 24 (1998), 191–294.
57   Mosheim, *Ecclesiastical History*, transl. Maclaine, 1: 464; missing from Wesley,
Ecclesiastical History, 2: 84. See Richard Landes, 'The Birth of Heresy: A Millennial
Phenomenon', *JRH* 24 (2000), 26–43.
58   Mosheim, *Ecclesiastical History*, transl. Maclaine, 1: 545; missing from Wesley,
Ecclesiastical History, 2: 151. Forty years later another Protestant historian who was
engaged in a far more radical redaction of Mosheim's work did not hesitate to retain
this detail: Charles Trelawney Collins, *A Summary of Mosheim's Ecclesiastical History*, 2
vols (London, 1822), 1: 294.

cause and partly the pretext and which[,] in its consequences, was highly profitable both to the kings of France and to the Roman pontiffs'.[59] Wesley's alteration is subtle, but it is tempting to see it in the light of the accusations that his own order reflected the Cromwellian enthusiasm of the seventeenth century: 'And thus ended a war which in its consequences was highly profitable both to the kings of France and to the Roman pontiffs'.[60] The war was no longer civil and religion was no longer its cause.

That there was a medieval element to both the early Methodist and anti-Methodist polemics of the late eighteenth century has generally been overlooked by historians. Yet opening up the medieval past was rhetorically difficult for both sides. By attacking the Methodists on the grounds of their similarity to medieval Catholics, Anglican polemicists risked the counter-argument that it was they who were behaving like the persecuting Roman church of the Middle Ages. But in arguing that they were the true heirs of the noble medieval heretics, Wesley and his followers had to avoid the impression that they wanted to create political unrest and had fully to buy into the prevailing idea that the Albigensians and Waldensians had been doctrinally smeared by European Catholics. For the historian observing these debates it would be easy to make the accusation that the authors under discussion deliberately manipulated and distorted religious history in the service of confessional polemic. To avoid such a simplistic analysis is to understand that for John Wesley, Thomas Green and George Lavington historical truth was informed by religious identity and shaped by the turbulence of England's recent past.

University of Exeter

---

59   Mosheim, *Ecclesiastical History*, transl. Maclaine, 1: 701.
60   Wesley, *Ecclesiastical History*, 2: 279.

REPRESENTING AND MISREPRESENTING THE HISTORY OF PURITANISM IN EIGHTEENTH-CENTURY ENGLAND[*]

by ROBERT G. INGRAM

An Englishman living during the mid-eighteenth century would have known that his country had been, at least since the late sixteenth century, a decidedly and, for the long-foreseeable future, an unalterably Protestant nation. But what sort of Protestant nation? One that needed a legally established church? And, if so, what sort of church should that church as established by law be? Did it, for instance, necessarily require a certain kind of church government? In its relation to the English state, did the church need to be the senior, equal or junior partner? And what rights, if any, should those not conforming to the established church have? These were vexing questions, and the mid-seventeenth-century civil wars had mostly been an intra-Protestant fight over them. Yet neither those internecine religio-political wars nor the subsequent political revolution of the late seventeenth century had resolved definitively any of the fundamental questions about church and state raised originally by the sixteenth-century religious Reformations. Those who had lived through the Sacheverell crisis, the Bangorian controversy or the fiercely anti-clerical 1730s recognized this all too well: historians, alas, have not.

The English Reformation and the bloody events it spawned during the seventeenth century haunted the eighteenth-century English. They, to borrow John Pocock's evocative description, 'lived with the memory of the civil wars as a nightmare from which [they were] struggling to awake, or if you prefer, to go to sleep again'.[1] For many in eighteenth-century England, the past was not dead; it was not even past. And forgetting, memorializing, manipulating, refashioning and taming that not-past was

[*] I thank Bill Gibson, Tony Claydon, Jeremy Gregory, Bill Bulman, Jason Peacey, Noah Millstone and Alex Barber for their advice. Unless otherwise noted, the place of publication is London.
[1] J. G. A. Pocock, 'Within the Margins: Definitions of Orthodoxy', in Roger D. Lund, ed., *The Margins of Orthodoxy: Heterodox Writing and Cultural Response, 1660–1750* (Cambridge, 1995), 33–53, at 38.

the eighteenth-century's great project. This article examines how eighteenth-century English historians made sense of their nation's religious and political history and, more importantly, to what end they made sense of it. It approaches the subject by way of the debate over Daniel Neal's four-volume *History of the Puritans* (1732–8). Neal (1678–1743) was a prominent London Dissenting minister and a prolific historian of Anglo-American religious Nonconformity, and the debate which his *History of the Puritans* initiated was one which dealt explicitly with the Reformation's legacy.[2] It reveals quite clearly the practical political significance which both sides saw in printed polemical engagement during the mid-eighteenth century. But the Neal debate was not anomalous in grappling with the consequences of the hugely disruptive sixteenth-century religious Reformations. Indeed, scratch not that far beneath the surface of many of the eighteenth century's most spirited polemical engagements prior to the American Revolution and one finds lurking there the Reformation and its progeny.

Neal's *History*, he promised, would 'preserve the Memory of those great and good Men among the Reformers, for attempting a further Reformation of its Discipline and Ceremonies; and ... account for the Rise and Progress of that Separation from the National Establishment which subsists to this Day'.[3] His study of English puritanism proved to be the most influential history of its subject written during the eighteenth century, and some still commend it for its accuracy.[4] Yet, as his own description suggests, Neal's was a polemical history with a practical purpose, and its publication spawned a small debate that drew into the fray some of the established Church of England's most prominent figures. None of the participants in that debate, of course, would have described their own works as polemical history: on the contrary, they repeatedly – incessantly – described themselves as 'impartial' or 'disinterested' historians, untainted by 'party principles'. That self-description, though, hints at the ultimate purpose of their historical scholarship – mobilization. For history-writing during

---

[2] For a brief survey of Daniel Neal's life and career, see *ODNB*, *s.n.* 'Neal, Daniel (1678–1743)'.

[3] Daniel Neal, *The History of the Puritans, or Protestant non-conformists*, 4 vols (1732–8), 1: iii.

[4] John Seed, *Dissenting Histories* (Edinburgh, 2008), 41; Laird Okie, 'Daniel Neal and the "Puritan Revolution"', *ChH* 55 (1986), 456–67, at 456.

this period was not an end in itself, but a means to an end: its aims were practical, not theoretical. Achieving those ends required historians to treat and present evidence in ways that would shift opinion in their favour. And while metaphysical debate during the period might mostly have been about logical exactitude, at the primary site of eighteenth-century polemical divinity – historical scholarship – debate was usually about using and misusing, representing and misrepresenting the past for present-day political purposes. The polemical historian did not so much aim to be right as to convince his audience that he was right.

Yet it would be wrong to suggest that polemical historians were cynics or casuists – much less were they relativists – who intentionally distorted the truth. Rather they believed in the truth of their cause and in the need to do their utmost to promote or defend that cause. Put another way, eighteenth-century polemical historians conceived of themselves, to use one of their own recurring metaphors, as fighting a kind of 'warfare on earth', one whose origins stretched back, at the very least, to the Reformation. And the point of that war was to win it. As such, authors thought very carefully about what they should include or exclude from their works, who would buy their books or pamphlets, and what they hoped to achieve by publishing them. If we are to understand the war which they believed they were fighting, we need, then, to understand their aims and their rules of engagement. All this might seem to state the obvious. But in historiographical terms it is to sail between the Scylla of Knights and the Charybdis of Pocock, between those who argue increasingly forthrightly that late seventeenth- and early eighteenth-century print culture made debates about the truth relativistic and those who argue for situating works in their various contexts, which in practice means situating them primarily within their various linguistic contexts.[5]

So, why did Daniel Neal publish his *History of the Puritans* when he published it? And what did he want it to do? The context is clear. Neal, who had previously published a two-volume *History of New England* (1720), wrote his *History of the Puritans* within the

---

⁵ See, e.g., Mark Knights, 'Public politics in England c.1675–c.1715', in Nicholas Tyacke, ed., *The English Revolution c.1590–1720* (Manchester, 2007), 169–84; J. G. A. Pocock, 'Historiography as a Form of Political Thought', *History of European Ideas* 37 (2011), 1–6.

context of the fiercely anti-clerical 1730s; his was one of the most prominent voices in the Dissenting campaign for greater religious liberties. The push for repeal in the early 1730s rode a cresting wave of anti-clericalism, with the Parliament of 1727–34 taking on something of the character of the Reformation Parliaments of the 1530s. Beginning in 1730, the Church of England faced a series of anti-clerical bills in the House of Commons, a body filled with Robert Walpole's supporters. From the perspective of Edmund Gibson, the chief architect of the church-Whig alliance and the man commonly known as Walpole's 'Pope', Walpole lacked the conviction, though not the power, to stop these blatant attacks on the church's legal privileges.[6]

From the early 1730s, there also emerged a highly organized campaign by Dissenters to repeal the Test and Corporation Acts, which together deprived Dissenters of full civil liberties by limiting public office-holding to religious conformists.[7] In addition to the establishment in 1732 of a board of Protestant Dissenting Deputies whose aim was 'to apply for a Repeal of the Test and Corporation Acts', a coordinated publishing campaign began to highlight the injustice of these acts. That Dissenting print campaign for repeal, of which Neal's work was a self-conscious part, had two central strands, each of which reinforced the other. Firstly, Dissenting

---

[6]   Edmund Gibson (*c*.1669–1748) served as bishop of London 1723–48, and was the clerical architect of the church-Whig alliance under Sir Robert Walpole's administration. His aim was to promote to ecclesiastical office those who were both Walpolean loyalists and theologically orthodox: Stephen Taylor, 'Whigs, Tories and Anticlericalism: Ecclesiastical Courts Legislation in 1733', *PH* 19 (2000), 329–55; Norman Sykes, *Edmund Gibson* (Oxford, 1926), 149–61. During the eighteenth century *orthodoxy* and *orthodox* were, at once, recognizable analytical categories and contested labels. On the one hand, both friend and foe reckoned that the *orthodox* accepted the Nicene and Athanasian Creeds, the Church of England's episcopal ecclesiology and the need for penal laws against religious Nonconformists. Where the orthodox and their opponents disagreed was over whether orthodoxy was true and promoted social and political order or whether it was crypto-popish and persecutory. On eighteenth-century orthodoxy, see Pocock, 'Within the Margins', 33–53; Robert G. Ingram, '"The Weight of Historical Evidence": Conyers Middleton and the Eighteenth-Century Miracles Debate', in William Gibson and Robert Cornwall, eds, *Religion, Politics and Dissent, 1660–1832* (Aldershot, 2010), 85–109; idem, *Religion, Reform and Modernity in the Eighteenth Century: Thomas Secker and the Church of England* (Woodbridge, 2007), esp. 1–18, 71–113.

[7]   Richard Burgess Barlow, *Citizenship and Conscience: A Study in the Theory and Practice of Religious Toleration in England during the Eighteenth Century* (Philadelphia, PA, 1962), esp. 15–97.

polemicists argued that the established Church of England was 'popish' because it had a view of religious authority that was anathema to 'consistent Protestantism'.[8] Rather than countenance the right of private judgement – a right that, Dissenters insisted, was both natural and inherent to any true religion – orthodox churchmen countered that any civil state worth its name must be capable of establishing a religion and, hence, of trumping such 'natural rights' as that of private judgement.[9] Allied to the argument for the right of private judgement was the argument from history. Despite the legal protection afforded by toleration since the Glorious Revolution, Dissenters had nonetheless suffered – and continued to suffer – from civil disabilities and occasional, but no less real, petty ignominies.[10] They also, perhaps more importantly, had a vivid collective memory of the abuses with which their religious forebears had been afflicted during the sixteenth and seventeenth centuries, abuses propagated by the established church, abuses which, by direct implication, undermined the credibility of that very same established church in the early 1730s.[11]

That collective Dissenting memory of mistreatment at the hands of established churchmen, no less than the antinomies of 'Protestant popery' and 'consistent Protestantism', had, however, been consciously and carefully built.[12] Dissenting clerical historians such as Richard Baxter and Edmund Calamy had written polemical histories, ones which aimed at accuracy, but accuracy in the service of a greater cause. When Calamy famously detailed the nearly two thousand ministers ejected in 1662, for instance, he was simultaneously preserving a record of their ejections, factually rebutting the aspersions of Samuel Parker, and constructing a

---

[8] Andrew Thompson, 'Popery, Politics and Private Judgment in Early Hanoverian Britain', *HistJ* 45 (2002), 333–56; idem, 'Contesting the Test Act: Parliament and the Public in the 1730s', *PH* 24 (2005), 58–70.

[9] Edmund Gibson, *The dispute adjusted* (Dublin, 1733), 8–10.

[10] David Wykes, '"So bitterly censur'd and revil'd": Religious Dissent and Relations with the Church of England after the Toleration Act', in Richard Bonney and David Trim, eds, *Persecution and Pluralism* (Oxford, 2006), 294–314.

[11] See esp. James E. Bradley, 'Anti-Catholicism as Anglican Anticlericalism: Nonconformity and the Ideological Origins of Radical Disaffection', in Nigel Aston and Matthew Cragoe, eds, *Anticlericalism in Britain, c.1500–1914* (Stroud, 2000), 67–92.

[12] Peter Lake, 'Antipopery: The Structure of a Prejudice', in Richard Cust and Ann Hughes, eds, *Conflict in Early Stuart England* (1989), 72–106; Mark Knights, 'Occasional Conformity and the Representation of Dissent: Hypocrisy, Sincerity, Moderation, and Zeal', *PH* 24 (2005), 41–57.

Dissenting identity of 'an embattled minority who were victims of a historical injustice, martyrs for the principles of conscience and religious liberty'.[13] Neal aimed for similar results.[14] Consider, for instance, the very title of his work – *History of the Puritans, or Protestant Non-Conformists* – in which he equated puritanism and Dissent, giving a false, if appealing, coherence to both and at the same time providing a genealogy for eighteenth-century Dissent that was problematic at best.[15] Likewise, connecting his four volumes was a narrative spine which recounted the persecution of puritans and which cast them as the authentic guarantors of Christian liberty. Moreover, for Neal the persecutory rot had set into the Church of England at the time of the Elizabethan religious settlement: rather than being the queen who saved England from popery, Elizabeth became, in Neal's hands, the monarch who legally established an ecclesiology and liturgy that was crypto-popish. While Neal's argument might not have been wholly at peace with its evidence, it was nevertheless designed to appeal to the broadest audience possible, including those critics of 'priest-craft' who were not themselves Protestant Dissenters.

Neal's was not a lone Dissenting voice on these issues. His argument for the relatively seamless evolution of sixteenth-century puritanism into post-revolutionary Dissent mirrored a larger movement among Protestant Dissenters in the early 1730s to paper over their denominational differences and band together in organizations such as the Protestant Dissenting Deputies to work for repeal of the Test and Corporation Acts.[16] And, just as Neal

---

13 John Seed, 'History and Narrative Identity: Religious Dissent and the Politics of Memory in Eighteenth-Century England', *JBS* 44 (2005), 46–63, at 61; see also David L. Wykes, '"To let the memory of these men dye is injurious to posterity": Edmund Calamy's *Account* of the Ejected Ministers', in R. N. Swanson, ed., *The Church Retrospective*, SCH 33 (Woodbridge, 1997), 379–92. Samuel Parker, bishop of Oxford under James II, was an indefatigable opponent of religious toleration and a prolific anti-Nonconformist polemicist of the late seventeenth century: *ODNB*, *s.n.* 'Parker, Samuel (1640–1688)'.

14 Neal had originally intended to collaborate with John Evans (1679/80–1730) to write a comprehensive history of English Protestant Nonconformity, with Evans covering the period until 1640 and Neal picking up the story from there. Evans's declining health during the late 1720s and his death in 1730 forced Neal to write the entire work himself.

15 Peter Lake, 'The Historiography of Puritanism', in John Coffey and Paul Lim, eds, *The Cambridge Companion to Puritanism* (Cambridge, 2008), 346–71.

16 James E. Bradley, 'The Public, Parliament and the Protestant Dissenting Depu-

had emphasized the persecution of puritans by 'popish Protestants', so too were other Dissenting historians, like Samuel Chandler, hammering home that the Church of Rome – and, by implication, the Church of England – had a long history of persecution.[17] Likewise, Neal joined with Chandler and others in 1734–5 to deliver a set of lectures at London's Salters' Hall on the iniquity of popery. Neal's contribution addressed the papacy's 'usurpation' of civil and religious authority and concluded with a dig at Archbishop Laud for having undermined the English 'battle' against 'the Devil' and the 'foreign tyrant' who tempted the English people to abandon their allegiance to the English Crown.[18] Neal left it to his readers to draw the lines of connection between Laud and his eighteenth-century clerical successors.

Yet, if mid-eighteenth-century Dissenters rallied around a shared history of persecution, so too did many orthodox churchmen also collectively remember past abuse at the hands of puritans. They too were haunted by the seventeenth century. The traumatic events of that century were recollected and given order and meaning by polemical historians such as Peter Heylyn, Jeremy Collier and John Walker, who told the story of the political and religious anarchy unleashed by puritans in the mid-seventeenth century. These orthodox historians likewise wrote in the service of a greater cause. When Walker published his *Sufferings of the clergy of the Church of England* (1714), for instance, he was doing so in an era when many claimed that the church was 'in danger'; his work provided a martyrology offering evidence that the Church of England had always been in danger from the very people held up for admiration by Baxter, Calamy and other Dissenting historians.[19]

If the Dissenting political and polemical campaign against the Test and Corporation Acts from the 1730s was coordinated, so too were the political and polemical responses of orthodox churchmen. The London clerical polemicist William Webster (1689–1758) and

---

ties, 1732–1740', *PH* 24 (2005), 71–90.

[17] Samuel Chandler, Introduction to Philippus van Limborch, *The history of the Inquisition*, 2 vols in 1 (1731), 1: 1–125. Chandler would later publish *The history of persecution* (1736), to which William Berriman and Zachary Grey responded at length; see, e.g., Zachary Grey, *An examination of … Chandler's History of persecution* (1736).

[18] Daniel Neal, *The supremacy of St. Peter* (1735), esp. 39–40.

[19] Matthew Neufeld, 'The Politics of Anglican Martyrdom: Letters to John Walker, 1704–1705', *JEH* 62 (2011), 491–514.

Edmund Gibson, in particular, conceived the initial orthodox response to Neal's historical project. At the time when Neal published the first instalment of his *History of the Puritans* in the winter of 1732, Webster was planning the commencement of his hyper-orthodox *Weekly Miscellany*, a newspaper he published pseudonymously for nearly a decade as 'Richard Hooker of the Inner Temple'.[20] Webster had long held an interest in sixteenth- and seventeenth-century English history, his first publication being an introduction to Thomas Skinner's life of George Monck. It was Webster who seems to have introduced Zachary Grey to Gibson.[21] A Bedfordshire rector, Cambridge resident, protégé of Daniel Waterland and sometime researcher for John Walker, Grey had, since the early 1720s, written reams of polemical histories in response to John Oldmixon and other Dissenting historians. His conclusions rested on his undeniable mastery of early modern English printed sources, to which he had access both in Cambridge's University Library and in his own substantial collection. But what distinguished Grey's work from the early 1730s onwards was the incredibly rich range of archival material on which he drew in his books. Grey had unfettered access to John Nalson's famous manuscripts, which included transcriptions of original documents and unreturned state papers. The Nalson manuscripts were at that time owned by Grey's good friend Philip Williams, fellow and later president of St John's College, Cambridge.[22] In an age when historians were increasingly expected to adduce factual evidence to bolster their claims, Grey's access to the Nalson cache proved a polemical boon. In Grey, Gibson had someone who was both a committed orthodox polemicist and a first-rate researcher. Gibson would, in turn, pass Grey's research materials about the history of

---

[20] On Webster, see *ODNB*, *s.n.* 'Webster, William (1689–1758)'; C. John Sommerville, *The News Revolution in England* (Oxford, 1996), 142; Michael Harris, *London Newspapers in the Age of Walpole:: A Study of the Origins of the Modern English Press* (Cranbury, NJ, 1987), 183–4. Webster's pseudonym evoked the sixteenth-century English theorist of the Church of England's purported *via media* between Rome and Geneva: cf. Diarmaid MacCulloch, 'Richard Hooker's Reputation', *EHR* 117 (2002), 773–812.

[21] Stephen Taylor, '"Dr. Codex" and the Whig "Pope": Edmund Gibson, Bishop of Lincoln and London, 1716–1748', in Richard W. Davis, ed., *Lords of Parliament* (Stanford, CA, 1995), 9–27, esp. 22–7.

[22] For Williams's possession of the Nalson collection, see London, BL, Add. MS 5841, fol. 4v.

English puritanism to Isaac Maddox, Queen Caroline's clerk of the closet. Among those materials was Grey's heavily annotated interleaved edition of Neal's *History of the Puritans*, which survives today in the library of St John's College, Cambridge.[23] Gibson's choice of his protégé Maddox to respond to Neal was astute since Maddox was himself a former Dissenter who had studied at the University of Edinburgh before returning to England and conforming to the established church there in the early 1720s. Maddox was one of the two dozen or so Dissenting apostates whom Calamy lamented losing to the Church of England, noting that they 'were, generally, persons of sobriety and unblemished character'.[24] So Grey provided the ordnance; Maddox chose, at least initially, where to lob it.

Maddox's *A vindication of the government, doctrine, and worship of the Church of England* (1733) attacked the foundations of the argument of Neal's first volume and the credibility of his evidence in order to make an argument that had unmistakable contemporary resonance. (Readers of Webster's *Weekly Miscellany* also received a distilled version of Maddox's argument in a front-page story around the same time as Maddox's book appeared, so his views had popular as well as scholarly impact.)[25] Maddox opened his book by blaming schism for popery's rise during Elizabeth I's reign: popery, he argued, thrived thanks to Protestant disunity, disunity that arose from Dissenters' undue attention to the 'external and disputed Parts of Religion, in Place of true Doctrine and real Goodness'.[26] Maddox's counter-history of the puritans highlighted puritan intolerance and the inherently schismatic tendencies of non-conforming Protestants from the very beginnings of the Reformation. Elizabeth I, he insisted, had inherited a 'universally Popish' nation, and she was, from her reign's very outset, beset by popish threats at home and from abroad.[27] In crafting her reli-

---

[23]   Cambridge, St John's College, shelfmarks Q.13.5, 7–9, 10. Gibson described the Grey materials that he forwarded from Grey via Webster to Maddox as 'Observations upon Mr. Neal's History, and lately, the Book relating to it': London, LPL, MS 2029, fol. 24: Gibson to Grey, [September 1732].

[24]   Edmund Calamy, *Historical Account of my own life*, ed. John Towill Rutt, 2 vols (1830), 2: 503–5.

[25]   *Weekly Miscellany*, no. 24 (26 May 1733).

[26]   Isaac Maddox, *A vindication of the government, doctrine, and worship of the Church of England* (1733), 4.

[27]   Ibid. 17.

gious settlement Elizabeth had needed to lure in papists while at the same time creating a church that would comprehend within it 'the greatest Number of Protestants'.[28] Yet far from all English Protestants' helping and supporting the young queen in the face of the popish menace, the puritans, especially those who had spent their Marian exile in Geneva, would not relent until the 'Genevan Plan' had been established in England, despite the fact that episcopal ecclesiology had both biblical and primitive precedents and was, in Maddox's words, the 'happy medium between Calvinists and Lutherans'.[29] Indeed, Maddox went even further, insisting that it was the puritans who were actually persecutory, noting that they had even hounded John Foxe and his son for being insufficiently Protestant.[30] Moreover, Elizabethan puritans were profoundly insincere, since they dubbed 'every thing ... Popery which [they] did not relish'.[31] That insincerity extended to their political theology, for Maddox hammered home the idea that Neal had cherry-picked his evidence regarding puritan loyalism. ' 'Twas easier for him to celebrate their Loyalty, when he thus carefully omitted all Instances of the Contrary', Maddox contended. Indeed Elizabethan puritans were actually committed anti-monarchists: 'The State ... was to be reduced to the same Form. Their comitial, provincial, or national Assemblies, the whole frame of their Church Government was perfectly Popular or Republican.'[32] Maddox left it to his readers to draw the lines of connection between the Elizabethan puritan crypto-republicans and their eighteenth-century Dissenting descendants.

Maddox's rebuttal of Neal primarily took the form of a thematic narrative. In order to convince his readers that he was treating Neal's argument fairly, he pre-emptively agreed only to cite historians of whom Neal approved (Thomas Fuller, for instance) and not to bring to bear evidence from those of whom he disapproved (Heylyn and Collier, for instance).[33] While the body of Maddox's book proceeded thematically, his 163-page appendix took the form of the line-by-line rebuttal favoured by many at the time.

---

28 Ibid. 32.
29 Ibid. 105.
30 Ibid. 140.
31 Ibid. 120, 124.
32 Ibid. 210.
33 Ibid. 12, 251.

That the appendix's tone – biting, sarcastic, ridiculing, unrelenting – differed from the main body is unsurprising since the appendix was little more than a cleaned-up cut-and-paste of the marginalia from Grey's annotated interleaved edition of Neal's work.[34]

Why would Edmund Gibson not simply have asked Grey to respond to Neal's first volume? The probable answer is not just that Grey was a first-rate researcher but a fourth-rate writer, but also that Grey habitually wrote not to convince waverers but to steel true believers. From Gibson's perspective this approach would have become increasingly unattractive as the 1730s wore on and Parliament took up anti-clerical measures such as the Ecclesiastical Courts Bill, the Mortmain Act and the Quakers' Tithe Bill.

Not only did Gibson not tap Grey to respond to Neal in 1732; Maddox did not even acknowledge Grey's assistance to him, something which angered the combustible Webster. 'I have not sent your MS to Maddocks', he wrote to Grey upon the appearance of Neal's second volume of the *History of the Puritans*. 'A Parcel of Scrubs! Why should we help them to Credit, when they will neither return the Civility, nor own it. They did not so much as acknowledge your Assistance.' Instead, urged Webster, 'Your MS, with a Preface, will make a Vol[ume]'.[35] London's booksellers, as it would turn out, might have offered conflicting advice. Even had Maddox properly thanked Grey for his research, Maddox's promotion to the episcopal bench in 1736 would have made him wary of engaging in a knock-down print battle with Neal. Sitting bishops – even seasoned polemical divines such as Thomas Sherlock or Benjamin Hoadly – tended to keep their powder dry, and when they did enter into the arena of public debate, they did so with weighty works such as Sherlock's *Tryal of the Witnesses* (1729) or Hoadly's *Plain Account* (1736). So from Gibson's perspective Daniel Neal was worth seeing off, but he was not worth Maddox sullying his reputation, especially in the midst of the febrile anti-clericalism of the 1730s.

Grey, though, had little to lose. He was who he was and would

---

34   Cambridge, St John's College, shelfmarks Q.13.5, 7–9, 10.
35   BL, Add. MS 5831, fol. 208, Webster to Grey, October [1735/6]; cf. ibid., fols 207–8, Webster to Grey, [1736], in which Webster asked for Grey's notes on the second volume of *History of the Puritans*, which had first appeared in mid-November 1735: *London Evening Post*, no. 1248 (15 November 1735).

never rise above his comfortable rectorship. To him, then, fell the orthodox job of refuting the last three volumes of Neal's *History of the Puritans*, with Gibson and Maddox urging him on from the sidelines.[36] In those refutations, he questioned Neal's very competence as a historian. Little escaped his notice, including Neal's use of 'MS' rather than 'MSS' to denote 'Manuscripts'.[37] More seriously, though, he accused Neal of being prejudicially selective with his evidence,[38] which helps to account for Grey's ostentatious appendices that provided full transcriptions of Nalson manuscript papers. Neal might, according to Grey, play hide-the-ball, but Grey, as he signalled to his readers, had nothing to hide.

Grey made his argument by way of the line-by-line format, taking the points with which he disagreed and rebutting them in sequence. The relentless – and, in Grey's case, wholly artless – litany of evidence was supposed to destroy Neal's credibility. Yet embedded within that litany was an argument which would have surprised no one familiar with Grey's anti-Dissenting outpourings from the 1720s. Throughout his three volumes, Grey hammered home the themes of Maddox's volume: Daniel Neal, the puritans he venerated, and the Protestant Dissenters who succeeded them were intolerant, schismatic and ruinous to the nation's political health. Without too much oversimplification, Grey's argument may be summarized thus: Wentworth good, Laud better, Charles I the best; Jacobean puritans bad, Caroline puritans worse, Oliver Cromwell the worst.

Whatever the merits of Grey's argument, his prosecution of it was, quite literally, unprofitable. In the summer of 1738, the nonjuror John Lindsay reported back to him that the London booksellers were refusing to print his third instalment:

> The truth is, that, after divers meetings and advances made towards the publication of your present work, when I had reason to think there was nothing more to do but to report to you the conclusion of a contract, no sooner did we come to the point, but I found, the taste of the times is such, that the

---

[36] BL, Add. MS 5831, fol. 157, Gibson to Grey, 24 March 1737. Maddox encouraged Grey to write a short synopsis of his three volumes in response to Neal: ibid., fols 165–6, Maddox to Grey, 15 April 1740.

[37] Zachary Grey, *An impartial examination of the third volume* (1737), 19.

[38] Zachary Grey, *An impartial examination of the second volume* (1736), 4, 404.

three former parts of the same work did not answer in trade; and therefore I have no hopes of dealing for it, unless you will print it at your own hazard.[39]

That the book eventually did appear in print seems to have been thanks to Grey promising the bookseller private subscriptions, and within a few months his friends were relaying reports back to him about their efforts to drum up subscribers for the new work and to peddle unsold volumes of his first two responses.[40] Even so, John Lewis would report in March 1739 that he was having trouble finding a copy of Grey's third refutation, since 'I believe no Bookseller will print them'.[41]

Why were booksellers reluctant to publish this work? Lewis's explanation turned on clerical habits. 'Our Clergy have something else to do: at Day, to hunt &c; & at night, to meet in Clubs, to drink & game 'till Midnight', he lamented to Grey, '& they who mind their Studies & their Cures, are treated with Sneer & Neglect, & their Company avoided.'[42] Lewis's explanation, appealing though it surely is to mainstream eighteenth-century historians, falls short of the evidence, for polemical divinity dominated eighteenth-century booksellers' catalogues, making up between one-quarter and one-third of all 'religious' titles (narrowly conceived); that percentage is likely to be significantly higher if we account for the fact that some titles which might not seem religious (histories, for example) were centrally concerned with such subjects as the history of the church. As Grey's experience itself shows, booksellers were unlikely to print what they could not sell: theirs was no public charity. Two other explanations, then, suggest why booksellers might have been initially loath to print Grey's third instalment. Firstly, his tendentious and, from our perspective, tedious line-by-line refutations of Neal compared poorly with the narrative histories that were becoming increasingly popular during the mid-eighteenth century. Perhaps more importantly, though, booksellers were unwilling to

---

[39] John Nichols, ed., *Literary Anecdotes of the Eighteenth Century* (1812), 1: 734, Lindsay to Grey, 20 July 1738.

[40] John Nichols, ed., *Illustrations of the Literary History of the Eighteenth Century* (1822), 4: 309–10, Thomas Doughty to Grey, 28 August 1738; BL, Add. MS 5831, fol. 175, Daniel Waterland to Grey, 12 January 1739.

[41] Ibid., fols 128–9, Lewis to Grey, 16 March 1739.

[42] Ibid.

flog polemical books in a one-sided fight. Maddox's *Vindication* (1733) had clearly irked Daniel Neal, eliciting from him a stand-alone refutation in which he protested that he had not, as Maddox had asserted, advocated the 'Geneva Plan' nor had he let off the Elizabethan puritans lightly for their own flaws.[43] In contrast, Neal produced no such response to any of Grey's volumes. Whether that was because Neal's health was declining rapidly, or whether he simply decided that ignoring was bliss, matters little. Either way, polemical divinity was premised on the idea of duelling polemicists: if one of the duellists refused to show up for the fight, so too were printers and booksellers likely to stay away. They, like the polemical divines they sometimes published, had a bottom-line goal. Acknowledging both of those bottom lines and accounting for them is essential if historians are properly to appreciate either the aims or the means by which eighteenth-century polemicists continued to fight England's long Reformation.

Ohio University

---

[43] Daniel Neal, *A review of the principal facts* (1734).

ARCHBISHOP TAIT, THE HUGUENOTS AND THE FRENCH CHURCH AT CANTERBURY

by ANDREW SPICER

Archibald Campbell Tait was enthroned as archbishop of Canterbury in February 1869. It was an inauspicious time to assume the primacy of the Church of England, which was riven by internal conflicts and religious differences. Furthermore, Gladstone had recently swept to power with the support of the Nonconformists. The new prime minister had a mandate to disestablish the Irish church and his political supporters sought to challenge the privileges and status of the Church of England. As primate, Tait attempted to defend the Church of England as the established church and restrict those parties that held particularly narrow and dogmatic beliefs, regardless of whether they were Evangelicals or Ritualists. The archbishop strove to straddle these religious differences and to achieve his aims through a policy of compromise and tolerance, but some of his actions served to cause further divisions within the Anglican church. Tait's efforts to restrict elaborate ceremonial and services through the Public Worship Regulation Act (1874) alienated the Ritualists, for example. Many more clergy were opposed to his concessions to Nonconformists in the Burials Bill (1877), which would have allowed them to be interred in parish churchyards.[1] Amidst the wider religious tensions and political conflicts that marked his primacy, the archbishop also took a close interest in the French Protestant Church at Canterbury, whose history he regarded as reflecting some important attributes of the Church of England, its past, and its current status in the world.

In 1860, Tait had commented in a parliamentary speech that 'in

---

[1] O. Chadwick, *The Victorian Church*, 2 vols (London, 1970), vol. 2; M.A. Crowther, *Church Embattled: Religious Controversy in Mid-Victorian England* (Newton Abbot, 1970), 13–39; G. I. T. Machin, *Politics and the Churches in Great Britain 1869 to 1921* (Oxford, 1987); P. T. Marsh, 'The Primate and the Prime Minister: Archbishop Tait, Gladstone and the National Church', *Victorian Studies* 9 (1965), 113–40; idem, *The Victorian Church in Decline: Archbishop Tait and the Church of England 1868–1882* (London, 1969); J. P. Parry, 'Religion and the Collapse of Gladstone's First Government, 1870–1874', *HistJ* 25 (1982), 71–101.

the centre of the metropolitan cathedral of Canterbury there was a place of worship which was occupied by French Protestants'.[2] *The Times* also drew attention to this historical survival in its report on the archbishop's enthronement:

> Conspicuous among the clergy was a French Protestant Minister who, in his black gown and fur collar, looked exactly like the old Huguenot divine and contrasted strangely with the sea of white [surplices] by which he was surrounded. It may be remembered that the Queen Elizabeth gave to the French and Flemish refugees who fled to England in 1561 [*sic*] permission to worship in the cathedral, and this privilege they still enjoy.[3]

Although an anomaly, the historical associations of the French Church appealed to Tait as it provided an important symbol of the past tolerance of the Church of England. During his primary visitation to Canterbury Cathedral, he spoke of 'the traditions of this place, which offered a sanctuary in time of danger to the persecuted Protestants of the Continent'.[4] The small community was also important because it demonstrated the links that the Anglican church had with Protestant churches overseas. It illustrated the 'historical connection' between French Protestantism and the cathedral and diocese of Canterbury.[5] It was the symbolism of the French Church and its history that led Tait to defend it from those who sought to dissolve the institution and redistribute its funds.

The archbishop's support for the French Church coincided with a growing interest during the mid-nineteenth century in the history of the Huguenot diaspora. This culminated in the commemoration of the bicentenary of the Revocation of the Edict of Nantes in October 1885, recalling Louis XIV's persecution of French Protestants and his abolition of the religious privileges granted to them at the end of the sixteenth-century wars of religion. These events also celebrated the economic and material contribution that Huguenot immigrants brought to the

---

2 *Hansard's Parliamentary Debates* (ser. 3), vol. 158, col. 125, 26 April 1860.
3 *The Times*, 5 February 1869.
4 A. C. Tait, *The Present Position of the Church of England* (London, 1873), 16.
5 A. C. Tait, *The Church of the Future* (London, 1880), 10.

countries where they settled during the 1680s.[6] Popular interest in their history had been stimulated by Giacomo Meyerbeer's opera *Les Huguenots*, first performed at Covent Garden in 1842, and by Sir John Everett Millais's painting *The Huguenot*, exhibited at the Royal Academy a decade later.[7] The subject also appealed to Victorian authors, resulting in a series of novels which tended to focus on the Huguenots' hazardous flight from persecution to seek exile in England.[8] An account of the French service in the crypt of Canterbury Cathedral even provided a turning point in Dinah Maria Craik's *A Brave Lady*, where the heroine rediscovered the religious principles of her Huguenot ancestors.[9]

Besides this general interest in the Huguenots, historical research was also undertaken into the communities established by French Protestants in early modern England.[10] The first published research on these immigrants was John Southerden Burn's *The History of the French, Walloon, Dutch and other Foreign Protestant Refugees settled in England* (1846). Although a rather anecdotal study, this volume examined the communities which had been founded in the mid-sixteenth century by refugees escaping the economic disorder and religious persecution associated with the French wars of religion and the Dutch Revolt, as well as those established in the wake of the Revocation of the Edict of Nantes.[11] This later migration was the focus of Charles Weiss's *Histoire des Réfugiés Protestants de France depuis la Révocation de l'Édit de Nantes*, which appeared in English translation in 1854. It provided a more academic study

6   See A. Spicer, '1885: French Protestantism and Huguenot Identity in Victorian Britain', in P. Benedict, H. Daussy and P.-O. Léchot, eds, *Histoire, mémoire et identités en mutation: Les huguenots en France et en diaspora (XVIᵉ–XXIᵉ siècles)* (Geneva, forthcoming).

7   R. Gwynn, 'Patterns in the Study of Huguenot Refugees in Britain: Past, Present and Future', in I. Scouloudi, ed., *Huguenots in Britain and their French Background, 1550–1800* (Basingstoke, 1987), 217–35, at 225, 233–4; Tessa Murdoch, *The Quiet Conquest: The Huguenots 1685–1985* (London, 1985), 313–15.

8   C. F. A. Marmoy, 'The Historical Novel and the Huguenots', *Proceedings of the Huguenot Society* 23 (1977–82), 69–78; Spicer, '1885'.

9   [Dinah Maria Craik], 'A Brave Lady', *Macmillan's Magazine*, February 1870, 294–7; eadem, *A Brave Lady* (London, 1870), 256–8, 261; see also A. Spicer, 'Victorian Vignettes of the French Church at Canterbury', *Proceedings of the Huguenot Society* 29 (2008–12), 716–18.

10   Spicer, '1885'.

11   J. S. Burn, *The History of the French, Walloon, Dutch and other Foreign Protestant Refugees* (London, 1846).

of immigration and placed the English refugee communities in a broader international context.[12] Undoubtedly the most popular work was Samuel Smiles's *The Huguenots: Their Settlements, Churches and Industries in England and Ireland* (1867), which was followed by his *The Huguenots in France after the Revocation of the Edict of Nantes* (1873). There were a number of editions of both works and even a French translation of *The Huguenots*.[13] Smiles admitted that he was less interested in the causes of the Huguenot diaspora than in its impact on English industry and history.[14] These publications and others heightened public awareness and academic interest in the establishment and history of the exile communities.

These works provided a partial history of the French Church at Canterbury. Burn's study largely relied on Edward Hasted's *The History and Topographical Survey of the County of Kent* but included extracts from the city records and also from the French Church's registers. These registers had passed through Burn's hands as he was responsible for collecting non-parochial registers following the introduction of civil registration in 1837. An engraving of 'The Entrance to the French Church in the Undercroft of Canterbury Cathedral' provided the frontispiece to Burn's work.[15] Smiles published a short article in the Evangelical magazine *Good Words*, which considered the Canterbury community in its wider context, but in his monograph he devoted a mere seven pages to the congregation, much of which described the cathedral crypt. Smiles similarly drew on local antiquarian sources, in particular William Somner's *The Antiquities of Canterbury*, first published in 1640 with an enlarged edition appearing in 1703.[16] A more thor-

[12] C. Weiss, *Histoire des réfugiés protestants de France depuis la révocation de l'Édit de Nantes jusqu'à nos jours*, 2 vols (Paris, 1853); idem, *A History of the French Protestant Refugees from the Edict of Nantes to our own days* (Edinburgh, 1854). A separate American translation was published in New York in 1854.

[13] S. Smiles, *Les huguenots: Leurs colonies, leurs industries, leurs églises en Angleterre* (Paris, 1870). In the preface, the translator Athanase-Laurent-Charles Cocquerel emphasized the importance of the links between the two nations as well as the memory of the persecution of the Huguenots and 'the warm fellowship of English brothers': ibid. vi–vii.

[14] S. Smiles, *The Huguenots: Their Settlements, Churches and Industries in England and Ireland* (London, 1867), vii.

[15] Burn, *History*, 38–53; Edward Hasted, *The History and Topographical Survey of the County of Kent*, 12 vols (Canterbury, 1797–1801), 11: 91–8; *ODNB*, s.n. 'Burn, John Southerden (1798–1870)'.

[16] S. Smiles, 'The French Church in Canterbury Cathedral', *Good Words* 7 (April

ough *Sketch of the History of the French Refugee Church of Canterbury* was provided by the church's minister Joseph Auguste Martin as an extensive appendix to his sermon *Christian Firmness of the Huguenots.* Published in 1881, Martin's *Sketch* provides an overview of the Canterbury congregation from its foundation to the nineteenth century, in the form of a series of documents with his observations upon them. The account perpetuated the myth that the French Church in Canterbury had gathered in the cathedral crypt for worship since the reign of Edward VI. In fact, while there may have been a congregation founded in the town around 1548/9, it is unlikely that they were granted permission to use the crypt. Furthermore it was wrongly assumed that, like the French and Dutch Churches in London, the congregation had also been sanctioned by the letters patent granted by the king to John a Lasco in July 1550.[17] (It was only in 1899 that the church recognized that it had been founded in 1575.)[18] Martin's account was rather different from earlier histories of the community. While he was keen to stress the ancient foundation of the French Church, his *Sketch* gave particular weight to the congregation's more recent history and in particular to the support provided by Archbishop Tait. The tract also looked to the future, appealing for funds to keep 'alive that shining spark of the sacred fire lit by the glorious fire of the Reformation' and asserting its 'opposition to the Romanising tendencies of the time'.[19]

The archbishop's involvement in the affairs of the French Church stemmed from an investigation by the Charity Commissioners into the congregation and its finances. By the mid-nineteenth century, the church was in serious decline; the *pasteur* Jean François Miéville served the congregation from 1789 until his death in 1840, but he was blind for the last twenty-three years of

---

1866), 253–8; idem, *Huguenots*, 120–7.

[17] J. A. Martin, *Christian Firmness of the Huguenots and A Sketch of the History of the French Refugee Church of Canterbury* (Canterbury, 1881), 35–40; F. W. Cross, *A History of the Walloon and Huguenot Church at Canterbury*, Huguenot Society Quarto Series 15 (London, 1898), 3–10.

[18] Canterbury, French Church, 'Actes du Consistoire de l'Eglise Française de Canterbury. 18 Février 1877 – 13 September [*sic*] 1946', 99. I am grateful to the consistory of the French Church in Canterbury and Michael Peters for making these records available to me. See A. M. Oakley, 'The Canterbury Walloon Congregation from Elizabeth I to Laud', in Scouloudi, ed., *Huguenots in Britain*, 56–71, at 56–9.

[19] Martin, *Christian Firmness*, 95.

his ministry. Therefore a layman read the liturgy every Sunday, no sermon was preached, and the minister officiated to the best of his ability at the quarterly communion services. Following Miéville's death, a replacement could not be found and so a minister came down from London, initially quarterly and then monthly, to administer the Lord's Supper.[20] In 1870, the Inspector of Charities 'very strongly condemned the relief given to the present recipients, and stated that it was quite clear that they attended the Church solely for the purpose of receiving the charity as scarcely any of them understood one word of the French language'.[21] Following their investigation:

> The Charity Commissioners considered that on three Sundays out of four the service at the Church was (to say the least) an anomaly, the English evening Common Prayer being read in French by an English layman to a congregation of seven persons, six of whom understood French imperfectly, if at all; though the larger congregation present on the fourth Sunday made the anomaly less apparent. The Commissioners considered that there was no sufficient reason for keeping on foot a French service for English-speaking people, or for preserving the shadow of a charity which has long since failed for want of objects.[22]

Proposals were drawn up for a more appropriate use of the French Church's charitable funds, such as the establishment of French scholarships at the King's School, Canterbury, and when this did not find favour with the school, for it to be divided between the infirmaries at Canterbury and Margate.[23]

In August 1875, Archbishop Tait asked the Lord President of the Council, the Duke of Richmond, in the House of Lords whether a scheme had been prepared by the Charity Commis-

[20] Ibid. 87–9; see also P. B. Nockles, 'Aspects of Cathedral Life, 1828–98', in P. Collinson, N. Ramsay and M. Sparks, eds, *A History of Canterbury Cathedral* (Canterbury, 2002), 256–96, at 276–8; A. Spicer, '"A Survival of a Distant Past": J. A. Martin and the Victorian Revival of the French Church at Canterbury', *Southern History* 34 (2012), 101–39.

[21] Canterbury, French Church, 'Livre des comptes de l'église Française Wallonnes de Cantorbery', 19 May 1870.

[22] London, LPL, Tait Papers, vol. 217, fols 373r–376v, Charity Commissioners to Robert Payne Smith, 7 April 1876.

[23] Tait Papers, vol. 206, fols 374r–375r, Charity Commissioners to Tait, 30 July 1875.

sioners 'for diverting to other objects the funds at present available for a French Protestant service in Canterbury Cathedral'. Tait also spoke of the important symbolism and need to preserve the French Church. He recognized that the congregation was now very small and that the minister did not live in Canterbury, but argued that 'the same might be said in respect of the services in many of the churches of the City of London'.[24] The duke reiterated the Charity Commissioners' findings about the poor state of the church and 'the necessity of something being done'.[25] The archbishop later expressed the hope that his intervention 'may stop their [the Charity Commissioners'] meddling plan, or rather may cause the service to be preserved in a more decorous form, while the charity money is better bestowed'.[26]

The parliamentary question prompted Martin to write to *The Times*, thanking the archbishop for his 'rebuke and protest against the meddling and muddling proclivities of the Charity Commissioners' and correcting 'the Duke [who] unconsciously spoke of a time which, happily, is no more. The Church of which they gave so sad and disheartening a description' was now 'a flourishing church'. This great change was due 'to the now permanent residence of the pastor among his flock, and the regular performance of the service, with the sermon, every Sunday'. Martin went on to argue that the commissioners had no jurisdiction over the church's funds:

> the small funds of the French Church of Canterbury, just sufficient to maintain the worship and give a little assistance to the poor, are derived from a source over which the Charity Commissioners have no control whatever. These funds are simply the proceeds of the poor box and the offertories of members of the congregation ...[27]

The duke's assertions about the lamentable state of the French Church were also challenged by a minister who had been asked to deliver the service and preach there.[28]

[24] *Hansard's Parliamentary Debates* (ser. 3), vol. 226, col. 726, 9 August 1875.
[25] Ibid., col. 727.
[26] R. T. Davidson and W. Benham, *Life of Archibald Campbell Tait*, 2 vols (London, 1891), 2: 315.
[27] *The Times*, 13 August 1875.
[28] Tait Papers, vol. 206, fols 379r–380v, William Chastel de Boinville to Tait, 11

The dispute continued into the late 1880s. In response to the archbishop's expressed wish that French services should continue, the commissioners put forward a proposal that would allocate two-thirds of the church's income to charitable purposes and the remainder to the maintenance of the ministry. Martin protested that this would mean that the French services would cease to be viable: 'This is an ingenious way of sustaining life, by drawing blood out of the body!'[29] The commissioner undertook a further investigation into the church and its finances in 1882 and again Tait was vigorous in his defence. Martin successfully argued that the church's revenue came from property purchased through money raised from donations and was not the result of legacies to the poor. Furthermore the discipline or church order of the French churches allowed them to merge the funds for the maintenance of the church and poor relief into one. A board was formed to manage the church's funds with the archbishop of Canterbury, his suffragan, the dean of Canterbury, and the pastor and treasurer of the French Church amongst the trustees.[30] A further attempt by the Charity Commissioners to address the issue of the French Church resulted in an exasperated response from the dean: 'it is annoying to find those commissioners lying by until late Archbishop Tait dies and then trying it on again'.[31] After Tait's death in 1882, his successor Edmund White Benson replied to the commissioners that he was 'entirely at one with the opinion of Abp Tait upon the subject' of the French Church.[32] The matter was finally settled with a report on the administration of the church's charitable funds in 1888.[33]

★ ★ ★

For Archbishop Tait one of the most important reasons for the preservation of the French Church was its historical associations.

August 1875.

[29]   Martin, *Christian Firmness*, 130–1.

[30]   Tait Papers, vol. 280, fols 232r–233r, Charity Commissioners to Tait, 1 February 1882; ibid., fols 236r–237v, Robert Payne-Smith to Tait, 23 February 1882; *The Times*, 18 January 1883.

[31]   LPL, Benson Papers, vol. 55, fols 361r–366v, Robert Payne Smith to Archbishop Benson, 30 November 1887.

[32]   Ibid., fols 367r–368v, Benson to Charity Commissioners, 1887.

[33]   Ibid., fols 378r–382v, Charity Commissioners Report, 1888.

In the House of Lords, he referred to how from 'the time of the Reformation downwards there had been in the Canterbury Cathedral a service for the French Protestants conducted in the French language, and it continued to the present time'. These services, he added, recalled the protection provided during the reigns of Edward VI and Elizabeth I for foreign Protestants persecuted for their faith.[34] He elaborated further on this in a sermon at Canterbury in 1876:

> I do not forget that in this cathedral, though in an obscure corner of it, there remains a memorial of those days when the Church of England, looked to as the mother of the Protestant Churches of Europe, gave an asylum to our persecuted Protestant brethren who came from other lands. This memorial of the past may have become now little more than a sentiment, but it is a sentiment not to be thought lightly of ... So that here there is something to remind us of our connexion with those who in distant lands maintain under great disadvantages the truths for which the Reformers were content to die.[35]

Tait's belief in the symbolic importance of the congregation was not a unique view. Following his speech in the House of Lords, one correspondent expressed the hope that 'some means might be devised for saving from oblivion the footprints of Huguenot faithfulness and English charity within the very precincts of the most interesting of the ecclesiastical edifices of this country'.[36] Smiles had also written earlier that 'though the church has become reduced to a mere vestige and remnant of what it was, it nevertheless serves to mark an epoch of memorable importance to England'.[37]

The archbishop's belief in the historical importance and symbolism of the French Church was certainly shared by the indefatigable Pastor Martin. In a lengthy letter to Tait in July 1876, he expressed the view that:

> Though that church, as a church may still be very useful, its

---

[34] *Hansard's Parliamentary Debates* (ser. 3), vol. 226, cols 725–7, 9 August 1875.

[35] A. C. Tait, *Some Thoughts on the Duties of the Established Church of England as a National Church* (London, 1876), 5–6.

[36] Tait Papers, vol. 206, fols 379r–380v, William Chastel de Boinville to Tait, 11 August 1875.

[37] Smiles, *Huguenots*, 127.

necessity as an institution for Foreign worshippers has now ceased. It can only be kept up as an living monument. And as such deserves to be kept. As an established monument embodying the history of the persecuted refugees and of their kind entertainers, with what great clouds of witnesses it is compassed about, from kings and queens to all estates of men in the world and in the church. To be historical, it must be kept with all the lustre of its charters, privileges, immunities etc., which constitute the essence of its existence and establish its autonomy. It must be a living monument of the largeness of heart of both church and state, and the incorporation of the glorious proviso contained in the Act of Uniformity. The French Church, brought by this standard, which is but its birth-right, acquires an historical significance, alike glorious to itself, to the Established Church, and to England.[38]

Martin seems to have developed further the historical associations of the French Church by initiating two annual services of commemoration.[39] The first was held on the fourth Sunday in July to mark the granting of letters patent by Edward VI to John a Lasco in 1550; this was recorded in the consistory minutes as the anniversary of the French Church's foundation. The second principal celebration was the 'Festival of the Reformation', 'in memory of the greatest event for God, which in the dispensations of God had ever been brought about since the first publication of the Gospel'.[40]

Even allowing for the mistaken beliefs concerning the date of its foundation, amongst the foreign Protestant churches the French congregation in Canterbury continued to worship in the same place as their sixteenth-century forebears. This was not true of the more senior French Church in London, which had been established in 1550. The Threadneedle Street church had been destroyed during the Great Fire of London in 1666; the church had been rebuilt but the congregation had been forced in 1842 to move to the church of St Martin-le-Grand.[41] As Martin explained:

---

38 Tait Papers, vol. 216, fols 138r–140r, Joseph Martin to Tait, 10 July 1876.
39 These anniversaries only appear in the consistory minutes after Martin had become pastor.
40 Martin, *Christian Firmness*, 98.
41 A. Spicer, '"A Place of refuge and sanctuary of a holy Temple": Exile Communi-

Of the two Refugee Churches now left of the many which once graced this Protestant land, this one especially, by its unbroken chain of religious Services and ministration in one and the same place, not less than by its faithful demonstration, for nearly three centuries and a half, of the vital energy and power of faith, and of the excellence of institutions firmly based on Scriptural principles, justly claims to possess all the conditions which a special Monumental Memorial of this nature should embody ...[42]

However, Martin was being disingenuous to a degree because, although its survival was fitful, the French Church in Southampton still continued to worship in God's House Chapel which had been granted to the congregation at its foundation in 1567.[43] It none-theless served the minister's purposes to emphasize the historical traditions and importance of the Canterbury church by focusing attention on its unbroken record of worship in the cathedral since the sixteenth century.

The archbishop also believed that it seemed 'undesirable that there should be any unnecessary interference with the French service in Canterbury Cathedral' at a time when 'there was a widespread desire to preserve any old building which was a link of connection between the past and the present'.[44] On several occasions he had drawn attention to the importance of the cathedral as a 'storehouse of religious and historical associations' and its 'very venerable fabric', and to being 'in the midst of the monuments of very old time, amid memorials of the history of our country, over the graves of great men who have done great works in former days'.[45] Furthermore, the cathedral fabric itself contained reminders of the use that had long been made of the crypt by the French Church. Visitors observed 'the French Prot-estant texts written on the ancient Norman pillars', which the

---

ties and the Stranger Churches', in N. Goose and L. Luu, eds, *Immigrants in Tudor and Early Stuart England* (Brighton, 2005), 91–109, at 93–4, 98–9, 104; Burn, *History*, 24–7.

[42] Martin, *Christian Firmness*, 133.

[43] Spicer, '"Place of refuge"', 94–6; *The Minute Book of the French Church at South-ampton, 1702–1939*, ed. E. Welch, Southampton Records Series 23 (Southampton, 1979), 9, 124–55.

[44] *Hansard's Parliamentary Debates* (ser. 3), vol. 226, col. 726, 9 August 1875.

[45] Tait, *Present Position*, 14; Tait, *Church of the Future*, 170–1.

congregation had been permitted to do 'so that they might not feel too much like strangers in the land to which persecution for their faith had driven them'.[46] The cathedral's historical association with the French community, and the fact that many of the inhabitants of Canterbury were Huguenot descendants, even led to proposals in the 1870s that the restoration of the chapter house should 'commemorate the union of the two great Western nations (the English and French alliance)'.[47] However, the Anglo-French Commercial Treaty of 1872, to which this probably referred, was not ratified by the National Assembly and the restoration was not completed for another twenty years.[48]

Besides preserving this 'memorial of the past', the French Church was also an important symbol in broader contemporary debates and affairs. The archbishop had a particular interest in the Church of England's role in 'that wider Church of Christ which belongs to all ages and to all countries'.[49] In the wake of the second Lambeth conference (1878), he reflected on how Lambeth, through the role of the primate and the decennial gathering of bishops, was increasingly becoming the centre to which the whole Anglican Communion looked and how 'that communion seems … to be more and more every year becoming itself a centre for all the Churches of Christendom which protest against Roman usurpation', as well as how the service held in Canterbury Cathedral had reminded the bishops attending the conference of 'the association which bound them to the birthplace of what we commonly call Anglo-Saxon Christianity'.[50] The cathedral's honorary canons also

---

[46] *Hansard's Parliamentary Debates* (ser. 3), vol. 158, cols 1639–40, 24 May 1860; R. E. Prothero, *The Life and Correspondence of Arthur Penrhyn Stanley,* 2 vols (n.pl., 1893), 1: 428; Anon., *A Handbook for Travellers in Kent and Sussex* (London, 1858), 177; R. J. King, *Handbook to the Cathedrals of England: Southern Division* (London, 1861), 385.

[47] *The Standard*, 29 May 1878; *Morning Post*, 31 May 1878; *Manchester Guardian*, 1 June 1878.

[48] Agatha Ramm, 'Granville', in Keith M. Wilson, ed., *British Foreign Secretaries and Foreign Policy; From Crimean War to First World War* (London, 1987), 94; Bryan Coutain, 'The Unconditional Most-Favoured-Nation Clause and the Maintenance of the Liberal Trade Regime in the Postwar 1870s', *International Organization* 63 (2009), 139–75; Nockles, 'Cathedral Life', 282–3. When the restored chapter house was opened by the Prince of Wales in May 1897, it marked the 1300th anniversary of St Augustine's mission: *Morning Post*, 31 May 1897.

[49] Tait, *Some Thoughts*, 4.

[50] Tait, *Church of the Future*, 2–3; P. V. Norwood, 'A Victorian Primate', *ChH* 14 (1945), 3–16, at 15–16.

provided evidence of the links with this wider Anglican community as they included a number of bishops of dioceses overseas, so
that there was 'no danger of forgetting that the Church of which
we are members has duties as wide as the world'.[51]

Tait, however, looked beyond the Anglican communion and
recognized the historical links dating back to the Reformation
which had led to 'a bond of cordial union, independent of outward
forms, uniting the wisest spirits of the Church of England with the
literary and theological labours of German, French, and Swiss Protestants'. The basis of this bond was the asylum that English Protestants had found during the reign of Mary Tudor.[52] Even while
he had been bishop of London in the 1860s, Tait had pointed to
the French Church in Canterbury as well as the German Lutheran
Church in the Chapel Royal of the Savoy in London as evidence
of 'the principles of the Church of England in recognizing that
there were such persons as Lutherans, and in affording them that
accommodation which since the Reformation it had been the
habit of one Protestant Church to extend to another'.[53] He argued
that, through their common adherence to the principles of the
gospel, 'the boundaries of separation' between the faiths should
'fade to an indistinct line' and the great Protestant churches, episcopal and non-episcopal, should 'feel that their cause is indissol-
ubly united with our own'.[54]

One of the consequences of Tait's public defence of the French
congregation was a reaffirmation of the association of the Church
of England and the Reformed Church in France, which had been
re-established at the time of the French Revolution following
the Edict of Tolerance (1787). In May 1876, following his House
of Lords' speech, he received a letter from Paris signed by some
seventy leading members and pastors of the French Reformed

---

[51] Tait, *Some Thoughts*, 6–7.
[52] Tait, *Church of the Future*, 12.
[53] *Hansard's Parliamentary Debates* (ser. 3), vol. 158, col. 125, 26 April 1860. Although
the French Reformed Church and the German Lutheran Church represented
different religious confessions, the latter had been established according to the same
terms outlined in the letters patent granted in 1550 to the Reformed congregations
in London: see A. Spicer, 'Lutheran Churches and Confessional Identity', in idem, ed.,
Lutheran Churches in Early Modern Europe (Farnham, 2012), 1–15, at 5–8; S. Steinmetz,
*Deutsche Evangelisch-Lutherische St.-Marien-Kirche London / St Mary's German Lutheran
Church London, 1694–1994* (London, 1994).
[54] Tait, *Church of the Future*, 12–13.

Church. They expressed their profound thanks to the archbishop for his intervention and the favour that had been shown to French refugees over the centuries in allowing them to worship in the cathedral crypt. Furthermore they greatly appreciated the proof that these actions provided of the Christian affection felt towards them by '[t]he Anglican Church, in recognising the Reformed Church of France as a sister church, at heart attached to the same fundamental doctrines'.[55] In responding, Tait emphasized the importance of the French Church as a symbol of the churches' association:

> The connection between that branch of the Church of Christ and the Established Church of England has always appeared to me to be expressed in a very interesting manner by the maintenance in the Metropolitical Cathedral of England, of that Reformed French service which has existed from the time of king Edward VI and I beg to assure you of my conscious desire to use whatever influence I possess to maintain fraternal relations between the Church of which I am a Primate and Protestant brethren in France.[56]

Tait also referred to the importance of maintaining good relations with the French Protestants in a terse letter to the Charity Commissioners in 1882: 'I have very distinct views as to the propriety and even necessity of maintaining the Ecclesiastical part of this foundation and its old historical connexion with Canterbury Cathedral which I know is highly valued by the French Protestants in all parts of the World.'[57] These sentiments reached a wider audience through the publication of the letters in several newspapers.[58]

The archbishop's positive attitude towards French Protestantism may be linked to his friendship with leading figures such as Eugène Bersier and Edmond de Hault de Pressensé, prominent

---

[55] Tait Papers, vol. 217, fols 363r–364v, Ministers of the French Reformed Church to Tait, 6 May 1876.

[56] Ibid., fol. 367r–v, Tait to ministers of the French Reformed Church, 30 May 1876.

[57] Tait Papers, vol. 280, fol. 234r–v, Tait to Charity Commissioners, 4 February 1882.

[58] *Pall Mall Gazette*, 13 June 1876; *Manchester Guardian*, 14 June 1876; *Blackburn Standard and North East Lancashire Advertiser*, 17 June 1876.

Evangelical theologians and ministers in Paris, but it was not a view shared by many other churchmen.[59] The French Reformed Church was little known in England and a doleful impression of its divisions, ineffectiveness and services was painted in *The Congregationalist*.[60] Within the Church of England, the *Church Quarterly Review* attacked French Protestantism because the 'sacraments are depreciated and administered by those who have no more right to such a ministry than any layman in England might'. This high church journal went on to condemn the fact that Socinianism was 'openly preached in many French Protestant chapels, that doubts should be cast upon the truth of the miracles, upon the articles of the Apostle's Creed, upon the divinity of our Lord'. The article also criticized those English Dissenters who cooperated with the church.[61]

Tait was concerned that the Church of England should also stand as the church of the nation. Only the established church, through its connection with the state and its 'power of influencing the whole social life of the nation', was in a position to make a 'national protest for God and for Christ, for goodness and for truth'.[62] Nonetheless, while it was possible for the Church of England to be seen as part of a brotherhood of Protestant churches, a less charitable view was taken of 'the existence of dissent from the National Church'.[63] In order to make the established church more representative of the nation, the archbishop adopted a conciliatory stance towards Nonconformity.[64] For some churchmen, the French Church at Canterbury had provided evidence of the possible coexistence of the Church of England and Nonconformity.[65] The foreign congregations were

---

[59] Tait, *Church of the Future*, 10–11, 40–1, 208; Davidson and Benham, *Life of Tait*, 2: 514–15.

[60] 'Free Churches in France. Sketches of Worship and Life', *The Congregationalist* 3 (1874), 305–9; 'The French Reformed Church', *The Congregationalist* 5 (1876), 27–32; D. Johnson, 'L'attitude des protestants britanniques aux débuts de la Troisième République', in A. Encrevé and M. Richard, eds, *Les protestants dans les débuts de la Troisième République (1871–1885)* (Paris, 1979), 491–534.

[61] 'English Churchmen on the Continent', *CQR* 5 (1877), 371. Socinianism is the rejection of the doctrines of the Trinity and divinity of Christ.

[62] Tait, *Some Thoughts*, 3–4, 98–100. See Marsh, 'Primate and Prime Minister', 113–40; idem, *Victorian Church*, 94–7.

[63] Tait, *Church of the Future*, 17.

[64] Marsh, *Victorian Church*, 245–51.

[65] 'I discover with satisfaction that the two most illustrious Canons of Canterbury

not, however, Nonconformist churches, as Martin explained to Tait: they had been 'established by the side of the English Church, [and] were in brotherly relation with it', and 'the intent of the Act of Uniformity was to crush & annihilate dissent and uphold the two Establishments, the English and the Foreign'.[66] It was a distinction which even the *Church Quarterly Review* recognized in an article attacking English Nonconformity.[67] Nonetheless it was still possible for a later correspondent to *The Times* to argue:

> It is, of course, true that many English churchmen view with dislike the survival of the French Protestant worship in the crypt of our cathedral church because it gives to a Nonconforming community a foothold in the mother Church of the Anglican communion. But it is equally true that many Nonconformists desire to maintain this worship, not because it has any rational object or satisfies any religious needs, but simply and solely because it gives them this foothold.[68]

The survival of the French Church, therefore, remained controversial even after the archbishop's death. Tait does not appear to have been criticized directly for supporting the church, although there was certainly some opposition amongst the cathedral clergy to its continued existence and to Pastor Martin in particular.[69] Even Walter Farquhar Hook, who in his biography of Archbishop Laud implicitly accused Tait of being despotic in relation to the Public Worship Regulation Act, discussed the struggle between the seventeenth-century archbishop and the foreign congregations without reference to the present primate and his support for the French Church.[70] Generally, Tait's personal tragedies and ill-

---

were, one a layman, the other a minister of the Dutch Church – Casaubon and Saravin [*sic*]; and that Arnold's much-abused theory of having different sects worship in the same church is here fulfilled even to exaggeration, inasmuch as a Presbyterian service is carried out in the Crypt at the same hour as the Cathedral service above': Prothero, *Life and Correspondence*, 428.

[66] Tait Papers, vol. 216, fol. 138r, Joseph Martin to Tait, 10 July 1876.
[67] 'Is the Church of England Protestant?', *CQR* 7 (1879), 261–304, at 277.
[68] *The Times*, 22 February 1895.
[69] Tait Papers, vol. 216, fols 131r–133v, 'E. D.' [Edward Parry, Bishop of Dover?] to 'C.' [Crauford Tait?], 21 June 1876; Nockles, 'Cathedral Life', 277.
[70] W. F. Hook, *Lives of the Archbishops of Canterbury*, 12 vols (London, 1860–76), 11: 254–6; Timothy Lang, *The Victorians and the Stuart Heritage: Interpretations of a Discordant Past* (Cambridge, 1995), 158–9.

health seem to have spared him from criticism during his primacy and even an attack on him in the *Church Quarterly Review* shortly before his death in 1882 was carefully qualified.[71] However, even high churchmen who criticized French Protestantism were able to recognize the unique position occupied by the foreign congregations. Furthermore, nineteenth-century histories of the Huguenots emphasized the material benefits that had accrued to the nation from the hospitality and tolerance afforded to those continental Protestants who had been persecuted for their beliefs. Tait regarded the French Church in Canterbury as a tangible reminder of this past that should be preserved. However, his defence of the congregation should not be seen in solely historical terms but also as an important symbol of 'that brotherhood which the Church of England claimed with Protestants throughout Europe'.[72]

Oxford Brookes University

[71] *ODNB*, *s.n.* 'Tait, Archibald Campbell (1811–1882)'; 'Charles Lowder', *CQR* 14 (1882), 57–68, at 62.
[72] *Hansard's Parliamentary Debates* (ser. 3), vol. 158, col. 1640, 24 May 1860.

MEMORIALIZING 1662: HAMPSHIRE CONGREGATIONALISTS AND THE 250TH ANNIVERSARY OF THE GREAT EJECTION*

by ROSALIND JOHNSON AND ROGER OTTEWILL

Edwardian Congregationalists regarded 1662 as their *annus mirabilis*, to be venerated and celebrated in equal measure. For them it was the year when all that they revered, such as the enthronement of conscience, had been thrown into sharp relief by the Great Ejection. This event, which helped to shape the identity of historically minded Congregationalists, had acquired a mythical quality and become part of the denomination's folk lore.[1] The Ejection involved the removal of 'some 2,000 ministers ... from their livings because they could not swear their "unfeigned assent and consent to ... everything contained and prescribed" in the new Prayer Book, or meet some of the other requirements of the new Act of Uniformity'.[2] Many ejected ministers attracted followers, who became the founding members of Dissenting congregations which later evolved into self-governing Congregational churches.

With the 250th anniversary of the Great Ejection due in 1912 there was a strong desire among Congregationalists that such an evocative event should be memorialized as it had been fifty years earlier. Two aspects of this engagement with the past are particularly germane. One concerns the nature of claims made about the Great Ejection and the other the justifications for its commemoration. In what follows, each aspect is considered in the light of evidence from Hampshire, where Congregationalism was well entrenched with thirteen churches: Above Bar in Southampton,

*   Thanks are due to Hugh McLeod and the editors of Studies in Church History for their constructive comments on earlier versions of this essay.
    1   Roger Ottewill, 'Representations of Congregational Identity in Edwardian Hampshire', *Local Historian* 41 (2011), 149–60, at 150–1.
    2   Timothy Larsen, 'Victorian Nonconformity and the Memory of the Ejected Ministers: The Impact of the Bicentennial Commemorations of 1862', in R. N. Swanson, ed., *The Church Retrospective*, SCH 33 (Woodbridge, 1997), 459–75, at 459. Also known as 'Black Bartholomew's Day', the Ejection took place on 24 August 1662, the feast of St Bartholomew.

Alton, Andover, Basingstoke, Christchurch, Fordingbridge, Gosport, Odiham, Ringwood, Romsey, Tadley, Whitchurch and Winchester, all tracing their lineage back to the mid-seventeenth century.[3] As Robbins suggests, it is at the local level that '"church history" really comes to life'.[4] Such an approach also redresses the balance of Larsen's study of the 1862 celebrations, which focused on the national scene, and affords insights into a relatively neglected field of Congregational history.[5]

The Hampshire Congregational Union (HCU) took the lead in alerting Congregationalists to the importance of 1912. As the Executive Committee noted in its annual report for 1911:

> We shall be commemorating ... [in 1912] the 250th anniversary of the Ejectment of 1662, an event which was fraught with grave peril to many of our forefathers, but out of which owing to the heroism displayed, there came an enrichment of life ... We cherish the memory of men and women who faced ridicule, opposition, and starvation rather than surrender at the bidding of a hostile power their high vision of truth and the sacred rights of conscience ... The knowledge of what they did calls for a like service on our part ... [We] would therefore urge that in every Church steps are taken to make clear the significance of this event ...[6]

Such exhortation reflected a tendency amongst leading Congregationalists to enlist the past when seeking to rally the faithful. At the 1908 spring gathering of the HCU, the chairman, Henry March Gilbert, speaking on 'Our Past and Present', reminded his audience that 'they had entered into a glorious heritage', and that if their forefathers had been present on that occasion they would have said: 'We too with great sums of fines, persecutions, impris-

---

3   Whitchurch, Christchurch and Gosport celebrated their 250th anniversaries in 1908, 1910 and 1913 respectively and the others in 1912.
4   Keith Robbins, *England, Ireland, Scotland, Wales: The Christian Church 1900–2000*, OHCC (Oxford, 2008), 22.
5   Larsen, 'Victorian Nonconformity'; see also Alan P. F. Sell, ed., *The Great Ejectment of 1662: Its Antecedents, Aftermath, and Ecumenical Significance* (Eugene, OR, 2012).
6   Winchester, Hampshire Record Office, 127M94/62/56, *Annual Report of the Hampshire Congregational Union for 1911* (Southampton, 1911), 23–4.

onments, tortures, and even with giving up life itself obtained for you this freedom which is yours today.'[7]

Hampshire Congregationalists also drew inspiration from what was happening at a national level. This received extensive coverage in the religious press, with the *British Congregationalist* publishing a succession of articles on 1662 and assiduously reporting commemorative events, and in secular newspapers. A notable exposition of the legacy of 1662 was an address by Walter Adeney, the new chairman of the Congregational Union of England and Wales (CUEW), at its annual assembly in May 1912, entitled 'The More Excellent Way'. Adeney encouraged his audience, 'whose fathers laboured long and hard and suffered many hardships for liberty and truth and the spirituality of the faith', to ensure the triumph of 'these superb ideas'.[8] It was in this spirit that Hampshire Congregationalists approached their commemorations.

'SUCH A NOTABLE DAY'

In offering 'the very heartiest congratulations to the members of … Tadley Congregational Church on their celebration of such a notable day', George Saunders, pastor of Above Bar Church, echoed what many Congregationalists felt about 1662.[9] In making this value-judgement, however, they were co-opting the past for their own ends and were equating history-as-account with history-as-event.[10]

Sometimes dramatic language was used when referring to the sacrifices to which the anti-Dissenting laws of Restoration England had given rise and on which various histories of the period written from a Dissenting perspective placed considerable emphasis.[11] At the 1912 autumn gathering of the HCU, J. D. Jones, Congregational statesman and pastor of the prestigious Richmond Hill Congregational Church in Bournemouth, argued: 'One of the most brilliant among the many brilliant pages in English history was that when 2,000 of the godliest men of the Established Church went out, facing poverty in many cases, and without reckoning

---

7 *Hampshire Post*, 1 May 1908, 2.
8 *British Congregationalist*, 9 May 1912, 325.
9 *Hants and Berks Gazette* [hereafter: *HBG*], 20 July 1912, 8.
10 Michael Stanford, *A Companion to the Study of History* (Oxford, 1994), 11.
11 For examples, see John Seed, *Dissenting Histories* (Edinburgh, 2008).

their lives if only they could accomplish their course.'[12] Similarly, in Basingstoke's Congregational Church magazine it was stated that the ejected ministers 'gave up their homes and faced poverty and hardship rather than do violence to their conceptions of the teachings of God's Word, and came out singly — not as an organized arrangement — thereby showing their own unbiased judgment, that come what will they could do no other'.[13] Binfield has written of the 200th anniversary: 'the Great Ejectment's bicentenary ... focused the mind on the minister as martyr, his people as saints'.[14] This was still the case. What might be considered a tragedy for all concerned was deemed a triumph.

It was also implied that the Great Ejection was qualitatively different from what had gone before. In placing in the foreground the events of 1662, Congregationalists often failed to give due weight to their historical context and in particular to the indignities which many clergy had faced during the 1640s. Cyril Edwards, rector of Mottisfont and honorary secretary of the Church Defence Association, took exception to the use of the word 'persecution' by speakers at Romsey's 1912 celebrations, and argued that it was necessary to 'look back a few years prior to ... [1662] ... to get at the truth'.[15] For 'just as the clergy had resigned in 1645 sooner than give up their faith' so in 1662 '2000 ... resigned in their turn'.[16] Thus, the past was, as it had been in 1862, 'contested territory', with Anglicans claiming that Nonconformists were 'misusing history'.[17]

The situation in the early 1660s was more complex. Some clergy were ejected in 1660 or 1661 when a sequestered minister was restored. The Declaration of Breda in 1660 had promised 'a Liberty to tender Consciences' in matters of religion.[18] Moderate Presbyterians had been encouraged by the Worcester House Declaration

---

[12] *Hampshire Telegraph* [hereafter: *HT*], 4 October 1912, 10.

[13] *Basingstoke & District Congregational Magazine*, June 1912, 3.

[14] Clyde Binfield, 'Victims of Success: Twentieth-Century Free Church Architecture', in Jane Shaw and Alan Kreider, eds, *Culture and the Nonconformist Tradition* (Cardiff, 1999), 142–81, at 143.

[15] *Romsey Advertiser* [hereafter: *RA*], 31 May 1912, 8.

[16] Ibid.

[17] Larsen, 'Victorian Nonconformity', 459, 462.

[18] Tim Harris, *Restoration: Charles II and his Kingdoms 1660–1685* (London, 2006), 52.

later that year.[19] But the Cavalier Parliament, elected in March 1661, sought to re-establish an episcopalian church.[20] The Act of Uniformity was but one item of legislation designed to avoid the 'factions and schisms' which it was believed had resulted from the previous situation.[21] Nevertheless, as Speed has observed, the experience of persecution following ejection was subject to local variation, and, as A. G. Matthews noted, Roman Catholics suffered more.[22] It may have been, as Ronald Hutton has written, that later Congregational churches owed their establishment to 'only a fraction' of those who were ejected, but the result of the Ejection was, as Eamon Duffy has remarked, 'a parting of the ways as momentous as any event since the break with Rome'.[23] Michael Watts nonetheless sees the break as ultimately positive, for while its immediate effect was persecution and suffering, it can be seen 'as a step towards the eventual and permanent liberation of Dissent'.[24]

At the time, the 1912 celebrations also afforded '1662 churches' opportunities for substantiating claims about their lineage. Given the turbulence of the post-Restoration period this was not necessarily a straightforward task. It was acknowledged, for example, that the 'records of the early history of the Congregational Church in Winchester ... [were] very scanty'.[25] Thomas Robilliard, the pastor at Tadley, admitted that 'owing partly to the neglect in recording their early transactions and partly to the loss of Church books it cannot now be precisely said at what time the dissenting congregation at Tadley was first formed'.[26] As Charles Surman, collator of information about Congregational pastors and churches, has shown, there was sometimes conflicting evidence as to the precise

[19] The Declaration offered concessions to Presbyterians, but did not reach the statute book: Michael R. Watts, *The Dissenters: From the Reformation to the French Revolution* (Oxford, 1978), 217–18.

[20] Harris, *Restoration*, 52–3.

[21] Owen Chadwick, 'Introduction' to Geoffrey F. Nuttall and Owen Chadwick, eds, *From Uniformity to Unity 1662–1962* (London, 1962), 1–18, at 11.

[22] Speed, *Dissenting Histories*, 4–5; A. G. Matthews, *Calamy Revised* (Oxford, 1934), lix.

[23] Ronald Hutton, *The Restoration: A Political and Religious History of England and Wales 1658–1667* (Oxford, 1985), 180; Eamon Duffy, 'The Long Reformation: Catholicism, Protestantism and the Multitude', in Nicholas Tyacke, ed., *England's Long Reformation, 1500–1800* (London, 1998), 33–70, at 53.

[24] Watts, *Dissenters*, 220.

[25] *Hampshire Chronicle* [hereafter: *HC*], 23 November 1912, 5.

[26] *HBG*, 13 July 1912, 8.

year in which a church was founded and which ejected minister was its first pastor.[27]

Nonetheless, surviving churchwardens' presentments of the period 1662 to 1689, conventicle returns of 1669 and licences issued under the Declaration of Indulgence of 1672, would suggest that most of Hampshire's thirteen '1662 churches' could justifiably point to a foundation date no later than 1669, albeit in many cases as a Presbyterian rather than an Independent congregation. Moreover, evidence supports some churches' claims regarding the identity of their first pastor, including Nathaniel Robinson of Above Bar, ejected from the living of All Saints, Southampton, in 1662;[28] Samuel Sprint, ejected minister of South Tidworth, who preached at Andover;[29] and Thomas Warren, ejected rector of Houghton, whom Romsey Congregationalists considered to be the founder of their church.[30]

Elsewhere, however, the situation was more opaque. In recounting the history of Alton Congregational Church the pastor, Harry Lewis, claimed that following the ejection of the Rev. J. Ferrol (or Farroll) from the living of Selborne he 'became an Independent preacher in Alton, and initiated the work to which that church owed its origin'.[31] Yet, the 1669 returns record that at a Presbyterian meeting kept at the house of Lawrence Geale, the regular preacher was Mr Marshall.[32] Moreover, Calamy notes that after leaving Selborne, Farroll retired to Guildford.[33] At Basingstoke, the 1669 returns refer to James Terry and James Marryot as preachers.[34] However, for the 1912 celebrations the pastor, Rocliffe Mackintosh, incorporated in the form of a catechism the assertion that: 'The Congregational Church at Basingstoke was formed as the result of ... the Rev John Hook leaving the Anglican Church

---

[27] Charles Surman, *Outline Notes on Three-Hundred Years of Congregational Ministry in Hampshire, with many Presbyterian Antecedents* (Birmingham, 1961), unpaginated.

[28] In Matthews, *Calamy Revised*, 413, it is recorded that by 1669 he was 'head of a conventicle of Independents at Southampton'.

[29] London, LPL, MS 639, Miscellanies Ecclesiastical, fol. 261r; see also Matthews, *Calamy Revised*, 456.

[30] G. Lyon Turner, *Original Records of Early Nonconformity under Persecution and Indulgence* (London, 1911), 1039.

[31] *Hampshire Herald and Alton Gazette* [hereafter: *HHAG*], 2 November 1912, 7.

[32] LPL, MS 639, fol. 263r.

[33] Matthews, *Calamy Revised*, 191–2.

[34] LPL, MS 639, fol. 261v.

in order that he might be free and lead others in what he believed to be the way of truth.'[35] Yet, as Surman observes, Hook does not appear to have commenced his ministry in Basingstoke until 1686.

Thus, for certain churches direct association with the Ejection was perhaps more a case of wishful thinking than historical accuracy. Their motivation was to obtain some of the kudos arising from their members' being seen as 'living representatives' of those who refused to conform in 1662.[36]

'Worthy of Admiration'

One justification for memorializing 1662 was to commemorate what Edwardian Congregationalists construed to be the defining moment of their denomination. As R. Murray Hyslop, treasurer of the CUEW, put it when speaking at the Above Bar celebrations: '[He] was sure they would all agree that there were many events in the history of their church which stood out in bold relief ... But all these paled into comparative insignificance when compared with the historical event they were called upon to commemorate on the present occasion.'[37]

Congregationalists were also expressing pride both in their collective past and that of local congregations. At Romsey's celebrations George Saunders claimed 'that [there] were few instances in the history of the country that were more worthy of admiration than that which they were celebrating that day',[38] while a visiting speaker at Odiham's celebrations commented 'that there was something to be proud of in a church with such a history'.[39]

Alongside remembrance and pride, speakers sought to emphasize that 1662 was meant to motivate, with Congregationalists being encouraged to emulate examples from the past. Here they were displaying the need for role models and a desire 'to use history to make a moral point'.[40] Speaking at the 1912 autumn gathering of the HCU, J. D. Jones contended that some of the 'heroism, devotion and sacrifice' displayed by the ejected ministers needed to be

35 *HBG*, 26 October 1912, 6.
36 Seed, *Dissenting Histories*, 3.
37 *Hampshire Independent* [hereafter: *HI*], 23 November 1912, 4.
38 *RA*, 24 May 1912, 8.
39 *HBG*, 26 October 1912, 6.
40 Beverley Southgate, *Why Bother with History* (Harlow, 2000), 33.

reproduced by Congregationalists of the early twentieth century.[41] In so doing, he was echoing the references to 'manliness', 'love of truth' and 'fortitude' at the 1862 celebrations.[42]

Others used the commemorations to remind Congregationalists that their primary allegiance was to Christ and not to any worldly authority. Speaking at Basingstoke, William Legg, pastor of Redhill Congregational Church, drew on a quotation from Philip Henry, 'one of the greatest of the ejected heroes of 1662', to animate his listeners:'To the command of my superior, who may be my king, I oppose the command of my Supreme, the King of Kings.'[43] Legg went on to argue that 'they were looking forward, led by the inspiration of the past'.[44]

Clearly, by the Edwardian era the situation was very different from that which had prevailed in the past, with leading Congregationalists often being as much part of the local establishment as Anglicans. Thus, at Andover and Winchester commemorative services were attended by the mayor and other civic dignitaries.[45] Nonetheless, when circumstances demanded, Congregationalists were still prepared to protest and invoke historical antecedents to legitimize extreme behaviour in making their point. A good example from the Edwardian era was the campaign of passive resistance against the highly controversial Education Act of 1902 which was often justified in terms reminiscent of 1662. Nonconformists were particularly upset because Anglican schools, while maintaining their distinctive denominational ethos, would have access to funding from the local rates. Resisters saw themselves as promoting the cause of freedom of conscience and making a sacrifice through having their goods seized and, in extreme cases, being imprisoned, for refusing to pay their rates in full.[46] Indeed, at the opening meeting of the passive resistance campaign in Whitchurch, the chairman, James Richards, pastor of Overton Congre-

---

[41] *HT*, 4 October 1912, 10.
[42] Larsen, 'Victorian Nonconformity', 464.
[43] *HBG*, 26 October 1912, 6.
[44] Ibid.
[45] *Andover Advertiser*, 26 July 1912, 1; *HC*, 23 November 1912, 5.
[46] See D. R. Pugh, 'English Nonconformity, Education and Passive Resistance', *History of Education* 19 (1990), 232–49.

gational Church, 'reminded the audience of the persecution that their fathers had had to put up with in the past'.[47]

In 1912 the challenges were less clear-cut but in some ways more daunting. As Murray Hyslop claimed, 'today it was not religious liberty which was at stake, but their very religion itself'.[48] Somewhat apocalyptic perhaps, but this was a recognition of the pervasiveness of secular counter-attractions with which churches were now having to contend and a prelude to a call to emulate 1662 with 'a new consecration of spirit and a new devotion to principle'.[49]

A further justification for memorializing 1662 concerned the distinctiveness of Congregationalists. As J. D. Jones explained, although all Nonconformists could 'lay claim to the noble Two Thousand as their progenitors ... [they] gave to Congregationalism the strength and dignity of a national movement'.[50] Nonetheless, the commemorations were often characterized by displays of solidarity with fellow Nonconformists, some of whom, such as the Presbyterians, had an even stronger case for looking to 1662 for inspiration. At Alton, for example, the anniversary meeting was attended by the ministers of Holybourne Presbyterian Church and the local Wesleyan Methodist Church.[51]

Speakers such as George Darlaston, pastor of Crouch End Congregational Church, preaching at Winchester, argued for greater toleration across all the denominations:

> It came down to the present day, to State and Free Churchmen alike, to encourage a better spirit of forbearance and patience, and frankness. All that controversy did was to define one's position, and it was desirable that they should all strive for that state of mind which refused to doubt the honour of the opposing party, and for that mutual respect which allowed all to live according to the light that was in them.[52]

Similarly, Charles Dickinson, a former pastor of Winchester Congregational Church, made it clear that 'they were not antago-

47 *HBG*, 17 October 1903, 7.
48 *HI*, 23 November 1912, 4.
49 Ibid.
50 *British Weekly*, 8 February 1912, 553.
51 *HHAG*, 26 October 1912, 4.
52 *HC*, 23 November 1912, 5.

nistic to the Church of England ... [and that] there was much [in it] ... which they appreciated; and in which they rejoiced'.[53] Their stance resonated with that of Dr J. M. McClure, headmaster of Mill Hill School in London. At a major commemorative rally in the Free Trade Hall, Manchester, he argued that the actions of the ejected ministers 'made toleration inevitable ... [and it] had now advanced to the dignity of a great moral principle which had done much to mould the higher life of the nation'.[54]

Nonetheless, some contributors at anniversary events continued to display their antipathy towards the Church of England. Vincett Cook, pastor of Bitterne Congregational Church, speaking at the 'United Congregational Church Demonstration' held as part of Above Bar's celebrations, 'thought the whole story of the ejectment was one of the most forcible arguments that could be used for the Disestablishment of the Anglican Church. A Church that could not find room for such men as those of the Ejectment had no right to be called a national church.'[55] Moreover, for some the ritualism which had permeated certain parts of the Church of England meant that Nonconformists in general and Congregationalists in particular were seen as protectors of the nation's Protestant heritage. In the words of an editorial from the *British Congregationalist*: 'Mediaevalism has swept over the Church like a flood. Sacerdotalism is rampant. Protestantism is at a discount ... and that is why we remain Nonconformists still.'[56] In the main, however, the 1912 celebrations avoided much of the unpleasantness of 1862, when the commemorations had resulted in a 'deepening of the divide between Church and Dissent' and given an impetus 'to strident Dissent, both in its theological and political forms'.[57]

A final and more prosaic justification for celebrating 1662 was to exploit it for fund-raising purposes, as had been the case fifty years earlier. As Larsen observes, '[t]he practical work which the Congregationalists undertook must ... take its place as part of the enduring impact of the bicentenary.'[58] In 1912, a leading Congregationalist, Silvester Horne, was of the opinion that 'it would be an

53 Ibid.
54 *Manchester Guardian*, 16 October 1912, 6.
55 *Southampton Times and Hampshire Express*, 23 November 1912, 7.
56 *British Congregationalist*, 5 September 1912, 639.
57 Larsen, 'Victorian Nonconformity', 472.
58 Ibid. 461, 471.

ill thing if … celebrations of the past should evaporate with mere verbiage. Some definite provision should be made that the future of the denomination should be secured.'[59] At national level the celebrations were used to promote the Central Fund for Ministerial Support, an initiative for ensuring that all ministers received a stipend of at least £120 per annum.

In Hampshire ambitions were more modest. At Above Bar funds were raised for much-needed repairs to the fabric of the church and for special projects, such as the completion of the Robinson Memorial Hall, dedicated to the first pastor of the church, Nathaniel Robinson. At Christchurch members 'celebrated their 250th birthday by cleaning the church, renovating the organ, and changing the choir seats … [and] thanks to the liberal gifts of many of the friends of the church, the money needed had come in remarkably well'. [60] However, at other churches shortfalls occurred which may indicate that 1662 had lost something of its power to motivate, at least from a financial perspective. Nonetheless, the HCU's Executive Committee still felt that: 'The gifts of such sums of money, in connection with these celebrations, in addition to the amounts required to meet the ordinary work of the Churches … [were] a witness to the vitality of the Church's life.'[61]

CONCLUSION

From the attention given to the 250th anniversary of the Great Ejection in Hampshire it is clear that Edwardian Congregationalists saw the past as a potent instrument in their quest to maintain a vigorous witness at a time when 'religious indifference' was being debated by the CUEW and, in Robbins's colourful phrase, 'Mammon was rampant'.[62] For Congregationalists in Hampshire, as elsewhere, the sacrifices of 1662 served as a rallying cry for the faithful and an impetus for stirring the consciences of the lukewarm. As Thomas Evans, pastor of Bitterne Park Congregational Church in Southampton, highlighted at Romsey's 249th anniversary, there was a need for greater effort on the part of those who

[59] *British Congregationalist*, 17 October 1912, 743.
[60] *Christchurch Times*, 29 April 1911, 5.
[61] Hampshire Record Office, 127M94/62/57, *Annual Repo.t of the Hampshire Congregational Union for 1912* (Southampton, 1912), 20.
[62] Keith Robbins, *History, Religion and Identity in Modern Britain* (London, 1993), 123.

'were lacking in zeal and had lost their moral enthusiasm'.[63] By memorializing 1662 it was hoped to galvanize whole congregations and move into the future renewed and invigorated. However, any subsequent quickening of the pace of church life was soon thrown into question by the traumas of the First World War.

University of Winchester
University of Birmingham

[63] *RA*, 12 May 1911, 1.

THE CHURCH OF ENGLAND IN THE DIOCESE OF LONDON: WHAT DOES HISTORY HAVE TO OFFER TO THE PRESENT-DAY CHURCH?

by JOHN WOLFFE

On 21 February 1900 in St Paul's Cathedral Bishop Mandell Creighton delivered his first, and what proved to be his last, visitation charge to the clergy of the diocese of London.[1] He began by reflecting briefly on the particular challenges of his own position and of London itself, but quickly moved on to focus on current ecclesiastical controversies, especially the nature of holy communion and the practice of confession. Creighton had been a historian long before he became a bishop, and it was therefore natural that his response to contemporary issues should rapidly move into an insightful lecture on Reformation history. His analysis was both specific and general. For example, he pointed out that breakfast was not normally eaten in medieval and early modern societies and so congregations naturally came fasting to a late morning communion service. In changed social circumstances it would be inappropriate 'to revive this custom as an absolute law'.[2] More broadly, he observed:

> Antiquity has a charm to many minds, especially when it can be viewed from a safe distance and is seen through the haze of sentiment. It is hard to distinguish between what upholds and what weakens the permanent elements of character, between truth and fancy, between what is necessary to explain the truth and what fritters away its supreme claim on the intelligence as well as on the feelings. On the other hand, it is easy to attempt the impossible task of avoiding past dangers, by the apparently simple process of cutting oneself adrift from the past altogether, and hoping to remake human nature by starving its finer side out of existence.[3]

---

[1] Mandell Creighton, *The Church and the Nation: Charges and Addresses*, ed. Louise Creighton (London, 1901), 287–323.

[2] Ibid. 308–9.

[3] Ibid. 297.

Creighton for his part advocated the upholding of a *via media* of the 'true temper of the Church of England', which could only be ascertained by careful enquiry.[4]

Creighton's observations well encapsulate an ambivalence in the Church of England's attitude to history that still rings true a century later. This essay, however, draws on the experience of recent collaboration between historians and church leaders in Creighton's own diocese to inform reflection on the current relationship between academic church history and practitioners on the ground. A lack of effective integration remains apparent despite the distinguished tradition of church historical study by Anglican clergy and committed lay people. Clergy, most notably the Chadwick brothers, have continued to scale the heights of academic recognition, while conversely serious historians, from Henry Hart Milman in the mid-nineteenth century to W. M. Jacob in our own day, have held senior positions in the Church of England.[5] As archbishop of Canterbury, Rowan Williams has been an eloquent advocate for the importance of history in contemporary Christian thinking.[6]

On the other hand, the indications are that insights from such scholarship do not readily permeate into the thinking of the Church of England, or indeed that of other denominations, at the grass roots. In theological and ministerial training, church history often appears something of a Cinderella subject, sometimes taught by non-specialists and struggling to maintain its foothold in the curriculum. There is an interesting contrast here with the training of army officers. The Royal Military Academy Sandhurst website describes 'modern military history' as a key component of an army officer's training and one of the institution's three main departments is War Studies, with fourteen members, most of whom are historians. The course includes a two-day trip to Normandy during which cadets examine 'real tactical-level scenarios from the 1944 campaign'. Twentieth-century specialisms predominate among the staff, but there are some with interests extending back to the Revolutionary and Napoleonic wars and even the medieval

---

4   Ibid. 298.
5   As dean of St Paul's and archdeacon of Charing Cross respectively.
6   Most notably in Rowan Williams, *Why Study the Past? The Quest for the Historical Church* (London, 2005).

era.[7] If the British army has deemed it useful for officers shortly to be commanding units in contemporary Afghanistan to have a detailed on-the-ground understanding of battles fought over sixty years ago, and at least some awareness of more remote military history, this would seem to be suggestive of the potential for more mainstream and practical applications of history in the contemporary church.

It was with such considerations in mind that in 2007 John Wolffe (Open University) and Arthur Burns (Kings College, London), in partnership with the diocese of London and Lambeth Palace Library, submitted an application to the Arts and Humanities Research Council's Knowledge Transfer scheme, for a project on 'Modern Religious History and the Contemporary Church'. Funding was subsequently awarded, enabling the project to commence in autumn 2008 and run until late 2011. The focus was on the Church of England in London, but with the object of generating ideas and methodologies that had a potentially much wider application. The diocese of London seemed an especially appropriate partner for such a venture, in view of its strategic location, rich history of innovation and recent record of significant church growth, against the trend of continuing overall Anglican decline. The focus of the project was the nineteenth and early twentieth centuries, reflecting both the expertise of the applicants and a sense that significant and meaningful analogies could be drawn with the present, especially in respect of the impact of large-scale migration on religious life in the metropolis. The venture also received enthusiastic support from the diocesan bishop, Richard Chartres, and committed day-to-day involvement from Archdeacon Bill Jacob. Lambeth Palace Library was involved as a further partner as the main depository for the papers of successive bishops of London, although much relevant archival material is also held by the Guildhall Library and by the London Metropolitan Archives.

There have been two main strands of activity. First, an online resource guide has been developed, designed to provide accessible guidance for those with historical interests but without formal historical training, who want to investigate London church history for its own sake, or in order to contextualize a present-day situa-

---

7   RMA   Sandhurst,   <http://www.army.mod.uk/training_education/training/17057.aspx>, accessed 12 August 2011.

tion or problem. The initial primarily Anglican material has subsequently been enhanced by information relating to the history of other denominations.[8] Users are encouraged to begin with easily accessible activities, such as 'reading' the building of their local church, before plunging into the archives.[9] The resource guide is complemented by material prepared by Neil Evans, Director of Professional Development for the diocese, on what have been termed 'history audits' for parishes. A history audit is not a systematic parish history, but rather a focused endeavour to uncover historical issues and themes that remain relevant to contemporary ministry. For example, the physical situation of church buildings imposes specific opportunities and constraints that may well be usefully understood in a historical context; there are indications that patterns of congregational behaviour in attitudes to clergy, money or neighbouring churches may unwittingly be transmitted across the generations.[10]

Second, the web-based material has been complemented by a series of face-to-face presentations and discussions. Members of the team visited a majority of the twenty-three deaneries in the diocese, and have also contributed to a variety of clergy and lay training events. There was a presentation to the Diocesan Synod in December 2009, and a presentation on interim insights to a gathering of invited senior clergy in December 2010. During the final phase of the project in 2011 there were three regional presentations to other dioceses, and a final London event exploring the religious diversity of the East End and seeking to apply the insights gained to other Christian and non-Christian religious traditions.

What follows will summarize the key points made in presentations to church audiences, thus also offering a short survey of relevant literature, and then reflect on the implications of the experience for academic ecclesiastical history. A particular focus

---

[8]   This development has been facilitated by further 'Follow-On' funding from the AHRC in 2012–13. Their essential support through both grants is most gratefully acknowledged.

[9]   'Building on History: The Church in London', <http://www.open.ac.uk/arts/building-on-history-project/resource-guide/about.htm>. It is intended that in the longer term this material will be maintained on the LPL website.

[10]   <http://www.open.ac.uk/arts/building-on-history-project/resource-guide/history-audit.htm>; Neil Evans and John Maiden, *What Can Churches Learn from their Past? The Parish History Audit* (Cambridge, 2012).

in discussions with church leaders has been on questioning the narrative of secularization, at least as presented in its starkest form, notably by Steve Bruce.[11] Attention has been drawn to the evidence that church attendance was never in the last two centuries anything approaching universal, at least not in London.[12] Audiences have also been given examples of significant religious vitality in the period, notably the massive church-building and home mission initiatives undertaken during the episcopates of Charles Blomfield (1828–56) and Archibald Campbell Tait (1856–68) and the later Forty-Five Churches Fund, providing places of worship for newly suburbanized north-west London in the 1920s and 1930s.[13] Such initiatives, they have been reminded, need to be evaluated in an informed historical context, rather than by potentially anachronistic twenty-first century criteria, or by judgements on long-term legacies that obscure substantial medium-term achievements. Moreover, popular attitudes have been characterized as not wholly secular, but rather as manifesting a 'diffusive Christianity', 'vicarious religion' and non-specific supernaturalism that was conducive to maintaining residual links with the churches through rites of passage and potentially responsive to effective mission.[14] Hence the church presence has been presented as one of change and fluctuation rather than of inexorable decline. Attention has thus been drawn to the historical importance of individual agency in determining the trajectories of parishes which sometimes looked very different from those of near neighbours with similar socio-economic conditions. Present-day leaders have therefore been

---

[11] Steve Bruce, *God is Dead: Secularization in the West* (Oxford, 2002).

[12] House of Commons Parliamentary Papers 1852–3 [1690], *Census of Great Britain, 1851: Religious Worship, England and Wales, Report and Tables* (London, 1853); Richard Mudie-Smith, ed., *The Religious Life of London* (London, 1904).

[13] Important recent studies are Arthur Burns, ed., '"My unfortunate parish": Anglican Urban Ministry in Bethnal Green, 1809–c.1850', in Melanie Barber and Stephen Taylor, eds, intro. Gabriel Sewell, *From the Reformation to the Permissive Society*, Church of England Record Society 18 (Woodbridge, 2010), 269–393; Rex Walford, *The Growth of 'New London' in Suburban Middlesex (1918–1945) and the Response of the Church of England* (Lampeter, 2007). The Tait phase is the focus of Open University doctoral research by Sarah Flew; see, in this volume, eadem, 'Money Matters: The Neglect of Finance in the Historiography of Modern Christianity', 430–43.

[14] Jeffrey Cox, *The English Churches in a Secular Society: Lambeth, 1870–1930* (New York, 1982), 93–5; Grace Davie, *Religion in Modern Europe: A Memory Mutates* (Oxford, 2000); S. C. Williams, *Religious Belief and Popular Culture in Southwark, c.1880–1939* (Oxford, 1999).

urged to see themselves as more the masters of their own destiny than the victims of events and social forces beyond their control. Indeed it has been suggested that the perception of failure among clergy led to a self-fulfilling crisis of morale in the earlier twentieth century, while in the 1960s and 1970s the diocese's sense that it was managing decline led to premature and short-sighted closures of churches.[15] Granted that the later twentieth-century cultural changes characterized by Callum Brown as 'the death of Christian Britain' have reinforced a sense of challenge to traditional church structures, the argument that an alternative narrative is possible has been given plausibility in London by the substantial rise in electoral roll membership since 1990.[16]

A linked point has been encouragement to reflect on the historical contingency of current structures. For example, it has been pointed out that the diocese of London in its present form is something of an accident of history. Since ancient times, the Thames has marked the southern boundary of the diocese, an arrangement that had some logic in the medieval era when there was little urban development south of the river, but which in more recent centuries has militated against any overall ecclesiastical strategy for the metropolis as a whole. In the nineteenth century there were various proposals for reorganizing diocesan structures, including a widely canvassed idea in the mid-1850s for creating a new Anglican diocese of Westminster. Hence there was no inevitability about the eventual structures that emerged, with the creation of the dioceses of St Albans in 1877, Southwark in 1905 and Chelmsford in 1914. These had the collective effect of relieving London of its original substantial Essex and Hertfordshire rural hinterland, while reinforcing the division of the metropolis at the Thames, and introducing a further dividing line, by placing substantial parts of north-east London in the diocese of Chelmsford.[17] There is a legitimate debate to be had

---

[15]   Cox, *English Churches*, 272–3; Walford, *Growth of 'New London'*, 213–14.

[16]   Callum G. Brown, *The Death of Christian Britain: Understanding Secularisation 1800–2000*, 2nd edn (London, 2009); Bob Jackson and Alan Piggot, 'Another Capital Idea: Church Growth and Decline in the Diocese of London 2003–2010', online at: <http://www.london.anglican.org/CapitalIdea>, accessed 23 August 2012.

[17]   Arthur Burns, *The Diocesan Revival in the Church of England c.1800–1870* (Oxford, 1999), 192–215; P. S. Morrish, 'County and Urban Diocese: Nineteenth-Century Discussion on Ecclesiastical Geography', *JEH* 26 (1975), 279–300; R. T. Davidson and

as to whether this arrangement serves the Church of England in contemporary London better than a single enormous metropolitan diocese would do, but such a discussion can be usefully informed by an awareness of the context and rationale for the original decisions regarding the current structure. Similar points can be made at the local level, where legal and personal factors made it much easier in the nineteenth century to plant new churches by division and subdivision within existing parishes rather than by more strategic reorganization involving two or more parishes. Hence, for example, the north-west London suburb of Cricklewood lacks any Anglican church on its main street, which is the A5 arterial road and the historic boundary between the ancient parishes of Hendon and Willesden.[18]

A further emphasis has been on the value of looking at past controversies as a means of inducing a sense of proportion in current internal Anglican arguments over (particularly) women bishops and homosexual clergy. It tends to come as a surprise to current leaders that passions in the nineteenth century ran quite as high over the theology of baptism (in the Gorham case from 1847 to 1850) and then over ritualism, which was seen by its opponents as subverting the essential character of the Church of England.[19] There is also a consistency in frustration regarding the pastoral consequences of such disputes. Creighton's words in 1900 have a strikingly contemporary resonance:

> Whatever may be your opinion about the importance of the points at issue, or about the need for controversy, you will all

W. Benham, *Life of Archibald Campbell Tait, Archbishop of Canterbury*, 2 vols (London, 1891), 1: 201–2.

[18] In 1850 Bishop Blomfield suggested to the vicar of Willesden that he should collaborate with the vicar of Hendon in the development of a new church for Cricklewood: London, LPL, Blomfield Papers, vol. 51, fols 330–1, Blomfield to Rev. R. W. Burton, 18 August 1851. However, the idea was not pursued, and church extension proceeded through division of the two existing parishes.

[19] Bishop Phillpotts's famous threat to break communion with Archbishop Sumner should he institute Gorham over his head (*A Letter to the Archbishop of Canterbury from the Bishop of Exeter* [London, 1850], 252) was indicative of the passions aroused by the Gorham case: see Owen Chadwick, *The Victorian Church: Part I, 1829–1859* (London, 1966), 250–71. On ritualism, see James Bentley, *Ritualism and Politics in Victorian Britain: The Attempt to Legislate for Belief* (Oxford, 1978); Dominic Janes, *Victorian Reformation: The Fight over Idolatry in the Church of England 1840–1860* (New York, 2009); Martin Wellings, *Evangelicals Embattled: Responses of Evangelicals in the Church of England to Ritualism, Darwinism and Theological Liberalism 1890–1930*, SEHT (Carlisle, 2003).

agree with me in thinking that the diversion of energy from practical work, and the appearance of disunion and dissension, are in themselves disastrous; and that true wisdom demands that we should consider how suspicion can be allayed, and the Church be able to resume its proper task of working peacefully for the highest interests of the people.[20]

History does not offer straightforward models for conflict resolution, but it does offer ample illustration of the negative consequences of introverted preoccupation with internal arguments, and also, more positively, of the propensity of Anglicans eventually to learn to live creatively with even quite radical differences.

Finally, the project has highlighted the potentialities of history for raising the profile of churches in their communities, through collaboration with local historians. The online resource guide has been designed to support such activity, and was complemented in October 2010 by a well-attended workshop for this constituency. The endeavour has been to encourage good practice in the writing of parish history, through, in particular, awareness of the wider historiographical context of academic church history and encouragement of wide community involvement. For example, young people might be enlisted to conduct oral history interviews with older members of congregations, or a whole village participate in research endeavours, as was the case in a particularly impressive project at Littlebury in Essex.[21] Church schools offer a further channel for wider community engagement, with encouragement to see the church building itself as a valuable resource for teaching about Christian and community history, an idea successfully piloted at Christ Church, Hampstead.[22]

What then are the implications of this experience for academic historians of Christianity? The potential dangers should first be acknowledged. There is an obvious tension between the academic insistence on balance and nuance and the understandable interest of clergy on the ground in gaining clear-cut insights into immediate pastoral and practical problems. Awareness of the risks was

---

[20] Creighton, *Church and Nation*, 290.
[21] Parish of Littlebury Millennium Society, *Littlebury: A Parish History* (Littlebury, 2005).
[22] See <http://www.open.ac.uk/arts/building-on-history-project/schools/index.html>.

heightened when one west London clergyman apparently told his local paper that the project showed that churchgoing is as popular at the present time as in the Victorian era, a seriously distorted representation of the evidence presented at the seminar he attended.[23] More subtly, it proves difficult to get busy people to move on from taking away a single 'big idea', such as the importance of clergy leadership or the problematic nature of the conventional secularization narrative, to spending time on developing a more informed engagement with history.

There is also the prima facie objection that an aspiration for historians actually to assist the work of the contemporary churches risks compromising their objectivity and detachment. Such thinking, however, would surely seem strange to colleagues in university engineering departments who see direct connections between their work and actual construction projects, and also, in a more cognate field to church history, to art historians who are used to collaborating with galleries and museums. If there is a difficulty for church historians, it surely lies not on a level of principle, but rather on one of practical experience in establishing the ground rules for such associations in a way that is responsive to the needs and capabilities of all parties. The prospect that research in British universities will in future be assessed for its 'impacts on the economy, society and/or culture' constitutes a further incentive to the grasping of this nettle.[24]

However, this line of development also offers exciting potential to stimulate new thinking about the history of the churches. There is intriguing potential to build on conversations with present-day church leaders to form new hypotheses about institutional and organizational constraints on historical development, which can then productively be explored and tested in the archives. For example, a recent study of church growth in London links historical to contemporary experience. Analysis of the role of church buildings in Finchley links archival research on their original construction and nineteenth-century development to consideration of their present-day utilization.[25] Moreover, it is hoped that if

[23] 'Church Membership is on the Rise in Ealing', *Ealing Gazette*, 7 December 2010.
[24] REF 2014, *Assessment Framework and Guidance on Submissions* (Bristol, 2011), 6.
[25] John Wolffe and Bob Jackson, 'Anglican Resurgence: The Church of England

the project succeeds in its aim of stimulating and facilitating more rigorous community-based research at the parish level, this will in years to come provide building blocks for academic analysis of grass-roots church life that is more sensitive than hitherto to the rich tapestry of varied local experience. A development of the project to encompass not only other Christian traditions but also Jews and Muslims has further extended the potentialities for gaining fresh understanding of the historic roles of religion in local communities.

Above all such conversations offer potential for better understanding of the dynamics of the relationship of churches to their own history. Past historians, from John Foxe to Richard William Church, have been highly influential in fostering partisan readings of history, alongside the liberal Anglican tradition represented by Mandell Creighton, which has sought to provide historical legitimacy for claims of Anglican comprehensiveness. More recent historians, whether churchmen or academics, conscious of the constraints of modern scientific history, have tried to avoid such ulterior agendas.[26] Arguably, however, while church history has gained in objectivity it has lost in obvious relevance to the needs of clergy and committed laity. Institutional loss of memory in the later twentieth-century churches is itself a historical phenomenon worthy of study, and may well provide a worthwhile perspective on the wider sense of terminal religious crisis characteristic of the period. However the deficiency is also one that is worth seeking to correct in the future, by emphasizing the value of history, not as a resource for perpetuating past battles but rather as one for stimulating creative innovation in pastoral and community engagement.

It is important not to have the illusion that the task is a straightforward or short-term one. The 'Modern Religious History and the Contemporary Church' project has benefited from substantial public funding, an able and committed team, enthusiastic collaborators, and the direct personal interest of both the bishop of London and the archbishop of Canterbury. Nevertheless, after

in London', in David Goodhew, ed., *Church Growth in Britain 1980–2010* (Aldershot, 2012), 23–39; John Wolffe, 'The Chicken or the Egg? Building Churches and Building Congregations in the Diocese of London', forthcoming in *Material Religion* 9 (2013).

²⁶ *Pace* John Kent, who in *The Unacceptable Face: The Modern Church in the Eyes of the Historian* (London 1987) argues that church history has remained inappropriately subordinate to theological and ideological agendas.

three years' work, it has done more to pose questions and chart a direction of travel, than to achieve widespread change in the Church of England's attitude to history. There is much more to be done, particularly in seeking to embed its ideas in the training and thinking of future clergy and lay leaders, and in applying such thinking to other denominations, tasks that will require the wider commitment of ecclesiastical historians as well as of the churches themselves.

The Open University

PART II

CHANGING PERSPECTIVES ON CHURCH HISTORY

WHAT DID WOMEN DO FOR THE EARLY CHURCH? THE RECENT HISTORY OF A QUESTION

by JUDITH M. LIEU

The question posed in the title deliberately reverses one that has accompanied me through my academic career: what did the early church do for women? The reversal signals what will prove to be an underlying theme of what follows, namely the role of women in history as objects or as the subjects of action and of discourse. Yet already the question as conventionally phrased highlights different points of stress that reflect where it belongs within reflective historiography, the subject of this volume. Firstly, '*What* did the early church *do*?' The coming of early Christianity, it is implied, brought blessings or perhaps curses, evoking a way of writing church history which goes back to Eusebius and which continues both through Edward Gibbon and through those who still portray the social and religious context of the time as one of the inarticulate search for alternative conceptions of the divine or for alternative social values that Christianity would answer. Secondly, 'for *women*': thus, a deliberate rejection of any universalizing interpretation of such effects; a recognition, or at least a suspicion, that any apparently universalizing claim is actually spoken from a 'normal' that is already gendered as male; an invitation to ask how women's experience could be recovered, what the sources would look like, and, indeed, whether it can be recovered from the extant sources. Thirdly, 'the *early* church', chosen here not just because that happens to be the period of my own work but because the origins of the church have a claim for a particular authority, at least for most traditions within the Christian church herself, and because, whatever may have happened thereafter, and whether the thereafter is portrayed as a story of advance or of decline, beginnings matter. Hence in some circles the early church is itself the problem and the question is focused more sharply: what did Jesus do for women? What did Paul do for women? Therefore, fourthly, the 'women' of the initial question are not only those of the period itself, but also those of subsequent generations, particularly if not only within the Christian church. It is not surprising, then, that many of those who have asked the question, and who have sought to answer it, have been women, a first step in justifying the reformulation of the question as posed here.

It is not only the bias of a biblical scholar that would trace the history of such questions back through, although not simply to, *The Woman's Bible* (1895–8), edited by Elizabeth Cady Stanton.[1] Cady Stanton's team, consisting entirely of women, subjected initially the opening books of the Bible to a merciless, if to our eyes a somewhat naïve, critique of their representation and expectations of women; but their target was no less those who used the Bible – and indeed who had used it on the one hand to support the campaign for the abolition of slavery and, on the other, simultaneously to exclude women from the platform in that campaign. Cady Stanton herself dismissed any divine authority claimed by the Bible, and she was pessimistic about attitudes to women in all organized religion, but, she wrote, 'the most bitter outspoken enemies of woman are found among the clergymen and bishops of the Protestant religion'.[2]

Her enterprise was controversial, and not only among those clergymen and bishops. Cady Stanton states that a number of deeply sympathetic women scholars felt forced to exclude themselves from her team for fear of losing any standing they had in the academic community – not an unreasonable fear considering the obstacle-strewn biographies even of some more recent women scholars. Indeed, publication of *The Woman's Bible* was followed by a contentious formal repudiation by the National American Woman Suffrage Association in 1896. Thus the question was already posed: what does it mean to interpret as a woman and who is served by so doing?

The Woman's Bible was republished in 1985 when it became something of an icon for the renewed wave of what may loosely be termed 'feminist scholarship on the Bible', an ever more disparate conglomerate of questions and methods.[3] It provided such

[1] Elizabeth Cady Stanton, *The Woman's Bible* (New York, 1895, 1898; repr. with intro. by Dale Spencer, Edinburgh, 1985).
[2] Ibid. 13.
[3] For its range already in 1985, see Letty M. Russell, ed., *Feminist Interpretation of the Bible* (Oxford, 1985); Adela Yarbro Collins, ed., *Feminist Perspectives on Biblical*

scholarship with its own history in opposition to those who dismissed it as driven purely by contemporary fashion, and it heralded studies of other nineteenth-century interpreters of the Bible who were women. The context of feminist scholarship in the 1980s shared some elements with that of Cady Stanton. By then a number of Protestant churches had embraced the ordination of women, with some consciously reclaiming aspects of their own distinctive historical heritage; however, debates particularly within the Church of England and the Roman Catholic Church on the question continued to appeal to the Bible and to the practice of the early church. For some the goal was to find and demonstrate support therein for whatever position they championed, for others the exercise provoked or reinforced their questioning of the authority accorded to 'origins', whether these were scripturally or ecclesially inscribed. This preoccupation with office-holding skewed, and arguably still sometimes continues to skew, the scholarly concerns concerning women, leaving unexamined or unchallenged the historical and theological presuppositions of the underlying arguments.[4] Yet the broader focus was still largely the invisibility of women in so many standard accounts of the biblical and ecclesial record; hence the primary task was still to go woman-hunting, exemplified by the starting point of many a workshop, 'name three women prophets, three women disciples'.

For some this 'act of recovery' was all that was needed to redress the imbalance: the voice of optimism is well represented by Dorothy Pape's triumphant conclusion, written in 1977: 'perhaps the most remarkable instance of Christ's confidence in women was when he gave the first revelation of his risen life to one or more women' – an assertion that well illustrates the persistent question of where agency lies.[5] Too often such optimism relied on a negative contrast: for example, claiming that Paul gave women more

Studies (Chico, CA, 1985). The explosion of bibliography since means that only key or representative examples will be cited in what follows.

4 See, e.g., the tendency to see the primary question as that of the roles or functions women could fulfil: e.g. Mary Hayter, *The New Eve in Christ: The Use and Abuse of the Bible in the Debate about Women in the Church* (London, 1987); Susanne Heine, *Women and Early Christianity: Are the Feminist Scholars Right?* (ET London, 1987); Ben Witherington III, *Women in the Earliest Churches*, SNTS Monograph Series 59 (Cambridge, 1988), 3, 219–20; see nn. 24 and 32 below.

5 Dorothy Pape, *God and Women: A Fresh Look at what the New Testament says about Women* (London, 1977), 57; see the discussion in Judith Lieu, 'The Women's Resurrec-

status than did Graeco-Roman thought where a woman was, in Aristotelian terms, a misbegotten male, or that Jesus spoke even to women, something a Jewish rabbi would (on this account) never do; Pape's 'Christ's confidence' presupposes the much-repeated generalization that in the first century the testimony of Jewish women was not trusted. By the 1990s the unreflective anti-Jewishness of much feminist scholarship was being catalogued; such denigrations of Jewish attitudes grew out of the anxiety to be able to demonstrate that Jesus or early Christianity was not just different but superior to its peers, and it arose from the failure to read the so-called background sources with the same critical eye as was dedicated to the Christian ones.[6]

A more critical, and sombre, note was sounded by Elisabeth Schüssler Fiorenza in 1983. Her formative *In Memory of Her* counselled a 'hermeneutic of suspicion', a method of reading the sources that questioned any assumption that they straightforwardly replicated 'how it was'.[7] Women, she argued, have been erased from the record by the conventions of a scholarship that ignores their presence or that turns Phoebe from a 'deacon' (as the Greek is translated elsewhere) to a mere 'servant' or even an ecclesiastically more admissible 'deaconess', and from being Paul's patroness to his 'good friend' (Rom. 16: 1); they have been erased by the patterns of textual transmission and translation that reassigned the apostle Junia's gender as Junias (Rom. 16: 7); they have been erased by the rules of oral tradition and written formulation that ensured that the woman must remain nameless of whom Jesus said, 'wherever the Gospel is proclaimed in the whole world, what she has done will be told in remembrance of her' (Mark 14: 9); and they have been erased by the processes of authorization which

tion Testimony', in *Resurrection: Essays in Honour of Leslie Houlden*, ed. Stephen Barton and Graham Stanton (London, 1994), 34–44.

6 See Katharina von Kellenbach, *Anti-Judaism in Feminist Religious Writings* (Atlanta, GA, 1994); Luise Schottroff and Marie-Theres Wacker, eds, *Von der Wurzel getragen: christlich-feministische Exegese in Auseinandersetzung mit Antijudaismus*, Biblical Interpretation Series 17 (Leiden, 1996). The contribution of Jewish women New Testament scholars to the debate has been particularly important, e.g. Amy-Jill Levine, 'Second Temple Judaism, Jesus, and Women: *Yeast of Eden*', *Biblical Interpretation* 2 (1994), 8–33; Levine is also editor of the Feminist Companion to the New Testament and Early Christian Literature series (London, 2001–).

7 Elisabeth Schüssler Fiorenza, *In Memory of Her: A Feminist Theological Reconstruction of Christian Origins* (New York, 1983).

excluded from the canon the tale of Paul's feisty disciple, Thecla, while including Paul's injunction to Timothy, 'Let a woman learn in silence with full submission' (1 Tim. 2: 11).[8] Schüssler Fiorenza's work, in which the hermeneutic of suspicion was to be followed by a critical recovery and remembering of women's stories, if necessary through the use of historical imagination, set a pattern taken up by many since.[9] Initially much of this work was pursued in anglophone settings; however, before long German scholars, although not all in established posts in faculties of theology, were advocating the recovery of 'Lydia's impatient sisters', albeit with less emphasis on a 'hermeneutic of suspicion'.[10] Particular note should be made of one of the early projects of the Institute for Ecumenical Research established for Hans Küng in the University of Tübingen after he lost his authority to teach within the Catholic faculty, 'Frau und Christentum', among whose outcomes was a detailed analysis of Greek and Latin sources on early Christian women by Anne Jensen, *Gottes selbstbewusste Töchter. Frauenemanzipation in frühen Christentum?*[11]

However by the 1980s biblical studies, like its sister disciplines,

---

[8] Thecla is the 'heroine' of a series of episodes within the second-century *Acts of Paul*; these chapters are often treated as an independent unit, 'The Acts of (Paul and) Thecla', although their separate circulation and expansion appears to be a later secondary development: see W. Schneemelcher, 'Acts of Paul', in E. Hennecke, *New Testament Apocrypha*, ed. W. Schneemelcher, 2 vols (ET London, 1965), 2: 326, 353–64; Jeremy W. Barrier, *The Acts of Paul and Thecla: A Critical Introduction and Commentary*, WUNT II, 270 (Tübingen, 2009). A critical edition of the Greek text is awaited.

[9] A parallel course was followed in the recovery of Jewish women; see, e.g., Tal Ilan, *Mine and Yours are Hers: Retrieving Women's History from Rabbinic Literature*, Arbeiten zur Geschichte des antiken Judentums und des Christentums 41 (Leiden, 1997); eadem, *Integrating Women into Second Temple History*, Texte und Studien zum antiken Judentums 76 (Tübingen, 1999).

[10] Luise Schottroff, *Lydias ungeduldige Schwestern* (Gütersloh, 1994), ET *Lydia's Impatient Sisters: A Feminist Social History of Christianity* (Louisville, KY, 1995); the reference is to Acts 16: 11–15. See Luise Schottroff, Silvia Schroer and Marie-Theres Wacker, *Feministische Exegese: Forschungserträge zur Bibel aus der Perspektive von Frauen* (Darmstadt, 1995), ET *Feminist Interpretation: The Bible in Women's Perspective* (Minneapolis, MN, 1998), who also trace the history back to *The Woman's Bible* (ibid. 3–7), and (ibid. 25) identify the first German scholarly monograph of feminist biblical exegesis as Elisabeth Moltmann-Wendel, *Ein eigener Mensch werden: Frauen um Jesus* (Gütersloh, 1980), ET *The Women around Jesus: Reflections on Authentic Personhood* (London, 1982).

[11] Anne Jensen, *Gottes selbstbewusste Töchter. Frauenemanzipation in frühen Christentum?*, Frauenforum (Freiburg, 1992), ET in an abbreviated form as *God's Self-Confident Daughters: Early Christianity and the Liberation of Women* (Louisville, KY, 1996); the difficulties Dr Jensen faced in furthering her scholarly career after the closure of the institute are well documented.

was already experiencing the destabilizing of the unquestioned claims to pure objectivity within the classical 'historical-critical' approach – an approach that was fundamental to Cady Stanton's own enterprise and that had still been normative for those trained in the 1960s and early 1970s, rooted in the exposition of the Bible as a linguistically, culturally and historically circumscribed text. Influences from the social sciences had already endeavoured to position it within a broader social context of practices and ideas, a social context within which women, sometimes categorized along with slaves, animals and inanimate topics such as war or wealth, could be located and analysed. From a more theoretical perspective, the social sciences could also provide models for interpreting changing patterns of authority within which women had become the victims of a perhaps inevitable institutionalization or routinization. At the same time, a newly academically respectable sensitivity to the 'Bible as literature', influenced by narratology in literary studies, looked beyond the text as an imprint of 'how it was' and invited the lifting of female characters out of its pages, scrutinizing the roles to which they were assigned or seeking to give them names and a voice where the text failed to do so; this approach proved particularly well suited to Old Testament narratives but was also, as shall be seen, to be applied to early Christian ones.[12] Perhaps most incisively there was not simply the acknowledgement that all interpretation is from somewhere, as if this were something of which the interpreter must purge herself, but the celebration of this locatedness. In particular, those who interpreted as women could find their own voice and permission to acknowledge their subjectivity. Thus there was the blossoming of ideological readings, political, post-colonial, feminist, queer, and intersections between these;[13] for such readings the focus of the interpretative lens was the rhetoric or persuasive effect of the texts, whether explicit or implicit, actual or potential, played out in the history of reception and of application, or available for appropriation. On the one hand these ways of reading have taught a greater sensitivity to

---

[12] Biblical scholars have favoured their own term, 'narrative criticism', for this analysis focused on literary strategies within the text.

[13] For an overview of these methods in general, see G. Aichele et al. ['The Bible and Culture Collective'] *The Postmodern Bible* (New Haven, CT, 1995), esp. the essay on 'Feminist and Womanist Criticism': ibid. 225–71. Essays in 'The Feminist Companion' Series (see n. 6 above) illustrate the various approaches discussed in this paragraph.

the power structures, including the interpretative power structures, which affect all women's lives; on the other, as scholars have come to acknowledge their own locatedness, western white women do not presume to speak for Latin-American women, or for Korean or for Afro-Caribbean women, nor they for each other. Within these other settings this has often offered mechanisms for those working within the churches to read the texts and to claim from them alternative narratives to that historically associated with the Western church.[14]

In this overview, biblical studies has proved useful terrain for outlining the navigational skills demanded by the question with which we started, not least because it is methodologically a highly self-reflective discipline, focused on the close reading of texts. Our access to the early church is almost exclusively through the texts it produced and preserved, although it was part of a world that is much more richly available through material remains and through other textual sources. Answering that initial question, therefore, remains a matter of reading, of how we read, and from where – as well as what we read. In recent decades the interest in what lies outside the conventional boundaries of 'the history of the church', understood as a relatively linear and unfolding narrative centred on institutions, has coincided with the discovery of texts which themselves belong outside those ecclesial (or 'orthodox') bound-aries. These, especially the so-called 'gnostic', texts have allowed the exploration of what once seemed mysterious and yet either threatening or seductive territory, although they have sometimes revealed that it is less threatening and less seductive than those within the church had portrayed it.[15]

In what follows, the effect of these conceptual and methodo-logical developments as applied to the study of women in the early church, together with the role of women scholars in them, will be explored through three case studies. The first of these is the claim that the benefits that early Christianity offered women, the 'good it did for' them, are attested by the significant numbers of women attracted to it, starting with Phoebe and Junia already mentioned.

---

[14] See, e.g., Musa W. Dube, *Postcolonial Feminist Interpretation of the Bible* (St Louis, MO, 2000).

[15] In particular the texts discovered *c.*1945 at Nag Hammadi: see James M. Robinson, ed., *The Nag Hammadi Library in English* (Leiden, 1977).

At the beginning of the twentieth century, in his *Expansion of Christianity in the First Three Centuries*, Adolf von Harnack had dedicated a chapter to the spread of Christianity among women.[16] Harnack had some notable predecessors on whom he could draw. The second-century philosopher Celsus charged Christians with targeting women: 'In private houses also we see wool-workers, cobblers, laundry-workers and the most illiterate and bucolic yokels, who would not dare to say anything at all in front of their elders and more intelligent masters. But when they get hold of children in private and some stupid women …'.[17] Celsus goes on to imply that these 'victims' are taught to reject the authority of their elders and betters. Similarly, in Minucius Felix's *Octavius*, the Roman opponent, Caecilius, complains that Christians collect together the most illiterate of society and 'credulous women who give way with the weakness natural to their sex'.[18] It is striking that in response Christian apologists do not deny the principle: Athenagoras mimics the categories when he underlines a contrast with the philosophers who delight in syllogisms, etymologies and ambiguities: 'Among us you will find ordinary people, artisans, and old women, who if they are unable to establish by argument the benefit from the teaching, do demonstrate by deed the benefit from the exercise of will'.[19] Such references, taken at face value, easily inspired more complex reconstructions of the past. In 1996 Rodney Stark, adopting a sociological perspective, still quoted Harnack to affirm 'the general truth that Christianity was laid hold of by women', and deduced a 2:1 imbalance of women to men in early Christianity; to this, together with the Christian rejection of abortion and infanticide, he attributed the rapid increase of the number of Christians in society.[20]

Alongside or behind all this ran a debate as to the explanation for this predominance of women: whether they had least to

---

[16] Adolf von Harnack, *The Expansion of Christianity in the First Three Centuries*, 2 vols (ET London, 1904–5), 2: 217–39.

[17] Origen, *Contra Celsum* 3.44, transl. Henry Chadwick (Cambridge, 1953), 158.

[18] Minucius Felix, *Octavius* 8.4, in Tertullian, *Apology, De Spectaculis*, transl. T. R. Glover / Minucius Felix, *Octavius*, transl. Gerald H. Rendall, LCL 250 (London, 1953), 335.

[19] Athenagoras, *Legatio* 11.3–4, in idem, *Legatio* and *De Resurrectione*, ed. and transl. William R. Schoedel, OECT (Oxford, 1972), 25. Other apologists continue this theme.

[20] Rodney Stark, *The Rise of Christianity: A Sociologist Reconsiders History* (Princeton, NJ, 1996), esp. 95–128.

lose, most to gain, or indeed whether it was to be attributed to what Caecilius called 'the weakness natural to their sex' and to what some since have seen as a natural affinity between women and religion.[21] Earlier scholarly accounts were content to appeal to the offer of equality inherent in the teaching of Jesus or Paul, often, as already seen, reinforced by a negative reading of Jewish and Graeco-Roman attitudes to women.[22] Applying sociological theory to the Pauline letters, Wayne A. Meeks used theories of status dissonance as a primary model for explaining the number of 'upwardly mobile' members of the churches mentioned therein; among these were women who found in Christianity avenues towards the status that the conventions of Roman society denied them.[23] Such views also coalesced with the then strong interest in the household as the primary context of early Christian association and in an (often over-simplistic) modelling of the private, the sphere of women, versus the public. They enabled the argument that it was as the church moved in to the public sphere, or became consciously sensitive to its public perception, that opportunities for women became progressively curtailed, and that such anxieties may already be identified within some New Testament texts (e.g. 1 Tim. 5: 3–16; 1 Pet. 3: 3–6).[24] It is striking that this attempt to negotiate through social theory the conventional boundaries of the canon partly mimics the theological concerns in the 1950s and 1960s, particularly within German Protestant New Testament study, over the emergence of 'early catholicism' (*Frühkatholizismus*), identified as the move beyond the 'apostolic age' to the idea of

---

[21] On this and what follows, see further Judith M. Lieu, 'The "Attraction of Women" in/to Early Judaism and Christianity: Gender and the Politics of Conversion', *JSNT* 72 (1998), 5–22, repr. in eadem, *Neither Jew nor Greek: Constructing Early Christianity* (Edinburgh, 2002), 83–99.

[22] So, e.g., Ben Witherington III, *Women in the Ministry of Jesus: A Study of Jesus' Attitude to Women and their Roles as Reflected in his Earthly Life*, SNTS Monograph Series 51 (Cambridge, 1984); idem, *Women in the Early Church*.

[23] Wayne A. Meeks, *The First Urban Christians: The Social World of the Apostle Paul* (New Haven, CT, 1983), 16–23; 70–3.

[24] See, e.g., Susan Heine, *Women and Early Christianity*, 124–46; Karen Jo Torjesen, *When Women were Priests: Women's Leadership in the Early Church and the Scandal of their Subordination in the Rise of Christianity* (New York, 1993), 155–76; Ulrike Wagener, *Die Ordnung des 'Hauses Gottes': Der Ort von Frauen in der Ekklesiologie und Ethik der Pastoralbriefe*, WUNT II, 65 (Tübingen, 1994). A more nuanced picture of the early period is presented by Carolyn Osiek and Margaret MacDonald with Janet H. Tulloch, *A Woman's Place: House Churches in Earliest Christianity* (Minneapolis, MN, 2006).

the church as institution and as agent of salvation, and evident, according to some, already within parts of the New Testament.[25]

Yet attention to the deliberate rhetorical fashioning of these texts cautions against citing them too quickly as evidence for the position of women; they belong within explicit polemic or apologetic, and they draw on what were established and unquestioned *topoi*. Women, it is assumed, are by definition irrational and gullible; from the polemical perspective of Celsus or of Caecilius, they are, therefore, hardly good advertisements for the intellectual or social credentials of the new religion. More importantly, in Roman thought the control of women in private is not a private matter: entrapping them in private households undermines the proper ordering of society, while according them status is a recipe for social collapse; an appeal to women is a potent symbol of subversion. Conversely, for its apologists, women represent the accessibility of the Christian message and its preachers' refusal to rely on the sophistry often criticized in popular philosophical teachers; they also represent its practicability – it leads to action, and women can act, their behaviour demonstrating its practical and beneficial effect, in a manner that some contemporaries were also claiming for women's study of philosophy. These women do not belong to the world of head-counting but to that of polemical point-scoring, and it is the apologetic negotiation of conventional values that first demands exploration.

A second case study develops and complicates such a picture, taking as its representative the account of the martyrdom of Perpetua and Felicitas in North Africa at the beginning of the third century.[26] This martyrdom account, widely seen as near-contemporary, is not only conventionally named after the two women, even though it also tells of the deaths of their male companions, but also incorporates the diary of Perpetua told in the first person; this has often been treated as authentically representing a woman's voice, a rarity in the ancient, as well as in the not-so-ancient,

---

[25] For this deliberate renegotiation of canonical boundaries, see Elisabeth Schüssler Fiorenza, ed., *Searching the Scriptures: A Feminist Commentary*, 2 vols (New York, 1993–4), which includes forty 'Christian' texts.

[26] Most commonly cited is the convenient, albeit not critical, Latin text and English translation by Herbert Musurillo, *The Acts of the Christian Martyrs*, OECT (Oxford, 1972), 106–31; see now the detailed study with text and translation by Thomas J. Heffernan, *The Passion of Perpetua and Felicity* (New York, 2012).

world.[27] Herbert Musurillo may have had this story particularly in mind when he wrote in the introduction to his corpus of Martyr Acts:

> Foremost, of course, is the portrayal of the martyrs' courage in the face of the most vicious torture and humiliation, a courage shared by both sexes, by both slave and free, as though in fulfilment of Paul's pronouncement in Galatians (3: 28), *For you are all one in Christ Jesus* ...[28]

This appeal to the conventional model of female liberation was echoed by William Frend in 'Blandina and Perpetua: Two Early Christian Heroines' (1978): 'Christianity provided scope for the human need of achievement and daring for a cause. Those who joined found themselves in a close-knit society without social or sexual distinction ... In the equality practised by the Christians many women found their chance of self-fulfilment'.[29] In recent studies, Perpetua and that other eponymous heroine, Thecla, have become iconic both of early Christian women and for contemporary women in the church, as is witnessed by the number of popular as well as of scholarly translations and discussions of the texts.[30] For many they embody the role of women in the early church, and what 'the church did for women'. Conventionally they have been prime examples for 'recovery and remembering' as advocated by Schüssler Fiorenza, offering an alternative memory or narrative for women; such a view was encouraged by the readiness to accept Perpetua's diary as authentic, and by the attempts to discover within the 'Acts of Paul and Thecla' and other Apocry-

---

[27] *The Martyrdom of Saints Perpetua and Felicitas* 3–10 (Musurillo, *Acts*, 108–19); see Patricia Wilson-Kastner et al., *A Lost Tradition: Women Writers of the Early Church* (Washington, DC, 1981), 1–32; Peter Dronke, *Women Writers of the Middle Ages: A Critical Study of Texts from Perpetua (†203) to Marguerite Porete (†1310)* (Cambridge, 1984); so largely still Joyce E. Salisbury, *Perpetua's Passion: The Death and Memory of a Young Roman Woman* (New York and London, 1997); and, with due caution, Heffernan, *Passion of Perpetua*.

[28] Musurillo, *Acts*, liii; as is frequently the case, the Pauline 'neither Jew nor Greek' is dropped.

[29] William Frend, 'Blandina and Perpetua: Two Early Christian Heroines', in J. Rougé and R. Turcan, eds, *Les Martyrs de Lyon (177)*, Colloques internationaux du Centre national de la recherche scientifique 575 (Paris, 1978), 167–77, at 175.

[30] This was the motivation of Wilson-Kastner, *Lost Tradition*; see also Elizabeth A. Clark, *Women in the Early Church* (Collegeville, MN, 1983), 78–88 (Thecla), 97–106 (Perpetua). For scholarly editions see nn. 8 and 26 above.

phal Acts motifs of folklore and oral transmission that might point to circles of women tradents and so to the recovery of women's voices.[31] However, for many others, rather than embody Galatians 3: 28 they stand at a turning point after the first flush of liberation brought to women by Jesus and perhaps sustained by Paul. Instead they represent the paths, the only paths on this view, along which supposedly 'real women' were able to achieve status within the church once access to the formal leadership roles, perhaps occupied by Phoebe or by Junia, had been firmly locked against them.[32]

The first of these paths was that of martyrdom: along with Perpetua is Felicitas, who in addition to being a woman was also a slave; eight months pregnant, by the grace of God (as the account has it) she gave birth prematurely, and so did not have to miss her appointment with martyrdom. A little earlier, at Lyons there was the slave-woman Blandina of Frend's article and a certain Biblis.[33] Elsewhere the aptly named Agathonike ('good victory') spurns the crowd when they reinforce her gender and proper role: 'Have pity on yourself and on your children'.[34] Positivists here will, with Musurillo, note this prominence of women, and, if indeed the blood of the martyrs was seed, their significance for the growth of the church; certainly their names are preserved, unlike those of so many other women, and they are promised an equal crown of glory. There are hints in the account of Perpetua that they too shared in the extraordinary power to bring about reconciliation

---

[31] So, e.g., Stevan L. Davies, *The Revolt of the Widows: The Social World of the Apocryphal Acts* (Carbondale, IL, 1980), 95–109; Virginia Burrus, *Chastity as Autonomy: Women in the Stories of the Apocryphal Acts* (Lewiston, NY, 1987). Beate Wehn, *'Vergewaltige nicht die Sklavin Gottes': Gewalterfahrungen und Widerstand von Frauen in der frühchristlichen Thekla-Akten* (Königstein, 2005), 51–3, still largely follows Burrus. On the title of 'the Acts', see n. 8 above.

[32] See n. 24 above. Others, maintaining the primary concern with office-holding, have argued that evidence for women fulfilling roles of recognized authority can be uncovered for several centuries, although often masked by ambiguous terminology or by negative polemic: Ute E. Eisen, *Amtsträgerinnen im frühen Christentum: Epigraphische und literarische Studien*, Forschungen zur Kirchen- und Dogmengeschichte 61 (Göttingen, 1996), ET *Women Office-holders in the Early Church: Epigraphical and Literary Studies* (Collegeville, MN, 2000).

[33] In the account of the 'Martyrs of Lyons and Vienne' preserved by Eusebius, *Historia ecclesiastica* 5.1.3–2.1 (text and translation in Musurillo, *Acts*, 62–85).

[34] *The Martyrdom of Carpus, Papylus, and Agathonike* 43 (Greek), 6 (Latin) (Musurillo, *Acts*, 22–37, at 28–9, 34–5). For the motif of an appeal to a mother's compassion for her children, see *Martyrdom of Perpetua* 6 (Musurillo, *Acts*, 113–14); 2 Macc. 7: 25–9; 4 Macc. 8: 20; 14: 11 − 16: 25; Luke 23: 28.

or to offer forgiveness that was accorded to the confessors, those imprisoned to await martyrdom.[35]

The second path, on this model, was that of asceticism. Perpetua only tangentially represents this, for she is married and the mother of a child; however, she does reject conventional expectations, not only by denying her father's authority but also by readily surrendering her child for others to care for, while, strangely, her husband is entirely absent from the narrative. Thecla serves as a better example. After eavesdropping on Paul's preaching, a message of self-denial and of hope of resurrection, almost literally entranced she resolutely rejects her fiancé and all other attempts at physical domination, and, after many an adventure and, some would say, an increasing independent subjectivity (including baptizing herself), she adopts a celibate lifestyle, perhaps even the style and dress of a man, and spends her future as an itinerant teacher. In her ascetic vocation she would in subsequent generations have many heirs (or heiresses), as through a range of narratives and then other testimonies women maintained their independence and acquired status through their embrace of celibacy and asceticism. Such narratives become particularly significant from the fourth century, where they have become the subject of close study, although there are dangers in assimilating second-century concerns to those of this later period.[36]

Thirdly there is the path of ecstatic behaviour, in time perhaps of mysticism. Perpetua herself is the recipient of prophetic and transformative visions; however, such behaviour was particularly associated with the second-century prophetic movement, originating in Phrygia, among whose founders were two women, Priscilla and Maximilla.[37] Subsequently the movement ('Montanism') was named after their male associate, Montanus, but, at least in the eyes of some, it maintained a reputation for the recognition it gave women. Other women credited with visionary experiences, which gave them authority as teachers of divine revelations,

---

[35] *Martyrdom of Perpetua* 13 (Musurillo, *Acts*, 121–3).

[36] See Elizabeth A. Clark, *Ascetic Piety and Women's Faith* (Lewiston, NY, 1986); Kate Cooper, *The Virgin and the Bride: Idealised Womanhood in Late Antiquity* (Cambridge, MA, 1996). On Thecla's heritage, see Stephen J. Davis, *The Cult of St Thecla: A Tradition of Women's Piety in Late Antiquity*, OECS (Oxford, 2001).

[37] See Christine Trevett, *Montanism: Gender, Authority and the New Prophecy* (Cambridge, 1996).

included Philumene, to be discussed below. Prophetic inspiration is not easily constrained by ecclesiastical legislation, and some have traced the phenomenon (or 'problem') back to the women whose veiling Paul tortuously demanded (1 Cor. 11: 2–16).[38] From a social-scientific perspective, comparisons have also been drawn with other examples of the manipulation of non-institutionalized power by women in male-dominated societies with tacit male consent, through claims to visions, contact with the spirit-world, frenzied behaviour or supernatural powers.[39]

As might be expected, the comparative benefits for women of these three – martyrdom, monastic asceticism and charismatic exuberance – as channels for female self-expression and self-determination in the early church can be evaluated in negative as well as positive terms.[40] However, they also provide a bridge to the third case study, often seen as an alternative route, namely the path beyond the boundaries of the emergent or what many now call the proto-orthodox church. Two women may serve as initial representatives; the first would be the nameless virgin who, according to the heresiologist Epiphanius, was corrupted by the second-century arch-heretic Marcion, who 'cheated her of her hope' and thus initiated his headlong fall from grace.[41] The second, also a virgin, would be Philumene, whose 'revelations' persuaded an erstwhile pupil of Marcion, Apelles, to yet further error.[42] These two women are but the tip of an iceberg: polemics against other marginalized, or 'heretical', groups, particularly those more recently lumped

---

[38] On the situation in Corinth, see Antoinette Clark Wire, *The Corinthian Women Prophets: A Reconstruction through Paul's Rhetoric* (Minneapolis, MN, 1995); Jorunn Økland, *Women in their Place: Paul and the Corinthian Discourse of Gender and Sanctuary Space*, JSNT Supplement Series 269 (London, 2004).

[39] For social-scientific analysis of the phenomenon, see I. M. Lewis, *Ecstatic Religion: A Study of Shamanism and Spirit Possession* (London, 1989).

[40] So already Gail Corrington, *Her Image of Salvation: Female Saviors and Formative Christianity* (Louisville, KY, 1992); Ross Shepard Kraemer, ed., *Maenads, Martyrs, Mystics, Matrons: A Sourcebook of Women's Religions in the Greco-Roman World* (Philadelphia, PA, 1988; 2nd edn, *Women's Religions in the Greco-Roman World: A Sourcebook* [Oxford, 2004]).

[41] Epiphanius, *Panarion* 42.1.4, in *Epiphanius II*, ed. Karl Holl, 2nd edn, ed. Jürgen Dummer, GCS (Berlin, 1980), 94.

[42] For texts and discussion, see Roman Hanig, 'Der Beitrag der Philumene zur Theologie der Apelleianer', *Zeitschrift für antikes Christentum / Journal of Ancient Christianity* 3 (1999), 240–77, who notes how she, too, shares the fate of other women, as her independent contribution is forgotten in later tradition.

together under the label 'gnosticism', routinely charge them with the seduction, intellectual and physical, of women, as well as with advocating unbridled sexual licence. Again, some have taken this at face value. Robin Lane Fox writes: 'Tales of promiscuity of heretical teachers enjoyed a wide currency and the theme became a standard accusation. They were a distinctive Christian slander, as women were particularly prominent in Church life, but perhaps we should not always dismiss them. The afternoons were long in a Gnostic's company.'[43] Others, however, have probed more deeply; some have asked what it was about 'gnostic' ideology that accommodated and attracted women, whereas others have suggested that, conversely, it was precisely their defence of female roles that helped damn as heresy an otherwise theologically innocuous movement such as Montanism.[44] Once again there is a complex analogical relationship between the sense among many contemporary women, including academic theologians and church historians, of marginalization within current ecclesiastical structures, and the renewed fascination with sources representing these marginalized forms of early Christian experience.

Taken at face value, each of these roles open to and adopted by women – martyrdom, asceticism, and charism, if not heretical flight – could well be construed not as what the church did for women but as what women did for the church; through them women sustained possibilities of countering what some would decry as a burgeoning and stultifying monochrome institutionalization. Rather than Schüssler Fiorenza's 'memory of her' it might appear preferable to speak of 'her memorializing of other possibilities'. Yet is it possible to take these women and their stories at face value, recovered, reclaimed and recelebrated? Even within the framework of more historical approaches, assumptions such

---

[43] R. Lane Fox, *Pagans and Christians* (Harmondsworth, 1986), 311; it is unclear whether we are to imagine a long lazy afternoon, the male (?) Gnostic teacher surrounded by his adoring female devotees, or the sexual dalliance that would be a welcome relief from long philosophical disquisitions – although why should only women be likely to succumb to either?

[44] On the dynamics of the association between heresy and women, see Ross Shepard Kraemer, 'Heresy as Women's Religion: Women's Religion as Heresy', in eadem, *Her Share of the Blessings: Women's Religions among Pagans, Jews, and Christians in the Greco-Roman World* (New York, 1992), 157–73; Wagener, *Die Ordnung*, 219–21. On the later period, see Virginia Burrus, 'The Heretical Woman as Symbol in Alexander, Athanasius, Epiphanius, and Jerome', *HThR* 84 (1991), 229–48.

as those regarding the accessibility of women's voices behind the
Apocryphal Acts or the *Martyrdom of Perpetua* have proved difficult
to sustain in the light of the complexities of textual transmission
or of close readings attentive to the dominant point of view.[45]
Recognition of the rhetorical strategies at play, as already seen in
the first case study, militates against treating polemical writers such
as Epiphanius as neutral commentators offering reliable historical information, while study of the 'gnostic' texts themselves has
shown them to be no more women-friendly than their 'orthodox'
counterparts.[46]

Moreover, a more substantial challenge has come from approaches
influenced by Michel Foucault, as mediated through Peter Brown,
and developed in particular by scholars (often women) in North
American departments of religion.[47] As they have emphasized, each
of these early Christian women bears not only the weight of their
personal histories (if indeed these can be recovered), but that of
the multiple fundamental perceptions about women which intersect in their representation and most particularly in their bodies.
For what holds together the different 'paths to female self-realiza-
tion' is their focus on the bodies of women; their empowerment
comes about through their mastery over, or their rejection of, their
bodies, through their emancipation from them, even to the extent

---

[45] The issues are well illustrated by the range of highly nuanced readings in Jan
N. Bremmer and Marco Formisano, eds, *Perpetua's Passions: Multidisciplinary Approaches
to the* Passio Perpetuae et Felicitatis (Oxford, 2012). Particularly influential in recent
reconsideration has been recognition of the structural and thematic, and so, potentially, the generic, similarities between these writings and the Hellenistic novels of the
same period, which increasingly have been interpreted not as 'women's literature' but
as reinforcing conventional values: see Virginia Burrus, 'Mimicking Virgins: Colonial
Ambivalence and the Ancient Romance', *Arethusa* 38 (2005), 49–88; Judith Perkins,
The Suffering Self: Pain and Narrative Representation in the Early Christian Era (London,
1995).

[46] The role of women in the sects he denounces is a recurring *topos* in Epiphanius, and he routinely transfers such claims between different groups when his earlier
sources are silent. On the place of women in 'gnostic' texts, see Karen L. King, ed.,
Images of the Feminine in Gnosticism (Philadelphia, PA, 1988); for more recent nuancing,
see Anne McGuire, 'Women, Gender, and Gnosis in Gnostic Texts and Traditions', in
Ross Shepard Kraemer and Mary Rose D'Angelo, eds, *Women and Christian Origins*
(Oxford, 1999), 257–99; Trevett, *Montanism*, 151–97, is cautious about the evidence that
women had more status in Montanism.

[47] Peter Brown, *The Body and Society: Men, Women, and Sexual Renunciation in Early
Christianity* (New York, 1988). Included here would be a number of those whose
work is cited in footnotes to this essay: Elizabeth Clark, Virginia Burrus and Elizabeth
Castelli, and from the UK Averil Cameron and Kate Cooper.

of the elimination of the feminine body and of the acquisition of a male persona, through experiences which are at once 'out of the body' and yet perceived as dangerously and excessively bodily. Sensitivity to the narrative strategies reveals how as readers we are not allowed to avoid this: the watching crowd are moved by horror as they observe Perpetua and Felicitas, 'one a pampered young girl, the other fresh from child birth, her breasts still dripping milk', just as they are by the beauty of Agathonike after she has removed her clothing; as Perpetua hastens to cover her thighs exposed by the heifer's ripping of her tunic, because she is more concerned for her modesty than for any pain, readers are sucked into the voyeurism of the text.[48] Perpetua rearranges her dishevelled hair, while Thecla offers to cut hers in response to Paul's anxieties about the temptations her beauty will bring her; there is a studied ambiguity in the authorial comment that through Blandina 'Christ demonstrated that what among men is considered cheap, ugly and contemptible merits great glory before God'.[49]

Reading the narratives from this perspective locates them, and their women, not (just) within a Christian trajectory but within the history of ideas, not confined to patristics but within the study of late antiquity. They exemplify and manipulate the conventional association within Greek thought of the male with the rational, and of women with the irrational, with the passions, and with domination by the body. Yet the apparent simplicity of such a binary model is deceptive and could mask deep ambiguities: men may act as if controlled by the body and may become feminized, while no less dangerous is the woman who becomes deceptively masculinized. Hence recent study has increasingly recognized that for (the invariably male) authors of antiquity discourse about women is not 'just' about women. In the words of Lévi-Strauss, taken up by a number of historians of late antiquity since, men use women to think with.[50] Within text and ideology construc-

---

[48] *Martyrdom of Perpetua* 20.1–5; *Martyrdom of Carpus* (Latin) 6.4–5 (Musurillo, *Acts*, 129, 35 respectively).

[49] For Perpetua, see n. 27 above; 'Acts of Thecla' 3.25 (*Acts of Paul*, ed. Schneemelcher, 359–60). For Blandina, see *Martyrs of Lyons* 1.17 (Musurillo, *Acts*, 67).

[50] On the use of Lévi-Strauss, see Ross Shepard Kraemer, *Unreliable Witnesses: Religion, Gender, and History in the Greco-Roman Mediterranean* (Oxford, 2011), 128–9. For the broader polemical application of such gendered associations, see Jennifer Wright Knust, *Abandoned to Lust: Sexual Slander and Ancient Christianity* (New York, 2006).

tions of woman are inextricably implicated in constructions of the normative self, i.e. the masculine self. Yet, consequently, they are no less implicated in shaping the in-group and identifying outsiders; this ranges from the way women behave or are controlled, seen as a mark of the character of society, through to language of sexual fidelity and (in)appropriate sexual relationships as a metaphor and measure of national integrity, and to the exploitation of the endangered woman or unwomanly woman as providing a space within which the possibilities of resistance or negotiation open to a minority group are explored (as in the biblical cases of Esther and Judith). If narratives of early Christian women provide fruitful material for analysis within this literary and ideological framework, those women themselves begin to lose their hard-won subjectivity as individual historical actors.[51]

This development should not be seen as the triumph of 'Hellenism over Hebraism', either within early Christian thought or in the primary allegiance of its modern scholars. The sensitivities of feminist biblical study again may provide a further interpretative lens, just as Scripture itself undoubtedly made its own contribution to early Christian ideologies of women. Of particular importance is the pervasive association within the Scriptures, Jewish and then Christian, of women with both sexual infidelity and religious infidelity, themes that are themselves inextricably intertwined both as supposed cause and effect and as reciprocally informing metaphors: Solomon's wives; folly touting her wares in the market place in the wisdom literature; the errant wife whom the prophet Hosea or God will brutally strip bare for her infidelities; Jezebel in 2 Kings; and her later colleague, the whore of Babylon. It is as heir to this tradition that the virgin seduced by Marcion should be placed, through a line that includes another virgin described two centuries before Epiphanius by Hegesippus when he introduced his account of the roots of heresies: 'For this reason they used to call the Church a virgin, for it was not yet defiled by vain reports'.[52] From the same stock, in the account of the martyrdoms at Lyons, the church is the virgin mother – that most ambivalent of impossible ideals – a mother who experiences no pain at the

---

[51] See Elizabeth A. Castelli, *Martyrdom and Memory: Early Christian Culture Making* (New York, 2004), 61–7, 138–43.

[52] Eusebius, *Historia ecclesiastica* 4.22.4.

death of her offspring but only at their failure to embrace death; those who recanted are described as miscarriages or abortions, those who finally renew their faith are 'reborn': 'the Virgin mother experienced great joy as she received again living those whom she had aborted dead'. Metaphor and person coalesce in the opposite direction when Blandina, tortured and executed after many of her fellows, is herself described as 'like a noble mother encouraging her children'.[53] 'Virginity as Metaphor', to quote the title of an essay by Averil Cameron, draws on (in both senses of the verb) the bodies of women, although not only on those of women.[54]

In the midst of her torture Blandina is tied, spreadeagled, to a stake. Those who watch, in the words of the account, see in the form of their sister, 'he who was crucified for them'.[55] Does Blandina become male, as Perpetua did in her dream, and as (in a different way) does Thecla, or does Christ lose gender specificity, incarnated in her? Accounts of martyrdom also describe the tortured and disfigured bodies of the male Christians, although without any comparable attention to their masculine features. The submissive body, not just marked by physical weakness but openly embracing weakness and suffering, was within Graeco-Roman culture, and perhaps not only there, deeply ambiguous. It has often been noted that the women martyrs are eulogized for their 'manly' bravery – the terms share a common root; Blandina is pointedly likened to 'a noble athlete'.[56] This does not only, as often supposed, open a door, even promotion, for women, but it also provokes a radical reimagination of the recognizable signs of the pre-eminent athlete and of the physical manifestation of their prowess. Once again this can be understood as 'men using women to think with': the women of these narratives provide a less threatening space for reconceptualizing masculinity as well as femininity within early Christian discourse.

[53] *Martyrs of Lyons* 1.45, 55 (Musurillo, *Acts*, 77, 79). Such imagery of the church also draws on biblical traditions of Jerusalem as barren mother whose children are restored, and of the church as bride (Isa. 54; Rev. 21: 2). It also intersects with the topos of expected motherly love noted above (n. 34).

[54] Averil Cameron, 'Virginity as Metaphor: Women and Rhetoric in Early Christianity', in eadem, ed., *History as Text: The Writing of Ancient History* (Chapel Hill, NC, 1989), 181–205.

[55] *Martyrs of Lyons* 1.41 (Musurillo, *Acts*, 74).

[56] Ibid. 1.18; subsequently (1.42) she is said to 'have put on Christ, that mighty and invincible athlete' (Musurillo, *Acts*, 67, 75).

Therefore, if the question with which we started has broadened out into the study of masculinity and indeed of constructions of gender, it is not only following the trend from women's studies to gender studies;[57] nor is it adding further topics to a shopping list of discrete items – along with animals, money and war – as sometimes treated in other, including ecclesial, settings. It has become ever more evident that the question of women belongs to the inner logic or deep grammar of the church's self-understanding. With this we have moved from what the church did for women to what women, past and present, have done for the church.[58]

Given the theme of this volume as the church's interpretation of its past, some reflection is merited, not least because many of the later stages of the journey here traced have been trodden mainly outside of confessedly ecclesial settings. Even where the particular association of women with martyrdom, asceticism, charismatic behaviour and perhaps life on the margins of the church has been treated as a window on their real experience, there has been vigorous debate regarding whether and in what ways these women did provide for their contemporaries, or do provide for subsequent generations, models of liberation, or whether they merely reinscribe definitions of femininity that need to be challenged. Seeing them as at every turn characterized by their bodies can only intensify such debate. There can be no doubt in subsequent church history, and even to the present, that the valorization of suffering and anxiety about woman's body have been deeply ambivalent for women (and not only for women); such valorization has given (real or supposed) meaning to an often enforced submission or passivity, but it has also demanded acquiescence in the face of various kinds of abuse and of easily inspired guilt about any protest against it.[59]

Finally, many have followed the journey through with increasing anxiety: having started with the desire to rescue women from the

[57] Here again studies of Christian and also Jewish material were embraced in a move that was already taking place in classics; see, e.g., Lin Foxhall and John Salmon, eds, *When Men were Men: Masculinity, Power, and Identity in Classical Antiquity* (London, 1998); Maria Wyke, ed., *Gender and the Body in the Ancient Mediterranean* (Oxford, 1998).

[58] A further dimension that cannot be explored here would be the multiple intersections with the gendered ways in which God is conceptualized.

[59] See already Susan Brooks Thistlethwaite, 'Every Two Minutes: Battered Women and Feminist Interpretation', in Russell, ed., *Feminist Interpretation*, 96–107.

obscurity if not erasure in which they had been submerged and by which they had been silenced for centuries, have we – particularly women scholars – returned them there, the real women at any rate?[60] Arguably the discussion has not simply returned to the position challenged by Schüssler Fiorenza's hermeneutic of suspicion, namely of tacit acceptance of the erasure of women by male authors, transmitters, translators and scholars.[61] Neither does the recognition that the authors of our sources are (almost exclusively) men, and that the women of their texts are *their* women, equate to the naïve and dismissive truism that 'they did not know about feminism and so it is pointless looking for it there', for that mantra is to resort to a narrow proof-texting attitude to Scripture and to the past. If the concern is with 'real women' there is something to be learned both from and for contemporary debates about whether, or how far, we acknowledge and affirm the decisions of women who by our criteria submit to male-dominated norms and values; how far we dismiss them as disempowered, oversocialized into submission; and how we recognize female agency and the multiple ways in which women negotiate society's expectations, contribute to these, and manipulate, reinforce or transform them.

What have women done for the church? They have posed the question and they have shown that the answer still lies ahead of us.

University of Cambridge

---

[60] See Elizabeth Clark, 'The Lady Vanishes: Dilemmas of a Feminist Historian after the "Linguistic Turn"', *ChH* 67 (1998), 1–31. Several of the scholars cited in these notes have become increasingly cautious about attempting historical recovery in their more recent publications: see the review of scholarly development and a personal perspective in Kraemer, *Unreliable Witnesses*, 3–28.

[61] One very patent by-product has been the increased sensitivity to gender issues in translation of the Scriptures as well as in scholarly analysis.

CHANGING HISTORICAL PERSPECTIVES ON THE ENGLISH REFORMATION: THE LAST FIFTY YEARS*

by DIARMAID MacCULLOCH

In 1971 and early 1972, as a final-year Cambridge undergraduate, I turned to the study of the English Reformation, under the able supervision of Felicity Heal, while attending the lectures of a wonderfully rackety and quirkily learned Fellow of Selwyn College, the late and much lamented patron of the Cambridge Footlights, Harry Porter. The course was entitled 'Thought and Religion in England 1500 to 1650', and it was fairly cutting-edge by the standards of its day: a genuine effort to reach across the divide then standard between the history and divinity faculties. It also tried to integrate England with mainland Europe – what in those days, we would routinely call with sublime and literal insularity 'the Continent'.[1]

It helped that one of the great figures in Cambridge's Divinity Faculty was Gordon Rupp, a historian of the Reformation who had long taken seriously the integration of England's Reformation history with that of the rest of Europe: witness his little compilation of his essays in 1947, still well worth reading, *Studies in the Making of the English Protestant Tradition*. Indeed, it was perhaps a major factor in delaying an update in English Reformation studies that Rupp largely turned away from the English Reformation after 1947. Rupp had wide-ranging interests which produced a perceptive study of Martin Luther's theology and a superb volume on English religion in the eighteenth century,[2] but there was one particularly important element in his broad vision: he was a

---

* I gave an earlier version of this article at a colloquium on 30 April 2011 to honour Dr Felicity Heal on her retirement. In view of her central place in Reformation studies in the last half-century, it has not been necessary to remove very many of the original references to Felicity, and I am happy to celebrate her ongoing career with this present augmented version.

[1] I will not repeat my sarcasm on this usage of 'Continent': see D. MacCulloch, M. Laven and E. Duffy, 'Recent Trends in the Study of Christianity in Sixteenth-Century Europe', *RQ* 59 (2006), 697–731, at 697–8.

[2] E. G. Rupp, *The Righteousness of God: Luther Studies* (London, 1953); idem, *Religion in England 1688–1791*, OHCC (Oxford, 1985).

Methodist minister, and thus existentially at one remove from the prevailing narrative of what the English Reformation had been about. What was this hegemonic narrative? It was of course, Anglican; and not just Anglican, but high church Anglican. There had once been a rival Evangelical Anglican hegemonic story, which could look back to the pioneering primary source research of two very clever seventeenth-century bishops, John Williams of Lincoln and York and Gilbert Burnet of Salisbury (Burnet being perhaps the greatest of Anglican historians), plus the decidedly less stellar but extremely hardworking perpetual curate of Low Leyton, John Strype. Williams, Burnet and Strype had created a narrative of the Reformation which was robust and actually resembled its reality.[3] But Victorian Evangelicals had largely abandoned their interest in high culture, which had once been considerable, and they shunned the 'humanities' sector in higher education just as it was developing in the 1880s.[4] By and large, they had not concerned themselves with the newly established and godless history departments of late Victorian universities, or with university theology departments which they would have regarded as even more pernicious in their teachings.

As a result, during the later nineteenth century adherents of the Oxford Movement or wider Anglo-Catholicism were dominant in the practice of religious history at university level, and they continued to be, well into the twentieth century. There is still a ghost of this in the undergraduate history syllabus of my own Theology Faculty in Oxford. A theology undergraduate interested in church history can study the early church, the medieval church, the Reformation and the nineteenth century. Note no eighteenth century, so that you cannot find out about the Enlightenment, at least if you want to be examined on it in Finals. The medieval church has until recent years been a bit of an afterthought, so the

---

3   For one fatal lapse on Strype's part, see my 'Foxes, Firebrands and Forgery: Robert Ware's Pollution of Reformation history', *HistJ* 54 (2011), 307–46. On Williams, whose scholarship has been in my view underrated, see B. Williams, ed., *The Work of Archbishop John Williams*, Courtenay Library of Reformation Classics 14 (Appleford, 1980); for another healthy revision of Williams's reputation, see S. Hampton, 'The Manuscript Sermons of Archbishop John Williams', *JEH* 62 (2011), 707–25.

4   On Victorian Evangelicals and culture, see D. Rosman, *Evangelicals and Culture* (London, 1984).

three big beast periods are those which Anglicans have always been supposed to know about: the early church, to study the Fathers on which Anglicanism likes to think itself as based; the nineteenth century, because that is when the Oxford Movement happened; and the Reformation, in order to wrestle with the embarrassment that the Reformation happened at all.

For Anglo-Catholics found the English Reformation embarrassing or distasteful. Much of their research and analysis minimized its revolutionary character and stressed how different it was from the Reformation on the 'Continent'. Self-confident heirs of the Oxford Movement felt somewhat nonplussed when they were ushered into its company. Unaccountably it failed to share many of their passionately held beliefs, and yet it had created the Church of England in which their beliefs were now expressed and put into practice. Such historians played down, deplored or ignored the reign of Edward VI, the most obviously militant phase of change; they looked for 'Catholic' tendencies in the Elizabethan Settlement, and thereafter they saw the coming of Arminianism or Laudianism as a natural product of earlier, Tudor phases of a church of the *via media*. They treated puritans as outsiders to and opponents of the established church, closely allied with post-1662 'Dissent' or Nonconformity. It was a useful polemical strategy which *a priori* relegated the puritans to the margins, doing their best up to 1642 to rock the boat from the inside, but leaving for the lifeboats after 1662, allowing 'Anglicanism' to sail serenely on its way.

The agenda for this was set in the mid-seventeenth century in the deeply polemical writings of Peter Heylyn, Archbishop Laud's chaplain. Heylyn's narrative was opposed vigorously (and, I would judge, very successfully) by Gilbert Burnet, but it was continued by the nonjuror historians of the late seventeenth and early eighteenth centuries, and it was then perpetuated by the Oxford Movement.[5] It can be encountered red in tooth and claw in Canon R. W. Dixon's monumental *History of the Church of England from the Abolition of the Roman Jurisdiction* (6 volumes, 1884–1910), whose very title stressed a break with the medieval past which was jurisdic-

---

[5]   A. Milton, *Laudian and Royalist Polemic in 17th-century England: The Career and Writings of Peter Heylyn* (Manchester, 2007). A fine overview is provided by P. Nockles, 'A Disputed Legacy: Anglican Historiographies of the Reformation from the Era of the Caroline Divines to that of the Oxford Movement', *BJRL* 83 (2001), 121–67.

tional rather than theological. The standard reference work to which I would have turned in my undergraduate years was the *Oxford Dictionary of the Christian Church,* edited by a canon of Christ Church, F. L. Cross. It was then in its first edition, published in 1957 but first conceived before the Second World War. That first edition well exemplified the Anglo-Catholic dominance of historiography, to the point of downright misrepresentation of the English Reformation; latterly, under the rigorous editorship of Dr Elizabeth Livingstone, its treatments of that subject have steadily moved away from the initial emphases to more inclusive and balanced perspectives.[6]

In other words, at the end of the 1960s the English Reformation was still shackled by instrumental history: the story of the past told in order to justify the present. We have already recalled the work of Gordon Rupp; it is more than coincidence that before the Second World War another Cambridge Methodist, Herbert Butterfield, had rumbled the same instrumental strategy more widely applied in English historiography, and called it the 'Whig' interpretation of history.[7] It may seem historically inept to align Anglo-Catholic historiography with Whiggery, an association which would have infuriated Tractarians fighting the Whigs in the 1830s, but the principle is the same: the past is used to justify the present, and to explain how it was inevitable that we got to where we are today. It is the historiography of a complacent establishment in every age.

Nonetheless, much of the reading to which my undergraduate supervisor perfectly properly directed me in 1972 was from that tradition. I remember perhaps the least satisfactory essay which I produced for her, and the one which produced more tactful comments from her about its drawbacks than any other in the sequence, was one entitled 'What contribution did the first generation of English reformers make to Protestant theology?' I was frankly puzzled, as well as bored, by much of what I read, and I now realize that it was boring because it was not true. It was indeed

---

[6]   For examples (in which I must confess to having a hand), compare successive entries across editions of *ODCC, s.vv.* 'Browne, Robert' (no longer 'clearly mentally unstable'); 'Real Presence' (now without a mendacious attribution of the doctrine to Hugh Latimer); 'Stubbs, John' (no longer a 'fanatic').

[7]   H. Butterfield, *The Whig Interpretation of History* (London, 1931). An enlightening portrait of Butterfield is M. Bentley, *The Life and Thought of Herbert Butterfield: History, Science and God* (Cambridge, 2011).

making strenuous and elaborate efforts to avoid the truth. Among my reading was Clifford Dugmore's *The Mass and the English Reformers*, a misconceived work devoted to proving that Thomas Cranmer was not really a Protestant and that he, Ridley and the like were trying to synthesize the work of Catholics and Reformers.[8] At least I did not buy that theory even then. Another book which bored me a great deal was volume 1 of Horton Davies's *Worship and Theology in England*. Davies (1916–2005) was a Welsh Congregationalist, who spent most of his teaching career in the USA at Princeton. Despite this Reformed Protestant consciousness, in the first part of what eventually became a six-volume work, published only two years before I wrote my essay, he had apparently completely swallowed the Anglo-Catholic view of the English Reformation.

At the root of the problem with volume 1 was Davies's decision to describe a mainstream tradition in the Tudor church as 'Anglican'. Davies never really explained where this tradition came from, except that it seemed to have emerged fully armed at the break with Rome in 1534. Thereafter it contended with a rival Protestant tradition which Davies described as 'Puritan', and these traditions appeared to be sufficiently identifiable as to warrant a detailed analysis listing their differences. It was strange, then, that the sixteenth-century individuals who belonged particularly to the 'Anglican' tradition seemed so indeterminate. Thomas Cranmer appeared to be one of them at one point, but on the basis of a wholly misleading citation of his homilies;[9] otherwise, Anglicans in the flesh seemed suspiciously anonymous before Richard Hooker, and this first volume culminated in a case study which enlisted in their ranks John Bruen of Stapleford Bruen (Cheshire), 'a devout Anglican layman'. Bruen, the archetypal puritan, who named his son Calvin, would have been baffled by this unwanted compliment, and furious if Davies had explained to him what it meant. Earlier in the volume, a list of Elizabethan 'Anglican' preachers consisted of those which elsewhere in the same volume Davies described

[8]   C. Dugmore, *The Mass and the English Reformers* (London, 1958). To be fair to Dugmore, in the journal which he himself edited, he published a polite but distinctly sceptical review of his work by that acute ecclesiastical historian, Norman Sykes: *JEH* 10 (1959), 246–8.

[9]   H. Davies, *Worship and Theology in England*, 1: *From Cranmer to Hooker, 1534–1603* (Princeton, NJ, 1970), 54.

as 'Calvinists' and 'Puritans', which seemed rather to overturn the possibility of distinguishing Anglicanism in the sixteenth century.[10] Most remarkable of all was Davies's account of Cranmer's two Prayer Books, in which he described the first of 1549 as 'the norm' for the nature of Anglican worship.[11] It is odd that Davies should take as a norm a book which within three years was discarded and replaced by one which has survived barely modified at the centre of the Church of England's liturgy ever since.

Having shaken our heads in sorrow at volume 1, we can observe that Davies's volume 2 began unobtrusively to correct the balance. Dealing with the seventeenth rather than the sixteenth century, this was published in 1975 as the last in his sequence of five (a sixth volume was to appear, rounding off a new edition in 1996); by 1975 Davies seemed to have picked up a change in the Zeitgeist. A technical theological term which appeared to be quite important in the eucharistic discussion of volume 1, 'virtualism', occurred only once in the whole span of volume 2: a welcome absence, since it appears to have been invented by Victorian high churchmen in order to make sixteenth-century Reformed Protestant eucharistic thought sound more like their own.[12] Moreover, Davies's general framework of interpretation became less contentious or tendentious as it dealt with the aftermath of 1662, for there it represented realistically the great fault-line which opened up within English Protestantism between the established church and Dissent after the Restoration of Charles II. Davies was now describing the tradition from which he himself had sprung.

This characteristic of Davies's work conveniently illuminates a further instrumentalism in the traditional tale of the English Reformation. Alongside the Anglican narrative were other, parallel stories of the English Reformation which were equally denominational, and which flanked it in triptych fashion. One was Roman Catholic, the other Free Church. To that extent, this triptych of independent religious historiographies paralleled the way that a very different variety of Reformation was taught in Germany, and indeed with notable and honourable exceptions, often still is: in

---

[10] Davies, *From Cranmer to Hooker*, 440, 236.
[11] Ibid. 34.
[12] H. Davies, *Worship and Theology in England, 2: From Andrewes to Baxter and Fox, 1603–1690* (Princeton, NJ, 1975), 159.

German historical writing on the Reformation, there is a Lutheran story, a Reformed story and a Catholic story, and the practitioners of those histories rarely cross the boundaries.[13] There is an institutional difference, however, between England and Germany; in Germany, each historiography can be practised in a university, in theological faculties established for Catholics or Protestants. In England, though not in Ireland, there have been virtually no university-level institutions or theological faculties specifically devoted to cultivating the non-Anglican stories. The exceptions were institutions significantly placed in institutional terms on the edge of the major universities: in the case of Oxford, the permanent private halls, such as St Benet's Hall for the Benedictines, Mansfield College for the Congregationalists, or Regent's Park College for the Baptists.

Because of this, the Roman Catholic narrative, which had been begun within the established church of Mary Tudor by the clients of Cardinal Pole and which persisted through many trials ever since, was until very recent years sustained by writers outside the academy, such as Cardinal Aidan Gasquet at the end of the nineteenth century. It was tribal history, and particularly tribal when Gasquet lost the scholarly assistance of his very able literary collaborator Edmund Bishop, a convert from Anglicanism. The culmination of the tradition was the three-volume *The Reformation in England* by Fr Philip Hughes.[14] In many ways, this is a fine work of synthesis, based on a remarkable sweep of the available primary source material. I was directed in my *Thought and Religion* course to the section in Hughes's second volume on Mary Tudor's England, and at the time this was undoubtedly the best account of the period available, looking past the traditional Protestant picture of it as failure twinned with cruelty and ineptitude. Hughes anticipated the picture of Marian England so ably delineated by Eamon Duffy in *The Stripping of the Altars* and *Fires of Faith*.[15] But you could not mistake it for anything else than history written by a Roman

---

[13] There are of course honourable exceptions in Germany, and one particular witness of this, arguably pioneering in its concern to reach over divides, is a volume of essays (to which I contributed): D. Wendebourg, ed., *Sister Reformations / Schwesterreformationen: The Reformation in Germany and in England – Die Reformation in Deutschland und in England* (Tübingen, 2010).

[14] P. Hughes, *The Reformation in England*, 3 vols (London, 1950–4).

[15] E. Duffy, *The Stripping of the Altars: Traditional Religion in England 1400–1580* (New

Catholic, with an apologetic aim: most notably, that section which I read and assiduously noted on Marian England. The shining exception to this generally polemical character of Catholic historiography on the Reformation appeared in the same decade as Hughes's work: it was the great trilogy by David Knowles, which projected beyond his normal medieval field into the Reformation, in his magnificent *The Religious Orders in England*.[16] If anything, Knowles was not celebratory enough of early Tudor monasticism, famously suggesting that his readers might see his account as 'the description of a falling day and lengthening shades' after 'the splendours of the dawn and noonday'.[17] James Clark has shown us in recent years more life and creativity in the period than we had suspected.[18] But Knowles's willingness to criticize while retaining a deep empathy with his fellow regulars was a mark of the particular position of the man: a monk who had created a delicate distance between himself and his community life, and whose creative genius benefited accordingly.[19]

Like their Roman Catholic mirror images, the Free Church narratives were largely tribal, speaking to their own various constituencies and telling them stories about themselves. It was significant that after spending some years at Mansfield College, Oxford, the Congregationalist Horton Davies found his eventual home for half a century in a great American university which did have an institutional Reformed Protestant tradition, Princeton. Often, in an unacknowledged collaboration with the high church Anglicans, the Free Church historians, especially Presbyterians, Congregationalists and Baptists, annexed the story of Elizabethan and early Stuart puritans to their own narratives. That was of course the strategy behind Horton Davies's narrative, which had led directly

Haven, CT, 1992), 524–63; idem, *Fires of Faith: Catholic England under Mary Tudor* (New Haven, CT, 2009).

[16] D. Knowles, *The Religious Orders in England*, 3 vols (Cambridge, 1948, 1955, 1959).

[17] Ibid. 3: 464; cf. ibid. 460: 'With the exception of the Carthusians, the Bridgettines and the Observant Franciscans, the religious life in England was humanly speaking easier and less spiritually stimulating in 1530 than it had been a century earlier.'

[18] J. G. Clark, 'The Culture of English Monasticism', in idem, ed., *The Culture of English Monasticism* (Woodbridge, 2007), 1–18.

[19] See C. Brooke's delicate and engaged meditation on Knowles's career, 'Dom David Knowles and his Vocation as a Monastic Historian', *Downside Review* 110 (1992), 209–25.

to his unholy collusion with the Anglican myth in volume I of his history. His book admittedly did illustrate something else more positive and admirable. Although often just as interested in structures and institutions as the Anglicans, Roman Catholics and Free Churchmen had something of a tendency to take investigations of historical theology more seriously; after all, it was their attention to theology which compelled them not to be Anglicans.

All this had begun to break down in the years around 1970 when I was an undergraduate. The ecumenical movement and the relaxation around the Second Vatican Council had encouraged churchmen to talk to each other across denominational boundaries (they were of course indeed practically all men then). There was a certain amount of comparing notes on denominational stories. Instrumentalist, tribal history might at least be questioned more, in the name of a new instrumentalism: breaking down the barriers – although actually the high church Anglican hegemonic narrative was also rather useful for these ecumenists, since its aim had always been to minimize the differences between Rome and Canterbury. One of its strongholds has remained the history presented in ecumenical documents produced by the Anglican-Roman Catholic International Commission (ARCIC).[20]

But quite separate developments were beginning to impinge on the practice of Reformation history which had been building up elsewhere for decades. The focus of religious history had long been on national affairs, which had been reinforced in the nineteenth century by the new availability of primary source material concentrated mainly in London, the records of Westminster government and the antiquarian collections in the British Museum, exemplified for instance in the monumental collections published by J. S. Brewer and his successors as *Letters and Papers, Foreign and Domestic, of the Reign of Henry VIII*.[21] Only gradually during the twentieth century did it become clear that equal archival riches lay in the provinces, as local record offices began to open: the first in Bedfordshire in the 1920s, but followed by many more county

[20] For an incisive analysis of one example of this tendency in ARCIC documents, see J. Maltby, 'Anglicanism, the Reformation and the Anglican-Roman Catholic International Commission's Agreed Statement *Mary: Grace and Hope in Christ*', *Theology* 110 (2007), 171–9.

[21] J. S. Brewer et al., eds, *Letters and Papers, Foreign and Domestic, of the Reign of Henry VIII, 1509–47*, 21 vols and 2 vols addenda (London, 1862–1932).

record offices from the 1950s. Alongside the Bedfordshire initiative came stirrings in the universities: the establishment of a research fellowship in local history at Reading as early as 1908 (though it proved short-lived), while a full-scale department of local history in the University of Leicester appeared in 1947.

Suddenly what had for centuries been antiquarianism became something else. But what? In 1950 G. M. Trevelyan, in a supremely patronizing retrospective on A. L. Rowse's best book, *Tudor Cornwall*, saw local history as an apprenticeship for real historians: he 'believed that Mr A. L. Rowse had it in him to become an historian of high rank if he would lay aside lesser activities and bend himself to the production of history on the grand scale'.[22] I more than suspect that my own doctoral supervisor Sir Geoffrey Elton took a similar attitude to my doctoral project on Suffolk in 1973. That particular enterprise was given at least a certain respectability in his eyes because of the fact that I spent most of my time viewing Suffolk through the proper primary sources, in other words, those to be found in the Public Record Office, thanks to peculiar local poverties in my local county record office sources. In fact one distinguished practitioner of local and indeed East Anglian history, Victor Morgan, tried to discourage me from tackling Suffolk; he said that the sources simply were not up to it.

Others were more fortunate than me as they sifted through what the local record offices were beginning to accumulate. The county archivists came just in time to save many country-house collections, which were then being dispersed, although virtually too late for my own choice of county, Suffolk. They gradually gathered in the parish records, and lastly they acquired the diocesan and cathedral archives from previously rather possessive ecclesiastical custodians. It was these ecclesiastical records which turned local history into a serious investigation of the English Reformation: an alternative to the hegemonic narrative. In the year of my graduation, 1972, Felicity Heal, Claire Cross, Stephen Lander and their friends began turning local Reformation history into an industry led by an annual conference which was as central to the move-

[22] A. L. Rowse *Tudor Cornwall* (London, 1941); Trevelyan's remark in his *Sunday Times* review of Rowse's *England under Elizabeth: The Structure of Society* (London, 1950) is quoted in H. P. R. Finberg, *The Local Historian and his Theme*, Leicester University Department of English Local History Occasional Papers 1 (Leicester, 1952), 8.

ment as the early Socialist Internationals were to Marxism: the Colloquium for Local Reformation Studies. Was it a coincidence that some of the giants in the land in those days were women, Dorothy Owen and Margaret Bowker in particular? Perhaps they were doing the history which the boys disdained.[23]

Nevertheless, the pioneer from the 1930s in such studies had been a man, and an Anglican too: A. G. Dickens. Dickens, despite an affection for high church liturgy in later life, broke with the Anglo-Catholic consensus on the *Sonderweg* of England in the sixteenth century. With his deep love and first-hand knowledge of Germany, and his zest for the resources of the emerging local record offices, his perspective was both wider and more concentrated than the kingdom of England, as much international as local. While recognizing the crucial role of the Tudor monarchy in religious change, Dickens laid emphasis on the popular elements which worked alongside official change, and there was much for him to say in his classic textbook analysis of the mid-1960s, *The English Reformation*.[24] So did Patrick Collinson, whose first major publication soon after that, *The Elizabethan Puritan Movement*, started to reposition the puritans within the structures of the established Church of England, and thus simultaneously struck a blow at the Anglican and Free Church narratives of the English Reformation.[25] Once more, this new perspective was the work of an outsider to the English ecclesiastical establishment, a product of an astonishingly various experience of interdenominational English Free Church Protestantism, which Pat has lovingly recreated in his memoirs.[26]

One feature nevertheless remained constant within this brave new world of counties and dioceses: the new local history was resolutely uninterested in ideas. Dickens was perhaps a shining exception here, for as much as Rupp he was familiar with German Reformation history, where ideas were taken very seriously. But

---

[23]   That was certainly Sir John Neale's attitude to such subjects as prosopography, on which so much of his work on Parliament was based: that was left to women, whom he would not allow to progress beyond the degree of MA. On this, see P. Collinson, *The History of a History Man: Or, the Twentieth Century viewed from a Safe Distance* (Woodbridge, 2011), 78. At least Neale put Collinson on the road to his study of puritanism: ibid. 77–8.

[24]   A. G. Dickens, *The English Reformation* (London, 1964).

[25]   P. Collinson, *The Elizabethan Puritan Movement* (London, 1967).

[26]   Collinson, *History of a History Man*, 5–37.

one does not find too many theological disputes even in Dickens's local work. For him as for others, the avoidance was to a great extent because of the sort of sources we used: they were primarily administrative or legal, and it was easy to be satisfied with the extraordinary wealth of new perspectives which this threw up. In my case, the avoidance of ideas was actively encouraged by Sir Geoffrey Elton, whose experience of the horrors of mid-twentieth-century Europe inspired by ideologies made him deeply suspicious of anything which could be classified as an ideology.

Given that the Reformation had been inspired by a big idea, this was a mistake, and the sources magnified the effect of that mistake. Administrators produce more paper on the subject of conflict and failure than they do on anything else, while legal papers are almost by definition the products of conflict and failure. This became the picture of the English Reformation which began emerging from the sources: most notably in the hugely influential picture of Lancashire painted by Christopher Haigh which was published in 1975.[27] It was a perspective which permeated my own first book on Tudor Suffolk in the mid-1980s. By then this stance had been christened 'revisionism', and no more so than in the collected essays which Haigh published with the significant title *The English Reformation Revised*.[28] Dickens was not among the contributors. It became difficult to see why there had been a Reformation at all, given how few people seemed to have wanted it. The conclusion might be rather like that of the old Anglican and hegemonic narratives; it was all down to the Tudors wanting institutional change, and getting their way, because the Tudors usually did.

A fresh ingredient to the mix of revisionism, which had not been a prominent feature of the first wave of local studies, was a newly assertive Roman Catholicism. That it was a separate ingredient is neatly demonstrated by the fact that the organizers of the Colloquium for Local Reformation Studies seriously debated in the mid-1970s as to whether they should include researchers on recusant history among their invitees; their conclusion was in favour.[29] Now that Roman Catholics had moved into the centre

---

[27] C. Haigh, *Reformation and Resistance in Tudor Lancashire* (Cambridge, 1975).
[28] C. Haigh, ed., *The English Reformation Revised* (Cambridge, 1987).
[29] I am grateful to Felicity Heal for this reminiscence: the year appears to have

of national life, not least into the centre of university history and theology departments, this was hardly surprising. J. J. Scarisbrick's Ford Lectures, given in 1982 and published soon afterwards, were a beautifully concentrated distillation of what the local historians had brought home from the fields, and a powerful affirmation of the vitality of late medieval English Catholicism.[30] To that would be added soon the works of Eamon Duffy, and so a trinity was born of Haigh, Scarisbrick and Duffy, names which soon tripped off sixth-form and undergraduate tongues as easily as an earlier generation might have spoken of Wilson, Keppel and Betty or Groucho, Chico and Harpo. These hypostases were never in as Chalcedonian a relationship as novices might fantasize; and we have all moved on over the decades as historians do, constantly revising our revisions – we do not always destroy, but we always enrich. But now we might not unquestioningly sign up to the famous formulation now two decades old, 'The English Reformation: a premature birth, a difficult labour and a sickly child', maybe not even its author.[31]

Although local studies and revisionism did much to shift the interests of historians, local historians did not have the materials in their preferred primary sources to tackle the theological sleight of hand represented by the old hegemonic narratives exemplified in Dugmore and Davies. That work of theological revision was going on for a long time rather separately from the local history revolution, although one or two personalities had a foot in both camps. One lone voice early on in the 1960s could be heard in an incisive little study by Peter Newman Brooks on Cranmer's eucharistic theology, which cut through much obfuscation to reveal three phases in his sacramental thinking, the last of which was unquestionably Reformed Protestant, after what amounted in the second phase to Lutheranism.[32] It is no coin-

been 1974, in anticipation of the 1976 colloquium.

30 J. J. Scarisbrick, *The Reformation and the English People* (Oxford, 1983).

31 C. Haigh, 'The English Reformation: A Premature Birth, a Difficult Labour and a Sickly Child', *HistJ* 33 (1990), 449–59, an extended review article of key texts over the previous few years. Haigh's latest work might be said to celebrate the effectiveness of the Reformation: C. Haigh, *The Plain Man's Pathways to Heaven: Kinds of Christianity in Post-Reformation England* (Oxford, 2007).

32 P. N. Brooks, *Thomas Cranmer's Doctrine of the Eucharist* (London, 1965; rev. edn, Houndmills, 1992). For my critical remarks about the terminology which Brooks used

cidence that Brooks's first mentor was Rupp, who contributed a foreword to the original edition (Collinson did the honours for the second). After that, it was yet another student of Rupp, Peter Lake, who through his doctoral work and subsequent publication of it, revealed that there were people in Elizabethan Cambridge who actually had a coherent theological position which was both puritan and yet not determinedly subversive of the Church of England. Why should that have been a puzzle? The Church of England, despite many features of which these 'moderate puritans' disapproved, was a Reformed Protestant church, to set alongside the churches of Scotland, Geneva, the Northern Netherlands, Hungary or Poland.[33]

This was the dirty little secret which high church Anglicans had been trying to hide since the time of Peter Heylyn. And it was that which had eluded me in my undergraduate essay on early English Protestants. I had spotted that they had not said anything especially original, but I had not yet been able to form a narrative of how their thoughts were being pulled away from an initial Lutheranism towards the Reformed, as part of the periphery of a wider Protestant story. And this process was not the work of John Calvin, but predated any influence he might have had.[34] So it has become more and more apparent in the last two decades that the word 'Calvinist' was nearly as redundant as 'Anglican' during the whole period of the English Reformation, and that the label 'Reformed Protestant' did the job much better.

And so divinity faculties and history faculties began to talk to each other fruitfully about the Reformation; and English faculties began doing so at much the same time. One could explore what

---

to characterize the change, see D. MacCulloch, *Thomas Cranmer: A Life* (New Haven, CT, 1996), 182–3, 392.

[33] P. Lake, *Moderate Puritans and the Elizabethan Church* (Cambridge, 1983).

[34] D. MacCulloch, 'The Importance of Jan Laski in the English Reformation', in C. Strohm, ed., *Johannes a Lasco: Polnischer Baron, Humanist und europäischer Reformator. Beiträge zum internationalen Symposium vom 14.–17. Oktober 1999 in der Johannes a Lasco Bibliothek Emden*, Spätmittelalter und Reformation n.s. 14 (Tübingen, 2000), 325–45; idem, 'Peter Martyr Vermigli and Thomas Cranmer', in E. Campi et al., eds, *Peter Martyr Vermigli: Humanism, Republicanism, Reformation / Petrus Martyr: Humanismus, Republikanismus, Reformation*, Travaux d'Humanisme et Renaissance 365 (Geneva, 2002), 173–202 ; idem, 'Heinrich Bullinger and the English-speaking World', in P. Opitz and E. Campi, eds, *Heinrich Bullinger (1504?–1575): Leben, Denken, Wirkung*, Zürcher Beiträge zur Reformationsgeschichte 24 (Zürich, 2006), 891–934.

that meant in terms of plays, poetry and prose, but rather I will pursue the theological theme.[35] I offer three crucial works of the new theological eye on the English Reformation which clinch the arguments I have laid out. One is the brilliant essay by my former student Alec Ryrie, 'The Strange Death of Lutheran England', which encapsulates the argument in the monograph based on his doctoral thesis that early English Protestantism (or better 'evangelicalism') speedily moved in the early 1540s from a more or less Lutheran phase to a positive alignment with Reformed Protestantism, in response to an erratically conservative turn in Henry VIII's religious policy.[36] A second is a superb account of the Reformed Protestantism of Transylvania by Graeme Murdock, which shows just how intimately enmeshed with the theology of early Stuart England the religious politics of that faraway place became. Who could forget the sad story of the eager Hungarian student who tried to use his Latin in the London docks to find his way to Cambridge University, and ended up not in *Cantabrigia* but in Canterbury? Nothing insular about him, or about the university at which he eventually and ruefully arrived.[37] The last exhibit is a beautifully forensic account of English Reformation eucharistic theology by Bryan Spinks. By juxtaposing the soteriology and sacramental theology of Richard Hooker and William Perkins, Spinks not only underscores their common Reformed Protestant heritage, but he also makes the point that Perkins, the archetypal 'puritan' in the Anglican hegemonic narrative, was more representative of the pre-Civil War Church of England than was Hooker. Spinks's last chapter describes the circumstances in which this order was reversed after 1660: then, a remodelled Hooker took his place in the subtly rewritten story of an Anglicanism which hardly existed before Charles II's Restoration. The agent of that

---

35 To appreciate one fine example of the usefulness of juxtaposing a deep understanding of the English Reformation with literature, see D. Womersley, *Divinity and State* (Oxford, 2010).

36 A. Ryrie, 'The Strange Death of Lutheran England', *JEH* 53 (2002), 64–92; idem, *The Gospel and Henry VIII: Evangelicals in the Early English Reformation* (Cambridge, 2003).

37 G. Murdock, *Calvinism on the Frontier 1600–1660: International Calvinism and the Reformed Church in Hungary and Transylvania* (Oxford, 2000), 65. The title of the book might be said to be its least happy feature, since Murdock is describing something much wider than 'Calvinism'.

particular realignment was the 'docufiction' of Izaak Walton's *Life of Hooker*.[38]

Yet Hooker's new role in the church's historiography and identity was also part of a wider story, much of which we hardly suspected at all until recent years. The extraordinary comeback of an episcopal Church of England with a refurbished version of the Book of Common Prayer after 1660 was not just a matter of high politics but was fuelled by a groundswell of popular support. Evidence for this lies in the steady build-up before the Civil Wars of a persistent affection for the Prayer Book; but even more surprisingly, during the Interregnum itself (as we now know, thanks to the great digital project of the Church of England Clergy Database), there was a quite unexpected clandestine commitment by very many clergy to seeking out the episcopal ordination which the Commonwealth's religious settlement had abrogated.[39] After that, the Reformed Church of England really did steadily become the Anglican Church of England, though it would have to wait until the nineteenth century before anyone unselfconsciously called it that.

So with this theological work added to the revolution in local studies, the stage was set for an overarching interpretation of the English Reformation which includes this new and more soundly evidenced Anglican historiography, and which could tritely be called post-revisionist. It was significant that the Colloquium for Local Reformation Studies has become simply the Reformation Studies Colloquium, and it was one of the main instigators of that conference who created the first extended statement in print of that new reality: Felicity Heal, with her volume in the Oxford History of the Christian Church, *Reformation in Britain and Ireland*.[40] What the local Reformation studies industry freed

[38] Bryan D. Spinks, *Two Faces of Elizabethan Anglican Theology. Sacraments and Salvation in the Thought of William Perkins and Richard Hooker* (Lanham, MD, 1999); see also W. B. Patterson, 'William Perkins as Apologist for the Church of England', *JEH* 57 (2006), 252–69. On Walton, see J. Martin, *Walton's Lives: Conformist Commemorations and the Rise of Biography* (Oxford, 2001).

[39] See J. Maltby, *Prayer Book and People in Elizabethan and Early Stuart England* (Cambridge, 1998); K. Fincham and S. Taylor, 'Vital Statistics: Episcopal Ordination and Ordinands in England, 1646–60', *EHR* 126 (2011), 319–44. The database is accessible online at <http://www.theclergydatabase.org.uk>.

[40] F. Heal, *Reformation in Britain and Ireland*, OHCC (Oxford, 2003). I can testify that my attendance in 2000 at Felicity Heal's preliminary seminar paper laying out

us to do was to get beyond the idea of the kingdom, still less the nation, as the only natural stage on which our investigations should take place, and go to stages both greater and smaller. We could indeed look at smaller units, as we had done from the 1960s. At first, we were probably too preoccupied with counties and dioceses (because those were the boundaries within which Tudor bureaucrats and judges worked and created archives), rather than thinking of the geographical or economic areas which actually shaped most people's lives. But we could also expand beyond one kingdom to think of larger units, and see how they interacted. So Heal's *Reformation in Britain and Ireland* took its title seriously and treated properly what I have termed, not without opposition, the 'Atlantic Isles' dimension.[41] Regardless of the name, this is essential to understanding the dramatic changes of the sixteenth century. Scotland provides a Reformed Protestant Reformation in purer and more clearly articulated form than England, while Ireland affords the unique spectacle in Europe of a Counter-Reformation coming to fruition despite the efforts of the central government, an achievement of resistance more generally associated with Protestantism.

Then we can run kingdoms together, as the Stuart monarchs tried to do before us, to see what consequences might follow. I think particularly of Haigh's ground-breaking study of Tudor Lancashire, which book exemplifies the religious story for a region which remained peculiar in its religious practice in terms of the rest of England, not just in the sixteenth but into the twentieth century. What happens if we lay Lancashire not against what might be happening in Suffolk or Kent, but against its real neighbours, the Pale of Dublin and north Wales?[42] This was a region of sea-coasts, bordering the Irish Sea, and that might have been as great

how she was proposing to structure this book impelled me to give up a similar writing project, which I felt would simply be duplicating the excellent prospectus which she presented.

[41] On the 'Atlantic Isles', see Diarmaid MacCulloch, *A History of Christianity: The First Three Thousand Years* (London, 2009), 13–14.

[42] On Wales, we await the published work of Katharine Olson, and so are still dependent on G. Williams, *Wales and the Reformation* (Cardiff, 1997). On the Pale in its relationship to the rest of Ireland, see C. Lennon, *The Lords of Dublin in the Age of the Reformation* (Dublin, 1989); H. A. Jefferies, *The Irish Church and the Tudor Reformation* (Dublin, 2010); J. Murray, *Enforcing the English Reformation in Ireland: Clerical Resistance and Political Conflict in the Diocese of Dublin, 1534–1590* (Cambridge, 2009).

a reality as whatever Tudor administrative units sought to impose their will on these regions. Given the problems or opportunities of transport in the sixteenth century, it would have been less trouble in 1541, when the diocese of Chester was founded, to get from Chester to Dublin than from Chester to York. Do we see these three societies acting in similar ways? Yes, we do: three anglophone elites who mostly refused to accept the Reformation, to the largely impotent annoyance of the English government in Westminster. And we might think of ways in which we might try to reconstruct this society of the Irish Sea and test its little foibles.

Here I draw your attention to another way in which that which was once merely antiquarian is now part of a newly holistic approach to the Reformation and what went before it. Now we are free to draw on the lessons of material culture. Andrew Spicer and Alexandra Walsham have made mainstream the study of parish churches and of sacred places, when before these were merely guilty pleasures for some of us.[43] I think of my own youthful enthusiasm for monumental brasses and sepulchral monuments: I did sneak some references to them into my doctoral thesis, though I do not think that Sir Geoffrey approved. To start a line of enquiry on the society of the Irish Sea, I would note the enthusiasm for monumental brasses in lowland England, but also in Yorkshire; contrast that with their striking virtual absence in the Pale of Dublin and North Wales, and their significant rarity in Lancashire. These regions commemorated their dead monumentally, certainly, but they did so in other mediums, some of which, such as the alabaster tombs made in the English Midlands which can be found in Wales, would have been just as inconvenient to import there as the products of London marblers.[44] What other commonalities might we find in the region, once we start thinking in this lateral way?

Those of us who have explored the importance of material culture have also inevitably been drawn to absences, in other words, to the vigorous efforts made in the Reformation to smash up other

[43] See esp. A. Spicer, *Calvinist Churches in Early Modern Europe* (Manchester, 2007); A. Walsham, *The Reformation of the Landscape: Religion, Identity and Memory in Early Modern Britain and Ireland* (Cambridge, 2011).

[44] See a very suggestive little discussion: R. Biebrach, 'Conspicuous by their Absence: Rethinking Explanations for the Lack of Brasses in Medieval Wales', *Transactions of the Monumental Brass Society* 18 (2009), 36–42.

people's material culture. Here our patron saint is Margaret Aston, who first rescued iconoclasm from the misrepresentations in parish church guidebooks, which habitually presented it as perpetrated by a roving gang of mindless thugs called the puritans, led by a thug called Oliver Cromwell. Suddenly we found that bishops and churchwardens had done a lot of it after all. In many case, the iconoclasts were far from mindless, but deliberately left fragments half-destroyed in their original place as 'monuments of ... indignation and detestation against them': in other words, symbols of victory over the Catholic past.[45]

Even more dramatic symbols are abbey ruins, and one out of many complex reasons that we still have abbey ruins from four centuries ago is that Protestants liked to keep them there to gloat. I think of a fascinating if adventurously speculative paper from Paul Everson and David Stocker on the building activity in Lincoln-shire by Charles Brandon, Duke of Suffolk, favourite of Henry VIII, who in 1537 set Brandon up as an informal lieutenant in that recently rebellious county. Brandon's grand new Lincolnshire houses contain some clear visual statements that he was a viceroy for Henry VIII's new religious dispensation, but Everson and Stocker note that at two of these houses, Kirkstead and Barlings, Brandon seems deliberately to have left substantial monastic ruins standing explicitly as ruins in the new ensemble – even 'ruin gardens' – as a symbol of godly victory: an ideological statement which one could parallel in other Tudor rebuildings to provide great houses for gentlemen at Hailes Abbey (Gloucestershire) and Newstead Abbey (Nottinghamshire).[46]

And to return to my old preoccupation with Anglo-Catholic myth-making, I will point out for you a beautiful piece of applied Reformation archaeology by Niall Oakey, which shows that some of the biggest iconoclasts were Victorian Anglo-Catholics. Oakey took a sample set of counties to see exactly when medieval rood screens were destroyed in parish churches. It turned out that thirty to forty per cent of surviving medieval screenwork disappeared in Norfolk churches during the nineteenth century, and no less than

45 M. Aston, 'Public Worship and Iconoclasm', in D. Gaimster and R. Gilchrist, eds, *The Archaeology of Reformation 1480–1580* (Leeds, 2003), 9–28, at 16–17.
46 P. Everson and D. Stocker, 'The Archaeology of Vice-regality: Charles Brandon's Brief Rule in Lincolnshire', ibid. 145–58.

forty to fifty per cent in Dorset. A high proportion of this was the work of Anglican high churchmen who convinced themselves that their church 'restorations' were undoing the harm of the Reformation by concentrating the eyes of congregations on eucharistic consecration at the high altar.[47] How about that for the myth of the English Reformation?

Felicity Heal was constrained by the plan of the Oxford History to end her story of the Reformations in the Atlantic Isles around 1600, and she was thus perforce unable to survey what it has become fashionable to see as a 'Long Reformation' stretching into the seventeenth or even the eighteenth century. Yet she was able to make a virtue of this necessity, arguing that by the end of the sixteenth century, after much variety, adjustment and growing self-definition, there was finally 'little cultural space' anywhere in the islands to be anything else but Romanist or Protestant, and so there is some point to making an end at this juncture.[48] This makes sense: 1600 was a watershed moment, a prelude to the greatest proof of the effectiveness of the English Reformation. When 1642 brought civil war to England, and Englishmen were prepared to fight and kill fellow Englishmen, it was not another War of the Roses, when Catholic had fought Catholic, just to propel into power a different upper-class twit from the royal family tree. Now Protestant fought Protestant, for the future shape of the Protestant church in England, and to decide the most effective means of defending the realm from popery. That is the measure of how much the English Reformation was a howling success.

One of the great results of half a century of development in Reformation studies has been one of liberation both to look closely and to look broadly. We have not forgotten or laid aside national stories, ours or others, but we also see the context of microcosm and macrocosm, region and continent. We have pluralized Reformations, as Christopher Haigh has taught us to do, in the interests of more intelligently discussing Reformation. We have

---

[47] N. Oakey, 'Fixtures or Fittings? Can surviving Pre-Reformation Ecclesiastical Material Culture be used as a Barometer of Contemporary Attitudes to the Reformation in England?', ibid. 58–72. This ideological destruction with a 'Catholic' agenda is of course widely paralleled in the Counter-Reformation rearrangement of churches across Europe: see E. C. Tingle, 'The Catholic Reformation and the Parish: The Church of Saint Thégonnec (Finistère, France) 1550–1700', ibid. 44–57.

[48] Heal, *Reformation in Britain and Ireland*, 478.

identified urban Reformations and rural Reformations next door to each other, and seen their differences: understood better how different Reformations link to each other. We have listened to humble people arguing about Reformation, tried to understand the objects and the landscape which they would have known. We have also remembered that clever people said significant things about Reformation, and were perfectly capable of getting across their messages to those without an Oxbridge education.[49] And we have tried above all to see the Reformation in its own terms and not what people in our own age would like it to have been. The end result is that Reformation history and religious history generally are taken much more seriously by other historians than they were fifty years ago: and that is something to celebrate.

St Cross College, Oxford

[49] For some of the ways in which they achieved that, see I. Green, *The Christian's ABC: Catechisms and Catechizing in England c.1530–1740* (Oxford, 1996); T. Watt, *Cheap Print and Popular Piety* (Cambridge, 1991); R. A. Leaver, *'Goostly Psalmes and Spirituall Songes': English and Dutch Metrical Psalms from Coverdale to Utenhove, 1536–1566* (Cambridge, 1991); L. Dixon, 'Richard Greenham and the Calvinist Construction of God', *JEH* 61 (2010), 729–45.

HISTORIOGRAPHY OF THE SCOTTISH REFORMATION: THE CATHOLICS FIGHT BACK?*

by STEPHEN MARK HOLMES

In 1926 the Revd James Houston Baxter, Professor of Ecclesiastical History at the University of St Andrews, wrote in the *Records of the Scottish Church History Society*: 'The attempts of modern Roman Catholics to describe the Roman Church in Scotland have been, with the exception of Bellesheim's *History*, disfigured not only by uncritical partisanship, which is perhaps unavoidable, but by a glaring lack of scholarship, which makes them both useless and harmful.'[1] The same issue of the journal makes it clear that Roman Catholics were not welcome as members of the society.[2] This essay will look at the historiography of the Scottish Reformation to see how the Catholics 'fought back' against the aspersions cast on them, and how a partisan Protestant view was dethroned with the help of another society founded ten years before the Ecclesiastical History Society, the Scottish Catholic Historical Association (SCHA).

A Contested History

The writing of history was an important weapon in the Reformation debates, as can be seen from Luther's autobiographical preface to his collected works.[3] The historiographical roots of this twentieth-century conflict reach back to John Knox's *History of the Reformation in Scotland* (1587), which was produced that 'posterity to come may be instructed how wondrously hath the light of Christ Jesus prevailed against darkness'.[4] Knox had been an actor

---

* An earlier version of this essay was delivered at the 2011 conference of the Scottish Catholic Historical Association in Edinburgh. I thank Owen Dudley Edwards for his comments on it.

[1] J. H. Baxter, 'Some Desiderata in Scottish Medieval History', *RSCHS* 1.4 (1926), 200–8.

[2] *RSCHS* 1.4, vii.

[3] *WA* 50, 657–61; cf. Melanchthon's funeral oration on Luther: *CR* 11, 726–34.

[4] *John Knox's History of the Reformation in Scotland*, ed. William Croft Dickinson, 2 vols (Edinburgh, 1949), 1: 6; a new critical edition is to be published by T. & T. Clark

in many of the events; the crucial years were written up soon after them, and he preserved important documents. However, not all posterity wished to be so instructed by one of the victors in the revolution of 1559–60. There is an alternative Catholic narrative in the polemical writings of Ninian Winzet (1518–92) and the *History of Scotland* of Bishop John Lesley (1527–96). Like Knox they emphasized the defects of the pre-Reformation church in Scotland, but their aim was to explain how so perfect a religion could have fallen so easily.[5] Later Catholic exiles such as Thomas Dempster (1579–1625) and David Chalmers (*c.*1580–1641) wrote to glorify the Scottish Catholic past, but the work of Dempster and the manuscript *Monasticon Scoticum* of the Scottish Benedictine Marianus Brockie (1687–1755) contain so much fiction that Baxter's words might be seen as restrained.[6] There was, however, another more scholarly Catholic historical tradition, in dialogue with Protestant antiquarians, represented by two Scottish priests who knew the great French Benedictine historian Jean Mabillon, Thomas Innes (1662–1744) and Richard Augustine Hay (1661–1736).[7]

After Knox, Scottish Protestantism, which had already produced the distinctly partisan *Rerum Scoticarum Historia* of George Buchanan (1506–82), developed its own tradition of historical writing about the Reformation.[8] In the seventeenth century the histories of

---

in 2013: *John Knox's History of the Reformation in Scotland*, ed. James Kirk and Margaret Sanderson.

5   Ninian Winzet, *Certaine Tractates, together with the book of four score and three questions and a translation of Vincentius Lirinensis*, ed. James King Hewison, 2 vols, Scottish Text Society 15, 22 (Edinburgh, 1888, 1890; first publ. 1562); idem, *De origine, moribus, et rebus gestis Scotorum* (Rome, 1578); idem, *The history of Scotland, from the death of King James I. in the year M.CCCC.XXXVI. to the year M.D.LXI*, ed. Thomas Thomson, Bannatyne Club (Edinburgh, 1830); idem, *The historie of Scotland wrytten first in Latin by the most reuerend and worthy Jhone Leslie, bishop of Rosse, and translated in Scottish by Father James Dalrymple ... 1596*, ed. Elphege George Cody, 2 vols, Scottish Text Society 19, 34 (Edinburgh, 1888, 1895).

6   Thomas Dempster, *Historia ecclesiastica gentis Scotarum* (Bologna, 1627); David Chalmers, *De Scotorum Fortitudine* (Paris, 1631); Edinburgh, Scottish Catholic Archives [SCA], SK/9–12, Marianus Brockie, *Monasticon Scoticum*; Henry Docherty, 'The Brockie Forgeries', *InR* 16 (1965), 79–127.

7   *ODNB, s.nn.* 'Hay, Richard (1661–1736)', 'Innes, Thomas (1662–1744)', online at <http://www.oxforddnb.com/view/article/12735 and 14432>, accessed 8 August 2011.

8   George Buchanan, *Rerum Scoticarum Historia* (Edinburgh, 1582); online edition and translation at <http://www.philological.bham.ac.uk/scothist/>.

David Calderwood (1575–1650) and John Spottiswoode (1565–1639) represented the views of the Presbyterian-covenanting and royalist-episcopalian tendencies in the Reformed Church of Scotland respectively.[9] After the disestablishment of the Scottish bishops in 1689, an alternative episcopalian Protestant history is found in works such as those of Bishop Robert Keith (1681–1757), whose history of Scotland from 1542 to 1568 was based on extensive original research and who was assisted by Thomas Innes in compiling his catalogue of Scottish bishops.[10] Two key works for the dominant modern Presbyterian narrative were the lives of John Knox and Andrew Melville by Thomas McCrie (1772–1835), a noted opponent of Catholic Emancipation. These were scholarly hagiographies designed to counter the Enlightenment hostility of writers such as William Robertson and David Hume to the 'fanaticism' of the reformers.[11] This new narrative of Protestant inevitability, a Presbyterian counterpart to the Enlightenment doctrine of 'progress', found expression in various statues of Knox erected during the following century and in written form in *The Reformation in Scotland* by David Hay Fleming (1849–1931), who came from the same fissiparous tradition of Presbyterian secessions from the Church of Scotland as Thomas McCrie.[12] For Fleming the Reformation was caused by the preaching of the word of God in a country marked by clerical ignorance, credulity, rapacity and depravity (illustrated by a long list of clerical bastards). He attempted to answer critics such as Andrew Lang by engaging with such charges as that the

---

[9] David Calderwood, *The True History of the Church of Scotland* (Edinburgh[?], 1678); John Spottiswoode, *History of the Church and State of Scotland* (London, 1655).

[10] Robert Keith, *History of the Affairs of Church and State in Scotland* (Edinburgh, 1734); idem, *A Large New Catalogue of the Bishops of the Several Sees within the Kingdom of Scotland* (Edinburgh, 1755).

[11] William Robertson, *The History of Scotland, During the Reigns of Queen Mary and of King James VI*, 2 vols (London, 1759); David Hume, *The History of England* (London, 1754–62); Thomas McCrie, *Life of John Knox* (Edinburgh, 1812); idem, *Life of Andrew Melville* (Edinburgh, 1819).

[12] David Hay Fleming, *The Reformation in Scotland: Causes, Characteristics, Consequences* (London, 1910). Statues of Knox were erected, for example, at the Glasgow Necropolis (1825); the 'Hall of Heroes' in the Wallace Monument, Stirling (1869); the Mound, Edinburgh, now in New College quadrangle (1896); and the Royal Mile, Edinburgh, now inside St Giles' Cathedral (1904). On Fleming, see *ODNB, s.n.* 'Fleming, David Hay (1849–1931)', online at < http://www.oxforddnb.com/view/article/33165>, accessed 24 July 2012.

Reformers destroyed books, art and buildings.[13] Though rooted
in the sources, it was a simplistic story of a nation moving under
God's guidance from the darkness of superstition into the light of
true religion, freedom and good education. This vision is still alive
in such popular works from the last decade as Roderick Graham's
John Knox: Democrat and Harry Reid's *Reformation: The Dangerous
Birth of the Modern World.*[14]

When the Scottish National Portrait Gallery was built in
the 1880s there was a statue of Knox on the façade; however, a
committee of Edinburgh Catholic women also commissioned a
statue of Mary Queen of Scots for its east wall.[15] Nineteenth-
century antiquarianism, romantic medievalism and the publication
of medieval sources encouraged a more positive view of Catholicism, and Catholics played a part in this, especially the Benedictine
monks of Fort Augustus.[16] Despite this, the prevailing picture of
the Scottish Reformation by the time of its four hundredth anniversary in 1960 was still what Alec Ryrie has called the 'heroic
Protestant narrative', and the main sites for university education in
church history were the divinity faculties of the four ancient Scottish universities, which trained, and were largely staffed by, Presbyterian ministers.[17] This situation may be compared to England,
with its own national myths of the English Reformation associated
with its national church and a revived Catholic alternative seen, for

---

[13] Andrew Lang, *John Knox and the Reformation* (London, 1905).

[14] Roderick Graham, *John Knox, Democrat* (London, 2001); Harry Reid, *Reformation: The Dangerous Birth of the Modern World* (Edinburgh, 2009).

[15] S. Karly Kehoe, *Creating a Scottish Church: Catholicism, Gender and Ethnicity in
Nineteenth-Century Scotland* (Manchester, 2010), 165.

[16] Paschal Downs and Alasdair Roberts, 'Dom Odo Blundell OSB (1868–1943): A
Different Kind of Historian', *InR* 56 (2005), 14–45. Two examples of the contribution
of Fort Augustus monks are Oswald Hunter Blair's translation of Alphons Bellesheim's
Geschichte der katholischen Kirche in Schottland (2 vols, Mainz, 1883), *History of the Catholic
Church in Scotland*, 4 vols (Edinburgh, 1887–90); and Elphege Cody's edition of Bishop
Lesley's history for the Scottish Text Society.

[17] Alec Ryrie, *The Origins of the Scottish Reformation* (Manchester, 2006), 5. In
1979 the General Assembly of the Church of Scotland opposed the appointment
of a Roman Catholic to the chair of theology in the divinity faculty of Edinburgh
University: S. J. Brown, 'Presbyterians and Catholics in Twentieth-Century Scotland',
in idem and G. Newlands, eds, *Scottish Christianity in the Modern World* (Edinburgh,
2000), 255–81. The chair of church history at Edinburgh was held by ministers until
1988, but even in the 1970s the subject was described as 'a secular discipline within a
divinity Faculty': David Wright and Gary Badcock, *Disruption to Diversity: Edinburgh
Divinity 1846–1996* (Edinburgh, 1996), 181, 109.

example, in the works of the Benedictine Francis Aidan Gasquet (1846–1929).[18]

REVISIONISM AND THE SCOTTISH CATHOLIC HISTORICAL ASSOCIATION

Outside the Scottish university system a small group of Catholic historians met in 1949 near Falkirk; a Scottish Catholic Historical Committee was elected to organize a conference in 1950 and to investigate the possibility of publishing a journal. This committee of eleven was required to be 'approved by the Roman Catholic Hierarchy'.[19] Only two were university lecturers, J. H. Burns of Aberdeen (politics) and Donald Nicholl of Edinburgh (history). The others included priests, schoolteachers, religious and a librarian.[20] At the 1949 meeting the Dominican Anthony Ross gave a programmatic paper entitled 'Some Scottish Catholic Historians' which sited the work of the new committee in the alternative historical tradition of Lesley and Dempster. He started with the pre-Reformation histories of John Major and Hector Boece, thus hinting that Protestant historiography was a deviation from the national tradition, and emphasized scholarly and eirenic figures who played a part in national life despite their religion, such as Thomas Innes.[21] This was the genesis of the *Innes Review* and the SCHA (originally called the 'Thomas Innes Society'), which were to study 'the part played by the Roman Catholic Church in the Scottish Nation'.[22]

---

[18] Diarmaid MacCulloch, 'The Myth of the English Reformation', *JBS* 30 (1991), 1–19; idem, 'Putting the English Reformation on the Map', *TRHS* ser. 6, 15 (2005), 75–95; David Knowles, *The Historian and Character* (Cambridge, 1963), 240–63; John Vidmar, *English Catholic Historians and the English Reformation, 1585–1954* (Brighton, 2005), 95–111, 116–22. On the criticisms of Gasquet's work by G. G. Coulton, see, in this volume, Alec Corio, 'The Development of G. G. Coulton's Critique of a Roman Catholic School of History', 417–29.

[19] SCA, GD 13/1/1/1, 'Constitution of the Scottish Catholic Historical Association 1950–1951'.

[20] 'Miscellany: The Scottish Catholic Historical Committee', *InR* 1 (1950), 67. They were: Fr Anthony Ross OP; Fr David McRoberts; Fr John McKee, archivist at Blairs junior seminary; Br Clare (Dr James Handley); Dr J. H. Burns; Dr Donald Nicholl; Anna Macdonald, Dowanhill Training College; Anthony Hepburn, the Mitchell Library; Peter Anson; and John Durkan and James Moffat, schoolteachers from Glasgow: John Durkan, 'Our First Half-Century', *InR* 50 (1999), i–vi.

[21] Anthony Ross, 'Some Scottish Catholic Historians', *InR* 1 (1950), 5–21.

[22] SCA, GD 13/1/2/1, 'Proposed Constitution of the Thomas Innes Society'; 'Constitution 1950–1951'; cf. 'Miscellany', 67.

This task involved providing a scholarly basis for a more balanced view of the medieval church, but about a third of the articles in the first decade of the *Innes Review* were devoted to the Reformation period. These had three significant emphases. The first concerned neglected evidence; for example, 'Early Scottish Libraries' by Anthony Ross and John Durkan listed about a thousand extant books owned by Scots before 1560.[23] The second was that this was an eirenic project; already in 1951 we find Durkan altering 'phrases likely to annoy the sympathetic Protestant reader' in an article by Fr Barry.[24] Thirdly, the SCHA aimed to critique the 'heroic Protestant narrative' on purely historical grounds; in the second issue, Durkan and Ross challenged the scholarship of two recent books on the Reformation: William Croft Dickinson's edition of Knox's *History* and *John Knox in Controversy* by Hugh Watt, Principal of New College, Edinburgh, who was told that he would have saved himself from basic errors had he paid a quick visit to the *Dictionnaire de théologie catholique*.[25]

The 1959 issues of the *Innes Review* contained articles on the Scottish church in the Reformation period, most of which were republished in 1962 in a volume edited by David McRoberts, *Essays on the Scottish Reformation 1513–1625*.[26] The committee had invited non-Catholic contributors and hoped to 'avoid controversy'.[27] They also, with the encouragement of their bishops, asked the Moderator of the General Assembly of the Church of Scotland for 1960, John Burleigh, to write a foreword, but this never happened and Burleigh's own *A Church History of Scotland* (1960) largely ignored the modern Roman Catholic Church.[28] By studying the 'long Reformation' from 1513 to 1625, the essays were able to give weight to Catholic reform and Catholic life before 1560. They covered such topics as bishops, parishes, hospitals, religious houses, literature, reforming councils and the destruction caused by the

---

[23] John Durkan and Anthony Ross, *Early Scottish Libraries* (Glasgow, 1961), first published in *InR* 9 (1958), 1–167.

[24] SCA, GD 13/226/14, John Durkan to David McRoberts, 26 December 1951.

[25] *InR* 1 (1950), 158–63.

[26] David McRoberts, ed., *Essays on the Scottish Reformation 1513–1625* (Glasgow, 1962).

[27] SCA, GD 13/2/3/1/8, SCHA committee meeting minutes, 9 February 1957.

[28] SCA, GD 13/239/15; 13/239/17, 18; John H. S. Burleigh, *A Church History of Scotland* (Oxford, 1960).

Reformation. Recalling the collaboration between Thomas Innes and Robert Keith, an Episcopalian contributor to the volume was Gordon Donaldson (1913–93), whose own book for the anniversary of 1560, *The Scottish Reformation*, was based on his 1957–8 Cambridge Birkbeck lectures. Donaldson also challenged the Presbyterian consensus, this time in terms of polity, by emphasizing continuity beyond 1560 and the late arrival of Presbyterianism (his mind was on the discussions during the 1950s concerning reunion between the Church of Scotland and the Scottish Episcopal Church, a project which was rejected by the former in 1959).[29] Donaldson acted as a reader for the SCHA, for example writing nine pages of critical comments on McRoberts's article in *Essays on the Scottish Reformation*, which dealt with 'Material Destruction caused by the Scottish Reformation'.[30]

In the two volumes by McRoberts and Donaldson we see historians working closely with the sources and refuting a particular denominational view, but with their own denominational agendas. In 1982 Ian Cowan rightly identified the two books as a turning point in the study of the Scottish Reformation, 'a triumph of scholarship over partisanship'.[31] It was as if this clash between established and disestablished historiographies cleared the ground for a new synthesis. This process was also parallel to similar developments elsewhere in Europe. Hans Hillerbrand's study of Reformation historiography argues that 'the Reformation was institutionalised as Protestant sacred space': a historical event or period became crucial for the self-understanding of the different Protestant confessions and the nations or regions which constructed their identity on the basis of Protestantism.[32] In the mid-twentieth century, however, he notes a new non-polemical Roman Catholic interest in Reformation history, associated with scholars such as Joseph Lortz and Otto Pesch, which broke down

---

[29] Gordon Donaldson, *The Scottish Reformation* (Cambridge, 1960). J. D. Mackie, Donaldson's predecessor as Historiographer Royal, wrote that Donaldson's aim was 'to debunk some cherished beliefs of Presbyterians and to suggest that Episcopalianism is a better thing': review of *The Scottish Reformation*, *EHR* 76 (1961), 715–17.

[30] SCA, GD 13/238/6.

[31] Ian B. Cowan, *The Scottish Reformation: Church and Society in Sixteenth-Century Scotland* (London, 1982), ix.

[32] Hans J. Hillerbrand, 'Was there a Reformation in the Sixteenth Century?', *ChH* 72 (2003), 525–52, at 527.

confessional barriers and, together with the work of sympathetic Protestant historians such as Heiko Oberman, re-examined the late medieval background to the Reformation.[33] The work of the SCHA historians had more in common with this movement than with 'the last truly Ultramontanist history' of the English Reformation by Philip Hughes, published in 1954.[34]

Four Scottish Catholic Historians

The origin of the SCHA and its reaction against the dominant historiography of the Scottish Reformation ensured that the historians associated with it had, despite their different interests and emphases, a certain common approach. Anthony Ross OP (1917–93) was editor of the *Innes Review* from 1950 to 1951 and chairman of the SCHA from 1961 to 1982. His *Early Scottish Libraries*, compiled with John Durkan, shows a pre-Reformation clergy in touch with intellectual currents from all over Europe, deeply influenced by Erasmus and with an interest in the latest Catholic reforming movements. A similar conclusion can be drawn from the 1953 *Catalogue of Scottish Medieval Books and Fragments* by David McRoberts (1912–78), which showed that the reformed Quiñones Breviary, an influence on Cranmer's Book of Common Prayer, was used in Scotland.[35] McRoberts's Rhind lectures on pre-Reformation church art and furnishings (1970) also argued that Scotland was not a cultural backwater, although he sometimes overstated his case.[36] McRoberts had studied for the priesthood in Rome, was Keeper of the Scottish Catholic

---

33 Ibid. 531–2.

34 Philip Hughes, *The Reformation in England*, 3 vols (London, 1950–4); Vidmar, *English Catholic Historians*, 2.

35 David McRoberts, 'Catalogue of Scottish Medieval Liturgical Books and Fragments', *InR* 3 (1952), 49–63, 131–5 (repr. Glasgow, 1953); idem, 'Some Sixteenth-Century Scottish Breviaries and their Place in the History of the Scottish Liturgy', *InR* 3 (1952), 33–48. On the Quiñones Breviary, see *Breviarium Romanum a Francisco Cardinali Quignonio*, ed. J. Wickham Legg (Cambridge, 1888); *The Second Recension of the Quignon Breviary*, ed. J. Wickham Legg, 2 vols, Henry Bradshaw Society 35, 42 (London, 1908, 1912); H. Jedin, 'Das Konzil von Trient und die Reform der liturgischen Bücher', *Ephemerides liturgicae* 59 (1945), 5–37. McRoberts's 'Catalogue of Scottish Medieval Liturgical Books and Fragments' has been replaced by Stephen Mark Holmes, 'Catalogue of Liturgical Books and Fragments in Scotland before 1560', *InR* 62.2 (2011), 127–212.

36 Published as David McRoberts and Stephen Mark Holmes, *Lost Interiors: The Furnishing of Scottish Churches in the Later Middle Ages* (Edinburgh, 2012).

Archives and editor of the *Innes Review* from 1952 to 1978. John Durkan (1914–2006) was a schoolmaster and a member of the SCHA committee from its beginning, serving as chairman from 1982 to 1986. His vast corpus of work is based on a remarkable familiarity with primary source material from all over Europe.[37] His publications on George Buchanan, sixteenth-century Scottish humanism, universities and education, libraries, hospitals and friars are of enduring value and often contain hints for further research that have still to be followed up, as with his article of 1950 on Archbishop Wauchope, which mentioned in passing connections during the 1530s and 1540s between Scots and the early Jesuits.[38] Leslie Macfarlane (1914–2006) is unusual in this group as having been a university lecturer, at Aberdeen University from 1953 to 1981. He was secretary of the SCHA between 1966 and 1988. His monumental 1985 biography of Bishop William Elphinstone gave a definitive picture of flourishing church reform in the diocese of Aberdeen in the years before 1513.[39] By paying attention to the sources and being honest about abuses, these writers contradicted Fleming's picture of a church marked by ignorance and depravity, and showed that its best elements were in contact with continental Catholic reform. The work of these four historians gave a more nuanced picture of sixteenth-century Scotland; it was supported and continued by the publications of other members of the SCHA committee, such as Mark Dilworth OSB (1924–2004) of Fort Augustus on Scottish monasticism and Michael Lynch of the University of Edinburgh on the Reformation in Edinburgh, the first Scottish example in book form of those local studies that have been so fruitful for the understanding of the English Reformation.[40]

37   For a bibliography of his works, see *The Renaissance in Scotland: Studies in Literature, Religion, History and Culture offered to John Durkan*, ed. A. A. MacDonald, Michael Lynch and Ian B. Cowan (Leiden, 1994), 417–28.

38   John Durkan, 'Robert Wauchope, Archbishop of Armagh', *InR* 1 (1950), 48–66.

39   Leslie Macfarlane, *William Elphinstone and the Kingdom of Scotland 1431–1514* (Aberdeen, 1985).

40   Mark Dilworth, *Scottish Monasteries in the Late Middle Ages* (Edinburgh, 1995); idem, *Monasteries and the Reformation in Scotland* (Edinburgh, 2010); Michael Lynch, *Edinburgh and the Reformation* (Edinburgh, 1981). On Scottish studies of the Reformation in the localities, see Ian Cowan's Historical Association pamphlet, *Regional Aspects of the Scottish Reformation* (London, 1978); Margaret Sanderson's preface to her *Ayrshire and the Reformation: People and Change, 1490–1600* (East Linton, 1997).

What enabled these Catholic historians to perform this successful exercise in revisionism from outside the academic establishment in a country which has remained marked by sectarian tension?[41] It helped that they were not working alone; for example Annie I. Dunlop (1897–1973) also laboured in the field of pre-Reformation Scottish church history, attending the Scots kirk in Rome while studying in the Vatican archives and later presenting a copy of her book on Bishop James Kennedy to Pope Pius XII.[42] Factors within the Scottish Roman Catholic community included the rise of an education-conscious Catholic middle class in the wake of the generous provisions for Catholic schools in the 1918 Education (Scotland) Act; the existence of an alternative institutional base in seminaries, religious houses and (from 1958) the Scottish Catholic Archives; and a new openness and confidence in Catholic culture associated with the Second Vatican Council.[43] Elements in broader Scottish culture were also favourable to the work of the SCHA. There was a growing dissatisfaction with old myths, expressed in the anti-Calvinism of writers such as Edwin Muir, Fionn MacColla, Hugh MacDiarmid and George Mackay Brown, and the development of a nationalism sympathetic to the older Scotland of Wallace and Bruce.[44] There is a 'cultural nationalist' dimension to McRoberts's work, seen in his Rhind lectures and his article 'The Scottish Church and Nationalism in the Fifteenth Century', recently critically examined by David Ditchburn.[45]

---

[41]   T. M. Devine, ed., *Scotland's Shame? Bigotry and Sectarianism in Modern Scotland* (Edinburgh, 2000); Steve Bruce et al., *Sectarianism in Scotland* (Edinburgh, 2004); Scottish Executive, *Sectarianism: Update on Action Plan on Tackling Sectarianism in Scotland* (Edinburgh, 2007). See also the Offensive Behaviour at Football and Threatening Communications (Scotland) Act 2012, of the Scottish Government.

[42]   'Annie I. Dunlop: A Memoir by Dr Ian B. Cowan', in *Calendar of Papal Letters to Scotland of Clement VII*, ed. Charles Burns (Edinburgh, 1976), ix–xviii.

[43]   Of the early years of the SCHA, Durkan wrote that 'the approach owed something to Vatican Council II', which was announced in 1959 and used the results of the non-polemical Catholic historical theology of thinkers such as Yves Congar and Henri de Lubac: 'Father Anthony Ross, O.P.: A Memoir', *InR* 44 (1993), 113–18, at 116.

[44]   Catholicism in Scotland, like the law, education and the Presbyterian and Episcopal Churches, is organized on a Scottish rather than British basis. Ross was a friend of MacDiarmid, co-authoring with him and Campbell Maclean *John Knox* (Edinburgh, 1976), and he also allowed George Mackay Brown to put on plays in the basement of his Edinburgh priory: Durkan, 'Anthony Ross'.

[45]   McRoberts and Holmes, *Lost Interiors*; David McRoberts, 'The Scottish Church and Nationalism in the Fifteenth Century', *InR* 19 (1968), 3–14; David Ditchburn, 'The "McRoberts Thesis" and Patterns of Sanctity in Late Medieval Scotland', in Steve

Catholicism itself, influenced by Aquinas and Vatican I, gave these historians a confidence that scholarship led by unbiased reason could not conflict with their faith and it also made them at home in continental scholarship and archives.

On the other hand their religion could cloud their eyes so that, for example, they followed Bishop Lesley in seeing Catholicism as the only true heir of pre-Reformation Scottish Christianity, thus missing both the strangeness of the Auld Kirk and the continuities with it in Protestantism. McRoberts's catalogue of pre-Reformation liturgical books included Catholic books up to 1696 but ignored Protestant liturgy except for two volumes containing Catholic elements: Murdoch Nisbet's Lollard New Testament, produced in the 1520s with a list of mass readings; and the 1587 Book of Common Order, which included Catholic feasts in its calendar. Another weakness was the acceptance of the polemical inheritance of moral criticism of pre-Reformation Catholicism.[46] Macfarlane painted a glowing picture of Elphinstone but in an *ODNB* article unjustly criticized his successor Bishop Gordon, who was in office in 1560.[47] Failure to see that Protestant and Catholic reform came from the same roots meant, for example, an inability to understand John Winram's sudden conversion to Protestantism in 1559.[48]

Beyond Denominational History

After Donaldson's book came many political studies of the Scottish Reformation and a certain neglect of theology. J. H. Burns, though publishing in other fields, also had a great influence on younger scholars working on the politics of the Scottish Reformation, such

---

Boardman and Eila Williamson, eds, *The Cult of Saints and the Virgin Mary in Medieval Scotland* (Woodbridge, 2010), 177–94.

[46] This is Alec Ryrie's criticism of McRoberts's 'otherwise splendid collection of *Essays on the Scottish Reformation*': *Origins of the Scottish Reformation*, 6. It was also an aspect of the contemporary 'new Catholic historiography' of the Reformation elsewhere in Europe: Hillerbrand, 'Was there a Reformation?', 531.

[47] *ODNB*, *s.n.* 'Gordon, William (*d.* 1577)', online at <http://www.oxforddnb.com/view/article/11085>, accessed 8 August 2011.

[48] McRoberts described him as 'an able man without any specific religious convictions who was intent on making his career in the church be it Catholic or Calvinist': *Essays on the Scottish Reformation*, xix. McRoberts's opinion is criticized by Linda Dunbar, *Reforming the Scottish Church: John Winram (c.1492–1582) and the Example of Fife* (Aldershot, 2002), 4.

as Jane Dawson and Roger Mason. The 1962 SCHA volume, *Essays on the Scottish Reformation 1513–1625*, however, was also programmatic both for Catholic historians and for the academy in several ways.

Firstly, it took seriously Catholic reform, central to the 1962 volume and to Macfarlane's *Elphinstone*.[49] Later work, such as that of James Cameron and Alec Ryrie, has included considerations of Catholic reform, and Linda Dunbar has written a fine study of John Winram. However, much remains to be done, not least a deeper examination of the varieties of Catholic reform in St Andrews and Aberdeen and a development of Durkan's work on continental influences and connections.[50]

Secondly, it attacked the myth of pre-Reformation Scotland as a cultural backwater and argued that 'Renaissance' is a fair description of Scottish culture from the late fifteenth century. It is not surprising that the Durkan *Festschrift* was entitled *The Renaissance in Scotland*, and he contributed to the currently flourishing interest in Scottish Renaissance literature. McRoberts also made an important contribution in this area in his works on religious art and architecture. The revival of interest in Tudor Latin polyphony at the start of the twentieth century played a role in the overthrow of a narrowly 'Anglican' historiography; it is not surprising that the *Innes Review* was among the first to publish on Scottish Renaissance polyphony, anticipating the recent revival of interest.[51] Lingering doubts about this early Scottish Renaissance are a legacy of the 'darkness to light' view of the Reformation rebutted in recent years by Jane Stevenson, Peter Davidson and Ian Campbell.[52]

---

[49] See nn. 26, 39 above.

[50] James K. Cameron, 'Catholic Reform in Germany and in the pre-1560 Church in Scotland', *RSCHS* 20 (1979), 105–17; idem, 'The Cologne Reformation and the Church of Scotland', *JEH* 30 (1979), 39–64; Alec Ryrie, 'Reform without Frontiers in the Last Years of Catholic Scotland', *EHR* 119 (2004), 27–56; idem, *Origins of the Scottish Reformation*; idem, 'Paths not Taken in the British Reformations', *HistJ* 52 (2009), 1–22; Dunbar, *Reforming the Scottish Church*.

[51] Benjamin Davies, 'The Historiography of the Reformation, or the Reformation of Historiography', *Early Music* 29 (2001), 263–72; Arthur Oldham, 'Scottish Polyphonic Music', *InR* 13 (1962), 54–61; D. James Ross, *Musick Fyne* (Edinburgh, 1993); Isobel Woods Preece, *Our awin Scottis use* (Glasgow, 2000).

[52] Jane Stevenson and Peter Davidson, 'Ficino in Aberdeen: The Continuing Problem of the Scottish Renaissance', *Journal of the Northern Renaissance* 1 (2009), 64–87; Ian Campbell, 'A Romanesque Revival and the Early Renaissance in Scotland,

Thirdly, McRoberts, through his study of late medieval church furnishings and liturgical books, opened up the rich world of pre-Reformation Scottish devotion. There have been some studies in this area, such as a major project funded by the Arts and Humanities Research Council on dedications to saints and Audrey-Beth Fitch's 2009 *The Search for Salvation* on lay devotion, but there is need for at least two major studies to complement Margo Todd's *The Culture of Protestantism in Early Modern Scotland*, one on pre-Reformation devotional life in general and the other specifically on liturgy, rooted in McRoberts's *Catalogue*.[53]

The history of the Scottish Reformation was very different from that of England, although they were closely linked in many ways. The work of the SCHA historians, in their close reading of the sources, abandonment of historical polemic and acceptance of pre-Reformation ecclesial decadence, resembled that of the Benedictine David Knowles (1896–1974). However, the effect of their work on Scottish Reformation historiography is perhaps better compared to that of more recent English revisionists such as Christopher Haigh, Jack Scarisbrick and Eamon Duffy, although it began earlier and its effect has been less thorough. Responding to the charge that English revisionism represents 'the unfortunate revival of confessional history', Duffy has noted that a number of those involved in this tendency are Roman Catholic and attributes this partly to the effects of the English 1944 Education Act 'which led to a postwar flood of Catholics into higher education' and 'the heightened and self-consciously religious preoccupations of a minority group'. He remarks: 'it seems extraordinary to me that before the recent debates no one appears to have thought it worth comment that most British Reformation historians were in fact practicing, or at least cultural, Protestants', and argues that a Catholic background can be an advantage to the historian of

---

c.1380–1513', *Journal of the Society of Architectural Historians* 54 (1995), 302–25; idem, 'The Peripheries Strike Back: Romanesque and Early Gothic Revival as a Reaction to Fourteenth-Century Marginalisation in Scotland, Ireland and Italy', in Stephan Hoppe, ed., *Stil und Bedeutung in der nordalpinen Renaissance* (Regensburg, 2008), 238–62.

53   Survey of Dedications to Saints in Medieval Scotland, online at <http://www.shca.ed.ac.uk/Research/saints/>, accessed 8 August 2011; Audrey-Beth Fitch, *The Search for Salvation: Lay Faith in Scotland* (Edinburgh, 2009); Margo Todd, *The Culture of Protestantism in Early Modern Scotland* (New Haven, CT, 2002).

this period, enabling them to see late medieval religion as 'more coherent and less repellent than may be the case for historians formed in a different religious tradition'.[54] Despite the disadvantages noted above, such as accepting the recusant Catholic polemicists' low view of the pre-Reformation church and an inability to appreciate continuities with the pre-Reformation church within Scottish Protestantism, this has been true for the SCHA historians.

In Scottish Reformation historiography there is a sense that the Catholics have fought back and 'won' in the sense that a partisan Protestant historiography of the Scottish Reformation is no longer accepted by serious historians, but this was simply by good scholarship and not by combative denominational polemics. Totally detached history is not possible and a distinct viewpoint can, if combined with rigorous scholarship, break down anachronistic orthodoxies and reveal hidden aspects of the past. It will also introduce its own blind spots, and so the writing of history is an endlessly reiterative process. The work of the SCHA historians was not the last gasp of sectarian historiography. They were, whatever their own hidden denominational intentions, the creators of a programme of research on sixteenth-century Scotland that, having demolished its partisan Presbyterian target and escaped its Roman Catholic origins, is still in its early stages.

University of Edinburgh

---

[54] Eamon Duffy, 'The English Reformation after Revisionism', *RQ* 59 (2006), 720–8, at 723. In the same issue, Diarmaid MacCulloch remarks on the advantage to a Reformation historian of being 'without confessional commitment': 'Protestantism in Mainland Europe: New Directions', 698–706, at 705.

PATRICK BOYLE, THE IRISH COLLEGES AND THE HISTORIOGRAPHY OF IRISH CATHOLICISM

by LIAM CHAMBERS

More than forty Irish colleges were established in France, Spain, Portugal, the Italian States and the Austrian Empire between the 1580s and 1690s to cater for a diverse range of Irish Catholic students and priests who had travelled to the continent to pursue higher education. The colleges were a significant feature of Irish Catholicism, most obviously in the early modern period, and they have therefore attracted substantial attention from historians. The first modern attempts to write their histories appeared in the later nineteenth century and were heavily influenced by a Rankean emphasis on primary sources, as well as contemporary Irish Catholic nationalism. If the dominant historiography of the period emphasized the persecution of the 'penal era', then the existence of a network of Irish colleges producing redoubtable clergy for the Irish mission helped to explain how the Catholic Church survived in Ireland. In this paradigm, the production of priests was the main role bestowed on the colleges. This essay examines the foremost early historian of the colleges, and of the viewpoint just outlined, the Vincentian priest and superior of the Irish College in Paris, Patrick Boyle. In 1901 he produced the first book-length history of an Irish college: *The Irish College in Paris from 1578 to 1901*.[1] Over the following three decades he published a series of important articles on the history of the Irish colleges and Irish migrants to continental Europe.[2] This essay provides the first assessment of Boyle's historical scholarship, placing it in the context of his long-running battle to secure the survival of the Irish College in Paris during an especially turbulent

---

[1]   The full title is *The Irish College in Paris from 1578 to 1901, with a Brief Account of the Other Irish Colleges in France: viz., Bordeaux, Toulouse, Nantes, Poitiers, Douai and Lille; and a Short Notice of the Scotch and English Colleges in Paris* (London, 1901).

[2]   These is no complete bibliography of Boyle's works, though an incomplete listing is available in Anon., 'Patrick Boyle's Writings', *Colloque: Journal of the Irish Province of the Congregation of the Mission* [hereafter: *Colloque*] 11 (Spring 1985), 391–3; additions in T[homas]. D[avitt]., 'Patrick Boyle', *Colloque* 17 (Spring 1988), 397–8.

period between the late 1880s and the 1920s. Boyle deliberately highlighted the significance of his college to Irish Catholicism, particularly in the preparation of clergy for the Irish mission. This emphasis had a strong influence on the historiography of the Irish colleges until as late as the 1980s, when Boyle's assumptions were finally and fundamentally challenged, a development which has in turn opened up the history of the colleges for fresh investigation. The essay concludes by pointing to the ongoing reconceptualization of the Irish colleges taking place within discussions concerning Irish Catholic student mobility, identity formation and migration, as well as ecclesiastical organization and development.[3]

BOYLE's IRISH COLLEGE

Born in County Derry in 1849, Patrick Boyle studied at a seminary in Cambrai before completing his clerical formation in Ireland. Following ordination as a Vincentian priest and postings in Dublin and in Lanark in Scotland, he was appointed principal of St Patrick's College, Armagh, in 1878. In 1887 he moved to St Patrick's College, Maynooth, as a spiritual director, before leaving two years later to take up the position of superior at the Irish College, Paris. Boyle was an energetic administrator, a committed teacher and a strong advocate for the college. He maintained an extensive network of correspondents, among them members of the Irish hierarchy, notably Cardinal Michael Logue, archbishop of Armagh and a former member of staff at the Irish College. Boyle finally retired in 1926, though he continued to teach at the college until 1932 and he died there the following year.[4]

While in Paris, Boyle emerged as a prolific ecclesiastical historian. He decided that a full history of the college was desirable, having earlier considered reprinting Thomas Murphy's short work of 1866.[5] Boyle was, of course, ideally placed to undertake the

---

3 The key challenge to Boyle appeared in L. W. B. Brockliss and P. Ferté, 'Irish Clerics in France in the Seventeenth and Eighteenth Centuries: A Statistical Study', *Proceedings of the Royal Irish Academy Section C* 87/9 (1987), 527–72.

4 This draws on accounts of Boyle's life and personality presented by John McGuinness and John Oakley respectively in *Colloque* 11 (Spring 1985), 382–9, as well as Boyle's diary: Paris, Irish College Paris Archives [hereafter: ICPA], MS A3.b46. An extensive collection of Boyle's papers is held in the ICPA: MSS A3.b1–47.

5 [Thomas Murphy], 'The Irish College, Paris', *IER* 2 (1866), 180–5, 252–62. Like Boyle, Murphy was a member of the college staff.

necessary research in the college archives, as well as in a number of important Parisian libraries, and he stressed that his work drew on 'official and authentic documents'.[6] The resulting book presented the history of the college in four sections, from its origins in the community of Irish priests who established themselves in Paris in 1578 to the date of publication (1901). In addition, it sketched the history of the other Irish colleges in France, as well as the English and Scots Colleges in Paris. Finally, it provided a series of primary sources (rules, official documents and biographical lists) in eighteen lengthy appendices.[7]

Boyle's *Irish College* offered a source-based history which reflected the concerns of the author. Most importantly, it established the historical credentials of the college, particularly for the sparsely documented early period: 'we have a chain of evidence extending over the greater part of the seventeenth century as to the existence of the Irish seminary'.[8] Boyle argued that the college had been created in response to religious persecution in Ireland and had made a vital contribution to overcoming its consequences:

> [The College] is also proof of the undying attachment of the Irish to the Catholic faith. The young men who could brave exile and poverty to obtain ecclesiastical education, and when they had won academic honours could return to live in the mountains and glens of Ireland, were truly witnesses of the faith, martyrs in preparation of heart, as many of them afterwards became martyrs in fact.[9]

Accordingly, the book placed a particular emphasis on missionaries and martyrs, as well as scholars and bishops.

Boyle also had other concerns. As a Vincentian priest, he was naturally keen to emphasize Vincent de Paul's connections with the Irish in Paris, as charitable benefactor and ideological friend.[10] Moreover, he wanted to highlight the college's theological orthodoxy. Without explicitly addressing the issue, Boyle was at pains to

---

6   Boyle, *Irish College*, vii.
7   Ibid. 141–233.
8   Ibid. 7.
9   Ibid. 111.
10   Ibid. 10–11, 16–17, 22; Boyle's work on Vincentian history included *St Vincent de Paul and the Vincentians in Ireland, Scotland and England, A.D. 1638–1909* (London, 1909); *Some Irish Vincentians in China in the 18th and 19th Centuries* (Dublin, 1918).

emphasize the ultramontane sympathies of the college throughout its history. Therefore he devoted considerable attention to an anti-Jansenist declaration penned by a group of Irish students in Paris (working, conveniently, with Vincent de Paul) in 1651.[11] He cited evidence from the 1730s to show that the Irish were not infected with 'the poison of error' (Jansenism) but had positive relations with the Jesuits.[12] During the revolutionary period, Boyle portrayed the college as a centre for refractory activity, for which it suffered during the Terror.[13] More recently, in 1860, the staff and students of the college had addressed Pius IX to express 'their attachment to his temporal sovereignty and their detestation of the attacks made upon it'.[14] A further feature of Boyle's *Irish College* was its emphasis on the clerical nature of the institution. Boyle was presumably well aware, from his reading of documents in the college archives, that the *Ancien Régime* Irish colleges in Paris had catered for a diverse mix of students – ordained priests, clerical students and students destined for professional careers. The foundation documents establishing bursaries for students made this clear.[15] However, by the time Boyle arrived it had long assumed the character of a nineteenth-century seminary.[16] Therefore he duly underlined the clerical nature of the institution throughout its history. Conscious that there had been complaints that few of the 'clerical' students persevered to ordination in the early eighteenth century, Boyle carefully noted that the Irish College established exclusively for younger students in 1776 'was a fully organized ecclesiastical seminary'.[17] Following the irregularities of the Napoleonic period, the superior appointed by the bishops, Paul Long, set out 'to restore the college to its exclusively ecclesiastical character'.[18] In

[11] Boyle, *Irish College*, 15–18, 22–4; for an up-to-date account, see Thomas O'Connor, *Irish Jansenists, 1600–70: Religion and Politics in Flanders, France, Ireland and Rome* (Dublin, 2008), 219–26.
[12] Boyle, *Irish College*, 34–5, 39.
[13] Ibid. 61–4.
[14] Ibid. 90.
[15] Liam Swords, ed., 'History of the Irish College, Paris, 1578–1800: Calendar of the Papers of the Irish College, Paris', *AH* 35 (1980), 2–233, at 47, 51, 110–15, 127, 133–4, 145, 148–9, 151, 163, 179.
[16] A number of students attempted to challenge this clericalizing tendency in the nineteenth century, but without success. See, e.g., ICPA, MS A2.e53, Seamus Foley to Abbé Caire, 31 July, 27 August 1852.
[17] Boyle, *Irish College*, 42.
[18] Ibid. 75.

effect, Boyle retrospectively clericalized the Irish colleges, whereas in reality the student population had been more diverse before the 1820s. Finally and unsurprisingly, Boyle sanitized the history of the college. He presented a one-sided account of the 1651 disputes (mentioned above). He glossed over the tumultuous problems of the 1730s and 1740s, when would-be reformers attempted to eject older students who were already ordained priests in favour of the younger *écoliers*.[19] Boyle also omitted the events of the 1850s, when the weak administration of John Miley caused a crisis in the college.[20] Boyle's college was therefore historically legitimate, theologically sound, clerical in character and conveniently Vincentian. Above all, it had made an outstanding contribution to Irish Catholicism in a period of violent repression.

Boyle's *Irish College* was only the beginning of the author's prolific scholarly career. From 1901, he published books, book-length translations, pamphlets and dozens of articles on the history of the Irish colleges and related matters, as well as on Vincentian history, pastoral theology, the priesthood and ecclesiastical politics. Many of his historical articles appeared either in the influential *Irish Ecclesiastical Record* or in the pioneering sources journal *Archivium Hibernicum*. In the pages of these periodicals, Boyle expanded on the history of the Irish College in Paris, assessed the contribution of heroic, scholarly and prominent individuals (John Baptist Walsh, Charles Kearney, Michael Moore, Thomas Hussey) and made available lists of students and other important primary sources for the first time.[21] He also contributed an important article on the 'Irish Colleges on the Continent' to the *Catholic Encyclopaedia*, where,

---

[19] See Liam Chambers, 'Rivalry and Reform in the Irish College, Paris, 1676–1775', in Thomas O'Connor and Mary Ann Lyons, eds, *Irish Communities in Early Modern Europe* (Dublin, 2006), 103–29.

[20] In 1932 Boyle commented to John McGuinness that the problems of the 1850s were 'more serious than I imagined', which suggests that limited information was available to him in 1901. See Boyle to McGuinness, 10 October 1932, in *Colloque*, 11 (Spring 1985), 389–91. On the 1850s, see Liam Chambers, 'Paul Cullen and the Irish College, Paris', in Daire Keogh and Albert McDonnell, eds, *Cardinal Paul Cullen and his World* (Dublin, 2011), 358–76; Gerard Moran, 'John Miley and the Crisis at the Irish College, Paris, in the 1850s', *AH* 50 (1996), 113–25.

[21] See n. 2 above. In addition, Boyle's translation of Pius X's encyclical *Notre Charge Apostolique* (1910), which attacked the French Le Sillon movement, should be noted. It appeared as *Some Errors Respecting the Rights of Democracy: Letter of His Holiness Pope Pius X to the Archbishops and Bishops of France on the Subject of the 'Sillon'* (Dublin, 1911). Marc Sangnier had established Le Sillon in 1894 to promote closer relations between

in stark terms, he articulated his view of the significance of the colleges:

> The history of the Irish colleges on the Continent is a manifest proof of the tenacity with which Ireland has clung to the Catholic faith. Without the succession of priests prepared in these colleges, the preservation of the faith in Ireland in the seventeenth and eighteenth centuries would have been impossible.[22]

THE CONTEXTS

Irish Catholic ecclesiastical history-writing in the late nineteenth and twentieth centuries was dominated by clergy with the interest, the understanding of church dynamics and the access to archival material necessary to undertake detailed research. This undoubtedly influenced the development of the subject into the early twentieth century, and, as James Kelly has pointed out in the case of diocesan history-writing, 'if the Church did not sponsor and churchmen did not write, or at the very least oversee the writing of diocesan history, it would largely be left unwritten'.[23] Boyle's work on the Irish College in Paris and related topics integrated well with the themes then dominant in Irish Catholic historiography, as articulated in the influential work of Laurence Renehan, Patrick Francis Moran, W. P. Burke and others, as well as the series of important and detailed diocesan histories which appeared from the 1860s.[24] Ecclesiastical historians of this period, including Boyle, focused largely on the institutional church, emphasized the persecution of Irish Catholicism in the early modern period and assumed the natural adherence of Irish Catholics to their faith. Neither was

---

the Catholic Church and the Third Republic; the movement disbanded following condemnation in *Notre Charge Apostolique*.

[22] Patrick Boyle, 'Irish Colleges on the Continent', *Catholic Encyclopedia*, 15 vols (New York, 1907–12), 8: 158–63, at 163.

[23] James Kelly, 'The Historiography of the Diocese of Dublin', in idem and Daire Keogh, eds, *History of the Diocese of Dublin* (Dublin, 2000), 1–19, at 8.

[24] Laurence Renehan, *Collections on Irish Church History* (Dublin, 1861); P. F. Moran, *Spicilegium Ossoriense: Being a Collection of Original Letters and Papers Illustrative of the History of the Irish Church from the Reformation to the Year 1800*, 3 vols (Dublin, 1874–84); W. P. Burke, *Irish Priests in the Penal Times (1660–1860)* (Waterford, 1914). Boyle singled out the influence of Alphons Bellesheim, *Geschichte der katholischen Kirche in Irland: Von der Einführung des Christenthums bis auf die Gegenwart*, 3 vols (Mainz, 1890–1): Boyle, *Irish College*, vii.

Boyle alone in his researches on the continental colleges. William M'Donald, the superior of the Irish College in Salamanca, had already produced a similar historical interpretation, with a parallel ecclesiastical agenda, in a series of articles also published in the *Irish Ecclesiastical Record* in the 1870s. Like Boyle, M'Donald had drawn heavily on his own college archive. However, he had concentrated on the early seventeenth century when the Spanish colleges were most significant and his work exhibited a more militantly Catholic nationalist tone than Boyle's comparatively more measured scholarship.[25]

Boyle had agendas other than simply adding to a dominant historiographical viewpoint. He was writing at a critical moment for the Irish College and was effectively drawing on the past to make a case for the college's future existence. Following serious problems in the early and mid-nineteenth century, the Irish Vincentians stabilized the college after they took over day-to-day management in 1858.[26] However, the events of 1870–1 and the political seachange which followed placed the college in a more uncertain position. In 1873 the French government established (or, more accurately, re-established) a *Bureau* to oversee the management of college finances.[27] The college authorities and Irish bishops were naturally apprehensive, but the *Bureau* proved to be more pliable than expected and Boyle deliberately praised it in his *Irish College*, noting the firm Catholic credentials of its leading members.[28] In fact, the financial position of the college was a more pressing issue, particularly in the late 1880s and early 1890s, just as Boyle took up his post. The need to carry out extensive repairs resulted in a reduction in the number of student rooms by the *Bureau*, which the Vincentian authorities deemed to be an unwarrantable intervention in the internal affairs of the college. Whilst the work was necessary, Thomas McNamara, the superior, and the Irish bishops

---

[25] e.g. William M'Donald, 'Irish Ecclesiastical Colleges since the Reformation: Salamanca I', *IER* 10 (1873), 353–66, at 356–7.

[26] For discussion, see Liam Chambers, 'Paul Cullen and the Irish College, Paris', in Keogh and McDonnell, eds, *Cardinal Paul Cullen*, 358–76.

[27] ICPA, MS A2.b74, Documents concerning the establishment of the Bureau Gratuit, 1873.

[28] Boyle, *Irish College*, 105–7; Paris, Archives nationales, F¹⁷ 17546, 'Fondations Catholiques Irlandaises: Procès Verbaux des Séances du Bureau Gratuit', tome 1: 1873–1895.

were disturbed by the dramatic nature of the move.[29] In 1892, the situation deteriorated further when the *Bureau* decided to reduce temporarily the number of bursary places from eighty-three to just fifty, in order to raise sufficient finances to fund further repairs and to pay off debts. Boyle, although seriously worried, attempted to assure the Irish bishops that the members of the *Bureau* were 'not influenced by any feeling hostile to religion'.[30] From a high point in 1887 when 104 students were housed at the college, numbers declined steadily and never fully recovered.[31] The reservations of the Irish bishops were magnified following the 1905 French law on the separation of the churches and the state. In the confusion about the legal standing of the Irish College, it was threatened with confiscation by the state and Boyle was forced to spearhead a lengthy battle to ensure that it remained open, enlisting the support of the British government.[32] In doing so he drew heavily on his historical researches. In 'A Plea for the Irish College in Paris' (1907) published in the *Irish Ecclesiastical Record*, he outlined the dangers to the college and made a case for its continued existence, but added:

> For ourselves, if the work of destruction cannot be averted, we shall quit France without a murmur. We shall even feel proud that we have been found worthy of sharing the persecution, which has laid waste the religious houses and plundered the ecclesiastical seminaries and despoiled the church of France.[33]

By 1908 the threat of closure had receded and the following year Boyle published a pamphlet on *The Irish Catholic Foundations in France*, in which he once again used his archival skills to demonstrate the Irish and ecclesiastical character of the investments made for the support of Irish students in the eighteenth century, funding which continued to form the bulk of the sums available in the

---

29 ICPA, MS A2.b111, *Report of the Irish College, Paris, for the Year 1888–89*; MS A2.b111, Thomas McNamara to the Archbishops and Bishops of Ireland, 24 September 1889.
30 ICPA, MS A2.b143, *Report of the Irish College, Paris, for the Year 1891–92*.
31 Figures derived from ICPA, MS A2.c4, 'Registre des élèves entrés au collège entre 1858 et 1938'.
32 Boyle, Diary, 1–37.
33 Patrick Boyle, 'A Plea for the Irish College in Paris', *IER* 21 (1907), 285–99.

early twentieth century.[34] While the college survived the potential consequences of the 1905 legislation, war forced its closure in 1914, but Boyle's advocacy was a crucial reason for its reopening in 1919.[35] It is clear that Boyle's historical scholarship developed in a particularly challenging period, during which the status and even the survival of the Irish College was frequently uncertain. His work not only underlined its historical significance to the Irish Catholic church, but made a compelling case for its continued existence addressed primarily to the Irish bishops. In short, the emphasis on the priest-producing Irish colleges of the penal era not only fitted the prevalent historiographical mood, it also established the credentials of the Irish College in Paris during a period of protracted uncertainty.

INFLUENCES AND NEW DIRECTIONS

Patrick Boyle and William M'Donald, with their dual commitment to archive-based history and the edification of the faithful, heavily influenced the historiography of the Irish colleges in the twentieth century.[36] Their interpretations clearly marked James O'Boyle's attempt to write a full history of the college networks, *Irish Colleges on the Continent*, which appeared in 1935. By the end of the 1930s, the Irish colleges in both Salamanca and Paris were closed to Irish students, effectively suspending historical research and ensuring that the work of Boyle and M'Donald went unchallenged for decades. In the meantime, Irish history underwent a dramatic transformation as a new generation of historians sought to professionalize scholarship along the lines they had encountered in Britain and elsewhere.[37] The relationship of ecclesiastical history to this process has not yet been the subject of close scrutiny, but it is clear that the mid-twentieth century saw the emergence of a new generation of historians (clerical and lay) working

[34] Patrick Boyle, *The Irish Catholic Foundations in France* (Dublin, 1909).

[35] Boyle, Diary, 57–60; see also Boyle's strong case for reopening, addressed to the Irish bishops, in ICPA, MS A2.b179, *Report of the Irish College, Paris, for the Year 1918–19*.

[36] By comparison, the researches of Boyle's contemporary, Georges Daumet, appear to have had little impact in Ireland: 'Notice sur les établissements religieux anglais, écossais et irlandais fondés à Paris avant la révolution', *Mémoires de la Société de l'Histoire de Paris et de l'Ile-de-France* 37 (1910), 1–184; 39 (1912), 1–224.

[37] Ciaran Brady, ed., *Interpreting Irish History: The Debate on Historical Revisionism* (Dublin, 1994).

on aspects of Catholic religious history, who were influenced by the changes taking place in Irish historical scholarship and who brought new standards to bear on the study of the Irish colleges and the related migration to continental Europe.[38] In 1973 T. J. Walsh published a major study of what he called *The Irish Continental College Movement*, which exhibited a less partial analysis than M'Donald or Boyle, while drawing on new research in French regional archives.[39] However, for many ecclesiastical historians the importance of the colleges was still conceptualized in terms which Boyle had pioneered. For example, Cathaldus Giblin wrote in 1971:

> Without the colleges on the continent, efforts on the part of the government to stamp out the Catholic faith in Ireland might well have been successful. These colleges served as supply stations, providing clergy to lead, guide and instruct the people ... the priests trained abroad kept the faith pure and in line with the teaching and practice of the Roman church.[40]

By the 1970s, a new interest in the history of the Irish College in Paris, dormant since the 1930s, was emerging. The college archives were rediscovered, catalogued and deployed by Brendan Devlin, Liam Swords and others.[41] A crucial historiographical turning point is to be found in the *Annales*-inspired research of Laurence Brockliss and Patrick Ferté on Irish students at the universities of Paris and Toulouse in the seventeenth and eighteenth centuries, which appeared in 1987. Their work revealed that, in fact, only a minority of students (perhaps as few as thirty per cent) returned to Ireland on completion of their studies in France. While this research was not primarily concerned with the Irish colleges, it

---

[38] Despite major advances and important publications, Benignus Millet was correct when, in 1990, he reiterated John Silke's observation that 'much of the history of the colleges remains to be investigated': Benignus Millet, 'The Seventeenth Century', in Réamonn Ó Muirí, ed., *Irish Church History Today* (Armagh, 1991), 42–62, at 56.

[39] T. J. Walsh, *The Irish Continental College Movement: The Colleges at Bordeaux, Toulouse and Lille* (Cork, 1973).

[40] Cathaldus Giblin, *A History of Irish Catholicism*, 4/3: *Irish Exiles in Catholic Europe* (Dublin, 1971), 63.

[41] Liam Swords, ed., *The Irish-French Connection, 1578–1978* (Paris, 1978). Robert Amadou's exhaustive study of the Collège des Lombards, which was the main Irish College in Paris from 1677 to the 1790s, has had less impact, but merits attention: 'Saint-Ephrem des Syriens du Collège des Lombards à nos jours', *Mémoires de la Féderation des Sociétés Historiques et Archéologiques de Paris et l'Ile de France* 37 (1986), 6–152.

nonetheless begged an obvious question: if the colleges were not, as Boyle and others had argued so strongly, primarily important for the formation of clergy who returned to Ireland, why were they important, if at all? Brockliss and Ferté suggested that Irish Catholic families sent their children to France to enter the church there, which offered greater prospects of social mobility than did the Irish church. As they put it: 'sending a son to be a priest in France was the ecclesiastical equivalent of sending another to join the Irish brigade'.[42] Of course, this does not mean that the Irish colleges were not important for the supply of priests to the Irish mission. It was certainly the case that the colleges facilitated the creation of a well-educated Irish Catholic clergy, in touch with continental European varieties of Catholic reform, who were able to reconstruct church structures in the early seventeenth century and the early eighteenth. From David Rothe to Cornelius Nary to John Thomas Troy, the Irish Catholic church was led by men educated on the Continent, usually (as with this trio) with strong links to the Irish college networks. However, it is also the case that Brockliss and Ferté's research challenged the overly enthusiastic views of earlier writers on the Irish colleges, specifically Boyle's work, and therefore encouraged historians to examine the Irish colleges afresh.

Some of the consequences are already emerging. The increasing publication of extensive prosopographies of Irish students at Paris and Leuven, as well as Alcalá de Henares, Lisbon, Santiago and Antwerp, in addition to the lists of Irish ordinations in Rome, Lisbon, Malines and Bordeaux, used in conjunction with relational databases, will permit historians insights into long-term trends concerning student and clerical migration.[43] The colleges (with perhaps the exception of the regular colleges) were not simply for the formation of priests and religious; they also provided pathways to alternative careers in medicine, law and the military, to take three obvious examples.[44] Nor were they isolated exile outposts; their connectedness was evident, if not highlighted, in the work

---

[42] Brockliss and Ferté, 'Irish Clerics in France', 550.

[43] The Irish in Europe Project based at the National University of Ireland, Maynooth, has been at the forefront of much recent research and has pioneered the use of relational databases in this field. See the project's website: <http://www.irishineurope.com/>.

[44] Swords, ed., 'Irish College, Paris', 179.

of Boyle in particular. Recent scholarship has emphasized that they were focal points for Irish migrant communities, bound into family networks running through Ireland, continental Europe and beyond.[45] As much recent research has convincingly shown, the migration of tens of thousands of Irish Catholic students, priests, merchants, soldiers, professionals and others to the Continent in the seventeenth and eighteenth centuries was a crucial feature of the period. The integration of the colleges, and those who resided in them, into the developing work on migration will recast them as more dynamic institutions than traditionally supposed.[46] The collapse of Boyle's analysis also begs questions about the intellectual influence of the colleges. To what extent did they shape the thinking of clergy and laity in Ireland? Closer attention to some of those issues passed over quickly or avoided altogether by Boyle, such as the disputes in Paris in the 1730s and 1740s, reveal that the Irish College played a controversial role in the early debates about reform of the church in the eighteenth century, as reformers on the Continent attempted to encourage transformation in the face of a hesitant episcopacy.[47]

While research since the 1980s has been significant, it is clear that much work on the colleges is required if we are to develop a comprehensive understanding of their place in the 'Irish in Europe' experience. Three examples will suffice. The financial, material and social histories of Irish student migration, though they have never been overlooked entirely, provide obvious subjects for further research.[48] The financial history of the colleges had a bearing on

---

[45] For an illuminating case study, see Priscilla O'Connor, 'Irish Clerics and Jacobites in Early Eighteenth-Century Paris, 1700–1730', in Thomas O'Connor, ed., *The Irish in Europe, 1580–1815* (Dublin, 2001), 175–90. Oscar Recio Morales has emphasized the political importance of the colleges in 'Not only Seminaries: The Political Role of the Irish Colleges in Seventeenth-Century Spain', *History Ireland* 9/3 (Autumn 2001), 48–52.

[46] For recent approaches to the 'Irish in Europe', see O'Connor, ed., *Irish in Europe*; Thomas O'Connor and Mary Ann Lyons, eds, *Irish Migrants in Europe after Kinsale, 1602–1820* (Dublin, 2003); eidem, eds, *Irish Communities*; eidem, eds, *The Ulster Earls and Baroque Europe: Refashioning Irish Identities* (Dublin, 2010).

[47] Chambers, 'Rivalry and Reform', 103–29.

[48] Indeed Patrick Boyle pioneered work on these subjects in 'Glimpses of Irish Collegiate Life in Paris in the Seventeenth and Eighteenth Centuries', *IER* ser. 4, 11 (1902), 432–50. The material history of the colleges has recently attracted attention: J. McDonnell, 'From Bernini to Celtic Revival: A Tale of Two Irish Colleges in Paris', *Irish Arts Review* 18 (2002), 165–75; Ana Castro Santamaría and Nieves Rupérez

the impact they had on Ireland – which is, surprisingly, another neglected issue. The challenge is to connect the lives of students at colleges and universities on the Continent with the careers of the seventeenth- and eighteenth-century clergy, elite and 'middling sort'. Exploration of the relationship between the Irish colleges and the English and Scots colleges in Flanders, France, Spain, Rome and elsewhere is also in its infancy. Interactions offer one subject for further research; more generally, a comparative dimension to the study of the colleges (and, indeed, to similar institutions on the Continent) would enrich our understanding of all of them.

CONCLUSION

Where late nineteenth-century Irish Catholic ecclesiastical historians emphasized the apparent blanket persecution of the early modern period, their contemporary successors are more likely to find themselves explaining the surprising vitality of Irish Catholic communities in the same period.[49] In this task, the role of the colleges is clearly important, if not yet fully understood. Beyond their priest-producing 'institutional' histories, it is becoming clear that the colleges facilitated student mobility, the development of dynamic migrant communities, the construction and adaptation of Irish identities, and the re-creation and reform of ecclesiastical structures. In short, while Boyle was correct to highlight the importance of the Irish colleges, and pioneering in his source-based approach, his analysis was understandably coloured by his struggle to preserve the Irish College in Paris. Future research on the colleges must take account of the work of Boyle, M'Donald and others, but should move beyond them to conceptualize afresh both the colleges and their place in the history of Irish Catholicism.[50]

Mary Immaculate College, University of Limerick

Almajano, 'The Real Colegio de San Patricio de Nobles Irlandeses of Salamanca: Its Buildings and Properties, 1572–1768', in O'Connor and Lyons, eds, *Ulster Earls*, 223–41.

[49] See, e.g., Ian McBride, *Eighteenth-Century Ireland: The Isle of Slaves* (Dublin, 2009), 215–45.

[50] For a historiographical survey with some important parallels, see Thomas Bartlett, '"Ormuzd Abroad ...Ahriman at Home": Some Early Historians of the "Wild Geese" in French Service, 1840–1950', in *Franco-Irish Connections: Essays, Memoirs and Poems in Honour of Pierre Joannon*, ed. Jan Conroy (Dublin, 2009), 15–30.

THE EVANGELICAL DISCOVERY OF HISTORY*

by DAVID W. BEBBINGTON

'From some modern perspectives', wrote James Belich, a leading historian of New Zealand, in 1996, 'the evangelicals are hard to like. They dressed like crows; seemed joyless, humourless and sometimes hypocritical; [and] they embalmed the evidence poor historians need to read in tedious preaching'.[1] Similar views have often been expressed in the historiography of Evangelical Protestantism, the subject of this essay. It will cover such disapproving appraisals of the Evangelical past, but because a high proportion of the writing about the movement was by insiders it will have more to say about studies by Evangelicals of their own history. Evangelicals are taken to be those who have placed particular stress on the value of the Bible, the doctrine of the cross, an experience of conversion and a responsibility for activism. They were to be found in the Church of England and its sister provinces of the Anglican communion, forming an Evangelical party that rivalled the high church and broad church tendencies, and also in the denominations that stemmed from Nonconformity in England and Wales, as well as in the Protestant churches of Scotland. Evangelicals were strong, often overwhelmingly so, within Methodism and Congregationalism and among the Baptists and the Presbyterians. Some bodies that arose later on, including the (so-called Plymouth) Brethren, the Churches of Christ and the Pentecostals (the last two primarily American in origin), joined the Evangelical coalition. These dynamic groupings spread over the parts of the globe inhabited by people of British stock. From the outbreak of the Evangelical Revival in the eighteenth century onwards, they obeyed their own imperative of preaching the gospel. By the second half of the nineteenth century they were culturally dominant in Britain, the United States and other lands of British settlement. Although their ascendancy subse-

---

* I am very grateful to Mark Noll for his comments on this essay and to other friends for discussion of topics in this field.

[1] James Belich, *Making Peoples: A History of the New Zealanders: From Polynesian Settlement to the End of the Nineteeenth Century* (Auckland, 1996), 135.

quently decayed in most areas of the British Isles, there was ample compensation in the extension of their influence into many other regions of the world though the missionary movement.[2] Evangelicals also penetrated the European continent, affecting the religious life of most of its countries. Excellent work has been done on some branches of the Evangelical movement on the Continent,[3] but this essay concentrates on history written about its adherents in the English-speaking world and the missions it generated. It offers an evaluation of the work written about Evangelicals of all types during the period since the foundation of the Ecclesiastical History Society in 1961.

Before the 1960s Evangelicals were generally averse to history. Many of them suffered from a disinclination to explore the life of the mind, preferring to concentrate on the more pressing task of evangelism.[4] The present, not the past, was the time in which people were converted. The eschatology most favoured amongst conservative Evangelicals, a form of premillennialism, encouraged belief in the imminent return of Christ to earth. If the second advent was likely at any time, scholarly enterprise appeared a waste of energy.[5] Furthermore there was an aspect of the Evangelical worldview that inhibited specifically historical work. The time that mattered was that of the earliest church. The first century provided, through the New Testament, authoritative teachings to obey and noble examples to follow. Subsequent Christian generations were notoriously inclined to degeneration and so, for many, were barely worth attention. Consequently when in the 1940s a group of British Evangelicals did create a centre for scholarly research, Tyndale House, Cambridge, it concentrated on biblical

---

[2]   The series 'A History of Evangelicalism' is the most convenient source for an overview. So far it contains three volumes: Mark A. Noll, *The Rise of Evangelicalism: The Age of Edwards, Whitefield and the Wesleys* (Leicester, 2004); John Wolffe, *The Expansion of Evangelicalism: The Age of Wilberforce, More, Chalmers and Finney* (Nottingham, 2006); and David W. Bebbington, *The Dominance of Evangelicalism: The Age of Spurgeon and Moody* (Leicester, 2005). Two further volumes on the twentieth century are in preparation.

[3]   e.g. Sébastien Fath, *Une autre manière d'être chrétien en France: Socio-histoire de l'implantation baptiste (1810–1950)* (Geneva, 2001); W. Reg Ward, *The Protestant Evangelical Awakening* (Cambridge, 1992); Gregory L. Nichols, *The Development of Russian Evangelical Spirituality: A Study of Ivan V. Kargel* (Eugene, OR, 2011).

[4]   Mark A. Noll, *The Scandal of the Evangelical Mind* (Grand Rapids, MI, 1994).

[5]   Timothy Weber, *Living in the Shadow of the Second Coming: American Premillennialism, 1875–1925* (New York, 1979). The same premillennial school of thought predominated long after 1925.

studies and effectively excluded church history from its purview.[6] One of its moving spirits, F. F. Bruce, who was to go on to occupy the Rylands Chair in Biblical Criticism and Exegesis at Manchester from 1959, was exceptional in writing three historical volumes on early Christianity, but even he had declared ten years before that 'if Church History teaches one thing more than another, it is that there is a constant tendency to deterioration'.[7] History was, if anything, at even more of a discount in the United States, where a strident Fundamentalism displaying overt hostility towards the academy had made a far greater impact on the Evangelical world. Although by the 1940s a number of 'neo-Evangelicals' were inching their way back towards greater engagement with scholarship, progress was especially slow in the discipline of history. As late as 1982 Mark Noll, a leading American Evangelical historian, was deploring 'the generally weak sense of history among most evangelical groups'.[8] Even the past of the Evangelical movement itself was alien territory.

Yet over the years beginning in 1961 the situation was transformed. Evangelicals – or at least a growing number of scholars in their ranks – became interested in their own past. Books were published, organizations formed and conferences held. By 1994 Harry S. Stout, Professor of History at Yale, could claim that, whereas in the 1970s 'evangelicalism was not a field of scholarly inquiry', by 1994, when he was writing, 'it certainly has become one'.[9] Stout was considering the United States alone, but his comment applied also to Britain, Australia and elsewhere. Although there were important contributions from outside the Evangelical movement, the achievement was largely the fruit of exploration by Evangelicals of their past. They had made a discovery of their own history. This essay examines the process. It considers first the

---

6   Thomas A. Noble, *Research for the Academy and Church. Tyndale House and Fellowship: The First Sixty Years* (Leicester, 2006).

7   Frederick F. Bruce, 'Church History and Its Lessons', in *The Church: A Symposium*, ed. J. B. Watson (London, 1949), 178, quoted by Tim Grass, *F. F. Bruce: A Life* (Milton Keynes, 2011), 73.

8   Wheaton, IL, Wheaton College, Billy Graham Center, Archives of the Institute for the Study of American Evangelicals [hereafter: ISAE], 'Proposal for a Planning Grant: An Institute for the Study of American Evangelicalism' (typescript, Wheaton, IL, 1982), 1. I am grateful to Eric Brandt for his assistance with research in these archives.

9   ISAE, Harry S. ['Skip'] Stout to ISAE Advisors, 29 May 1994.

state of the historiography of the Evangelical movement in the years preceding the upsurge of interest. Earlier historical work on aspects of the Evangelical world did exist, but much of what was produced was popular and unscholarly. The second topic is the ways in which existing patterns of writing were changed from the 1960s onwards; the general trend was towards markedly higher standards of scholarship. Then there will be a discussion of the major innovations in writing about the Evangelical movement over the period. So, thirdly, there will be assessment of the impact of religious developments on Evangelical historiography. The fourth section will analyse changes in historical fashion that affected writing about Evangelicals. The overall aim will be to explain the reasons for the growth and character of Evangelical historical studies over the last half-century.

In the first place, the prevailing model in the study of the Evangelical past before 1961 was denominational history. In Britain history societies had existed within the various Nonconformist bodies since around the opening of the twentieth century. The Baptist Historical Society, for example, had been founded in 1908 for the purpose, among others, of 'holding Meetings to Discuss Obscure Points'.[10] There was a similar pattern in America, where the equivalent Baptist organization had been formed as long before as 1853. Methodists, Congregationalists, Presbyterians and even Huguenots possessed their counterparts. Quakers, on the fringe of the Evangelical movement, and Unitarians, definitely beyond the fringe, had their own organizations too. The aim of these historical agencies was to defend the principles of their parent bodies. Evangelical Anglicans, though possessing no historical society, fitted the mould by reissuing in 1951 G. R. Balleine's history of the Evangelical party, first published in 1908, with a preface expressing the hope that the book would remain 'a vindication of the historic Evangelical tradition in the Church of England'.[11] There was therefore a longstanding custom of, as it were, slicing the history of Protestantism longitudinally, by denomination.

---

[10] Circular announcing a meeting to establish the Baptist Historical Society, April 1908, quoted by Faith Bowers, 'Centenary History of the Baptist Historical Society: Part 1: 1908–2008', *Baptist Quarterly* 42 (2008), 325–39, at 325.

[11] G[eorge]. R. Balleine, *A History of the Evangelical Party in the Church of England* (London, 1951), v.

The rarity of horizontal slicing into different periods meant that the common ground occupied by Evangelicals in the relatively recent past was obscured. Methodists, who owed their existence to the Evangelical Revival, focused their historical interest almost exclusively on John Wesley, with perhaps a side-glance for his brother Charles. Thus the Methodist denominational association was (and is) called the Wesley Historical Society. Consequently, at least down to the 1950s, there was little attention to the decades after Wesley's death in 1791. The chief exceptions were the four ground-breaking but rather uncritical studies of the relationship of Methodism to labour history by the minister Robert Wearmouth, published between 1937 and 1957.[12] In America William Warren Sweet, though himself a Methodist minister, deliberately tried to counteract the same dominance of confessional history by refusing to allow his graduate students at the University of Chicago to write dissertations about their own denominations, thereby producing a generation of scholars with a broader vision who flourished in the third quarter of the twentieth century – Robert Handy, Winthrop Hudson, Sidney Mead.[13] Among them there were signs, as in Handy's volume about the United States and Canada in the Oxford History of the Christian Church series, that religious history could be illuminated by treating Evangelicals as a distinct sector.[14] Yet the institutional pattern of higher education in America, whereby most church history was taught and written in seminaries and departments affiliated to specific religious bodies, meant that the subject retained its overwhelmingly confessional stance. History was treated as a branch of denominational apologetics.

Biography was another common feature of Evangelical historical work in the middle years of the twentieth century. The practice of commemorating the recently dead persisted, often generating

---

[12] Robert F. Wearmouth, *Methodism and the Working-Class Movements of England, 1800–1850* (London, 1937); idem, *Methodism and the Common People of the Eighteenth Century* (London, 1945); idem, *Methodism and the Struggle of the Working Classes, 1850–1900* (Leicester, 1954); idem, *The Social and Political Influence of Methodism in the Twentieth Century* (London, 1957).

[13] Sidney E. Mead, 'Professor Sweet's Religion and Culture in America: A Review Article', *ChH* 32 (1953), 33–49, at 41–2; James L. Ash Jr, *Protestantism and the American University: An Intellectual Biography of William Warren Sweet* (Dallas, TX, 1982), 103.

[14] Robert T. Handy, *A History of the Churches in the United States and Canada*, OHCC (Oxford, 1976).

anecdotal volumes with such titles as *Passion for Souls*.[15] Figures from the remoter past attracted some attention, with Wesley predictably looming large. Wesley was manipulated to fit the preconceptions of his Methodist biographers so that their twentieth-century priorities could bask in the glow of his authority. Thus the most popular American biography of Wesley in the 1950s was written by Francis J. McConnell, a bishop in the Methodist Episcopal Church whose mind had been moulded by the school of philosophy sometimes labelled 'personalism', according to which personality is the ultimate metaphysical principle. In his book Wesley is described as having been 'profoundly interested in human values' and eager for the 'release of higher human possibilities'.[16] Even when historical work aspired to higher scholarly standards, it was often cast in biographical form. The most telling study of Evangelical Anglicanism published around mid-century, though not presented as a biography, illustrates the point. G. C. B. Davies's book *The Early Cornish Evangelicals* (1951), despite its title, was almost exclusively concerned with Samuel Walker of Truro.[17] There were symptoms of change, for there was already the start of a tendency to examine the theology of Wesley in its intellectual context. Harald Lindström's *Wesley and Sanctification* (1946), though concentrating again on the single individual, is an early instance of a series of fruitful studies of the thought of the founder of Methodism.[18] When L. E. Elliott-Binns, a broad-minded Evangelical clergyman who had also written on Erasmus and Pope Innocent III, published in 1953 an account of the eighteenth-century revival, he expressed dismay that his source biographies were often 'the works of pious admirers, lacking in critical ability and with no apparent desire to verify their statements'.[19] He was not going to add to their number, but his scrupulosity was unusual. Biography, often tending to hagiography, remained a living genre among Evangelicals.

That was true of a specific department of Evangelical historical

[15] Kenneth Hulbert, *Passion for Souls: The Story of Charles H. Hulbert, Methodist Missioner* (London, 1959).

[16] Francis J. McConnell, *John Wesley* (New York, 1939), 310, quoted by Richard Heitzenrater, *The Elusive Mr. Wesley*, 2 vols (Nashville, TN, 1984), 2: 203.

[17] G[eorge]. C. B. Davies, *The Early Cornish Evangelicals, 1735–60* (London, 1951).

[18] Harald Lindström, *Wesley and Sanctification* (London, 1946).

[19] L[eonard]. E. Elliott-Binns, *The Early Evangelicals: A Religious and Social Study* (London, 1953), 5.

writing, missionary studies. Biographies depicting the heroic deeds
of their pioneering subjects were almost as much the norm in the
middle of the twentieth century as they had been in the middle
of the nineteenth. In 1947 A. G. Pouncy published an account of
the career of Henry Martyn, the scholar who left Cambridge at
the opening of the nineteenth century in order to blaze a gospel
trail into Iran. An Evangelical publisher issued it with the subtitle
'The First Modern Apostle to the Mohammedan'.[20] Complementing the biographies were institutional histories published by
the various agencies, denominational and undenominational. The
Bible Churchmen's Missionary Society, for example, published a
record, again in 1947, of its first quarter-century. The tone of the
book can be gauged from the foreword's explanation that the society's missionaries were eager to 'get to grips with the devil in the
strongholds of paganism by unsheathing therein the sword of the
Spirit'.[21] Although the book did include descriptions of setbacks,
it was primarily a story of successive triumphs designed to foster
further support for the society. The one major work that broke
out of the constrictions of missionary advocacy was Kenneth
Scott Latourette's magisterial *History of the Expansion of Christianity* (1937–47). Latourette, a Baptist minister on the faculty of Yale
Divinity School, discussed the advance of the faith over its two
thousand years in seven volumes, allocating the sixth to the nineteenth century and the seventh to the twentieth.[22] His expertise
in Chinese history ensured that he treated missions in the context
of their host cultures far more than his contemporaries. In general,
however, the history of the worldwide spread of Evangelical religion remained an intellectual backwater.

The place of Evangelicalism in mainstream historiography was
marginal, particularly in Britain. It is true that the eighteenth-
century Evangelical Revival claimed a place in British textbooks
just as the contemporary Great Awakening was discussed in their
American equivalents. G. M. Young, a fellow of All Souls College,

[20] A[nthony]. G. Pouncy, *Henry Martyn, 1781–1812: The First Modern Apostle to the Mohammedan* (London, 1947).
[21] Daniel H. C. Bartlett, Foreword to W[alter]. S. Hooton and J. Stafford Wright, *The First Twenty-Five Years of the Bible Churchmen's Missionary Society (1922–47)* (London, 1947), ix.
[22] Kenneth S. Latourette, *A History of the Expansion of Christianity*, 7 vols (New York, 1937–47).

Oxford, also gave weight to the formative influence of Evangelical religion over Victorian England in his luminous study, *Portrait of an Age* (1936). A boy born in 1810, he pointed out on his opening page, 'found himself at every turn controlled, and animated, by the imponderable pressure of the Evangelical discipline'.[23] It became conventional to acknowledge the role of Evangelical faith in the temper of the era. A post-war collection of BBC talks on the Victorian age included two, by Charles Smyth of Cambridge and Gordon Rupp, later of the same university, on the Anglican and Nonconformist varieties of Evangelicalism.[24] Acknowledgement, however, did not lead on to analysis. In the 1950s the Victorian era, still languishing under a shadow of sneering disapproval, was accorded only limited academic scrutiny. The place of Evangelicals in nineteenth-century Britain remained shrouded in obscurity, with few apart from Lord Shaftesbury receiving attention.[25] The twentieth century, according to leaders of historical opinion, was a period for recollection rather than record. Since the United States possessed so much shorter a past, the centuries when Evangelicals were active were more carefully researched. Eminent historians such as Richard Hofstadter of Columbia University could not fail to take account of the movement, so that, for example, his study of *Anti-Intellectualism in American Life* (1963) treats the Evangelical spirit as 'the most powerful carrier' of the phenomenon he examines.[26] More sympathetic accounts could also be found in mainstream history. In 1959 William G. McLoughlin Jr of Brown University successfully argued in his *Modern Revivalism* that the religious revivals beloved by Evangelicals had been 'more significant than social historians have yet acknowledged'.[27] The most thorough coverage of Evangelicalism in a national history, however, was to be found in the first volume of Manning Clark's

[23] G[eorge]. M. Young, *Victorian England: Portrait of an Age*, 2nd edn (London, 1957), 1.

[24] Charles Smyth, 'The Evangelical Discipline', and Gordon Rupp, 'Evangelicalism of the Nonconformists', in *Ideas and Beliefs of the Victorians: An Historic Revaluation of the Victorian Age* (London, 1949), 97–104, 105–12.

[25] The frequently reprinted J[ohn]. L. and Barbara Hammond, *Lord Shaftesbury* (London, 1923), had put Shaftesbury on the intellectual map.

[26] Richard Hofstadter, *Anti-Intellectualism in American Life* (London, 1964), 47.

[27] William G. McLoughlin Jr, *Modern Revivalism: Charles Grandison Finney to Billy Graham* (New York, 1959), vi.

massive *History of Australia*, appearing in 1962.[28] Clark, as the unbelieving son of an angular Evangelical Anglican clergyman,[29] saw Evangelicalism as one of the three great contending forces in the Australian past alongside the Enlightenment and Roman Catholicism. Yet the internal history of the movement was little illuminated either in Clark's volumes or elsewhere. Although in lands outside Britain there was rather more recognition of the role of the Evangelical movement in the national past, the detail of its life usually seemed beneath serious academic notice.

The second section of this essay can usefully address the ways in which the mid-twentieth-century legacy of historiography relating to Evangelicalism was adapted in later years. The existing pattern – high on denominational history, life stories and missionary successes but low in mainstream history – certainly persisted in the decades from the 1960s onwards, but with striking modifications. Denominational studies became notably more scholarly. The transformation was most obvious in Methodist history, where a new edition of Wesley's works achieved much higher standards of precision from the appearance of the first volume in 1975.[30] Reg Ward, the editor of the journals in Wesley's works, John Wigger, David Hempton and others wrote works that put Methodism – British, American and global – squarely within the parameters of conventional history.[31] *A History of the Methodist Church in Great Britain*, published in four volumes between 1965 and 1988, included chapters of great quality, perhaps the most valuable being a study in volume 1 by John Walsh, fellow of Jesus College, Oxford, who also wrote illuminatingly on the broader Evangelical movement.[32] Congregationalism was similarly served in England by

[28] Manning Clark, *The History of Australia*, 6 vols (Parkville, Vic., 1962–87).

[29] Manning Clark, *A Historian's Apprenticeship* (Parkville, Vic., 1992), ch. 1.

[30] John Wesley, *The Appeals to Men of Reason and Religion and Certain Related Open Letters*, ed. Gerald R. Cragg, *The Works of John Wesley, Vol. 11* (Oxford, 1975). The series continues.

[31] W[illiam]. R. Ward, *Religion and Society in England, 1790–1850* (London, 1972); John H. Wigger, *Taking Heaven by Storm: Methodism and the Rise of Popular Christianity in America* (New York, 1998); David Hempton, *Methodism: Empire of the Spirit* (New Haven, CT, 2005).

[32] John Walsh, 'Methodism at the End of the Eighteenth Century', in Rupert Davies, A. Raymond George and Gordon Rupp, eds, *A History of the Methodist Church in Great Britain*, 4 vols (London, 1965–88), 1: 275–315; J[ohn]. D. Walsh, 'Origins of the Evangelical Revival', in *Essays in Modern English Church History in Memory of Norman Sykes*, ed. G[areth]. V. Bennett and J[ohn]. D. Walsh (London, 1966), 132–62.

Clyde Binfield, whose long editorship of the *Journal of the United Reformed Church Historical Society* ensured a succession of perceptive articles. There were authoritative monographs on the Presbyterians of North America by, for example, Mark Noll on the leaders of Princeton Seminary and Richard Vaudry on the Free Church in Canada.[33] Baptists were particularly well served by a series of nearly twenty publications on the Baptist Heritage in Atlantic Canada issued from 1979 under the inspiration of Jarold K. Zeman, who had received an academic formation at Charles University in Prague before the Communist takeover of Czechoslovakia forced him to emigrate.[34] Newer religious bodies also began to attract their historians: Harold Rowdon on the Brethren in England, Edwin Harrell on the Disciples of Christ in America and Walter Hollenweger on the Pentecostals worldwide opened fresh paths where others have followed.[35] At the same time denominational loyalties were fading,[36] so that Evangelical history relating to more than one denomination seemed a more natural unit of historical study. Yet writing about specific denominations did survive, and, while much of it continued to be designed for internal consumption and some of it tolerated low standards of research, several historians were engaging powerfully with the issues raised by a wider historiography.

Biography has also been affected by an improvement in scholarly standards. It must be admitted once more that a great deal of more popular writing has remained immune to the trend. A biography of Charles Haddon Spurgeon, the greatest of Victorian preachers, appeared in 1992. The author, Lewis Drummond, formerly president of Southeastern Baptist Theological Seminary in North Carolina, provided a full scholarly apparatus and conceded that his subject had weaknesses, but he was eager to draw lessons, turned aside to vindicate the miracle of the feeding of the five

---

[33] Mark A. Noll, *Princeton and the Republic, 1768–1822: The Search for a Christian Enlightenment in the Era of Samuel Stanhope* (Princeton, NJ, 1989); Richard W. Vaudry, *The Free Church in Victorian Canada, 1844–1861* (Waterloo, ON, 1989).

[34] Jarold K. Zeman, *Open Doors: Canadian Baptists, 1950–1990* (Hantsport, NS, 1992).

[35] Harold H. Rowdon, *The Origins of the Brethren, 1825–1850* (London, 1967); David Edwin Harrell Jr, *A Social History of the Disciples of Christ*, 1: *Quest for a Christian America: The Disciples of Christ and American Society to 1966* (Nashville, TN, 1966); Walter J. Hollenweger, *The Pentecostals* (London, 1972).

[36] Robert Wuthnow, *The Restructuring of American Religion: Society and Faith since World War II* (Princeton, NJ, 1988).

thousand and even gave an account, without any sense of anomaly, of the entry of Spurgeon into heaven.[37] Yet a growing number of biographers have illuminated whole areas by writing about individuals. One of them, John Pollock, an Evangelical Anglican clergyman, managed to bridge the gulf between the popular and the academic in his well-rounded study of William Wilberforce.[38] Henry Rack of the University of Manchester performed the same feat to produce the standard life of John Wesley in 1989.[39] Eighteenth-century Methodists have fared better than most other categories of Evangelical: Charles Wesley, John Fletcher and Francis Asbury have all received penetrating biographical treatment in the recent past.[40] The high proportion of attention to the eighteenth century, in some measure reflecting a general preoccupation of historians in the early twenty-first century, is nowhere better illustrated than by the scholarship lavished on Jonathan Edwards, the New England Puritan divine who is often hailed as 'America's theologian'. The Yale edition of the works of Edwards, begun in 1959, spawned a cottage industry of conferences, colloquia and collections on Edwards, culminating in the masterly biography by George Marsden.[41] There are also excellent biographies of later figures such as the leader of the Free Church of Scotland, Thomas Chalmers, the nineteenth-century American evangelist D. L. Moody, his twentieth-century successor Oral Roberts and the British social gospeller Hugh Price Hughes, but they are less thick on the ground than for the earlier period.[42] Biographical work, especially on the eighteenth century, has greatly improved over the last fifty years.

37 Lewis Drummond, *Spurgeon: Prince of Preachers* (Grand Rapids, IL, 1992), 715, 44, 771 respectively.

38 John Pollock, *Wilberforce* (London, 1977).

39 Henry D. Rack, *Reasonable Enthusiast: John Wesley and the Rise of Methodism* (London, 1989).

40 Gareth Lloyd, *Charles Wesley and the Struggle for Methodist Identity* (Oxford, 2007); Patrick Streiff, *Reluctant Saint? A Theological Biography of Fletcher of Madeley* (Peterborough, 2001); John H. Wigger, *American Saint: Francis Asbury and the Methodists* (Oxford, 2009).

41 George M. Marsden, *Jonathan Edwards: A Life* (New Haven, CT, 2003).

42 Stewart J. Brown, *Thomas Chalmers and the Godly Commonwealth in Scotland* (Oxford, 1982); James F. Findlay Jr, *Dwight L. Moody: American Evangelist* (Chicago, 1969); David Edwin Harrell, *Oral Roberts: An American Life* (Bloomington, IN, 1985); Christopher Oldstone-Moore, *Hugh Price Hughes: Founder of a New Methodism, Conscience of a New Nonconformity* (Cardiff, 1999).

The academic revolution in the historiography of Evangelicals is nowhere more evident than in missionary studies. The prime agent of change was Andrew Walls, successively of Aberdeen, Edinburgh and Liverpool Hope universities, who, as an ex-missionary himself, realized the need to remodel the history of Christian missions. Its focus was to be less on the missionaries than on the peoples being evangelized and their subsequent creation of an indigenous Christian culture. Walls never composed a monograph, his favoured form of expression being the essay, but the two collections of his short pieces, in conjunction with his supervision of postgraduates, his sponsorship of the biennial Yale-Edinburgh conferences on missionary history and his collection of an archive of primary sources at Edinburgh, laid the foundations for the turning of missionary history into a thoroughly academic subdiscipline.[43] Much of the superstructure was added during the 1990s by the North Atlantic Missiology Project and its successor the Currents in World Christianity project, funded by the Pew Charitable Trust in the United States. Both projects sponsored sequences of seminars and larger international conferences that led to published collections of papers. Perhaps the most significant outcome was the account of the world missionary conference of 1910 by Brian Stanley, the coordinator of the projects and Walls's successor but one at Edinburgh.[44] Meanwhile Andrew Porter, Rhodes Professor of Imperial History at the University of London, was examining the rapports between missions and overseas expansion, the result being his telling *Religion versus Empire?* (2004).[45] Twentieth-century world Christianity, drawn to general attention by Philip Jenkins's *The Next Christendom* (2002), has become a vibrant research field. This upsurge of scholarship embraced Roman Catholic, Anglo-Catholic and liberal Protestant missions, but its chief focus was on Evangelical agencies and the churches they created.

Over the last fifty years mainstream history has sometimes given the Evangelical movement its due, though often it has not.

[43] Andrew F. Walls, *The Missionary Movement in Christian History: Studies in the Transmission of Faith* (Edinburgh, 1996); *The Cross-Cultural Process in Christian History: Studies in the Transmission and Appropriation of Faith* (New York, 2002).

[44] Brian Stanley, *The World Missionary Conference, Edinburgh, 1910*, Studies in the History of Christian Missions (Grand Rapids, MI, 2009).

[45] Andrew Porter, *Religion versus Empire? Protestant Missionaries and Overseas Expansion, 1700–1914* (Manchester, 2004).

Even accomplished church historians have at times misrepresented Evangelicals. Thus Adrian Hastings, once a colleague of Walls at Aberdeen before moving to the chair of theology at Leeds, marred his otherwise admirable volume of the Oxford History of the Christian Church on Africa by presenting early nineteenth-century Evangelicals as making 'millennialist assertions', whereas in reality, as post-millennialists, they were almost uniformly opposed to expectations of the imminent end of the world.[46] Perhaps the most influential study giving prominence to Evangelicals has been *The Age of Atonement* (1988) by Boyd Hilton of Trinity College, Cambridge. Although Hilton disclaimed any wish to examine Evangelicals themselves, he aimed to give much greater depth to the generalizations made in the wake of G. M. Young about the sway of the movement over the culture of the earlier Victorian years. Hilton persuasively argued that attitudes relating to the central Evangelical teaching about the cross conditioned social thought and public policy.[47] The role of Evangelicalism in moulding public affairs in North America has also received greater attention. Richard Carwardine, of Sheffield and then Oxford, showed how, as he put it, 'evangelical Protestants were amongst the principal shapers of American political culture in the middle years of the nineteenth century'.[48] In Canada, partly because of Richard Allen's book *The Social Passion* (1971), it became historical orthodoxy that the shift of Evangelical religion towards the social gospel was the primary factor in the move in the direction of welfare legislation during the earlier twentieth century.[49] Thus general historians have contributed to putting the role of Evangelical religion on the map of broader affairs. It is another way in which the treatment of Evangelicals has rolled forward during the last fifty years.

In many respects, however, there have been more fundamental changes in the historiography of the Evangelical movement. It is not merely that the subject has become more academically serious; it is also that alterations in the ecclesiastical landscape have affected

[46] Adrian Hastings, *The Church in Africa, 1450–1950*, OHCC (Oxford, 1994), 271.

[47] Boyd Hilton, *The Age of Atonement: The Influence of Evangelicalism on Social and Economic Thought, 1785–1865* (Oxford, 1988).

[48] Richard J. Carwardine, *Evangelicals and Politics in Antebellum America* (New Haven, CT, 1993), ix.

[49] Richard Allen, *The Social Passion: Religion and Social Reform in Canada, 1914–28* (Toronto, ON, 1971).

writing about the movement, especially by Evangelicals themselves. The third section of this essay will accordingly be devoted to innovations flowing from religious developments of the post-war era. A basic conditioning factor was the growing strength of Evangelicalism. That may sound odd as a comment on a period in British history marked by a collapse of churchgoing. In the single decade between 1989 and 1998 the proportion of the English population worshipping on a given Sunday fell from 9.9 per cent to 7.5 per cent. Over the same years, however, the Evangelical share of churchgoers increased from 30 to 37 per cent.[50] Although there was a decline in absolute numbers of Evangelical worshippers, they had become a larger proportion of the Christian community at prayer. Likewise in the United States the mainline churches lost ground to those identifying themselves as Evangelical. Awareness of Evangelicals as a sector of the American population made rapid strides after Jimmy Carter, elected president in 1976, was identified as coming from their ranks. Evangelicals began to enjoy salience as a political constituency to be courted or reviled.[51] There was also a growing consciousness that the burgeoning Protestants of the Third World, the long-term fruit of the missionary movement, were overwhelmingly Evangelical by conviction. Hence Evangelicals as a grouping enjoyed much more prominence than in the past. The public, especially in America, wanted to read about them and mainstream publishers became keen to issue books on Evangelical themes. A milestone was the publication in 1980 by Oxford University Press in New York of George Marsden's *Fundamentalism and American Culture*, a study of the warping of popular Evangelicalism into hardline Fundamentalism in the United States.[52] The huge success of Marsden's path-breaking book helped ensure that Oxford in New York welcomed titles on Evangelical subjects for the rest of the period. Other academic presses followed suit, with McGill-Queen's University Press in Canada, for instance, generating a long sequence of 'Studies in the History of Religion', many with Evangelical subject-matter. The expansion of Evangelicalism

[50] Peter Brierley, *The Tide is Running Out: What the English Church Attendance Survey Reveals* (London, 2000), 27; idem, ed., *UK Christian Handbook, Religious Trends No. 2* (London, 1999), 12.3.

[51] Wuthnow, *Restructuring of American Religion*, ch. 8.

[52] George M. Marsden, *Fundamentalism and American Culture: The Shaping of Twentieth-Century Evangelicalism, 1870–1925* (New York, 1980).

in the later twentieth century undergirded the growth of historical work on the movement.

At the same time Evangelicals discovered history as a career option. The movement had long fostered entry to the ministry and the other professions, but, with the expansion of higher education after the Second World War, rapid in North America but also happening elsewhere after some delay, academia offered fresh opportunities. A generation of American graduate students with backgrounds in conservative denominations pursued history as a vocation. Timothy L. Smith, who composed the first major work in the efflorescence of Evangelical historiography, *Revivalism and Social Reform* (1957), was a minister of the Church of the Nazarene, a Holiness denomination.[53] George Marsden was the son of a minister of the Orthodox Presbyterians who had split from mainline Presbyterianism in the wake of the Fundamentalist disputes the historian chronicled. Mark Noll came from a Conservative Baptist home.[54] Martin Marty at Chicago, William Hutchinson at Harvard and Sydney Ahlstrom at Yale all provided supervision on Evangelical topics for doctoral candidates, who in due course went on to mentor a further generation of aspirants in the field. In Britain a key agency was the Inter-Varsity Fellowship (IVF) that bound together Christian Unions, groups of Evangelical students, in the universities. It launched professional groups for graduates, the Christian Medical Fellowship being the largest, and added one in the early 1960s for historians. Although for many years the Historians' Study Group did little more than hold a couple of small gatherings a year, it fostered the idea that historical research and teaching could be a sphere for Christian enterprise. One of the earliest pieces of writing to explore Evangelical history as a distinct genre was an unpublished Cambridge prize essay of 1962 by Haddon Willmer, later Professor of Theology at Leeds, on the Evangelical movement in England between 1785 and 1835.[55] Willmer, the son of a conservative Baptist minister, was active at university in the Cambridge Inter-Collegiate Christian Union. The

---

[53] Timothy L. Smith, *Revivalism and Social Reform: American Protestantism on the Eve of the Civil War* (Nashville, TN, 1957).

[54] Maxie B. Burch, *The Evangelical Historians: The Historiography of George Marsden, Nathan Hatch and Mark Noll* (Lanham, MD, 1996), 5, 3.

[55] Haddon Willmer, 'Evangelicalism, 1785 to 1835', Hulsean Prize essay, University of Cambridge (1962).

IVF, which established equivalents in most other countries in the Commonwealth and some beyond, also nurtured scholars in other parts of the world. At an international conference on Evangelical history in Sydney in 1997, nearly all the dozen people round the table found that they had IVF backgrounds.[56] The rise of Evangelical historical scholarship, which was parallel to the advance of conservative Protestants in several other academic disciplines,[57] was a global phenomenon.

Their enterprise established a number of institutional bases. The Historians' Study Group in Britain evolved into the autonomous Christianity and History Forum with its own bulletin, its sixth issue publishing in 2010 articles on Evangelical interactions with the Huguenots, the novel and the empire.[58] The Forum paled in significance, however, by comparison with its sister organization in North America, the Conference on Faith and History, founded in 1968 by Richard V. Pierard and Robert D. Linder, graduate students at the University of Iowa. The Conference could draw on the network of Christian colleges in North America as well as the smaller number of Evangelicals holding posts in secular institutions and so grew to number over six hundred members.[59] Its periodical, *Fides et Historia*, existed primarily to 'stimulate or provoke dialogue among evangelical Christian historians' rather than to encourage research on any sector of religious history,[60] but from its earliest years it generated papers on the history of the Evangelical movement and their proportion grew over time. In Australia an Evangelical History Association, sharing the American organization's concern with fellowship but more centrally focused on the history of the movement, was launched in 1987 under Stuart Piggin, soon to become master of Robert Menzies College at Macquarie University in Sydney.[61] It issued the periodical *Lucas*, produced an

[56] Personal experience.

[57] D. Michael Lindsay, *Faith in the Halls of Power: How Evangelicals joined the American Elite* (New York, 2007), chs 3–4.

[58] *Christianity and History Bulletin*, no. 6 (Summer 2010), 7–43.

[59] 'The Conference on Christianity and History', <http://www.huntington.edu/cfh/fides.htm>, accessed 1 August 2011.

[60] Robert D. Linder, 'Editorial', *Fides et Historia* [hereafter: *FH*] 2 (1969), 2.

[61] Geoffrey R. Treloar, 'History as Vocation: Stuart Piggin as Evangelical Historian and Historian of Evangelicalism', in *Making History for God: Essays on Evangelicalism, Revival and Mission in Honour of Stuart Piggin, Master of Robert Menzies College, 1990–2004*, ed. Geoffrey R. Treloar and Robert D. Linder (Sydney, 2004), 3–34, at 14.

Australian Dictionary of Evangelical Biography and published collected volumes of papers. Most important of all was the Institute for the Study of American Evangelicals at Wheaton College, Illinois. Originating as no more than informal meetings between young friends in academia such as Mark Noll and Nathan Hatch, in 1979 the group held a successful conference at Wheaton on the Bible in America, afterwards publishing the papers, and three years later set up the Institute to organize more gatherings.[62] The momentum of the series of conferences, which regularly led to volumes published with academic imprints, was sustained by annual consultations that doubled as holidays *en famille* on the coast of New England complete with games of softball. The result, as George Marsden put it, was the creation of 'an informal network of colleagues who have become the closest of friends and hence have accomplished by concerted effort what none of them could have done alone'.[63] The emergence of Evangelical history probably owes as much to family games as to high-level intellectual developments.

Nevertheless, innovations in the sphere of theology did have an impact on historical studies. Evangelicals had been accustomed to repudiate tradition, seeing it as a sinister force undermining a pure biblicism. Gradually during the period some of their leaders became more friendly towards the concept. F. F. Bruce realized 'the prevalence of tradition' among Brethren assemblies which believed themselves to be free from its influence and so expounded the value of early Christian traditions in a lecture series of 1968.[64] The Baptist Barrie White, principal of Regent's Park College, Oxford, was willing, in a booklet of 1976, to treat tradition as a condensing of the work of the Holy Spirit in the past and thus as carrying a measure of authority for subsequent practice.[65] In the United States, where the Evangelical school in the Episcopal Church had long been in eclipse, there was from the 1970s a novel upsurge of enthusiasm for liturgy that drew many towards the traditional. Robert E. Webber of Wheaton College was the central figure, joining an Episcopal congregation and urging a rediscovery of the common

---

[62] Nathan O. Hatch and Mark A. Noll, eds, *The Bible in America: Essays in Cultural History* (New York, 1982).

[63] ISAE, George Marsden, 'ISAE: Retrospect and Prospect – June 1994'.

[64] F[rederick]. F. Bruce, *Tradition Old and New* (Grand Rapids, MI, 1970), 9.

[65] B[arrington]. R. White, *Authority: A Baptist View* (London, 1976), 23–6.

roots that bound Evangelicals to the church's past.[66] Although he was the son-in-law of Harold Lindsell, the author of *The Battle for the Bible* (1976) and champion of a stern inerrancy designed to buttress the sole authority of the Bible, Webber published an influential series of books commending high church worship as the correct complement to Evangelical belief. Addressing the common fear of Evangelicals that the venture might elevate tradition over Scripture, he pointed out that tradition meant no more than 'passing on', whether a truth or a practice. The proper perspective on Christ, the church, worship and spirituality was within what Webber called 'the paradigms of history', how each of them had been viewed in the past.[67] A fascination with the links between the New Testament and the present, a form of history-mindedness, was springing up. In such a context the Evangelical past itself could not fail to exert a stronger appeal over minds associated with the movement.

A more specific set of intellectual influences played over the growth of Evangelical historiography. The Conference on Faith and History, together with its organizational equivalents in other lands, was centrally preoccupied in its early years with the relationship of theology to the discipline of history. 'Is there a Christian approach to history?', asked an article in the second volume of *Fides et Historia* in 1969.[68] The aim was to bridge the gulf between an Evangelical allegiance and the academic enterprise. At one level the object was the typical Evangelical desire to witness to the faith; at another it was to develop what came to be called a 'Christian mind'. The most significant theological stimulus in this direction came, perhaps remarkably, from the Netherlands. A number of Dutch neo-Calvinist theologians developed a school of thought that called for the subjection of all areas of human activity to the lordship of Christ. Its leading exponent, Abraham Kuyper, founder of a separatist Dutch Reformed movement in 1892 and Prime Minister of the Netherlands from 1901 to 1905, set out his vision in the Stone Lectures of 1898 at Princeton Seminary, published as

---

[66] Robert E. Webber, *Common Roots: A Call to Evangelical Maturity* (Grand Rapids, MI, 1978).

[67] Robert Webber, *Ancient-Future Faith: Rethinking Evangelicalism for a Postmodern World* (Grand Rapids, MI, 1999), 180–1, chs 4, 8, 11, 14.

[68] Charles J. Miller, 'Is there a Christian Approach to History?', *FH* 2 (1969), 3–15.

Lectures on Calvinism.[69] The impact of this point of view on English speakers was hugely reinforced by American exponents, especially the theologian Cornelius Van Til, a son of Dutch immigrants to the United States who contended for the importance of presuppositions in intellectual exploration. It followed that believers must adopt distinctively Christian premises when undertaking any discipline such as history.[70] The school of Kuyper shaped the thought of C. T. McIntire of the Institute for Christian Studies at Toronto, at one time a leading theorist of history in Evangelical circles.[71] Van Til deeply swayed George Marsden, who believed that 'the very facts of history differ for the Christian and the non-Christian historian'.[72] Calvin College, where Marsden taught, was a bastion of this point of view. During the 1970s a small Christian Studies Unit propagated the same standpoint in Britain, but its deepest influence was always felt in the Netherlands itself, helping in 1989 to inspire the creation there of an Association of Christian Historians.[73] Although this ideological position was applicable to all genres of history, political and economic as much as religious, and although several advocates, including Marsden, modified their loyalties over time, it fostered self-confidence among Evangelical historians. They came to believe that they could study their own past with an emphasis on what they themselves considered important, the theological and the spiritual. Neo-Calvinism was a potent reinforcer of Evangelical history.

Yet Calvinism also generated opposition to the rise of academic historiography among Evangelicals. During the second half of the twentieth century there was a striking resurgence of specifically Reformed theology in the English-speaking world. Under the leadership of Martyn Lloyd-Jones and J. I. Packer, confessional Calvinism gathered force, first in Britain, and then, partly through the *Banner of Truth* magazine and publishing house, across the globe. The editor of the magazine, Iain Murray, once Lloyd-Jones's assistant minister, believed that history books ought to subserve the twin

---

[69] Abraham Kuyper, *Lectures on Calvinism* (Grand Rapids, MI, 1931).

[70] John Frame, *Cornelius Van Til: An Analysis of His Thought* (Phillipsburg, NJ, 1995).

[71] C. T. McIntire, 'The Focus of Historical Study: A Christian View', *FH* 14 (1981), 6–17, esp. 10, 11.

[72] George M. Marsden, 'The Spiritual Vision of History', *FH* 14 (1981), 55–66, at 56.

[73] *Christianity and History: An International Newsletter*, no. 2 (1991), 1–3.

causes of advancing spiritual religion and promoting Reformed orthodoxy. He preferred history with heroes, as a book of his with that title published in 2009 confirmed.[74] Murray was championing a more traditional style of Evangelical historiography. In 1994–5 there was an instructive controversy about how history should be written. In a review in the *Banner of Truth*, Murray censured Harry S. Stout of Yale, a regular participant in the programmes of the Institute for the Study of American Evangelicals, for having embraced the norms of social and cultural history and so having surrendered to the 'unregenerate mind'.[75] Another reviewer in the magazine criticized Stout's biography of the evangelist George Whitefield for 'being obsessed with finding the slightest flaw in the character of a spiritual giant'.[76] Stout, himself a firm Calvinist, replied vigorously that he and professionals like him followed the evidence, not dwelling on 'devotional or hagiographic themes'. The Bible itself did not hide the faults of its characters. If social and cultural history was illegitimate, 'there is no room for Christians in the secular academy'.[77] Murray responded that 'to write the lives of eminent Christians with minimum notice of the things which meant *most* to them, and without which their lives cannot be understood, is to mislead'.[78] It was an issue of priorities. For Murray, selecting the achievements of Evangelicals was designed to edify and evangelize; for Stout, portraying Evangelicals in their totality was a contribution to scholarship. By 1995 there was no doubt that the second brand of Evangelical historiography had come to stay.

Ecclesiastical developments of the period also conditioned the type of writing produced by scholarly historians. Among the most important phenomena of the later twentieth century was the ecumenical movement. The organized rapprochement between the churches had long been suspect in most Evangelical eyes because it neglected the existing unity of true believers and seemed to augur compromise with Rome. From the 1960s, however, there was a thaw in the ecclesiastical climate. The Second Vatican Council

---

74 Iain H. Murray, *Heroes* (Edinburgh, 2009).
75 Iain H. Murray, in *Banner of Truth*, July 1994, 8.
76 David White, in *Banner of Truth*, March 1994, 29.
77 Harry S. Stout, in *Banner of Truth*, March 1995, 7–10, at 7, 8.
78 Iain H. Murray, in *Banner of Truth*, March 1995, 10–11, at 11.

suggested that Rome was not, after all, *semper eadem*. Ecumenical contacts, multiplying from that decade onwards, steadily reduced suspicions. For a few Evangelical historians the Ecclesiastical History Society was one of the agencies that disarmed their fears. Joint historical efforts, however, were easiest where there was least ecclesiastical distance to bridge. In 1993, for example, Alan Sell, a dedicated ecumenist in the United Reformed Church, brought together previously separate English and Welsh Nonconformist bodies in the quaintly named Association of Denominational Historical Societies and Cognate Libraries.[79] Dr Williams's Centre for Dissenting Studies, set up in 2004, fulfilled a similar function in promoting the history of all the Nonconformist denominations, Evangelical and non-Evangelical. Both were responsible for publishing several valuable collections of papers. The ecumenical climate, however, undoubtedly had wider results, affecting the style of writing about Roman Catholics and Anglo-Catholics. In the past Evangelical historians would have concentrated on chronicling Protestant resistance to Catholic designs, and as late as 1979 Peter Toon could still write a book celebrating the Evangelical critique of the Oxford Movement.[80] Evangelicals, however, were now capable of writing dispassionately about their own anti-Catholic past, as in John Wolffe's *The Protestant Crusade in Great Britain* (1991).[81] John Maiden's study of the Prayer Book controversy of 1927–8 discussed the two sides, the catholicizing forces and their Evangelical opponents, with scrupulous even-handedness.[82] For most Evangelicals who were attracted to historical writing, the Catholic Church and its Anglican imitators no longer constituted the opposition.

The ecumenical impulse meant not just closer interdenominational relations but also stronger international awareness. Advances in communications, especially flights by air and messages by e-mail, revolutionized possibilities of global cooperation during the period. This trend was reflected in Evangelical historiography

---

[79] 'Association of Denominational Historical Societies and Cognate Libraries', <http://www.adhscl.org.uk/>, accessed 2 August 2011.

[80] Peter Toon, *Evangelical Theology, 1833–1856: A Response to Tractarianism*, Marshall's Theological Library (London, 1979).

[81] John R. Wolffe, *The Protestant Crusade in Great Britain, 1829–1860* (Oxford, 1991).

[82] John Maiden, *National Religion and the Prayer Book Controversy, 1927–1928* (Woodbridge, 2009).

too. The World Methodist Historical Society, affiliated to the World Methodist Council, held three-yearly conferences in various countries.[83] Similar series of peripatetic Baptist, Brethren and Pentecostal world conferences, largely historical in their concerns, were launched. For generic Evangelical history a crucial event was a conference on Transatlantic Evangelicalism at Wheaton College, Illinois, in 1992, giving rise to two collections of published essays, *Evangelicalism* and *Amazing Grace*.[84] Representatives from much of the English-speaking world attended, setting up a short-lived International Association for the Study of Christianity and History. Although this fledgling body managed to do little more than circulate a newsletter, bonds forged at the Wheaton conference remained strong and led to other ventures.[85] The same international approach led to the publication by the Inter-Varsity Press, an Evangelical imprint, of a five-volume 'History of Evangelicalism'.[86] The *oeuvre* of one individual, however, was probably the most valuable contribution to scholarship arising from the internationalization of Evangelical history. Reg Ward, professor of history at Durham until 1986, wrote in retirement *The Protestant Evangelical Awakening* (1992), delineating for the first time some of the rapports between continental revivals and the subsequent developments in North America and the United Kingdom, following it up fourteen years later with *Early Evangelicalism: A Global Intellectual History*.[87] His appreciation of pan-European linkages, possible because of Ward's command of German, unusual among English-speaking historians, transformed the context in which the genesis of the Evangelical movement must be situated.[88] Reg Ward demonstrated that Evangelical history has to be international in scope.

A further tendency in the churches of the period, especially

---

[83] 'World Methodist Historical Society', <http://www.gcah.org/site/pp.aspx?c=g hKJIoPHIoE&b=3761527>, accessed 2 August 2011.

[84] Mark A. Noll, David W. Bebbington and George A. Rawlyk, eds, *Evangelicalism: Comparative Studies of Popular Protestantism in North America, the British Isles and Beyond, 1700–1990* (New York, 1994); George A. Rawlyk and Mark A. Noll, eds, *Amazing Grace: Evangelicalism in Australia, Britain, Canada and the United States* (Montreal, 1994).

[85] *Christianity and History: An International Newsletter*, nos 1–8 (1991–4).

[86] See n. 2 above.

[87] W[illiam]. R. Ward, *The Protestant Evangelical Awakening* (Cambridge, 1992); idem, *Early Evangelicalism: A Global Intellectual History, 1670–1789* (Cambridge, 2006).

[88] See John Walsh, 'Profile: W. R. Ward: Methodist Historian and Historian of Methodism', *Epworth Review* 22 (1995), 41–6.

strong among Evangelicals, was a rising eagerness to relate the Christian gospel to its cultural setting. Missiologists, among whom Andrew Walls was the most historically informed, took the initiative in relating the spread of the faith to the attitudes of its recipients, hoping to reveal the best ways of maximizing converts.[89] It was the genius of Lesslie Newbigin, a United Reformed Church minister who had served as a bishop in the Church of South India, to relate this body of thinking to the circumstances of the West. In his brief but powerful book, *The Other Side of 1984*, published by the British and World Councils of Churches in 1983, Newbigin argued that the Western churches must penetrate behind the debilitating effects of the Enlightenment if they were to recover their missionary vigour in articulating public truth.[90] His summons led to the Gospel and Our Culture movement which held a conference at Swanwick in 1992, published the conference papers and maintained an ongoing network.[91] The interaction of gospel and culture was becoming a central topic for reflection among Evangelicals and a wider Christian constituency. Historiography displayed similar symptoms. George Marsden's *Fundamentalism and American Culture* had already, in 1980, shown by its very title an appreciation of the need to locate Evangelical developments in their broad setting.[92] Hymns attracted attention, notably in Sandra Sizer's *Gospel Hymns and Social Religion* (1978), as a key way in which Evangelicals expressed themselves in an art form.[93] On the other side of the Atlantic, my *Evangelicalism in Modern Britain* (1989), though perhaps best known for its effort to define the word 'Evangelical', attempted to show how the movement had been shaped by the changing cultural ambience.[94] Regent's

---

[89] See n. 43 above.

[90] Lesslie Newbigin, *The Other Side of 1984: Questions for the Churches* (London, 1983).

[91] Hugh Montefiore, ed., *The Gospel and Contemporary Culture* (London, 1992); 'The Gospel and Our Culture', <http://gospel-culture.org.uk/intro.htm>, accessed 3 August 2011.

[92] See n. 52 above.

[93] Sandra S. Sizer, *Gospel Hymns and Social Religion: The Rhetoric of Nineteenth-Century Revivalism* (Philadelphia, PA, 1978).

[94] D[avid].W. Bebbington, *Evangelicalism in Modern Britain: A History from the 1730s to the 1980s* (London, 1989). On the thesis of ch. 1 of this book, see Michael G. Haykin and Kenneth J. Stewart, eds, *The Emergence of Evangelicalism: Exploring Historical Continuities* (Nottingham, 2008), published in the United States as *The Advent of Evangelicalism: Exploring Historical Continuities* (Nashville, TN, 2008).

Park College, Oxford, set up a Centre for the Study of Christianity and Culture, its first conference in 1996 taking 'Culture and the Nonconformist Tradition' as its theme. The resulting book, according to one of the editors, reported on the experience of Nonconformists in 'balancing their absorption of the culture of their time, with the creation of their own distinctive subcultures'.[95] Popular culture was not neglected in subsequent writing, with such studies as an account of the enormously popular Cornish Methodist fiction by the three Hocking siblings, Silas, Joseph and Salome.[96] The two-way process of culture influencing religion and religion influencing culture became a common historical theme.

A final trend in the churches took place in the area of spirituality. Its normative form among many Evangelicals had long been that propagated by the Keswick movement, according to which holiness was to be discovered through the exercise of faith. The hold of Keswick teaching, however, slackened during the 1960s, when there arose an entirely different model of piety associated with charismatic renewal, encouraging free expression in worship, a search for bodily wholeness, close personal relationships and a willingness to embrace authentic living in the secular world.[97] The topic of spiritual practice became a major preoccupation. A whole series of pamphlets, the Grove Spirituality booklets, explored the subject from an Anglican Evangelical standpoint from 1982 onwards.[98] Historians affected by renewal naturally paid attention to religious experience in the past. Ian Randall, tutor at the Baptist Spurgeon's College in London and the author of *Evangelical Experiences* (1999), an account of inter-war English Evangelical spirituality, had himself been touched by the charismatic movement.[99] Likewise in America a new and thorough account of

---

[95] Jane Shaw, 'Introduction: Why "Culture and the Nonconformist Tradition"?', in eadem and Alan Kreider, eds, *Culture and the Nonconformist Tradition* (Cardiff, 1999), 6.

[96] Alan M. Kent, *Pulp Methodism: The Lives & Literature of Silas, Joseph & Salome Hocking, Three Cornish Novelists* (St Austell, 2002); Martin Wellings, '"Pulp Methodism" revisited: The Literature and Significance of Silas and Joseph Hocking', in Peter Clarke and Charlotte Methuen, eds, *The Church and Literature*, SCH 48 (Woodbridge, 2012), 362–73.

[97] D[avid]. W. Bebbington, 'Holiness in the Evangelical Tradition', in Stephen C. Barton, ed., *Holiness Past and Present* (London, 2003), 298–315, at 308–14.

[98] The first was Peter Adam, *Living the Trinity* (Bramcote, 1982).

[99] Ian Randall, *Evangelical Experiences: A Study in the Spirituality of English Evangelicalism, 1918–1939* (Carlisle, 1999).

the Great Awakening was written by Thomas S. Kidd, a member of a Baptist church with a distinctly charismatic ethos. Unlike many previous commentators, Kidd laid particular stress on the radical Evangelicals who went in for dreams and portents.[100] Revivalism was increasingly studied for its own sake rather than for the light it cast on such themes as social control. A leading historian of eighteenth-century Canada, George Rawlyk, drew attention to the formative role of the revivalist Henry Alline in the country's Maritime provinces.[101] Rawlyk, who was a core member of the circle around the Institute for the Study of American Evangelicals, became fascinated by religious experience in the past and wrote *Canada Fire* (1994) to show the radical credentials of revivalists from his home country.[102] Janice Holmes demonstrated the importance of revivals in late nineteenth-century Britain and Ireland and a range of scholars of Evangelicalism swamped the 2008 volume of Studies in Church History with accounts of revivalism in the modern period.[103] Spirituality and revival were in the air; they also appeared increasingly in the historiography. It was another way in which religious developments affected the writing of Evangelical history in the period.

The historiography of the movement, however, was also shaped by broader trends in the world of scholarship. To this, the fourth aspect of the subject, we now turn. The long-term twentieth-century shift of history towards techniques and concepts drawn from the social sciences necessarily had a major impact. Some of the best work on religion in the modern world was achieved by applying sociological methods. In England the *oeuvre* of Hugh McLeod, beginning with *Class and Religion in the Late Victorian City*

---

[100] Thomas S. Kidd, *The Great Awakening: The Roots of Evangelical Christianity in Colonial America* (New Haven, CT, 2007).

[101] George A. Rawlyk, *Ravished by the Spirit: Religious Revivals, Baptists and Henry Alline* (Montreal, 1984); idem, *Henry Alline: Selected Writings*, Sources of American Spirituality (New York, 1987).

[102] George A. Rawlyk, *The Canada Fire: Radical Evangelicalism in British North America* (Montreal, 1984). On Rawlyk, see Mark A. Noll, 'George Rawlyk's Contribution to Canadian History as a Contribution to United States History: A Preliminary Probe', *FH* 32 (2000), 1–17, also in Daniel C. Goodwin, ed., *Revivals, Baptists, and George Rawlyk*, Baptist Heritage in Atlantic Canada 17 (Wolfville, NS, 2000), 29–51.

[103] Janice Holmes, *Religious Revivals in Britain and Ireland, 1859–1905* (Dublin, 2000); Kate Cooper and Jeremy Gregory, eds, *Revival and Resurgence in Christian History*, SCH 44 (Woodbridge, 2008).

(1974), showed how much could be revealed about religion when the central category of analysis was class and there was copious use of statistics.[104] Few Evangelical historians practised this type of history, although one, Nigel Scotland, contributed to the adjacent subdiscipline of labour history by writing a study of agricultural labourers' trade unionism in East Anglia in the later nineteenth century. It was notable for giving ample space, as labour historians rarely did, to the ideas of the Primitive Methodists who formed the trade union vanguard.[105] A social scientific theory much in vogue during the 1960s and 1970s, the notion of manipulation of the lower classes by the upper classes, was applied to Evangelical religion. 'Revivals', wrote Paul E. Johnson in an influential study of early nineteenth-century Rochester, New York, that appeared in 1978, 'provided entrepreneurs with a means of imposing new standards of work discipline and personal comportment upon themselves and the men who worked for them, and thus they functioned as powerful social controls.'[106] Likewise an account of the Clapham Sect around William Wilberforce by Ford K. Brown, published in 1961, dwelt on its efforts to discipline the lower orders and, most famously, E. P. Thompson in his *Making of the English Working Class* two years later depicted Methodist preachers as using 'emotional violence' to turn converts into docile workers and loyal subjects.[107] Those with Evangelical sympathies found this picture far from compelling. Two of them were responsible for powerful ripostes. Reg Ward showed in *Religion and Society in England, 1790–1850* (1972) the extent to which Methodism in early industrial England was a radical force, sapping the foundations of church and state, and Nathan O. Hatch, in his book *The Democratization of American Christianity* (1989), laid bare the populism of Evangelical and related movements in the early national period of the United States that caused alarm to the new country's elites.[108]

[104] Hugh McLeod, *Class and Religion in the Late Victorian City* (London, 1974).

[105] Nigel Scotland, *Methodism and the Revolt of the Field: A Study of the Methodist Contribution to Agricultural Trade Unionism in East Anglia, 1872–1896* (Gloucester, 1981).

[106] Paul E. Johnson, *A Shopkeeper's Millennium: Society and Revivals in Rochester, New York, 1815–1837* (New York, 1978), 138.

[107] Ford K. Brown, *Fathers of the Victorians: The Age of Wilberforce* (Cambridge, 1961); E[dward]. P. Thompson, *The Making of the English Working Class* (Harmondsworth, 1968; first publ. 1963), 418.

[108] Ward, *Religion and Society*; Nathan O. Hatch, *The Democratization of American Christianity* (New Haven, CT, 1989).

Although the first of these works was less effective than the second in redirecting the flow of historical writing, both struck powerful blows at the model of social manipulation by religion. The theory of social control was a symptom of the permeation of Marxist ideas into academia. Thompson, though coming from a Methodist background, had embraced a sophisticated form of Marxism with a strong cultural component.[109] A few other British historians with Marxist convictions wrote about aspects of the Evangelical movement. A. Allan Maclaren, for example, published in 1974 a study of religion in Aberdeen at the time of the Disruption of the Scottish church from that standpoint.[110] Its claims about the dearth of working-class involvement in Presbyterianism were later to be undermined by Peter Hillis.[111] Although research findings moulded by Marxist premises rarely endured, the legacy of Karl Marx played a significant role in the emergence of Evangelical historiography. Perhaps surprisingly, Marxism acted as a beacon for Evangelical historians. Those Evangelicals who gave any thought to historical theory in the 1960s and even in the 1970s normally accepted uncritically the prevailing objectivist model of history being the patient collection of brute facts from relevant sources.[112] According to John Warwick Montgomery of Trinity Evangelical Divinity School, Deerfield, Illinois, probably the best known exponent of an Evangelical philosophy of history at the time, Marxist rewritings of history were 'gross examples' of the solipsistic fallacy that 'there is no objective reality outside myself'.[113] For the younger generation who were discovering history as a vocation, however, Marxist successes in the academy showed that committed history was acceptable. 'If neo-Marxists can write neo-Marxist history', asked George Rawlyk in 1993, 'why should not evangelical Christian historians ... write from an evangelical Christian

[109] On Thompson, see David Hempton and John Walsh, 'E. P. Thompson and Methodism', in Mark A. Noll, ed., *God and Mammon: Protestants, Money and the Market, 1790–1860* (New York, 2002), 99–120.

[110] A. Allan MacLaren, *Religion and Class: The Disruption Years in Aberdeen* (London, 1974).

[111] Peter Hillis, 'Presbyterianism and Social Class in Mid-Nineteenth-Century Glasgow: A Study of Nine Churches', *JEH* 32 (1981), 47–64.

[112] Peter Novick, *That Noble Dream: The 'Objectivity Question' and the American Historical Profession* (Cambridge, 1988).

[113] John Warwick Montgomery, *The Shape of the Past: A Christian Response to Secular Philosophies of History* (Minneapolis, MN, 1975), 8.

perspective?'[114] The ideas of Marx began to be treated temperately in Evangelical writing about history. C. T. McIntire, for instance, wrote appreciatively of Marx's insight into human culture-making capacity and in my *Patterns in History* (1979) there is a sympathetic appraisal of the Marxist view of history.[115] Marxist historical scholarship blazed a trail which Evangelicals were eager to follow.

The rise of women's history, followed by gender history, was one of the most striking phenomena of historiography during the late twentieth century. Accounts of women's part in religious history began to flow from the press, though sometimes it was accused of being, especially in America, more committed to feminism than to scholarship. In Britain, however, the earliest significant study of an Evangelical topic was written by Olive Anderson of Westfield College, London, precisely to show that female preaching in the 1860s owed more to pre-millennialism than to feminism.[116] The best monograph in the field was actually by a man, Frank Prochaska, whose *Women and Philanthropy in Nineteenth-Century England* (1980) documented the work of Evangelical societies.[117] The publication of Leonore Davidoff and Catherine Hall's *Family Fortunes* (1987), examining religious as well as other roles of men and women in nineteenth-century households, already marked a shift towards a more sophisticated gender history.[118] Evangelicals themselves lagged behind in Britain, not publishing illuminating critical history about women until the eve of the twenty-first century.[119] Part of the explanation lay in the division of opinion among Evangelicals about the role of women, crystallized over the issue of female ordination. My commissioned article on nineteenth-century Evangelical women appearing in 1984 in the journal circulating among graduates from Christian

[114] George A. Rawlyk, 'Writing about Canadian Revivals', in Edith L. Blumhofer and Randall Balmer, eds, *Modern Christian Revivals* (Urbana, IL, 1993), 208–26, at 219.

[115] McIntire, 'Focus of Historical Study', 12–13; David Bebbington, *Patterns in History* (Leicester, 1979), ch. 6.

[116] Olive Anderson, 'Women Preachers in Mid-Victorian Britain: Some Reflexions on Feminism, Popular Religion and Social Change', *HistJ* 12 (1969), 467–84.

[117] F[rank]. K. Prochaska, *Women and Philanthropy in Nineteenth-Century England* (Oxford, 1980).

[118] Leonore Davidoff and Catherine Hall, *Family Fortunes: Men and Women of the English Middle Class, 1780–1850* (London, 1987).

[119] Linda Wilson, *Constrained by Zeal: Female Spirituality among Nonconformists, 1825–1875* (Carlisle, 2000).

Unions carefully avoided taking sides in the debate.[120] The theme first occurred on the conference schedule of the Institute for the Study of American Evangelicals in 1993.[121] In the following year there appeared Susan Juster's *Disorderly Women*, an account of the prominence of women among New England Free Baptists in the Revolutionary era, and three years later Catherine Brekus's *Strangers and Pilgrims*, exploring female preaching in America down to 1845.[122] Women became and remained central to historiography about Evangelicals. Men considered as male fared less well, in that the rising theme of masculinity was rarely examined on either side of the Atlantic. Two studies of the representation of men in the writings of the Victorian preacher Charles Haddon Spurgeon and William Booth, the founder of the Salvation Army, are exceptions.[123] Despite the small inroads into masculinity, the content of writing about Evangelicalism was transformed in the area of gender during the period.

So too was discussion of Evangelicals and race. In the United States the civil rights movement prompted a sustained reassessment of the place of racial divisions in the national past. The scrutiny of slave religion led to novel findings such as the extent of black preaching to whites and the prevalence of mixed black and white worship before the Civil War.[124] The intertwining of the subsequent racial discrimination in the South with the Evangelical religion of the oppressors and of the oppressed was freshly explored.[125] Perhaps the most striking development in the historiography was a turn from treating the civil rights movement as a

---

[120] D[avid]. W. Bebbington, 'Evangelicals and the Role of Women, 1800–1930', *Christian Arena* 37 (1984), 19–23.

[121] ISAE, 'ISAE History Research: Consultations', 14–15.

[122] Susan Juster, *Disorderly Women: Sexual Politics and Evangelicalism in Revolutionary New England* (Ithaca, NY, 1994).

[123] Laura Lauer, 'William Booth: Saint or Charlatan?', and Andrew Bradstock, '"A Man of God is a Manly Man": Spurgeon, Luther and "Holy Boldness"', in Andrew Bradstock et al., eds, *Masculinity and Spirituality in Victorian Culture* (Basingstoke, 2000), 194–208, 209–25.

[124] Mechal Sobel, *Trabelin' On: The Slave Journey to an Afro-Baptist Faith* (Princeton, NJ, 1979), 190–9; John B. Boles, ed., *Masters & Slaves in the House of the Lord: Race and Religion in the American South, 1740–1870* (Lexington, KY, 1988).

[125] Paul Harvey, *Redeeming the South: Religious Cultures and Racial Identities among Southern Baptists, 1865–1925* (Chapel Hill, NC, 1997); idem, *Freedom's Coming: Religious Culture and the Shaping of the American South from the Civil War through the Civil Rights Era* (Chapel Hill, NC, 2005).

largely secular phenomenon to emphasizing, as Mark Noll put it in 2008, 'the strength of the African-American religion that drove the movement'.[126] More generally, black studies became more widespread, producing such classics as Evelyn Brooks Higginbotham's *Righteous Discontent: The Women's Movement in the Black Baptist Church, 1880–1920* (1993).[127] Works on indigenous peoples, including Native Americans and Australian Aborigines, increasingly engaged with the role of Evangelical missionaries among them.[128] In British historiography the issue of race focused mainly on the subject of the abolition of the slave trade. Traditionally this was a topic where the Evangelicals came to the fore as the leaders, under Wilberforce, of the campaign against the trade. They still appeared in that role in the probing analysis by Roger Anstey, professor at the University of Kent at Canterbury and a Methodist, in 1975.[129] The subsequent growth in coverage of the topic, however, had the effect of stressing the agency of other groups and circumstances, even in a collection of essays in memory of Anstey.[130] It was only with the appearance of Christopher Leslie Brown's *Moral Capital* (2006) in time for the bicentenary of abolition that the Evangelicals were reinstated to prominence, though it was now an earlier group and with more carefully delineated motives.[131] At a more popular level William Hague's biography of Wilberforce (2007), with the sub-title 'the life of the great anti-slave trade campaigner', and even more the film *Amazing Grace* (2006) helped consolidate the place of Evangelical religion in the process of abolition.[132] The Evangelical record on issues surrounding race relations was increasingly valued in America and intermittently stressed in Britain.

---

[126] Mark A. Noll, *God and Race in American Politics: A Short History* (Princeton, NJ, 2008), 135.

[127] Evelyn Brooks Higginbotham, *Righteous Discontent: The Women's Movement in the Black Baptist Church, 1880–1920* (Cambridge, MA, 1993).

[128] e.g. William G. McLoughlin Jr, *Cherokees and Misssionaries, 1789–1839* (New Haven CT, 1984); John W. Harris, *One Blood: 200 Years of Aboriginal Encounter with Christianity: A Story of Hope*, 2nd edn (Sutherland, NSW, 1994).

[129] Roger Anstey, *The Atlantic Slave Trade and British Abolition, 1760–1810* (London, 1975).

[130] *Anti-Slavery, Religion and Reform: Essays in Memory of Roger Anstey*, ed. Christine Bolt and Seymour Drescher (Folkestone, 1980).

[131] Christopher Leslie Brown, *Moral Capital: Foundations of British Abolitionism* (Chapel Hill, NC, 2006).

[132] William Hague, *William Wilberforce: The Life of the Great Anti-Slave Trade Campaigner* (London, 2007).

DAVID W. BEBBINGTON

There was again a transatlantic difference over the theme of
nationhood. For Americans, the question of how the diverse
elements in a new land were forged into a nation was a matter
of perennial importance; British historians of the recent past, by
contrast, long left the equivalent issue to the medievalists and early
modernists. A longstanding American tradition saw Evangelical
religion as an agent of social integration in the early republic.
Its hold on the historiography was, if anything, strengthened
during the period. Mark Noll's *America's God* (2002) recounted
how the Second Great Awakening exercised a pervasive influence
on society, so that, for example, in 1840 there were more than
twice as many Methodist sermons heard per capita as letters delivered.[133] Daniel Walker Howe's volume on the years 1815–1848 in
the Oxford History of the United States confirmed the general
verdict that the Evangelical movement brought 'civilization and
order' to America.[134] In Britain the subject of national identity
became a popular theme only as the devolution debate gathered
momentum and particularly after the publication of Linda Colley's
Britons (1992), a book which attributed a primary role to Protestantism in integrating the diverse parts of the United Kingdom
during the eighteenth century. Already, however, the question
had been broached in volume 18 of Studies in Church History,
which was devoted to the theme of *Religion and National Identity* (1982).[135] The president of the Ecclesiastical History Society
who chose that theme, Keith Robbins, subsequently delivered a
series of Ford Lectures touching on the topic, issued a collection
of essays about it and wrote the volume of the Oxford History
of the Christian Church on twentieth-century Britain with the
title *England, Ireland, Scotland, Wales* (2008).[136] Evangelicalism had
its place in Robbins's analyses, but it was far more prominent in
R. Tudur Jones's study of Wales between 1890 and 1914, *Faith and*

---

[133] Mark A. Noll, *America's God: From Jonathan Edwards to Abraham Lincoln* (New
York, 2002), 201.
[134] Daniel Walker Howe, *What God Hath Wrought: The Transformation of America,
1815–1848*, Oxford History of the United States (New York, 2007), 188.
[135] Stuart Mews, ed., *Religion and National Identity*, SCH 18 (Oxford, 1982).
[136] Keith Robbins, *Nineteenth-Century Britain: Integration and Diversity* (Oxford,
1988); idem, *History, Religion and Identity in Modern Britain* (London, 1993); idem,
England, Ireland, Scotland, Wales: The Christian Church, 1900–2000, OHCC (Oxford,
2008).

the Crisis of a Nation (1981–2; ET 2004).[137] A collection of essays on religion and national identity in Wales and Scotland confirmed that Evangelicalism was closely bound up with the sense of nationhood in each.[138] The amplest treatment of the Evangelical factor in nationhood, however, was in Callum Brown's book *The Death of Christian Britain* (2000). In a work of marked originality, Brown contended that Evangelicalism shaped the discourse, and therefore the identity, of the British people between 1800 and the sudden onset of secularization in the 1960s.[139] At a single bound, British historiography caught up with its American counterpart in relating Evangelical religion to national identity.

Advances in the history of ideas also impinged on Evangelical historiography. The discussion of Evangelical theology was in a backward state for much of the period. Bernard Reardon of the University of Newcastle, the author of the most frequently used text on nineteenth-century religious thought in Britain, confined Evangelicalism to an introductory section, pointing out its 'weaknesses'. 'Intellectually it was narrow', he wrote, 'and naïvely reactionary.'[140] That judgement reflected the paucity of research that had hitherto been undertaken in the field. America had been better served in the past with a series of monographs on the decline of Calvinism,[141] but even in the United States there was a dearth of up-to-date studies until Bruce Kuklick's *Philosophers and Churchmen* (1985).[142] Stimulus to further work came chiefly from three directions. In the first place, the historians of science found it essential to engage with theology. Thus in 1991 John Hedley Brooke, in pushing forward the study of religion and science in the eighteenth and nineteenth centuries, explored Evangelical themes in some detail.[143] Four years

---

[137] R. Tudur Jones, *Faith and the Crisis of a Nation: Wales, 1890–1914* (Cardiff, 2004; first publ. in Welsh 1981–2).

[138] Robert Pope, ed., *Religion and National Identity: Wales and Scotland, c.1700–2000* (Cardiff, 2001).

[139] Callum Brown, *The Death of Christian Britain: Understanding Secularisation 1800–2000* (London, 2001).

[140] Bernard M. G. Reardon, *Religious Thought in the Victorian Age: A Survey from Coleridge to Gore* (London, 1980; first publ. 1971), 29.

[141] Frank H. Foster, *A Genetic History of the New England Theology* (Chicago, IL, 1907) and Joseph Haroutunian, *Piety versus Moralism: The Passing of the New England Theology* (New York, 1932) are the classic studies.

[142] Bruce Kuklick, *Philosophers and Churchmen: From Jonathan Edwards to John Dewey* (New Haven, CT, 1985).

[143] John Hedley Brooke, *Science and Religion: Some Historical Perspectives* (Cambridge,

later a conference under the auspices of the Institute for the Study of American Evangelicals brought together historians of science, including Brooke, and historians of theology to produce a collection of essays on *Evangelicals and Science in Historical Perspective* (1999).[144] Secondly, the history of political thought, the main genre in the study of ideas normally encountered by historians, prompted some of them to take a parallel interest in the history of religious thought. In particular, the novel methods in the history of political thought entailing placing authors in their intellectual milieu championed by Quentin Skinner at Cambridge inspired a few to apply similar techniques to Evangelical theologians. A collection of papers on the subject, showing an awareness of the limitations as well as the potential of Skinnerian methods in the intellectual history of religion, appeared in 2009.[145] And thirdly some historical theologians, with Alan Sell prominent among them in Britain and E. Brooks Holifield in America, laid bare hitherto unexplored dimensions of Evangelical thought.[146] One of the most illuminating, because it opened up non-Anglican Evangelical theology with unprecedented clarity, was Mark Hopkins's *Nonconformity's Romantic Generation* (2004).[147] Sell, Hopkins and others began to fill up the gaps left by Reardon. Earlier Evangelical ideas were at last coming into their own.

It has to be admitted that the most radical historical approaches of the age did not take root in Evangelical studies. Apart from Callum Brown, few students of Evangelical history drew on postmodernist practice. That is primarily because so many of the specialists in the field were themselves Evangelicals. In general the Evangelical world reacted with horror at the challenge of postmodernism to cherished assumptions. In particular its characteristic denial of any single intended meaning in texts alarmed those who saw the Almighty as the primary author of Scripture. Evangelicals published such works as *Truth Decay: Defending Christianity*

1991).

[144] David N. Livingstone, D. G. Hart and Mark A. Noll, eds, *Evangelicals and Science in Historical Perspective* (New York, 1999).

[145] Alister Chapman, John Coffey and Brad S. Gregory, eds, *Seeing Things Their Way: Intellectual History and the Return of Religion* (Notre Dame, IN, 2009).

[146] Alan F. Sell, *Defending and Declaring the Faith: Some Scottish Examples, 1860–1920* (Exeter, 1987), and many subsequent titles; E. Brooks Holifield, *Theology in America: Christian Thought from the Age of the Puritans to the Civil War* (New Haven, CT, 2003).

[147] Mark Hopkins, *Nonconformity's Romantic Generation: Evangelical and Liberal Theologies in Victorian England*, SEHT (Carlisle, 2004).

against the Challenges of Postmodernism.[148] Only a handful of bolder souls in the Evangelical movement, such as Robert Webber, were willing to endorse a postmodern understanding of the world, and virtually none of them was a historian.[149] Nevertheless the postmodern questioning of received practice constituted a stirring of the historiographical waters. In 2010 there appeared a collection of essays, *Confessing History*, which asked whether faith needed to be applied more drastically to the study of the past. Perhaps, the authors suggested, history had been unduly limited by its confinement to a professional straitjacket.[150] In due course that point of view was likely to produce more drastic reassessments of the Evangelical past. The period under review, however, had already, as we have seen, witnessed at least two significant advances in method associated with the Evangelical discovery of history. One was a recognition that history is a matter of perspectives on the past; the other was fresh attention to culture as a subject for historical investigation. Both innovations, though showing little or no postmodern inspiration, were parallel to the postmodernist enthusiasms for perspectives and culture, and sometimes they were put into practice even in advance of contemporary fashion. So the practitioners in the Evangelical school of history were by no means retrogressive in their methodological assumptions.

There was, therefore, a transformation of Evangelical history over the half-century between 1961 and 2011. At the opening of the period Evangelicals themselves neglected their history, producing chiefly denominational apologias, edifying biographies and missionary hagiographies. Evangelicals in Britain, and in some measure those elsewhere, did not figure prominently in mainstream historical literature. These patterns altered over the fifty years, with denominational, biographical and missionary studies all becoming much more scholarly and Evangelicalism sometimes (though by

---

[148] Douglas Groothuis, *Truth Decay: Defending Christianity against the Challenges of Postmodernism* (Downers Grove, IL, 2000).

[149] Webber, *Ancient-Future Faith*, esp. 29–34. An exception was Stanley Grenz, an Evangelical who was sympathetic to postmodernism and, although primarily a theologian, also wrote history.

[150] Eric Miller, 'Introduction: A Tradition Renewed? The Challenge of a Generation', in John Fea, Jay Green and Eric Miller, eds, *Confessing History: Explorations in the Christian Faith and the Historian's Vocation* (Notre Dame, IN, 2010), 9. I am grateful to Andy Tooley for this reference.

no means consistently) occupying an enhanced position in general histories. Religious changes affected the volume of Evangelical history, with Evangelicals increasing as a proportion of the church-going population, adherents of the movement pursuing careers in history and some of them creating effective institutional bases. The acceptance of tradition and the influence of neo-Calvinism helped promote their study of the past, though not without criticism from the Calvinist camp. Broader religious developments impinged on the type of history they wrote: the ecumenical imperative led to more cooperative studies and less anti-Catholic content; global links fostered international coverage; the theme of gospel and culture rose to prominence and equally spirituality came to the fore. At the same time scholarly trends shaped the way the history of Evangelical movements was written. Methods and models from the social sciences were applied to the Evangelical past while Marxism both impinged on written history and showed committed schol-arship was possible. The rise of women's and gender history, race issues and national identity changed the content of Evangelical studies, each of these themes attracting historians from outside the movement to explore aspects of its record. The history of Evangelical ideas began to be nourished by advances in the history of science, the history of political thought and historical theology. And if postmodernism exerted little effect, Evangelical historians could claim to have anticipated its twin concerns for perspectives and culture. By the end of the period, historians in general were paying growing attention to the history of the Evangelical move-ment, though there was much scope for further growth. Among Evangelical scholars themselves, the previous neglect of their past was over: they had made a discovery of history.

University of Stirling

INSIDER AND OUTSIDER HISTORY:
THEORIES OF QUAKER ORIGINS FROM THE NINETEENTH AND TWENTIETH CENTURIES*

by ROSEMARY MOORE

In the words of a modern Quaker historian, 'Friends are an historical people, and we derive much of our identity from our tradition'.[1] During the past hundred and fifty years the history of Quaker beginnings has several times been reinterpreted, as different Quaker theologies have risen to prominence and been given historical underpinning, and the interpretations themselves then subjected to historiographical reflections by later scholars. Much of this process has been 'insider' history, written by Quakers, but in the second half of the twentieth century Quaker beginnings became for a time a preoccupation of mainstream secular history, which has greatly changed the understanding of early Quakerism.

Following early nineteenth-century schisms, American Quakers began to investigate their history, seeking support for their own positions.[2] A reaction against Macaulay's dismissive attitude to George Fox and William Penn may have been a factor in the increasing interest in Quaker history.[3] Modern Quaker historical study, however, is generally taken to derive from the situation of British Friends in the mid-nineteenth century, when they were seriously diminishing in numbers. An essay competition in 1858–9, set up to investigate the causes of their decline, produced no clear solution, except for a general agreement that early Friends had been very successful evangelists, and that a study of Quaker origins might help in finding a solution to current problems. The first result, in 1868, was William Tallack's *George Fox, the Friends, and Early Baptists*, which showed the similarities between early Quak-

* I am grateful to Stephen W. Angell, Pink Dandelion, J. William Frost and John Punshon for their comments on earlier versions of this essay.

[1] John Punshon, 'The End of (Quaker) History', in Pink Dandelion, ed., *The Creation of Quaker Theory: Insider Perspectives* (Aldershot, 2004), 32–42, at 37.

[2] Notably the work of the Hicksite Friend, Samuel M. Janney, *History of the Religious Society of Friends from its Rise to the Year 1828*, 4 vols (Philadelphia, PA, 1859–60).

[3] T. B. Macaulay, *The History of England from the Accession of James II, vol. 1* (London, 1849), 17 (Fox), 297–300 (Penn).

erism and contemporary Baptist ideas and practices. In 1876 came a more comprehensive work, *The Inner Life of the Religious Societies of the Commonwealth,* by Robert Barclay of Reigate, so called to distinguish him from his ancestor, the seventeenth-century Quaker theologian, author of *The Apology for the True Christian Divinity.* The nineteenth-century Barclay set about a major programme of study, corresponding with German and American scholars on Anabaptist and Mennonite history, and reading numerous early Quaker documents. His conclusion, that Fox was influenced by the religious atmosphere of the mid-seventeenth century, has been confirmed by many later students of Quakerism, but his belief that Friends were influenced by continental mystical or spiritual sects has been less universally accepted. He also thought that Quakerism led directly to Methodism and other forms of Evangelicalism, and, since virtually all British Quakers and many in America were at that time Evangelical in theology, his book was well received on both sides of the Atlantic.[4]

During the fourth quarter of the nineteenth century, knowledge of biblical criticism and Darwinian theory was percolating through society, and British Quakerism began to move on.[5] Books appeared putting forward approaches to Christianity that would accommodate modern thought. It was suggested that 'an evolutionary interpretation of outward nature may be true', that the Old Testament might contain 'an admixture of the legendary and of survivals from a previous heathendom', that the substitutionary doctrine of the atonement was not to be found in the Bible, and that religious faith and practice should be based on reason and conscience.[6] British Friends grew concerned that their young people, attracted to modern thought, would see nothing to hold them in the rather dull and staid Evangelical Quakerism of that day. And if the young people were to be lost, it would be a death sentence for British Quakerism, for in those days the Religious

---

4   See Thomas Hamm, 'George Fox and the Politics of Late Nineteenth Century Historiography', in Dandelion, ed., *Creation of Quaker Theory,* 11–18, for a full account of this period.
5   For these developments, see Thomas C. Kennedy, 'An Angry God or a Reasonable Faith: The British Society of Friends 1873–1888', *JFHS* 57/2 (1995), 183–98.
6   Francis Frith, William Pollard and William Edward Turner, *A Reasonable Faith* (London, 1885); Edward Worsdell, *The Gospel of Divine Help: Thoughts on some First Principles of Christianity* (London, 1886), 14.

Society of Friends was maintained from generation to generation by Quaker families breeding more Quakers. During the last years of the nineteenth century the proponents of a more liberal faith gained ground.

In 1895, a conference was held in Manchester to discuss the future of the society, and among the participants was a young man named John Wilhelm Rowntree, eldest son of Joseph Rowntree of the chocolate company. He laid out a vision for a future Quakerism which would not be afraid to confront modern science: 'If the age of the faith which comes by tradition and authority is gone and men can no longer believe without knowing why they believe … then such a change will bring as its ultimate result not weakness but new strength.'[7] Quakers needed to learn about their origins, but also something of modern thought and the hope of progress which was characteristic of the late nineteenth century. Rowntree planned to start the process by writing a book on Quaker history.

Then in 1897 Rufus Jones, an American Quaker philosopher from the Quaker college of Haverford, took a European holiday. As a student, Jones had been attracted by his reading of Emerson to the study of mysticism, and had come to conclusions regarding Quaker origins which were similar to those reached by Robert Barclay of Reigate.[8] He met Rowntree at Mürren in Switzerland and wrote later that, as they climbed the Schilthorn, 'I unfolded to him my growing plan to write the history of Christian mysticism and to trace back the roots of Quakerism to those spiritual movements before the birth of George Fox. We both saw in a flash that our two proposed historical lines of study complemented one another'.[9]

Together, Jones and Rowntree planned a series of books on Quaker history, 'treating it as an experiment in spiritual religion'.[10]

---

[7] From John Wilhelm Rowntree's address to the Manchester Conference, 'Has Quakerism a Message to the World Today?', in *The Society of Friends: Report of the Proceedings of the Conference … in Manchester … 1895* (London, 1896), 75–83, at 82.

[8] Rufus Jones, *The Trail of Life in College* (New York, 1929), 89–91. Jones's interest in mysticism developed independently of the British movement associated with Friedrich von Hügel and William Inge. However, the preface to his *Studies in Mystical Religion* (London, 1909), vi, acknowledges Inge as among the people who 'read and criticised some of the chapters'.

[9] Ibid. 196; see also Thomas C. Kennedy, 'History and Renaissance: The Vision of John Wilhelm Rowntree', *JFHS* 55/2 (1984), 35–56.

[10] Jones, *Studies in Mystical Religion*, v–vii.

Quaker renewal was in the air; the Friends Historical Society and the Woodbrooke Quaker Study Centre in Birmingham were both founded in 1903. Then in 1905 Rowntree died suddenly of pneumonia. Revised plans had to be made for the books, which were named the Rowntree Histories in memory of John Wilhelm, and funded by Rowntree money. The authors were Rufus Jones and William Charles Braithwaite, who was by profession a lawyer and banker. The first two books of the series, Jones's *Studies in Mystical Religion* and *The Quakers in the American Colonies*, were published in 1909 and 1911 respectively. In *Mystical Religion* Jones demonstrated similarities between Quakers and other sects of the Commonwealth period, and traced lines of influence from medieval mystics, for he considered that Quakerism was 'part of a very much wider religious movement, which had for many years been gaining volume and intensity'.[11] The first Quakers had believed that God had revealed himself directly within them, and their faith was both mystical and prophetic. Belief in direct inspiration from God chimed very well with the idea that religion should be a matter of reason and conscience. However, Jones did not follow Barclay in welcoming the succession from early Quakerism through quietism to its later Evangelicalism. The Rowntree historians considered this a regrettable aberration.[12]

The third book in the series, Braithwaite's *The Beginnings of Quakerism*, came in 1912. It ends with a flourish, demonstrating the hopes of the Rowntree authors:

> We have too readily assumed that the first vitality attending a new spiritual movement is essentially visionary and transitory. The wonder and glow of the fresh revelation cannot, indeed, be repeated, but the light itself may come with perennial power to successive generations of disciples ... In this great revitalising of Christianity, which is already beginning, the Quaker faith may play a worthy part.[13]

Braithwaite's book is a detailed and thorough study of the history

---

[11] Rufus Jones, Introduction to William C. Braithwaite, *The Beginnings of Quakerism* (London, 1912), xxv–xliv, at xxv.

[12] Alice Southern, 'The Rowntree Histories and the Growth of Liberal Quakerism', *Quaker Studies* 16 (2011), 7–73, gives numerous examples of the Rowntree historians' evident disapproval of later Quaker developments.

[13] Braithwaite, *Beginnings*, 529.

of early Quakerism, and is still important. The fate of Jones's works on mysticism has been different. A direct link between continental spiritual movements and Quakerism cannot be demonstrated, and Jones's use of the word 'mysticism' itself attracted criticism, despite his insistence that he was using a broad definition according to which 'mysticism' meant 'any type of religion which insists upon an immediate inward revelation of God'.[14] Moreover, the theological climate changed. British Quakerism had become almost universally liberal before World War I, and remained so, but after that war the easy optimism of the Edwardian era was no longer possible and liberal theology, which had never been adopted by the majority of American Quakers, was in retreat. There was a revival of puritan studies, and puritans began to appear in a more favourable light than had been admitted by the Rowntree historians.[15]

Geoffrey Nuttall's *The Holy Spirit in Puritan Faith and Experience* (1946) approached Quakerism in a new way.[16] Nuttall, who was not a Quaker, emphasized the importance of the Holy Spirit in puritanism, showing its operation, successively, in Presbyterians, Independents, Baptists and Seekers, with Quakerism as the logical outcome. Quaker historians recognized the importance of Nuttall's work; consequently, when a second edition of Braithwaite's *Beginnings* came out in 1955, Jones's introduction was removed, and replaced by a short note explaining that 'recent studies have, in the minds of a number of scholars, put Quakerism in a rather different light'.[17] It was fortunate that Braithwaite had left the study of the supposed mystical origins of Quakers to Jones, so that the introduction could be removed without affecting the rest of Braithwaite's book. However, there are letters showing that Braithwaite was entirely in agreement with Jones about Quaker mystical antecedents, and he might not have been happy to see his book being used in connection with an entirely different theory.[18]

When Braithwaite's second volume of Quaker history, *The Second Period of Quakerism,* was reissued in 1961, Jones's intro-

---

[14]   Ibid. xxxiv.
[15]   e.g. William Haller, *The Rise of Puritanism* (New York, 1938).
[16]   Geoffrey F. Nuttall, *The Holy Spirit in Puritan Faith and Experience* (Oxford, 1946; repr. with new introduction by Peter Lake, Chicago, IL, 1992).
[17]   L. Hugh Doncaster, new Foreword to Braithwaite, *Beginnings*, 2nd edn, ed. Henry J. Cadbury (Cambridge, 1955), vii.
[18]   Southern, 'Rowntree Histories', 24.

duction was again taken out, and this time it was replaced by a lengthy new paper supporting the puritan origins of Quakerism and written by Frederick B. Tolles, Professor of Quaker History at Swarthmore College, Pennsylvania, a major centre of Quaker studies.[19] He had previously written: 'Quakerism in England had flowered out of Puritan soil. Geoffrey Nuttall has shown us that it was not a revolt against Puritanism, as we used to think ... but a special development, a distinctive element within the Puritan tradition, and in a very real sense the fulfilment of it'.[20] Tolles also considered that early Quakers accepted 'traditional Protestant doctrines of the Trinity, the Deity of Christ, the Vicarious Atonement, and the plenary inspiration of Scripture', which were not part of Nuttall's research.[21]

The next contribution to the study of Quaker origins, and also influenced by Nuttall and the revival of puritan studies, came in 1964 with Hugh Barbour's *The Quakers in Puritan England*. Barbour, Professor of Religion at another Quaker institution, Earlham College, Richmond, Indiana, accepted the derivation of Quakerism from puritanism. In the preface to the first edition he wrote: 'It is hoped that this book may open the way for deeper discussions between liberal and conservative Quakers, as well as between Friends and non-Friends'.[22] This was the era of the ecumenical movement, and the search was on for common ground between denominations, which for Quakers meant emphasizing their connections to the puritans.

Sixty years after the appearance of the Rowntree series, and thirty years after the publication of Nuttall's seminal book, the time was ripe for a reassessment of the work of Rufus Jones. The American academic Melvin B. Endy Jr was not a Quaker, and 'had no personal Quaker theological axe to grind'.[23] He noted the influence of the ecumenical movement:

[19] Frederick B. Tolles, new Introduction to Braithwaite, *Second Period*, 2nd edn, ed. Henry J. Cadbury (Cambridge, 1961), xxv–xxxvi.

[20] Frederick B. Tolles, *The Atlantic Community of the Early Friends* (London, 1952), 21.

[21] Frederick B. Tolles, *Quakers and the Atlantic Culture* (New York, 1960), 109.

[22] Hugh Barbour, *The Quakers in Puritan England* (New Haven, CT, 1964; repr. with new preface, Richmond, IN, 1985), xi.

[23] E-mail from J. William Frost, Professor Emeritus, Swarthmore College, 8 February 2011, quoted with permission.

It is surely the case that the recent insistence on the Puritan and hence mainstream Christian roots of the Friends was not unaffected by the intellectual respectability brought to Reformation theology by Protestant Neo-orthodoxy and by the Friends' desire to participate in an ecumenical movement pervaded by Neo-orthodox themes.[24]

Endy considered that Rufus Jones's use of the word 'mysticism' had been misunderstood, and that Jones had also been handicapped by a now-outdated view of puritanism. It was a fact that Quakers shared many of the ideas of the continental spiritual reformers that had been current in England during the seventeenth century. Likewise, there had been bitter disputes on matters of Scripture, Christology and the atonement between Quakers and puritan ministers, throwing doubt on statements by those such as Tolles and Barbour that Quakers were sound on traditional Christian theology. Endy concluded that the early Quakers should rather be classed with groups such as Diggers, Familists and some Ranters, whom he called Spiritualists, as their faith was based on the indwelling Christ and a direct relationship with God.

Meanwhile, barely noticed by professional historians, yet another contribution to theories about Quakerism had appeared during the middle years of the twentieth century. In 1943 a tiny pamphlet called *Prophetic Quakerism* by one Lewis Benson was published privately in America, and in 1951 it was reissued in Britain 'as a personal contribution to thought about the present position of the life of the Society of Friends'. It became enormously influential, especially among the Young Friends of that generation, of whom I was one. Benson's thesis was that the Quakerism of George Fox was not mystical, evangelical, liberal or puritan, but something else entirely different: briefly, that when George Fox said, 'Christ is come to teach his people himself', he meant just that.[25] Benson's ideas were later developed by Douglas Gwyn, well known among

---

[24] Melvin B. Endy Jr, 'The Interpretation of Quakerism: Rufus Jones and his Critics', *Quaker History* 70 (1980–1), 3–21, at 4. He expanded these ideas in 'Puritanism, Spiritualism and Quakerism', in Richard Dunn and Mary M. Dunn, eds, *The World of William Penn* (Philadelphia, PA, 1986), 281–301. For Barbour's views on similarities between early Quaker and puritan theology, see *Quakers in Puritan England*, 133–6.

[25] Lewis Benson, *Prophetic Quakerism* (London, 1951); idem, *Catholic Quakerism* (Philadelphia, PA, 1968). See also Dandelion, *Creation of Quaker Theory*, 3.

Quakers as a writer and teacher on the early years of the movement. In my own research, Benson's work has made me especially
alert to the element of realized eschatology in early Quaker writings.

So far discussions about Quaker origins had been confined
to theological ideas, but early Quakerism was now attracting the
attention of a new school of secular historians. The first stirrings
were in evidence in 1895, predating the Rowntree series, in the
writing of the German Marxist Eduard Bernstein.[26] Presumably
because he was both German and Marxist, he had little influence on Quaker historians, though Braithwaite knew his work and
commented on it.[27] In 1950, J. F. Maclear pointed out in an article
that Quakers participated in 'the common messianic excitement
and the political unrest' of the Interregnum, and this was followed
in 1955 by Alan Cole's dissertation, 'Quakers and Politics'.[28]
However, this work largely passed Quaker historians by. Then, in
1973, Christopher Hill published *The World Turned Upside Down*,
and for the first time all the many references in early Quaker and
anti-Quaker pamphlets that demonstrate Quaker political radicalism were put together and analysed.[29] This was followed by
other works by historians of the same ilk, notably by Barry Reay's
The Quakers in the English Revolution, with its detailed discussion
of the influence of Quakers on the events of 1659.[30]

The second edition of Barbour's *The Quakers in Puritan England*,
which came out in 1985, had a new preface acknowledging recent
progress made in Quaker historical studies, which included 'inten-
sive new studies of English radical Puritans' by, among others,
Christopher Hill. But it took the work of one Quaker historian
in particular to persuade other Quaker historians to take serious
account of the work of the materialist school. This was Larry Ingle,

---

[26] Eduard Bernstein, 'Die Vorlaufer des Neueren Sozialismus', in *Die Geschichte des
Sozialismus, 1/2: Von Thomas More bis zum Vorabend der französischen Revolution* (Stutt-
gart, 1895), 507–718; seventeenth-century section transl. H. J. Stenning as *Cromwell and
Communism: Socialism and Democracy in the Great English Revolution* (London, 1930; repr.
New York, 1966).

[27] Braithwaite, *Second Period*, 565 n.5.

[28] J. F. Maclear, 'Quakerism and the End of the Interregnum: A Chapter in the
Domestication of Radical Puritanism', *ChH* 19 (1950), 240–70; Alan Cole, 'Quakers
and Politics' (Ph.D. thesis, Cambridge University, 1955).

[29] Christopher Hill, *The World Turned Upside Down* (London, 1973), 231–58.

[30] Barry Reay, *The Quakers in the English Revolution* (London, 1985).

author of several strongly worded articles on the limitations of Quaker insider history, and of a notably revisionist biography of George Fox.[31] He wrote:

> Debates over historical issues can become quite arid, nearly the sole property of an insider group most familiar with the arcane contours of the discussion ... one can read the works of two of the main participants in the debate [Jones and Barbour] and hardly realise that two civil wars and a revolutionary upheaval formed a violent backdrop for the rise of Quakerism.[32]

It is perhaps significant that, unlike Jones, Tolles and Barbour, Ingle was not attached to a Quaker foundation, but was Professor of History at the University of Tennessee at Chattanooga.

Most Quakers do not read academic journals, and twenty years ago the materialist revision of early Quaker history was still little known to them. However, in 1991, the tercentenary of Fox's death, the Friends Historical Society invited Christopher Hill to give a lecture in Friends House, London.[33] Entitled 'Quakers and the English Revolution', it contained nothing new or surprising to historians. But this was an audience of ordinary London Quakers, interested in history but unacquainted with recent developments. I well remember the frisson of horror as Hill told of Fox's belief that a Quaker soldier was worth seven non-Quakers, and stated that Quakers were negotiating with army leaders in the chaos of 1659 and that Fox was not the sole leader of the Quakers in the 1650s. This was perceived as an attack on the foundations of Quakerism; touch George Fox or the 'Quaker Peace Testimony' at your peril!

Doubts remained in some Quaker circles as to whether the secular historians' approach should be considered a full-blown theory of Quaker origins. In 1994 Wilmer A. Cooper, dean of the Earlham School of Religion, identified four hypotheses, which he associated with Rufus Jones, Geoffrey Nuttall, Lewis Benson and John Punshon. (The last, found in Punshon's short history of Quakerism, *Portrait in Grey*, should probably rather be consid-

---

[31] H. Larry Ingle; *First among Friends: George Fox and the Creation of Quakerism* (New York, 1994).

[32] Larry Ingle, 'From Mysticism to Radicalism: Recent Historiography of Quaker Beginnings', *Quaker History* 76/2 (Fall 1987), 79–94, at 79.

[33] Christopher Hill, 'The Quakers in the English Revolution', *JFHS* 56/3 (1992), 166–79.

ered as an early attempt at an all-inclusive theory.)[34] Cooper did
not include Christopher Hill's theory, saying that the origins of
Quakerism were 'more complex' than Hill admitted.[35] This is true,
but Cooper's was nevertheless an ostrich-like position. A corresponding and opposing stance existed among non-Quaker historians, as I discovered in 1998 when the anonymous peer reviewer
of a manuscript of mine referred to Reay's *The Quakers in the
English Revolution* as 'the standard work on early Quakerism'. This
was equally perverse.

When I began work on Quakerism in 1989, finding myself
confronted with several mutually incompatible theories of Quaker
origins, I devised a study of the Quaker pamphlet literature using
a computerized database, then a novelty, with the hope that this
would reduce the element of personal bias. It appeared from this
study that early Quakerism had many facets, and that all theories
were to a degree correct. There were similarities with other radical
religious movements both in Britain and on the Continent, but
Quakerism was different in its heightened sense of the presence
of Christ in the believer and in its distinctive practices, both of
which aspects related to the powerful personality of George Fox.
The main thrust of Quaker teaching was at odds with conventional theology, and yet Quaker authors frequently protested that
they belonged within the Christian mainstream, and later in the
century Quakers did indeed creep under the Trinitarian bar of the
1689 Toleration Act. The radical political thread was there, but not
as pervasive as suggested by Hill and Reay.[36]

In recent years, Quakers have become more comfortable with
the notion that their forebears were political revolutionaries, a
development which has been helped by new historical studies
suggesting that the 1650s, and Quakers with them, were perhaps

[34] John Punshon, *Portrait in Grey: A Short History of the Quakers* (London, 1984).
Cooper did not mention Richard Bailey, *New Light on George Fox and Early Quakerism:
The Making and Unmaking of a God* (San Francisco, CA, 1992). Bailey suggests that
Fox actually saw himself, and was seen by his followers, as divine. This is probably best
taken as an extreme example of the 'Benson' theory.

[35] Wilmer A. Cooper, 'The Legacy of Rufus Jones', in *Practice n the Presence: Essays
in Honour of T. Canby Jones*, ed. D. Neil Snarr and Daniel L. Smith-C hristopher (Picken,
IN, 1994), 15–35.

[36] Rosemary Moore, *The Light in Their Consciences: Early Quakers in Britain 1644–
1666* (University Park, PA, 2000).

not quite as revolutionary as once thought.[37] Equally, the work of G. H. Williams and Mennonite scholars on the Magisterial and Radical Reformations has made the similarity of early Quakers to continental Anabaptists and such groups look less alarming.[38] It is now accepted by all serious Quaker scholars that these were important aspects of the origins and early history of the movement. There is no indication that developments in mainstream history are likely to cause further revision of Friends' interpretations of their traditions in the near future.

This does not, however, mark the end of controversy. While important advances in Quaker studies have been made by scholars who were not themselves Quakers, the fact remains that many, if not most, contributors to theorizing about Quaker origins have been 'insiders'. This account of Quaker historiography over the past hundred and fifty years has included a number of examples of Quaker traditions being viewed through particular Quaker theological spectacles, a tendency that continues. It is too early to make a proper appraisal of twenty-first-century contributions to Quaker historiography, but Carole Dale Spencer's *Holiness: The Soul of Quakerism* must be mentioned. This book attempts to demonstrate the dominance of holiness theology throughout Quaker history, a controversial viewpoint. It has received a fiercely antagonistic review from a Quaker of a different theological stripe.[39] Thus there is still potential for sharp disagreement regarding the nature of Quakerism.[40]

The mid-seventeenth century has been thoroughly dissected, so it may be that the focus of Quaker history will move to later periods, which should impinge less on Quaker traditions of their

---

[37] David Underdown, *A Freeborn People* (Oxford, 1996), 68–9, has a summary of historians' views of the mid-seventeenth century as they then stood.

[38] G. H. Williams, *The Radical Reformation* (Philadelphia, PA, 1962; 3rd edn, Kirksville, MO, 1992); Guy F. Hershberger, *The Recovery of the Anabaptist Vision* (Scottdale, PA, 1957).

[39] Carole D. Spencer, *Holiness: The Soul of Quakerism* (Milton Keynes, 2007), reviewed by Chuck Fager, *Quaker Theology*, no.16 (Fall/Winter 2009), 73–83; see also the debate between Thomas Hamm and Spencer, 'An Exchange on *Holiness: The Soul of Quakerism*', in the same issue, 55–72.

[40] See John Punshon, 'The Significance of the Tradition: Reflections on the Writing of Quaker history' [presidential address to the Friends Historical Society], *JFHS* 60/2 (2004), 77–96, at 95, where he suggests that divisions in American Quakerism are such that 'no grand narrative of Quakerism can be established unless it is firmly based on the reality of the divisions'.

origins. There may also be more to come on specific aspects of early Quakerism, notably the 'peace testimony', which, as has been shown, is a sensitive matter for many Quakers and has recently been under discussion.[41] The future will show.

Centre for Postgraduate Quaker Studies in association with the University of Birmingham

[41] Meredith Baldwin Weddle, *Walking in the Way of Peace: Quaker Pacifism in the Seventeenth Century* (Oxford, 2001) describes variations in Quaker pacifism. Gerard Guiton, *The Growth and Development of Quaker Testimony, 1652–1661 and 1960–1994* (New York, 2009), takes a more traditional Quaker view, that Quakers were pacifist from their beginnings.

376

HISTORIES OF HETERODOXY: SHIFTING APPROACHES TO A MILLENARIAN TRADITION IN MODERN CHURCH HISTORY

by PHILIP LOCKLEY

In 1956, the Society for the Promotion of Christian Knowledge published a work chronicling a subject billed as 'an unrecorded chapter of Church history'.[1] The author was an elderly Anglican clergyman, George Balleine. The book was *Past Finding Out: The Tragic Story of Joanna Southcott and her Successors*.

Before Balleine, the early nineteenth-century figure of Joanna Southcott, and her eventually global religious movement, had garnered scant mainstream attention.[2] The most extensive work was Ronald Matthews's rudimentary analysis of Southcott and five other 'English Messiahs' in a 1936 contribution to the psychology of religion.[3] Southcott had not, in fact, claimed to be a messiah herself; rather, she was the prophet of a coming messiah named 'Shiloh'.[4] Southcott's followers (variously labelled 'Southcottians', 'Christian Israelites' 'Jezreelites', among other names) believed that she and certain later figures were inspired by God to signal the imminence of the Christian millennium. Claimants to be the actual Shiloh messiah occasionally featured within this particular tradition of biblical interpretation, inspiration and theodicy. The splinter-prone movement spread through Britain, Australia, New Zealand and North America, and retained a few thousand members in the twentieth century.

Balleine's study reflected the publishing conventions of its

---

[1] George Balleine, *Past Finding Out: The Tragic Story of Joanna Southcott and Her Successors* (London, 1956), ix.

[2] Between 1900 and 1950, many publications on Joanna Southcott were produced by followers, most notably Alice Seymour, *The Express*, 2 vols (London, 1909); eadem, *The Voice in the Wilderness: The Gospel of the Holy Spirit as given to Joanna Southcott by the Spirit of Truth* (Ashford, 1933).

[3] Ronald Matthews, *English Messiahs: Studies of Six English Religious Pretenders, 1656–1927* (London, 1936).

[4] On 'Shiloh' and interpretations of Gen. 49: 10, see Gordon Allan, 'Southcottian Sects from 1790 to the Present Day', in Kenneth Newport and Crawford Gribben, eds, *Expecting the End: Millennialism in Social and Historical Context* (Waco, TX, 2006), 213–36, at 219.

time, and the professional concerns of its author. Its hundred and fifty pages featured no references, despite clearly originating from some first-hand sources, some perhaps still in Southcottian hands.[5] Balleine, an Oxford history graduate, claimed an objective stance towards his subject, insisting that the book would only 'record the facts and let them speak for themselves'.[6] Despite such claims to neutrality, the voice of the clerical professional resounded throughout this 'tragic story'. To Balleine, Southcott and her early followers were 'devout' church people, much misled by their religious experience.[7] Their story deserved a place in the annals of the Church of England, serving an instructive purpose: to caution those 'dazzled by the thought of a life that yields itself wholly to the guidance of the Spirit'.[8] Mapping what Balleine called the 'queer byways' of mid-nineteenth-century Southcottianism, he saw a movement ruinously loosed from its Anglican anchor, subject to the whim of autocratic prophets.

In 2011, Jonathan Cape and Yale University Press published a history of a single Southcottian group in the twentieth century, *Octavia, Daughter of God*.[9] The author was again an Anglican priest, Jane Shaw (also an Oxford historian of religion), the subtitle likewise descriptive – 'the story of a female messiah and her followers'.

Ten years before, Shaw had first read about the figure of 'Octavia', alias Mabel Barltrop, a vicar's widow who died in 1934, and the Panacea Society, the community that had accepted Barltrop as Southcott's Shiloh messiah in 1919. Visiting in 2001, Shaw found the Panacea Society's once thriving community in Bedford reduced to single figures. Shaw became the first scholar allowed into the society's extensive uncatalogued archive, recording both its own history and that of many earlier Southcottian groups. From this mass of material, Shaw painstakingly recovered a biograph-

---

5   Balleine's unacknowledged sources were most likely rare printed collections available to him locally as vicar of Bermondsey in London (a historic Southcottian haunt) during the 1930s. He may also have consulted material already deposited in the British Museum (later forming part of the British Library collection). I am indebted to Andrew Atherstone for insights into Balleine's clerical career and Southcottian interests.

6   Balleine, *Past Finding Out*, xi.

7   Ibid. ix, 2–4, 7, 10, 19–22, 24–5.

8   Ibid. x.

9   Jane Shaw, *Octavia, Daughter of God: The Story of a Female Messiah and her Followers* (London, 2011).

ical history of Octavia and her inter-war community. The earlier archives, dating back to the 1790s, were made available to a team of Oxford theologians and historians.[10]

Shaw's study of the Panacea Society is a history of religion, culture and gender. It is also church history. Throughout her narrative, Shaw discusses the insular beliefs, interests and actions of her unorthodox subjects in relation to wider church life, especially that of the Church of England, during the early twentieth century. In part, the individual biographies of these mostly female millenarians dictated this approach, as so many had Anglican backgrounds and adopted religious roles denied them as women in conventional churches.[11] Yet many other aspects of Panacea Society life further required Shaw to define a concept with the ring of an ecclesiastical oxymoron – an Anglican millennium. Members of the Panacea Society described themselves as 'C of E plus', a designation that led Shaw to ponder whether any priest really knew what their parishioners were quietly believing.

Fifty-five years separate the works of Balleine and Shaw. In this time diverse studies have discussed the Southcottian millenarian tradition, in passing and in detail. From the 1960s to the early 1980s, Southcottians attracted the attention of social historians, including John Saville and E. P. Thompson, whose *Making of the English Working Class* condescendingly sought to rescue 'even the deluded follower of Joanna Southcott, from the enormous condescension of posterity'.[12] Come the heyday of 'popular religion' – when 'official' or 'learned' Christianity was juxtaposed to autonomous popular cultures within which orthodox authorized beliefs were 'mediated' or 'refashioned' – early Southcottianism attracted two detailed social studies, by J. F. C. Harrison and James Hopkins.[13] Presenting opposing arguments, these studies were notably based on specific

---

[10] This team all belonged to an Oxford interdisciplinary research project, the Prophecy Project, convened by Dr Jane Shaw and Professor Christopher Rowland from 2003 to 2010.

[11] Shaw, *Octavia*, 80–3.

[12] E. P. Thompson, *The Making of the English Working Class*, rev. edn (Harmondsworth, 1968), 13, 420–8; John Saville, 'J. E. Smith and the Owenite Movement, 1833–1834', in Sidney Pollard and John Salt, eds, *Robert Owen: Prophet of the Poor* (London, 1971), 115–44.

[13] J. F. C. Harrison, *The Second Coming: Popular Millenarianism, 1780–1850* (London, 1979); J. K. Hopkins, *A Woman to Deliver Her People: Joanna Southcott and English Millenarianism in an Era of Revolution* (Austin, TX, 1982). Essays challenging distinc-

public archives, so superseding much of Balleine's narrative. In the 1980s, gender historians assumed the mantle of interest in Southcott and her followers; from the 1990s this passed to literary scholars and historians of print culture.[14] Across this expanse of time and scholarship, however, one group remained prodigiously uninterested in Southcottianism: church historians.

In this essay, I want to account for this disinterest and indicate ways that the field of church history may be made richer by attending to the sources and the stories of groups commonly considered 'heterodox'. The modern historiography of Southcottianism is, I believe, instructive. It does not represent the fate of all forms of Christian heterodoxy among church historians. For instance, the comparable millennial tradition founded by Emmanuel Swedenborg has received occasional attention in Studies in Church History;[15] the emergence of what became the Catholic Apostolic Church in the 1830s has also intrigued scholars from a range of church traditions.[16] Yet, to a remarkable degree, the shifts in scholarly approaches to Southcottianism just outlined have covered almost all historiographical fashions. Even allowing for ecclesiastical historians' legendary immunity to fashion – sartorial and scholarly – why the dearth in Southcottian interest within church history until so very recently?

Since 2005, I have been one of the Oxford University researchers granted access to the Bedford archives of the Panacea Society to research nineteenth-century Southcottianism. I have written a

tions between elite and popular religion notably feature in Kate Cooper and Jeremy Gregory, eds, *Elite and Popular Religion*, SCH 42 (Woodbridge, 2006).

[14] See esp. Barbara Taylor, *Eve and the New Jerusalem: Socialism and Feminism in the Nineteenth Century* (London, 1983); Anna Clark, *The Struggle for the Breeches: Gender and the Making of the British Working Class* (Berkeley, CA, 1995); Jon Mee, *Romanticism, Enthusiasm, and Regulation: Poetics and the Policing of Culture* (Oxford, 2003); Susan Juster, *Doomsayers: Anglo-American Prophecy in the Age of Revolution* (Philadelphia, PA, 2003); Eitan Bar-Yosef, *The Holy Land in English Culture 1799–1917: Palestine and the Question of Orientalism* (Oxford, 2005).

[15] W. R. Ward, 'Swedenborgianism: Heresy, Schism or Religious Protest', in Derek Baker, ed., *Schism, Heresy and Religious Protest*, SCH 9 (Cambridge, 1972), 303–10; P. J. Lineham, 'Restoring Man's Creative Power: The Theosophy of the Bible Christians of Salford', in W. J. Sheils, ed., *The Church and Healing*, SCH 19 (Oxford, 1982), 207–23.

[16] Columba Graham Flegg, *'Gathered under Apostles': A Study of the Catholic Apostolic Church* (Oxford, 1992); Sheridan Gilley, 'Edward Irving: Prophet of the Millennium', in Jane Garnett and Colin Matthew, eds, *Revival and Religion since 1700: Essays for John Walsh* (London, 1993), 95–110; Tim Grass, *The Lord's Watchman: Edward Irving*, SEHT (Milton Keynes, 2011).

study of this millenarian tradition, based on material in Bedford and other archives, which revises existing social, cultural and gender histories.[17] My own approach has combined elements of social and cultural history with theology, seeking to take articulated beliefs seriously as a motivational and meaningful basis for behaviour. The longstanding neglect of Southcottianism within church history has caused me much reflection. Just as Jane Shaw found with her twentieth-century subject, for me nineteenth-century Southcottians were difficult to write about without reference to the wider Christian church.[18] There was, again, the need to consider the denominational background of millenarian converts. Yet there was also the question of how far the formation, spread, persistence and renewal of Southcottian groups mirrored contemporary trends in wider Protestantism over significant time. Going beyond the work of Balleine and Shaw, my research raises questions about the ways that this millenarian tradition may have generated the historical consciousness of a church, aware of its own posterity – yet one whose resulting story is absent from the wider church's modern narrative.

My research and reflections lead me to two conclusions regarding the past and future of how ecclesiastical historians approach subjects such as Southcottianism, and so how they write histories of heterodoxy. These distinct yet ultimately connected conclusions relate to 'archives' and 'otherness'. Here, they are explored and explained in turn.

In the last fifty years, the archives of the mainstream Christian churches have undergone a degree of consolidation. Within British Nonconformity, in particular, two established centres, the John Rylands University Library in Manchester and Dr Williams's Library in London, have exerted a gravitational pull on outlying collections, though other denominational foci remain, not least the Oxford Centre for Methodism and Church History. Anglican centralizing tendencies have been felt at the Lambeth Palace Library and the Borthwick Institute in York. Local and regional public archives have also attracted deposits in the wake of piece-

---

[17] Philip Lockley, *Visionary Religion and Radicalism in Early Industrial England* (Oxford, 2013).
[18] My reflections on this subject were further influenced by close involvement with Shaw's study as a research assistant.

meal church retrenchment, closure and a welcome awareness that paper records do not live long in leaky vestries. The upshot, it may be argued, has been that church historians have enjoyed a boon in archival access to their subject, with ever greater amounts of material available in ever fewer locations.

This access is, of course, predominantly an evidential window on institutional Christianity. These are the archives of churches, dioceses, chapels, connexions, missionary bodies and theological colleges. They are the papers of church leaders, administrators and lawyers. Not that these collections do not record the religious lives of laity, or the commitments of the common Christian. Phyllis Mack's recent work in the John Rylands Methodist Archives surely demonstrates the rich insights into religious experience that such material can afford.[19] Nevertheless, the perennial dual question remains: whose archive? whose history?

Over the same period, substantial deposits of material generated by the Southcottian religious tradition have been steadily accrued by particular archival institutions in both Britain and America. These institutions notably differ from those typically attracting church archives. With the exception of the Panacea Society's Bedford archives, built up from its members' own inherited papers and acquisitions and retained under private control, the wider availability of Southcottian material in recent times has been the result of one cause: mortality. Since the 1950s, as Southcottians have died, their beliefs have, to an unprecedented extent, died with them. Families who once carefully passed on papers, books and records from one believing generation to the next, in the sure and certain hope that their faith was of immense significance to a future world, now looked askance at such bundles of old papers. For a time, many were donated to the British Library, the London Metropolitan Archives or local historical societies. Between the 1960s and 1980s, however, an international market in Southcottian sources became a little-known by-product of the oil bonanza: the University of Texas acquired seven separate manuscript collections (of varying size) from London auctions. Since 1990, Princeton

---

[19] Phyllis Mack, *Heart Religion in the British Enlightenment: Gender and Emotion in Early Methodism* (Cambridge, 2008).

University Library has added English Southcottian material to its unrivalled collections on American millennialism.[20]

A significant characteristic applies universally to these collections: each acquisition reflects its origins as the deliberate conscious construction of Southcottians themselves. The shape and scope of these deposits – or, in the case of the Panacea Society, the entire archive – is of single unified bodies of historical material. In other words, these bundles of books and papers began as Southcottians' own archives, a record of what they thought important to record and keep. These are their 'church archives', and they remain, in large part, just that. The common collective labels for most deposits are 'Southcott Collection' or 'Southcottian Papers'.[21]

All this, I suspect, has had the notable effect of isolating such sources from their wider archival surroundings. What has been the result? Only scholars seeking the subject out, with a prior interest, have consulted Southcottian material.[22] Until recently, the most studied sources – those in London and a proportion in Texas – were apparently only accessed by historians already intrigued by Southcottianism and committed to writing a focused study of the subject.

Keeping this insight of the 'separation of archives' in mind, we turn now to the related idea of 'otherness'. My argument is, essentially, that church historians have treated forms of Christianity designated 'heterodox', such as Southcottianism, in a manner that reflects their appearance in the ecclesiastical archives that they typically consult. That is to say, they do not see them, ignore them, or otherwise consider them in an exclusionary way, rendering them outside the boundaries of their subject, rendering them 'other'.

---

[20] The principal deposits for American varieties of Southcottianism are the University of Michigan and Hamilton College, New York State. The tendency for Southcottian material to migrate across the Atlantic has been recently countered by a substantial deposit of 'Jezreelite' material (1870–1900) in the Medway Archives, Rochester. My Oxford colleague, Ruth Windscheffel, has made extensive use of this new collection in her forthcoming study of James and Esther Jezreel.

[21] Eugene Wright, *A Catalogue of the Joanna Southcott Collection at the University of Texas* (Austin, TX, 1968).

[22] Before Jane Shaw's discovery of the Panacea Society collections in 2001, and the Oxford Prophecy Project that followed, the only archive-based studies since Balleine to feature any Southcottian papers were the social histories of Harrison and Hopkins. Subsequent gender, literary and cultural studies made minimal reference to primary evidence.

An example from the work of the eminent historian of Methodism, David Hempton, serves to illustrate my point here. On more than one occasion, Hempton has applied the epithet 'bizarre' to nineteenth-century Southcottianism, defining such popular millenarianism as a 'bizarre sub-culture', centred on 'religious psychotics'.[23] One notable use of the term appears in a discussion of the Victorian 'Pope of Methodism', Jabez Bunting.[24] Revisiting Bunting's 'formative years', before becoming president of the Wesleyan Connexion in 1820, Hempton quotes a moderately lengthy reference from Bunting's papers in 1803, in which Bunting makes clear his contempt for 'the notorious Joanna Southcote'. After detailing his own perceptions of her claims, Bunting compares her success to the appeal of the devil, and juxtaposes her message to that of true 'faith and repentance'.[25] Hempton displays an admirably even-handed approach to his principal subject – Bunting – a figure with ample historical 'baggage' himself. However, I do not believe an equivalent even-handedness is achieved by Hempton's labelling of Southcottianism as 'bizarre' when introducing the quotation. The conclusion I draw, however, is that Hempton's terminology was influenced by Bunting's description of Southcott, by the record of Southcottians thus existing within the Methodist Church's own archives, and so, beyond that, the record of such beliefs available in church historians' default research institutions, such as the John Rylands University Library, home of the Bunting Papers.[26]

To my mind, Hempton replicates the 'otherness' that a Methodist leader such as Bunting applied to the Southcottian movement in an historical context of rumour and miscommunication, mistrust of women's religion, and, above all in Bunting's case, the overwhelming desire to police the boundaries of orthodoxy and institutional obedience. Southcottian archives present a

---

[23] David Hempton, 'Evangelicalism and Eschatology', *JEH* 31 (1980), 179–94, at 182; idem, *Methodism and Politics in British Society, 1750–1850* (London, 1984), 95.

[24] David Hempton, *The Religion of the People: Methodism and Popular Religion, c.1750–1900* (London, 1996), 94.

[25] The reference for this quotation from Bunting's journal is given as T. P. Bunting, *The Life of Jabez Bunting, D.D. with Notices of Contemporary Persons and Events* (London, 1887), 182.

[26] Manchester, John Rylands University Library, Methodist Church Archives, Papers of Jabez Bunting.

rather different picture of Southcott's influence among Methodist congregations in the north of England at the precise time that Bunting wrote. Late in 1803, Southcott visited various chapels from County Durham to Cheshire, where 'many hundreds if not a thousand' were reported crowding to hear her. 'At Stockport', Southcott herself wrote, 'there is a division amongst the Methodists'; 'those that believe in my writings and the near approach of Christ's Kingdom gave up their chapel to me'.[27] The image thus conjured of 'millenarian Methodists' is surely one to intrigue historians of Methodism and related churches.

Let us now consider two further examples of how material found in Southcottian archives may be related to wider nineteenth-century church history, and so indicate how such 'heterodoxy' is mistakenly overlooked or regarded as unconnected to the 'orthodox' mainstream.

The first example demonstrates the potential that lies in the obsessive detail that millenarians could include in their own records. For Southcottians, compiling lists of their names, perhaps with addresses or family details, was an important exercise in witnessing their belief before God and each other.[28] Cross-referencing this kind of exclusively Southcottian evidence with more general ecclesiastical records reveals traces of Southcottian religious activities previously invisible. Between roughly 1805 and 1820, Southcottians licensed their meeting spaces as Protestant dissenting chapels. In the York archdiocese, a condition of each application for such a licence was twelve signatures of men or women representing the specific religious body. Many of these applications, now kept in York's Borthwick Institute, detail the denomination – chiefly 'Methodist' or 'Baptist' during the early nineteenth century. A significant number of applications, however, feature no such designation, just an address and twelve names. Comparing the contents of contemporary Southcottian lists with surviving licence applications allows us to identify in numerous cases, and for the first time ever, the specific brand of 'Protestant

---

[27] London, BL, Add. MS 47794, fol. 14.
[28] For such lists, see Bedford, Panacea Society, PN 240 fol. 20; PN 243, fol. 81; Austin, TX, University of Texas, Harry Ransom Research Center, Joanna Southcott Collection, 370–2.

dissent' being licensed: millenarianism.[29] By 1806, eight Southcottian meetings were licensed in the Leeds, Bradford and Halifax region alone.[30] By 1812, there were further chapels and licensed rooms in York, Sheffield, Doncaster and numerous other Yorkshire locations.[31]

A second example illuminates something of the religious 'ecology' within which Southcottianism spread, beyond the examples of 1803 already given. In the 1820s and 1830s, one of Southcott's prophetic successors, John Wroe, oversaw the expansion of the millenarian tradition, commissioning itinerant missionaries to preach throughout the British Isles. Very little material in ecclesiastical archives would give any indication of the scope or success of this endeavour which so closely resembled the activities of popular revivalist Protestants. Surviving Southcottian sources testify to the connections existing between revivalists and the millenarian 'other'. Two of Wroe's more prominent itinerants, William Cooke and Archibald McPhail, had been Methodist and Baptist preachers respectively, before converting to Southcottianism in the mid-1820s.[32] Each preacher utilized their prior training to convert others to millennial expectancy. McPhail, for instance, is recorded as travelling through Scotland, employing revivalist techniques and evoking familiar responses from urban crowds. In Aberdeen in 1829, McPhail first held 'forth the word at the most public place that I could get'– the market cross.[33] He 'stood up and preached to about a thousand people', returning to the same spot several days in a row, until a group was willing to commit themselves publicly to belief.[34] Among these, McPhail wrote, was 'one of the head singers among the Methodists', so that 'we all marched out to the streets, and sung, and got a great congregation in a few minutes. On the

---

[29] Harry Ransom Research Center, Joanna Southcott Collection, 372.

[30] York, Borthwick Institute of Historical Research, Records of the Diocesan Administration of the Archbishop of York, Dissenters Faculty Book 3 (1793–1816), fols 342, 346, 392, 396, 404, 409, 414, 422.

[31] Ibid., fols 603, 608–10, 613, 622, 636–7, 642–3.

[32] John Wroe, *The Life and Journal of John Wroe, with Divine Communications* … , 2nd edn, 3 vols (Ashton-under-Lyne, 1900), 1: 96–121, 319; Anon., *Extracts of Letters and Other Writings of the Israelite Preachers 1823* (Wakefield, 1840), 8–9; Anon., *Extracts of Letters and Other Writings of the Israelite Preachers 1827* (Wakefield, 1840), 8.

[33] Anon., *Extracts of Letters and Other Writings of the Israelite Preachers 1829* (Wakefield, 1840), 9.

[34] Ibid. 10.

11th day, I preached four times; a great many people attended, and were much affected, with tears flowing down their cheeks'.[35]

To conclude, George Balleine called the story of Southcottianism 'an unrecorded chapter of Church history'. It is not unrecorded; ample archives of its own making survive. Balleine's idiosyncratic attempt to write the chapter that he had in mind, with the material he had to hand, was subsequently bettered by social historians. None achieved much recognition among church historians, who appear to have assumed such a 'chapter' worth skipping or omitting. In time, further Southcottian archives were discovered and, as Jane Shaw's recent study indicates, this material allows such millenarian beliefs to be inserted within given sections of the church's story.

Yet the nature of Southcottian sources, including those uncovered in my own work, may in fact point to this not really being a 'chapter of Church history' at all. Such material, scattered and gathered in its own 'church archives' grants a new perspective to an abiding religious phenomenon: the informal dynamics of popular Protestant dissent. Viewed in a longer-term light, such forms of acknowledged heterodoxy – in this case, a religious movement centred on the authority of claims to modern prophecy rather than on institutions or Scripture – seem more like strands that run through the narrative of the modern church, persisting and mutating through the nineteenth and twentieth centuries. Church historians have not paid nearly enough attention to the presence of such strands. Nor have they fully appreciated the extensive scope of the archives of the 'heterodox', or their pertinence to the more immediate 'straight' strands of the 'orthodox'. When it is recalled that sixty-four different sects (Southcottians among them) featured under the designation 'other isolated Congregations' in the Census of Religious Worship carried out in March 1851 – with over one hundred thousand attendances recorded on the census day – a glimpse of the potential field for research, in one country, in one period, is given.[36]

---

35 Ibid.
36 Horace Mann, *Religious Worship in England and Wales: Abridged from the Official Report made by Horace Mann* (London, 1854), 53–4; K. D. M. Snell and Paul S. Ell, *Rival Jerusalems: The Geography of Victorian Religion* (Cambridge, 2000), 404, 423–4. This is not to claim that all such census sects would be considered as 'heterodox' as South-

It is for church historians to choose to trace the full and comprehensive texture of the Christian experience of the past. To recover the breadth of people's responses to the Christian message, to acknowledge the assortment of expressions generated, is to feel the thickness of straight and wayward strands to the story of Christianity. Pursuing this approach requires a sensitivity to the distinctive nature of all church archives – formal and informal, public and private – kept to carry on the particular Christian interpretation their owners imposed upon their historic experience. Following the wayward strands can certainly sometimes lead to strange places: Bedford, for instance.

University of Oxford

cottianism by church historians; my point is to hint at a compellingly unchartered hinterland awaiting adequate exploration.

RE-VISIONING THE PAST AND RE-SOURCING THE FUTURE: THE UNRESOLVED HISTORIOGRAPHICAL STRUGGLE IN ROMAN CATHOLIC SCHOLARSHIP AND AUTHORITATIVE TEACHING

by KENNETH L. PARKER

During twenty years of teaching at a Jesuit university in an ecumenical Ph.D. programme focused on historical theology, I have observed a profound unresolved problem in Roman Catholic theological scholarship. Framed very simply, it is this: since the rise of historical consciousness among Roman Catholics during the nineteenth century, conflicting historiographical assumptions about the Christian past have led to tensions and divisions among Roman Catholic scholars and church authorities. My purpose here is to diagnose this unresolved challenge and propose a mode of analysis for intra-ecclesial dialogue.

Four historiographical metanarratives[1] will be discussed, which in my observation characterize four divergent assumptions about the Christian past found in Roman Catholic discourse. These metanarratives will be referred to as successionism, supercessionism, developmentalism and appercessionism. Successionism claims that Christian truth was received by the apostles and has

---

[1] Jean-François Lyotard brought the current use of the term 'metanarrative' into intellectual discourse in the late 1970s, in his 'postmodern' critique of 'modern' master narratives. Lyotard used 'modern' to designate any science that seeks legitimation through a grand narrative, applied universally. For Lyotard, 'en simplifiant à l'extrême', postmodern refers to 'l'incrédulité à l'égard des métarécits': Jean-François Lyotard, *La condition postmoderne: Rapport sur le savoir* (Paris, 1979), 7. This incredulity is above all a rejection of metanarratives that assert the totalizing nature of any transcendent or universal truth – except of course the universal, totalizing truth of its own scepticism. 'Metanarrative' has become a virtual synonym for 'metahistory'. 'Metahistory' gained currency through R. G. Collingwood's use of it to describe the work of philosophers of history, and refers to overarching totalizing theories of history like those of Hegel, Marx or Spengler. Hayden White has sought to displace the pejorative taint with which early twentieth-century historians regarded 'metahistory': Hayden White, *Metahistory: The Historical Imagination in Nineteenth-Century Europe* (Baltimore, MD, 1973). It is now recognized by most historians that historical scholarship inevitably requires narrative ordering – an ordering informed by assumptions about the past that the scholar applies either consciously or unconsciously.

been preserved by their successors unaltered by time and circumstance. Supercessionism ascribes to ancient Christianity a privileged normative quality, identifies a period – or periods – of corruption that distorted Christian teaching, and looks to a later era when primitive Christian truth is rediscovered and restored. Developmentalism identifies in early Christianity nascent expressions of doctrinal teaching, yet assumes that organic growth – in human time and experience – results in a deeper, more expansive understanding of truths that may take centuries of struggle and debate to discern. Appercessionism, unlike the other three metanarratives, does not privilege earlier Christianity, but looks to the heightened consciousness of the current age to critique former Christian teaching and practice, chart a new way forward and reshape Christianity in light of newly realized values. More complete definitions of these metanarratives will be provided in the course of this essay.

Tension over the use of these metanarratives is not a twentieth-century phenomenon, but has been evident at least since events surrounding the First Vatican Council (1869–70). Indeed the two Vatican councils can be viewed as bookends of a major shift in the rise of historical consciousness among Roman Catholics. My purpose here is not to value one metanarrative over the others, but rather to encourage identification of their use as a mode of analysis that may permit more productive dialogue among Roman Catholics. Much of what I propose could equally apply to the study of the Anglican Communion or other ecclesial communities. My hope is that, by focusing on the challenge faced by Roman Catholics, the value of this approach will be evident by analogy.

★ ★ ★

The year 1961 not only marked the founding of the Ecclesiastical History Society, but also a crucial year of preparation for the Second Vatican Council. The first session of the council began in October 1962, just three months after Dom David Knowles delivered the first presidential address to the Ecclesiastical History Society at Peterhouse, Cambridge.

Like its nineteenth-century predecessor, Vatican II altered the trajectory of Roman Catholic scholarship in ways no one foresaw in 1961 and 1962. Of particular interest for this essay is the draft document, *De fontibus revelationis*. Prepared by Holy Office theologians under the supervision of Cardinal Alfredo Ottaviani, the text maintained a successionist metanarrative when explaining the foundations for Roman Catholic truth claims.[2] On 20 November 1962, just weeks after the council began its first session, bishops rejected this draft by a significant majority. Pope John XXIII appointed a new commission of theologians, some only recently rehabilitated after years of suspicion and censure for their engagement with modern biblical scholarship and criticism of neoscholastic thought. They drafted a new text.[3] This new document included an explicit endorsement of historical-critical methods for correct interpretation of Scripture.[4] In the closing days of the council, on 18 November 1965, *Dei Verbum* was passed by 2,344 votes to 6.[5] Like other documents promulgated by the council, *Dei Verbum* highlighted Vatican II's dramatic 're-visioning' of the Christian past and the council's 're-sourcing' of the ongoing study of Roman Catholic truth claims.

Roman Catholic authorities had long treated the rise of historical consciousness in western culture with suspicion. Indeed, since 1910 the Anti-Modernist Oath required all priests and seminary professors to denounce 'the error of those who affirm that the faith proposed by the Church can be repugnant to history, and that Catholic dogmas, in the way they are understood now, cannot accord with the truer origins of the Christian religion'. The oath included the statement, 'I flatly reject the heretical invention of the evolution of dogmas'. Affirming the 'unwavering charisma of the truth', candidates declared that Roman Catholic teaching 'has existed and will always exist in the succession of bishops from the Apostles', is not 'adapted to the culture of each age', and is 'absolute and unchangeable'.[6]

The documents of Vatican II up-ended that dominant successionist metanarrative of the Christian past, by locating the church's understanding of revealed truth in the context of human history,

---

[2] This approach had become normative in the wake of Leo XIII's revival of Thomism in the later nineteenth century through his encyclical *Aeterni Patris* (1879).

[3] Fergus Kerr, *Twentieth-Century Catholic Theologians: From Neoscholasticism to Nuptial Mysticism* (Oxford, 2007), 37.

[4] *Dei Verbum*, §12. All references and quotations from the documents of the Second Vatican Council are drawn from the official English translations online at: <http://www.vatican.va/archive/hist_councils/ii_vatican_council/>, accessed 26 March 2012 and subsequently.

[5] Joseph Prior, *The Historical Method in Catholic Exegesis* (Rome, 1999), 146.

[6] Kerr, *Twentieth-Century Catholic Theologians*, 223–5.

and valuing the methods and tools of modern historical research. Council documents also highlighted a diversity of historiographical metanarratives, using three other visions of the Christian past to frame conciliar teaching. *Dignitatis Humanae*, the decree on religious liberty, explicitly invoked doctrinal development.[7] *Perfectae Caritatis*, the declaration on renewal of religious life, called for a return to the original sources of religious orders to achieve revitalization, thus making use of a supercessionist metanarrative.[8] *Gaudium et Spes*, the pastoral constitution on the church in the modern world, acknowledged the recent heightened consciousness of women and their demand for equity with men in society – an equity that had been denied women in the Christian past – and in so doing appealed to the apperceptive metanarrative.[9]

These other metanarratives of the Christian past – which had been marginalized in early twentieth-century Roman Catholic scholarship but woven into the teaching of conciliar documents – have, frankly, led to tensions and conflict. Fifty years after the Second Vatican Council an open question remains: can Roman Catholic scholars and church authorities find a historiographical consensus on how to frame the Christian past?

I will begin by examining the successionist metanarrative inherent in neo-scholasticism (the officially sanctioned theological movement that sought to apply medieval scholastic thought to modern intellectual needs in the late nineteenth and early twentieth centuries). Attention will then turn to the alternative metanarratives evident during the period between Vatican I and Vatican II. I will then analyse how these metanarratives have been used by Roman Catholics in the post-Vatican II era, giving two examples of how they have been sources of tension in Roman Catholic thought. The last section will focus on statements by Joseph Ratzinger, as professor, prefect and pope, to demonstrate the complexity of this ongoing struggle for consensus on how best to re-vision the Christian past and re-source the ongoing study of Roman Catholic truth claims.

---

[7] *Dignitatis Humanae*, §1.
[8] *Perfectae Caritatis*, §2.
[9] *Gaudium et Spes*, §29.

SUCCESSIONIST METANARRATIVE

In his 1965 novel, *The British Museum is Falling Down*, David Lodge recounted a day in the life of a twenty-five-year-old married Catholic man studying English literature at the University of London during the Second Vatican Council (1962–5). Adam Appleby's morning began with amorous musings as his wife measured her body temperature and recorded it on a church-sponsored calendar to determine her 'safe period', while their three young children toddled about, reminding him of the consequences of impetuous marital union.[10] When his wife reported symptoms of morning sickness, Adam was filled with dread.

As he scootered his way to the British Museum for a day of research, Adam encountered his parish priest, Fr Finbar, and offered him a lift. Just after a near-accident on a busy London street – Adam's attention distracted by fearful thoughts of a fourth pregnancy after four years of marriage – he blurted out to the good Irish priest: 'Do you think the Council will change the Church's attitude on Birth Control?' Fr Finbar stiffened and responded with absolute certainty: 'The Church's teaching never changes … on that or any other matter'. Being an educated layman, Adam countered with John Henry Newman's theory of doctrinal development. To this Fr Finbar reacted: 'Newman, wasn't he a Protestant?'[11]

While Fr Finbar's reaction may provoke amusement among ecclesiastical historians in the twenty-first century, he accurately articulated convictions popularized in Britain by the notable Oxford Movement convert, Henry Edward Manning, during his long tenure as archbishop of Westminster. Even as an Anglican in 1846, Manning condemned Newman's recently published *Essay on the Development of Christian Doctrine* (1845), observing: 'the Tridentine Doctors would have severely censured the modern theories of development, or gradual rise as false, and dangerous'.[12] Manning's commitment to a scholastic understanding of dogmatic truth only

---

[10] David Lodge, *The British Museum is Falling Down* (New York, 1965), ch. 1.

[11] Ibid. 30.

[12] Oxford, Bodl., MS Eng. Lett.c.662, fol. 68r, Manning to unknown correspondent, 10 March 1846. To William Gladstone he wrote: 'I am a long way off from Development.' He expressed doubts about the viability of Newman's theory of development, and asserted that whatever its influence, the impact would not be seen soon, 'Certainly not for a long time': Atlanta, GA, Emory University, Pitts Library, Manning Papers, Box 1, Folder 22, Manning to Gladstone, 6 March 1846.

deepened in the wake of his conversion in 1851. Fourteen years later, shortly after becoming archbishop of Westminster in 1865, Manning stated: 'the divine action of the day of Pentecost is permanent, and pervades the world so far as the Church is diffused, and pervades all ages, the present as fully as the past, today as fully as in the beginning'.[13] One should not look to the past for knowledge of the faith, for 'the enunciation of the faith by the living Church of this hour, is the maximum evidence, both natural and supernatural, as to the *facts* and the *contents* of the original revelation'.[14]

The successionist metanarrative of the Christian past – which links the absolute and changeless nature of Christian truth claims with the apostolic succession of bishops – stretches back at least to Eusebius of Caesarea in the fourth century. The scholasticism of Luis de Molina, Francisco Suarez, Gabriel Vasquez and John de Lugo linked the absolute certainty of dogma to this successionist metanarrative.[15] After Vatican I, Manning declared that the conciliar definition of papal infallibility represented the triumph of dogma over history. He stated: 'The scientific historian reads the history of the Catholic Church in one sense, the Catholic Church reads its own history in another. Choose which you will believe.'[16] In the era of Vatican II, Fr Finbar had church authority on his side – or did he?

DEVELOPMENTAL METANARRATIVE

Adam Appleby's appeal to Newman's theory of doctrinal development had a distinguished lineage as well. While the successionist vision of Christian truth cherished by Manning dominated public Roman Catholic discourse up to the eve of Vatican II, Newman's theory of development had already taken root in the imagination of Roman Catholic theologians and bishops during the First Vatican Council. In February 1870, as council fathers struggled

---

[13] Henry Manning, *The Temporal Mission of the Holy Ghost: Or, Reason and Revelation* (New York, 1887; first publ. 1865), 83.

[14] Ibid. 205 (emphasis in the original). This argument is also found in the pre-papal publications of Gregory XVI (Mauro Cappellari); see Mauro Cappellari, *Il Trionfo della Santa Sede e della Chiesa contro gli assalti de' novatori respinti e combattuti colle stesse loro armi* (Rome, 1799), 19.

[15] See Anthony Kemp, *The Estrangement of the Past: A Study in the Origins of Modern Historical Consciousness* (Oxford, 1991), 3–65; Owen Chadwick, *From Bossuet to Newman: The Idea of Doctrinal Development* (Cambridge, 1957), 1–48.

[16] Henry Manning, *Religio Viatoris*, 4th edn (London, n.d.), 80.

for consensus on how to define papal infallibility, Bishop David Moriarty of Kerry observed in a letter to Newman:

> Strange to say, if ever this definition comes you will have contributed much towards it. Your treatise on development has given the key. A Cardinal said the other day – 'We must give up the first ten centuries, but the infallibility is an obvious development of the supremacy.' Of course development was ever at work in the Church, but you brought it out and placed it on a pedestal.[17]

Though Newman grumbled and complained at this news, by 1871 his theory was proving crucial in efforts to reconcile himself and others to a definition he contended had been foisted on the Church by an 'aggressive insolent faction'[18] – a faction led by Archbishop Manning and other neo-ultramontane Oxford Movement converts.[19] Newman consoled a troubled disciple with an appeal to development:

> Looking at early history, it would seem as if the Church moved on to perfect truth by various successive declarations, alternately in contrary directions, and thus perfecting, completing, supplying each other. Let us have a little faith in her, I say. Pius is not the last of the Popes. ... Let us be patient, let us have faith, and a new Pope, and a re-assembled Council may trim the boat.[20]

Newman's developmental metanarrative did not simply appeal to primitive Christian belief and practice as the static standard of a 'golden age'. Rather he contended that while truth is whole and complete – in God – full understanding of that truth might span centuries, as humans struggled toward complete comprehension of dogmatic truth under the providential guidance of the Holy Spirit. He rejected the fixed vision of truth found in successionism,

---

[17] John Henry Newman, *Letters and Diaries*, ed. C. Stephen Dessain et al., 32 vols (London, 1961–), 25: 58 n. 2.

[18] Ibid. 18–19; see also 17.

[19] Kenneth L. Parker, 'Historical Consciousness and Papal Infallibility: Manning, Döllinger, Newman, and Acton's Uses of History in Defense of Truth', in idem and Erick Moser, eds, *The Rise of Historical Consciousness among the Christian Churches* (Lanham, MD, 2012), 89–122.

[20] Newman, *Letters and Diaries*, 25: 310.

and argued for a living tradition, organically growing, flowering and bearing fruit. Because he did not localize Christian truth claims in a distant past that required reappropriation and restoration, he could acknowledge historical data that indicated shifts and alterations in Christian teaching. This development – or growth – in the Christian doctrinal tradition occurred despite periods of controversy, corruption and disorder. To account for this Newman created criteria for analysing true and false development.[21]

So when Adam Appleby – eager to fulfil his marital duty without fear – appealed to Newman's developmental metanarrative on a crisp November morning in the early 1960s, he had reason to hope that the church's attitude on birth control could 'develop' – or could it?

SUPERCESSIVE METANARRATIVE

To complicate matters further, what neither of Lodge's characters posited was the possibility of a corrupted church tradition that required correction, adjustment, or – dare I say – reformation. Yet that was precisely the premise of the *ressourcement* movement, or what its neo-scholastic critics called *la nouvelle théologie*.[22] Étienne Gilson expressed this explicitly in a letter to Henri de Lubac on 8 July 1956: 'Our only salvation lies in a return to Saint Thomas himself ... before [the Thomism] of Cajetan, whose famous commentary is in every respect the consummate example of a *corruptorium Thomae*. ... Salvation lies in returning to the real St. Thomas ... accept no substitute!'[23]

When Yves Congar published his *True and False Reform in the*

[21] John Henry Newman, *An Essay on the Development of Christian Doctrine* (London, 1845).

[22] *Ressourcement* theologians reacted against early twentieth-century neo-scholasticism, with its exclusive emphasis on scholastic modes of reasoning, rejection of modern forms of intellectual discourse, and resistance to constructive engagement with other faith traditions. They sought to restore Catholic theology to its original purity of thought and expression, and argued that this required a 'return to the sources', or '*ressourcement*'.

[23] Étienne Gilson, *Lettres de M. Étienne Gilson addressées au P. Henri de Lubac* (Paris, 1986), 19–20. Jean Daniélou, in notes on criticism received for his article, 'Les orientations présentes de la pensée religieuse', *Études* 79, no. 249 (avril–mai 1946), 1–21, wrote, 'le nèo-thomisme représente une forme sclérosée et durcie de la pensée du Docteur Angélique': Paris, Archives de la Province de France de la Compagnie de Jésus, Q Ly 521/1. I am grateful to Erick Moser for this reference.

Church in 1950,[24] the papal nuncio to Paris, Archbishop Angelo Roncalli – the future Pope John XXIII – wrote in his copy of the book, 'A reform of the Church – is it possible?'[25] Congar was one of the first theologians summoned by John XXIII after he announced that a second Vatican council would be convened – this despite Congar's angst-filled exile to the damp fenlands of Cambridgeshire in 1956.[26] Judging from the decrees promulgated, Congar's work informed crucial documents of Vatican II.[27] Yet Congar stood on the shoulders of many early twentieth-century Roman Catholic scholars, who collectively became known as participants in the *ressourcement* movement.[28] Marie-Dominique Chenu, Henri de Lubac and Louis Bouyer are a mere sampling of these influences on Congar. Dom David Knowles's engagement should not be overlooked, for his inaugural presidential address to the Ecclesiastical History Society in August 1962, entitled 'Some Recent Work on Early Benedictine History', was an assessment of *ressourcement* scholarship on the Rule of Saint Benedict.[29]

While scholars identified with this movement also employed other metanarratives in their theological argumentation, the supercessive metanarrative dominated their rhetorical appeals to the Christian past. This historiographical model posited a period of decline, corruption or atrophy, primarily with reference to the manualist tradition that over a three-hundred-year period had created a 'secondhand' understanding of scholasticism, dominated by an emphasis on magisterial teaching and canon law. This decline – as *ressourcement* theologians perceived it – could only be reversed by a return to original or classic sources to gain new insights and rejuvenate the faith. These scholars denounced the neo-scholasticism of the early twentieth century as lacking the vitality and

---

[24] Yves Congar, *Vrai et fausse réforme dans l'Église* (Paris, 1950).

[25] Elizabeth Therese Groppe, *Yves Congar's Theology of the Holy Spirit* (Oxford, 2004), 22.

[26] For the circumstances which led to this period, see Yves Congar, *Journal d'un théologien: 1946–1956* (Paris, 2005), 412–41.

[27] *Apostolicam Actuositatem, Unitatis Redintegratio* and *Lumen Gentium* are three examples. For further details, see n. 4 above.

[28] Marcellino D'Ambrosio, '*Ressourcement* Theology, *Aggiornamento*, and the Hermeneutics of Tradition', *Communio* 18 (1991), 530–55, at 531.

[29] David Knowles, 'Some Recent Work on Early Benedictine History', in C. W. Dugmore and Charles Duggan, eds, *Studies in Church History* 1 (London, 1964), 35–46.

relevance needed to address the concerns of Christians in the twentieth century. Their work influenced a younger generation of scholars who helped prepare documents at the council. Karl Rahner, Eduard Schillebeeckx, Hans Küng, Joseph Ratzinger (the future Pope Benedict XVI) and many others looked to *ressourcement* scholarship in their formative years. Although their lives and scholarship took them in different directions after the council, this common bond must not be forgotten.

The success of the twentieth-century *ressourcement* movement at Vatican II should not obscure the fact that this metanarrative had been employed during the 1860s papal infallibility debate leading up to the First Vatican Council. Indeed, to express this anachronistically, it was *ressourcement*-like scholarship that Ignaz von Döllinger advocated in his famous manifesto delivered at the Munich Congress in 1863. The new *wissenschaftliche* theology he envisioned would 'reverse the analytic method of the Middle Ages' and focus on the historical roots of theological knowledge.[30] His call for theology grounded in archival research and critical historical scholarship was denounced in Pius IX's *Tuas libenter* in December 1863. The Syllabus of Errors in 1864 explicitly condemned key elements of Döllinger's theological agenda to revitalize Roman Catholic theology.[31]

Döllinger's *The Pope and the Council* and *Letters from Rome* argued that forged documents in the ninth and thirteenth centuries had corrupted all subsequent teaching on papal authority.[32] He called for a return to the sources of ancient Christian teaching on papal authority, in order to ask of these sources new questions raised

---

[30] In 1863 Ignaz von Döllinger invited a number of German theologians to explore how the Roman Catholic Church should engage modern ideas. His address has been described as an apology for liberal Catholicism, and an assault on the ultramontane theory and the reasoning that supported it. For an English translation of Döllinger's speech, see John Acton, 'Munich Congress', *Home and Foreign Review* 4 (January 1864), 228–35, quotation at 234. For the German text, see Ignaz von Döllinger, 'Die Vergangenheit und Gegenwart der katholischen Theologie', in idem, *Kleinere Schriften* (Stuttgart, 1890), 161–97, at 193.

[31] Franz Xaver Bischof, *Theologie und Geschichte: Ignaz von Döllinger (1799–1890) in der zweiten Hälfte seines Lebens* (Stuttgart, 1997), 95–105.

[32] Janus [Ignaz von Döllinger], *The Pope and the Council* (London, 1869), 94–150; Quirinus [Ignaz von Döllinger], *Letters from Rome on the Council*, 2 vols (London, 1870), 1: 249–50, 259–65.

by the pressing circumstances of the latter part of the nineteenth century. Because he refused to submit to the new definition after the council, Döllinger was excommunicated in 1871.[33]

This contrast in conciliar reception of the supercessive metan-arrative – at Vatican I and Vatican II – is a striking illustration of the readiness of twentieth-century Roman Catholic scholars and church authorities to ground Catholic truth claims in historicized conceptions of tradition. It demonstrated a consciousness of the need for reform, correction, adaptation and renewal. While de Lubac, Congar, Chenu and other *ressourcement* scholars suffered the ire of influential neo-scholastics such as Cardinal Ottaviani prior to the council, it was their historical scholarship that sparked the imagination of a future pope and laid the groundwork for crucial documents during Vatican II.[34]

APPERCEPTIVE METANARRATIVE

In 1958 Pope John XXIII called for *aggiornamento* (updating or renewal), and announced plans for a second Vatican council. When asked why a council was needed, he is widely reported to have expressed the desire 'to throw open the windows of the Church so that we can see out and the people can see in'. Yet when the windows of the church were opened at the council, new vistas – not rooted in the sources of church tradition, but manifested in contemporary culture – attracted some theologians and bishops. A perceived new and heightened consciousness concerning a range of contempo-rary issues seemed to call for a radical departure from teachings of the past, because of the signs of the times.[35] This quest for relevance ultimately estranged former allies in the *ressourcement* movement from one another.

Yet even Pope John XXIII hinted at the need for change grounded in a contemporary heightened consciousness rather than in ancient or 'classic' precedents. Concerning women's roles, the pope stated in *Pacem in Terris*, issued on 11 April 1963, 'Since women are becoming ever more conscious of their human dignity,

---

33 Bischof, *Ignaz von Döllinger*, 275–94.
34 'To a very great degree, in all sectors touched by the Council ... *aggiornamento* was made possible by the patristic renewal of the last fifty years': Henri de Lubac, *Mémoire sur l'occasion de mes écrits* (Namur, 1989), 319–20.
35 *Gaudium et Spes*, §4.

they will not tolerate being treated as mere material instruments, but demand rights befitting a human person both in domestic and in public life'.[36] Certain Vatican II documents manifested a conscious embrace of shifts that had no precedent in the Christian past but were rooted in the heightened consciousness of the age. Again concerning women, *Gaudium et Spes* acknowledged in its introduction: 'Where they have not yet won it, women claim for themselves an equity with men before the law and in fact'.[37] The document went further and stated:

> For in truth it must be regretted that fundamental personal rights are not yet being universally honored. Such is the case of a woman who is denied the right and freedom to choose a husband, to embrace a state of life, or to acquire an education or cultural benefit equal to those recognized for men.[38]

This vision of the Christian past – a past open to critique and censure – reflects what I call the apperceptive metanarrative. 'Apperception', a term that gained currency through Leibniz in the late seventeenth century and used since the nineteenth century by educational psychologists, refers to the assimilation of new information and insights that require in turn a critical reassessment of previously assumed truth claims in light of a rising or heightened 'consciousness'.[39] It was this trend, already nascent in texts of papal and conciliar documents, that proved unsettling for certain *ressourcement* scholars. Yet, again, this was not a mid-twentieth-century innovation. Appercessionism had its roots in the later nineteenth century and can be discerned in the reaction to

---

36 Pope John XXIII, *Pacem in Terris*, §41, cf. §43; see n. 4 above for more details.

37 *Gaudium et Spes*, §9.

38 Ibid., §29.

39 Conscious apperception was defined by Carl Jung as 'a process by which the subject of himself, from his own motives, consciously and attentively apprehends a new content and assimilates it to another content standing in readiness'. Passive apperception Jung defined as 'a process in which a new content from without (through the senses) or from within (through the unconscious) presses through into the consciousness and, to a certain extent, compels attention and apprehension upon itself'. Both elements of Jung's definition are at work in my use of the term. However, the latter emphasis on 'new content' that compels a reconsideration of an older 'content' is what I am most concerned to emphasize here: Carl Jung, *Psychological Types, or The Psychology of Individuation*, transl. H. G. Baynes (London, 1946), 524. I am grateful to Jonathan King for his helpful comments and observations.

Vatican I of Lord Acton, who, although still in his thirties, functioned as an informal lay whip of the bishops opposing a definition
of papal infallibility at the council. Acton's unprecedented engagement in the politics of the council proceedings – and his devotion to nineteenth-century liberal values of liberty, democracy and
progress – gave him a unique perspective from which to analyse,
and judge, that historic event.

Herbert Butterfield, citing Acton's most famous aphorism –
'Power tends to corrupt and absolute power corrupts absolutely'
– observed that while it had the ring of wisdom, he sensed that 'it
was a truth more dear to the heart of the liberal that was in him
[Acton] than to the mind of the Roman Catholic [in Acton]'.[40]
Butterfield noted Acton's refusal to privilege the past in any way;
and Acton's own words confirm this insight: 'The canonisation
of the historic past [is] more perilous than ignorance or denial,
because it would perpetuate the reign of sin and acknowledge the
sovereignty of wrong.'[41]

Acton's suspicion of the powerful may well have been nurtured
in conversation with Newman. During a controversy with church
authorities over the *Rambler* in the late 1850s, Acton described an
astonishing three-hour meeting, in which Newman candidly spoke
of the 'natural inclination of men in power to tyrannize, [and the]
ignorance and presumption of our would be theologians'.[42]

Acton's understanding of the Christian past also grew out of
his experience of archival research with his mentor, Ignaz von
Döllinger, as well as the extraordinary opportunity to engage in
the internal workings of Roman Catholic ecclesiastical politics at
Vatican I. As a young layman, free of the ethical turmoil created

---

[40] Herbert Butterfield, *The Whig Interpretation of History* (London, 1931), 110. The
original context for that aphorism is a letter written by Acton to Bishop Mandell
Creighton, concerning his history of the papacy: CUL, Add. MS 6871, fol. 59v, Acton
to Creighton, 5 April 1887.

[41] John Acton, 'Inaugural Lecture on the Study of History', in John Neville Figgis
and Reginald Vere Laurence, eds, *Lectures on Modern History* (London, 1906), 26.

[42] John Acton and Richard Simpson, *The Correspondence of Lord Acton and Richard
Simpson*, ed. Josef Altholz and Damian McElrath, 3 vols (Cambridge, 1971), 1: 116. This
comment was made with specific reference to Henry Manning, William Ward and
John Dalgairns, all of whom were Oxford Movement converts and advocates of the
neo-ultramontane cause. Newman's reaction was visceral, for Acton reported that he
'moaned for a long time rocking himself backwards and forwards over the fire, like an
old woman with the tooth ache': ibid.

by vows and oaths required of the hierarchy, Acton's self-appointed role as lay whip of the minority bishops at Vatican I gave him a unique position from which to evaluate – and to judge – the behaviour of ecclesiastical leaders and the decision-making process of the council.[43] The experience marked his life and altered his scholarship.

Acton's loyalty to the Roman Catholic Church was only equalled by his commitment to the liberal principles of his day. As he affirmed to his future wife in 1865: 'The one supreme object of all my thoughts is the good of the Church.'[44] Owen Chadwick noted that Acton's massive book collection was focused on two themes: liberty and the history of the papacy.[45] Acton sought to wed the liberal moral principles of his day – and the truth that could be gleaned through scientific historical research – to the divine mission of the Catholic Church. In notes that post-dated the council, he described his commitment to liberal moral principles that reflected liberty, democracy and scientific progress (which included historical scholarship) in this way:

> In reality, it [Acton's liberal morality] is a new departure, a renovation.[46] It depends on ideas which not all men share. It casts out a number of men in the present; still more in the past. It is a view created by new discoveries – the peculiar certitudes of science, opening of archives, [and] accuracy of research.[47]

In direct response to arguments put forth by Manning, Acton declared: 'Historians, who have to judge dead popes like other mortals, cannot acknowledge in the living pope any superiority to criticism. A science of history would not exist under such a system. Popes and Saints would be exempt from the ordinary laws of historical reasoning and judgment.'[48] Elsewhere Acton explained:

[43] Roland Hill, *Lord Acton* (New Haven, CT, 2000), 192–225.

[44] Damian McElrath, *Lord Acton: The Decisive Decade, 1864–1874* (New York, 1970), 64.

[45] Owen Chadwick, *Acton and History* (Cambridge, 1998), 252.

[46] From the late medieval period through to the nineteenth century, 'renovation' was used in theological discourse to describe renewal wrought by the Holy Spirit.

[47] CUL, Add. MS 5647, fol. 60r. The notebook from which this is drawn contains notes Acton made in preparation for a biography of Ignaz von Döllinger. It was one of his many unfinished book projects.

[48] CUL, Add. MS 5542, fol. 27v. This comment is drawn from a notebook that

'My own doctrine must be clear, no dependence on great names, say good and evil impartially. Don't admit a presumption for your own side.'[49] In his system, humanity's capacity for evil was only equalled by its capacity to discern the good and ascertain truth. His confidence in human reason and scientific inquiry, so typical of nineteenth-century European intellectuals, privileged no time, no person and no institution – except his own era, his own rational judgement and the discipline of history as he understood it. Because new knowledge gained through archival research heightened awareness of hitherto unacknowledged injustices, even the earliest Christians were open to criticism and their actions censurable.

In an ecclesiastical ethos that treated liberal principles as antithetical to Roman Catholic teaching and *wissenschaftliche* history as a challenge to the Christian faith, Acton faced unavoidable conflict. His passionate liberal belief in human progress – with its assumptions of the inevitability of greater liberty in society and democracy in politics – clashed with contemporary liberal assumptions about Roman Catholicism on the one hand and the prevailing Roman Catholic rejection of liberalism on the other. Indeed, as Oliver Richardson observed in 1905, Acton was the most Catholic of liberals and the most liberal of Catholics.[50]

Yet in the early 1960s Pope John XXIII and the Second Vatican Council up-ended previous assumptions. Like *ressourcement* scholarship – which had suffered recrimination and derision from neo-scholastics before it became a guiding principle in the drafting of conciliar documents – Acton's cherished liberal values moved from the margins to the centre of ecclesial discourse on key issues at the council. Papal and conciliar authority endorsed concepts of liberty and human dignity that animated John Acton's life of scholarship.

The repercussions of Vatican II's shift toward a historicized understanding of tradition are still being felt in biblical studies, moral teaching and doctrinal debates. The metanarratives introduced in its documents have played an essential, if at times unacknowledged, role in Roman Catholic discourse. Indeed, even as

---

contains his reflections on the First Vatican Council.

49 CUL, Add. MS 5647, fol. 59v.

50 Oliver H. Richardson, 'Lord Acton and his *Obiter Dicta* on History', *Sewanee Review* 13 (1905), 129–42, at 135.

the council concluded in December 1965, storm clouds of conflict were evident – and tension over how to engage the Christian past has proved to be the essential background to the theological debates of the last half-century.

★ ★ ★

It is not possible here to recount numerous examples of how this has played out over the last fifty years. Instead, two much debated issues have been chosen to illustrate how these metanarratives created challenges for Roman Catholic scholarship and authoritative church teaching. In both cases, participants in the debates have understood well the historiographical issues at stake, and have consciously engaged in a tug of war over how to re-vision the Christian past and re-source future studies of Roman Catholic truth claims.

The Papal Commission on Birth Control and *Humanae Vitae*

Perhaps the most striking example of tensions over conflicting metanarratives of the Christian past has focused on the question of contraception. Adam Appleby's fictitious turmoil over birth control resonates with Roman Catholics of a certain age who lived through the council and the first years of the post-Vatican II era. Popes John XXIII and Paul VI reserved the question of birth control to themselves during the council and created commissions to study contraception.

In his 1965 study, *Contraception: A History of its Treatment by the Catholic Theologians and Canonists*, John Noonan Jr, a lay consultant to Paul VI's commission, explicitly invoked the theory of development to describe the history of the Roman Catholic Church's teaching on birth control.[51] From 1964 to 1966, the commission's deliberations entered public discourse through the media; and when the commission's majority report was submitted to Paul VI in 1966, its conclusions and recommendations were leaked to the press.

Paul VI's seventy-one-member commission recommended that church teaching should permit the use of contraceptives, denied

---

[51] John T. Noonan Jr, *Contraception: A History of its Treatment by the Catholic Theologians and Canonists* (Cambridge, MA, 1965), 491–533.

that contraceptives (as the commission defined them) were always intrinsically evil, and affirmed that their recommendation was in basic continuity with tradition and with declarations of the magisterium.[52] During the commission's concluding deliberations in the summer of 1966, Cardinal Shehan of Baltimore – not known for his progressive views – reportedly observed (23 June 1966): 'The Church develops, and the *sensus fidelium* [sense of the faithful] plays a big role in that development. The Church must recognize how marriage is lived today'.[53]

However, this argument – using developmentalism to ground it – was not accepted by Paul VI. Three days after the majority report was presented to the pope, a minority report, prepared by four clerical moral theologians on the commission, rejected these conclusions and recommended maintaining the prohibition on contraceptives, based on existing magisterial declarations affirming procreation as the primary end of marital intercourse.[54] Employing language that paraphrased the successionism of Vincent of Lérins, implicit in his maxim that Catholic teaching is that which has been believed always, everywhere and by everyone (*quod semper, quod ubique, quod ab omnibus creditum est*), the minority report warned that a change in church teaching on contraception would undermine the moral tradition of the church and the authority of the magisterium. Citing the historical survey found in Noonan's book, the minority report authors observed:

> History provides fullest evidence ... that the answer of the church has always and everywhere been the same, from the beginning up to the present decade. One can find no period of history, no document of the church, no theological school, scarcely one Catholic theologian, who ever denied that contraception was always seriously evil.[55]

The minority report stated that contraception is always intrinsically evil, 'because the Catholic church, instituted by Christ to

52 Clifford Longley, *The Worlock Archives* (London, 2000), 232; Robert McClory, *Turning Point: The Inside Story of the Papal Birth Control Commission* (New York, 1995), 99, 127.

53 McClory, *Turning Point*, 124.

54 Ibid. 129–37; Leslie Woodcock Tentler, *Catholics and Contraception: An American History* (Ithaca, NY, 2004), 227–8.

55 Robert G. Hoyt, ed., *The Birth Control Debate* (Kansas City, MO, 1968), 30.

show men a secure way to eternal life, could not have so wrongly erred during all those centuries of its history'.[56] Arguments from development, used in the majority report, were criticized[57] for failing to affirm the stability of natural law and for applying faulty reasoning to the data of history.[58] Expressing grave concerns about the implications for the magisterium's teaching authority on other moral issues if church teaching was altered, the minority report observed that many would conclude 'that the assistance of the Holy Spirit was lacking in her'.[59]

In 1966 an eager laity awaited news of a shift in Roman Catholic teaching on birth control. They waited another two years. In July 1968, Pope Paul VI ended the suspense and promulgated the encyclical *Humanae Vitae*. The pope rejected the majority report as 'unconvincing' and incorporated key elements of the minority report into his encyclical. Contraceptive use continued to be prohibited because the majority report had used criteria that 'departed from the moral teaching on marriage proposed with constant firmness by the teaching authority of the Church'.[60] The pope went further and stated: 'The pastors of the Church enjoy a special light of the Holy Spirit in teaching the truth. And this, rather than the arguments put forward, is why you are bound to such obedience.'[61]

The ensuing controversy is well known and need not be recounted here.[62] What is important to note for this study is that the minority report from the commission, *Humanae Vitae* itself, and subsequent studies of the commission's majority report made explicit reference to the developmental metanarrative and how it

---

[56] Ibid. 37.

[57] Ibid. 40–3.

[58] Ibid. 50–5.

[59] Ibid. 61.

[60] *Humanae Vitae*, §6, online at: <http://www.vatican.va/holy_father/paul_vi/encyclicals/documents/hf_p-vi_enc_25071968_humanae-vitae_en.html>, accessed 5 April 2012.

[61] Ibid., §28.

[62] For the best studies of this issue, see Robert Blair Kaise , *The Politics of Sex and Religion: A Case History in the Development, 1962–1984* (Kansıs City, MO, 1985); McClory, *Turning Point*; and, for an assessment after twenty years, John T. Noonan Jr, *Contraception: A History of its Treatment by Catholic Theologians and Canonists* (enlarged edn, Cambridge, MA, 1986), appendices.

clashed with the successionist metanarrative of the minority report and *Humanae Vitae*.[63]

In Robert Blair Kaiser's study of the period from 1962 to 1984, he described a pre-Vatican II church in which the issue of birth control seemed so settled that the subject did not even appear in the *postulata* (wishes for changes) submitted by bishops. He went on to observe: 'not more than four years later, a papal commission would urge that the pope change the church's traditional teaching on birth control'. Kaiser noted that Archbishop Heenan of Westminster, in the wake of the promulgation of *Humanae Vitae*, observed to a British journalist: 'It's too late'. He cited polls conducted in 1968 which showed that the vast majority of Roman Catholics of the North Atlantic nations already practised contraception, and did so with a clear conscience. Kaiser framed this experience of the 1960s debate as an extraordinary manifestation of doctrinal development. 'The process helped those privy to it see how changes in church practice, almost imperceptible in ages past, could unfold much faster in a mass mediated world.'[64]

My own analysis is rather different. The minority report and *Humanae Vitae* rightly criticized the majority report's appeal to the developmental metanarrative. As Noonan acknowledged and Kaiser later confirmed, what had 'developed' in ecclesial deliberations had taken less than a decade, rather than centuries. To use Acton's language, it was a 'renovation'. The recommendations did represent a departure from previous magisterial teaching – and significantly altered the received understanding of church teaching on contraception.

I would argue that they were in fact employing an argument that reflected an apperceptive metanarrative of the Christian past. Recent scientific innovations in birth control technologies had opened up new and effective means of managing reproductive decisions. An informed Roman Catholic laity struggled over how to reconcile their fidelity to magisterial teaching with their desire to use new and efficient forms of birth control. Cardinal Leo Joseph Suenens spoke directly to this point in his famous critique of *Humanae Vitae*

---

[63] Noonan's recent study treats this clash of successionism and developmentalism in more detail: John T. Noonan Jr, *A Church that Can and Cannot Change: The Development of Catholic Moral Teaching* (Notre Dame, IN, 2005).

[64] Kaiser, *Politics of Sex and Religion*, 5–7.

in 1968. He questioned whether moral theologians sufficiently accounted for scientific progress concerning 'what is according to nature'. He concluded: 'I beg you my brother bishops, let us avoid a new "Galileo affair." One is enough for the Church'.[65]

While Paul VI's successors have remained steadfast in their support of *Humanae Vitae*, the laity has largely disregarded this magisterial teaching. Is it, as Cardinal Suenens asserted, another Galileo moment in the history of Roman Catholicism? Has continuity been preserved and the integrity of Roman Catholic moral teaching been vindicated? Or is it too soon to say whether this doctrinal stance will not – or cannot – develop? What is clear – from the arguments of the minority report and the text of *Humanae Vitae* – is that church authorities shrank from employing developmentalism as the basis for alterations in church teaching on contraception, and reasserted successionism as the basis for defending Roman Catholic moral teaching in this matter.

THE ROLE OF WOMEN IN THE CHURCH

While John XXIII's *Pacem in Terris* and Vatican II's *Gaudium et Spes* addressed directly the heightened consciousness of women and their changing roles in society, the practice of the council did not reflect this heightened consciousness. Mary Daly described her own evaluation and judgment of this disparity in autobiographical reflections added in 1975 to the second edition of her book, *The Church and the Second Sex* (1968). She recounted her observation of a council session in this way:

> I saw in the distance a multitude of cardinals and bishops – old men in crimson dresses. In another section of the basilica were the 'auditors': a group which included a few Catholic women, mostly nuns in long black dresses with heads veiled. The contrast between the arrogant bearing and colorful attire of the 'princes of the church' and the humble, self-deprecating manner and somber clothing of the very few women was appalling. ... Although I did not grasp the full meaning of the scene all at once, its multileveled message burned its way deep into my consciousness.[66]

65 Peter Hebblethwaite, *Paul VI* (New York, 1993), 394.
66 Mary Daly, *The Church and the Second Sex* (New York, 1985), 10.

Daly acknowledged appreciatively the statements made by John XXIII and positions taken by the council. She noted that church authorities were aware of the heightened consciousness of women, and the need to promote equitable treatment of women and encourage their changing roles in society. However, she criticized the 'static world-view' of scholastic theology, which impeded these alterations: 'The frame of mind which it engenders is hardly open to theological development and social change'.[67] Daly's critique has been amplified over the decades, as generations of theologians have pursued the question of women's roles in the Roman Catholic Church. Employing an apperceptive metanarrative, Daly and others have argued for the need to correct past injustices and act on the heightened consciousness of this era. Among other issues, debates about the ordination of women to the priesthood have been vigorous and contentious.

Because controversy over the ordination of women mounted during the 1970s, 1980s and early 1990s, Pope John Paul II sought to clarify magisterial teaching in 1994. In his letter *Ordinatio Sacerdotalis*, the pope stated that he lacked authority to ordain women priests because Christ himself selected only men as apostles and the church, following Christ's example, had never ordained women. John Paul II concluded that this was to be 'definitively held by all the faithful.'[68] Joseph Ratzinger, then prefect of the Congregation for the Doctrine of the Faith, followed up with a *responsum ad dubium* (a formal request for clarification) in 1995 in which he used language suggestive of the successionist metanarrative as it had been expressed by Vincent of Lérins in the fifth century:

> This teaching requires definitive assent, since, founded on the written Word of God, and from the beginning constantly preserved and applied in the Tradition of the Church, it has been set forth infallibly by the ordinary and universal Magisterium … Thus, in the present circumstances, the Roman Pontiff, exercising his proper office of confirming the brethren (cf. Lk 22: 32), has handed on this same teaching by a formal

---

[67] Ibid. 118–46, 183.
[68] *Ordinatio Sacerdotalis*, §4, online at: <http://www.vatican.va/holy_father/john_paul_ii/apost_letters/documents/ hf_jp-ii_apl_22051994_ordinatio-sacerdotalis_en.html>, accessed 5 April 2012.

declaration, explicitly stating what is to be held always, everywhere, and by all, as belonging to the deposit of the faith.[69]

These documents did not have the desired result. Roman Catholic scholars have continued to explore the question of women's ordination, despite the efforts of John Paul II and Cardinal Ratzinger to bring a definitive end to the debate with magisterial declarations.

In *The Hidden History of Women's Ordination: Female Clergy in the Medieval West* (2007), Gary Macy, a Roman Catholic professor now at Santa Clara University, employed the supercessive metanarrative in a manner resembling *ressourcement* scholarship. He argued that a hidden – or rather a forgotten – tradition of ordaining women existed in the early medieval west. Macy stated: 'This study is concerned first and foremost with the historical question [of] whether women were ordained in the past, that is to say, whether they were considered ordained by their contemporaries according to the definition of ordination used at that time'.[70] Macy traced evidence of women's ordination in the medieval west, a practice that he documented from the sixth to the twelfth centuries. He found a shift in this practice in the twelfth and thirteenth centuries, and explored evidence of an emerging theological argument dating from that period that not only excluded women from ordination, but also asserted that women had never received ordination of any kind. Macy used historical evidence to demonstrate that a later theological tradition altered church practice. By reclaiming this historically grounded earlier tradition, theologians have argued for reform and renewal of ecclesial life – based on a recovered earlier tradition.

Here again a controverted theological question has been approached using three different historiographical metanarratives to argue in favour of, or against, the ordination of women. Those who argue from appercessionism – the heightened consciousness of the age – see in the Christian past much to censure in the treatment of women and the need to redress injustices that stretch back into the earliest centuries of Christianity. Pope John

---

[69] 'Responsum ad Dubium, Sacred Congregation for the Doctrine of the Faith October 28, 1995', online at: <http://www.newadvent.org/library/docs_df95os.htm>, accessed 5 April 2012.

[70] Gary Macy, *The Hidden History of Women's Ordination: Female Clergy in the Medieval West* (New York, 2007), 5.

Paul II and Cardinal Ratzinger based their magisterial teaching on successionism – claims to a constant and unbroken tradition of male ordinations since Christ appointed the apostles. Macy, while protesting that he is doing the work of a historian – and not arguing a theological position – nevertheless has used an approach that reflects the supercessionism employed by early twentieth-century *ressourcement* scholars.

What is of interest here is not whether the ordination of women would be a 'renovation', as Acton might have framed it, or the restoration of an earlier tradition, as *ressourcement* scholars might argue from the data of historical research, but whether there is room in Roman Catholic theological discourse for the apperceptive and supercessive metanarratives on this controverted subject. To date, church authorities have relied on the successionist metanarrative to defend the exclusion of women from priestly ordination. It remains to be seen whether Newman's appeal to the developmental metanarrative in 1871 might not apply to this contemporary Roman Catholic debate: 'Let us be patient, let us have faith, and a new Pope, and a re-assembled Council may trim the boat'.[71]

THE CASE OF POPE BENEDICT XVI

Pope Benedict XVI's own struggles to come to terms with these differences in his writings as a scholar, cardinal and pope illustrate this unresolved tension in Roman Catholic scholarship and authoritative teaching. Professor Joseph Ratzinger boldly stated in the opening pages of his *Introduction to Christianity* (1968) that Giovanni Battista Vico's argument against the static scholastic concept of truth, *verum est ens* ('being is truth'), and Vico's assertion that *verum quia factum* ('truth is what is made'), ended the apologetical power of the 'old metaphysics' and required Christians to think *historically* about their faith.[72] Thomas Aquinas was not mentioned anywhere in this book and Ratzinger notably did not appeal to natural theology as envisioned by Pius X's twenty-four Thomistic theses, which were intended to be foundational for all Roman Catholic theological discourse. In the post-Vatican II ethos of his publication, Ratzinger sought to wean his targeted student

---

71 Newman, *Letters and Diaries*, 25: 310.
72 Joseph Ratzinger, *Einführung in das Christentum* (Munich, 1968), 34–8; ET *Introduction to Christianity* (New York, 1969), 31–4.

audience away from the neo-scholasticism of the pre-conciliar era, and to reorient them towards a new apologetical strategy, which employed the council's emphasis on anthropology and the history of religions. This break with pre-conciliar norms of Roman Catholic thought is striking and suggests respect for historical-critical approaches to understanding the faith that are incompatible with the successionist metanarrative of neo-scholasticism.[73]

Professor Ratzinger's critique of successionism was even more incisive in his 1969 commentary on *Dei Verbum*, the Dogmatic Constitution on Divine Revelation. After reviewing the conciliar debate over Vincent of Lérins' text − which Trent and Vatican I had canonized in their documents − Ratzinger explained why *Dei Verbum* had excluded it. He noted that Vincent's text 'no longer appears as an authentic representative of the Catholic idea of tradition'. He went on to observe: 'Vincent of Lérins' static *semper* no longer seems the right way of expressing this problem.' In an analysis that suggests an embrace of appercessionism − at least with reference to the rise of historical consciousness − Ratzinger stated that our 'new orientation simply expresses our deeper knowledge of the problem of historical understanding, which is no longer adequately expressed by the simple idea of a given fact and its explanation'.[74]

In 1982, a year after he became prefect of the Congregation for the Doctrine of the Faith, Cardinal Ratzinger published a refashioned version of his 1969 work *Theologische Prinzipienlehre* (Principles of Catholic Theology). In it he contrasted Martin Luther's *Heilsgeschichte* ('salvation-history'), which he concluded was characterized by 'discontinuity', with earlier understandings of the continuity of Christian history. Apostolic succession was the safeguard of this continuity. While seeking an alternative vision of history that might affirm the principle of historical continuity which he valued, Ratzinger condemned the political theology of scholars such as Johann Baptist Metz. Their approach, he argued, marked a new form of discontinuity, which focused salvation on the future, 'hope' and 'the work to be done'. In Ratzinger's assessment, these political theologians rejected the past and suspended

---

[73] Kerr, *Twentieth-Century Catholic Theologians*, 190–1.
[74] Herbert Vorgrimler, ed., *Commentary on the Documents of Vatican II*, 4 vols (New York, 1969), 3: 187–8.

'all reference to tradition'. For him, their way of 'thinking "historically" becomes thinking anti-historically'.[75]

While the cardinal affirmed the priority of a historicized tradition, his vision of a 'historical' tradition necessarily served the apologetics of continuity and eschewed contemporary critiques of church tradition that might require change or departure from previous magisterial teaching. Yet his own 1969 rejection of the Vincentian canon, despite its enshrinement at Trent and Vatican I, suggests that he himself had engaged in similar exercises of critique and correction of previous expressions of Catholic tradition. Whether this example is characterized as a developmental or apperceptive argument, Ratzinger's apparent rejection of successionism is a striking departure from the metanarrative reflected in the Anti-Modernist Oath he had taken as a priest and professor.

In 1986, in an article on the ecclesiology of Vatican II, Ratzinger praised Newman's concept of development, described it as one of the 'decisive and fundamental concepts of Catholicism' and noted that Vatican II 'had the merit of having formulated it for the first time in a solemn magisterial document'. He criticized those who clung to a literal test of Scripture or patristic teaching for banishing Christ to the past, and characterized their practice as 'either an entirely sterile faith that has nothing to say to the present, or an arbitrary act that skips over two thousand years of history, throwing them into the waste-bin of failures'.[76] This striking endorsement of developmentalism, and critique of successionism and certain applications of the supercessionist metanarrative, suggest that the cardinal had appropriated the developmental metanarrative as a middle way which could maintain the principle of continuity that he valued. Yet it also suggests something new – a change in church teaching that critiqued previously revered assumptions about authentic church teaching. As the first twentieth-century prefect of the Congregation for the Doctrine of the Faith who was not a doctrinaire neo-scholastic theologian, his critique could be read as a repudiation of views cherished by his predecessors. Acton might have called this a 'renovation', or the grafting of a new and heightened consciousness into the intellectual life of the Catholic

---

75 Joseph Ratzinger, *Principles of Catholic Theology* (San Francisco, CA, 1987), 159.
76 Joseph Ratzinger, 'The Ecclesiology of the Second Vatican Council', *Communio* 13 (1986), 239–52, at 241–2.

Church. Alternatively, Newman could justifiably have regarded it as a final vindication of his theory of development.

In December 2005 Pope Benedict XVI delivered his first Christmas address and confronted directly the struggle over the historical legacy of the Second Vatican Council. He described two interpretative models at work: the 'hermeneutic of discontinuity and rupture' and the 'hermeneutic of reform'. The pope explained that the first had 'availed itself of the sympathies of the mass media, and also one trend of modern theology'. The latter hermeneutic − where applied − had borne new life and new fruit, and achieved 'renewal in the continuity of the ... Church which the Lord has given to us'. Employing explicitly the language of development, he noted that the council had focused on anthropology, and had as its agenda 'to determine in a new way the relationship between the Church and the modern era'.

Briefly recounting the church's struggle with modernity, starting with Galileo, Benedict acknowledged that by the 1960s it was necessary to engage with the modern era in new ways. One key element of this engagement involved redefining 'the relationship between faith and modern science'. He stressed that this did not simply refer to the natural sciences but also to 'historical science for, in a certain school, the historical-critical method claimed to have the last word on the interpretation of the Bible and, demanding total exclusivity for its interpretation of Sacred Scripture, was opposed to important points in the interpretation elaborated by the faith of the Church'. While acknowledging that documents produced during the second half of the council might suggest − and even affirm − discontinuity with the past, Benedict nevertheless explained that after 'the various distinctions between concrete historical situations and their requirements had been made, the continuity of principles proved not to have been abandoned'. Strikingly the pope made observations that resonate with the developmental claims of the majority report on birth control in 1966, and resemble apperceptive assumptions articulated by Mary Daly and other feminist theologians:

> It is precisely in this combination of continuity and discontinuity at different levels that the very nature of true reform consists. In this process of innovation in continuity we must learn to understand more practically than before that the Church's decisions on contingent matters − for example,

certain practical forms of liberalism or a free interpretation of the Bible – should necessarily be contingent themselves, precisely because they refer to a specific reality that is change-able in itself.[77]

Acknowledging the necessary discontinuity in historically contingent matters is a crucial step toward reconciling the diver-gent metanarratives used in Roman Catholic discourse. Like Ratzinger's affirmation in 1969 of the heightened historical consciousness of twentieth-century Catholics, it appears to leave room for the supercessive, developmental and apperceptive metan-arratives to play a role in Roman Catholic scholarship and author-itative teaching. The documents of Vatican II seem to support this conclusion. The only metanarrative that historical contingency appears to exclude is successionism.

CONCLUSION

Leo XIII opened the Vatican Archives in 1879, and the palaeo-graphical school attached to it adopted a motto endorsed by him: *Nihil est quod ecclesiae ab inquisitione veri metuatur* ('The church has nothing to fear from the quest for truth').[78] John Paul II reaffirmed this pontifical conclusion in 1999. During his noteworthy apology for the execution of Jan Hus in 1415 the pope stated: 'Faith has nothing to fear from historical research.'[79] Yet Roman Catholic experience in the twentieth and twenty-first centuries demon-strates that this is an eschatological hope rather than a settled reality. The root cause is not the data of historical research, but the conflicting metanarratives applied to the data. Acknowledging shared – and divergent – historiographical assumptions about the Christian past is a crucial starting point for dialogue about contro-verted matters. While overt acknowledgement of these historio-

77 Benedict XVI, 'Address of His Holiness Benedict XVI to the Roman Curia, 22 December 2005', online at: <http://www.vatican.va/holy_father/benedict_xvi/speeches/2005/december/documents/hf_ben_xvi_spe_20051222_roman-curia_en.html>, accessed 5 April 2012.
78 Owen Chadwick, *Catholicism and History: The Opening of the Vatican Archives* (Cambridge, 1978), 143.
79 John Paul II, 'Address of the Holy Father to a Symposium on John Hus, 17 December 1999', online at: <http://www.vatican.va/holy_father/john_paul_ii/speeches/1999/december/documents/hf_jp-ii_spe_17121999_jan-hus_en.html>, accessed 5 April 2012.

graphical differences will not resolve tensions, it is a step towards recognizing that – despite differing understandings of the Christian past – there is a shared love for the Roman Catholic Church.

In 1846 Philip Schaff concluded: 'Romanism cannot give up the principle of stability, without unsettling its own foundations.'[80] Cardinal Alfredo Ottaviani, whose coat of arms bore the motto, *Semper Idem* ('Always the Same'), strove in vain to retain that principle in documents of the Second Vatican Council. Instead, young theologians such as Joseph Ratzinger embraced the need for a historicized understanding of tradition and acknowledged a vital role for historical research in theological discourse.

While this apperceptive – or developmental – incorporation of historical consciousness into the Roman Catholic dogmatic tradition was enshrined in documents of Vatican II, the council left unresolved the diversity of historiographical metanarratives used by Roman Catholic theologians and church authorities. Indeed, in the two post-Vatican II examples presented here, church authorities maintained the successionist metanarrative in defence of nineteenth- and twentieth-century magisterial teaching, rejecting arguments to alter church teaching based on one or more of the other historiographical metanarratives.

Although the young Joseph Ratzinger's theological imagination was nurtured by *ressourcement* scholarship, and his writings as prefect of the Congregation for the Doctrine of the Faith extolled the developmental metanarrative as a 'fundamental concept of Catholicism', his 2005 pontifical statement leaves open to interpretation the application of these metanarratives in theological discourse. The pope's experience and writings mirror the complexity of this issue for Roman Catholic scholars and church authorities. Recognizing and naming the metanarratives at work in Roman Catholic theological debates is a place to start. To face without fear the need to re-vision the Christian past in order to re-source the future study of Christian truth-claims may be an eschatological hope, but for Roman Catholics it is a work that must be done.

Saint Louis University

---

[80] Philip Schaff, *What is Church History? A Vindication of the Idea of Historical Development* (Philadelphia, PA, 1846), 47n.

THE DEVELOPMENT OF G. G. COULTON'S CRITIQUE OF A ROMAN CATHOLIC SCHOOL OF HISTORY

by ALEC CORIO

Coulton tells the Cambridge youth
That Roman Catholics doctor truth:
While Abbot Aidan Gasquet cries:
Your English History's packed with lies![1]

This essay focuses on the polemical historical writing of G. G. Coulton (1858–1947), chiefly his attacks on Francis Aidan Gasquet (1846–1929), whom he believed was the leading member of a mendacious and well-organized Roman Catholic school of history.[2] Apart from the personal animosity which grew up between them as a result of Coulton's aggressive attitude, this was an ideological and historiographical conflict between the progressive values of an agnostic Anglican priest turned Cambridge academic and the romanticized medievalism of an English Benedictine who was eventually elevated to the rank of cardinal. Coulton accused Gasquet of falsely appropriating the authority of 'scientific' history to advance the position of the contemporary Roman Catholic Church in England, and of using the rhetoric of primary source research to sweeten the lies he told about the glories of the pre-Reformation church. Gasquet never openly answered Coulton, but the fact that he did not correct or modify his conclusions, and the manner in which Roman Catholic writers defended them, led Coulton to believe that the spirit of the Roman Catholic Church itself was opposed to historical accuracy. The growing influence of Gasquet's views over academic and popular constructions of the

---

[1]   'Cambridge Squib', quoted in Shane Leslie, *Cardinal Gasquet: A Memoir* (London, 1953), 103.

[2]   Other studies of the conflict between Coulton and Gasquet include Gerald Christianson, 'G. G. Coulton: The Medieval Historian as Controversialist', *CathHR* 57 (1971), 421–41; David Knowles, *Cardinal Gasquet as an Historian* (London, 1956); idem, *The Historian and Character*, ed. Christopher Brooke and Giles Constable (Cambridge, 1963), 240–63; Leslie, *Gasquet*, 103–34; Michael Bentley, *Modernizing England's Past* (Cambridge, 2005), 59–60.

national past also suggested to Coulton that England was willing to be deceived about the trustworthiness of the methods underlying historical research, and the importance of its Reformation heritage. Coulton initially criticized Gasquet and then castigated Roman Catholicism in increasingly strident publications, and suggested radical changes to the way that historical debate should be conducted and adjudicated, in order to defend his understanding of the Reformation's commitment to truth, crystallized in his rigid adherence to empirical primary source research. A study of this inter-religious polemic demonstrates the influence of the idea of 'scientific' historical authority over the religious thought of the early twentieth century and on understandings of the place of the Roman Catholic Church in English society. It also deepens our knowledge of how the boundaries of the increasingly professionalized historical discipline were defended at the intersection of intellectual and popular culture.

In the late nineteenth and early twentieth centuries, Protestants and Roman Catholics alike tried to substantiate the claim that their confession embodied virtue and continuity – and therefore deserved to exercise public influence – by creating exclusionary narratives of the nation's past. Polemical historical writers attempted to define the nation in terms of a characteristic confessional spirit, either Catholic or Protestant, which had historically expressed the true essence of England. Some also adopted the impressive scholarly authority of the new discipline of 'scientific' history, claiming the inspiration of Leopold von Ranke, to support these constructed pasts.[3] Gasquet was the first Roman Catholic writer to do this successfully, gathering a wide constituency of non-Catholic readers. Gasquet's claims challenged the Protestant teleology of England's past, which for three hundred years had dominated the nation's cultural identity.[4] In the opinion of an American student writing in 1920, Gasquet's historical work

---

[3]   On the nationalizing authority of 'scientific' history, see Georg G. Iggers, *Historiography in the Twentieth Century: From Scientific Objectivity to the Postmodern Challenge* (Middletown, CT, 1997), 23–30; idem, 'Nationalism and Historiography, 1789–1996: The German Example in Historical Perspective', in Stefan Berger et al., eds, *Writing National Histories: Western Europe since 1800* (London, 1999), 15–29, at 19.

[4]   Persuasively argued in D. Hempton, *Religion and Political Culture in Britain and Ireland: From the Glorious Revolution to the Decline of Empire* (Cambridge, 1996), 176–7.

... has helped to remove from the minds of the conventional those many prejudices which barred the English people from doing justice to the Catholic Church. His work on the Pre-Reformation period has done more than that of any one man to bring the Catholic tradition of history before the attention of the public.[5]

Gasquet's positive portrayal of pre-Reformation life was adopted with enthusiasm by Roman Catholics, especially popular writers such as Hilaire Belloc and G. K. Chesterton. It was also influential in shaping later scholarship in the field of late medieval history.[6] Gasquet's major works all argued that the pre-Reformation church had offered holiness and hope to the English people, and that the Reformation was not a consequence of monastic depravity, overweening papal authority or the discovery of biblical truth. Nor was it the basis of England's future greatness. He claimed that substantial primary source research supported his understanding of the beneficial role of the medieval English church in society, and implied that both the true essence of England and the spirit of 'scientific' historical enquiry found their fulfilment in the modern Roman Catholic Church.

Gasquet's first monograph, *Henry VIII and the English Monasteries,* set out to convince his readers of his 'scientific' credentials by denouncing the 'historical romances' of the best-known historian of Tudor England, J. A. Froude.[7] Gasquet claimed that, instead of exercising his creative faculties like Froude,

> the facts speak strongly enough for themselves, and I have endeavoured to add as little as possible of my own to the story they tell. All I desire is that my readers should judge from the letters, documents and opinions, which will be found in the following pages, whether bare justice has hitherto been done to the memory of the monastic order in England.[8]

---

[5]   J. Lloyd Mecham, *An Evaluation of the Work of Cardinal Gasquet in the Field of Pre-Reformation History* (Berkeley, CA, 1920), 15–16.

[6]   Knowles, *Historian and Character*, 259, 262.

[7]   Francis Aidan Gasquet, *Henry VIII and the English Monasteries*, 2 vols (London, 1888–9), 1: 290.

[8]   Ibid. 1: xi. Gasquet's claim simply to present archival material to show the truth of the past was a conscious attempt to identify himself with the 'scientific' movement in history categorized as modernism by Bentley, *Modernizing England's Past*, 11–13.

Gasquet's claim to embody 'scientific' detachment was at the heart of his work's appeal and influence: 'Newspapers of all ranks and shades of opinion – secular and religious, daily and weekly, Protestant and Catholic – have conspired to speak highly not merely of the author's patience in research, his skill in grouping facts, and the finish of his literary style, but of his strict historical impartiality.'[9] His collaborator, Edmund Bishop, believed that 'no book has appeared of late years by a Catholic, or any other than Cardinal Newman's, which has found access among Protestants – like Fr Gasquet's; it is the good temper, the candour, the fairness that strikes everyone'.[10]

Gasquet argued that a plain reading of facts culled from the archives demonstrated the continuity of the Roman Catholic Church's mission in England, and that Catholic and English civilization had reached a high point in the glories of a pre-Reformation 'Age of Faith', when 'Religion overflowed, as it were, into popular life, and helped to sanctify human interests ... [and] was to the English people as the bloom upon the choicest fruit'.[11] He maintained that the Reformation had been carried out by the rich for their own selfish ends, and as a result of the deprivation of the church the commonwealth had suffered:

> [Viewing] the innumerable miseries entailed upon successive generations by that wholesale appropriation of the property of the Church and the poor ... it is impossible not to see in the spoliation and destruction of the monasteries the fount and origin of many of those appalling sores in the body of the nation ... the sacred heritage of the English poor was eaten up by the house of Tudor.[12]

By attempting to show how Roman Catholicism had underpinned the most cherished institutions of English history, and had maintained a charitable civil order from which present social conditions were a tragic decline, Gasquet implied that the Roman Catholic Church, particularly in its heritage of monasteries and guilds, embodied ancient virtues which could again benefit the national community. Gasquet's portrait of the Middle Ages was a historical

---

9   'Literary Notices', *The Liverpool Mercury*, 20 June 1888, 7.
10 Nigel Abercrombie, *The Life and Work of Edmund Bishop* (London, 1959), 146.
11 F. A. Gasquet, *The Eve of the Reformation* (London, 1919; first publ. 1900), 285.
12 Gasquet, *Henry VIII*, 1: 493–4.

apologetic, which aimed to persuade modern England to embrace the enduring merits of the Roman Catholic Church. Through Hilaire Belloc's political writings, Gasquet's medieval manifesto for social justice influenced the policies of the Liberal Party, and was arguably the unifying principle of the English Roman Catholic community in the inter-war period.[13]

Coulton's attacks on Gasquet were motivated initially by a desire to expose the inaccuracies of Gasquet's scholarship, and to demonstrate that Gasquet had adopted the rhetoric of primary source research to dignify incompetent and biased work. When Coulton noticed apparent errors in Gasquet's publications, he wrote to ask him for details of the sources he had used. Receiving no reply, Coulton searched through Gasquet's footnotes and found them to be surprisingly lacking in manuscript references.[14] Coulton also accused Gasquet of not having the basic skills necessary for historical research: 'The Cardinal has betrayed, at different times, an ignorance of Latin, and of the Vulgate in especial [*sic*], almost as startling as his inaccuracies in matters of fact ... In this he follows the modern traditions of his Church'.[15] He believed that Gasquet misunderstood and misused the evidence he cited, and that he concentrated on anachronistic and irrelevant material that could be twisted to meet his purposes: 'these are documents on which Dr. Gasquet lays special stress, to the exclusion ... of the most definite and irrefragable evidence ... It is not enough for him to build upon such worthless hole-and-corner documents; but he must also misread them in order to get the results he needs!'[16] In response to the continued publication of Gasquet's error-laden texts and his powerful position within the Roman Catholic Church, and because of his increasing influence over academic and popular ideas of medieval history, Coulton decided to expose Gasquet's weaknesses in print. From 1905 to 1937, eight years after Gasquet's death, Coulton published controversial works

---

[13] On Belloc's distributionism, but not Gasquet's influence on it, see James R. Lothian, *The Making and Unmaking of the English Catholic Intellectual Community, 1910–1950* (Notre Dame, IN, 2009), 54, 70, 122–7.

[14] G. G. Coulton, *Medieval Studies No. 1: The Monastic Legend: A Criticism of Abbot Gasquet's 'Henry VIII and the English Monasteries'* (London, 1905), 2.

[15] Coulton, *Medieval Studies No. 14: The Roman Catholic Church and the Bible* (London, 1921), 23.

[16] Coulton, *Medieval Studies No. 1*, 11.

which accused Gasquet, and what he eventually came to believe was a Roman Catholic school of history, of 'disparag[ing] modern civilization in comparison with a purely imaginative and unhistorical idea of medieval life', in order to increase the prestige of the contemporary Roman Catholic Church in England.[17] Coulton saw the 'immoral principles' of Roman Catholicism revealed by this manipulation of history.[18]

Gasquet avoided any direct confrontation with 'the modern malleus monachorum'.[19] According to Ethelbert Horne, 'the Cardinal always held Coulton in contempt, & would never notice anything he said as he was too low down in his methods ... The [Downside] community have never cared to defend the Cardinal's memory, as they knew he would not wish it, seeing he always despised Coulton as an historian'.[20] In 1906, Gasquet did disparagingly mention a 'literary chiffonier' in the preface to a new edition of *Henry VIII and the English Monasteries*.[21] Coulton believed this was a reference to him, '(in the French of Stratford attë Bowe,) as a literary ragman'.[22] The dismissal of his wide familiarity with primary sources, in terms that suggested he gathered unrepresentative scraps and passed them off as true history, enraged Coulton, since this was what he believed Gasquet and his imitators were doing. Coulton provided factual evidence for accusing Gasquet of misusing the documents he had looked at: as an appendix to *Ten Medieval Studies*, he printed a fifty-eight page 'rough list of Misstatements and Blunders in Cardinal Gasquet's writings'.[23] Gasquet's refusal to correct or to justify these mistakes led Coulton to conclude that he knew of the weaknesses in his work, and kept silent to avoid exposure.

When Gasquet admitted that he had made an occasional error, such as lending his support to J. B. Mackinlay's contention that St Edmund's bones had been transferred to Toulouse before the

---

[17] Ibid., title verso.

[18] G. G. Coulton, *Medieval Studies No. 17: Roman Catholic Truth: An Open Discussion* (London, 1924), 48.

[19] London, Archives of the English Province, Society of Jesus, Thurston Papers, 39.3.5.5, Letter from David Knowles, 15 November 1937.

[20] Ibid., Ethelbert Horne to Thurston, 3 November 1938.

[21] Gasquet, *Henry VIII*, viii.

[22] G. G. Coulton, *Medieval Studies No. 6: The Truth about the Monasteries* (London, 1906), 16.

[23] G. G. Coulton, *Ten Medieval Studies* (Cambridge, 1930), 203–61.

destruction of the shrine at Bury St Edmunds, Coulton thought this was hardly good enough.[24] He believed Gasquet had always known that the bones which were intended to be installed in Westminster Cathedral could not have belonged to Edmund, but had wanted to support the foundation of a cult centred on misattributed relics. Coulton thought that Gasquet had concealed the truth until refusing to admit his mistake would have damaged his reputation and that of his church even further. This period of 'eight years' silence encouraged his co-religionaries to climb to that height of self-deception from which they so suddenly fell'.[25] Gasquet's theories about the orthodoxy of the pre-Reformation Bible had likewise been debunked by a series of scholars; however, he persisted in them. Coulton viewed this maintenance of error as pragmatic deceit, 'a stage of impenitence at which what was mere mis-statement must be christened *falsehood*, and a still further stage of hardened deliberation when the only fitting word is *lie*'.[26]

Coulton argued, in contrast to Gasquet's view, that primary sources clearly demonstrated that the Middle Ages had been a time of deprivation and general gloominess. He believed that the repression of the church had stifled individual and national potential. Coulton's sympathies were engaged only by those exceptional men and women who had struggled against the 'dead weight of tradition'.[27] He saw them as precursors to our age, in which freedom from ecclesiastical authority might allow godliness to flourish:

> ... the development of mankind since the Reformation ... is part of a world-process to which we must do homage. And we shall best and most sympathetically study our ancestors of the Middle Ages ... if we regard them not as men who enjoyed higher privileges which they were unable to transmit to us,

---

[24] J. B. Mackinlay, *Saint Edmund, King and Martyr: A History of his Life and Times, with an Account of the Translations of his Incorrupt Body* (London, 1893). Coulton dealt imaginatively with the controversy in his time-travelling fantasia, *Friar's Lantern* (London, 1906), 80–7.

[25] Coulton, *Medieval Studies No. 14*, 8.

[26] G. G. Coulton, *Fourscore Years* (London, 1945), 332.

[27] G. G. Coulton, *Five Centuries of Religion*, 2: *The Friars and the Dead Weight of Tradition* (Cambridge, 1927).

but as men who struggled hard to become what we (if only we will) may be.[28]

This progressivism was remarked on in Coulton's lifetime. Alfred H. Sweet commented: 'He is firmly convinced that things modern are better than things medieval, and the dark colours in which he paints the past are applied ... that there may stand out in sharper contrast the advantages of the luminous present'.[29] If anything, Sweet's assessment underrates Coulton's condemnation of the Middle Ages. Gerald Christianson's more recent claim that Coulton was a Cartesian, a pure intellect who judged the past solely on the basis of what he found while weighing primary sources, also underestimates the importance of Coulton's progressivism as a religious impulse.[30] This was rarely explicitly articulated in his work, because in argument he preferred to concentrate on the discussion of primary source material rather than abstract concepts. However, Coulton undoubtedly understood that a 'scientific' approach to the pursuit of truth was justified by its recognition of transcendent values in the past, and in the process of studying the past. This was his religious object. Coulton feared that the idealization of a medieval utopia and a return to Roman Catholic values would stifle the increase of intellectual liberty and limit humanity's potential for spiritual growth. In addition, Coulton believed that maintaining historical error was sinful; openness to criticism and the correction of error was the path to God. If Coulton seemed *'pitiless toward certain errors, it is because these are still unblushingly defended.* According to my creed, this world and the next belong not to those who have never blundered but to those who can repent and amend'.[31] He believed that polemical historical debate was a valuable spur to

---

[28] G. G. Coulton, *Medieval Studies No. 13: The Plain Man's Religion in the Middle Ages* (London, 1916), 12.

[29] Alfred H. Sweet, 'Coulton as an Interpreter of the Middle Ages', *The Historian* 2 (1939), 28–40, at 34. This article was originally submitted to the Jesuit journal *Thought*, which refused publication after contacting Herbert Thurston: Thurston Papers, 39.3.5.5, Letter from Samuel K. Wilson (president of Loyola University, Chicago, IL), 29 March 1937.

[30] Christianson, 'G. G. Coulton: The Medieval Historian as Controversialist', 427, 436, 439. On Coulton's view of justice and providence, see G. G. Coulton, *Medieval Studies No. 19: Mr Hilaire Belloc as Historian* (London, 1930), 3–5.

[31] G. G. Coulton, *Medieval Studies No. 15: More Roman Catholic History* (London, 1921), 14.

repentance, and part of the search for truth. Through the 'scientific' process, in Coulton's view, humanity grew toward a closer union with the Creator.

Coulton's attacks on Gasquet's historical reputation were rebutted, chiefly by Herbert Thurston, Hilaire Belloc and G. K. Chesterton, on the grounds that Coulton was prejudiced against Roman Catholics, and that this prevented him from seeing that Gasquet's historical work rested on sound documentary foundations and offered an accurate interpretation of England's Catholic past. Coulton unconvincingly dismissed this accusation by referring to the Roman Catholic students who freely attended his classes in Cambridge.[32] Coulton's talent for discovering medieval sources was also turned against him in the press: it was suggested that the extensive material Coulton printed as proof of the cruelty of medieval society could have been discovered only by searching desperately for evidence against Gasquet's views.[33] This criticism was echoed by non-partisan and established academics, who believed that Coulton's method of collecting huge numbers of extracts from disparate primary sources showed a lack of moderation which was far from 'scientific': 'the crushing accumulation of more than a hundred pages of hostile citation … tend[s] to defeat his own purpose … The reader will be provoked into thinking that a great institution … can never have deserved, or received, so universal a condemnation'.[34] Thurston suggested that these attempts to argue his opponents into silence were a polemical proof of Coulton's inveterate anti-Catholicism: when Coulton was losing a debate he shifted his ground to discuss another manuscript, in order to continue his attacks on the Roman Catholic Church.[35] Coulton's response to Thurston acknowledged the Jesuit's own talents for controversy: 'My only "shifts" have been that, standing always on that ground, I have faced squarely in turn every fresh excuse of his, and thus boxed the whole compass'.[36]

---

[32] Coulton, *Medieval Studies No. 19*, 9.

[33] G. G. Coulton, *The Scandal of Cardinal Gasquet* (Taunton, 1937), 3, quoting James Patrick Broderick.

[34] E. W. Watson, Review of *Five Centuries of Religion*, *EHR* 43 (1928), 621–3, at 623.

[35] Thurston Papers, 39.3.5.5, undated copy of letter to the editor of the *Western Morning News*.

[36] Ibid., Newspaper clipping, 'Letters', *Western Morning News and Mercury*, 13 July, no year marked.

Coulton's claim that Gasquet represented a Roman Catholic school of history whose members defended Gasquet's conclusions to 'avoid a shock to their paper currency' was based on his observation of Gasquet's influence despite his inaccuracies.[37] The experience of meeting the unscholarly yet subtle Thurston, Belloc and Chesterton in debate convinced Coulton that the Roman Catholic hierarchy had decided to defend Gasquet in order to maintain the reputation that his publications had gained for their church, but they knew they could not do so on truly 'scientific' historical grounds. Coulton accused Belloc of affecting ignorance of the true facts of history when it was convenient, and attributed his 'impenitent maintenance of exploded error' to 'the slippery slope upon which many so-called Catholic things stand, and which often tempts, little by little, to liberties which the historian would not dream of taking in commercial life or at a game of cards'.[38] Coulton came to believe that this attitude was inculcated by the structures of the Roman Catholic Church. His knowledge of papal pronouncements on the dogmatic limitations to be placed on historians, the censorship of respected scholars, and the condemnation of the Vatican's approach to history by Lord Acton and Cardinal Newman, all led him to the conclusion that the Roman Catholic Church wanted to limit the scope of historical studies so that they only served a propagandistic purpose:[39]

> ... in this totalitarian religious State, an atmosphere is created not merely sectarian, but even ultra-sectarian, practically parochial. Inside the vast world-domain of History in general, Leo XIII marks out this fenced-off park of Roman Catholic History ... There is no other religious organisation in the world which shows, in the very highest places, such frequent

37 G. G. Coulton, *Sectarian History* (Taunton, 1937), 7.
38 Coulton, *Medieval Studies No. 19*, 7; idem, *Sectarian History*, 13; idem, *Scandal*, 6.
39 Coulton frequently cited Leo XIII's letter on the education of the clergy, *Depuis le Jour* (Rome, 1899), which called for greater scientific and historical training of clergy, within limits, as 'a magnificent and conclusive demonstration of the truth and divinity of Christianity': online at <http://www.vatican.va/holy_father/leo_xiii/encyclicals/documents/hf_l–xiii_enc_08091899_depuis–le–jour_en.html>, accessed 5 January 2012; he also quoted Acton's criticisms of papal infallibility and Newman's statement that to be a good Roman Catholic one must doctor truth: G. G. Coulton, *Romanism and Truth* (London, 1930), 7–8, 9, 10.

and serious historical error and, too often, such blind impenitence.[40]

There were two potential consequences, Coulton believed, if
the 'bad ingrained tradition' of Roman Catholic historiography
was not checked by credible 'scientific' historians.[41] The Roman
Catholic attitude to historical truth might confine Roman Catholics in England to an intellectual ghetto.[42] It would certainly limit
their capacity for spiritual growth. Alternatively, the advocacy of
the Roman Catholic historical school might convert the wider
population, first to the idealization of a false past, and perhaps then
to a false religion. Coulton felt that the influence of the Roman
Catholic Church was insidious: '"Rome as unreformed" still
poisons truth at source; still maintains punitive theories immoral in
principle ... She *acted* immorally while she could; impotent now,
she still *asserts* immoral principles'.[43] Coulton's polemical writings asserted what he believed to be true about the past, and true
history, more importantly, served a moral cause in which he deeply
believed. To establish defensible boundaries against false historical
claims, in 1932 Coulton suggested that the British Academy should
establish tribunals to adjudicate on disputed historical facts. This
was a revolutionary and rather authoritarian development in the
way that historians might think about validating their scholarship
and enforcing its liberal credentials:[44]

Here in this island, we are most favourably situated to understand and to judge, for in our Established Church one man
may be practically a Roman Catholic, another practically a
Unitarian, and neither, fortunately, able entirely to eliminate

---

[40] Coulton, *Sectarian History*, 61.

[41] Coulton, *Scandal*, 6.

[42] Ibid. 6, 7. Coulton thought that their immorality justified the legal supervision
of Roman Catholic clergy. Only in 'Protestant countries' and 'under a system of law
and police such as no man even dreamt of in the Middle Ages' did they observe a pure
life: Coulton, *Medieval Studies No. 6*, 12. On the regulation of monasteries in Victorian
England, see Walter L. Arnstein, *Protestant versus Catholic in Mid-Victorian England: Mr.
Newdegate and the Nuns* (Columbia, MO, 1982).

[43] Coulton, *Medieval Studies No. 17*, 48.

[44] Coulton's suggestion was also an aggressive development of the value which the
historical profession had begun to place on collaborative works of historical scholarship, such as the *Cambridge Modern History*, through which the collective purpose and
credibility of the historical community was asserted.

the other. Do we not therefore bear ... responsibility for maintaining the moral currency in history ... ?[45]

Ironically, the recent historiography of the Reformation period has been based on the kind of methodological grasp shown by Coulton, but its conclusions about medieval religion and social stability are closer to those drawn by Gasquet: there is an eirenic consensus that the pre-Reformation church in England, though imperfect, was active and well loved.[46] Yet the historical profession has largely forgotten both the antagonists of this study. Their legacies are entrenched in the techniques and foci of medieval research, but their rhetoric and aspiration to 'scientific' authority resting on technical expertise, indeed the historical profession's claim to possess any absolute narrative authority, have long been abandoned. This study has focused on a period when the authority of 'scientific' historical scholarship was assumed, but its ownership was disputed by Roman Catholics, keen to return their church to a fuller place in the nation's public life, and liberal progressives, alarmed by the authoritarian associations of Roman Catholicism. As the natural affection of Roman Catholic historical writers for an age before their church had been libelled and suppressed became increasingly influential, Coulton felt compelled to 'emphasise even to weariness the damning evidence' that he perceived existed against the Roman Catholic Church.[47] The polemical conflict between Coulton and Gasquet's defenders was not simply epistemological, focusing on the difficulties of writing about religion and historical authority; it exposed societal anxiety over the

---

[45] G. G. Coulton, 'Some Problems in Medieval Historiography', *PBA* 18 (1932), 155–90, at 172.

[46] The 'revisionism' of J. J. Scarisbrick and Eamon Duffy now sets the tone for the historiography of the late medieval church, notwithstanding the criticism of some of Duffy's conclusions by Ethan Shagan. Generally speaking, contemporary writers on the pre-Reformation church emphasize its strength rather than its vulnerability, which creates obvious difficulties in explaining the eventual popularity of Protestantism in England. They also focus on the importance of lay devotion and the parish, rather than – as Gasquet did – viewing monasticism as the fullest expression of Catholic Christianity. However, the use of parish records, sermons and visitation reports to trace the reception of religious instruction among the laity, and the vibrancy of their devotional lives, utilizes archival sources whose investigation was pioneered by both Gasquet and Coulton. See in this volume, Dairmaid MacCulloch, 'Changing Historical Perspectives on the English Reformation: The Last Fifty Years', 282–302

[47] Coulton, *Medieval Studies No. 6*, 19.

decline of the Anglican confessional state and a newly assertive spirit in Roman Catholicism. By arguing for the value of continuity between medieval and modern ideals, Gasquet struck at the foundations of both the Anglican hegemony and Coulton's beliefs in progress in history. There was an irreconcilable conflict between the Roman Catholic romanticization of 'the Age of Faith' and Coulton's progressive teleology.

The Open University

MONEY MATTERS: THE NEGLECT OF FINANCE IN THE HISTORIOGRAPHY OF MODERN CHRISTIANITY

by SARAH FLEW

The subject of religion and finance is seriously neglected within the historiography of the church during the modern period. This essay explores the pioneering 'Financing of American Religion' project and suggests possible fruitful avenues of research into the financing of British religion. By way of a case study, it analyses the size of the religious voluntary sector as a whole and then, within that, the individual finances of a range of Anglican voluntary organizations, all home missionary organizations within the diocese of London. Historians of religion have shown a certain reluctance to grapple with the columns of figures and minutiae of detail contained in cash books, general ledgers and annual reports. This essay serves as a brief taster of the wealth of material contained in such sources.

HISTORIOGRAPHY: THE EXISTING LITERATURE

Daniel Howe, an American historian, comments on this reluctance by church historians to engage with economic issues:

> Despite its importance, there has been little written on the topic, even by professional historians of religion. The two most potentially embarrassing subjects to discuss are sex and money, and it has taken longer for historians of American religion to bring themselves to address the latter. The clergy know well that their congregations often show even more reluctance to hear about money from the pulpit than to hear about sex. Scholars seem to have shared some of this sensitivity.[1]

In recent years, American religious historians have made a concerted effort to initiate a dialogue on this 'sensitive' issue. In the 1990s, a project on the 'Financing of American Religion' was carried out by the Institute for the Study of American Evangeli-

---

[1] Daniel Walker Howe, 'Afterword' to M. A. Noll, ed., *God and Mammon: Protestants, Money, and the Market, 1790–1860* (Oxford, 2002), 295.

cals at Wheaton College.[2] The stimulus was a perceived financial crisis in American religion during the late 1980s and early 1990s. One of the core purposes of the project was to research individual giving in a variety of ways: the relationship between giving and income; the relationship between giving and involvement; the connection between giving and pledging; denominational differences in individual giving; and historical trends in giving (in absolute and per capita terms).[3] The project principally examined a range of topics associated with the financial issues facing religious groups at that time but it also sought to historicize the issue of religious finance by embedding currently experienced problems in historical research into the infrastructure and tradition of voluntary giving that emerged in the nineteenth century.[4]

The subsidiary historical project concentrated on a historical examination of American Evangelical religion. The output of this component of the project was principally in the form of two edited collections: *More Money, More Ministry: Money and Evangelicals in Recent North American History* (2000), edited by Larry Eskridge and Mark Noll; and *God and Mammon: Protestants, Money, and the Markets, 1790 to 1860* (2002), edited by Mark Noll. *God and Mammon* is littered with references to the lack of scholarly attention to the issue of church and finance in the United States. In Noll's view, '[e]ven basic questions about the economic dimensions of the Protestant churches and voluntary societies remain unanswered',[5] and 'despite what is known about the existence of these diverse ways of raising money for Protestant enterprises, serious studies with full details on the mechanics of fund-raising and on its meaning for the religious and cultural lives of the churches remain rare'.[6]

In contrast to these recent American investigations, British historians have been reticent about initiating a similar dialogue, very little work having been done to initiate a British historiography on the mutually complex inter-relationship of church and finance.

---

[2] Mark Chaves, 'The Financing of American Religion Initiative Evaluation: Final Report' (unpublished report, Institute for the Study of American Evangelicals, November 1997), 1.
[3] Ibid. 6–10.
[4] Ibid. 13.
[5] Noll, *God and Mammon*, 7.
[6] Ibid. 10.

If American religious historians bemoan their lack of knowledge regarding this topic, the state of the British historiography is even more lamentable. British religious historians have approached this subject matter in five different ways. Firstly, Boyd Hilton's classic book *The Age of Atonement* (1986) examines the central influence of Evangelicalism on social and economic thought. Secondly, G. F. A. Best's *Temporal Pillars* (1964) is an examination of Church institutions, studying Queen Anne's Bounty and the Ecclesiastical Commissioners. Thirdly, the Ecclesiastical History Society's volume on *The Church and Wealth* (1987) discusses the problem of the acquisition of wealth, as both a burden and responsibility, by both the church and the individual. Michael Wilks, in his presidential address, seems openly apologetic regarding the topic of the volume: 'The theme "The Church and Wealth" ... in many ways... could hardly seem less appropriate to that institution whose founder commanded his followers to take neither silver nor gold'.[7] Fourthly, David Jeremy's two books, *Capitalists and Christians* (1990) and *Religion, Business and Wealth* (1998), explore the relationship between business and religion. Regarding *Capitalists and Christians*, Jeremy writes: 'this study has attempted to open up to further enquiry and public interest the important but neglected topic of interactions between business and religion in a world in which ideology and economics regularly intersect'.[8] Finally, J. P. Ellens's book *Religious Routes to Gladstonian Liberalism: The Church Rate Conflict in England and Wales, 1832–1868* (1994) examines the religious and political climate which led to the abolition of the church rate in 1868. However, none of these approaches in major works have put finance at the centre of the issue being debated.[9]

NEW APPROACHES

The aim of this essay is to initiate an examination of the relation-

---

7 Michael Wilks, 'Thesaurus Ecclesiae', in W. J. Sheils and D. Wood, eds, *The Church and Wealth*, SCH 24 (Oxford, 1987), xv–xlv, at xv.

8 D. J. Jeremy, *Capitalists and Christians* (Oxford, 1990), 419.

9 See two papers which do discuss the financial efficiency of pew rents: S. J. D. Green, 'The Death of Pew Rents, the Rise of Bazaars, and the End of the Traditional Political Economy of Voluntary Religious Organisations: The Case of the West Riding of Yorkshire, *c.*1870–1914', *Northern History* 27 (1991), 198–235; Callum G. Brown, 'The Costs of Pew-renting: Church Management, Church-going and Social Class in Nineteenth-Century Glasgow', *JEH* 38 (1987), 347–61.

ship between religious adherence and the financing of religion and to discover how this changed during the period from 1860 to 1914. This is regarded as the pivotal period in terms of the conventional narrative of religious decline. Both Jeremy Morris and Stephen Yeo argue that voluntary organizations were in difficulty from the 1890s due to the withdrawal of support by the middle and upper classes; this affected both financial support and practical involvement through such means as sitting on committees.[10] Academic writing on the topic of philanthropy has generally been more concerned with the issues that philanthropy set out to remedy: health, poverty, prostitution, alcohol abuse, education and housing. David Owen, in his classic work *English Philanthropy: 1660–1960*, states openly that he has deliberately 'largely ignored' the topic of specifically religious philanthropy.[11] This academic preoccupation with bodily, rather than spiritual, welfare has resulted in a rather skewed historiography of philanthropy that underplays the role of religion and religious motivation. Peter Dobkin Hall, referring to the state of American historiography on philanthropy, admits: 'Quite clearly, the scholarship of philanthropy has given religion short shrift'.[12] This statement could equally be made for the state of British scholarship on philanthropy.

The following case study will explore the relationship between religious adherence and the financing of religion by analysing the available sector income figures for religious voluntary organizations.[13] A number of charitable directories for London were produced in the second half of the nineteenth century; the most useful for the purposes of analysing income to religious voluntary groups is *The Classified Directory to the Metropolitan Charities*, published by William F. Howe annually between 1876 and 1919. Howe helpfully classifies the charity entries into two divisions ('Spiritual Welfare' and 'General Welfare') which are then subdi-

[10] Stephen Yeo, *Religion and Voluntary Organisations in Crisis* (London, 1976); J. N. Morris, *Religion and Urban Change: Croydon 1840–1914* (Woodbridge, 1992).

[11] D. E. Owen, *English Philanthropy: 1660–1960* (Cambridge, 1965), 3.

[12] Peter Dobkin Hall, 'The History of Religious Philanthropy in America', in R. Wuthnow and V. A. Hodgkinson, eds, *Faith and Philanthropy in America: Exploring the Role of Religion in America's Voluntary Sector* (San Francisco, CA, 1990), 38–62, at 38.

[13] Rare examples of this approach include Jane Garnett, 'Gold and the Gospel: Systematic Beneficence in Mid-Nineteenth-Century England', in Sheils and Wood, eds, *The Church and Wealth*, 347–58; S. J. D. Green, *Religion in the Age of Decline* (Cambridge, 1996), ch. 3.

vided. The figures included in Howe's directory are in no way comprehensive for the religious charitable sector as a whole; they do not include amounts distributed in relief by church and chapel congregations or informally raised for specific projects such as the building of a church. The value in Howe's figures, however, is that they provide the income figures specifically for voluntary organizations based in London, and also that his categorization was consistent throughout the period. Owen, who criticizes many of the directories, considers that Howe's guide produced 'the least unsatisfactory London figures'.[14]

An examination of the summary figures included in Howe's directory (see Table 1) shows that reported charity income for the period from 1874 to 1914 in absolute figures rose overall by 112%, that of welfare charities rising by 101% and that of religious charities by 128%. During this period, the number of charity entries in the spiritual category remained quite level.[15] The bulk of these financial increases occurred within the mission categories (Class II): income reported by home missions societies rose by 172%, that of home and foreign mission societies by 357% and that of foreign missions by 127%. However, over this period the proportion of charity income going to religious charities rose only slightly, from 42.5% to 45.7%.

In the home mission category, reported income rose by over £700,000 during this period. By examining the specifics of this sector's income, it is possible to ascertain that most of this increase in income can be attributed to five organizations. Four of them were established during the period; of these the most significant newcomer was the Church Army (established in 1882) whose income in 1914 was £280,000. The other three new organizations were all sister organizations to the Bishop of London's Fund: the Bishop of St Albans' Fund (established in 1878), the South London Church Fund (established in 1878) and the East London Church Fund (established in 1880). The fifth organization, which was already in existence at the start of the period, was Dr Barnardo's Home for Orphans and Destitute Children (established in 1866) whose income in 1914 was £245,000. Howe lists its income in

---

14 Owen, *English Philanthropy*, 477.
15 There were 118 entries in 1874 and 120 in 1914.

the 1874 directory as £12,440.[16] In summary, nearly 80% of the increase in reported home mission income can be accounted for by receipts from new organizations and the spectacular financial success of Dr Barnardo's. On the whole, the income levels for the remaining home missionary societies either remained level or rose slightly.

In the home and foreign mission category, reported income rose by over £450,000. Virtually all of this increase can be assigned to five organizations, all of which existed before the Howe series of directories started. Two reported throughout the period and made steady increases within it; the other three started reporting later.[17] In relation to these three, it is the addition of the Salvation Army's income that has the most dramatic impact on this section's figures; their reported income in 1914 was £288,000. Although the Salvation Army did not submit an entry to Howe's directory until 1884, its income in 1875 (when it was still known as the Christian Mission) was only £2,178.[18] It can, therefore, be stated that the increase in income in this category was mainly due to the increasing financial success of organizations that were already in existence before the commencement of the Howe directory series. The increments within this sector, therefore, were not due to the establishment of new organizations.

In the foreign mission category, income rose by an impressive figure of nearly £1,000,000. Of this amount, £600,000 can be accounted for by the entries of seven organizations. Three of these were founded within the period and explain £100,000 of the increase, while the steady financial success of the other four generated £500,000: the Baptist Missionary Society (established in 1792), the Church Missionary Society (established in 1799). the London Missionary Society (established in 1795) and the Society for the Propagation of the Gospel in Foreign Parts (established in 1701). The rest of the increase in income can be accounted for

[16] The entry for 1874 is listed under its initial name of the East End Juvenile Mission.

[17] Four of the societies, as listed in the directories, were the British and Foreign Sailors' Society (established 1833), the Mission to Seamen (established 1856), the Presbyterian Missions (established 1847) and the Church Extension Association (established 1864). The fifth was the Salvation Army (established 1865 as the Christian Mission).

[18] *Christian Mission Magazine*, July 1876, 172.

firstly by smaller organizations making steady financial progress through the period, and secondly by organizations that existed before the commencement of Howe's charity directory but which chose not to submit entries until a later date. In summary, the majority of the increase in this category is a result of the increasing financial success of organizations that predate the commencement of the series of Howe directories.

This analysis highlights a number of research possibilities. Firstly, it indicates that the financial health of religious voluntary organizations (as a sector) was quite buoyant in the late nineteenth and early twentieth centuries, and that the income of this sector had seen greater increases than that of the welfare sector. Secondly, in terms of trends, the majority of financially successful new organizations fell within the category of home mission. Thirdly, it highlights the issue of competition. For example, what impact did the foundation of the Church Army have on the finances of other Anglican home mission organizations? Fourthly, it raises the question of how the long established foreign mission organizations sustained their impressive financial record over such a long period. Finally, how can the relative successes and failures of the period be analysed in denominational terms?

Case Studies

What does this analysis of charitable income say about public support of religious organizations? In the nineteenth century, as now, religious voluntary organizations competed for public support between themselves and with welfare agencies. Within this period, some voluntary organizations merged, some folded, some persisted and became stronger, and some newly formed organizations quickly became established and very successful. To form a more nuanced picture of the financial state of the religious sector, it is necessary to look in detail at the financial health of a few specific religious voluntary organizations. In London, a number of new Anglican voluntary organizations were established in the first few years of Bishop Tait's episcopate (1856–68). We shall examine the finances of three of these as case studies; they all fall within the home mission category, and their annual income figures are shown in Table 2.

The first is the London Diocesan Home Mission (LDHM) which was established in 1857. Its aim was to undertake immediate and emergency mission work without the delay entailed by the erection of a church. Its method was to 'employ a certain number of clergy, under the Bishop's direction, for distinctly evangelistic or "aggressive" work in crowded districts, with a view in most cases to the ultimate formation of new parishes'.[19] Taken at face value the income figures for the LDHM indicate a stability of income throughout the period.[20] However, closer inspection reveals that its most consistent source of funding throughout the period came from an annual block grant of between £1,500 and £2,000 from the Bishop of London's Fund. This grant represented approximately 30% of the LDHM's annual income. Before the establishment of the Bishop of London's Fund in 1863, income came from subscriptions, donations and church collections: by 1914 income from these sources had fallen to a negligible 1% of annual income. The principal source of income (in the region of 60%) after 1882 was dividend income from invested legacies.

The second case study relates to the Bishop of London's Fund (BLF). Its purpose was to raise the money that would finance the work of other organizations in the diocese. In its first fifty years to 1913, it paid out £1.5 million in grants. The objectives of the Fund were the support of missionary clergy or additional curates, Scripture readers and 'mission women'; the provision of clergymen's residences, schools and mission rooms or school churches; the endowment of old or new districts and of curacies; and the building of churches. During the initial decade income declined, because although the number of contributions remained consistent (in the range of 2,000 to 2,500 payments annually), the average size of these contributions was larger in the first few years. Income then stagnated and then fell to its lowest levels in the late 1870s and early 1880s. The number of annual contributions dropped by more than half between 1873 and 1878.[21] The BLF's golden jubilee report

---

[19] R. T. Davidson, *The Life of Archibald Campbell Tait*, 2 vols (London, 1891), 1: 261–2.

[20] The printed annual reports of the LDHM can be found at the British Library and Lambeth Palace Library. The information has been supplement by details from the LDHM general ledgers (London Metropolitan Archive, DL/A/H/020/MS31994).

[21] The printed annual reports of the BLF can be found at the British Library, Bodleian Library, Cambridge University Library, Lambeth Palace Library and the National Archives (CRES 40/103). Figures are extrapolated from BLF Annual Report subscription lists. The number of donors and subscribers in 1873 was 2,135; that for 1878 was 812.

stated that after the slump of the early 1880s it had experienced continuous growth in the number of supporters. However, it also stressed that receipts had 'been greatly affected by the passing away of old and very large contributors'.[22] However, this report also recorded the extent of the Fund's success compared with other organizations: 'It has been by far the largest Diocesan Institution of the kind, and instead of gradually dying out, as so many have done, it has shown in the latter half of its existence considerable signs of growth'.[23] This success can be analysed through the subscription lists in the 1912 annual report. The number of contributions had surpassed the numbers experienced during the society's first few years, having risen to 2,712. However, within the period, the profile of the typical funder had changed from being a man (in the 1865 subscription list) to being a woman (in the 1912 subscription list). In addition to this gender switch, the size of the typical contribution had also declined. In 1865, 68% of contributions had been of sums below £10 per annum; the comparative figure for 1912 was 91%. In conclusion, analysis confirms the assertions of the jubilee report that the level of financial support (in terms of the number of contributions) had indeed increased but that there had been a decline in the number and amount of larger contributions.

The third case study relates to the London Diocesan Deaconess Institution (LDDI) which was founded in 1861 by Miss Elizabeth Ferard and the Revd Thomas Pelham Dale, with the official approval of Bishop Tait. The deaconess order had recently been revived on the continent; the LDDI was modelled on the German Protestant Deaconess Institution at Kaiserswerth, which had been founded in 1838. Initially the principal work of the LDDI was nursing, but as time progressed the work of the deaconesses expanded to encompass visiting, conducting clubs, holding mothers' meetings, helping at schools, running classes of all kinds and general parish work.[24] The LDDI annual income figures demonstrate a high degree of steadiness and consistency throughout the period. The sources of

---

[22] *The Origin of the Bishop of London's Fund ... and its Work for 50 Years* (London, 1913), 5–6.

[23] Ibid. 9.

[24] *The Official Yearbook of the Church of England* (London, 1883), 175; Henrietta Blackmore, ed., *The Beginning of Women's Ministry: The Revival of the Deaconess in the Nineteenth-Century Church of England*, Church of England Record Society 13 (Woodbridge, 2007).

funding, however, changed considerably. There was a shift away from relying on public support to being financed principally by the sisters and the missions in which they worked. Virtually all income came from four sources: payments from deaconesses, payment from missions, dividend income and voluntary donations. In 1865 the LDDI received no money from dividend returns on investments, but by 1914 dividends made up 12% of its income. Payments from missions rose from 5% of its income in 1865 to 29% in 1914. Likewise contributions from deaconesses rose from 20% of its income in 1865 to 52% in 1914. These last two sources compensated for diminishing donations and subscriptions from the general public: in 1865 subscriptions and donations accounted for 66% of annual income, but by 1914 they had fallen to only 5%.[25]

In summary, all three organizations maintained their income levels after an initial period. However, the financial accounts of two of them showed a marked decline in donations and subscriptions from the general public. The BLF avoided this decline by gaining new support, mainly from women. These findings demonstrate that, whilst all three organizations sustained their income levels during the period, each had adapted and had become reliant upon new sources of funding. These initial findings suggest that the buoyant public financial support of Anglican religious voluntary organizations experienced in the third quarter of the nineteenth century had stalled by the beginning of the twentieth century.[26]

CONCLUSION

These initial results highlight the need for further research in this area. The Final Evaluation Report of 'Financing of American Religion' laid out the project's initial findings and indicated a number of areas for further study. The project found that the denominations that had the higher per capita income did so not because individuals had higher income but because of the way that giving was institutionalized by that denomination. So, by way of example, denominations that had a tradition of pledging had higher per

---

[25] A virtually complete but uncatalogued run of LDDI printed annual reports is held in the London archive of the Community of St Andrew (formerly the LDDI).

[26] A full statistical analysis of the subscription lists will be found in my Open University doctoral thesis, provisionally entitled 'Philanthropy and Secularisation: The Funding of Anglican Voluntary Religious Organisations in London, 1860–1914'.

capita income than those that did not. Linked with this, differences in denominational practice (such as the use of pledging or tithing) were related to theological differences.[27] It was found, for example, that levels of Catholic giving were lower than those for Protestant giving because Protestant churches placed more emphasis on the concept of Christian stewardship and therefore were more likely to institutionalize this concept in practices such as the signing of annual pledge cards.[28] It also indicated that the perceived religious financial crisis of the 1980s and 1990s might actually represent a return to normal levels of income, and that the post-World War II boom America of the 1950s had skewed religious groups' expectations of levels of income. Another avenue of research indicated was the correlation between involvement and finance, that financial decline more accurately indicated a decline in church membership or involvement. The project recommended that further research be done in several areas: how voluntary giving becomes institutionalized in different denominations; the different mix of funding streams in different denominations; an examination of individual giving across a range of religious voluntary organizations; the business side of running a religious group in a receipts and expenditure analysis (in other words, an examination of how religious bodies manage their financial affairs, in terms of both income and expenditure); how religious organizations respond to the professionalization of fundraising; the influence of gender on voluntary giving; and the relationship between geographical location and giving.[29]

The aim of the 'Financing of American Religion' project was to 'create a discourse focused on the financing of American religion'. It is time for British historians to initiate their own discourse. This essay, which evaluates the income of religious voluntary organizations, is but a small step towards initiating this important dialogue. There are many interesting and fruitful avenues of research that could be pursued in the future: an examination of the factors linked to sustaining organizational longevity; an analysis

---

[27] Chaves, 'Financing of American Religion', 15–16.

[28] Dean R. Hoge et al., 'Giving in Five Denominations', in Mark Chaves and Sharon L. Miller, eds, *Financing American Religion* (Walnut Creek, CA, 1999), 3–10. For more information on the importance of teaching the doctrine of Christian stewardship in relation to levels of giving, see Flew, 'Philanthropy and Secularisation'.

[29] Chaves, 'Financing of American Religion', 19–29.

of corporate donations to religious organizations; an exploration of how competition, in the form of new organizations, affected the finances and fortunes of existing organizations; a consideration of how the availability of funding shaped the form of mission work; an analysis of the trends in charitable bequests given to religious organizations; an exploration of how religious organizations responded to the professionalization of fundraising; an examination of the different mix of funding streams in different denominations and how these funding streams shifted over time; a study of the influence of gender on voluntary giving; an analysis of demographic shifts in giving; an examination of motivation behind giving financial donations anonymously; and finally a study of the implicit tension between running a religious organization as a well-managed financially viable business concern whilst also maintaining the belief that God will look after the financial security of the organization. That is a considerable list of fruitful avenues of new research for modern religious historians. All we need to do now is to overcome our very British reticence to talk about money.

The Open University

Table 1: Charity Income, 1874 to 1914 (£)

	1874	1880	1885	1890	1895	1900	1905	1910	1914
Religious Societies									
Bible Societies	228,418	206,518	210,245	217,804	222,441	226,572	236,973	258,565	304,134
Book & Tract Societies	87,241	79,750	78,736	95,923	88,383	93,220	88,147	80,854	81,271
Home Missions	414,010	466,651	521,678	669,952	738,217	820,685	935,302	1,072,953	1,127,730
Home & Foreign Missions	126,765	128,537	248,495	156,248	387,944	262,237	539,409	604,472	579,740
Foreign Missions	761,000	779,656	802,426	962,878	1,044,127	1,289,070	1,427,704	1,638,886	1,728,789
Church & Chapel Building	71,730	29,583	31,483	14,731	13,047	14,454	37,654	39,066	36,156
Religious Societies Subtotal	1,689,164	1,690,695	1,893,063	2,117,536	2,494,159	2,706,238	3,265,189	3,694,796	3,857,820
Welfare Societies	2,286,417	2,430,851	2,554,373	2,801,116	3,144,111	3,724,824	4,268,063	4,366,000	4,585,311
Total	3,975,581	4,121,546	4,447,436	4,918,652	5,638,270	6,431,062	7,533,252	8,060,796	8,443,131

Source: W. F. Howe, ed., *The Classified Directory to the Metropolitan Charities* (London, 1876–1919).

Table 2: Income Figures for a Sample of Anglican Religious Voluntary Organizations (£)

	London Diocesan Home Mission (LDHM)	Bishop of London's Fund (BLF)	London Diocesan Deaconess Institution (LDDI)
1865	5,300	48,248	1,176
1870	7,750	42,004	1,431
1875	5,528	27,007	1,665
1880	5,598	17,503	1,902
1885	4,977	18,408	1,666
1890	5,557	17,544	1,969
1895	5,619	22,243	1,714
1900	5,179	26,744	1,556
1905	4,668	31,822	2,064
1910	4,859	26,842	1,895
1914	5,156	25,417	1,790

Figures are taken from a variety of sources: *The Official Yearbook of the Church of England,* surviving general ledger books, Herbert Fry's *Royal Guide to the principal London and other Charities* and annual reports.

PART III

CHURCH AND STATE IN HISTORY

CHURCH AND STATE, RELIGION AND POWER IN LATE ANTIQUE AND BYZANTINE SCHOLARSHIP OF THE LAST FIVE DECADES

by CLAUDIA RAPP

Tackling issues of church and state is a tall order under any circumstances. Taking the metahistorical view and summarizing the scholarship on church and state makes it positively daunting, especially when the half-century under consideration spans the entire lifetime of the author. This task is made even more challenging when the societies and cultures under investigation are late antiquity and medieval Byzantium, the former (*c.*300–*c.*800, encompassing the entire Mediterranean) a paradigmatic period of religious change, the latter (330–1453, focusing on the Greek-speaking eastern half of the Roman empire and its subsequent history) emblematic of 'otherness' when compared to the Christian tradition in the West that has shaped our worldview to the present day.

GENERAL TRENDS IN HISTORICAL RESEARCH

Let me begin with general trends in historical research of late antiquity and the Middle Ages. The French *Annales* school cast its long shadow well into the 1970s, with its emphasis on doing history 'from below' and its focus no longer on 'dead white males' but on large numbers of people, their activities and the mentalities that these reveal. The attention to those groups of the population that do not themselves assume a voice in the written record prepared fertile ground for the three main lessons that scholarship in the last fifty years has learned to apply.

First, we should approach our sources with a healthy dose of scepticism, rather than taking them at face value. This is particularly challenging for medieval historians, as written narratives by individual authors are our main tools. Jacques Derrida's famous dictum regarding the 'death of the author' sent a ripple of shock waves through those branches of scholarship that, like medieval studies, depended on individual authors and their works. Hayden White's emphasis on the constructedness of narrative discourse has led to the investigation of 'master narratives' in medieval authors, particularly those aimed at constructing a historical past for a ruling group of people.[1] Especially relevant for Byzantinists was Edward Said's *Orientalism*, which alerted us to the danger of seeking in Byzantium a romanticized 'other' onto which it was possible to project nineteenth-century fantasies of a lusciously hyper-sensuous, viciously backstabbing, bizarrely bureaucratic and excessively autocratic imperial court, on the model of the Ottoman sultanate.[2]

The second lesson we have learned is to pay greater attention to larger groups within a culture and to investigate their conduct as an assertion of independent identity. This discovery has three roots, first among them cultural anthropology. Pierre Bourdieu's assertion that it is the 'habitus', the learned behaviour and the equally learned codes for its interpretation, that determines a culture, has reinserted an anthropological approach into our field and thus reinforced the focus on the aggregate population and directed attention to the unwritten rules that govern its conduct – a direction of inquiry that Gert Althoff has in recent decades applied to the Latin Middle Ages in his work on *Spielregeln*.[3]

A second root of this broader view of medieval societies is the 'feminist turn' of the 1970s, which restored agency to women, closely followed by a general turn towards the construction of gender and sexual orientation (that includes the 'queering' of texts) which has taught us to read our sources against the grain in order to uncover hidden agendas or disguised details about the life experience of men and women and its articulation, including their sexuality.[4]

[1] Hayden White, *The Content of the Form: Discourse and Historical Representation* (Baltimore, MD, 1987).

[2] Gabrielle M. Spiegel, *The Past as Text: The Theory and Practice of Medieval Historiography* (Baltimore, MD, 1997); Elizabeth A. Clark, ed., *History, Theory, Text: Historians and the Linguistic Turn* (Cambridge, MA, 2004); Edward Said, *Orientalism* (New York, 1978).

[3] Pierre Bourdieu, *Outline of a Theory of Practice* (Cambridge, 1977; first publ. Paris, 1972); Gerd Althoff, *Spielregeln der Politik im Mittelalter: Kommunikation in Frieden und Fehde* (Darmstadt, 1997).

[4] See, e.g., Judith Bennett, *History Matters: Patriarchy and the Challenge of Feminism* (Philadelphia, PA, 2006); and in this volume, Judith M. Lieu, 'What did Women do for the Early Church? The Recent History of a Question', 261–81. The study of sexuality in Byzantium has not yet grown much beyond its infancy, compared to scholarship on the western Middle Ages; see, e.g., Glenn Burger and Steven F. Kruger, eds, *Queering the Middle Ages* (Minneapolis, MN, 2001).

The third root, closely connected in genesis and outlook to feminist studies, is the wave of colonial and subaltern studies which has been influential in North America since the 1980s. It has sharpened our eyes for subversive strategies among disenfranchised social groups – strategies that function simultaneously as an expression of power 'from below' and as a destabilizing element within a political system, forcing it to assert itself in even more overt and oppressive ways.[5]

The third big lesson we have learned is to take material culture more seriously. This is a general shift which cannot be pinned down to individual scholars or books, but which has nonetheless had a deep impact on the scholarship especially of late antiquity and Byzantium. The appropriation of objects, artefacts and archaeological findings by historians of all fields for the purpose of studying a culture in all its manifestations may have made art historians nervous as they insist on their methodological monopoly for the correct interpretation of visual sources, but it has had the widespread effect of generating a revival of the kind of object-driven cultural history that had been practised in the late nineteenth and early twentieth century. One can seek the reasons for this greater valuation of material culture in various places: with the ever accelerating proliferation of visual media in the last fifty years through television, films and the internet, we have collectively become more attuned to the importance of objects and images as signifiers. Classical archaeologists have learned since the days of Heinrich Schliemann that the single-minded search for Troy VIIa, the Palace of Priam and his gold treasure, results in the destruction of layers of subsequent history and should be avoided. One very significant expression of this heightened interest in material culture is the recent wave of exhibitions on Byzantium that tend to attract large audiences, to the great delight of curators and the pleasant surprise of museum directors. To mention only those in the anglophone world: an important series at the Metropolitan Museum in New York began in 1977–8 with the milestone *Age of Spirituality* exhibition that singled out the art of late antiquity for the first time, followed by *The Glory of Byzantium* in 1997, *Byzantium: Faith and Power (1261–1557)* in 2004, and *Byzantium*

---

[5] See, e.g., Robert J. C. Young, *Postcolonialism: An Historical Introduction* (Oxford, 2001).

and Islam: Age of Transition in 2012.[6] The J. Paul Getty Museum in Los Angeles hosted *Holy Image, Hallowed Ground: Icons from Sinai* in 2006–7,[7] while London put on display *The Road to Byzantium: Luxury Arts of Antiquity* at the Courtauld Gallery in 2006,[8] and *Byzantium 330–1453* at the Royal Academy in 2008–9.[9] It could be argued that all of these exhibitions, in one way or another, diminish Byzantium by reducing it to Orthodox Christianity, but in view of the fact that most surviving material culture that is portable and hence suitable for exhibitions either stems from an ecclesiastical context or is infused with Christian iconography, that criticism would be unfair.

All of these new trends have affected late antique and Byzantine scholarship. We no longer talk exclusively about the church, but about church and people or church and society, or indeed take a close-up view of the religious experience of groups or individuals, and especially of women.[10]

HISTORICAL DEVELOPMENTS AND THEIR IMPACT

These trends in scholarship were themselves rooted in their own historical context, which was shaped by the aftermath of, and slow recovery (politically, economically, socially and intellectually) from, the horrors of the Second World War: in the late 1960s the hippies, the student movements and the Vietnam War protests made us realize the enormous potential for the unleashing of the collective power of the marginalized. We have witnessed an acute reminder of its enduring potential more recently in the 'Arab Spring'. These movements have called into question the permanence of the great institutions of power and thus have sharpened our perception of the articulation of power through institutions.

---

[6] Kurt Weitzmann, ed., *Age of Spirituality: Late Antique and Early Christian Art, Third to Seventh Century* (New York, 1979); Helen C. Evans and William D. Wixom, eds, *Glory of Byzantium: Arts and Culture of the Middle Byzantine Era, A.D. 843–1261* (New York, 1997); Helen C. Evans, ed., *Byzantium: Faith and Power (1261–1557)* (New Haven, CT, 2004).

[7] Robert S. Nelson and Kristen M. Collins, eds, *Holy Image, Hallowed Ground: Icons from Sinai* (Los Angeles, CA, 2006).

[8] Frank Althaus and Mark Sutcliffe, eds, *The Road to Byzantium: Luxury Arts of Antiquity* (London, 2006).

[9] Robin Cormack and Maria Vassilaki, eds, *Byzantium 330–1453* (London, 2008).

[10] e.g. Rosemary Morris, ed., *Church and People in Byzantium* (Birmingham, 1990).

On the level of global politics, the last five decades have seen shifts of tectonic magnitude. In the early 1960s, the Cold War between the Soviet Union (and the Warsaw Pact) and the USA (and NATO) was at its height. The Berlin Wall was constructed as a deliberate provocation of the Western allies in 1961, and in the following year the Cuban missile crisis brought the two super-powers to the brink of open war. Yet three decades later, by the early 1990s, the Warsaw Pact had ceased to exist, the Soviet Union had dissolved, the European Union had been formed and the USA had become embroiled in military operations in the Middle East. Instead of the two superpowers of the last decades of the twentieth century, global politics in the new millennium involves several major players, with further additions in the form of the newly prosperous Asian nations and the oil-rich countries of the Middle East. These developments have made us more aware of the global interconnectedness of historical events, so that scholars are more willing to engage in synchronic or comparative studies, or indeed to extend the chain of causality to consider domino or ripple effects and to seek the origin and consider the outcome of events in regions well beyond their original realm of investigation.[11]

It is not only our perception of the power of secular institutions and of states that has changed in the last half-century, but also our understanding of Christianity. The historians of the church who got into their stride in the 1960s had grown up within a strong confessional framework. They wrote as Catholics or Protestants, Anglicans or Orthodox, and many of them were monks or clerics themselves. The rapid secularization of Europe and the USA within the space of only two generations after the Second World War has opened up the scholarly field of church history to non-believers and to women. Most of all, it has allowed us to think about religion in terms of personal piety, as the result of individual choice, not as the inevitable consequence of the existence of an overpowering institution which determines the framework of one's upbringing and shapes one's understanding of the world. The recent resurgence in Fundamentalist Christianity in the USA and elsewhere and the public displays of Muslim faith, often with

---

[11] A good example is the series of conferences and edited volumes under the title 'Transformation of the Roman World' between 1992 and 1998, with funding from the European Science Foundation.

a political agenda, have further contributed to this new willingness to conceive of Christianity as articulated at the level of the individual rather than imposed by an institutional superstructure. This understanding of religion as a personal choice among a variety of different options has in the last two decades opened the way to a greater appreciation of the fluidity of the boundaries between Judaism and Christianity, on the one hand, and between orthodoxy and heresy, on the other, combined with a waning interest in the church as an institution. This trend also affects our understanding of paganism and Christianity, a point to which I will return later.

FROM LATE ANTIQUITY TO BYZANTIUM

These historical and historicizing generalizations are necessary to provide the backdrop to the scholarly treatment of the relation of church and state in late antiquity and Byzantium that will concern me in what follows. Church and state are deceptively simple categories, which serve as shorthand for other binary pairs: patriarch versus emperor; religious versus secular; or even private versus public. These are tightly packaged terms that are often used interchangeably when greater analytical differentiation would be more helpful to unravel the issues. Behind them lurks the inherited assumption, first articulated in the Enlightenment, that there should be a clear distinction between the two, with religion being the exclusive domain of the church and indeed best left out of the state.

Byzantium was the only empire that lasted for well over a millennium. The fate of its capital of Constantinople provides convenient chronological book-ends. In 330, eighteen years after Constantine the Great, with the help of the God of the Christians, had achieved the epoch-making victory that would make him ruler of Rome, he founded his New Rome on the site of the old city of Byzantion on the Bosphorus. By the end of the fifth century, the 'city of Constantine' became the permanent residence of the emperor and also of the patriarch of Constantinople, the head of Byzantine Christendom. It remained the central seat of government, with a hiatus of fifty-seven years of Crusader rule in the twelfth century (1204 to 1261), until it fell to the thunder of Ottoman cannon in 1453. And Istanbul, as the city was renamed under the Ottomans, is still today the seat of the Ecumenical Patriarchate of Constantinople, held in honour by a large number of Orthodox Christians throughout the world.

In the course of these centuries, internal developments as much as external challenges affected the position of church and state, and had consequences for their interaction. The early Byzantine period, which lasted until the seventh century (and is thus chronologically identical with 'late antiquity', the latter however covering the wider geographical spectrum of the entire Mediterranean), was the formative time that established the players and possibilities for later centuries. The precedent-setting nature of this period means that its attraction to scholars and the general public remains unabated. So it repays dwelling on here. The fundamental question is how the newly recognized religion of Christianity inserted itself into the pre-existing frameworks of the Roman Empire and of Greco-Roman culture.

Even those of us who are sceptical of the view that history is 'made' by 'dead white males' have to admit that Constantine's reign and specifically his support for the Christian religion represents a pivotal moment in the history of Europe and indeed the globe. Not surprisingly, the study of 'the first Christian emperor' has developed almost into a cottage industry of Constantine studies and biographies in different languages. The popularity of Constantine received further impetus from the 1700th anniversary exhibitions and conferences that began in the last decade. There was a major exhibition in York, where in 306 Constantine was proclaimed emperor by the troops of his father Constantius Chlorus, and a year later in Trier, the latter's headquarters on the Continent.[12] More events were planned for 2012, the anniversary of the Battle of the Milvian Bridge, and 2013, that of the Edict of Toleration. Constantine's relation to Christianity inevitably stands in the foreground of such enterprises. But already a backlash is beginning. Raymond van Dam's *The Roman Revolution of Constantine* deliberately plays down the emperor's religious measures and integrates them into a much broader study of his imperial politics. Van Dam insists that his analysis 'defines Christianity in terms of identity rather than beliefs'.[13]

---

[12] Elizabeth Hartley, Jane Hawkes and Martin Henig, eds, *Constantine the Great: York's Roman Emperor* (Aldershot, 2006); Alexander Demandt and Josef Engemann, eds, *Konstantin der Grosse* (Mainz, 2007).

[13] Raymond van Dam, *The Roman Revolution of Constantine* (Cambridge, 2007), 13.

So why this resurgence of interest? In this time of political awakenings in Middle Eastern countries and virulent (and often, unfortunately, violent) religious assertions of Islam around the globe, combined with an economic crisis that has made visible the fissures within the European system created by visionary politicians over the last three decades, it is perhaps not too far-fetched to surmise that it is the search for a specifically European identity that has generated this heightened interest in the common roots of a specifically Christian tradition, with the reign of Constantine as its bedrock. It is worth questioning the consequences of the adoption of such a line of thought. An over-emphasis on the Christian roots of Europe can easily lead to a paradigm of a 'Clash of Civilizations'[14] that pits a Christian Europe against an Islamic Middle East, a paradigm in which religious allegiance is the main marker of cultural, and hence also of political identity. Half a millennium after the Renaissance brought the discovery of the individual, three centuries after the Enlightenment began to question the necessity of an overarching ideological framework of Christianity, and more than two centuries after the French Revolution taught us the separation of religion and politics, of church and state, we may well ask about the consequences of a return to power politics and identity politics within a framework defined by religion.

A seminal book by Garth Fowden forcefully made this point: *Empire to Commonwealth* was published in 1993.[15] Written at the end of the Cold War, it is a product of its own time, yet bears re-reading for the larger issues it raises through its comparison of Christianity with Islam as political forces. Fowden argues the peculiarity of the Byzantine (and, by extension, medieval European) model, whereby a pre-existing political structure, the empire, was infused with a new religion, Christianity. This comes into sharp focus in comparison with the rise of Islam, in which religion, power and institutions grew relatively fast, simultaneously and in relation to one another.

[14] Samuel P. Huntington, *The Clash of Civilizations and the Remaking of World Order* (New York, 1996).
[15] Garth Fowden, *Empire to Commonwealth: Consequences of Monotheism in Late Antiquity* (Princeton, NJ, 1993).

CHRISTIANITY AND THE LATER ROMAN EMPIRE

With the reign of Constantine, Christianity was no longer forced to be a victim of a pre-existing political system, but empowered to act as a player in the empire. Given these historical conditions, the relationship between state and church can be conceptualized in a number of different ways.

1. *Decline.* From the point of view of the empire, the burning issue is that of decline. The imperial office in Rome expired in 476, until it was revived by Charlemagne in 800. The boundaries of the Roman Empire contracted under the influence of migration and aggressive military movement from the outside, and the social structures that had supported the machinery of empire and conquest were increasingly eroded from within. Did the rise of Christianity simultaneously with these developments undermine the power of the Roman Empire and contribute to its demise? Edward Gibbon, the great Roman historian of the Enlightenment, posed this question in such eloquent terms that his work still provides a satisfying foil and a convenient straw man for much of modern scholarship.

The issue of decline has largely been raised in cultural terms. The central question was how the minority religion of Christianity could be successful not only in finding imperial support, but in transforming the Greco-Roman culture, assumed to be superior, so thoroughly that it descended into the 'darkness' of the Middle Ages. In 1963, Arnaldo Momigliano set the stage for this line of inquiry when he edited a volume with contributions from scholars of ancient and Byzantine history and entitled it *The Conflict between Paganism and Christianity in the Fourth Century.*[16] Two years later came the publication of Eric Robertson Dodds's *Pagan and Christian in an Age of Anxiety.*[17] From then on, pagans and Christians were seen to be in conflict, a paradigm that still infused Robin Lane Fox's *Pagans and Christians.*[18] These were scholars trained in the classical tradition and their unspoken assumption was that Christianization was not merely a counterpoint but actu-

---

[16] Arnaldo Momigliano, ed., *The Conflict between Christianity and Paganism in the Fourth Century: Essays* (Oxford, 1963).

[17] Eric Robertson Dodds, *Pagan and Christian in an Age of Anxiety: Aspects of Religious Experience from Marcus Aurelius to Constantine* (Cambridge, 1965).

[18] Robin Lane Fox, *Pagans and Christians* (New York, 1987).

ally hostile to Greco-Roman culture and thus to be blamed for the disappearance of classical learning.

But there are exceptions. A few isolated efforts were made to write the history of religious and cultural change from the pagan viewpoint. It is only the voices of the elite literati that are preserved, rather faintly, due to the selective transmission of pagan authors in the Middle Ages, but those that do survive often sound a shrill note of despair at the perceived danger of cultural change. The attitude and responses of the non-literate majority of the population can only be guessed from the survival of pagan sanctuaries in the towns and especially in the countryside, or from the repeated urgent pleas of Christian clerics beseeching their flock to avoid participation in traditional religious rites and practices. Most remarkable in its intellectual scope is the short book by Bernard Chuvin, *Chronicle of the Last Pagans*.[19] Alan Cameron's *The Last Pagans of Rome* takes a slightly different approach, arguing not for pagan resistance against an increasingly dominant and muscular Christianity, but for slow apathy giving way to adjustment and finally conversion, as the only way that pagan aristocrats were able to maintain their privileged role in society.[20]

Another, more recent strand of scholarship still rides the wave of the pagan-Christian paradigm, but now directs its curiosity to the exact mechanisms and the pace at which conversions happened, often with a specific regional focus. Keith Hopkins investigated the process of conversion with statistical methods and showed that there was a snowball effect that reached its greatest rate of acceleration in the second half of the fourth century.[21] Frank Trombley traced the progression of the transformations of cities, towns and villages in the eastern Mediterranean under the impact of Christianity with the help of both literary and archaeological evidence.[22] Raymond van Dam applied the same method to Cappadocia, the homeland of the great fathers of the fourth century: Basil of

---

[19] Bernard Chuvin, *Chronicle of the Last Pagans* (Cambridge, MA, 1990; first publ. as *Chronique des derniers païens*, Paris, 1990).

[20] Alan Cameron, *The Last Pagans of Rome* (Oxford, 2011).

[21] Keith Hopkins, 'Christian Number and Its Implications', *Journal of Early Christianity* 6 (1998), 185–226, responding to Rodney Stark, *The Rise of Christianity: A Sociologist Reconsiders History* (Princeton, NJ, 1996).

[22] Frank Trombley, *Hellenic Religion and Christianization, c.370–529*, 2 vols, Religions in the Graeco-Roman World 115 (Leiden, 1993–4).

Caesarea, his brother Gregory of Nyssa and his friend Gregory of Nazianzus.[23] Stephen Mitchell showed on the basis of epigraphic and archaeological materials how Christianity gradually took hold of Anatolia.[24] Michele Salzman used funerary epigraphy to identify the slow pattern of conversion among the Roman aristocracy at the end of the fourth century, and thereby confirmed Kate Cooper's assertion that the influence of women in the Christianization of late Roman society was overstated by contemporary authors who regarded the new religion with scepticism or hostility, and hence by modern scholars who followed their lead.[25]

Most of these recent works signal the impact of archaeology and material culture on the study of the growth of Christianity within the prevailing Greco-Roman context. Studies of individual sites have revealed the slow pace at which Christianity made its presence visible and palpable within the fabric of the late Roman and early Byzantine city. We now know that the conversion of temples into churches was not an isolated phenomenon and that it took until the middle of the fifth century for new church buildings to be set up in the middle of towns and cities, rather than on their periphery.[26] More recent studies have added further complexity: Kim Bowes explored the role of the Roman aristocracy in the promotion of Christianity, not least as building patrons, against the framework of changing definitions in the public and private articulations of religion.[27] Ramsay MacMullen, who had engaged with patterns of Christianization in earlier monographs, recently turned his attention to Christian sites around the Mediterranean,

---

[23] Raymond van Dam, *Kingdom of Snow: Roman Rule and Greek Culture in Cappadocia* (Philadelphia, PA, 2002); idem, *Becoming Christian: The Conversion of Roman Cappadocia* (Philadelphia, PA, 2003).

[24] Stephen Mitchell, *Anatolia: Land, Men and Gods in Asia Minor*, 2 vols (Oxford, 1993).

[25] Michele Salzman, *The Making of a Christian Aristocracy: Social and Religious Change in the Western Roman Empire* (Cambridge, MA, 2002), Kate Cooper, 'Insinuations of Womanly Influence: An Aspect of the Christianization of the Roman Aristocracy', *JRS* 82 (1992), 150–64.

[26] A good introduction is Johannes Hahn, Stephen Emmel and Ulrich Gotter, eds, *From Temple to Church: Destruction and Renewal of Local Cultic Topography in Late Antiquity* (Leiden, 2008); see also Johannes Hahn, *Gewalt und religiöser Konflikt. Studien zu den Auseinandersetzungen zwischen Christen, Heiden und Juden im Osten des Römischen Reiches (von Konstantin bis Theodosius II)* (Berlin, 2004).

[27] Kim Bowes, *Private Worship, Public Values, and Religious Change in Late Antiquity* (Cambridge, 2008).

both the churches inside the cities and the Christian tombs and chapels outside the cities, concluding that in addition to the established institutional church in urban centres about which we are informed through texts composed by clergy, even larger numbers of people engaged in cults to commemorate the Christian dead outside the cities, thus constituting *The Second Church*, the title of his provocative book.[28]

The gradual process of Christianization which archaeological studies have brought to light stands in stark contrast to the concept of 'conversion' as a sudden, forceful and life-changing personal decision that led to almost instantaneous baptism, which had provided the prevailing paradigm since the 1930s. Modern scholars readily subscribed to this romanticized notion of the transformation of an individual on the basis of late antique texts, first and foremost Augustine in his *Confessions* but also hagiographical narratives, which were themselves tools designed to secure conversion, often with an apologetic undertone.[29] The mainstreaming of archaeology thus provides an important 'reality check' against the triumphalist narratives of Christian authors.

2. *Loss of Innocence*. From the point of view of the Christian message, the integration of the church with the empire can be regarded as a loss of innocence. Scholars of early Christianity have turned the question of the decline of empire or of Greco-Roman culture on its head and asked whether the transformation of Christianity from a persecuted minority cult to state religion changed its original, true character and led to the corruption of its message as it was forced to compromise its ideals for the sake of a share in political power. The German sociologist Max Weber posed this question in the 1920s in terms of the relationship between charisma and institution in the growth of religions. After the death of the charismatic founder of a religious movement, Weber observed, the creation of a structured institution was essential to enable subsequent generations to carry on the original message, despite the inherent danger that the founder's teaching may become subsumed

---

[28] Ramsay MacMullen, *The Second Church: Popular Christianity, A.D. 200–400* (Atlanta, GA, 2009).

[29] The seminal work is Arthur Darby Nock, *Conversion: The Old and the New in Religion from Alexander the Great to Augustine of Hippo* (London, 1933, repr. Lanham, MD, 1988); for a recent counterpoint, see Kenneth Mills and Anthony Grafton, eds, *Conversion in Late Antiquity and the Early Middle Ages* (Rochester, NY, 2003).

by the institution's drive to perpetuate itself. In a very influential work with the provocative title *The End of Ancient Christianity*, Robert Markus questioned how Christian thought and identity were affected by the new prominence that the religion had gained on the public stage in the post-Constantinian era and came to the conclusion that it had radically changed by the time of Gregory the Great in the sixth century. More recent studies have tackled this issue from a different angle, by asking about the relationship between monasticism (representing charisma) and the episcopate (representing the institution of the church in cooperation with the empire).[30] My study of the role of bishops in late antiquity attempted to go beyond the Weberian model that pitched spiritual against institutional authority by introducing the concept of ascetic authority as the middle ground which both defined and justified the bishop's extensive public role.[31]

3. *Interconnectedness.* Between the viewpoint of empire and decline, on the one hand, and that of church and the loss of innocence, on the other, is that of interconnectedness. Here, value judgements are suspended. Decline or loss is not part of the debate. The emphasis is rather on mutual influence and interdependence.[32] Interestingly, these studies tend to take as their starting point the perspective of empire, and more specifically imperial ideology as expressed in art, ritual and rhetoric.

The first milestone within the last half-century was Francis Dvornik's *Early Christian and Byzantine Political Philosophy: Origins and Background.*[33] This compilation of source texts with extensive commentary demonstrated how the Hellenistic ruler cult that had dominated the eastern Mediterranean for centuries provided fertile ground not only for the Roman imperial cult but also for the

---

[30] Philip Rousseau, *Ascetics, Authority and the Church in the Age of Jerome and Cassian* (Oxford, 1978; 2nd edn, Notre Dame, IN, 2010); Andrea Sterk, *Renouncing the World yet Leading the Church: The Monk-Bishop in Late Antiquity* (Cambridge, MA, 2004).

[31] Claudia Rapp, *Holy Bishops in Late Antiquity: The Nature of Christian Leadership in an Age of Transition* (Berkeley, CA, 2005).

[32] Daniel Boyarin, *Border Lines: The Partition of Judaeo-Christianity* (Philadelphia, PA, 2004); Adam H. Becker and Annette Yoshiko Reed, eds, *The Ways that Never Parted: Jews and Christians in Late Antiquity and the Early Middle Ages* (Minneapolis, MN, 2007); Jeremy M. Schott, *Christianity, Empire, and the Making of Religion in Late Antiquity* (Philadelphia, PA, 2008).

[33] Francis Dvornik, *Early Christian and Byzantine Political Philosophy: Origins and Background* (Washington, DC, 1966).

Christian conceptualization of Christ as 'Lord' and 'Saviour' (*kyrios* and *sōter* both being key terms in the adulation of rulers), thus paving the way for a specifically Christian view of the monarch as God's vicegerent that was to provide the foundation for the imperial ideology of the Byzantine Empire. Sabine MacCormack's *Art and Ceremony in Late Antiquity* showed how the *adventus* ceremonies for the arrival of emperors or their officers were adapted for use by Christian bishops or holy men, while Michael McCormick investigated *Eternal Victory: Triumphal Rulership in Late Antiquity, Byzantium and the Early Medieval West*.[34] Following this trajectory is one of the most challenging (and most challenged) books, Thomas Mathews's *The Clash of Gods*.[35] He revisited the chicken-and-egg question of whether imperial culture was Christianized or whether Christian art adopted for itself the pictorial repertoire of imperial art, and concluded that Christianity did not merely experience a passive 'loss of innocence' but actively engaged in promiscuity (to keep within the metaphor) in seeking to insert itself into the imperial framework.

Yet even in these studies of interconnectedness, an old paradigm prevails, which views a highly developed Roman, imperial culture with its long tradition (the state) in contrast to the crude expressions of a newcomer religion (the church) that was still fumbling to find the appropriate forms for its articulation in art and literature and could not help but borrow from its predecessors.

4. *Development in Dialogue*. This impasse was broken to some extent in the 1990s, under the influence of the discipline of religious studies and often articulated by scholars familiar with the Jewish traditions of late antiquity; Christianity was no longer seen as a fixed monolith that existed in immutable isolation from the beginning, but as one of many options available on the rich marketplace of religions at the time. Christianity was thus no longer pitched against 'paganism' but treated within a larger context that also included Judaism. In fact, one of the most remarkable developments of recent decades, as has already been noted, is a willingness

[34] Sabine G. MacCormack, *Art and Ceremony in Late Antiquity* (Berkeley, CA, 1981); Michael McCormick, *Eternal Victory: Triumphal Rulership in Late Antiquity, Byzantium and the Early Medieval West* (Cambridge, 1986).
[35] Thomas F. Mathews, *The Clash of Gods: A Reinterpretation of Early Christian Art* (Princeton, NJ, 1993; rev. edn 1999).

to assume the same degree of genuine religious sentiment among the followers of ancient cults that has been taken for granted in Christian believers. Hence the new political correctness in terminology that has replaced 'paganism' with 'Greco-Roman religion', thereby abolishing an old Latin expression that, when flowing from the pens of Christian theologians, was meant to be insulting and exclusionary.[36] Hence also the preference in modern scholarship to replace the discussion of ancient *'cults'* with 'Greco-Roman *religion'*, thus replacing an emphasis on ritual practice as characterizing ancient religion with an acknowledgement of belief and faith that had previously been considered to be the sole domain of Christianity.[37]

CONSTANTINE AND BEYOND

It is in the context of the reign of Constantine that issues of church and state find their most acute articulation. Because the favouritism that he showed to the new religion was of such novelty and would have such far-reaching consequences for the history of the Middle Ages down to the present day, his actions have been scrutinized under the microscope, as it were, to identify epoch-making precedents for the four paradigms I have just discussed. Was Constantine the unsuspecting emperor who yielded to the pressure of ambitious bishops? Or was he a clever ruler who seized the opportunity to marshal the forces of Christianity in order to secure his rule and the empire? Such studies are based on two presuppositions: that the emperor represents the 'state' and that there was such a thing as 'the church' in the early fourth century that the emperor would find it useful to exploit. They implicitly posit the existence of a well-oiled ecclesiastical administrative machine, with a fully developed hierarchy of offices and a well-managed territorial administration that inserted itself into the boundaries of Diocletian's reformed empire.

Among scholars in the last decade, there has been a strong tendency to assume that Constantine's motivations were political

---

[36] On the history of the word *paganus* and the new political correctness in avoiding it, see now Cameron, *Last Pagans of Rome*, 14–32.

[37] Hubert Cancik and Jörg Rüpke, eds, *Die Religionen des Imperium Romanum: Koine und Konfrontationen* (Tübingen, 2009). For a different, equally innovative attempt to undo the 'Christianizing assumptions' of earlier scholarship, see Clifford Ando, *The Matter of the Gods: Religion and the Roman Empire* (Berkeley, CA, 2008).

first and foremost, and that his religious allegiance and support of Christianity were secondary, and a private matter at that. In his *Constantine and the Bishops*, Harold Drake makes the point that Constantine was adept at exploiting Christianity for his own political purposes.[38] Such views have, however, not reached the mainstream of popularizing history or the media, and I myself would be the first to admit that it is easier to appeal to the curiosity of undergraduate students with stories of Visions of the Cross in the sky than it is to interest graduate students in questioning the motivations that Constantine's biographer Eusebius might have had in recounting this story. The *Life of Constantine* by Eusebius, bishop of Caesarea, the core text for our understanding of the emperor's religious politics, is a curious mixture of rhetorical praise, history and biography with a distinct hagiographical touch. Thanks to the work of Averil Cameron and Stuart Hall, it is now available in a good English translation with historical commentary.[39] Our dependence on this text, however, is something of an anachronism. In the Byzantine tradition, as Friedhelm Winkelmann has shown, it had a rather lukewarm reception.[40]

CHURCH AND STATE IN BYZANTIUM: CAESAROPAPISM?

With his legislation in favour of Christians, his convocation of the Council of Nicaea and his reliance on bishops for the administration of the empire, Constantine appears to have set the tone for the future of church-state relations in the Byzantine Empire.

The distinction between church and state, however, is highly problematic for Byzantium. Marie Theres Fögen noted in a brief but brilliant summary of Byzantine political ideology that Christianity provided the legitimation and rationale to both emperor and patriarch for their actions, resulting in endless constellations of collaboration and conflict. It was only in institutional terms that the Byzantines had the ability to conceive of the 'state' as distinct from the 'church', in the sense that the two had different

---

[38] Harold A. Drake, *Constantine and the Bishops: The Politics of Intolerance* (Baltimore, MD, 2000).

[39] Eusebius, *Life of Constantine*, intro., transl. and commentary by Averil Cameron and Stuart G. Hall, Clarendon Ancient History Series (Oxford, 1999).

[40] Friedhelm Winkelmann, *Die Textbezeugung der* Vita Constantini *des Eusebius von Caesarea* (Berlin, 1962).

administrative structures for the enforcement of their interests.[41] If, following Fögen, we discard as anachronistic the notion of a religiously neutral state as the counterpoint to the church as the exclusive domain of religion, this still leaves us with the question of the nature of the state in Byzantium.

Perhaps surprisingly, Byzantinists have not taken much interest in this issue. John Haldon is the only scholar to have critically engaged with the question of Byzantium as a 'state' in the modern, Marxist-influenced definition of an 'institution ... which above all others functions to maintain and reproduce class domination and exploitation'.[42] After explaining the state's dependence on the 'tributary mode' (a term deemed more appropriate than 'feudalism'), regardless of whether tribute is extracted in the form of taxation or as rent, Haldon goes on to detail the application of this mode by the three landholding powers in Byzantium: the emperor, the aristocracy, and the church and monasteries. Haldon's definition is based on the power of the institution and the exploitation of the population. Consequently, there can be no distinction between church and state, because the church forms part of the latter's exploitative system.

Most Byzantinists, however, are content to use 'state' as synonymous with empire, imperial rule and imperial administration, and to think about relations between state and church in terms of relations not between institutions but between emperor and patriarch. That the emperor embraced responsibility for the church and took charge of church affairs is evident in many ways: not only did he convene church councils, following the example set by Constantine at Nicaea, sometimes attending the sessions and even contributing to the discussion, he was also responsible for the appointment of the patriarch. Constantinople was the youngest among the pentarchy of patriarchates. The rank of the archbishop of Constantinople as equal in honour to that of Rome was recognized at the Council of Chalcedon in 451, and the use of the title of 'Patriarch' is firmly attested since the fifth century. By the ninth century, the patriarch's claims to territorial universality were

---

[41]   Marie Theres Fögen, 'Das politische Denken der Byzantiner', in Iring Fetscher and Herfried Münkler, eds, *Pipers Handbuch der Politischen Ideen*, 2 (Munich, 1993), 41–85, at 59.

[42]   John F. Haldon, *The State and the Tributary Mode of Production* (London, 1993), 1.

expressed by the adoption of the adjective 'Ecumenical' in his official titulature.

It was the emperor who selected his favourite candidate from a list of three which had been produced by the metropolitan bishops, although he also had the right to deviate from this list and to appoint his own favourite, who could even be a layman. Often enough, the emperor ensured that a patriarch who had become troublesome was deposed and another one appointed in his stead. Of the 122 patriarchs elected between 379 and 1451, 53 were deposed or forced to resign, and of these at least 36 did so at the instigation of the emperor.

It was also the emperor who acted as the instrument of God's will in the enthronement of a new patriarch, when he pronounced: 'Divine grace and the imperial rule that I have received from it brings forth this most pious patriarch of Constantinople.'[43] The emperor ruled by divine appointment, as the vicegerent of Christ. He was responsible for the welfare of the empire in its entirety, and since it was a Christian empire, his responsibility encompassed the church as well. He enjoyed special 'liturgical privileges', as they are called: together with the clergy, he was allowed to enter the sanctuary of a church, and like clergy, he was allowed to receive the eucharistic bread with his hands, rather than being fed with a communion spoon. Did this make him a priest or place him in the ranks of the clergy? Most scholarship continues to agree that this was not the case. For one thing, the emperor did not officiate at any sacramental liturgies.

There are, however, two key passages that seem to indicate an emperor's arrogation of priestly rank: Constantine called himself *episkopos tōn ektos*, when addressing the bishops at the Council of Nicaea, as his biographer Eusebius reports. Did he really mean to claim, as a literal translation of these words would suggest, that he was a 'bishop to those outside', thus arrogating clerical rank for himself and justifying an expansionistic Christianity-driven foreign policy of conquest by mission? Or did he perhaps intend to make a pun on the word *episkopos*, which at that time still retained its original meaning of 'overseer'? Or, as one recent study has argued, did his biographer Eusebius simply seize on this expression to

43 Hans-Georg Beck, *Kirche und theologische Literatur im byzantinischen Reich* (Munich, 1959; repr. 1977), 62.

reinforce a theme that runs through the entire *Vita Constantini*, namely that Constantine was a new Moses for his time who led the Christian church out of bondage into a new future, with his unlikely victory in the Battle of the Milvian Bridge as a re-enactment of the crossing of the Red Sea? Moses was, after all, regarded by Jews and Christians alike as the model of religious and political leadership, at one and the same time priest and lawgiver, and thus also as a model bishop.[44]

Four centuries later, Leo III, the instigator of Iconoclasm, reportedly referred to himself as 'emperor and priest' (*basileus kai hiereus*). Like the passage in Eusebius, this has generated lively discussion in scholarship, ostensibly not about the interpretation of the passage but regarding its authenticity – textual criticism always serves as a convenient tool to wipe an uncomfortable issue off the table.[45] For it is not a Byzantine source that reports these words, but a letter by Pope Gregory II that throws them back at the emperor in order to discredit him on account of his arrogance and his misguided removal of icons.[46]

Written and pictorial sources throughout the existence of the Byzantine Empire attribute a religious quality to imperial rule, but refrain from using these exact words. How, then, to conceive of the role of the emperor in relation to the church? Hans-Georg Beck in his excellent handbook *Kirche und theologische Literatur im byzantinischen Reich* expresses with characteristic bluntness a thought that is echoed, as noted above, by Marie Theres Fögen: 'in Byzantine thought about theology and the state, state and church are not distinguished and indeed cannot be distinct, but they are manifestations of the same Christianity, manifestations that are unthinkable one without the other. Thus the notion of a "theory of two swords" is inconceivable in Byzantium.' He then explains that 'the Emperor within Christendom here on Earth carries the Spirit in a special way, analogous to bishops and priests'. As a result, Beck insists, 'caesaropapism' cannot be an issue in Byzan-

---

[44] Claudia Rapp, 'Imperial Ideology in the Making: Eusebius of Caesarea on Constantine as "Bishop"', *Journal of Theological Studies* n.s. 49 (1998), 685–95.

[45] Franz Tinnefeld, 'Kirche und Staat im byzantinischen Reich', *Ostkirchliche Studien* 54 (2005), 56–78, at 67.

[46] Gilbert Dagron, *Emperor and Priest: The Imperial Office in Byzantium* (Cambridge, 2003; first publ. as *Empereur et prêtre: Étude sur le 'césaropapisme' byzantin*, Paris, 1995), 158–66.

tium, because that would presuppose competition between two independent institutions, one of which wishes to deny the other's independence.[47]

The mention of 'caesaropapism' has long been a red flag for scholars of Byzantium. It appeared as convenient shorthand employed dismissively by Western medievalists who did not sufficiently appreciate the complexities of the interplay between emperor and patriarch in its ever-changing historical constellations. But this changed with the publication of Gilbert Dagron's *Empereur et prêtre: Étude sur le 'césaropapisme' byzantin*, written by a Byzantinist at the height of his learning and wisdom, after a long and distinguished career at the Collège de France. Its title is inspired by the words attributed to Leo III, which are held to be genuine. Dagron considers a wealth of evidence, from imperial ceremonies to church architecture, from letters to acts of church councils, with a heavy dose of theological works, and concludes that modern Byzantine scholars ought to accept and embrace the fact that the emperor at the helm of the empire they study was indeed a priest-king on the model of Melchizedek. Near the end of the book, Dagron draws attention to the genesis of the term 'caesaropapism' in the mid-eighteenth century. It was put forth as an experiment by Iustus Henning Böhmer (1674–1749), a professor at Halle, in his *Manual of Protestant Law*, in order to bestow equal criticism on rulers who govern the church (*caesaro-papia*) and on ecclesiastical leaders who assume worldly powers (*papo-caesaria*), clearly an anti-Catholic jibe. 'This imprecise concept', Dagron observes, 'was above all a killer word'.[48] It was employed by Western medieval scholarship as a way to keep Byzantium at a comfortable and alienating distance, as a foil to allow the Western understanding of the 'theory of the two swords' to shine that much more brightly. By his own admission, Dagron was only able to conceive of his subject and to develop his approach at the end of the second millennium, after the pageantry of communist countries after the Second World War had reinforced the importance of ritual and sacrality for the consolidation and articulation of power, however secularly

---

[47] Beck, *Kirche und theologische Literatur*, 36.
[48] Dagron, *Emperor and Priest*, 283.

conceived. The recent funerary celebrations for the president of North Korea, Kim Jong-Il, are a reminder of this force.

From today's perspective, what does the future hold in store for scholarship? The strongest new trend will, I think, be globalization. The Byzantine Empire, its mechanisms of power as well as the ideologies that undergird these mechanisms, will no longer be studied synchronically within the same religious system of Christianity (Byzantium and the West), or diachronically within the same regional context (the survival of Orthodoxy and the Byzantine heritage), but there will be greater curiosity about Byzantium, not only within the larger world of the Mediterranean, but also as a hinge between the Greco-Roman world and the Islamic world and even Asia. Such comparative approaches will offer entirely new vantage points for the study of religion, and thus also affect our understanding of its role in politics. Byzantinists will continue to question the categories of church and state, patriarch and emperor, religious and secular from new angles, and perhaps one day rise to Dagron's challenge and be proud to affirm the uniqueness of caesaropapism.

University of Vienna

CHURCH AND STATE IN EARLY MODERN ECCLESIASTICAL HISTORIOGRAPHY

by ANTHONY MILTON

'Church and state' is a phrase that one rarely meets with in most early modern ecclesiastical history that has been written over the past fifty years. One major exception has been the United States of America, where the phrase even has its own journal. With regard to early modern English history, one rare exception very much proves the rule: Leo Solt's *Church and State in Early Modern England* (a synthetic work published in 1990) is the work of an American historian, who admits in his preface that he has chosen to interpret the relationship 'very broadly', and that the book 'might be more accurately entitled "Religion and Politics in Early Modern England"'.[1] The axiomatic status of the separation of church and state in the United States, and its continuing use as a political football, has given the phrase a prominence in public discourse that has naturally been reflected in American historiography, where figures such as Roger Williams invite the application of later terminology to the seventeenth century.[2] Where 'church and state' have not been separated (or at least had not been in the early modern period), the term seems to have been less appealing to historians, at least to those working on the period before the assault on established churches in the nineteenth century.

This is not to say that the relationship between religion and the relative powers of the secular magistrate has not continued to be an area of significant concern and intense interest for early modern historians. But it has tended to be subsumed within different historiographies and discussed in different terms, with a different terminology, under the rubric of scholarship on 'religion and politics' (where Solt almost placed his book), 'the politics of religion', or reli-

---

[1] Leo F. Solt, *Church and State in Early Modern England 1509–1640* (Oxford, 1990), vii–viii. The *Journal of Church and State* has carried articles on early modern England and Europe, but these tend not to be written by prominent historians in the field, and the journal itself is clearly focused more on nineteenth- and twentieth-century debates on secularism, public education and the First Amendment.

[2] See T. L. Hall, *Separating Church and State: Roger Williams and Religious Liberty* (Urbana, IL, 1998).

gious toleration. Different terminology is of course never a matter of a mere neutral juggling with words – it indicates different presuppositions, entails different framing devices, and also means that scholarship is not necessarily directly engaging with the ideas and nostrums of earlier historians who employed such terms. In many cases this has involved study which moves beyond that of ecclesiastical institutions – towards the study of religion and the state rather than that of church and state. It has also been accompanied by a far more wide-ranging and enriched sense of the sources and methodologies that church historians should use, ranging through the social and political sciences, including anthropology, ethnology and linguistics.[3] This trend can of course be observed across all historical periods, and raises the question of whether we should accept that this really amounts to religious history rather than church history, or whether ecclesiastical historians should seek to redefine their remit to include all this expanded range of religious history (although this is arguably to make 'ecclesiastical history' so capacious as to be meaningless as an intellectual category).

The changing scope of research and diversification of terminology have had significant implications for how church and state should be understood, and also for the precise role of the early modern period in their evolving relationship. The study of church and state in the early modern period is inevitably partly overshadowed by questions of modernity, and by the assumption that modernization is the story of how church and state become decoupled. Traditionally, rationalism and secularization are understood to have been both the modernizing forces driving this separation and the main beneficiaries of it: modernity can only truly develop once states are freed from the shackles of the church and can thereby in turn free their societies from such restraints. Religious toleration is thus itself viewed as a creation of the secularizing state, restraining persecuting state churches and ultimately disestablishing them. However, elements of this picture have been, if not challenged, then at least reconfigured, in some of the early modern scholarship of the last fifty years.

★ ★ ★

---

[3] See W. Frijhoff, 'Church History without God or without Faith?', *Concilium* 42/2 (2006), 65–75.

The main context in which European scholars have been rethinking early modern church-state relations has been that generated by the so-called 'confessionalization paradigm', and this will form the basic focus of this essay. An important precursor of the debate was the work of Ernst Walter Zeeden on what he termed *Konfessionsbildung* ('confessional formation'), first laid out in a famous article in *Historische Zeitschrift* in 1958. Zeeden emphasized that in the early modern period Catholicism, Lutheranism and Calvinism all began to build confessional churches centred on written confessions of faith, with identities that were tightly defined, and social and confessional boundaries that were strictly delimited.[4]

It was in the late 1970s and early 1980s, however, that Zeeden's work was taken up by the historian Heinz Schilling and transformed into what he later dubbed 'the confessionalization paradigm'. The distinction is important: not *Konfessionsbildung* (Zeeden's 'confessional formation') but *Konfessionalisierung* ('confessionalization'). In this rendering, the 'formation of confessions' is linked to a much broader political and social transformation: Schilling has described confessionalization as one of 'the driving elements of the early modern process of transformation, which re-shaped the status-structured social world of old Europe into modern democratic, industrial society'.[5]

Most famously, Schilling linked confessionalization and social discipline to the rise of nation-states and to the process of state-building. *Integration* is the key to the whole process. At the heart of confessionalization is a mutually reinforcing, functional alliance between the leaders of the state on the one hand, and the theologians and churchmen of the emerging state churches on the other. For the rulers, confessional reform provided an instrument of state-building, whereby their subjects could be transformed

---

4 E. W. Zeeden, 'Grundlagen und Wege der Konfessionsbildung in Deutschland im Zeitalter der Glaubenskämpfe', *HZ* 185 (1958), 249–99; idem, *Die Entstehung der Konfessionen: Grundlagen und Formen der Konfessionsbildung im Zeitalter der Glaubenskämpfe* (Munich, 1965).

5 T. A. Brady, 'Confessionalization – The Career of a Concept', in *Confessionalization in Europe, 1555–1700: Essays in Honor and Memory of Bodo Nischan*, ed. J. M. Headley, H. J. Hillerbrand and A. J. Papalas (Aldershot, 2004), 1–20, at 4–5, quoting and translating from H. Schilling, 'Die Konfessionalisierung von Kirche, Staat und Gesellschaft', in W. Reinhard and H. Schilling, eds, *Die katholische Konfessionalisierung: Profil, Leistung, Defizite und Perspektiven eines geschichtswissenschaftlichen Paradigmas* (Gütersloh, 1995), 11–49.

into a more coherent and obedient political unit, the fragmentary medieval community of privileged groups being converted into an equal body of regulated subjects. For the church, secular officials provided extra resources for fighting heresy and heterodoxy, and for imposing true religion in a more systematic fashion. The result was a sacralization of the monarch and state power. This alliance of territorial state-building and confessionalization also influenced social relations by the enforcing of greater social discipline among the population, through the cooperation of pulpit and administration ('magistracy and ministry' as its English variant has been dubbed). This mutually reinforcing combination of religious reform, state-building and social discipline – all imposed from above – generated a systematic process of social change that affected all areas of life and propelled society towards modernity.[6] The sociologist Norbert Elias had seen the monopoly of military force and taxation as the crucial factors in the process of state-building (which he saw essentially as a process of the monopolizing of public functions by the state). Schilling by contrast was emphatic that 'the monopoly of the church and religion, as enforced through the state's confessionalization, *preceded* and *facilitated* the monopolization of military force and taxation'.[7] In tying confessionalization to modernity and state-building, Schilling also significantly altered the older German idea that the Protestant Reformation initiated the full secularization of all institutional power, thus clearing the way for the growth of modern states.[8]

A further feature of this paradigm, which Schilling developed slightly later, was his insistence on the confessionalization of international relations in this period. Rather than 'reason of

---

[6] H. Schilling, *Konfessionskonflikt und Staatsbildung* (Gütersloh, 1981); idem, 'Confessional Europe', in T. A. Brady et al., eds, *Handbook of European History 1400–1600*, 2 vols (Leiden, 1995), 2: 641–75, esp. 656–9; idem, 'Die Konfessionalisierung im Reich: Religioser und gesellschaftlicher Wandel in Deutschland zwischen 1555 und 1620', *HZ* 246 (1988), 1–45, transl. as 'Confessionalization in the Empire: Religious and Societal Change in Germany between 1555 and 1620', in idem, *Religion, Political Culture and the Emergence of Early Modern Society* (Leiden, 1992), 205–45; idem, 'The Reformation and the Rise of the Early Modern State', in J. D. Tracy, ed., *Luther and the Modern State in Germany* (Kirksville, MO, 1986), 21–30.

[7] N. Elias, *The Civilizing Process*, transl. E. Jephcott, 2 vols (New York, 1977–82); Schilling, 'Reformation and the Rise', 27 (my italics).

[8] J. F. Harrington and H. W. Smith, 'Confessionalization, Community and State Building in Germany, 1555–1870', *JMH* 69 (1997), 77–101, at 78.

state' being determined by dynastic interest, Schilling has argued that confessional identities increasingly became a key element in foreign policy, embracing 'political identity and ideology, the style of politics, cultural representation of the princes and states, as well as the questions of alliance, legitimation and propaganda'. The confrontations that this created then provided the impulse for 'a fundamental change in the structure and functioning of international politics' by prompting the 'secularization' of foreign relations and 'the formation and rise of the modern international system of power states'.[9] Schilling himself has noted that this feature of his confessionalization paradigm has had less impact on early modern historians, but a heightened (albeit untheorized) awareness of the importance of religious convictions in early modern debates on foreign policy has been evident in scholarship for some decades, in England and elsewhere.[10]

One other notable feature of the work of Schilling and his followers has been their insistence on the inclusion of Roman Catholicism within this picture. This followed on from the work of Zeeden, and there are possible reasons for this that are located very much within modern German religious and political history, and the confessional allegiances of some of the scholars involved.[11] But this cross-confessional emphasis also partly reflects a more general shift among cultural and religious historians, who have increasingly tended to see Protestantism and Counter-Reformation Catholicism, below their surface differences, as being engaged in essentially the same process: the formalization and standardization (sometimes effectively the Christianization) of the culture of the people of early modern Europe. This is itself part of a broader process of

<hr>

[9] H. Schilling, 'Konfessionalisierung und Formierung eines internationalen Systems während der frühen Neuzeit', in H. Guggisberg and G. Krodel, eds, *Die Reformation in Deutschland und Europa: Interpretationen und Debatten* (Gütersloh, 1993), 597–613; idem, ed., *Konfessionalisierung und Staatsinteressen 1559–1660* (Paderborn, 2007); idem, *Early Modern European Civilization and its Political and Cultural Dynamism* (London, 2008), 67–86.

[10] e.g. T. Cogswell, *The Blessed Revolution: English Politics and the Coming of War, 1621–1624* (Cambridge, 1989); S. Pincus, *Protestantism and Patriotism: Ideologies and the Making of English Foreign Policy, 1650–1668* (Cambridge, 1996), 15–79; C. E. Harline, *Pamphlets, Printing and Political Culture in the Early Dutch Republic* (Dordrecht, 1987).

[11] H. Schilling, 'Confessionalization: Historical and Scholarly Perspectives of a Comparative and Interdisciplinary Paradigm', in Headley, Hillerbrand and Papalas, eds, *Confessionalization in Europe*, 21–36, at 22–3.

sociocultural change, as argued influentially in the work of Peter Burke and Jean Delumeau.[12] Moreover, while this work has made elite Catholicism seem more like Protestantism, in the work of Bob Scribner and others popular Protestantism has seemed much closer to Catholicism: rather than an antidote to Roman Catholic superstition, it can be seen as simply generating its own versions (with 'superstition' merely an 'other' against which all confessions defined themselves).[13] More generally, scholars have been grasping the degree to which the gaping theological chasms between the confessions that were posited by the polemicists of the age did not correspond to theological, intellectual or social reality. In Catholicism's inclusion within the confessionalization paradigm the crucial contributor has been the Roman Catholic scholar Wolfgang Reinhard. Although his arguments are commonly linked with those of Schilling, it must be stressed that Reinhard was fully conscious of the difficulties involved in associating Catholicism with Protestant forms of confessionalism. He conceived of a confessionalization of the church rather than of society, and drew up a catalogue of Catholic confessional peculiarities (or *propria*) which should be flagged up in qualifying the absorption of Catholicism within a model of confessionalization.[14]

Confessionalization was born in German Protestant historiography, where it is still enormously influential and continues to generate a dauntingly prodigious body of scholarly work. But Schilling is emphatic that this was a general European phenomenon, and the model has been tested by historians of a number of other countries, including those of central and eastern Europe, and to a lesser extent France, Spain and the Netherlands.[15] Schilling

---

[12] J. Delumeau, *Le Catholicisme entre Luther et Voltaire* (Paris, 1971); P. Burke, *Popular Culture in Early Modern Europe* (London, 1978).

[13] R. W. Scribner, 'Incombustible Luther: The Image of the Reformer in Early Modern Germany', *P&P*, no. 110 (1986), 36–68; idem and T. Johnson, eds, *Popular Religion in Germany and Central Europe 1400–1800* (Basingstoke, 1996). For a critical response to Scribner's arguments, see E. Cameron, *Enchanted Europe: Superstition, Reason and Religion 1250–1750* (Oxford, 2010).

[14] W. Reinhard, 'Was ist katholische Konfessionalisierung?', in idem and Schilling, eds, *Katholische Konfessionalisierung*, 419–52; idem, 'Gegenreformation als Modernisierung?', *ARG* 68 (1977), 226–52; Brady, 'Confessionalization', 8–10.

[15] For a brief summary, see U. Lotz-Heumann, 'Confessionalization', in D. M. Whitford, ed., *Reformation and Early Modern Europe: A Guide to Research* (Kirksville, MO, 2008), 136–57, at 146–9. Schilling's account of the European applicability of his

did not leave England out of his confessionalization model, but English historians characteristically have seemed to be completely unaware of this formulation. The one major early modern English religious historian who did at least briefly note the phenomenon was the late and much lamented Patrick Collinson. At a colloquium in 1996 he described having encountered at an Anglo-German conference in Munich the previous year 'a process called confessionalization ... which some historians see as highly relevant to the early modern process of state formation'. Collinson was at this time sceptical about whether this model could be applied to England because of 'the failure of the state church to define and underwrite Protestant orthodoxy'. Ten years later, however, at the 75th Anglo-American Conference of Historians, he had notably changed his mind: he declared unequivocally that 'Elizabethan England was a confessional state. If we follow the reasoning of Heinz Schilling, Wolfgang Reinhard and others, proponents of the currently fashionable notion of "confessionalisation", the English case was more typical than exceptional'.[16]

This re-evaluation echoed (perhaps unconsciously) some rethinking of the paradigm on the Continent, to which we shall return later. But it also reflected an increasing readiness among English Reformation and post-Reformation historians to recognize the role played by the state in the enforcement of religious orthodoxy. There has long been a fatal Anglican tendency to see the Church of England as essentially non-confessional, and this in a country which executed by burning more heretics in a shorter period of time than any other; which executed more Catholic martyrs than any other Protestant country; where every Protestant archbishop of Canterbury from Cranmer to the 1630s held that the pope was the Antichrist; a country that witnessed the bloodiest civil war fought among Protestants in early modern Europe; that experienced a further major reformation a century after its

---

paradigm seems more emphatic in his 1995 'Confessional Europe' than in his earlier articles 'Die Konfessionalisierung im Reich', 38; and 'Reformation and the Rise', 24.

[16] P. Collinson, 'Comment on Eamon Duffy's Neale Lecture and the Colloquium', in N. Tyacke, ed., *England's Long Reformation, 1500–1800* (London, 1997), 71–86, at 78–9; P. Collinson, *This England: Essays on the English Nation and Commonwealth in the Sixteenth Century* (Manchester, 2011), 38. For a brief discussion of the Church of England in relation to the confessionalization debate, see S. Ehrenpreis and U. Lotz-Heumann, *Reformation und konfessionelles Zeitalter* (Darmstadt, 2002), 103–4.

supposed settlement, along with two mass ejections of thousands of clergy within a twenty-year period – yet which still wants to see itself as uniquely moderate, stable and irenical, detached from the acrimonious confessional divisions of the Continent.[17] In recent decades English church historians, led by Collinson in the 1960s and reinforced by a host of subsequent scholars, have emphasized the degree to which the values of Reformed Protestantism had captured the elite of the Elizabethan church and state.[18] Contemporaries were convinced that the Church of England stood on the Reformed side of continental Protestantism (why else would it send delegates to the international Reformed Synod of Dort?). Its confession of faith constituted one of the most advanced Protestant confessions when it was first drawn up under Edward VI, and in the form of the Thirty-Nine Articles it notably endured without challenge, qualification or further elaboration for a great deal longer than most continental confessions did. Could it perhaps be the case that it is the very lack of challenges and revisions to the Thirty-Nine Articles that has misled Anglicans into seeing them as an uncontroversial and undogmatic formulation of agreed principles, rather than as an exceptionally successful confessional statement? In this context it seems far more natural to consider England alongside the confessionalizing developments of the Continent.

Another important influence has been the greater attention paid by mainstream English historians to the predicament of English Roman Catholics. No longer marginalized in the pages of the journal *Recusant History*, the last twenty years have seen a revolution in the study and understanding of English Catholics, and as a result the Elizabethan state has seemed less a benignly Anglican institution and more a sometimes ruthless participant in a fraught

---

[17] This sentiment can even infect discussions by non-English scholars. Thus at the Augsburg conference on 'Catholic confessionalization' in September 1993 the question was raised in discussion 'ob der Anglikanismus als Konfession gelten könne, oder vielmehr als eine nicht-konfessionalisierte Nationalkirche zu betrachten sei': Schilling, 'Die Konfessionalisierung von Kirche', 47.

[18] e.g. P. Collinson, *The Elizabethan Puritan Movement* (London, 1967); idem, *The Religion of Protestants* (Oxford, 1982); S. Alford, *The Early Elizabethan Polity: William Cecil and the British Succession Crisis, 1558–1569* (Cambridge, 1998); S. Adams, *Leicester and the Court: Essays on Elizabethan Politics* (Manchester, 2002); D. Crankshaw, 'Preparations for the Camterbury Provincial Convocation of 1562–63: A Question of Attribution', in *Belief and Practice in Reformation England: A Tribute to Patrick Collinson from his Students*, ed. S. Wabuda and C. Litzenberger (Aldershot, 1998), 60–93.

and potentially cataclysmic confessional stand-off, with France's religious wars an all-too-likely model for future events. William Cecil's claim that the state was not persecuting and executing Roman Catholics for their religion has at last been studied as a polemical assertion by a zealous Protestant rather than merely as a factual statement by a staid politician.[19] However, these English historiographical trends have not been inspired by, and have not engaged directly with, the confessionalization paradigm, and it is only now that a prominent historian of England's Reformation – Peter Marshall – has set himself the task of writing its history with the confessionalization model in mind.[20]

Few among non-German ecclesiastical historians (and not many even among German ones) have been particularly keen to follow the multidisciplinary approach of Schilling in linking religious with social, political and even economic developments. Historians of political science working on state development in the early modern period have sought to link political and cultural phenomena in explicating the rise of nation-states, but typically their emphasis has been on the impact of the military revolution and its unprecedented fiscal and administrative demands in promoting national integration. One of the few historians of this type who has sought to address confessional issues in this context is Mike Braddick, whose work on state formation includes a section on 'the confessional state'. But Braddick still maintains the pre-eminence of military-fiscal pressures in state formation, and while his treatment of 'the confessional state' tackles many of the themes that have been central to European scholarship on confessionalization, he does not engage with this work directly. Philip Gorski is a rare example of a historical sociologist who has engaged directly and extensively with the confessionalization paradigm, although his failure to discuss it alongside the military-fiscal dimension means that historians of state formation have tended to neglect

---

[19] Collinson, *This England*, 46. On the historiography of English Catholicism, see the introduction to E. H. Shagan, ed., *Catholics and the 'Protestant Nation': Religion, Politics and Identity in Early Modern England* (Manchester, 2005), 1–21.

[20] P. Marshall, '(Re)defining the English Reformation', *JBS* 48 (2009), 564–86, at 575–6. Professor Marshall's forthcoming Yale monograph (provisionally entitled *Heretics and Believers: A New History of the English Reformation*) will engage with the confessionalization paradigm in more detail.

his work.[21] Moreover, Gorski is not uncritical of the confessionalization paradigm itself, and it is to critiques of confessionalization that we must now turn.

Historians' reservations have focused on various aspects of Schilling's arguments.[22] His obsession with modernity has not prompted significant agreement or emulation beyond Reinhard's work. His insistence that confessionalization was the driving force behind a range of other contemporaneous social, cultural and economic phenomena has prompted the predictable response that the causal relationships are assumed rather than demonstrated, and that confessionalization is arguably best seen as one of a number of sometimes interlinked phenomena (or indeed as a *symptom* of a broader process of social change, rather than a cause of it).[23] The incorporation of Catholicism into the confessionalization process has never really been received terribly well, while the long catalogue of Catholic *propria* has also been matched by an insistence by other historians on the vital significance of the distinctive *propria* of Calvinism in theology, piety and spirituality. For some historians these have explained why only in Calvinism did the social discipline central to the confessionalization thesis truly emerge, while for others the 'individualism' and 'inward-looking quality' of Calvinism made it not 'an entirely appropriate instrument of confessionalization'.[24]

Most interesting for our purposes has been the critique of the confessionalization paradigm's interpretation of church–state relations. There are certainly some cases where the model of confessionalization works to perfection. But counter-examples, where

---

[21] J. Brewer, *The Sinews of Power: War, Money and the English State, 1688–1783* (London, 1989); M. J. Braddick, *State Formation in Early Modern England c.1550–1700* (Cambridge, 2000); P. S. Gorski, *Disciplinary Revolution: Calvinism and the Rise of the State in Early Modern Europe* (Chicago, IL, 2003).

[22] For overviews of these critiques, see Ehrenpreis and Lotz-Heumann, *Reformation*, 67–71; Lotz-Heumann, 'Confessionalization', 143–9.

[23] Lotz-Heumann, 'Confessionalization', 143–4.

[24] Ibid. 144–5; Brady, 'Confessionalization', 9–12; Gorski, *Disciplinary Revolution*, 19–22, 114–55; H. Schilling, ed., *Die reformierte Konfessionalisierung in Deutschland: Das Problem der 'Zweiten Reformation'*, Schriften des Vereins für Reformationsgeschichte 195 (Gütersloh, 1986), esp. 458–67; A. Pettegree, 'Confessionalization in North Western Europe', in J. Bahlcke and A. Strohmeyer, eds, *Konfessionalisierung in Ostmitteleuropa: Wirkungen des religiösen Wandels im 16. und 17. Jahrhundert in Staat, Gesellschaft und Kultur*, Forschungen zur Geschichte und Kultur des östlichen Mitteleuropa 7 (Stuttgart, 1999), 105–20, at 119–20.

rulers and churches struggled to impose confessional change on their people, or showed little enthusiasm for doing so, or where the local intensification of social discipline was not tied to state-building, have not been hard to find (as revealed in studies of Hesse-Kassel, Brandenburg, Anhalt, Transylvania and Ireland, among others).[25] These help to demonstrate that England's shortcomings as a confessional state were far from unusual, and were in some senses typical. It should also be stressed that Schilling himself always recognized that as religious reform and state-building could fuse, so could religious dissent and political opposition, and that confessionalization could threaten state integration just as much as it might promote it. There was indeed a dialectical relationship between integration and confrontation.[26] Inevitably, however, his work tended to concentrate on those cases where the central authorities were responsible for driving confessional integration.

The problem here has been not so much an unbalanced concentration on confessionalization's success stories, as a tendency to assume what is very much a top-down model of social and cultural life, being concerned with how the elites of state and church sought to regulate the laity. One of the oddities of the timing of the introduction of the confessionalization paradigm in the 1980s is that it was concurrent with a scholarship which was seeking to get away from the official reformation of state confessions and to address the extent to which this had actually had only a very limited and spasmodic influence on systems of popular belief. Most famously in the work of Bob Scribner, but also now in that of a generation of historians, there has been an emphasis not on formal confessions but on popular mentalities and their practical expression, on magic and folklore, on popular practice

---

[25] H. R. Schmidt, 'Sozialdisziplinierung? Ein Plädoyer für das Ende des Etatismus in der Konfessionalisierungsforschung', *HZ* 265 (1997), 639–82; B. Nischan, *Prince, People and Confession: The Second Reformation in Brandenburg* (Philadelphia, PA, 1994); W. Freitag, 'Konfliktfelder und Konfliktparteien in Prozeß der lutherischen und reformierten Konfessionalisierung', *ARG* 92 (2001), 165–94; L. Schorn-Schütte, 'Konfessionalisierung als wissenschaftliches Paradigma?', and K. Zach, 'Stände, Grundherrschaft und Konfessionalisierung in Siebenbürgen', in Bahlcke and Strohmeyer, eds, *Konfessionalisierung*, 63–77, 367–91; U. Lotz-Heumann, 'Confessionalization in Ireland: Periodization and Character', in A. Ford and J. McCafferty, eds, *The Origins of Sectarianism in Early Modern Ireland, 1500–1700* (Cambridge, 2005), 24–53.
[26] Schilling, 'Konfessionalisierung im Reich', 6, 38–9.

and ritual.[27] It is the persistence of communal tradition and the eclecticism of lay beliefs that have stood out in such studies. In England, some aspects of this approach have had a resonance that the scholarship on confessionalization has never matched, helped in part by the amount of relevant work available in the English language, its prominence in American Reformation scholarship and by Bob Scribner's residence in Cambridge. This approach was also able to build upon an independent English historiographical trend since the late 1960s which had sought to investigate variations in the local impact of the Reformation, and to question the extent of popular Protestantism and the speed with which changes in the official religion of the church were actually reflected at a local level. G. R. Elton's famous comment in 1977 that in 1553 England was almost certainly nearer to being a Protestant country than anything else was the last statement of an increasingly discredited tradition.[28]

While for some English historians this incomplete reformation process appeared to provide the basis for escalating confessional conflict, a number of historians in the 1990s sought instead to present it as the achievement of an instinctively non-confessional or indeed anti-confessional English people. Norman Jones's account of the English Reformation stressed the importance of charity, irenicism and pragmatism in the manner in which English society adapted to the Reformation. Christopher Marsh applauded the English 'layfolk' whose 'popular religion' was marked by 'flexibility', 'a syncretic instinct and a reluctance to abandon ... the middle ground'; this was a religiosity marked by tolerance of religious difference and an instinct to create a hybrid religion 'compounded of that which is best in both'. Here, I think, there is a dangerous slippage back to the conviction that the English are

---

[27] R. W. Scribner, 'The Impact of the Reformation on Everyday Life', in *Mensch und Object im Mittelalter und in der frühen Neuzeit: Leben, Alltag, Kultur. Internationaler Kongress, Krems an der Donau, 27. bis 30. September 1988*, ed. G. Jaritz, Veröffentlichungen des Instituts für Realienkunde des Mittelalters und der frühen Neuzeit 13 (Vienna, 1990), 315–43; T. A. Brady, 'Robert W. Scribner, a Historian of the German Reformation', in R. W. Scribner, *Religion and Culture in Germany (1400–1800)*, ed. L. Roper (Leiden, 2001), 9–28.

[28] R. O'Day, *The Debate on the English Reformation* (London, 1986), ch. 6; G. R. Elton, *Reform and Reformation: England 1509–1558* (London, 1977), 371.

instinctively anti-confessional – not so much 'woolly Anglicanism' as 'fluffy Anglicanism'.[29]

Attention to the extent of popular tolerance of religious difference and confessional coexistence (what has been dubbed by the Dutch scholar Willem Frijhoff 'the ecumenicity of everyday life')[30] may have been an expression of Anglican insularity in the work that I have just mentioned, but it has received more rigorous and empirical analysis on the Continent in particular over the last twenty years, and some of this work, such as that of Gregory Hanlon on Aquitaine, has engaged explicitly with confessionalization models.[31] This body of work has been brought together most helpfully by Benjamin Kaplan in his book *Divided by Faith: Religious Conflict and the Practice of Toleration in Early Modern Europe* (2007).[32] This is a study that is very self-consciously written in the aftermath of 9/11, and is anxious to give a positive answer to the question 'can people whose basic beliefs are irreconcilably opposed live together peacefully?' Kaplan believes that they can, and that the key to demonstrating this is to reveal the working of peaceful coexistence as a social practice and a pattern of interaction (getting away from the idea of it as a secularizing, Enlightenment concept) that is evident before, during and after the process of confessionalization.[33] Kaplan is confronting a traditional view of

---

[29] N. Jones, *The English Reformation: Religion and Cultural Adaptation* (Oxford, 2002); C. Marsh, *Popular Religion in Sixteenth-Century England* (Basingstoke, 1998), 212–13. Of the two types of 'Anglicanism' mentioned in the above text, I am taking the former to denote an intellectually engaged attempt to avoid ideological conflict through the pursuit of a deliberately indeterminate moderation in which obfuscation is seen as an inherently positive force, whereas the latter term is intended to refer to a sentimentalized view of English religious culture as inherently liberal and tolerant.

[30] W. Frijhoff, *Embodied Belief: Ten Essays on Religious Culture in Dutch History* (Hilversum, 2002), 37. The appropriate term for such coexistence remains a matter of dispute. Frijhoff's use of 'omgangsoekumene' has been followed by a number of historians. Kaplan has warned that this could be confused with modern–day ecumenism, although his preferred term of 'toleration' carries similar problematic modern associations: see B. Kaplan, *Divided by Faith: Religious Conflict and the Practice of Toleration in Early Modern Europe* (London, 2007), 11; idem, 'Religiously Mixed Marriage in Dutch Society' in idem et al, eds, *Catholic Communities in Protestant States: Britain and the Netherlands, c.1570–1720* (Manchester, 2009), 48–66, at 50.

[31] G. Hanlon, *Confession and Community in Seventeenth-Century France: Catholic and Protestant Co-existence in Aquitaine* (Philadelphia, PA, 1993).

[32] See n. 30 above, and also the important comparative discussion in A. Walsham, *Charitable Hatred: Tolerance and Intolerance in England, 1500–1700* (Manchester, 2006), ch. 6.

[33] Here the impulse to oppose the 'secularization' model arguably leads Kaplan

the relationship between religious toleration and modernity that was actually intensified by Schilling's model of confessionalization. Schilling declared unequivocally that confessional Europe ended 'around 1650', because 'the state had become strong enough to function effectively without the aid of church or religion' and as a consequence 'it could reject the maxim that "religion is the bond of society" and embrace a plurality of churches and worldviews'.[34] Religion, in other words, would always favour repression, whereas as soon as it was strong enough the state would favour toleration and pluralism instead. For Kaplan, by contrast, it was state interference through the process of confessionalization that generated the extremes of religious intolerance that followed, and these were overcome not so much by the rise of Enlightenment as by the decline of confessionalization, which enabled some of the practices of mutual forbearance to resume.

Ultimately, though, Kaplan's work offers a more subtle analysis of forms of local tolerance and intolerance than his framing devices would suggest. He paints a picture of local communities in which elaborate power-sharing schemes were combined with the turning of blind eyes to hidden and cross-border activities, and yet in which tension, anxiety and bitterness were never far away. Indeed, much of his evidence demonstrates how local religious communities in the most multi-confessional regions developed ever tighter and more exclusive confessional identities, and marked their confessional boundaries with increasing rigidity. Here Kaplan in some respects returns to a principal thread of his earlier book on Utrecht: the creation of multiple confessions. In this earlier study Kaplan had noted how all five religious communities in early modern Utrecht – Calvinists, Remonstrants (i.e. Arminians), Mennonites, Lutherans and Roman Catholics – experienced a rise of confessionalism, in the form of (re)building ecclesiastical structures, competing for the unaffiliated, and the religious disciplining of congregations.[35] Philip Benedict's work on Montpellier has

at times to overstate the religious credentials of other moderating social forces. For instance: 'Honor, loyalty, friendship, affection, kinship, civic duty, devotion to the common weal – these bonds have a sacred character that might reinforce or complicate an individual's confessional allegiance': Kaplan, *Divided by Faith*, 9.

34 Schilling, 'Confessional Europe', 667–8, 669.

35 B. Kaplan, *Calvinists and Libertines: Confession and Community in Utrecht, 1578–1620* (Oxford, 1995); cf. O. Mörke, 'Die politische Bedeutung des Konfessionellen im

similarly demonstrated how communities which had earlier coped with confessional division by exhibiting an impressive degree of cross-confessional tolerance gradually separated over the course of the seventeenth century.[36] Similar patterns have been found in the multi-confessional communities of east central Europe.[37]

These examples reflect a much broader development in the study of confessionalization, away from national confessions and state churches and towards what was arguably a much more widespread process of tighter integration on a local level of exclusive, individual confessional communities. This could of course often frustrate or complicate state formation. But it need not represent an explicit rejection of the confessional identity of the state: in some cases it reflected an intensification of it. Crucially, though, this was a process rooted not in any state-driven process of confessionalization but rather in the popular vitality and growth of lay piety on a local level. Especially influential here has been the work of Marc Forster in his study of the bishopric of Speyer and other small Catholic territories in south-western Germany. Forster and others have questioned the assumed link to state-building by noting the growth of Roman Catholic confessionalism without the existence of a strong state, and with no clear connection to the process of state-building (or to social or political modernity). Confessional formation is thus presented 'as a process more negotiated than imposed'.[38] This stress on the spontaneous formation (*Bildung*) rather than the state-led imposition of confessions echoes

Deutschen Reich und in der Republik der Vereinigten Niederlande', in R. G. Asch and H. Duchhardt, eds, *Der Absolutismus – ein Mythos? Strukturwandel monarchischen Herrschaft in West- und Mitteleuropa (ca.1550–1700)*, Münstersche historische Forschungen 9 (Cologne, 1996), 125–64.

[36] P. Benedict, 'Confessionalization in France? Critical Reflections and New Evidence', in idem, *The Faith and Fortunes of France's Huguenots 1600–85* (Aldershot, 2001), 309–25, at 313; see also J. R. Farr, 'Confessionalization and Social Discipline in France, 1530–1685', *ARG* 94 (2003), 276–93.

[37] Lotz-Heumann, 'Confessionalization', 147–8. More generally, see also C. Scott Dixon, D. Freist and M. Greengrass, eds, *Living with Religious Diversity in Early-Modern Europe* (Aldershot, 2009).

[38] M. R. Forster, *The Counter-Reformation in the Villages: Religion and Reform in the Bishopric of Speyer, 1560–1720* (London, 1992); idem, *Catholic Revival in the Age of the Baroque: Religious Identity in Southwest Germany 1550–1750* (Cambridge, 2001); Brady, 'Confessionalization', 14–15; Harrington and Smith, 'Confessionalization', 91. See also D. H. Shantz, 'Politics, Prophecy and Pietism in the Halberstadt Conventicle, 1691–1694', in F. van Lieburg, ed., *Confessionalism and Pietism: Religious Reform in Early Modern Europe* (Mainz, 2006), 129-47.

the approach of the historians of the early modern state who have preferred the term 'state-formation' to 'state-building' in recognition of the importance of local initiatives and the co-option of local agents in the process (although this may be a matter of historiographical coincidence rather than of a conscious influence).[39]

One of the recurring observations in these studies of what Philip Benedict has dubbed 'weak confessionalization' (with the term 'strong confessionalization' reserved for its state-led counterpart) is that these self-generated confessional identities were hardening over time, over the course of the seventeenth century and beyond. This in turn has led historians to a changed sense of the chronology of confessionalization. Schilling has stated emphatically that the state-run confessionalization that concerned him was over by 1650, and indeed German historians in the past (including Zeeden) traditionally assumed this to have been the case, as by the eighteenth century the rigid juridical structures of *cuius regio, eius religio* were breaking down.[40] More recently historians have continued to endorse much of this periodization, although with qualifications. Studies of monarchy and religion in the eighteenth century, for example, have charted the gradual process whereby this relationship was re-envisioned. While monarchs may have been desacralized, 'divine right' ideology still persisted, and religion continued to play a significant role in court life and political legitimation (even if it ceased to provide the *only* frame of reference for monarchical rule), while the sacrality of the monarch was increasingly transferred from his person to his office.[41] Similarly, studies of foreign relations have agreed that the confessional factor became less central to power relations by the eighteenth century, although here again some historians have noted the degree to which confessional concerns continued to be strongly aired and invoked, even if they were now competing with other ideological forces such as political economy and the perceived 'balance of power'.[42]

---

[39] e.g. Braddick, *State Formation*; S. Hindle, *The State and Social Change in Early Modern England* (Basingstoke, 2000). Braddick's use of the term 'state formation' reflected the influence of anthropologists and political scientists rather than of historians of confessionalization: personal e-mail to author, 17 March 2012.

[40] Zeeden, *Entstehung der Konfessionen*, 181; Schilling, 'Confessional Europe', 669.

[41] M. Schaich, 'Introduction' to idem, ed., *Monarchy and Religion: The Transformation of Royal Culture in Eighteenth-Century Europe* (Oxford, 2007), 1–40, at 5–6, 9, 25, 36–8.

[42] For an emphasis on the deconfessionalization of foreign relations, see the work

The periodization of confessionalization has seemed most askew, however, when historians have studied 'weak confessionalization'. A focus on *mentalité* rather than high politics and legal restrictions has revealed that 'weak confessionalization' was becoming stronger and reaching its height in the *eighteenth* century, and this forces a rethinking of the significance of the later dismantling of state-church structures. A landmark publication in this field twenty years ago was Etienne François's study of Catholics and Protestants in eighteenth-century Augsburg, entitled *Die unsichtbare Grenze* ('the invisible border'). François maintained that 'only because the confessional borders had become (firstly) an internalized border – and therefore largely independent of the institutional preconditions that led to their formation – could they survive the radical structural changes of the early nineteenth century' and continue to exist in a completely altered context.[43] The 'border' or 'boundary' of François's title is invisible because it is not judicial or political, but social.

François describes a world in which each confession has created its own self-sufficient and exclusive social system. This type of 'confessionalism' is the counterpart of what Dutch historians and sociologists have termed '*verzuiling*' or 'pillarization': the phenomenon in the nineteenth-century Netherlands in which each religious denomination developed its own political, social and cultural community, with its own political party, trade union, schools and youth organization, in a form of social and cultural apartheid (and there have been attempts to apply the concept of *verzuiling* to religious identity-formation in the seventeenth-century Netherlands and even England).[44] Here scholarship seems to have come full

---

of Steve Pincus, esp. his *Protestantism and Patriotism* and *1688: The First Modern Revolution* (London, 2009); also D. Onnekink and G. Rommelse, eds, *Ideology and Foreign Policy in Early Modern Europe (1650–1750)* (Farnham, 2011). For the continuing importance of religion in foreign policy discourse, see the articles in the same volume by B. Wagner-Rundell, S. Jettot and S. Rameix. See also T. Claydon, *Europe and the Making of England 1660–1760* (Cambridge, 2007); A. C. Thompson, 'Early Eighteenth-Century Britain as a Confessional State', in idem and I. McBride, eds, *Protestantism and National Identity: Britain and Ireland c.1650–c.1850* (Cambridge, 1998), 86–109, at 96–106.

43 E. François, *Die unsichtbare Grenze: Protestanten und Katholiken in Augsburg 1648–1806* (Sigmaringen, 1991), 242, quoted and translated in Harrington and Smith, 'Confessionalization', 91–2.

44 S. Groenveld, *Huisgenoten des geloofs: Was de samenleving in de Republiek der Verenigde Nederlanden verzuild?* (Hilversum, 1995); A. Milton, 'Religion and Community in

circle, and with the study of confessional boundaries we are back in the world of Zeeden's *Konfessionsbildung*. This increasing historiographical emphasis on multiple exclusive confessions might seem to imply that the historical concept of the confessional church-state is now a dead letter: there are so few examples of a simple convergence of church and state in a process of national integration. Nevertheless, it may be that there is still room for a church-state dimension. In recent years a number of scholars have argued that the process of confessional formation – even in the form highlighted in François's work – partly helped to confessionalize nineteenth-century German nationalism, and that the nineteenth century should be categorized as a confessional age.[45] The more that confessionalism is pushed into the nineteenth century, the more it can be argued to have made a contribution to the development of nationalism, if we move beyond the specific church-state dynamic and focus more on the generation of a confessionally charged national identity.

The move towards the study of confessionalized national identities which were not necessarily allied to the direct persecution of religious minorities takes us to another phenomenon that has been explored more in the work of Willem Frijhoff. While acknowledging that the majority of the early modern Dutch population were not full members of the Dutch Reformed church, Frijhoff has nevertheless drawn attention in a number of publications to the manner in which the broader community participated in the public rites over which the public church presided. The public church did not enforce attendance and allegiance according to the classic confessionalization model, but it nevertheless held a monopoly over determining Christian behaviour in the public sphere. For many people it simply provided the setting for the public organization of religion, of whatever denomination. Its

Pre-Civil War England', in N. Tyacke, ed., *The English Revolution c.1590–1720: Politics, Religion and Communities* (Manchester, 2007), 62–80.

45 Harrington and Smith, 'Confessionalization', 92–5; O. Blaschke, 'Das 19. Jahrhundert: ein zweites konfessionelles Zeitalter?', *Geschichte und Gesellschaft* 26 (2000), 38–75 (thanks to Michael Bentley for drawing this article to my attention); idem, ed., *Konfessionen im Konflikt. Deutschland zwischen 1800 und 1970: Ein weiteres konfessionelles Zeitalter* (Göttingen, 2002); C. Kretschmann and H. Pahl, 'Ein "zweites konfessionelles Zeitalter?" – Vom Nutzen und Nachteil einer neuen Epochensignatur', *HZ* 276 (2003), 369–92.

buildings belonged to the municipality, and they served multiple functions: as community edifices, as sites for public events and concerts organized by the corporation and other non-religious institutions, and as venues for rites of passage, including burial for all, including non-Protestants. The Reformed Church 'gradually integrated public values, including secular values' until the whole of public life in the Netherlands acquired what Frijhoff has called 'a sort of Calvinist coloration'.[46]

These observations can take us back to England, and to another debate that has been going on for the last twenty-five years, over whether eighteenth-century England should rightly be deemed a 'confessional state'. Traditionally, there was a belief that the so-called Toleration Act of 1689 marked the effective end of any confessional state. In 1975, Gareth Bennett's *Tory Crisis in Church and State* presented an account of the early eighteenth century in which there is a sense that not just the Tory party but also the Anglican church was decisively defeated with the failure of the attempts of the high church zealot Francis Atterbury and his supporters to reinforce the church's power to enforce orthodoxy and punish occasional conformity.[47] The implication is that a confessional state must necessarily be based on Atterbury's style of coercive high churchmanship (with specific penalties for occasional conformity) or none at all. But in 1985, in his controversial book *English Society 1688–1832*, Jonathan Clark claimed that eighteenth-century England was a confessional state after all. The 'Church-Whig alliance' meant that the Church of England, 'the ubiquitous agency of the State', enjoyed a 'social and doctrinal primacy', with established religion playing a dominant role in the period's public doctrine and discourse. Providential ideas still played a major role in political theology, and there was no widespread 'secularization'.[48] Clark's associated claim that Hanoverian England

[46] W. Frijhoff, 'Strategies for Religious Survival outside the Public Church in the United Provinces: Towards a Research Agenda', in *Wege der Neuzeit: Festschrift für Heinz Schilling zum 65. Geburtstag*, ed. S. Ehrenpreis et al., Historische Forschungen 65 (Berlin, 2007), 177–94, at 183–5; idem, *Embodied Belief*, 51; idem, 'Kalvinistische Kultur, Staat und Konfessionen in den Vereinten Provinzen der Niederlande', in P. C. Hartmann, ed., *Religion und Kultur im Europa des 17. und 18. Jahrhunderts* (Frankfurt, 2004), 109–42.

[47] G.V. Bennett, *The Tory Crisis in Church and State 1688–1730* (Oxford, 1975).

[48] J. C. D. Clark, *English Society 1688–1832* (Cambridge, 1985), 82, 89, 136, 137, 277 etc.

should be called an *ancien régime* generated the most academic attention and hostility. But some English religious historians were keen to embrace the concept of a confessional state, building on a body of scholarship gathering steam in the 1980s that had sought to rehabilitate the aims and achievements of the Hanoverian church.[49] Others have been more cautious. Stephen Taylor, who was prominent in restoring the reputation of the Hanoverian church, and who granted that it was 'an integral part of the domestic apparatus of the English State', has nevertheless stopped short of endorsing the term 'confessional state'. He has pointed out that, however much churchmen and politicians may have seen the institutions of church and state as parts of a single entity, nevertheless being a member of the established church was neither a mark of political allegiance nor a requirement for enjoying the rights and privileges of a subject. Moreover, English kings, concurrently electors of Lutheran Hanover and kings of Presbyterian Scotland, could not be regarded simply as 'Anglicans'.[50]

Characteristically for English historical scholarship, this was a debate which seemed generally unaware of pertinent European historiography, even though it used the term 'confessional state', and began at precisely the same time that Schilling's work was the focus of major European conferences.[51] There are plenty of ironies to savour here – not least that the confessionalization that Schilling and others saw as a route to modernity, Clark saw as a main bulwark *against* change. In a European context, the limited pluralism of the eighteenth-century English state seems less striking, the confessional elements of the regime more apparent. English historians' obsession with treating the Anglican/Dissenter division as fundamental has always meant that insufficient attention

---

[49] e.g. W. Gibson, *The Achievement of the Anglican Church, 1689–1800: The Confessional State in Eighteenth-Century England* (Lampeter, 1995).

[50] Ibid. 26–7; S. Taylor, 'Un état confessional? L'Église d'Angleterre, la constitution et la vie politique au XVIIIᵉ siècle', in A. Joblin and J. Sys, eds, *L'Identité anglicane* (Arras, 2004), 141–54.

[51] Whilst the revised version of Clark's book includes a short section entitled 'the confessional state' (*English Society 1660–1832: Religion, Ideology and Politics during the ancien régime* [Cambridge, 2000], 26–34), it still offers no definition of the term and makes no allusion to European debates. Clark does claim, however, that a confessional state does not require 'denominational uniformity', but only 'the dominance ... of certain ideas of what society's problems were and how they should be addressed': ibid. 34.

has been paid to the continuing strength of anti-Catholicism and the boundary-fixing that went with it. Given the political settlement of 1688, which had altered the royal succession in order to prevent the accession of a Catholic monarch, this was very much a *sichtbare Grenze*. Colin Haydon's work on eighteenth-century anti-Catholicism established this very clearly (complementing work done on this topic for the sixteenth and seventeenth centuries), and Haydon's arguments were supplemented by another work published at the same time. Linda Colley's *Britons*, published in 1992, had an enormous impact at a time when national identity was an increasingly sensitive issue politically. While accepting that 'Great Britain … was not a confessional state in any narrow sense', she pointed out that 'its laws proclaimed it to be a pluralist yet aggressively Protestant state'. But she also sought to present Protestantism in cultural rather than juridical form as a common and ameliorating bond transcending the divisions of the different kingdoms of Britain, acting as the crucial cement of a wider British nationhood. 'Protestantism determined how most Britons viewed their politics, [and] approached and interpreted their material life.'[52] This argument has drawn a sceptical response from many religious historians, concerned at the simplifications involved in Colley's rather literal treatment of notions of elect nationhood. They have stressed the ambivalent and contested nature of Protestant nationalism, seeing it as both stabilizing and disruptive, as offering a means for criticism and division rather than unity. Most obviously, of course, they have asked where Ireland fitted in.[53] Nevertheless, however overstated, this notion of a unifying and aggressive Protestant nationalism, while it might not work for Britain, would arguably work rather well for England, as some commentators have noted. Moreover, this cultural hardening of Protestant national identity fits with the models of Frijhoff and others rather well. Is this perhaps the 'Protestant coloration' of English public life to match the 'Calvinist coloration' in the Netherlands?

[52] L. Colley, *Britons: Forging the Nation, 1707–1837* (London, 1992), 18, 19; C. Haydon, *Anti-Catholicism in Eighteenth-Century England* (Manchester, 1993). For earlier anti-Catholicism, see esp. P. Lake, 'Anti-popery – The Structure of a Prejudice', in R. Cust and A. Hughes, eds, *Conflict in Early Stuart England* (Harlow, 1989), 72–106.
[53] e.g. Claydon and McBride, eds, *Protestantism and National Identity*, 11–12.

One other facet of this 'weak confessionalization' which is beginning to attract increasing attention is that of state prayers. The British State Prayers project – based at Durham University – is shedding important light and generating international research.[54] These state prayers could be very much an aid to the promulgation of an exclusive national identity (as Eamon Duffy argued some years ago for the Tudor period, and as some recent work on Scandinavian state churches would seem to imply), but they could also fit a model that stresses a broader Protestant national identity transcending the narrower identity of the established church.[55] There may be limits to the extent to which Dissenters were involved in these occasions, but probably only Quakers and Roman Catholics systematically refrained from participation. The ways in which these events could create a certain sense of broader national Protestant identity beyond the confines of the state church invite further study. Judicial structures and coercive forms may not be indispensable features for a confessional identity that inextricably binds religion and the nation. *Religio* can be *vinculum societatis* without the state's direct intervention; it did not cease to be that *vinculum* after 1650.

As should be clear from the foregoing analysis, future scholarship on church-state relations in the early modern period has a variety of possible avenues to explore. Several decades of a renewed scholarly emphasis on the importance of religion in the past are unlikely to be reversed, especially as historians are beginning not merely to challenge the assumed historical trajectory of secularization but also to regard 'secularization' itself as a misleading construct.[56] Historians of politics and political thought (apart from some members of the so-called 'Cambridge school' of Quentin

---

[54] As well as a two-volume edition of texts, the directors of the AHRC-funded project, 'British State Prayers, Fasts and Thanksgivings, 1540s–1940s' are completing a monograph: N. Mears, S. Taylor and P. Williamson, *The British Nations and Divine Providence: Public Worship and the State from the Reformation to the Twentieth Century* (forthcoming, Oxford, 2014).

[55] E. Duffy, 'The Shock of Change: Continuity and Discontinuity in the Elizabethan Church of England', in S. Platten, ed., *Anglicanism and the Western Christian Tradition* (Norwich, 2003), 42–64, at 50–1; N. Mears, 'Public Worship and Political Participation in Elizabethan England', *JBS* 51 (2012), 4–25; J. Östlund, 'Politics and Identity in Swedish Prayer Days, 1660–1730' (forthcoming).

[56] J. C. D. Clark, 'Secularization and Modernization: The Failure of a "Grand Narrative"', *HistJ* 55 (2012), 161–94.

Skinner and his supporters) seem to have accepted the need to integrate religion within their analysis.[57] The challenge remains of finding ways of understanding the prominence of religious themes within public discourse, and of religious actors on the public stage, without treating religion as an irreducible core of values resistant to other modes of thought or secular influences. It is to be hoped, therefore, that a recognition of the continuing significance of religious discourse and symbolism will be combined with a greater sensitivity to its changing meaning and significance. Sadly, religion and political science remain unwilling bedfellows, and each side's fears of the other's determinism run the risk of stymieing attempts to integrate the study of 'weak confessionalization' into the broader study of state-building, at least for the moment. The greatest danger for ecclesiastical history, though, will be if it ceases to listen to, to converse with and to learn from other disciplines.

University of Sheffield

---

[57] For a critique of Skinner's approach to religion, see John Coffey, 'Quentin Skinner and the Religious Dimension of Early Modern Political Thought', in Alister Chapman, John Coffey and Brad S. Gregory, eds, *Seeing Things Their Way: Intellectual History and the Return of Religion* (Notre Dame, IN, 2009), 47–74.

THE FALL AND RISE OF CHURCH AND STATE? RELIGIOUS HISTORY, POLITICS AND THE STATE IN BRITAIN, 1961–2011[*]

by MATTHEW GRIMLEY

In trying to trace the development of church–state relations in Britain since 1961, one encounters the difficulty that conceptions of both 'church' and 'state' have changed radically in the half-century since then. This is most obviously true of the state. The British state in 1961 was (outside Stormont-governed Northern Ireland) a unitary state governed from London. It still had colonies, and substantial overseas military commitments. One of its Houses of Parliament had until three years before been (a few bishops and law-lords apart) completely hereditary. The prime minister controlled all senior appointments in the established Church of England, and Parliament had the final say on its worship and doctrine. The criminal law still embodied Christian teaching on issues of personal morality.

But the nature of the British state was beginning to change in dramatic ways by 1961. Britain's application to join the European Economic Community in that year was a sign that its orientation was changing from empire to Europe. The decision of the Macmillan government to place limits on Commonwealth immigration (enacted the following year in the Commonwealth Immigrants Act) ended the open-door policy of immigration that had applied since 1948, a change caused by anxiety about racial tension in major cities. 1961 also saw the passing of the Suicide Act, which the legal philosopher H. L. A. Hart called a legislative 'landmark', because it was 'the first Act of Parliament for at least a century to remove altogether the penalties of the criminal law from a practice both clearly condemned by Christian morality and punishable by law'.[1] The foundation of *Private Eye* magazine the same year portended a more critical treatment of the institutions of church

---

[*] I am grateful to the audience and the other speakers at the EHS winter conference in January 2012 for their comments, and in particular to Sheridan Gilley, Perry Butler, David Thompson, Sarah Foot and the editors of this volume.

[1] H. L. A. Hart, *Law, Liberty and Morality* (London, 1963), Preface.

and state alike. The satirists who founded it took an ecclesiastical term, 'establishment', and stretched it into a critique of the whole elite power structure of Britain.

Harold Macmillan's choice of Michael Ramsey as archbishop of Canterbury in 1961, against the wishes of the outgoing primate, Geoffrey Fisher, also portended a major change in the established church's relationship with the state. Unlike Fisher, Ramsey's attitude to the state was angular and uneasy. A cradle Congregationalist, he retained a Nonconformist suspicion of establishment, saying in a television interview on the eve of his election as archbishop that 'if disestablishment were to come we would remember that our credentials come not from the State but from Christ'.[2] One of Ramsey's main aims as archbishop was to extricate the Church of England from the less satisfactory aspects of establishment. Since his ordination in the aftermath of the Prayer Book controversy of 1927–8, when Parliament had twice vetoed the church's attempts to rewrite the Prayer Book, Ramsey had keenly felt that the Church of England needed a more complete form of self-government, of the sort the Church of Scotland had secured in the Church of Scotland Act of 1929. In a series of reforms during the 1970s, including the creation of the General Synod in 1970 and the Church of England (Worship and Doctrine) Measure of 1974, Ramsey finally secured from Parliament what it had denied in 1927–8 – the Church of England's right to control its own liturgy and doctrine. Other legislation, recommended by the Chadwick Report in 1970 and implemented in 1977, gave the church more influence over the appointment of bishops via the Crown Appointments Commission.

Under Ramsey, the Church of England also seemed to be drawing back from the state in other ways. He campaigned for the rights of immigrants and refugees, chairing the National Committee for Commonwealth Immigrants and taking on the government over the plight of the Kenyan Asians in 1968. He also welcomed the process, begun by the 1937 Matrimonial Causes Act but resumed by the 1961 Suicide Act, by which certain forms of personal conduct, deemed sinful in Christian tradition, were decriminalized. Ramsey worked behind the scenes in the House of

---

2 *ODNB*, *s.n.* 'Ramsey, (Arthur) Michael (1904–1988)'.

Lords to ensure the passage of homosexual law reform in 1967, and (less successfully from his point of view) tried to engineer a reform of abortion and divorce law that would be mutually acceptable to church and state. [3]

The Church of England was also drawing away from the state by projecting a more internationalist and ecumenical identity. As the British Empire was dismantled, Anglicans increasingly perceived of themselves as part of a global Anglican Communion of equals, a sort of religious version of the Commonwealth (with the addition of the USA). Anglicans identified with the anti-apartheid movement, both in South Africa, where bishops Ambrose Reeves, Joost de Blank and Trevor Huddleston were among its leaders, and also in England. Christian movements for international reconciliation and ecumenism in post-war Europe sought to subsume national particularism in membership of larger communities. Within Britain, ecumenical projects for reunion with other churches – the first two phases of the Anglican-Roman Catholic International Commission (ARCIC) negotiations from 1967 and the plan for Anglican-Methodist reunion – seemed to portend the end of Anglicanism's role as a state church and a move towards a larger identity.

But the striking thing about the continuing gradual dismantling of what remained of the confessional state in the later twentieth century was that it did not lead to the formal separation of church and state that seemed to be its logical endpoint. As Simon Green has argued, once the established Church of England had ceased to be tainted by its privileges, it ceased to be objectionable, and so in some ways its position in the nation actually became stronger.[4] The movement for disestablishment of the Church of England had petered out in the 1920s and never revived after 1945. The stalling of plans for reunion with Methodism in 1972, and with Rome over a much longer period, meant that the established status of

[3] Matthew Grimley, 'Law, Morality and Secularisation: The Church of England and the Wolfenden Report, 1954–1967', *JEH* 60 (2009), 725–41; Jane Lewis and Patrick Wallis, 'Fault, Breakdown, and the Church of England's Involvement in the 1969 Divorce Reform', *20th Century British History* 11 (2000), 308–32.

[4] S. J. D. Green, 'Survival and Autonomy: On the Strange Fortunes and Peculiar Legacy of Ecclesiastical Establishment in the Modern British State, c.1920 to the Present Day', in idem and R. C. Whiting, eds, *The Boundaries of the State in Modern Britain* (Cambridge, 1994), 299–324.

the Church of England did not need to be reconsidered. Another reason why establishment was left intact was the repeated failure of attempts to reform the House of Lords, which if successful would have forced a discussion of the role of Anglican bishops in parliament.

As Green points out, the cultural changes of the 1960s only served to shore up establishment. It is true that a few radicals agitated for disestablishment, on the grounds that a truly counter-cultural church needed to be shorn of compromising ties with the state.[5] But many Anglican radicals defended establishment as a platform for social criticism and a connection (via the parochial system) with the poorest parts of society. Anglican campaigns on moral issues such as homosexual law reform were predicated on the church's established position. In *Soundings* in 1962, Alec Vidler defended establishment because 'it helps to keep the church aware of its obligation to serve the whole people in all areas of their need'.[6] In *Honest to God* in 1963, John Robinson defended it on the grounds that that 'anything that helps to keep its frontiers open to the world as the Church of the nation should be strengthened and reformed; anything that turns it in upon itself as a religious organization or Episcopalian sect I suspect and deplore'.[7] Robinson's defence of establishment hinted at another reason why liberal Anglicans supported it – it offered them a protected space, a guarantee that their liberal theology would be tolerated. This had been one reason why modernists (the precursors of liberal theologians like Robinson) had defended establishment earlier in the twentieth century.[8]

The recognition that Britain was now a multi-faith society dawned slowly, from the 1970s onwards. This change too might have been expected to have made establishment untenable. But that did not happen, partly because new discourses of multiculturalism themselves owed something to older rhetorical justifications of Anglican comprehensiveness and toleration. The idea of the

---

[5] See, e.g., Humphrey Green, 'Erastus rebutted – or, the Obstacle of Establishment', *Prism*, April 1958, 8–18; *Disestablishment and Unity*, *Prism* special issue, January 1959; Editorial, *Prism*, June 1959, 1.

[6] Alec Vidler, 'Religion and the National Church', in idem, ed., *Soundings; Essays Concerning Christian Understanding* (Cambridge, 1962), 241–63, at 261–2.

[7] John Robinson, *Honest to God* (London, 1963), 141.

[8] Alan Stephenson, *The Rise and Decline of English Modernism* (London, 1984).

established church as a defender of all religions gained currency among Muslims and other non-Christian religious minorities, especially after the Rushdie affair in 1989.[9] Although Prince Charles caused controversy in 1994 when he first said that he wished to be 'defender of faith' rather than 'defender of *the* faith', the Church of England increasingly justified itself as a defender of *all* faiths, an argument made by Charles's mother in a speech to multi-faith leaders at Lambeth Palace to mark her Diamond Jubilee in 2012. 'The concept of our established Church is occasionally misunderstood and, I believe, commonly under-appreciated', said the Queen. 'Its role is not to defend Anglicanism to the exclusion of other religions. Instead, the Church has a duty to protect the free practice of all faiths in this country.'[10]

Nevertheless, post-war immigration did have implications for all Christian churches, not just the established church. The arrival in Britain of new religious minorities, each with their own concepts of 'religion' and the 'state', and with different traditions of accommodation with the state in the British Empire and elsewhere, demanded a renegotiation of the relationship between religion and the state. Religious pluralism, traditionally conceived in Britain as a pluralism of Christian traditions, was now reconfigured as a pluralism of different global religious traditions. The development of multiculturalism as a policy involved a reformulation of the way religious education was taught that had implications for all denominations.[11] Demands were increasingly made for an extension of privileges enjoyed by Christian denominations, particularly in denominational schooling, to other religions. The Blasphemy Act, which had only protected the Church of

---

[9] Tariq Modood, 'Establishment, Multiculturalism and British Citizenship', *Political Quarterly* 65 (1994), 53–73.

[10] Queen Elizabeth II, speech at Lambeth Palace, 15 February 2012, online at: <http://www.archbishopofcanterbury.org/articles.php/2358/the-queen-attends-multi-faith-reception-at-lambeth-palace>, accessed 28 August 2012.

[11] Gerald Parsons, 'There and back again? Religion and the 1944 and 1988 Education Acts', in idem, ed., *The Growth of Religious Diversity: Britain from 1945*, 2: *Issues* (London, 1994), 161–98; Stephen Parker and Rob Freathy, 'Ethnic Diversity, Christian Hegemony and the Emergence of Multi-faith Religious Education in the 1970s', *History of Education* 41 (2012), 381–404; idem, 'Context, Complexity and Contestation: Birmingham's Agreed Syllabuses since the 1970s', *Journal of Beliefs and Values* 32 (2011), 247–63.

England, was repealed in favour of a law against religious hatred that covered all religions.

The continuance of establishment in England and (in qualified form) in Scotland did not preclude churches, both established and non-established, from confronting the state after 1961. This confrontation was often in the area of foreign policy, expressed through causes such as the Campaign for Nuclear Disarmament (from the Aldermaston marches through to the Greenham Common peace camps) and the anti-apartheid movement from the late 1950s to the 1980s, and later in the anti-debt and international development campaigns. But it also addressed domestic concerns, in particular Thatcherite economic and employment policies. The Church of England Board of Social Responsibility report *Faith in the City* (1985) was accompanied by a running commentary from bishops representing economically deprived areas such as Liverpool (David Sheppard) and Durham (David Jenkins).[12] Similar criticisms from the Church of Scotland brought a pointed rejoinder from Margaret Thatcher in her 'Sermon on the Mound' when she visited its General Assembly in May 1988. All mainstream Christian denominations were critical of aspects of Thatcherism, but it was the two established churches, the Church of England and the Kirk, which became Thatcher's key religious opponents in the 1980s. Opposition to the permissive legislation of the 1960s also created some strange bedfellows; from 1967, the year of the legalization of abortion and the first National Evangelical Anglican Congress at Keele, Evangelicals became increasingly vocal in their opposition to abortion, bringing them into an unprecedented alliance with Catholics. Under the informal leadership of Lord Longford and Mary Whitehouse, the two groups also collaborated on campaigns against obscenity in the 1970s. Christians' roles in challenging government policy in these very different ways paradoxically increased their political visibility during a period when almost all denominations were suffering degrees of numerical decline.

The Catholic Church also increased its political influence in

---

[12] Archbishop of Canterbury's Commission on Urban Priority Areas, *Faith in the City: A Call for Action by Faith and Nation* (London, 1985). For wider relations between the Church of England and the Thatcher governments, see Liza Filby, 'God and Mrs Thatcher: Religion and Politics in 1980s Britain' (Ph.D. thesis, University of Warwick, 2010).

other areas from the 1970s onwards. Catholic archbishops had long been making interventions on social questions, of course, but Cardinal Basil Hume (archbishop of Westminster from 1976) was particularly shrewd in picking particular issues such as international development and British miscarriages of justice. By allying itself with these progressive causes, the Catholic Church was trying to do two things: to retain the support of progressive, middle-class Catholics (who were in danger of falling away because of disaffection at church teaching on contraception) and to resonate with a wider public. This culminated in the Catholic Bishops' 1997 statement on the Common Good, which came close to endorsing Tony Blair's New Labour. Catholicism's coming in from the cold had already been symbolized by the visit of Pope John Paul II to Britain in 1982. The low-key nature of protest against the visit (except from the inevitable Ian Paisley) demonstrated the decline of sectarianism.[13] This was true even in Scotland, which was part of the papal itinerary; Orangeism had declined in the West of Scotland, and the increasingly prominent Scottish Nationalist Party was moving away from its sectarian roots.[14] Catholics were now prominent in all political parties; between 2001 and 2003, two out of three main British party leaders (Iain Duncan Smith and Charles Kennedy) were Catholics, while the third, Tony Blair, worshipped as a Catholic, was married to a Catholic and was himself shortly to convert. That Blair did not do so until after leaving office was perhaps a sign that vestigial traces of anti-Catholicism remained in British politics, though it probably had more to do with his squeamishness about discussing his religion as prime minister.

Changes in Historiography

It is, of course, difficult to prove a connection between the phases in church-state relations set out above and trends in historical writing

---

[13] Though for the argument that anti-Catholicism remained a force during and after 1982, see John Wolffe, 'Change and Continuity in British Anti-Catholicism 1829–1982', in Frank Tallett and Nicholas Atkin, eds, *Catholicism in Britain and France since 1789* (London, 1996), 67–83.

[14] Though just prior to the papal visit, the Scottish National Party president, William Wolfe, had spoken of the need to protect the Falkland Islands 'from the cruel and ruthless fascist dictatorship of a Roman Catholic State': quoted in Keith Robbins, *England, Ireland, Scotland, Wales: The Christian Church 1900–2000*, OHCC (Oxford, 2008), 434.

about church and state over the last half-century. Prosaic considerations such as the time taken to write and publish books make it hard to 'prove' that such and such a history book was influenced by such and such a contemporary event just because they appeared around the same time. Most historians are understandably wary of the accusation that their curiosity is merely driven by contemporary events. The trends in historical writing that I am tentatively sketching here were never universal: there were always some historians who remained resolutely impervious to the *Zeitgeist* (church historians perhaps more than most). Some historians' careers also spanned very long periods. George Kitson Clark published his first book in 1929 and his last, *Churchmen and the Condition of England*, in 1973. This raises the question of whether his last work should be seen as representative of the 1970s or of a historian who had been intellectually formed in the 1920s. But, even allowing for these difficulties, it is possible to discern some phases in historical writing about church and state in modern Britain. The remainder of this essay will chart the fall, and then the revival, of 'church and state' as a subject of study. Though there will be brief mention of works of medieval and early modern history written during this period, the main focus of the essay will be on books written since 1961 about nineteenth- and twentieth-century Britain.

In the two decades after the Second World War, historians continued to write traditional studies of church–state relations, most of which continued to give priority to the Church of England.[15] A few historians of ideas wrote less institutional accounts, arguing for the influence of theology on nineteenth-century political thought.[16] What characterized all these accounts was their confidence in the importance of their subject. But despite this apparent confidence, both 'church' and 'state' were already going out of fashion as subjects of academic study by the late 1950s. The decline of interest in the state was a partly a product of changing fashions in political philosophy. Idealist political philosophy had been discredited by the linguistic philosophers, and for a while there

---

[15] Olive Brose, *Church and Parliament: The Reshaping of the Church of England* (Stanford, CA, 1959); Geoffrey Best, *Temporal Pillars: Queen Anne's Bounty, the Ecclesiastical Commissioners and the Church of England* (Cambridge, 1964).

[16] Alec Vidler, *The Orb and the Cross: A Normative Study in the Relations between Church and State with Reference to Gladstone's Early Writings* (London, 1945); Duncan Forbes, *The Liberal Anglican Idea of History* (Cambridge, 1952).

was nothing to replace it. Jose Harris has pointed to the 'widespread silence that prevailed on the underlying nature, powers and purposes of the state' in British political thought from the early 1940s to the late 1960s.[17] In 1956, the historian Peter Laslett proclaimed that 'for the moment, anyway, political philosophy is dead', naming the culprits as linguistic philosophy, Marxism and sociology.[18] Political philosophy did revive thereafter, but in 1961 it was still possible for Isaiah Berlin to ask 'Does Political Theory still exist?'[19]

This loss of faith in the agency of the state had implications for historians as well as political theorists. In a 1963 article on St Augustine, Peter Brown argued that a key problem which 'we all have to face' was:

> to what extent is it possible to treat man as having a measure of rational control over his political environment? The discovery that this control is limited has revolutionized political theory. Half the world is committed to some form of Marxist determinism: and the other half, far from rallying to Hobbes, Locke and Rousseau, studies Freud, the social psychologists, and the sociologists.[20]

Under these influences, historians increasingly embraced what E. P. Thompson called 'history from below', turning away from the study of the state. Some of the proponents of this shift were Marxists like Thompson, but there was also a wider disciplinary move, influenced by the French *Annales* school, towards structural approaches garnered from sociology and anthropology.[21]

This shift had major implications for the study of ecclesiastical history. Already by the time the Ecclesiastical History Society was set up in 1961, the idea that ecclesiastical history had to be studied

[17] Jose Harris, 'Political Thought and the State', in Green and Whiting, eds, *Boundaries of the State*, 15–28, at 15.
[18] Peter Laslett, Introduction to idem, ed., *Philosophy, Politics and Society* (Oxford, 1956), vii–xv, at vii.
[19] Isaiah Berlin, 'Does Political Theory still exist?', in Peter Laslett and W. G. Runciman, eds, *Philosophy, Politics and Society (Second Series)* (Oxford, 1962), 1–33.
[20] Peter Brown, 'St Augustine', in Beryl Smalley, ed., *Trends in Medieval Political Thought* (Oxford, 1963), repr. in Brown, *Religion and Society in the Age of St Augustine* (London, 1972), 25–45, at 28.
[21] For a more detailed discussion of the 'turns' towards anthropology and sociology, see, in this volume, Sarah Foot, 'Has Ecclesiastical History Lost the Plot?', 1–25.

in its broader social context had gained force. An early statement of the society's aims promised that 'ecclesiastical history will be regarded in its widest sense, to include the social and economic background against which Christian movements have taken place throughout history'.[22] This widening was a salutary corrective to the narrowly institutional 'church and state' accounts that had dominated the discipline since the nineteenth century. But more worrying for ecclesiastical historians was that the rise of structural accounts – and in particular of the sociological twins, class analysis and the secularization thesis – threatened to short-circuit them altogether.

This short-circuiting could happen in two ways. First, the use of class analysis meant that religion could be reduced to an epiphenomenal role as an outgrowth of the interests of the ruling class. This was true of E. P. Thompson's *The Making of the English Working Class* (1963), with its famous denunciation of Methodism as 'the chiliasm of despair' and 'a ritualised form of psychic masturbation'.[23] The second sort of short-circuiting of ecclesiastical history came from secularization theory, which was hardly new but became highly influential in the 1960s. Books such as Bryan Wilson's *Religion in Secular Society* (1966) and Alasdair MacIntyre's *Secularization and Moral Change* (1967) were widely read, not just in the sociology departments of the new universities but also by historians and clergy.[24]

Even before Thompson, Wilson or Macintyre had put pen to paper, Ted Wickham, the founder of the Sheffield Industrial Mission, had short-circuited church history in both ways in *Church and People in an Industrial City* (1957), a historical account of religious decline that drew heavily on classical secularization theory. Although his topic was ostensibly the nineteenth-century churches his preoccupation was often with exploring the roots of religion's more recent decline and thus of the contemporary predicament of the Church of England. 'The weakness and collapse of the churches in the urbanised and industrialised areas of the country

---

[22] Stella Fletcher, '*A Very Agreeable Society*': *The Ecclesiastical History Society 1961–2011* (Southampton, 2011), 10.

[23] E. P. Thompson, *The Making of the English Working Class* (London, 1968 edn), 411, 405 respectively.

[24] Bryan Wilson, *Religion in Secular Society: A Sociological Comment* (London, 1966); Alasdair MacIntyre, *Secularization and Moral Change* (Oxford, 1967).

should be transparently clear to any who are not wilfully blind, as also the intractable and chronic nature of the missionary problem facing the Church in our modern society', he warned.[25] This was a contention that Wickham made not just in his historical writing but also in his leadership of the Sheffield Industrial Mission, which sought to circumvent the parochial system and reach people in an industrial context.

The culprit in Wickham's account of religious decline was the failure of the established church to transcend its own class interests and speak persuasively to the working classes. For Wickham, church leaders, like political leaders, were part of the elite; as he put it, 'the men of the Churches had their own vested interests and they were not those of the working class'.[26] (This made it uncomfortable for Wickham when Harold Macmillan made him a bishop.) Subsequent studies such as K. S. Inglis's *Churches and the Working Classes in Victorian England* (1963) followed Wickham in arguing that the whole structure of Anglican establishment had been an encumbrance in the nineteenth century.[27] As Jeremy Morris has recently pointed out, explanations that made class central to religious decline were attractive, because they 'struck a chord with social historians increasingly preoccupied with class analysis', and because they 'seemed to fit closely arguments which instrumentalised religion in class conflict by presenting it as an agent of social manipulation and control'.[28] In this respect they fitted into the broader anti-institutionalism that characterized much British culture from the later 1950s through to the 1970s. Few historians were any longer interested in studying fusty institutions such as churches and the state, except to depict them as outgrowths of class interest. Wickham was scathing about traditional church history, with its elite preoccupations, lamenting that 'unfortunately, "Church history", with few great exceptions, is invariably about the Church abstracted from society, about ecclesiastical institutions, personalities or movements, in which the world in which they are set seems quite incidental'.[29]

---

[25] E. R. Wickham, *Church and People in an Industrial City* (London, 1957), 11.
[26] Ibid. 198.
[27] K. S. Inglis, *Churches and the Working Classes in Victorian England* (London, 1963).
[28] Jeremy Morris, 'Secularization and Religious Experience: Arguments in the Historiography of Modern British Religion', *HistJ* 55 (2012), 195–219, at 198–200.
[29] Wickham, *Church and People*, 12.

In the 1970s historians began to produce detailed studies that largely endorsed the ideas of the secularization theorists. Hugh McLeod's *Class and Religion in the Late Victorian City* (1974) followed Wickham in making class central to its explanation. Alan Gilbert's *Religion and Society in Industrial England* (1976), while it nuanced classic accounts by introducing the idea of a time-lag between urbanization and secularization, nevertheless followed them in presenting industrialization as the motor of secularization.[30] By concentrating on social structure, neither account had much to say about politics.

This omission was equally true of the revisionist studies that began to question secularization in the 1980s. These books, often based on local case studies, argued that working-class culture was not as inimical to religion as earlier accounts had suggested. They demonstrated the vitality of self-generated forms of popular religion and emphasized regional diversity in patterns of religiosity. But what few of them did was to challenge the primacy of the 'popular' as a category in religious history, or to explore the way that it intersected with 'elite' forms of authority, clerical or secular.[31] In particular, they did not consider the intersection of religious and national identity or the role played by the state in providing conditions for religious innovation. There were some notable exceptions to this neglect. Jeffrey Cox and Jeremy Morris both explored the impact that the expanding sphere of local government had on the churches, though their local studies concentrated very much on municipal, rather than national, government.[32] Hugh McLeod's comparative work on world cities led him to emphasize local political culture as a determinant of religious observance and to consider the relationship of national identity and religion.[33]

[30] Hugh McLeod, *Class and Religion in the Late Victorian City* (London, 1974); Alan Gilbert, *Religion and Society in Industrial England: Church, Chapel and Social Change, 1740–1914* (London, 1976).

[31] For a more recent discussion of this relationship, see the essays in Kate Cooper and Jeremy Gregory, eds, *Elite and Popular Religion*, SCH 42 (Woodbridge, 2006).

[32] Jeffrey Cox, *The English Churches in a Secular Society: Lambeth, 1870–1930* (Oxford, 1982); Jeremy Morris, *Religion and Urban Change: Croydon, 1840–1914* (Woodbridge, 1992).

[33] Hugh McLeod, *Piety and Poverty: Working-Class Religion in Berlin, London, and New York 1870–1914* (New York, 1993); idem, 'Protestantism and National Identity 1815–1945', in Peter Van der Veer and Hartmut Lehmann, eds, *Nation and Religion: Perspectives on Europe and Asia* (Princeton, NJ, 1999), 44–70.

A second wave of revisionist accounts, notably Sarah Williams's *Religious Belief and Popular Culture in Southwark* (1999) and Callum Brown's *The Death of Christian Britain* (2001), emphasized the importance of subjective religious practice and the role it played in individual identity formation.[34] Both books made use of oral history as a source and drew on insights garnered from the 'linguistic turn', the shift by historians, under the influence of literary theory, towards a greater awareness of the contingent and changing meanings of language. This development was enormously liberating for historians who had become mired in the secularization debate, because it allowed them to escape from the assumption that 'religion' was reducible to formal religious observance. But Jeremy Morris observed in 2003 that it also had a downside, which was 'a certain constriction in the meaning and scope of religion'. Morris's particular complaint was that 'in the interests of avoiding so-called reductionist accounts of secularisation, historians have recently tended to refuse consideration of the intimate connections between religion and political life'.[35]

The Return of Church and State

However, the dominance of structural and social explanations of religious change was challenged by current events, both national and global. This process began with the eruption of politico-religious conflict in Northern Ireland from 1969. By the later 1970s, some sociologists were beginning to recognize that religion was not retreating from public and political life in the way that they had predicted. Though many continued to cleave to secularization theory, others began to argue for cyclical, rather than linear, patterns of religious change; Daniel Bell, for example, posited 'The Return of the Sacred' in 1977.[36] Events between the Iranian Revolution of 1979 and the collapse of the Soviet bloc in 1989 seemed to vindicate Bell's analysis. Political Islam became recognized as a global force in the Middle East, South Asia and, via episodes such

---

[34] S. C. Williams, *Religious Belief and Popular Culture in Southwark, c.1880–1939* (Oxford, 1999); Callum Brown, *The Death of Christian Britain: Understanding Secularisation 1800–2000* (London, 2001).

[35] Jeremy Morris, 'The Strange Death of Christian Britain: Another look at the Secularization Debate', *HistJ* (2003), 963–76, at 968.

[36] Daniel Bell, 'The Return of the Sacred? The Argument on the Future of Religion', *British Journal of Sociology* 28 (1977), 419–49.

as the Rushdie affair, in the West. The political power of Christianity also became more apparent through the rise of the religious right in the United States, the Solidarity protest movements in Poland and the charismatic global leadership of the Polish pope, John Paul II.

These political events forced historians to think more about the relationship between religion and political ideology. Some were explicit in reflecting on how recent events had changed their perspective. In 1988 the late-antique historian R. A. Markus wrote in a preface to the revised edition of his book *Saeculum* (1970) that historians needed to take account of recent

> ... changes in the climate of political thinking, apparent in the styles of thought about society and its problems adopted among Christian thinkers, political philosophers or theologians such as the theologians of 'Liberation', or writers on 'political theology'. There have been changes in the perception of political problems: the significance attached, for example, to social and political polarisation, to the menace of theocratic regimes, to social and cultural alienation, to terrorism, to poverty, especially in [the] third world, or in inner cities, to injustice embedded in political structures – to mention only a few of the themes that have moved towards a more central position in the spectrum of Western anxieties since 1968.[37]

Others were less explicit in connecting their historical writing with contemporary events. Nevertheless, there was a demonstrable shift towards the study of religion and politics. From the early 1980s, a number of historians sought to reinstate religion as a causal factor in events such as the English Civil War.[38] J. C. D. Clark argued for the survival of an Anglican *ancien régime* until 1832, while Boyd Hilton, Jonathan Parry, Richard Brent, Colin Matthew, David Bebbington and Michael Bentley all demonstrated the centrality of theology to nineteenth-century theories of economy and the state, and to the worldviews of politicians such

---

[37] R. A. Markus, *Saeculum: History and Society in the Theology of St Augustine*, rev. edn (Cambridge, 1988), viii–ix.

[38] See, e.g., John Morrill, 'The Religious Context of the English Civil War', *TRHS* ser. 5, 34 (1983), 155–78; Conrad Russell, *The Causes of the English Civil War* (Oxford, 1990).

as Gladstone and Salisbury.[39] It was probably not a coincidence that British historians began to do this during the 1980s, when, in addition to the global resurgence of religion cited above, there was also a revival of moralized political discourse, rooted in religious language, in the form of Thatcherism. By no means all these historians were personally attracted to Thatcherism, but it became more plausible to posit a connection between theology and economic and political thought against its backdrop; Boyd Hilton's *The Age of Atonement*, for example, perhaps struck a chord partly because it came out in 1988, the year of Thatcher's infamous 'Sermon on the Mound'. Hilton's argument that Evangelical theology had influenced the development of laissez-faire individualism in the early nineteenth century seemed particularly plausible and pertinent in the context of Thatcher's attempts to assert a similar link in the late twentieth.[40]

It took rather longer for historians to recognize the continuing role of religion in twentieth-century politics. But here too, a questioning of the assumption that class was the primary determinant of political allegiance (itself partly a consequence of the decline of Marxism as a political system, and partly of the linguistic turn) eventually led to a renewed recognition of the persistence into the mid-twentieth century of confessionally based voting patterns. Historians, led by Maurice Cowling but by no means all uncritical followers of his, also demonstrated the role of religion in the rhetoric and 'public doctrine' of twentieth-century politicians such as Stanley Baldwin and Winston Churchill.[41] There has also

---

[39] J. C. D. Clark, *English Society, 1688–1832* (Cambridge, 1985); Boyd Hilton, *The Age of Atonement: The Influence of Evangelicalism on Social and Political Thought, 1785–1865* (Oxford, 1988); Jonathan Parry, *Democracy and Religion: Gladstone and the Liberal Party* (Cambridge, 1986); Richard Brent, *Liberal Anglican Politics: Whiggery, Religion and Reform, 1830–1841* (Oxford, 1987); H. C. G. Matthew, *Gladstone*, 2 vols (Oxford, 1986–95); David Bebbington, *The Mind of Gladstone, Religion, Homer and Politics* (Oxford, 2004); Michael Bentley, *Lord Salisbury's World: Conservative Environments in Late-Victorian Britain* (Cambridge, 2001).

[40] Although, as Hilton pointed out, the parallel was 'tempting but misleading, for we are not really living in another Age of Atonement': *Age of Atonement*, 374.

[41] Maurice Cowling, *Religion and Public Doctrine in Modern England*, 3 vols (Cambridge, 1980–2001); Philip Williamson, 'The Doctrinal Politics of Stanley Baldwin', in *Public and Private Doctrine: Essays in British History Presented to Maurice Cowling*, ed. M. Bentley (Cambridge, 1993), 181–208; idem, *Stanley Baldwin: National Leadership and National Values* (Cambridge, 1999); idem, 'Christian Conservatives and the Totalitarian Challenge 1933–40', *EHR* 115 (2000), 607–42. For a discussion of the

been a renewed appreciation by historians of the amount of time that Parliament continued to spend addressing religious questions such as Welsh disestablishment or Prayer Book revision in the first decades of the twentieth century.[42] While Parliament increasingly thereafter turned its attention to other considerations such as the creation of a welfare state, the reform of education and the liberalization of law on personal morality, all these debates continued to be infused with religious perspectives, and they too have been a subject for historians (the present author included) in recent years.[43]

From the 1980s onwards, there was also renewed interest from historians in the role played by religion in national identity. The more general recovery of historians' interest in nationalism was itself partly a product of resurgent Celtic nationalism and of the Falklands War.[44] But by the end of the decade, the collapse of the Soviet bloc, and the role played by Christian churches in nationalist movements in its successor states, as well as the ongoing sectarian conflict in Northern Ireland, were leading historians to a greater recognition of the role of religion in nationalism. This was apparent in Linda Colley's *Britons*, which posited Protestantism as a key component in the creation of British identity in the eighteenth and early nineteenth centuries.[45] Although Colley's argument was open to the criticism that it elided denominational and geographical differences, it did prompt other historians to explore

influence of religion on the early Labour Party, see Peter Caterall, 'The Distinctiveness of British Socialism? Religion and the Rise of Labour, c.1900–1939', in Matthew Worley, ed., *The Foundations of the British Labour Party: Identities, Cultures and Perspectives, 1900–1939* (Farnham, 2009), 131–52.

[42] G. I. T. Machin, *Politics, Society and the Churches 1869–1921* (Oxford, 1987); idem, 'Disestablishment and Democracy. c.1840–1930', in Eugenio F. Biagini, ed., *Citizenship and Community: Liberals, Radicals and Collective Identities in the British Isles 1865–1931* (Cambridge, 1996), 120–47; John Maiden, *National Religion and the Prayer Book Controversy, 1927–1928* (Woodbridge, 2009); Matthew Grimley, *Citizenship, Community and the Church of England: Liberal Anglican Theories of the State between the Wars* (Oxford, 2004), ch. 4.

[43] Grimley, *Citizenship, Community and the Church of England*; S. J. D. Green, *The Passing of Protestant England: Secularisation and Social Change c.1920–1960* (Cambridge, 2011), ch. 6; Grimley, 'Law, Morality and Secularisation'.

[44] See, e.g., Raphael Samuel, ed., *Patriotism: The Making and Unmaking of British National Identity*, 3 vols (London, 1989). For an investigation of role of religion in national identity from the same period, see Stuart Mews, ed., *Religion and National Identity*, SCH 18 (Oxford, 1982).

[45] Linda Colley, *Britons: Forging the Nation, 1707–1837* (New Haven, CT, 1992).

the relationship between religion and the component national identities of the British Isles, and to trace the continuation of Protestant national identities in the later nineteenth and twentieth centuries.[46] The connections between religion and nationalism were further emphasized by the conflagration in post-communist Yugoslavia, a link directly drawn in the work of the church historian Adrian Hastings, whose own advocacy of the Bosnian cause during the Yugoslav wars led him to address the role of religion in shaping national identity in *The Construction of Nationhood* (1997).[47] A smaller but unexpectedly resonant tragedy, the death of Diana, Princess of Wales in 1997, and the extraordinary mixture of official and unofficial mourning rituals that followed it, also drew historians' attention to the historic role of the established church in choreographing national rituals and in the projection of monarchy.[48]

Some of the studies that have so far been cited here might seem to support the argument, variously advanced by David Nicholls on the left and Edward Norman on the right, that Christian churches in Britain have tended to support the agglomeration of state power since the eighteenth century.[49] But historians have also uncovered anti-statist traditions of religiously based political thought – as in Simon Skinner's work on Tractarian social thought or Nicholls's own work on Christian pluralists.[50] Imperial historians have increasingly challenged the assumption that missionaries were an unques-

[46] Tony Claydon and Ian McBride, eds, *Protestantism and National Identity, c.1650–c.1850* (Cambridge, 1999); McLeod, 'Protestantism and National Identity'; John Wolffe, *God and Greater Britain: Religion and National Life in Britain and Ireland 1843–1945* (London, 1994); Matthew Grimley, 'The Religion of Englishness: Puritanism, Providentialism and National Character 1918–1945', *JBS* 46 (2007), 884–906; Green, *Passing of Protestant England*.

[47] Adrian Hastings, *The Construction of Nationhood: Ethnicity, Religion and Nationalism* (Cambridge, 1997).

[48] John Wolffe, *Great Deaths: Grieving, Religion and Nationhood in Victorian and Edwardian Britain* (Oxford, 2000); idem, 'National Occasions at St Paul's since 1800', in Derek Keane, Arthur Burns and Andrew Saint, eds, *St Paul's: The Cathedral Church of London 604–2004* (New Haven, CT, 2004), 381–91; Arthur Burns, 'From 1830 to the Present', in Keane, Burns and Saint, eds, *St Paul's*, 84–110; Philip Williamson, 'The Monarchy and Public Values, 1910–1953', in Andrzej Olechnowicz, ed., *The Monarchy and the British Nation, 1780 to the Present* (Cambridge, 2007), 223–57.

[49] David Nicholls, *Deity and Domination: Images of God and the State in the Nineteenth and Twentieth Centuries* (London, 1989); Edward Norman, *Church and Society in England, 1770–1970: A Historical Study* (Cambridge, 1976).

[50] S. A. Skinner, *Tractarians and the Condition of England: The Social and Political*

tioning, unarmed wing of British imperialism, instead emphasizing their criticisms of government policy and their role in facilitating protest or nationalist movements.[51] Studies of the churches in both world wars have moved on from portraying senior clergy as cheerleaders or recruiting sergeants, and have demonstrated a more nuanced position in which broad support for the British cause did not preclude criticism of particular atrocities or of jingoism.[52] It has been demonstrated that successive archbishops of Canterbury (even that quintessentially establishment figure Geoffrey Fisher) criticized aspects of British foreign policy during the Cold War.[53] These studies have been important in undermining the assumption that church and state were always hand in glove.

The return of 'church' and 'state' as accepted and respectable themes of study has had an impact on the way historians of religion write synoptic histories. These now routinely incorporate national and imperial identities, the role of religion in party politics, and church–state relations. But here too there is still a difference between accounts of the nineteenth and twentieth centuries. Two recent volumes in Pearson Longman's 'Religion, Society and Politics series' illustrate this. As its title suggests, Stewart Brown's book, *Providence and Empire: Religion, Society and Politics in the United Kingdom, 1815-1914* (2008) addresses all these themes, emphasizing the connection between the religious and the political.[54]

Thought of the Oxford Movement (Oxford, 2004); David Nicholls, *The Pluralist State: The Political Ideas of J. N. Figgis and his Contemporaries*, 2nd edn (Basingstoke, 1994).

51 Hilary M. Carey, ed., *Empires of Religion* (Basingstoke, 2008); Jeffrey Cox, *The British Missionary Enterprise since 1700* (London, 2008); idem, 'From the Empire of Christ to the Third World: Religion and the Experience of Empire in the Twentieth Century', in Andrew Thompson, ed., *Britain's Experience of Empire in the Twentieth Century* (Oxford, 2011), 76–121; Andrew Porter, *Religion versus Empire? British Protestant Missionaries and Overseas Expansion, 1700–1914* (Manchester, 2004).

52 Stuart Bell, 'The First World War', in S. G. Parker and T. Lawson, eds, *God and War: The Church of England and the Armed Conflicts of the Twentieth Century* (Aldershot, 2012), 33–59; Andrew Chandler, *Brethren in Adversity: George Bell and the Crisis of German Protestantism* (Woodbridge, 2007); idem, 'The Church of England and the Obliteration Bombing of Germany during the Second World War', *EHR* 108 (1993), 920–46.

53 Sarah Stockwell, '"Splendidly leading the way": Archbishop Fisher and Decolonisation in British Colonial Africa', *Journal of Imperial and Commonwealth History* 36 (2008), 545–64; Matthew Grimley, 'The Church and the Bomb: Anglicans and the Campaign for Nuclear Disarmament, c.1958–1984', in Parker and Lawson, eds, *God and War*, 147–64.

54 Stewart J. Brown, *Providence and Empire: Religion, Society and Politics 1815–1914*

Callum Brown's volume for the twentieth century in the same series, though, is entitled *Religion and Society in Twentieth Century Britain*. Somewhere along the way, the word 'politics' has been dropped from the title. This is presumably deliberate, because the relationship between politics and religion does not feature much in Brown's narrative either. However, other histories of twentieth-century British Christianity have given much fuller coverage to the interaction of religion and politics.[55] So, more strikingly, have two recent general histories of post-war Britain (admittedly both by the same author) in the New Oxford History of England.[56]

Since the late 1970s, there has been a greater appreciation of the role of the institutions of church and state as agents of religious change in their own right. Here sociologists led the way, initially David Martin in his *General Theory of Secularization* (1978), then others such as Grace Davie and Jose Casanova.[57] Robin Gill argued that the nineteenth-century established church suffered a kind of overstretch, leading to over-provision of empty churches.[58] More recently, David Hempton has argued that establishment initially led to a religious revival in the nineteenth century, but that it turned into a liability thereafter.[59] J. C. D. Clark has similarly posited that Anglicanism's 'association with the state might be at some times (as during the French Revolution) a source of strength, at other times (as after 1918 and 1945) of weakness'.[60] The very categories of 'established churches' and 'secular states' have also been challenged by pan-European comparative studies that have demonstrated that no post-1945 western European state has been religiously neutral in the sense advocated by the American political

(Harlow, 2008).

55 Adrian Hastings, *A History of English Christianity 1920–1990*, rev. edn (London, 1991); Robbins, *England, Ireland, Scotland, Wales*.
56 Brian Harrison, *Seeking a Role: The United Kingdom 1951–1970* (Oxford, 2009); idem, *Finding a Role? The United Kingdom 1970–1990* (Oxford, 2010).
57 David Martin, *A General Theory of Secularization* (Oxford, 1978); Grace Davie, *Religion in Modern Europe: A Memory Mutates* (Oxford, 2004); Jose Casanova, *Public Religions in the Modern World* (Chicago, IL, 1994).
58 Robin Gill, *The Myth of the Empty Church* (London, 1993).
59 David Hempton, 'Established Churches and the Growth of Religious Pluralism: A Case Study of Christianisation and Secularisation in England since 1700', in Hugh McLeod and Werner Ustorf, eds, *The Decline of Christendom in Western Europe, 1750–2000* (Cambridge, 2003), 81–98.
60 J. C. D. Clark, 'Secularization and Modernization: The Failure of a "Grand Narrative"', *HistJ* 55 (2012), 161–94, at 188.

theorist John Rawls; rather, all states have allowed certain religions financial or educational privileges.[61] These studies have also indicated the persistence of religion in political ideology in much of post-war Europe, particularly through 'Christian democracy'.[62] Hugh McLeod has argued for the persistence of 'Christendom' – consisting of polities in which key political and social institutions were structured around religious adherence – in Western Europe until the late 1960s.[63] Seen from this comparative perspective, Britain's established churches seem less singular, and the binary distinction between secular and confessional states gives way to more of a spectrum.

What aspects of church-state relations remain to be explored by historians over the next fifty years? In an essay which appeared in 2003, Jeffrey Cox argued that an 'alternative master narrative' to secularization 'will focus on state and legal power and the origins of religious toleration rather than structural differentiation, urbanisation and industrialisation'.[64] The reference to law is suggestive here, because there has still been comparatively little consideration of the changing legal relationship between the state, churches and other religious groups. Recent controversies over the implementation of the 1998 Human Rights Act and the revision of charity law (which has implications for the legal status of religious groups) have emphasized the complexities and ambiguities of that legal relationship in Britain, and there is room for more historical study of this.[65] The question of how far modern multiculturalist discourses have been informed by older ideas of toleration and pluralism is another area that needs to be explored. And there is more to be said about the impact of the decline of Protestantism

[61] John Rawls, 'The Idea of Public Reason Revisited', in idem, *The Law of Peoples: With The Idea of Public Reason Revisited* (Cambridge, MA, 1999), 129–80. For a recent Christian critique of Rawls, see the essays in Nigel Biggar and Linda Hogan, eds, *Religious Voices in Public Places* (Oxford, 2009).

[62] Jytte Klausen, 'Europe's Uneasy Marriage of Secularism and Christianity since 1945 and the Challenge of Contemporary Religious Pluralism', in Ira Katznelson and Gareth Stedman Jones, eds, *Religion and the Political Imagination* (Cambridge, 2010), 314–35.

[63] Hugh McLeod, *The Religious Crisis of the 1960s* (Oxford, 2007); idem and Ustorf, eds, *Decline of Christendom*.

[64] Jeffrey Cox, 'Master-Narratives of Religious Change', in McLeod and Ustorf, eds, *Decline of Christendom*, 201–17, at 210.

[65] For recent discussion by a legal theorist, see Julian Rivers, *The Law of Organised Religions: Between Establishment and Secularism* (Oxford, 2011).

on national identity, and about its corollary, Catholicism's declining sense of separateness from the nation and the body politic. Another area has been opened up by recent debates about conceptions of the secular in western society. Philosophers and political theorists have written extensively on this subject, particularly since the 11 September 2001 attacks on the United States, but the question of how far western conceptions of the secular were themselves rooted in Christian categories is an important one for historians, too.[66] As Bernice Martin has put it, 'a secular Islamic or Confucian world would look very different from the one we inhabit'.[67] The apparent revival of aggressive secularism in Britain in the last decade has also drawn attention to how under-explored the history of modern British secularism has been.[68]

The eclipse of 'church and state' as a subject for historians of British religion from the 1950s to the early 1980s is peculiar, in that it was not paralleled in the historiographies of other countries. Thomas Kselman has pointed out that French religious history continued to be conceived in terms of church–state relations.[69] The same was true of the United States, where political controversies on 'church and state' issues meant that the terms retained their salience as a subject of historical study. Nor, although social theory affected British historians of all periods in Britain, did medievalists or early modernists go quite so far as modernists in embracing secularization theory (which could not easily be applied to their periods) or in rejecting the study of church and state. Simon Green's

[66] Talal Asad, *Formations of the Secular: Christianity, Islam, Modernity* (Stanford, CA, 2003); Charles Taylor, *A Secular Age* (Cambridge, MA, 2007); Michael Warner, Jonathan Van Antwerpen and Craig J. Calhoun, eds, *Varieties of Secularism in a Secular Age* (Cambridge, MA, 2010); Craig J. Calhoun, Mark Juergensmeyer and Jonathan Van Antwerpen, eds, *Rethinking Secularism* (Oxford, 2011). For a recent discussion of some of this literature by a historian, see Dominic Erdozain, '"Cause is not quite what it used to be": The Return of Secularisation', *EHR* 127 (2012), 377–400.

[67] Bernice Martin, 'The Non-Quantifiable Religious Dimension in Social Life', in Paul Avis, ed., *Public Faith? The State of Religious Belief and Practice in Britain* (London, 2003), 1–18, at 13.

[68] For exceptions, see Susan Budd, *Varieties of Unbelief: Atheists and Agnostics in English Society, 1850–1960* (London, 1977); David Nash, *Blasphemy in Modern Britain: 1789 to the Present* (Aldershot, 1999); Callum Brown, '"The Unholy Mrs Knight and the BBC": Secular Humanism and the Threat to the "Christian Nation", c.1945–1960', *EHR* 127 (2012), 345–76.

[69] Thomas Kselman, 'Challenging De-Christianization: The Historiography of Religion in Modern France', *ChH* 75 (2001), 130–9.

recent argument that 'a social history of religion has to be a political and intellectual history as well' might seem like a statement of the obvious to historians of earlier periods, who might never have dreamt that it could be anything else.[70] However, Green's assertion does underline how, for a time between the 1950s and 1980s, the social history of religion in Britain did indeed become separated from its political and intellectual history. As this article has tried to show, how and why this happened is now a subject for historical study in its own right.

Merton College, Oxford

---

[70] Green, *Passing of Protestant England*, 11.